Blackwell Companions to Literature and Culture

This series offers comprehensive, newly written surveys of key periods and movements and certain major authors, in English literary culture and history. Extensive volumes provide new perspectives and positions on contexts and on canonical and post-canonical texts, orientating the beginning student in new fields of study and providing the experienced undergraduate and new graduate with current and new directions, as pioneered and developed by leading scholars in the field.

A Companion to Shakespeare's Works

A COMPANION TO

SHAKESPEARE'S WORKS

VOLUME I

THE TRAGEDIES

EDITED BY **RICHARD DUTTON**
AND **JEAN E. HOWARD**

Blackwell
Publishing

Editorial material and organization copyright © 2003 by
Blackwell Publishing Ltd

350 Main Street, Malden, MA 02148-5018, USA
108 Cowley Road, Oxford OX4 1JF, UK
550 Swanston Street, Carlton South, Victoria 3053, Australia
Kurfürstendamm 57, 10707 Berlin, Germany

First published 2003 by Blackwell Publishing Ltd

Library of Congress Cataloging-in-Publication Data has been applied for.

ISBN 0-631-22632-X (hardback)

ISBN 1-405-10730-8 (four-volume set)

A catalogue record for this title is available from the British Library.

Set in 11 on 13 pt Garamond 3
by SNP Best-set Typesetter Ltd., Hong Kong
Printed and bound in the United Kingdom
by MPG Books Ltd, Bodmin, Cornwall

For further information on
Blackwell Publishing, visit our website:
http://www.blackwellpublishing.com

Contents

Notes on Contributors

Catherine Belsey chairs the Centre for Critical and Cultural Theory at Cardiff University. Her books include *The Subject of Tragedy: Identity and Difference in Renaissance Drama* (1985), *Desire: Love Stories in Western Culture* (1994), and *Shakespeare and the Loss of Eden: The Construction of Family Values in Early Modern Culture* (1999).

Philippa Berry is a Fellow and Director of Studies in English at King's College, University of Cambridge. She combines interdisciplinary research in English and European Renaissance culture with work on feminist and postmodern theory. She is the author of *Of Chastity and Power: Elizabethan Literature and the Unmarried Queen* (1989) and *Shakespeare's Feminine Endings: Disfiguring Death in the Tragedies* (1999), and co-editor of *Shadow of Spirit: Postmodernism and Religion* (1992) and *Textures of Renaissance Knowledge* (forthcoming).

Gordon Braden is John C. Coleman Professor of English at the University of Virginia. He is the author of *The Classics and English Renaissance Poetry, Renaissance Tragedy and the Senecan Tradition, The Idea of the Renaissance* (with William Kerrigan), and *Petrarchan Love and the Continental Renaissance*.

Jerry Brotton is Lecturer in Renaissance Studies at Queen Mary College, University of London. He is the author of *Trading Territories: Mapping the Early Modern World* (1997), *The Renaissance Bazaar: From the Silk Road to Michelangelo* (2002), and with Lisa Jardine, *Global Interests: Renaissance Art Between East and West* (2000). He is currently writing a book on the art collection of King Charles I.

Mark Thornton Burnett is a Reader in English at the Queen's University of Belfast. He is the author of *Masters and Servants in English Renaissance Drama and Culture: Authority and Obedience* (1997), the editor of *The Complete Plays of Christopher Marlowe* (1999) and *Christopher Marlowe: Complete Poems* (2000), and the co-editor of *New Essays* on *"Hamlet"* (1994), *Shakespeare and Ireland: History, Politics, Culture* (1997), and *Shakespeare, Film, Fin de Siècle* (2000). His forthcoming book is entitled *Constructing "Monsters" in Shakespearean Drama and Early Modern Culture.*

Rebecca W. Bushnell is Associate Dean for Arts and Letters and Professor of English at the University of Pennsylvania. Her books include *Prophesying Tragedy: Sign and Voice in Sophocles' Theban Plays* (1988), *Tragedies of Tyrants: Political Thought and Theater in the English Renaissance* (1990), and *A Culture of Teaching: Early Modern Humanism in Theory and Practice* (1996). She has just completed a study of early modern English gardening books.

Martin Coyle is Chair of the Board of Studies for English Literature at Cardiff University. He is joint general editor of the New Casebooks series.

Hugh Grady is Professor of English at Arcadia University in Glenside, Pennsylvania and the author of *The Modernist Shakespeare: Critical Texts in a Material World* (1991, 1994), *Shakespeare's Universal Wolf: Studies in Early Modern Modernity* (1996), and *Shakespeare, Machiavelli, and Montaigne: Power and Subjectivity from "Richard II" to "Hamlet"* (2003).

Kim Hall holds the Thomas F. X. Mullarkey Chair in Literature at Fordham University. The author of *Things of Darkness: Economies of Race and Gender in Early Modern England* (1995), she has published numerous articles on race in Renaissance/early modern culture and has lectured nationally and internationally on Shakespeare, race theory, Renaissance women writers, visual arts, material culture, and pedagogy. She is currently working on two books: *Othello: Texts and Contexts* and *The Sweet Taste of Empire: Gender and Material Culture in Seventeenth-Century England.*

Graham Holderness is Professor of English, Dean of the Faculty of Humanities and Education, and Director of Research at the Graduate School at the University of Hertfordshire. He has published extensively in modern and early modern literature and drama, being author, co-author, editor or co-editor of 30 books, 22 of which are on Shakespeare. These include *Shakespeare's History* (1985), *The Shakespeare Myth* (1988), *Shakespeare: The Play of History* (1988), *Shakespeare: Out of Court* (1990), *Shakespeare's History-Plays: Richard II to Henry V* (1992), *Shakespeare: The Histories* (2000), *Cultural Shakespeare* (2001), *Visual Shakespeare* (2001), and *Textual Shakespeare* (2002). His first novel, *The Prince of Denmark*, was published in 2001, and a poetry collection, *Craeft: Poems from the Anglo-Saxon*, was awarded the Poetry Book Society recommendation for summer 2002.

David Scott Kastan is Old Dominion Foundation Professor in the Humanities at Columbia University. He has written widely on Shakespeare, most recently *Shakespeare* *and the Book* (2001). He is a general editor of the Arden Shakespeare, and his edition of *1 Henry IV* for that series appeared in the autumn of 2002.

Bernice W. Kliman is Professor of English Emeritus, Nassau Community College, and coordinates the New Variorum Hamlet project for the Modern Language Association. She has authored or edited several books (most recently *Approaches to Teaching Hamlet*) and written many essays, reviews, and notes, mainly on performance and on editing, in journals such as *AEB (Analytic and Enumerative Bibliography)*, *Cahiers Elisabéthains*, *Shakespeare Bulletin*, *Shakespeare Newsletter*, and *Shakespeare Quarterly*.

Naomi Conn Liebler is Professor of English and University Distinguished Scholar at Montclair State University. She is the author of *Shakespeare's Festive Tragedy: The Ritual Foundations of Genre* (1995), co-editor of *Tragedy* (1998) an anthology of theoretical readings in the genre, and editor of *The Female Tragic Hero in English Renaissance Drama* (2002). She has published numerous essays on Shakespeare, other early modern English drama, and modern European and American drama, and is presently working on a critical edition of Richard Johnson's 1596–7 prose romance, *The Most Famous History of the Seven Champions of Christendom*.

Richard C. McCoy is Professor of English at Queen's College and the Graduate Center, City University of New York, and the author of *Sir Philip Sidney: Rebellion in Arcadia* (1979), *The Rites of Knighthood: The Literature and Politics of Elizabethan Chivalry* (1989), and *Alterations of State: Sacred Kingship in the English Reformation* (2002).

Kathleen McLuskie is Deputy Vice-Chancellor at the University of Southampton. She is editing *Macbeth* for Arden 3 and working on the commercialization of early modern culture.

Cynthia Marshall is Professor of English at Rhodes College in Memphis. She is the author of *The Shattering of the Self: Violence, Subjectivity, and Early Modern Texts* (2002) and editor of *Shakespeare in Production: As You Like It* (forthcoming).

Michael Neill is Professor of English at the University of Auckland, New Zealand; he is the author of *Issues of Death* (1997) and *Putting History to the Question* (2000). He has edited *Antony and Cleopatra* for the Oxford Shakespeare, and is currently editing *Othello* for the same series.

Sasha Roberts is a Lecturer in English at the University of Kent. Her publications include *Reading Shakespeare's Poems in Early Modern England* (2002), *Women Reading Shakespeare, 1660–1900: An Edited Anthology* (co-edited with Ann Thompson, 1997), *Romeo and Juliet* in the new Writers and Their Work series (1998), and articles on Shakespeare, early modern reading practices, and visual culture. She is currently researching a book on the formation of literary taste in early modern manuscript culture.

Kenneth S. Rothwell is Emeritus Professor of English at the University of Vermont, Burlington. He co-founded and co-edited with Bernice W. Kliman the *Shakespeare on Film Newsletter*, produced the Shakespeare on Film Festival in 1996 at the Los Angeles World Shakespeare Congress, and has most recently published *A History of Shakespeare on Screen: A Century of Film and Television* (1999), and "An Annotated Screenography" for the MLA, *Approaches to Teaching Shakespeare's Hamlet* (2001).

Katherine Rowe is Associate Professor of English at Bryn Mawr. Her publications include *Dead Hands: Fictions of Agency, Renaissance to Modern* (1999), as well as articles on Shakespeare, Renaissance drama, early modern psychology, and film. Her current projects include a co-edited anthology, *Reading the Early Modern Passions: Essays in the Cultural History of Emotion* (2003), and a study of contractual relations in Stuart drama.

Kiernan Ryan is Professor of English at Royal Holloway, University of London, and a Fellow of New Hall, University of Cambridge. His most recent publications include *King Lear: Contemporary Critical Essays* (1993), *New Historicism and Cultural Materialism: A Reader* (1996), *Shakespeare: The Last Plays* (1999), *Shakespeare: Texts and Contexts* (2000), and *Shakespeare* (3rd edn., 2002). He is currently completing a study of Shakespearean comedy and romance.

Jyotsna G. Singh is an Associate Professor of English at Michigan State University. She is the author of *Colonial Narratives/Cultural Dialogues: "Discoveries" of India in the Language of Colonialism* (1996) and the co-author of *The Wayward Sisters: Shakespeare and Feminist Politics* (Blackwell, 1994). Most recently, she co-edited *Travel Knowledge: European "Discoveries" in the Early Modern Period* (2000).

Ian Smith is Associate Professor of English at Lafayette College. He has published principally on Shakespeare and on postcolonial literature. He is currently preparing a book on race and barbarism in the Renaissance.

Introduction

The four *Companions to Shakespeare's Works* (*Tragedies*; *Histories*; *Comedies*; *Poems, Problem Comedies, Late Plays*) were compiled as a single entity designed to offer a uniquely comprehensive snapshot of current Shakespeare criticism. Complementing David Scott Kastan's *Companion to Shakespeare* (1999), which focused on Shakespeare as an author in his historical context, these volumes by contrast focus on Shakespeare's works, both the plays and major poems, and aim to showcase some of the most interesting critical research currently being conducted in Shakespeare studies.

To that end the editors commissioned scholars from many quarters of the world – Australia, Canada, France, New Zealand, the United Kingdom, and the United States – to write new essays that, collectively, address virtually the whole of Shakespeare's dramatic and poetic canon. The decision to organize the volumes along generic lines (rather than, say, thematically or chronologically) was made for a mixture of intellectual and pragmatic reasons. It is still quite common, for example, to teach or to write about Shakespeare's works as tragedies, histories, comedies, late plays, sonnets, or narrative poems. And there is much evidence to suggest that a similar language of poetic and dramatic "kinds" or genres was widely current in Elizabethan and Jacobean England. George Puttenham and Philip Sidney – to mention just two sixteenth-century English writers interested in poetics – both assume the importance of genre as a way of understanding differences among texts; and the division of Shakespeare's plays in the First Folio of 1623 into comedies, histories, and tragedies offers some warrant for thinking that these generic rubrics would have had meaning for Shakespeare's readers and certainly for those members of his acting company who helped to assemble the volume. Of course, exactly *what* those rubrics meant in Shakespeare's day is partly what requires critical investigation. For example, we do not currently think of *Cymbeline* as a tragedy, though it is listed as such in the First Folio, nor do we find the First Folio employing terms such as "problem plays," "romances," and "tragicomedies" which subsequent critics have used to designate groups of plays. Consequently, a number of essays in these volumes self-consciously examine the meanings and lineages of the terms used to separate one genre from another and to compare the way Shakespeare and his contemporaries reworked the generic templates that were their common heritage and mutually constituted creation.

Pragmatically, we as editors also needed a way to divide the material we saw as necessary for a Companion to Shakespeare's Works that aimed to provide an overview of the exciting scholarly work being done in Shakespeare studies at the beginning of the twenty-first century. Conveniently, certain categories of his works are equally sub-stantial in terms of volume. Shakespeare wrote about as many tragedies as histories, and again about as many "festive" or "romantic" comedies, so it was possible to assign each of these groupings a volume of its own. This left a decidedly less unified fourth volume to handle not only the non-dramatic verse, but also those much-contested cat-egories of "problem comedies" and "late plays." In the First Folio, a number of plays included in this volume were listed among the comedies: namely, *The Tempest*, *Measure for Measure*, *All's Well That Ends Well*, and *The Winter's Tale*. *Troilus and Cressida* was not listed in the prefatory catalog, though it appears between the histories and tragedies in the actual volume and is described (contrary to the earlier quarto) as a tragedy. *Cymbeline* is listed as a tragedy; *Henry VIII* appears as the last of the history plays. *Pericles* and *Two Noble Kinsmen* do not appear at all. This volume obviously offers less generic unity than the other three, but it provides special opportunities to think again about the utility and theoretical coherence of the terms by which both Shakespeare's contemporaries and generations of subsequent critics have attempted to understand the conventionalized means through which his texts can meaningfully be distinguished and grouped.

When it came to the design of each volume, the editors assigned an essay on each play (or on the narrative poems and sonnets) and about the same number of some-what longer essays designed to take up larger critical problems relevant to the genre or to a particular grouping of plays. For example, we commissioned essays on the plays in performance (both on stage and in films), on the imagined geography of different kinds of plays, on Shakespeare's relationship to his contemporaries working in a par-ticular genre, and on categorizations such as tragedy, history, or tragicomedy. We also invited essays on specific topics of current interest such as the influence of Ovid on Shakespeare's early narrative poems, Shakespeare's practice as a collaborative writer, his representations of popular rebellion, the homoerotic dimensions of his comedies, or the effects of censorship on his work, As a result, while there will be a free-standing essay on *Macbeth* in the tragedy volume, one will also find in the same volume a discussion of the same aspect of the play in Richard McCoy's essay on "Shakespearean Tragedy and Religious Identity," in Katherine Rowe's "Minds in Company: Shakespearean Tragic Emotions," in Graham Holderness's "Text and Tragedy," and in other pieces as well. For those who engage fully with the richness and variety of the essays available within each volume, we hope that the whole will consequently amount to much more than the sum of its parts.

Within this structure we invited our contributors – specifically chosen to reflect a generational mix of established and younger critics – to write as scholars addressing fellow scholars. That is, we sought interventions in current critical debates and examples of people's ongoing research rather than overviews of or introductions to a topic. We invited contributors to write for their peers and graduate students, rather than tailoring essays primarily to undergraduates. Beyond that, we invited a diversity of approaches; our aim was to showcase the best of current work rather than to advocate for any particular critical or theoretical perspective. If these volumes are in any senses a representative trawl of contemporary critical practice, they suggest that it would be premature to assume we have reached a post-theoretical era. Many lines of theoretical practice converge in these essays: historicist, certainly, but also Derridean, Marxist, performance-oriented, feminist, queer, and textual/editorial. Race, class, gender, bodies, and emotions, now carefully historicized, have not lost their power as organizing rubrics for original critical investigations; attention to religion, especially the Catholic contexts for Shakespeare's inventions, has perhaps never been more pronounced; political theory, including investigations of republicanism, continues to yield impressive insights into the plays. At the same time, there is a marked turn to new forms of empiricist inquiry, including, in particular, attention to early readers' responses to Shakespeare's texts and a newly vigorous interest in how Shakespeare's plays relate to the work of his fellow dramatists. Each essay opens to a larger world of scholarship on the questions addressed, and through the list of references and further reading included at the end of each chapter, the contributors invite readers to pursue their own inquiries on these topics. We believe that the quite remarkable range of essays included in these volumes will be valuable to anyone involved in teaching, writing, and thinking about Shakespeare at the beginning of the new century.

The editors did not commission a separate essay on Edward III, but several contributors have chosen to treat it as a Shakespearean text: please see the index. We did commission an essay on Henry VIII, but that appears in Volume IV: *Poems, Problem Comedies, Late Plays*. Other contributors have chosen to discuss it in both of these volumes.

1

"A rarity most beloved": Shakespeare and the Idea of Tragedy

David Scott Kastan

All words are pockets into which now this, now that is put, and sometimes many things at once.

Friedrich Nietzsche, *The Wanderer and his Shadow*

It is upon the pillars of the great tragedies – *Hamlet*, *Othello*, *King Lear*, and *Macbeth*[1] – that Shakespeare's reputation most securely rests, and indeed it is the tragic plays in general that seem most robustly to confirm Shakespeare's greatness. The tragedies arguably test the emotional resources of their readers and audiences more strenuously than the comedies or histories, confirming a generic bias that Shakespeare's own age often expressed. In the Induction to *A Warning for Fair Women* (1599), Tragedy, with whip in one hand and a knife in the other, appears on stage to insist upon her supremacy in the repertory: Comedy is but "slight & childish," designed merely "To tickle shallow iniudiciall eares," but Tragedy is made of sterner stuff. Its claim to "raigne as Queene / In great Apollos name and all the Muses" (Ind., 75–6) rests upon its ability to present

> passions that must moue the soule,
> Make the heart heauie and throb within the bosome,
> Extorting teares out of the strictest eyes,
> To racke a thought and straine it to his forme,
> Untill I rap the sences from their course.
> This is my office. (Induction, 44–8)

And although Comedy aggressively contests Tragedy's claim to generic preeminence, asserting the stultifying predictability of its plots ("some damnd tyrant to obtaine a crowne, / Stabs, hangs, impoysons, smoothers, cutteth throats"; 49–50), many would assent to Tragedy's aesthetic superiority, like Kyd's Heironomo, finding Comedy easy and self-indulgent, only "fit for common wits" (*The Spanish Tragedy*, 4.1.157).

Nonetheless, for all her critical praise, even Tragedy must admit that too often she "is scorned of the multitude," while Comedy and History hold the stage and are "Painted in playbills upon every post" (*A Warning*, Ind., 73). What we know about the repertory of Elizabethan theatre companies, mainly derived from Henslowe's account books (and a caveat must be that there is no reason to assume that every acting company followed the patterns of Henslowe's; his diary, however, is the only such document we have), confirms Tragedy's plaint. In the theatrical season of 1592–3, Lord Strange's men performed twenty-seven plays, only three of which – *The Spanish Tragedy*, *The Massacre at Paris*, and *The Jew of Malta* – were obviously tragedies; the following year, Lord Sussex's company performed twelve plays, only two of which were tragedies – *Titus Andronicus* and *The Jew of Malta*. What records we have confirm that comedies and histories made up the largest part of the acting companies' offerings; tragedies were significantly less often played, although nonetheless they were, as Roslyn L. Knutson has shown, "rare and valuable commodities."[2]

In Shakespeare's company, however, tragedies may well have been somewhat less rare, although no less valuable, than in the repertory of the Admiral's men, if only by virtue of Shakespeare's own playwrighting. As early as 1598 Francis Meres recognized Shakespeare as being "the most excellent" of all contemporary playwrights in both comedy and tragedy; and, although his list of six plays offered as evidence of Shakespeare's excellence in tragedy includes four (*King John*, *Richard II*, *Richard III*, and *1 Henry IV*) that would later be viewed as histories,[3] the classification suggests only how much more amorphous (and thus expansive) the early modern definition of tragedy was than our own.

By 1623 the Folio would neatly organize the thirty-five plays listed in the catalog (thirty-six plays are in the volume, but problems over the rights to *Troilus and Cressida* prevented it from making the table of contents) into the three familiar dramatic genres: "COMEDIES, HISTORIES and TRAGEDIES." The fourteen comedies are clearly linked by a conventional understanding of that genre: plays, mainly about love, which begin in emotional and social confusion and end in harmony. The ten histories are defined by their common dependence upon narrative accounts of English history and are arranged according to the chronology of their subject matter. With the eleven plays that make up the section of "TRAGEDIES," however, it is less easy to characterize the principle of organization.

Indeed, beyond the commonplace generic principle that tragedies should end in suffering and defeat (and *Cymbeline*'s notorious presence among the Folio's tragedies confounds even this seemingly inescapable principle), too little else obviously joins these plays together or separates them from a number of the histories, as Meres had already seen in 1598. Comedy and tragedy could be easily differentiated, usually on the simple contrasting principle, as Byron would later phrase it, that "all tragedies are finish'd by a death; / All comedies are ended by a marriage" (*Don Juan*, 3.9). Tragedy and history, however, were harder to distinguish, at least until the organization of the Folio itself began to fix the definition of the history play as a drama uniquely dependent upon the history of post-conquest England. The title pages of the early quartos of both *Richard II* and *Richard III* confidently label those plays tragedies: *The Tragedie of King Richard the second* and *The Tragedy of King Richard the third* (and each is called a "tragedie" in its entrance in the Stationers' Register, the first on August 29, 1597, the second on October 20 of that year). In 1615 the fifth edition of *Richard II* was published, still identifying the play as *The Tragedie of King Richard the Second*; and even as late as 1634, *Richard III* could once again be reissued as *The Tragedie of King Richard the Third*. Even the Folio seemed somewhat uncertain about this play, for, while the catalog lists it among the histories and titles it *The Life and Death of Richard the Third*, the head title (though not the running title) calls it *The Tragedy of Richard the Third* (sig. q5r).

But even if the publication of the 1623 Folio could be said more or less firmly to establish the history play as a separate genre,[4] the tragedies themselves as defined by the categorization of the Folio make up a not much less diverse set than Meres's earlier mixed grouping. Though the death of the titular character might seem to unify the Folio's tragic plays, they display remarkable differences in how that death is experienced: in *Julius Caesar* that death comes in the middle of the play, and indeed Caesar arguably is not the play's hero at all; in *Macbeth* the title character of course dies, but his death does not easily produce the same sense of loss we normally associate with tragedy, as his death seems neither unjust nor undesirable; in *Antony and Cleopatra* the deaths of the title characters are, at least in their own imaginations, fully compensated by the victory they celebrate in their worldly defeat; and although *Timon of Athens* traces the disintegration of its hero, it stops before the character's death. Even more disruptive is the appearance of *Cymbeline* at the end of the Folio's section of tragedies. Here too the title character does not die, but the action is that of wondrous renewal rather than decline. The play's location among the tragedies is justified perhaps only by the fact that in not driving toward a marriage it is in that sense no comedy and in not being about the post-conquest English political past, it is not a history play. *Cymbeline*'s presence in the section, then, suggests that Tragedy is the catch-all category. Even if the play's appearance among the tragedies is an editorial mistake (and certainly the play's marvelous conclusion defies any conventional understanding of tragedy), its location in the Folio merely confirms how insecure the very category of tragedy is.

It is no doubt unwise to put too much pressure upon the Folio's generic distinctions. The organization is almost certainly not Shakespeare's own. Most likely it represents the organizing impulses of the volume's two editors, his friends and fellow actors, John Heminge and Henry Condell, and it is probably pointless to work backwards from the Folio categorizations in search of Shakespeare's own generic understandings. Indeed, Shakespeare seems to have been genially suspicious of genre theory; Polonius's ludicrous inventory of dramatic kinds (*Hamlet*, 2.2.397–401) alone must warn us of the hazards and limited benefits of literary taxonomy. Certainly no concept of genre can be exclusive or precise, since the resemblances that we recognize in texts are not necessarily the only ones that exist, nor are our classifications the only ones that are possible. Still, if it matters little what we call these plays ("What's the use of them having names," sensibly asks the Gnat in *Through the Looking Glass*, "if they won't answer to them?"), some idea of genre underpins both the creation and the understanding of all literature; every act of reading and writing "originates" in a provisional idea of the text's genre.[5]

Tragedy, of course, had a rich critical history by the time Shakespeare wrote.[6] Aristotle's definition of tragedy in the *Poetics* (6.49b24–8) as the imitation of the fall of a noble man through some flaw or error (*hamartia*) which arouses and purges (through *catharsis*) pity and fear is well known now, if still imperfectly understood. Unquestionably, following Lorenzo Valla's translation of the *Poetics* into Latin in 1498, Aristotle's literary influence was increasingly felt in Renaissance Europe.[7] But Aristotle is largely a red herring in regard to Shakespeare. Aristotle's definition of the "best" kind of tragedy was not intended to be normative, and, in any case, there is no evidence that Shakespeare ever read the *Poetics* (or anything else by Aristotle). Indeed, Shakespeare's only two references to Aristotle (Hector's anachronism in *Troilus and Cressida* at 2.2.166, and Tranio's allusion in *The Taming of the Shrew* at 1.1.32) both seem to suggest that for the English dramatist Aristotle was no more than a usefully recognizable name for an ancient moral philosopher.

Shakespeare seems to have been unaware of (or willing to ignore) Aristotle's theorization or even of any of the many Renaissance commentaries on the *Poetics*. For Shakespeare, as for most of his contemporary dramatists, tragedy as a literary term simply named a particular plot structure, though his own use of the word suggests an even more imprecise sense of its meaning (not unlike what many teachers bewail today when "tragedy" is allowed to define some disastrous event – which might include anything from a natural catastrophe to the defeat of a favorite football team – rather than a literary genre). At the end of *Love's Labour's Lost* he invokes a relatively confident generic sense of comedy, as Berowne admits: "our wooing doth not end like an old play: / Jack hath not Jill. These ladies' courtesy / Might well have made our sport a comedy" (5.2.870–2). "Tragedy," however, is rarely used with even this level of generic specificity. *Henry V*'s reference to "Edward the Black Prince, / Who on the French ground played a tragedy" (1.2.105–6) means only that the English Edward wreaked devastation upon the French (at Crécy). In *Titus Andronicus* Tamora refers to the "complot of this timeless tragedy" (2.2.265) but, although the language is explicitly literary, the Queen of the Goths means no more by it than the "conspiracy that brought about the untimely calamity" of Bassanius' death. Even the play's later reference to "the tragic tale of Philomel" (4.1.47) carries little of the generic specificity of Berowne's use of "comedy." If this does explicitly recognize tragedy as a literary mode, it does little more than mark it as some lamentable action. In general, Shakespeare's use of "tragedy" or any of its cognates works similarly. At the end of *Othello* "the tragic loading of this bed" (5.2.365) could conceivably invoke generic norms or possibilities, but it means little more – though poignantly nothing less – than "devastating" or "appalling."

If any theoretical pressures existed to shape Shakespeare's understanding of tragedy they came more from medieval articulations of the genre than classical ones. Chaucer

was seemingly the first to use the English word "tragedy," in a gloss in his translation (ca. 1380) of Boethius's *De Consolatione Philosophiae*: "Tragedye is to seyn a dite
of a prosperite for a tyme that endeth in wrecchidnesse."[8] The felt need for a gloss
suggests that tragedy was then an unfamiliar concept in English, but quickly the idea
of tragedy as the fall from prosperity to wretchedness became commonplace. Chaucer's
definition is perhaps so limited as to seem obvious and unhelpful, especially in our
hypertheoretical age, but in its very simplicity it calls attention to tragedy's power,
marking it as universal and inexplicable. It defines the inescapable trajectory of the
tragic action but not its cause, and in its reticence about who or what is responsible
for the dire change of fortune it speaks tragedy's fearful incomprehensibility.

Although a number of literary models intervene between Chaucer's definition and
Shakespeare's plays – e.g., Chaucer's own *Troilus and Criseyde*, the *de casibus* tragedies
of *A Mirror for Magistrates*, and the early tragic plays of Kyd and Marlowe – Chaucer's
definitional reserve finds its most powerful analogue in the agonizing silences of
Shakespeare's tragedies. "Why should a dog, a horse, a rat have life / And thou no
breath at all?" (5.8.307–8), King Lear cries, holding his broken child. No answer is
forthcoming, though it lies in the incalculable murderousness of the world. And
directly questioning that world produces no more satisfying responses. "Is there any
cause in nature that makes these hard hearts?" (3.6.74–5).

These are the unanswered (perhaps unanswerable) questions of the tragic world.
Are there reasons for the intolerable suffering? Is the tragic motor human error or
capricious fate? Is the catastrophe a just, if appalling, retribution, or an arbitrary
destiny reflecting the indifference, or, worse, the malignity of the heavens? A textual
variant in *Hamlet* may uncannily focus the choice. At the end of both Q2 and Folio
Hamlet, Horatio offers to tell "How these things came about" (5.2.385). "So shall you
hear," he tells Fortinbras, "of carnal, bloody and unnatural acts, / Of accidental judge-
ments, casual slaughters, / Of deaths put on by cunning . . ." In Q2 (1604–5) he then
adds: "and for no cause" (sig. O2r). In the Folio (1623) Horatio says differently; there
it is "and forc'd cause" (TLN 3878). For "no cause" or for "forc'd cause." Are the dreadful events horrible accidents or fearful necessities?

For Shakespeare, anyhow, the uncertainty is the point. Characters may commit
themselves to a confident sense of the tragic world they inhabit; but the plays
inevitably render that preliminary understanding inadequate, and the characters
struggle unsuccessfully to reconstruct a coherent worldview from the ruins of the old.
And it is the emotional truth of the struggle rather than the metaphysical truth of
the worldview that is at the center of these plays. Shakespeare's tragedies provoke the
questions about the cause of the pain and loss the plays so agonizingly portray, and
in the refusal of any answers starkly prevent any confident attribution of meaning or
value to human suffering.

Perhaps here we can begin to discover the logic of Shakespeare's tragic practice.
Kenneth Muir's oft-quoted comment that "There is no such thing as Shakespearian
tragedy: there are only Shakespearian tragedies"[9] merely begs the question of how
"Shakespearian" modifies "tragedy," either as an individual exemplar or a group. If

Muir is only saying that Shakespeare does not seem to have written tragedy driven by a fully developed theoretical conception of the genre we can easily assent, but a coherent and powerfully compelling sense of tragedy can be seen to develop through the plays.

Tragedy, for Shakespeare, is the genre of uncompensated suffering, and as he writes in that mode the successive plays reveal an ever more profound formal acknowledgment of their desolating controlling logic. "What are tragedies," asks Thomas Kyd, "but acts of death?" (*Soliman and Perseda*, 1.1.7), but death alone is not enough to define the genre for Shakespeare. A play like *Everyman*, for example, is unmistakably an act of death, but its fundamental logic of radical consolation undoes the tragic force of Everyman's dying. The title of the Flemish version of the morality, *Den Spieghel der Salicheit van Elckerlijc* (The Mirror of Everyman's Salvation), attests to its essentially *comic* form. Located with the benevolent economy of Christian salvation, Death, however unwelcome, does not appall, for ultimately it results in Everyman's *Salicheit*, his salvation or bliss. In the context of the Christian promise to swallow up death "into victory," death indeed loses its "sting" (1 Corinthians 15: 51–5). As Everyman suffers the death "that we all endure" (l. 888), Knowledge announces, "Now hath he made an ending" (l. 890). The Angel recognizes, however, that such a death is actually a beginning: "Now shalt thou into the heavenly sphere / Unto the which all ye shall come / That liveth well before the day of doom" (ll. 899–900). There can be no tragedy in Everyman's death if he dies into a more authentic order of being and we, with Knowledge, can "hear angels sing / And make great joy and melody / Where Everyman's soul received shall be" (ll. 891–3).

In Knowledge's lines we may possibly hear anticipatory strains of Horatio's gracious response to Prince Hamlet's death: "let flights of Angels sing him to his rest" (5.2.349); but in the contextual differences between the two we may gauge the distance between the tragic universe and Christian comedy of the morality play. In *Everyman* the song of the Angels confirms the play's movement from *tristia* to *gaudium*. In *Hamlet* the lines confirm nothing except perhaps the failure of Hamlet's promise. Not only does Horatio's humanity itself serve to differentiate his authority from that of Knowledge, but also his statement lacks the confirmation from the play that Knowledge's receives in *Everyman*. At the end of the morality the Angel assures us that Everyman has indeed entered "into the heavenly sphere." God's redemptive love has wrought comedy from tragedy. In the tragedy, however, Horatio hopes for the song of angels, but what we hear is not the angelic choir he feels should welcome Hamlet into eternity but the martial music of Fortinbras's advancing troops. "Why does the drum come hither?" asks the puzzled Horatio, and the answer lies in the logic Shakespeare has discovered, The tragedies chronicle "the way to dusty death" (*Macbeth*, 5.5.23), but they take us no further. Unlike Everyman's, the ending made by the tragic agonists is final and rending. In their consuming rhythms, the tragedies uncompromisingly insist that death still has its sting.

Shakespeare's tragedies witness to the horror and mystery of human suffering. Pain and loss remain the central tragic facts, necessarily restricting a Christian perspective which would insist "that the afflictions of this present time are not worth the glory that shall be unto us" (Romans 8: 18). The promise of an afterlife of glory would indeed lead us to say with the distracted King Lear, "If it be so, / It is a chance which does redeem all sorrows / That ever I have felt" (5.3.266–8), but Shakespeare's tragedies pointedly withhold such redeeming knowledge. Within the boundaries of tragedy, Lear's conditional can never be made declarative. *King Lear* ends, and still "All's cheerless, dark and deadly" (5.3.291).[10]

Still, few today would expect tragedy (or indeed any other literary form) to offer the full compensation of Christian redemption. "Christian salvation opposes tragic knowledge," in Karl Jaspers's famous phrase,[11] but it did not need a twentieth-century existentialist to make the point. In *Twelfth Night* Feste proves Olivia a fool for her excessive grief over her brother's death: "The more fool, madonna, to mourn for your brother's soul, being in heaven" (1.5.67–8). An eternity of bliss is indeed a more than adequate compensation for any suffering in this vale of tears. But Shakespeare's tragedies refuse even lesser consolations, and indeed in that refusal lies their power and the deepest logic of their form. Tragedy for Shakespeare is the literary genre in which suffering is not only irreparable but is also neither compensated nor even effectively consoled. Understandably, many critics would have it otherwise. If they grant that the effects of tragedy are generally irreversible, they would find meaning, even value, in the experience of human suffering based on what it teaches; though plays seem to me far less confident that anything is finally learned beyond how intensely we feel the need to make suffering seem intelligible.

In this, *King Lear*'s Edgar anticipates the responses of many of the play's readers (spectators, interestingly enough, seem less likely to indulge in the rationalization of the play's spectacle of suffering). He has, as Michael Goldman has said, a "gift for confidently formulating some principle about the uses, limits, or significance of suffering only to have it shattered by succeeding events,"[12] and the remarkable resiliency to keep applying it. On the heath he discovers in Lear's suffering affective terms that seemingly enable him to bear his own:

> When we our betters see bearing our woes,
> We scarcely think our miseries our foes.
> Who alone suffers suffers most i' th' mind,
> Leaving free things and happy shows behind;
> But then the mind much sufferance doth o'erskip
> When grief hath mates, and bearing fellowship. (3.6.100–5)

Yet this perception, which momentarily makes his pain "light and portable" (106), is immediately tested and found wanting. Edgar comes face to face with his blind and embittered father, and though his grief now "hath mates," this new "fellowship" rudely increases his "sufferance." Edgar is led to confront the world's seemingly limitless capacity to inflict pain: "I am worse than e'er I was, / And worse I may be yet. The worst is not / So long as we can say 'this is the worst'" (4.1.26–8).

Relentlessly the play demonstrates that no intellectual formulation can be equal to the tragic necessity of human suffering, yet Edgar's confidence that suffering has moral significance cannot be shaken. Again and again he seeks some new way to make tragic experience intelligible and hence bearable, successively reformulating a perspective each time the action denies him the apparent consolation just discovered. Through his rationalizations not only is he "made tame to fortune's blows" (4.6.217) but also he would lead Gloucester to submit patiently to the will of the gods. He accompanies his despairing father to a place that Gloucester takes for the cliffs at Dover, and when Gloucester finds himself alive after his supposed fall, Edgar persuades him his "life's a miracle" (4.6.55). The "great opposeless wills" of the gods (38) can be happily submitted to as the heavens are shown just and the gods "ever gentle" (213).

But, of course, it is Edgar, rather than the merciful heavens, who has saved Gloucester. "Think that the clearest gods who make them honours / Of men's impossibilities have preserved thee" (73–4), Edgar says; and the emphasis must fall on "Think." Thinking does not make it so, however comforting or even necessary the thought might be. Nothing in the play confirms Edgar's vision of the clearest gods actively participating in human history and earning for themselves "honours / Of men's impossibilities". (This is not, of course, to say that Gloucester should have been left to his despair, but rather to insist that it is imperfect human love that ameliorates it rather than the gracious action of a perfect and perfecting providence.)[13] Edgar's language reflects Christ's reply to those who asked despairingly, "And who then can be saved?": "And he said, the things that are impossible with men, are possible with God" (Luke 18: 26–7). But in the tragic world of *King Lear* "the things that are impossible with men" are no more possible for any other agency. We discover not the clearest gods who would save man but the "eyeless rage" (3.1.8) of an anarchic nature that would annihilate him.

Still Edgar will not easily abandon his conviction that the play's spectacle of suffering is proof of the retributive action of providence. "The gods are just, and of our pleasant vices / Make instruments to plague us" (5.3.171–2). To Edmund he would rationalize even his father's hideous ordeal: "The dark and vicious place where thee he got / Cost him his eyes" (173–4). Edgar insists, like so many critics of tragedy, that suffering has moral meaning, and though Edmund confirms his brother's vision ("thou hast spoken right; 'tis true"), the example Edgar chooses in fact invalidates it. Edgar argues that Gloucester's adultery merits the "extrusion," to use Dr. Johnson's revealingly self-protective Latinate word, of his eyes; and indeed an English audience might have remembered that the homily "Agaynst Whoredome and Adulterie" claimed that "among the Locrensians the adulterers had both their eyes thrust out."[14] Yet Edgar's confident moral economics are undercut by the horrible scene of Gloucester's blinding. We are made to watch as Gloucester's eyes are viciously put out, and the monstrous cruelty of Regan and Cornwall cannot easily convince us that "the gods are just." In truth, Gloucester is not blinded for his lust, but most literally for his gratuitous act of kindness towards Lear that leads Cornwall to label him a "traitor." It is not the dark and vicious place where Edward was conceived that costs Gloucester his eyes but the dark and vicious place that is the play world.

Only in the last lines of the play (at least in the Folio text) does Edgar abandon his sententious moralizing. The grim parade of death inhibits him now from offering yet another formulation of how suffering might be borne or understood.

> The weight of this sad time we must obey,
> Speak what we feel, not what we ought to say.
> The oldest hath borne most; we that are young
> Shall never see so much, nor live so long (5.3.322–5)

Time is now "sad," and even the resilient Edgar must bow beneath its crushing "weight," no longer able to express any confidence greater than that the future will never experience comparable suffering. But even this limited confidence (however much it too is unearned) is expressed in unduly reassuring couplets, imposing a formal order on an action in which truly to speak what we feel would likely be to say nothing more than Lear's reiterated howls (255).

In its most fully developed form, tragedy, as Shakespeare comes to understand it, offers nothing to reassure us about the world of mortal accidents. As Lear desperately imagines that the dead Cordelia still breathes, he admits that "If it be so, / It is a chance which does redeem all sorrows / That ever I have felt" (263–5). But the feather does not stir and Cordelia does not live. Sorrows here are not redeemed, nor are they redemptive. No reconciliation is possible or even desirable with such a universe, and Lear's death comes as a welcome relief from the world's harrowing cruelty. Perhaps predictably, Edgar urges Lear, in words that significantly echo his phrase that initiates Gloucester's reconciliation with the universe, "Look up, my Lord" (311; cf. 4.6.59); yet this time, rather than occasioning a reaffirmation of faith by the suffering monarch, the line elicits Kent's rebuke: "Vex not his ghost; O, let him pass. He hates him / That would upon the rack of this tough world / Stretch him out longer" (312–14). In a merciless world the only mercy is to be allowed to leave it. The best we can say is that the destructive action comes to an end.

Critics, however, have regularly said more. The destructive action, we are told, instructs, even refines. In the spectacle of suffering reside the most profound truths of the human condition. Indeed, it is tragedy's presumed ethical intelligibility and utility that have inevitably served as the basis of its cultural prestige. We learn from its dreadful spectacle. Thus Sidney (who did know the *Poetics*)[15] tells us in *The Defence of Poesy* that tragedy "maketh kings fear to be tyrants, and tyrants manifest their tyrannical humours; that, with stirring the affects of admiration and commiseration, teacheth the uncertainty of this world, and upon how weak foundations gilden roofs are builded."[16] But the value (and the perplexing pleasure) of tragedy surely does not lie in its didactic impact, and in any case the humbling lessons of "the uncertainty of this world" are inevitably taught more memorably out of the theatre than in it. Indeed, one might say that for Shakespeare this kind of moralizing is more likely to be the bitter cause of tragedy than its reassuring effect. Tragedy would be far less harrowing if it were certain that humane truths can be learned by experiencing it.

Not unreasonably, one still might point precisely to *King Lear* for evidence that suffering does instruct and ennoble. Indeed, Lear comes to see in Poor Tom's ostentatious poverty a poignant sign of "how this world goes" (4.6.143–4), and if Tom's suffering is but mimed, it is nonetheless part of the process that leads Lear not only to recognize the moral challenge of the world's unmistakable disparities of wealth and power but also and more importantly to see them as signs not of an immutable social order but of an intolerable social injustice. The means of amelioration rest not with Heaven but with sympathetic human action. Those with a surplus of wealth must shake "the superflux" to provide for those in need, and that alone will "show the heavens more just" (3.4.35–6). "Distribution," as Gloucester says, "should undo excess / And each man have enough" (4.1.73–4).

Yet the sympathy Lear discovers to animate his leveling depends upon an experience the play insists is unique ("we that are young / Shall never see so much"). As Jonathan Dollimore writes, "in a world where pity is the prerequisite for compassionate action, where a king has to share the suffering of his subjects in order to 'care,' the majority will remain poor, naked and wretched."[17] But perhaps even more disturbing is that Lear's painfully learned compassion is so easily left behind as the tragic action appallingly intensifies. In a lacerating fifth act where so much that has happened before can either be dismissed, like the announcement of Edmund's death that is "but a trifle here" (5.3.294), or be temporarily lost to memory, like Albany's astonishing "Great thing of us forgot" (235) at the belated mention of King Lear, Lear's utopian social vision is itself abandoned without a second thought in the final agon. If the tragic experience indeed improved its sufferers, one might say of tragedy itself, as the gentleman does of Cordelia, that "Sorrow would be a rarity most beloved / If all could so become it" (4.3.23–4). But tragic suffering neither instructs nor improves; at best it numbs.

Lear dies with no final recognition. In the 1608 Quarto text Lear distractedly says "pray you vndo / This button, thank you sir, O, o, o, o" and then successfully wills his own death: "Breake hart, I prethe, breake" (sig. L4r). In the 1623 Folio text, before he dies he seemingly has some insight that he wishes to share: "Do you see this? Looke on her! looke her lips, / Looke there, looke there" (5.3.309–10; TLN 3282–3). But whatever he thinks he sees he is unable clearly to communicate, and if, as Bradley thought,[18] he dies in joy convinced Cordelia is alive, the terrible fact of her death, terrible both for the survivors and for the audience or readers of the play, must mock the idea that tragic suffering leads to knowledge (Aristotle's *anagnorisis*). The Folio ending is arguably darker than the Quarto version. The Quarto's exhausted Lear is replaced in the Folio by a hallucinatory one. In "the false anagnorisis at the end," as A. D. Nuttall sees, "Shakespeare makes his rejection of the final, classical insight completely inescapable."[19]

If Aristotle's theory of tragedy, especially in Sidney's neo-Aristotelian version, is based on its culturally stabilizing, even reforming, capacity, Shakespeare's a- (if not, as Nuttall would have it, anti-) Aristotelian tragic practice is far less comforting. It tells us that loss may teach nothing but the unspeakable murderousness of the world. If the endings of these plays display some form of the conventional tragic pattern in which the destruction of the hero is followed by some social or spiritual reintegration of the society, they are in these plays less a sign of what has been, however painfully, learned, than a mere acknowledgment that the catastrophic conclusion is not the "promised end" but merely the "image of that horror" (*King Lear*, 5.3.261–2). As metaphoric rather than actual apocalypse the ending cannot help but acknowledge human duration. Raymond Williams, in his attack upon the unconsidered individualism of post-Enlightenment Europe, insists that tragedy is not merely the story of "what happens to the hero" but is as much "what happens through the hero." But Shakespeare, anyway, is less interested in what survives the tragic agon than this suggests. Surely Williams is right that "Life does come back, life ends the play, again and again," but Shakespeare's tragedies offer little optimism about what "meanings are reaffirmed and restored."[20] What future is acknowledged by the plays offers little in the way of affirmation, only time (admittedly itself some consolation) "to have more talk of these sad things" (*Romeo and Juliet*, 5.3.307; cf. *Othello*, 5.2.370–1, where Lodovico announces his intention to head "straight abroad," that he may "to the state / This heavy act with heavy heart relate").

The conclusions of the tragedies quickly tie up the tragic matter and cast our attention back on the destructive events. Even in *Romeo and Juliet*, although the "ancient grudge" (Prologue, 3) has ended, our focus is not on the time of peace that is now at hand but on the disheartening action just concluded. Of course it is true that the doomed lovers "with their death bury their parents' strife" (8), but the play denies this accord restorative force. In addition to his son, Montague's "wife is dead tonight" (5.3.210), and the elder Capulet has lost his only child. At the end of act 1, Juliet's father had lamented that "Earth hath swallowed all my hopes but she" (1.2.14), but by the end of the play earth will cruelly swallow even this "hopeful lady" (15). The feud ends, then, not because the killing logic of hatred has been learned and eschewed, but because no one is left alive to continue it. Even the families' joint gesture of peace is at best valedictory rather than restorative; dumb, golden statues stand mockingly in place of the "quick, bright things [that have] come to confusion" (*A Midsummer Night's Dream*, 1.1.149). "Some shall be pardon'd, and some punished" (5.3.308), we are assured by the Duke, but no convincing principles of justice and responsibility have been discovered that might permit the reparatory actions of the state to seem particularly reassuring. And the final couplet rounds off the action and again fixes our attention back upon the tragic lovers: "For never was a story of more woe / Than this of Juliet and her Romeo" (309–10).

Some, however, have even found considerable consolation in this contraction and enclosure. Murray Krieger, for example, has argued that the tragedies' centripetal energy "brings us the assurances of form, presents its form, presents its formal order as a token, a security — something given in hand — to guarantee the cosmic order beyond the turbulence it has conquered."[21] But perhaps, as the broken rhythms of

Krieger's sentence might themselves suggest, there is something desperate in this assertion; it is almost literally whistling in the dark. Tragedy – at least tragedy as Shakespeare writes it – offers no convincing guarantees of an ultimately sustaining and reassuring order, either cosmic or civic. And in this his tragedies reveal how poorly they satisfy the theoretical conception of Aristotle, for whom even the most appalling examples of human self-destructiveness reveal an intelligibility that is ultimately ethical and "reclaimable for the polis."[22]

Shakespeare accepts, then tests and finally extends (perhaps even, explodes) the conventional understanding of tragedy, discovering its deepest logic precisely in the refusal of its offered consolations and exploring the necessary formal response to that understanding. The earliest tragedies – *Titus Andronicus* and *Romeo and Juliet* – are, in a radical sense, Shakespeare's masterpieces; the young playwright displays his mastery over inherited forms, declaring his ability to rework recognizable classical models, one Senecan, one Ovidian, into compelling contemporary plays. *Titus* is explicitly a classical play, an early example of Shakespeare's several explorations of Rome and *Romanitas*, but here in its most grotesque aspect. These Romans speak the familiar language of classical virtue and stoic self-control, but their actions display uncontrollable passions and an often hideous injustice; they are too much like the Goths they see as their enemies and opposites for "great Rome" (5.1.2) to be more than a tattered ideal. No play has more appalling images of human cruelty. Dr. Johnson lamented "the barbarity of the spectacles,"[23] but clearly they are exactly what Shakespeare insists we see. "*Enter . . . Lavinia, her hands cut off and her tongue cut out, and ravished* (2.3.0s.d.); *Enter a messenger with two heads and a hand*" (3.1.234s.d.); severed limbs, hands and heads, and "pasties" (5.2.189) made of human flesh, create the visual texture of the play's nightmare world. Bodies are "lopped and hewed" (2.4.17), just as the state itself is "By uproars severed" (5.3.67). But the real nightmare is that moral difference dissolves in the play's hideous rhythms of revenge. With the exception of the pitiable Lavinia, victims become tormentors in turn. Aaron may be a "ravenous tiger" (5.3.5), no less than is Tamora (195), but Rome itself, however much it imagines itself a bulwark against rapacious nature, reveals its moral kinship with what it loathes and fears. Rome is not the source and defender of civilized value but is itself "a wilderness of tigers" (3.1.54).

The play's gruesome spectacle provokes another of tragedy's anguished questions about a natural order that would permit such barbarism: "O why should nature build so foul a den, / Unless the gods delight in tragedy" (4.1.58–9), laments Marcus. And the limited restoration at the end offers no answer. The conventional culminating gestures of renewal are conspicuously muted here. In a hasty valedictory the new emperor, Lucius, assigns the Roman dead to their respective family monuments, and only finds a compelling voice in the final four lines as he denies Tamora funeral rites: "No mournful bell shall ring her burial, / But throw her forth to beasts and birds to prey: / Her life was beastly and devoid of pity, / And being dead, let birds on her take pity" (5.3.198–9). In the final two lines the awkward repetition of "pity," where one might expect a rhyme, accentuates pity's absence from the play and denies the ending even the limited formal satisfaction of a concluding couplet. As with the Romans and the Goths themselves, identity where one expects difference, disturbs.

Titus, in many ways, anticipates the fully realized pattern of the tragedies. Its grim spectacle of suffering is inadequately balanced by the small gathering of survivors at the end who, however determinedly, at most can punish but not prevent the atrocities of the play world. If this modestly recuperative ending is meant to be "a reflection of a more just moral and political order,"[24] it is a distressingly pale one, arguably only a little less unnerving in its smug ineffectuality than the hideous actions which have preceded it.

Play after play repeats this pattern. *Romeo and Juliet*, as we have seen, offers a more fully articulate effort to salvage something from the ruins of wasted lives, but its vision of renewed social harmony is finally no more satisfying than *Titus*'s concluding vision of remorseless hate. Neither play allows us to find in its images of continuity anything that will compensate us for what has been lost. *Macbeth*, however, is perhaps the most obvious exception to my generalization about the nature of Shakespeare's tragic structures. The end of the play indeed seems to establish a compelling restoration not merely of lineal right but of moral right as well. The destructive course of Macbeth's life is revealed, in De Quincey's phrase, as an "awful parenthesis" in the orderly progress of time. Malcolm's coronation restores the line of Duncan, ending the period of Macbeth's unnatural rule, and once again "the time is free" (5.8.55). Apparently this is a world in which "things" can indeed "climb upward / To what they were before" (4.2.24–5).

But such an upward climb would reverse the tragic trajectory, and *Macbeth* will itself refuse the desire to turn its action into a moral and political romance. This is, however, a desire given voice by the moral characters of the play. For them, the action is a reassuring demonstration of the resiliency of the natural order. They return to Scotland "to dew the sovereign flower and drown the weeds" (5.2.30), to purge aberrant evil and reestablish natural right. "March we on," says Caithness, "To give obedience where it is truly owed: / Meet we the med'cine of the sickly weal; / And with him pour we, in our country's purge, / Each drop of us" (25–9). For them, the action of the play is curative, but if that is indeed what the arc of the play defines, *Macbeth* hardly seems a tragedy at all. If we accept the understanding of the invading Scottish lords, the action is, in its transparent justness and seeming inevitability, a homiletic warning in an ultimately comic form.

But Macbeth is a tragedy; it is not the triumph of the moral world that compels us but the fall of the immoral Macbeth. The moral world sees nothing remarkable in his fearful actions, imaginatively reducing Macbeth in size so it can apply its conventional, though necessary, judgments. Angus insists at their approach to Macbeth's castle, "now does he feel his title / Hang loose upon him, like a giant's robe / Upon a dwarfish thief" (20–2). The proffered comic structure of the play with its orthodox moral teleology would insist that Angus is right, but the play gives us a Macbeth who resists even the transparent reasonableness of the moral judgments. Macbeth is no dwarf, but a giant, even in his callous brutality. When he is confronted by young

Siward, it is not the youth's innocence or goodness that thrills but Macbeth's gigantic presence. After his challenge on the battlefield, admittedly the boy does not shrink from Macbeth's terrifying identification, "My name's Macbeth" (5.7.7); but Siward is swiftly dispatched, and his opposition seems more callow than noble, more preposterous than sublime.

Siward's death is given a conventional valediction. His father is assured that his son died "like a man" (5.8.43). The boy, he is told, received his fatal wounds "on the front," and the father completes the line: "Why then, God's soldier be he" (5.8.47). Metrically and morally all is neatly settled. But not least in the ease with which Old Siward accepts his son's death (even Malcolm admits "He's worth more sorrow"), the play asks more searching questions about what it means to live or die "like a man."[25] Lady Macbeth has urged Macbeth to murder by challenging his manliness, and, though Macbeth asserts his willingness only to do "all that may become a man" (1.7.46), he transgresses those boundaries so he might become in her eyes "so much more the man" (51). Macbeth urges the murderers to act against Banquo by appealing to their sense of manliness (3.1.90–1). And, lest this be thought only the perverse misconstruction that produces the play's criminality, Malcolm similarly reforms Macduff's more humane conception of masculinity by turning his tears for his slaughtered family into the desire for revenge. "Dispute it like a man," Malcolm says; and he receives the appropriate rebuke from the grieving husband and father: "But I must also feel it like a man" (4.3.221). Nonetheless, in fewer than ten lines Macduff is led to "let grief / Convert to anger" (228–9), and, with his resolve to march against Macbeth, he is assured by Malcolm that "This tune goes manly" (235).

In the harsh world of the play, to be a man is to kill and be willing to be killed. If the play would humanize the definition by insisting that the cause for which one risks one's life or takes one matters, it also disturbingly blurs the very differences its stark morality demands. In part the play's resistance to its moral construction lies in the difficulty of discovering where "obedience . . . is truly owed." Nothing should be simpler. Macduff seemingly clarifies the issue, if it needs clarification, by calling Macbeth an "untitled tyrant bloody sceptred" (4.3.104), but, however bloody his scepter, Macbeth is, as Macduff knows well, *titled*. Although Macbeth is undeniably a murderer, he lawfully succeeds and is crowned. "Tis most like the sovereignty will fall upon Macbeth," observes Ross; and Macduff responds: "He is already named and gone to Scone / To be invested" (2.4.29–32). "Named" and "invested," Macbeth is legally king, and at least by the absolutist logic of King James's own imperial political philosophy, Macbeth is "truly owed" at least the passive obedience of his countrymen.[26]

But the complex political issues, perhaps of interest today more to historians than to literary critics or playgoers, find their parallel in the play's moral design, where again seeming right disturbingly blurs. Duncan's gracious sovereignty is set against Macbeth's willful brutality, but Duncan's rule depends upon – indeed demands – Macbeth's violence. The unexplained revolt that begins the play is put down by Macbeth's ferocious defense of Duncan's authority. Violent disruption is violently repaired. Certainly we are to distinguish Macbeth killing *for* the king from Macbeth's killing *of* the king. Killing for the king marks Macbeth as "valiant," a "worthy gentleman" (1.2.24); killing the king marks Macbeth as monstrous, an "abhorred tyrant" (5.7.11). But from the first the play undoes even these apparently unassailable oppositions, obscuring easy distinctions that would legitimize the state's monopoly on violence. Not merely does Macbeth's merciless treatment of "the merciless Macdonwald" (1.2.9) confound the crucial difference, but also the unanchored pronouns that literally confuse the two. Macbeth carves "out his passage"

> Till he faced the slave
> Which ne'er shook hands, nor bade farewell to him,
> Till he unseamed him from the nave to th' chops,
> And fixed his head upon our battlements. (1.2.20–3)

Only "our battlements" is clearly differentiated; the referents of the third person singular pronouns are as "doubtful" as the battle itself that the captain reports. All that is "fixed" is the head of a rebel.

Hero and villain, as Harry Berger has ingeniously demonstrated,[27] are throughout unnervingly intertwined and indistinguishable, as in the captain's image of the rebel troops and the king's forces as "two spent swimmers, that do cling together" (28). In the battle Macbeth fights bravely, but textual density and syntactic ambiguity uncannily dislocate his loyalties. Duncan "reads / [Macbeth's] personal venture in the rebels' fight" (1.3.91); he "finds [Macbeth] in the stout Norweyan ranks" (95). Macbeth confronts the invading King of Norway, who is "assisted by that most disloyal traitor / The Thane of Cawdor" (1.2.53–4), not with the certain authority of Duncan, "clear in his great office" (1.7.18), but only with confusing "self-comparisons, / Point against point, rebellious arm 'gainst arm" (1.2.56–7).

Though the play in part does insist upon stark moral distinctions to animate its moral comedy, it then carefully undoes them to make the play a tragedy. Malcolm and Macduff insist to the end that the action is reparative. Evil has been defeated and right triumphantly reestablished. Malcolm points proudly to "this dead butcher and his fiend-like Queen" (5.9.35) and ends inviting all assembled "to see us crowned at Scone" (41). But the assurances and the affirmations of the end are Malcolm's, not the play's. Certainly the play insists upon a more complex understanding of Macbeth and his Lady, both too sensitive in their awareness of evil to be reducible to the moral cartoon of Malcolm's judgment. And the action ends with unsettling echoes of its beginning: with an attack upon established rule from disloyal nobles and a foreign army, with the victorious nobility rewarded with new titles, and with the execution of a rebellious Thane of Cawdor. Malcolm is three times hailed as king exactly as Macbeth had been by the witches. Perhaps this is renewal, but it sounds too much like repetition. Maybe, as Malcolm would have it, the nation has been returned to moral and political health or maybe all that has happened is the establishment of the conditions for a new round of temptation and disorder (as in Roman Polanski's 1971 film of the play, which ends with Malcolm's brother, Donalbain, going off to seek the witches and his own crown, or, indeed, as in the chronicles themselves, where the historical Donal Bane turned rebel, allying himself with the King of Norway, killing Malcolm's son and successfully claiming the throne).

The play ends with a vision of futurity that is too weak to prevent Macbeth's reality from dominating what we have witnessed. Perhaps the moral world succeeds more impressively than it does in *Titus*, *Romeo and Juliet*, or *Othello*, but it never exerts a more powerful claim on our interests and sympathies than that over which it triumphs. Benedetto Croce acutely observed that "in *Macbeth*, the good appears only as the revenge taken by the good, as remorse, as punishment."[28] It is incapable of wresting attention or concern from Macbeth's tragic course. At the end of the play even Macbeth knows that his defeat is necessary and desirable, but although we share that knowledge morally, our dramatic distance from it is measured in that, if we inevitably feel relief at his defeat, we are never able truly to rejoice in the victory of his enemies. Though theatrical superstition insists on referring to the play as "The Scottish Play," it is pointedly the tragedy of Macbeth. "To the end," as Bradley observed, "he never totally loses our sympathy;"[29] and no less true is that to the end Malcolm never totally gains it. Even, then, in its unusual manner, *Macbeth* confirms the tragic pattern, tempting us with a restorative vision that it makes us refuse, forcing us to face frontally, as Macbeth himself must do, the terrible image of what he has become.

For Shakespeare, tragedy will not easily give way to the efforts to deny it. In its endings, the exhausted survivors will inevitably seek to convince themselves that the tragedy has not only passed but also that its causes have been banished and the experience has at least taught worthy lessons. But the plays insist that tragedy is something far less reassuring, as the most seemingly reassuring of them, *Macbeth*, makes us see. Tragedy tells us that human cruelty is terrible and its consequences are not easily contained. This is not to say that the vision of such a world where suffering is seemingly inevitable and where nothing is offered as effective compensation or consolation is true; it is only to say that such a vision is tragic.

A coda: this understanding of tragedy may explain something about both *Coriolanus* and *Timon of Athens* that has generally been seen as a limitation of those two late plays. After the metaphysical density and poetic richness of the so-called "great" tragedies, the harshness of these two classical plays often has been taken as evidence of a decline in Shakespeare's artistic powers or, less judgmentally, of a change in his conception of tragedy. But it seems to me that in their stylistic severity these two plays uncompromisingly display the fullest extension of Shakespeare's tragic understanding into the drama. If a play like *King Lear* devastatingly refuses any of the consolations it seemingly offers, from the happy ending promised by the historical material to the resignation that would at least leave Lear and Cordelia together "like birds i' the cage" (5.3.9), it still offers its readers and playgoers the not inconsiderable consolation of its remarkable artistic control, what Henry James called "the redemptive power of form." The old conundrum about the pleasure of tragedy is answered by recognizing not only, as Samuel Johnson saw, that it "proceeds from our consciousness of fiction"[30] but also that the fiction itself shows, in A. D. Nuttall's words, "the worst we can imagine ennobled by form."[31] But the two late classical plays refuse even that. Pushing the logic of tragedy as far as it can go, they insist that we witness the disintegration of their heroes without the ennobling comforts of Shakespeare's poetic imagination seemingly in play; they refuse even the consolations of art.

NOTES

1   For the Hegelian A. C. Bradley (1991), it was only these four plays that fully realized the characteristics of "pure tragedy" (p. 21), the representation of a world "travailing for perfection, but bringing to birth, together with glorious good, and evil which it is able to overcome only by self-torture and self-waste" (p. 51); see pp. 23–51.
2   Knutson (1998: 260).
3   Meres, *Palladis Tamia* (London, 1598), sig. OO2r.
4   The conceptualization of the subgenre was not, of course, completely dependent upon the Folio's practice. "History," of course, already appears as one of the genres personified in the Induction to *Warning For Fair Women* in 1598. But prior to the Folio it would be difficult to discover a widespread and coherent principle of generic definition.
5   Pleynet (1968), esp. pp. 94–126; for a valuable overview of Shakespeare's generic understanding, see Danson (2000).
6   For a useful survey of what ideas might have been available to Shakespeare and his contemporaries, see Kelly (1993). For a valuable selection of modern theorizations, see Drakakis and Liebler (1998).
7   See Bernard Weinberg's magisterial *A History of Literary Criticism in the Italian Renaissance* (1961), esp. chapter 9, "The Tradition of Aristotle's *Poetics*: I. Discovery and Exegesis," vol. 1, pp. 349–423.
8   Book II, Prose 2, 70–2; Robinson (1957: 331).
9   Muir (1972: 12).
10 For a fuller account of the formal characteristics of Shakespeare's tragedies, and from which some paragraphs here have been borrowed, see Kastan (1982), esp. pp. 79–101.
11 Jaspers (1952: 38). In the mid-twentieth century there was much discussion of the tensions between tragedy and Christian thought; see, for example, Laurence Michel's "The Possibility of Christian Tragedy" (1956: 403–28). Recent theorists of tragedy have largely been uninterested in the question, presumably as the incompatibility seems so apparent. But for an age in which religious thought was so central, even as the Reformation fractured the sense of security that it might offer, tragedy must have been viewed in some relation to the belief in a just and merciful God, if only as a heuristic model of an existence in God's absence.
12 Goldman (1972: 99).
13 For an important discussion of the relation of the imperfections of love to the play's notion of tragedy, see Stanley Cavell's brilliant "The Avoidance of Love", in his *Must We Mean What We Say* (1976): 267–353.
14 *Certain Sermons and Homilies Appointed to be Read in Churches* (1908: 137).
15 For an account of Sidney's familiarity with Aristotle, see Buxton (1964: 72).
16 Duncan-Jones (1989: 230).
17 Dollimore (1984: 191).
18 Bradley (1991: 291).
19 Nuttall (1996: 97).
20 Williams, "Modern Tragedy," in Drakakis and Liebler (1998: 155–6).

21 Krieger (1973: 4).

22 The phrase is Adam Phillips's in a review of Jonathan Lear, *Open-Minded: Working out the Logic of the Soul* (1998), first published in *The London Review of Books* and reprinted in his *Promises, Promises: Essays on Psychoanalysis and Literature* (2000: 172).

23 Woudhuysen (1989: 223).

24 Mehl (1986: 19).

25 On the play's complex construction of masculinity, see Adelman (1992: 130–47); and Kimbrough (1983: 175–90). There have been, of course, numerous studies of the centrality of the definition of manhood to the play, one of the earliest and most influential being Waith (1950: 262–73).

26 James had argued "very strongly and expresly against butchering euen of Tyrannical Kings" in his *Trew Law of Free Monarchies*, in McIlwain (1918: 64). For a fuller account of the complex politics of the play, see Kastan (1999: 165–82).

27 Berger (1997: 70–97); first published as "The Early Scenes of *Macbeth*: Preface to a New Interpretation", *ELH*, 47 (1980): 1–31.

28 Croce (1920: 229).

29 Bradley (1991: 305).

30 "[I]f we thought murders and treasons real, they would please no more," Johnson adds; in his "Preface to the Edition of Shakespeare's Plays" (1765), in Woudhuysen (1989: 136).

31 Nuttall (1996: 99).

REFERENCES AND FURTHER READING

Adelman, J. (1992). *Suffocating Mothers: Fantasies of Maternal Origin in Shakespeare's Plays, "Hamlet" to "The Tempest."* New York: Routledge.

Bayley, J. (1981). *Shakespeare and Tragedy*. London: Routledge and Kegan Paul.

Belsey, C. (1985). *The Subject of Tragedy: Identity and Difference in Renaissance Drama*. London: Methuen.

Berger, H. (1997). *Making Trifles of Terrors: Redistributing Complicities in Shakespeare*. Stanford, CA: Stanford University Press.

Bradbrook, M. C. (1952). *Themes and Conventions of Elizabethan Tragedy*. Cambridge: Cambridge University Press.

Bradley, A. C. (1991) [1904]. *Shakespearean Tragedy*. Harmondsworth: Penguin Books.

Buxton, J. (1964). *Sir Philip Sidney and the English Renaissance*. London: Macmillan.

Cavell, S. (1976). The Avoidance of Love. In *Must We Mean What We Say*. Cambridge: Cambridge University Press, 267–353.

Croce, B. (1920). *Ariosto, Shakespeare, and Corneille*, trans. D. Ainslie. New York: Holt.

Cunningham, J. V. (1951). *Woe or Wonder: The Emotional Effect of Shakespearean Tragedy*. Denver, CO: University of Denver Press.

Danson, L. (2000). *Shakespeare's Dramatic Genres*. Oxford: Oxford University Press.

Dollimore, J. (1984). *Radical Tragedy: Religion, Ideology and Power in the Drama of Shakespeare and his Contemporaries*. Brighton: Harvester.

Doran, M. (1954). *The Endeavors of Art: A Study of Form in Elizabethan Drama*. Madison: University of Wisconsin Press.

Drakakis, J. and Liebler, N. C. (eds.) (1998). *Tragedy*. London: Longman.

Duncan-Jones, K. (ed.) (1989). *Sir Philip Sidney: A Critical Edition of the Major Works*. Oxford: Oxford University Press.

Eagleton, T. (2003). *Sweet Violence: The Idea of the Tragic*. Oxford: Blackwell.

Eliot, T. S. (1932) [1927]. Shakespeare and the Stoicism of Seneca. In *Selected Essays, 1917–32*. London: Faber and Faber.

Everett, B. (1989). *Young Hamlet: Essays on Shakespeare's Tragedies*. Oxford: Clarendon Press.

Frye, N. (1967). *Fools of Time: Studies in Shakespearean Tragedy.* Toronto: University of Toronto Press.

Goldman, M. (1972). *Shakespeare and the Energies of Drama.* Princeton, NJ: Princeton University Press.

Jaspers, K. (1952). *Tragedy is Not Enough*, trans. K. W. Deutsch. Boston, MA: Beacon Press.

Johnson, S. (1989). *Samuel Johnson on Shakespeare*, ed. H. R. Woudhuysen. Harmondsworth: Penguin Books.

Kastan, D. S. (1982). *Shakespeare and the Shapes of Time.* London: Macmillan.

—— (1999). *Shakespeare After Theory.* New York: Routledge.

Kelly, H. A. (1993). *Ideas and Forms of Tragedy from Aristotle to the Middle Ages.* Cambridge: Cambridge University Press.

Kimbrough, R. (1983). Macbeth: The Prisoner of Gender. *Shakespeare Studies*, 16, 9, 175–90.

Knutson, R. L. (1988). Influence of the Repertory System on the Revival and Revision of *The Spanish Tragedy* and *Dr. Faustus. English Literary Review*, 18, 260.

Krieger, M. (1973) [1960]. *The Tragic Vision.* Baltimore, MD: Johns Hopkins University Press.

Liebler, N. C. (1995). *Shakespeare's Festive Tragedies: The Ritual Foundation of Genre.* London: Routledge.

Long, M. (1976). *The Unnatural Scene: A Study in Shakespearean Tragedy.* London: Methuen.

McIlwain, C. H. (ed.) (1918). *Political Works of James I.* Cambridge, MA: Harvard University Press.

Mans, K. (1995). *Inwardness and Theater in the English Renaissance.* Chicago, IL: University of Chicago Press.

Mehl, D. (1986). *Shakespeare's Tragedies: An Introduction.* Cambridge: Cambridge University Press.

Michel, L. (1956). The Possibility of Christian Tragedy. *Thought*, 31, 403–28.

Miola, R. S. (1992). *Shakespeare and Classical Tragedy.* Oxford: Clarendon Press.

Muir, K. (1972). *Shakespeare's Tragic Sequence.* London: Hutchinson.

Neill, M. (1997). *Issues of Death: Mortality and Identity in the Drama of Shakespeare and his Contemporaries.* Oxford: Clarendon Press.

Nuttall, A. D. (1996). *Why Does Tragedy Give Pleasure?* Oxford: Clarendon Press.

Phillips, A. (2000). *Promises, Promises: Essays on Psychoanalysis and Literature.* London: Faber and Faber.

Pleynet, M. (1968). *Théorie d'ensemble.* Paris: Seuil.

Poole, A. (1987). *Tragedy: Shakespeare and the Greek Example.* Oxford: Blackwell.

Reiss, T. (1980). *Tragedy and Truth: Studies in the Development of a Renaissance and Neo-classical Discourse.* New Haven, CT: Yale University Press.

Robinson, F. N. (ed.) (1957). *The Works of Geoffrey Chaucer*, 2nd edn. Boston, MA: Houghton Mifflin.

Snyder, S. (1979). *The Comic Matrix of Shakespeare's Tragedies.* Princeton, NJ: Princeton University Press.

Waith, E. (1950). Manhood and Valour in Two Shakespearean Tragedies. *English Literary History*, 17, 262–73.

Watson, R. (1994). *The Rest is Silence: Death as Annihilation in the English Renaissance.* Berkeley: University of California Press.

Weinberg, B. (1961). *A History of Literary Criticism in the Italian Renaissance*, 2 vols. Chicago, IL: University of Chicago Press.

Woudhuysen, H. R. (ed.) (1989). *Samuel Johnson on Shakespeare.* London: Penguin Books.

2

The Tragedies of Shakespeare's Contemporaries

Martin Coyle

I

Shakespeare's great tragedies – *Hamlet, Othello, King Lear, Macbeth, Coriolanus*, and *Antony and Cleopatra* – belong to the period around 1600–8. No tragedies which we consider great by anyone else have survived from those years. There were other dramatists writing tragedies during this time – Ben Jonson, *Sejanus, his Fall* (1603), John Marston, *Antonio's Revenge* (1604), George Chapman, *The Revenge of Bussy d'Ambois* (1604) – but none of these has ever replaced or seriously rivaled *Hamlet*, for example, in terms of critical attention. It is as if, for a number of years, the stage was simply overwhelmed by Shakespeare.[1] The question of Shakespeare's contemporaries, however, as might be expected, is a good deal more intriguing than this summary account suggests.

In terms of tragedy, Shakespeare's key contemporaries were Thomas Kyd, Christopher Marlowe, Thomas Middleton, and John Webster. Kyd and Marlowe belong to the 1590s (Kyd died in 1594, Marlowe in 1593), the period of *Titus Andronicus* and *Romeo and Juliet*, while Middleton, like Webster, was writing between 1602 and 1624, the period of the major tragedies, but also going on beyond them. As has often been noted, Kyd and Marlowe made Renaissance tragedy possible, changing the uninspiring drama of the 1580s into something new, at once exciting and daring. Middleton and Webster, like Jonson, Marston, Chapman, Thomas Heywood, John Ford, John Dekker, Francis Beaumont, and John Fletcher, were as much Shakespeare's rivals as contemporaries, competing for the same audience. Like Shakespeare, they were influenced by Kyd and Marlowe, but they were also influenced by Shakespeare. This in part explains why the relationship between the tragic dramatists of the Renaissance is a more complex matter than initially seems the case, something that becomes apparent if we look at the way in which the plays themselves engage in a discussion about the nature of tragedy as a genre. Indeed, Renaissance drama is perhaps best seen as constantly in the process of constructing a poetics of tragedy rather than as having any single notion of tragic form.

It is a "poetics," however, that differs markedly from the abstract theorizing of Sidney's *Defence of Poesie* (1595) where he writes of how tragedy

> openeth the greatest wounds, and showeth forth the ulcers that are covered with tissue; that maketh Kinges feare to be Tyrants, and . . . that, with sturring the affects of admiration and commiseration, teacheth the uncertainety of this world. (Watson 1997: 105)

Sidney offers one view of what tragedy might be. But the plays themselves, both implicitly and explicitly, debate their knowledge of the genre. We can see this in *Hamlet*, in Polonius's description of the traveling actors:

> The best actors in the world, either for tragedy, comedy, history, pastoral, pastoral-comical, historical-pastoral, tragical-historical, tragical-comical-historical-pastoral, scene individable, or poem unlimited. (2.2.392–5)[2]

Going beyond Sidney's definition, Polonius's description suggests that tragedy is as much a performance as a genre, a part of the established and expected repertoire of actors. But it also suggests that the boundaries between types of play are unfixed; that what, at one moment, is tragedy might become historical or pastoral, and that what is serious can be switched in an instant into something else. The most disturbing examples of this kind of switching are perhaps Iago's asides in *Othello*, where the audience may be unsure how to respond to his cynicism. But switching works in various other ways, too. At a structural level, we can instance the use of multiple plots for changing perspective, as in Middleton's *The Changeling*, or the interpolation of comic scenes in *Doctor Faustus*, while at a textual level there is the interrogative pastiche of *The Revenger's Tragedy* and its macabre dressing up of the dead.

Some of the most illuminating insights into the unfixed nature of Renaissance drama have been provided by Steven Mullaney in *The Place of the Stage* (1988). Mullaney's particular topic is the significance of the location of the theatres in the marginal space of the Liberties, outside the city of London, a place "where the contradictions of the community – its incontinent hopes, fears, and desires – were prominently and dramatically set on stage" (p. viii). More specifically, Mullaney speaks of how for John Stow, a sixteenth-century antiquarian and surveyor, London was "a palimpsest of the many who [had] lived and died within its confines" (p. 15). Throughout his analysis Mullaney returns to this idea of London as a palimpsest, as a text that is overlaid with ceremonies and rituals but also crisscrossed by the changing economic world transforming it. Tragedy and its central figure, I suggest, are not unlike the stage Mullaney describes, constantly overlaid with motifs, new signs, and new values in a shifting world where drama is reinventing itself as part of a burgeoning leisure industry and competing with other forms of popular entertainment such as bear-baiting.

One further implication of Mullaney's thesis is that Renaissance drama cannot readily escape its own historical conditions. He implies, without stating as much, that the plays are occasional rather than universal, that they belong to their particular historical moment. This, of course, runs counter to the familiar notion of tragedy as timeless and universal. It also suggests that we should not confuse the ability of later ages to respond to texts with the notion that there is something of great matter in tragedy, something outlasting its moment. That we think of tragedy in this way is prompted by the fact that it focuses upon that most universal of concerns: death. In that sense tragedy does, indeed, dramatize an issue of no small significance. But, paradoxically, death is also, as Michael Neill (1997: 13–22) observes, something insignificant, something that has no form, no essence. Death, as Hamlet says, is common (1.2.74), but through tragedy, as well as through rituals such as funerals and other representations, we invest it with a rich array of cultural meanings as if to limit its power or to give it a significance other than that which we fear most – that it has no meaning except itself.[3]

These paradoxes are foregrounded in Renaissance drama in various ways as it debates and discusses tragedy. They are so because, as Neill and Mullaney suggest, in the shifting, changing world of sixteenth- and seventeenth-century England, it is no longer possible to deal with death in a simple fashion. More specifically, it is no longer possible to contain the significance of death within the old religious, institutional framework. New ideas, new doubts, and new uncertainties undo the thinking that surrounds death and, with it, tragedy. The effect of Renaissance drama is thus to offer us a kaleidoscope of views about death and tragedy in which atheism jostles with bourgeois sentimentality, violence with philosophical speculation, the public with the private, and the grotesque with the comic and absurd. It is a drama that confronts the familiar issue of death in a much more fluid, open way, one that we misrepresent for the sake of coherence if we isolate Shakespeare for solitary consideration.

II

Much of what I have said so far can be summed up in the figure of Christopher Marlowe. Atheist, over-reacher, perhaps gay, Marlowe is the epitome of the new intellectual free-thinker and poet–dramatist. That image of the aspiring Renaissance figure is present in the opening of *Tamburlaine* (1587), but there is also something more than this in the language:

> From jigging veins of rhyming mother-wits,
> And such conceits as clownage keeps in pay,
> We'll lead you to the stately tent of war,

Where you shall hear the Scythian Tamburlaine
Threatening the world with high astounding terms,
And scourging kingdoms with his conquering sword.
View but his picture in this tragic glass,
And then applaud his fortunes as you please.
(The First Part of *Tamburlaine the Great*, Prologue)[4]

The lines self-consciously announce a new play: a tragedy, but also a history of war couched in a language of defiance, depicting the rise and triumph of the Scythian. It is, above all, a language conscious of its difference. That difference lies in its very form, the blank verse which replaces the jigging rhyme of the fourteen-syllable line (the "fourteener") used in the 1580s. As McMillin and MacLean (1998: 123–4) note, it is a dramatic language that is urgently different. There is now, thanks to Marlowe, a linguistic medium for tragedy; something new that can be heard and announces itself as new.

But the Prologue also formulates the tragic in terms of a complex, lingering irony. The play is to be a narrative of great events and battles, the struggle of a man against the odds. But it is a far from clear-cut narrative of great events and battles. Behind the action lies the sense of a providential scheme in which Tamburlaine is to serve as God's scourge of the world until it is time for his death. But, at the same time, there is also the heralding of a heroic, masculine discourse of a warrior culture, which, in turn, is set in the larger historical context of Elizabeth's feminine court. What perhaps most obviously cuts across all of this, however, is the sense of a world where men defy the powers that be.

Tamburlaine, it is clear, represents a radical type of questioning tragedy which Jonathan Dollimore (1989) has described, and which grows out of an intellectual culture of skepticism. Dollimore sees such questioning as part of subversion of power structures and of the inherited hierarchy of Elizabethan society, but it is also a questioning of what a play and what a tragedy might be. No longer merely a vehicle for moral lessons, tragedy in *Tamburlaine* aspires to move beyond a simple narrative of the fall of princes or tales of men overthrown by fortune. Indeed, as Wiggins (2000: 37) notes, that narrative of death does not happen. Tamburlaine is not overthrown and does not die at the end of the play, or at least the end of Part One.

The Prologue to *Tamburlaine* leaves it open to the audience to "applaud his fortunes" as they please. Evidently they did applaud, since Marlowe produced a sequel, the second part repeating the formula of a series of conquests ever more violent and brutal. The most memorable scenes visually, and those which later dramatists were to emulate, involve, in Part One, Bajazeth, the captured Emperor of the Turks, kept in a cage until he brains himself in despair, and, in Part Two, Tamburlaine's chariot being drawn by the kings he has defeated. This is the very stuff of spectacle, of the frightening reality of militaristic power divorced from any ethical consideration or sense of mortality. When death does finally come to Tamburlaine, it comes as a shock to the flesh that it cannot survive:

> What daring god torments my body thus,
> And seeks to conquer mighty Tamburlaine?
> Shall sickness prove me now to be a man,
> That have been term'd the terror of the world?
> (The Second Part of *Tamburlaine the Great*, 5.3.42–5)

Such speeches provide tragedy with one of its set motifs, as Tamburlaine becomes an example of the limits of human achievement encased in mortal flesh. There is, though, nothing here of the language of repentance or last minute deathbed confession which were to become stock resources of the drama (Neill 1997: 207). Instead, what we have is still the language of classical conquest, with death and the gods as the mortal enemy. Meanwhile on stage there is a gathering, a tableau, a huddling together around the body. The moment of death is thus also a visual moment, a feature that makes death oddly readable rather than mysterious, a matter of stage semiotics.

Death here, then, as Neill observes (ibid: 206), has to do with "the relation between mortal and narrative endings." For Neill, the ending of *Tamburlaine* is presented as "an occasion of profound anxiety" in which the hero's "self-consumption" is stressed (p. 207). This may be true, but the play also has to signal to its audience the dark moment of death when the actor will speak no more. It is a moment that is extended in *King Lear* and tested to its limits, yet it comes. And then an elegy takes place over the body – in *Tamburlaine* delivered by one of his sons – so that there is a sense of ritual which connects to other rituals outside the theatre even as the words themselves, as Neill points out (p. 207), question the ability to contain death in language or ceremony.

One implication of this analysis is that beginnings and endings are the formal stuff of tragedy; what appears in the middle may not be as we expect. The case of *Doctor Faustus* (1589) suggests this even more clearly. The play exists in two versions, with version A, containing fewer comic scenes, now taken as the preferred text. *Tamburlaine*, as we have seen, is in two parts, as if plays could be extended, or revised either by cutting or adding, without damage to the fabric of their tragic impact. There are, although outside the boundaries of this essay, variants of *King Lear* and *Hamlet* which also suggest how tragedy might, in essence, be nothing more than a play ending in death and presented in a certain kind of language, as defined by the play itself. Thus, for example, the beginning of *Doctor Faustus* rejects the heroic, warlike world of *Tamburlaine*:

> Not marching in the fields of Thrasimene,
> Where Mars did mate the warlike Carthigens,
> Nor sporting in the dalliance of love
> In courts of kings where state is overturned
> (Chorus, 1–4)

Instead, the Chorus continues, "we must now perform / The form of Faustus's fortunes, good or bad" (7–8). If the play's opening frame seems dismissive of the earlier heroic tragedy, there is nevertheless an overlap both in the mention of fortunes and in the allusion to Icarus (20), so that it is hard not to see the plays sharing a pattern. Like Tamburlaine, Faustus aspires to reach beyond limits, to move beyond the mundane and to achieve a power that makes him godlike and more than human.

The sense of overlap between *Faustus* and other plays from the period is evident elsewhere, most obviously in the use of the morality pattern of salvation and damnation, and in the use of the Good and Bad Angels. It is as if Marlowe wishes to bring different forms of tragedy into conflict so that, as Dollimore (1991: 130–1) suggests, what is exposed through Faustus's transgression is the limiting structure of his universe and the tyranny of a God that keeps such a universe in place. The death of Faustus is thus inevitable, but also powerfully moving despite the evident folly of his pact with the devil:

> My God, my God, look not so fierce on me.
> Adders and serpents, let me breathe awhile.
> Ugly hell, gape not, come not, Lucifer!
> I'll burn my books. Ah, Mephostophilis! (5.2.197–200)

The speech does not just convey the notion of wasted potential, something evident in many tragedies. It is also about the terror of life after death, a life which cannot be changed or altered. Whatever closure is provided by the play's ending, here we become aware that the tragedy runs on afterwards, that death is not the end. As Dollimore notes (1991: 131), plays after *Faustus* interrogate religious issues less directly, but they are no less haunted by the question of what lies beyond death, the question why death is not an end.

In *Faustus*, as in *Tamburlaine*, the keynote of tragedy is sounded at the beginning and the end. It is established through language and motifs that we come to identify as structural: the defying of limits, the overturning of conventional hierarchies, the aspiring mind, the will to power, the attempt to go beyond the merely human. But in *Faustus* tragedy also involves the idea of reaching towards a new understanding of the human subject as a text written upon. The great moment of the play is when Faustus binds himself in a pact only to see his blood freeze in horror, and then:

> *Consummatum est*: this bill is ended,
> And Faustus hath bequeathed his soul to Lucifer.
> But what is this inscription on mine arm?
> *Homo fuge!* Whither should I file? (1.5.73–6)

Faustus seeks to read himself as if a book, a book that, like the literal books at the start of the play, he only partly understands. It is a moment when the human subject seems rent between desire for knowledge and the outward control of authority, producing a new sort of inwardness in the tragic hero. What, however, is also evident in *Faustus* is the way in which Marlowe discovers not just an interior language for tragedy but also an interior for tragedy itself. In *Tamburlaine* there is a simple sense of tragedy as something with a beginning and an end. With *Faustus*, as with *Edward II* (1592), we begin to see a different pattern of tragedy emerge as each play takes up the implications of its predecessor and develops them further. In the case of *Edward II*, for example, the tragic focus is on the torture of the human body. Lightborn's killing of the homosexual king Edward by smothering him with a table and squashing him to death as a red-hot spit is inserted into his rectum is a moment of horror that turns tragedy into the grotesque. It is as if each play uncovers a further aspect of the tragic, each darker than the one before, so that tragedy becomes a narrative where there is an ever-increasing violence against those who transgress. But with that discovery there also comes a need to discuss, if only implicitly, the genre of tragedy itself.

III

If Marlowe provides us with one example of how the form of drama had to be reconsidered to admit new material, and, in turn, how the arrival of that new material changed again the form of tragedy, Thomas Kyd offers a particularly vivid example of the same process. Kyd is important for a number of reasons, not least because *The Spanish Tragedy* (1589)[5] makes *Hamlet* possible and therefore makes possible all the plays that live off *Hamlet*. Kyd provided a model of the plotting acumen so necessary for Renaissance revenge tragedy and is the master of multiple plotting and scenic form: witness, for example, the careful juxtapositions of the first three scenes of court and judgments; or the ironies of the stichomythic dialogue in the wooing of Horatio and Bel-imperia in 2.2; or the discovery of Horatio's hanged body in 2.4; or the series of trials, including that of Pedringano, henchman to the machiavellian Lorenzo; or, finally, the elaborate play-within-the-play, the last of the dramatic entertainments in a play filled with the spectacle of death (Smith 2001: 83).

Here is tragedy as a theatrical skill intended to keep the audience guessing what will happen next in terms of surprise and irony. There is, for example, the carnage of the ending, where the bodies on stage seem to suggest a sense of closure, only for the choric Ghost of Andrea, the first victim of the play's slaughter, and Revenge, his guide from the classical underworld, to come on stage to begin what Revenge calls the "endless tragedy" (4.5.48) of punishment for Andrea's foes. The labyrinth of plot and counter-plot in *The Spanish Tragedy* establishes the revenge tragedy play as a formula that could be quarried, copied, parodied, added to but not ignored. Much of Renaissance drama, indeed, becomes a rewriting of Kyd's enormously popular play. That popularity may, in part, be a function of its structure: the multiple plot and choric framing allow the audience sufficient distance to see the issues the play raises about justice, the operation of the law, the duty of government and the rights of citizens from a series of perspectives so that the action on stage becomes endlessly fascinating (Kinney 1999: 51).

Those issues are articulated, however, not just at a formal level through the multiplicity of viewpoints of the plots but also at the level of the suffering individual. If Marlowe provides the drama with a figure of the aspiring mind for tragedy, Kyd constructs, in the figure of Hieronimo, a hero who is much more passive and whose grief at the murder of his son pushes him into madness. Kyd provides, that is, the type of the suffering hero. The vehicle for this suffering is the soliloquy, which comes to serve as a sign both of tragedy and of the tragic protagonist, operating as a special moment in the play and as something distinctive to the genre, though not, of course, limited to it.

Part of the effect of the soliloquy, as has often been noted, is to create a sympathy with the central figure, but also, in the case of *The Spanish Tragedy*, to reposition the audience politically. Issues of law and violence, we see through Hieronimo's impassioned analyses, become the responsibility not of the state machine but of individual judgment (Kinney 1999: 49). A different view of the way in which the soliloquy functions is offered by G. K. Hunter (1982: 94), who suggests that Kyd presents a hero seeking to act within the framework of a Christian society, and that in the second half of the play he takes to individual action, but on the basis of an individualism that is questioned. What Kyd does, according to Hunter, is to set up a new relationship in which polarities are contained through the soliloquy within a single mind. Catherine Belsey (1985) suggests, however, that the soliloquy as a device is not so much the effect of an individual mind as constructed out of disparate voices played across the human subject, and that these voices contain traces of an earlier morality drama, as in the following lines from Kyd:

> No, no, Hieronimo, thou must enjoin
> Thine eyes to observation, and thy tongue
> To milder speeches than thy spirit affords. (3.13.39–41)

The body here is in fragments so that the speaker "is at once unified and discontinuous" (Belsey 1985: 46), present on stage as a human agent but divided severally in the speech itself. Such self-address and simultaneous splitting of the subject seems to operate as sign of the madness made visible elsewhere in the play by physical action, such as when Hieronimo is seen to be digging to fetch his son's body back from death (3.12.70–1). It is, however, primarily through the soliloquy that we are made aware of the crisis in the human subject.

That crisis deepens into madness, and it is with madness that Kyd opens up what might be called the otherness of tragedy, something we can also refer to as its radical politics. The hero finds the world so insufferable or incomprehensible that he runs mad. As Karin Coddon (1994: 390) has noted in connection with *Hamlet*, such madness provides a position outside the control of political authority and threatens its hegemony. As Coddon observes, "the discourse of madness becomes virtually indistinguishable from the discourse of treason" (p. 381), but also more ambiguous in that, as a "semiotic excess," it problematizes the closure that is "the object of the rites of punishment" inflicted by the state (p. 385). The mad hero "lingers in the dangerous, equivocal space of 'reason in madness'" (p. 390), undoing all attempts to fix meaning. In turn, the soliloquy becomes a moment that contains only irresolution, doubts, and questions, its conclusion endlessly deferred as one soliloquy follows another.

If the crisis of justice that Kyd explores in *The Spanish Tragedy* reinforces the link between tragedy, madness, and subjectivity, it also, as Molly Smith (2001) suggests, foregrounds the connections between stage, state, and scaffold. The stage in this view becomes a place not so much defiant of state power as a replication of the fear it produces, a fear made all the worse by the seeming absence of any providential scheme. Where Marlowe implies that heaven and hell are tools for divine control, in Kyd they seem no more than theatrical devices, tricks of the trade that will make a hit show. The figures of the Ghost and Revenge who remain on stage throughout *The Spanish Tragedy* appear to act on a different plane from the earthly characters, or to enfold the action in a further level of irony. Revenge may indeed know where the plot is leading, but such knowledge is not shared with the human characters on stage (Wiggins 2000: 40). While Kyd thus establishes some of the spectacular devices that will be used in later tragedy – the ghost, the suffering hero, madness, the play-within-the-play, the final mass killing – he also leaves the play seeming only to be about a kind of pain or fear without any hope – about being, in Revenge's word, endless. This is one of the ways in which Kyd influences Shakespeare: he shows how a well-made play can push things to the very edge of understanding, revealing the abyss that lies beneath the formal tragic structure.

IV

If we take Kyd and Marlowe together we can construct a diachronic model of how tragedy changed from, say, *Gorboduc*, a 1560s play about the tragic consequences of dividing the state, to *King Lear*, another play on the same theme. It is an attractive, evolutionary model, even though it omits complicating factors such as Shakespeare's early tragedies of *Titus Andronicus*, *Romeo and Juliet*, and *Julius Caesar*. As Lawrence Danson (2000: 116) suggests, these can be placed in a number of different categories, so that we might reasonably speak of a number of different developments or patterns of tragedy. This involves thinking about a more synchronic model in which there is interaction between plays by different authors as tragedy clusters around certain topics and certain historical moments either because they are new or because they involve a shift in the paradigm. One small but significant group of plays focuses on love and domestic life – the anonymous *Arden of Faversham* (1592) and Thomas Heywood's *A Woman Killed with Kindness* (1603) are the main texts, although we might also include some aspects of *Othello* here. The context for these domestic tragedies about marriage is provided by such works as Miles Coverdale's 1541 translation of Henry Bullinger's treatise on marriage, *The Christen State of Matrimonye* and, later, John Dod and Robert

Cleaver's *A Godlie Forme of Householde Government* (1598), as well as texts such as William Gouge's *Of Domesticall Duties* (1622). With these plays the emphasis moves away from the assumptions shared by Kyd and Marlowe and derived from Aristotle and Seneca that tragedy involves persons of consequence to figures who are caught up in the ordinariness of life.

We can see this in the anonymous *Arden of Faversham.*[6] At the play's center are a number of domestic concerns: the household, marriage, women's position. Domestic or private does not, however, mean nonpolitical. Indeed, by staging the murder of Arden (itself reported in Stow's *Annals* and elsewhere) the theatre is not merely reflecting "an intensification of the debate about marriage" (Belsey 1985: 130) but also announcing the domestic as fit for tragedy because it belongs to the audience's own time and interests. In the case of *Arden* this becomes clear in the way in which the tragedy is relational to the ordering of society: Arden is unbearable (the selfish entrepreneur of "amoral ambition," in Kinney's (1999: 99) description), but there is no escape from marriage into divorce, so that Alice's situation is intolerable; she cannot enjoy Mosby her lover's love freely, but he also seems unreliable, so that she will be betrayed whichever way she turns.

With this shift into the domestic as a topic there comes about a shift in the register of the tragic discourse. The opening of the play is a lament by Arden that Alice now loves Mosby, but it is fired by social and class concerns; the suggestion is that her adultery would be acceptable to Arden if Mosby were a gentleman. On the other hand, Alice is much more radical in her valuations of marriage; she argues that Arden would not have to die if she did not feel constrained. And marriage itself she sees as but words:

> Sweet Mosby is the man that hath my heart;
> And he usurps it, having nought but this –
> That I am tied to him by marriage.
> Love is a god, and marriage is but words;
> And therefore Mosby's title is the best. (1.98–102)

All of this comes in the long opening scene where the play sets out its thesis. Trapped by her sexual desire, Alice seeks the help of various figures to kill Arden. Arden, however, is not easily killed and we might struggle to see why. Neill (1997: 45) is obviously right when he argues that there is a constant dread of ending in tragedy, leading almost inevitably to delay, though the delay in *Arden* seems primarily because the villains hired to do it cannot accomplish their simple task. Black Will, for example, has a window fall on his head as he waits to kill Arden, while, later, he and Shakebag get lost in the mist and fall (emblematically as well as comically) into a ditch while pursuing Arden. After scene 13, however, it becomes possible for Arden to die. In this scene Arden turns down a plea for charity from Greene the sailor to restore his land, so that his death might seem an act of punishment by providence for his rapaciousness. But it is also possible that it follows from his turning against the advice of his companion, the Franklin, and his willingness to believe Alice's story about her relationship with Mosby. Arden dies, we might surmise, because he trusts his wife and ignores the advice of his male friend. There is little sympathy for him, it has to be said; certainly there is much more for Alice as both murderer and victim surrounded by men who conspire or who are foolish.

At the end Alice is sentenced to die, but, as Findlay (1999: 152) notes, her death is overshadowed in some way. The play lacks the formal ending we might expect of a tragedy and becomes a much more public affair rather than a question of individual resistance or grief. Instead, the focus at the end is on how everybody connected with the murder has to die, however remote the connection. Thus a figure such as Bradshaw, who simply carries a letter to Alice, dies, and no one is interested in his innocence or guilt. Tragedy here is a matter of how the social structure not only criminalizes people but also how that social structure preserves itself whatever the cost in human life.

Arden was published in 1592, but may have been written as early as 1588. It is thus contemporary with the plays of Marlowe and Kyd. The authors were in effect rivals for the attention of the growing Elizabethan play audience, offering their different kinds of tragedy. This variety of the plays itself suggests how new issues and new considerations were demanding attention as the secular was invading the once religious form of drama. But, in addition, in Kyd and in *Arden* there is a new interest in how to explore and exploit the dramatic space between the beginning and the end of tragedy, and, implicitly, with that new interest come new ideas about what happens in a tragedy. Those ideas attracted the criticism of Puritan writers such as Philip Stubbes in his *Anatomie of Abuses* (1583), denouncing the immoral excesses of the stage. Significantly, at the end of *Arden* the Franklin describes the play as a "naked tragedy," one without adornment or glamor. He claims for it a "simple truth" without "other points of glozing stuff," as if to criticize other more elaborate plays and their deceptive rhetoric, while defending this new form of tragedy (Epilogue, 14–18). The implicit struggle over the nature of tragedy in the plays was in this sense part of a larger struggle about the function of drama in the period and about the nature of the emerging social order, something evident again in *A Woman Killed with Kindness.*[7]

The play, dated 1603 and so close to *Othello*, begins by praising the newly married couple, Anne and Frankford, as partners in a perfect relationship:

> You both adorn each other, and your hands
> Methinks are matches. There's equality
> In this fair combination; you are both scholars,
> Both young, both being descended *nobly*. (1.65–8)

The opening stress is upon equality, but undermining that, as critics have noted, is an unevenness of power relations between the two, together with a further imbalance that attributes to woman a moral superiority but sexual weakness. There is already tension in the opening scene as Anne is sexualized through the discourse, and it is not long before she is seduced by the villain Wendoll.

What is more puzzling is what Wendoll is doing there in the first place. Like the Franklin and like Iago, Wendoll seems to be an example of male bonding and companionship. He also appears to represent an aristocratic pretentiousness on behalf of the bourgeois Frankford as he seeks to emulate court generosity. But there is also a political point here. Corruption of the marriage bed is seen to come from outside rather than inside the domestic family, and this is because the play's project appears to be to validate emerging middle-class values and to position them centrally on stage. This may tie in with the way the play sets out to gain a certain sympathy for Anne through her address to women in the audience, so establishing a special relationship between stage and the domestic world. Such moralizing may seem trite but it is also present, for example, in Emilia's speech to the audience in act 4 in *Othello*.

But Heywood is a lot more conservative than Shakespeare. Even if we read *A Woman Killed with Kindness* ironically, what he seems to be offering is a reinscription of value within the limited world of the domestic rather than in the heroic and dangerous world of *Othello*. At the end of the play Anne is brought on dying in her bed, having been encouraged to punish herself physically and psychologically. She becomes a martyr figure, but also a figure whose death reasserts the set ending of the dying tableau scene absent in *Arden*. The latter is much more open and subversive in its questions about who is dying and why; there is, however, no mystery in *A Woman Killed with Kindness* about death's work. Nor are there doubts (amongst the characters) about justice; Anne has seemingly got her just deserts even though everybody regrets her death. The play's title is deliberately echoed at the end in her epitaph: "here lies she whom her husband's kindness killed" (17.140). "Killed with kindness" suggests there is a naturalness to the death, so making the tragedy neither strange nor shocking. The domestication of the plot is also there in the domestication of the language of tragedy. It is as if the play claims that the domestic will resolve (through common sense, intellectual application, study, and hard work) those things that trouble heroic tragedy and their intellectual heroes; it will make everything safe and reasonable. Paradoxically, the function of tragedy in *A Woman Killed* is to make untragic, to sentimentalize, to make noble feelings viable in the home so that tragedy is not a matter of exceptional passion or excess but a matter of weeping and sadness, of everything being more or less under control.

This may be to misread *A Woman Killed*; Heywood's play may alienate or appall us so much that we reject its politics. But what is in part at issue is how domestic tragedy seems to be at odds with other representations of a similar topic. Even though there is no adultery in *Othello*, the play excites erotically. There is sex in *A Woman Killed*, but it is punished and woman's body is restored along with the family name. This is clearly not the case in *Othello*, where unfulfilled desire threatens to spill over even as Othello is about to kill Desdemona:

> It is the cause, it is the cause, my soul –
> Let me not name it to you, you chaste stars –
> It is the cause. Yet I'll not shed her blood,
> Nor scar that whiter skin of hers than snow
> And smooth as monumental alabaster. (5.2.1–5)

The sensuous image of alabaster skin elides the gap between death and desire, making Desdemona both present and absent but also eroticizing the murder. These complex effects *A Woman Killed* labors to make mundane, as if they are too shocking to be shown. Sex, therefore, is made comic through the servant Nicholas spying on Anne and Wendoll, while the death of Anne is made merely tearful. Constantly *A Woman Killed* seeks to reduce the tragic, including the language of tragedy, to the ordinary.

V

Arden of Faversham and *A Woman Killed with Kindness*, together with *Othello*, place woman at the center of tragedy in a new way. Marlowe and Kyd have women characters, but their plays are male and heroic. With 1600 we seem to see a shift of thinking about the subject of tragedy. In contrast to Shakespeare's history plays, where Jean Howard and Phyllis Rackin (1997: 137) see the early plays as initially including the recognition of women as powerful figures, but then, in later plays, being excluded, in tragedy women come more and more to find a place. This is not to ignore the problem of patriarchal representation; that women are primarily seen as dangerous or threatening or as betrayers, as if the stage is trying to take control of women at the center of the plays and the social nexus. But, as Alison Findlay (1999: 59) notes, Kyd's telling line in *The Spanish Tragedy*, where Hieronimo asks "what's a play without a woman in it?" (4.1.97), seems to suggest that the dramatists themselves were more than conscious of the need to recognize women as central in the tragic matrix. And while no actresses took part in public plays on stage, time after time plays return to Kyd's question, as social issues are negotiated around women. Indeed, it is possible to see later Renaissance tragedy in terms of a struggle or debate between a slightly old-fashioned heroic discourse and an increasingly powerful gender discourse, a debate that reflects the broader social shifts taking place outside the theatres as England moved out of an older set of political and religious codes into a more uncertain period of economic expansion and social reformation.

Not that that debate is restricted to domestic tragedy. Against the very English landscapes of *Arden* and *A Woman Killed with Kindness* we can set another, much larger and self-evidently much more significant, if more disparate, group of plays, including Webster's *The Duchess of Malfi* (1614) and *The White Devil* (1612), Ford's *'Tis Pity She's a Whore* (1625), and Middleton's *The Changeling* (1622) as well as *The Revenger's Tragedy* (1607), which take for their setting foreign courts and foreign countries. They

are, in essence, tragedies of excess, an excess both of violence and plotting that threatens the very form they dramatize. If they are projected images of the Jacobean world
at its darkest, however, they also show us dramatists prepared to extend the confines
of tragedy and to open up further those questions of marriage and authority which
remain unanswered by Heywood's play. In turn, they provide perhaps the most
complex interventions in the tragic nexus, unsettling our ideas of what tragedy is or
might be.

In contrast to the domestic plays considered above, *The Duchess of Malfi* associates
restriction with the poisonous world of its Italianate court symbolized in the actions
of the Duchess's brothers as they seek to restrain her. The note of regulation is there
in the opening of the play in the contrast between the order of the French court and
the corruption of Milan and Rome. Where the former is associated with the free-
flowing, glittering water of the fountain, the latter is compared to a prison. By contrast again, when the Duchess determines to marry Antonio she speaks of going into
a wilderness, beyond the confines of her brothers' rule, while also stressing the ambivalence of her action:

> The misery of us that are born great –
> We are forced to woo, because none dare woo us,
> And as a tyrant doubles with his words,
> And fearfully equivocates, so we
> Are forced to express our violent passions
> In riddles, and in dreams, and leave the path
> Of simple virtue which was never made
> To seem the thing it is not. (1.2.374–81)[8]

The speech is about the dilemma of heroic women having to act a part in language
that denies their virtue. Where in plays like *Arden* virtue seems a straightforward
matter, Webster gives us a discourse that questions such simple judgments about
women and desire. Of course, Webster is writing about aristocratic women and about
a widow and remarriage, so that strict comparisons with domestic tragedies are not
totally accurate, but the sense offered is of a world much more complicated than that
of the domestic writers for whom tragedy is a vehicle for everyday truths. In Webster
tragedy becomes more entangled. Thus judgment of the Duchess contrasts her
naturalness with her sexual appetite, so that the play seems to undermine our response
while leaving us in no doubt about the evil tyranny of her brothers.

In addition to its reappraisal of marriage and sexual desire the play also adds to its
claims of tragedy by other devices, especially torture. In the dark of her prison the
Duchess is presented first with a dead hand and then made to see the dead images of
her husband and children. The prison scenes of torture take us back into the world
of Marlowe and *Edward II* but also to *A Woman Killed*, as if tragedy itself is returning to those grotesque moments of punishing aberrant lovers. There is, of course,
torture in *King Lear* and *Titus Andronicus*, but in *The Duchess of Malfi* torture is also

an expression of Ferdinand's incestuous longing for his sister. The incest may be moti-vated by more than sexual desire. Frank Whigham (1991: 266) has argued that, in an economic context, Ferdinand is "a frightened aristocrat" and that his incestuous desire is "a *social posture* of hysterical compensation – a desperate expression of the desire to evade association with inferiors" which may be brought about by the Duchess's sexual relations with the lower classes. To that extent the play seems built on a faultline where we cannot readily separate individual psychological desire from economic and political factors.

The image of the faultline might itself serve as a metaphor for tragedy in general and how it opens up different levels that overlap and lead to different, yet often par-allel critical interpretations.[9] Thus, for some, the key to Webster's art is the strange dialogue throughout between the Duchess, Ferdinand, and Bosola, while for others it is the power of a single line such as the Duchess's "I am Duchess of Malfi still" (4.2.152), where she asserts her identity in the face of death, defying the court's attempts to reduce her to madness. "Still" here seems to become the keyword of the play, as perhaps "now" does in *Hamlet* or "nothing" in *King Lear*. It is as if the move-ment of the play throws up an insignificant, single word that takes on enormous emblematic significance in a chaotic world. Tragedy at this point is a use of language that is neither grand nor heroic but which, paradoxically, carries the weight of the action, only to reveal that language is ultimately inadequate to do so.

Implicit in this kind of use of language is a sophisticated awareness of tragic form, and how the play is adding to and adapting the meaning of tragedy. This is under-lined in Webster's allusiveness. Webster's art often draws upon other plays, leading to a rich intertextuality in his tragedies. Such is the case with *The White Devil*, where in the final act motif follows upon motif as death follows on death.[10] The play itself is overtly conscious of its piling up of allusions, something given visual form in the figure of the ghost in act 5:

> *Enter* BRACCIANO's Ghost, *in his leather cassock and breeches, boots, {and} a cowl, {in his hand} a pot of lily-flowers with a skull in't.* (5.4.124.s.d.)

This multilayered assemblage takes us back to the idea of the palimpsest and how tragedy becomes a layering effect of motifs, a potentially absurd repertoire the char-acters themselves seem aware of. Again in act 5, Lodovico, when discussing revenge, advises Francisco:

> O my lord!
> I would have our plot be ingenious,
> And have it hereafter recorded for example
> Rather than borrow example. (5.1.74–7)

Lodovico argues that their revenge needs ingenuity so that it will be "hereafter recorded," as if what matters about the tragedy is its difference from other plays. Mere borrowing will not serve; the new plot must be more memorable than well-worn examples.

Webster, then, opens up the question of whether tragedy is merely an imitation of another action by another dramatist or something else; of whether it has a set pattern or is merely a collection of motifs and devices; and, indeed, of where the tragic lies. Does it, for example, lie in the ending of *King Lear* with all its questions about Cordelia and the old king? Or is it in the elegiac note of Macbeth's words about Lady Macbeth:

> She should have died hereafter;
> There would have been a time for such a word? (5.5.17–18)

Or does the tragic lie, as in Webster, in a vision of hell where life is tortured and tormented? Or perhaps it is in the image of mist, the confusion where nothing is clear, but where at the end, the central characters nevertheless reassert a grasp on what has been achieved in defiance. So, for example, the end of *The White Devil*, where Flamineo points to his sister and their defiant bravery:

> Th' art a noble sister –
> I love thee now . . . (5.6.241–2)

Yet a few lines later Flamineo speaks of dying in a mist (5.6.260). What we see at the end of the play, then, is not the pattern of tragedy but rather the level of confusion or contradiction Webster generates. A similar confusion is visible at the end of *The Spanish Tragedy* in the play-within-the-play, but there it is part of Hieronimo's mad revenge plot. Here, in *The White Devil*, it seems to overwhelm any ordering shape or form, as if to suggest an elemental chaos.

VI

Webster's ending in *The White Devil* seems at once open and unclear as the complex plots and motifs come together in a long finale, almost as if tragedy itself has become too big for the stage, with too many motifs, ideas, and deaths. Middleton's plays are much tighter.[11] The key image of *Women Beware Women* (1614) is a game of chess. Livia invites Leantio's mother to come and play chess and then, later, sends for her daughter-in-law Bianca, recently married to her merchant's agent son. Like all Jacobean plots, the play's elaborations can seem excessive, but its terror comes out when, as the two women play chess, Bianca is raped by the Duke on the upper level of the stage. *Women Beware Women* might appear just another play of courtly corruption and sexual depravity, but that view becomes impossible to sustain in the face of Bianca's words when she returns, her body defiled:

> Now bless me from a blasting! I saw that now
> Fearful for any woman's eye to look on.
> Infectious mists and mildews hang at's eyes,
> The weather of a doomsday dwells upon him.
> Yet since mine honour's leprous, why should I
> Preserve that fair that caus'd the leprosy? (2.2.422–7)

As in Marlowe, hell is never far away, but where Faustus stares in amazement at his own body's revolt, Bianca here articulates the very penetration of damnation into the flesh and its corruption.

The play's elaborate games take on a further level of complication in the final scene, where Livia plots against the Duke and Bianca, but is outmaneuvered in a spectacular masque, only for Bianca's plot against the Cardinal to end with her accidentally poisoning the Duke before killing herself. The deadly corruption of the court is clearly embodied in its baroque plotting and bizarre murders, but we might wonder what it has to say about the shaping of tragedy. Is it that tragedy has become an ironic spectacle built on moral emptiness? Modern criticism finds itself admiring such plays perhaps because they come nearer to our own sense of a postmodern world of sexual depravity. Or to our sense of the powerful drives that urge human beings towards their own destruction and that of others. This might seem to be the case in Middleton and Rowley's *The Changeling*, with its riddling title challenging us to identify the changeling. In the event it is several people: it is Beatrice-Joanna who changes from the object of Alsemero's love into Deflores's lover; it is the foolish lovers who pursue Isabella in the madhouse while she herself plays the part of a changeling; and it is Deflores who for Beatrice-Joanna becomes a "wondrous necessary man" (5.1.90) who protects her honour by murdering her maid.

This multiplicity of figures suggests the way in which the play explores a disjunction of connections. *The Changeling* famously has two plots at different social levels; while Beatrice-Joanna is wooed in the mercantile world of Petrarchanism, Isabella helps her husband in the madhouse where he mistrusts her loyalty. The play sets up complementary but also competing perspectives. There seems little that is heroic here, however, and not much to sympathize with apart from Isabella. The passions the play exposes seem as fearful as the politics of the society that seeks to constrain people. Yet, having said that, we recognize something else in the final moments of the play. Deflores, the deflowering lover, stabs Beatrice-Joanna offstage; she returns, warning her father to avoid her lest she contaminate him:

> Oh come not near me, sir, I shall defile you.
> I am that of your blood was taken from you
> For your better health; look no more upon't,
> But cast it to the ground regardlessly. (5.3.149–52)

Few deaths are more compelling in their recognition of the corruption that runs through the body that, simply by the touch, will injure. Like Bianca, Beatrice-Joanna dies as if to purge the social body, yet we are aware that she is the victim of that social body's patriarchy and of its obsessions.

That is made clear in the virginity test in act 4, a test based on a mixture of science and control which highlights the fetish surrounding sexual purity. From the play's start there is an anticipation of Beatrice-Joanna's loss of chastity – her father speaks of her virginity as just a "toy" (1.1.193), a trifling matter – and of her subsequent punishment, foreshadowed perhaps in Marlowe's *Jew of Malta* in the death of the virgin nuns and in Tamburlaine's slaying of the virgins of Damascus. In each of these the stage seems to be enacting a murderous ritual which is not concerned with the human condition but with a voyeuristic violence against women, especially those who seem chaste or unobtainable, while tragedy has become a vehicle for sexual fantasy and gratification, defiled by the blood it spills.

The concern with taboos and virginity is nowhere more evident than in Ford's *'Tis Pity She's a Whore*.[12] The play could be described as a compendium of all the motifs looked at so far, reusing scenes and plots (Giovanni the young scholar is a version of Faustus, while the revenge theme has echoes of Kyd's *Spanish Tragedy*), though offered with a new extravagance, as if to push excess beyond its breaking limit in a bid for a new sensationalism. In 4.3 Soranzo, believing (correctly) that Annabella has betrayed him and is pregnant by someone else – it is, in fact, her brother, Giovanni – drags her across stage, while she sings defiantly of her love in Italian. The incident suggests how tragedy always flirts with a kind of decadent violence that, for all its emblematic force, is also calculated to be memorable for its own sake as spectacle. *'Tis Pity* is full of such moments, comic and otherwise. In 3.8 the innocent and foolish Berghetto is mistakenly ambushed and pierced with swords so that he seems to "piss forward and backward" (3.7.11), a figure of the leaky body associated with women but also the body in its death throes as blood begins to run out of it. And, as the play moves towards its ending, so the acts become more horrid, as in the ripping out of Putana's eyes. Such spectacular violence reaches its climax in the final scene where Giovanni brings in his sister's heart on his dagger, as if to symbolize both their incestuous love and his desire to possess her. Or as if, because he is playing the part of the martyr of love, the heart has become his own. The spectacle overrides our grasp of the events; those present are stunned by the monstrosity of what they behold.

Incest is no more than sexual desire for someone outside the allowed boundaries of love. Throughout the play, however, Giovanni debates its significance with the Friar, and its trail to damnation. But he also has to dupe Annabella and hide the truth from her. As Susan Wiseman (2001: 214) says, incest is a secret crime which hides itself in other languages; it is a love without a discourse of its own. Couched in various types of language, including that of romantic love, it has nothing that marks it out. In this way it might seem to double as a metaphor for tragedy; it, too, has no language of its own in the Renaissance but seems to search around, as Neill (1997: 29–48) argues, in the language of *memento mori*, funeral oration, confession, puns, doubts and uncertainties, the macabre, the dance of death and apocalypse.

It is, of course, convenient that incest in *'Tis Pity She's a Whore* should provide a kind of analogy for the language of tragedy, doing so in the same kind of way that other plays also seem to provide their own definition of how they conceive of tragedy and its discourse. In the case of *'Tis Pity*, however, the idea of analogy is further evident in the title, with its relabeling of the central act as prostitution rather than incest. The effect is to criminalize Annabella for sexual acts that society can recognize rather than those it wishes to hide. In addition, it suggests to the audience how simple moral judgments fall short of the complex reality of the interplay of sexual desire, violence, and the family. Tragedy in *'Tis Pity* thus takes the form of an undermining of those hidden assumptions and ideology of marriage that underpin domestic tragic plays.

A similar undermining of assumptions, though to very different effect, is evident in *The Revenger's Tragedy*.[13] This deals not with incest but with revenge and murder. The play starts with a famous skull scene, as Vindice addresses the remains of his poisoned love:

> Thou sallow picture of my poison'd love,
> My study's ornament, thou shell of death,
> Once the bright face of my betrothed lady,
> When life and beauty naturally fill'd out
> These ragged imperfections,
> When two heaven-pointed diamonds were set
> In those unsightly rings – then twas a face . . . (1.1.14–20)

Vindice's posture is borrowed from Hamlet in the graveyard, but it has also been learnt from paintings of young men which Roland Frye (1984) draws attention to in his discussion of *Hamlet*, paintings in which they are seen fondling a skull like a mother with child, as if to suggest that death is born of man. Or as if to present an image of the death that is yet to come, a *memento mori* that suggests how Vindice will also become a corpse.

The Revenger's Tragedy has a more literal corpse in 1.4. This is the wife of the lord Antonio. She has been raped and, consequently, killed herself; she now lies with two Bibles on her pillow. The effect of the opening scenes is thus like a transi tomb, with one corpse on top of another. But the play also has a third dead figure of woman when Vindice dresses up the skull to meet the Duke, her original poisoner, in 3.5. The flesh is then reimagined back onto the skull, with its lips poisoned. Here is the grotesque, horrid process of putrefaction hinted at in various plays: the process of the dying of the flesh slowly. *The Revenger's Tragedy* comes closer to the nightmare of tragedy that other plays, even *Hamlet*, hardly dare hint at. In most tragedies, the rotting flesh of death is replaced by a concern with sexual excess or sexual purity. Instead of the body dying we are given the body sexual. *The Revenger's Tragedy* undoes that reversal, returning tragedy to a more direct confrontation with death.

But not just that. The multiple deaths and disguises in *The Revenger's Tragedy* seem to be a version of the game of *fort/da* ("gone"/"there"), a playing with death, that

Catherine Belsey (1999) describes in her discussion of Hamlet.[14] The game involves both the mastery of death and a mocking of it. Its most evident form is when Vindice is hired to kill himself and leaves the poisoned Duke dressed in his clothes. Here death, however, also comes to be a sort of palimpsest, as does the play as a whole in its weaving of motifs. Incest, revenge, masques, thunder, disguise, irony, comedy, even pastoral, all are present. *The Revenger's Tragedy* is the most complex of the plays looked at, not simply because of its plotting but because of the way it makes explicit or pushes into prominence the clash between the reality of death and its representation in drama. At the same time it draws attention to the way in which tragedy is always on the edge of absurdity and mockery. In this it may have learned its craft from *King Lear* or *Hamlet* or from *The Spanish Tragedy* or even from Marlowe, but like them it has changed the genre by its dramatization of the issue of death. This is the defining feature of Renaissance tragedy: breaking the pattern even while conforming to it, by re-examining both the structure and subject matter of tragedy.

VII

It might be objected that what I have argued is simply a matter of the implications of plots, and also that I have fallen into the old trap of reading Shakespeare's contemporaries through Shakespeare. In some ways this is inevitable. We cannot pretend Shakespeare is not there. As Jan Kott (1964) observed many years ago, Shakespeare is our contemporary and we read the past through him, partly because of the way in which Shakespeare constructs us.

By that, I mean the way in which Shakespeare in *Hamlet* brings into being not just a different kind of tragedy but also a different kind of audience. In her book *Shakespeare and the Popular Voice* (1989) Annabel Patterson argues that the tone of *Hamlet* is "recognizably a *fin de siècle* malaise"; that "it is a play that marks the end, not the beginning of an era" (pp. 93–4). From the standpoint of revenge tragedy this may be so, but for most critics *Hamlet* is Shakespeare's most modern play, seen in the way in which, in the soliloquies, Hamlet searches out a new inwardness or presents human subjectivity in a new mode (Barker 1984). It is possible, however, to offer a slightly different view of the soliloquies and how they function in this most self-conscious of all tragedies.

That self-consciousness is seen, for example, in the rather odd summary of the plot Horatio offers at the end:

> So shall you hear
> Of carnal, bloody, and unnatural acts;
> Of accidental judgments, casual slaughters;
> Of deaths put on by cunning and forc'd cause;
> And, in this upshot, purposes mistook
> Fall'n on the inventors' heads – all this can I
> Truly deliver. (5.2.372–8)

It has often been noted how this summary might fit any tragedy of the period, and yet falls short of describing *Hamlet* itself. There are other places, too, where the play displays a metatheatrical awareness, most obviously in the play-within-a-play, in the references to *Julius Caesar* and in Hamlet's own antic disposition, as if to draw attention to its awareness that it knows all about revenge tragedy and what is expected.

At the same time we cannot help but be aware that there is, as it were, another play going on in *Hamlet*. Or, to put that another way, the most spectacular feature of the play is not its action. It has great scenes, and no one will deny that Shakespeare is as good as anyone at the standard business of tragedy, but Hamlet does not really act until the killing of Polonius. Instead, he talks. It seems almost naive to suggest it, but what distinguishes *Hamlet* from other tragedies is its structural and thematic use of the soliloquy, as if to suggest that tragedy is not so much a matter of ghosts and poison and incest as of talking.

Other dramatists, of course, such as Marlowe and Kyd, use the soliloquy, but Shakespeare uses it differently. That difference is a matter of address, of the direction of the soliloquy, of where it is going. And that is not just inwards, towards an exploration of Hamlet's feelings or thoughts or motives or identity, but outwards, towards the audience. The main thing about the soliloquy is its address, its inclusion of the audience in a single voice, in a single perspective and set of ideas:

> To be, or not to be – that is the question;
> Whether 'tis nobler in the mind to suffer
> The slings and arrows of outrageous fortune,
> Or to take arms against a sea of troubles,
> And by opposing end them? To die, to sleep –
> No more; and by a sleep to say we . . . (3.1.56–61)

What we perceive here is not just the thinking subject but a new kind of hero – university educated, witty, sensitive, but above all talking to us in a way that no one else does in Renaissance drama. Hamlet fills out the space of the stage not with action but with words, with soliloquies which are about "we." They are about, that is, the way in which the play binds the audience together, creating a new social group that distinguishes itself by its attitude to language and to the drama on stage. Something of this appears in the choruses of *Henry V*, in the addresses to "gentles all" (Prologue, 1.8), but in *Hamlet* there is a whole level of the play that is concerned with the way in which language marks out a social group that is interested largely in its own language, and which finds the ordinary stuff of tragedy – murder, adultery, corruption – at a remove from its own values.

Take the end of the first soliloquy, where Hamlet speaks of how he must hold his tongue (1.2.159). It is as if his speech is holding up the other play, the melodrama, the absurd play of death and incest that is going on and in which Hamlet is not really interested, apart from his mother's actions. These appall him, but he is also shocked, in his second soliloquy ("O, what a rogue and peasant slave am I!"; 2.2.543), that he does not respond like the Player who cries for Hecuba while he describes the killing of her husband; that he can say nothing about his father's death and that he finds his attempts at grief and passion to be mere rant. A similar issue occurs in the prayer scene (3.3), when Hamlet pauses to scan the language of revenge as illogical and in need of correction if it is to do its job.

In his last soliloquy[15] Hamlet contrasts the heroic deeds of Fortinbras and his own lack of action, wondering "Why yet I live to say 'This thing's to do'" (4.4.44). Hamlet cannot work out why he cannot take action, or what is holding him back. Why is he not like other revenge figures? What he cannot know is that he is in a play where he is the vehicle of something else happening in tragedy, something that is not evident in other plays. Through Hamlet we are hearing a new model of talk that regards other discourses with contempt because of their passion. It is a model that admires stoicism, but cannot be stoic; it is a model that wishes to be silent but always discusses and debates. It is a model of behavior, of filling the world with words, which we relate to in ways we have not yet fully understood. But because we do relate to *Hamlet* in a different way from other Renaissance plays, it means that we label the plays that both follow and precede it as the tragedies of Shakespeare's contemporaries rather than seeing Shakespeare as their contemporary, or, indeed, as seeing them as our contemporaries. In that sense, *Hamlet* stands between us and the past even as it links us to it.

NOTES

1   I owe this point to Richard Dutton. I am grateful to my colleagues Roger Ellis and John Peck for their suggestions in the writing of this essay.
2   References to Shakespeare are to Alexander (1951).
3   I draw here, as throughout, on Neill (1997), Wiggins (2000), and Howard (1999).
4   All quotations from the plays of Marlowe are taken from Steane (1969).
5   All quotations from *The Spanish Tragedy* are from Kinney (1999).
6   Quotations are from Kinney (1999).
7   Quotations are from Kinney (1999).
8   Quotations from *The Duchess of Malfi* are from Kinney (1999).
9   I have obviously borrowed the idea of the faultline from Alan Sinfield (1992), *Faultlines: Cultural Materialism and the Politics of Dissident Reading.*
10 All quotations are from John Russell Brown's (1997) edition of the play.
11 All quotations from Middleton's plays are from Loughrey and Taylor (1988).
12 Quotations are from Kinney (1999).
13 The play is now generally accepted as by Middleton rather than by Tourneur. Quotations are from Loughrey and Taylor (1988).
14 The game is from Freud's account of how his grandson, "who was 'greatly attached to his mother'," repeatedly threw a cotton reel on a string into his curtained cot, thus making it disappear, coincidental with his mother's absences (Belsey 1999: 166). The game is a reenactment of a frightening event or moment, but also a kind of gratification of the instinct for revenge (ibid: 107).

15 The soliloquy is omitted from the Folio and from modern editions such as the *Oxford Shakespeare* (Wells and Taylor, 1986), which uses the Folio as its control text.

REFERENCES AND FURTHER READING

Alexander, P. (ed.) (1951). *William Shakespeare: The Complete Works*. London: Collins.

Barker, F. (1984). *The Tremulous Private Body*. London: Methuen.

Belsey, C. (1985). *The Subject of Tragedy: Identity and Difference in Renaissance Drama*. London: Methuen.

——(1999). *Shakespeare and the Loss of Eden: The Construction of Family Values in Early Modern England*. Basingstoke: Macmillan.

Brown, J. R. (ed.) (1997). *The White Devil*. Manchester: Manchester University Press.

Callaghan, D. (ed.) (2000). *A Feminist Companion to Shakespeare*. Oxford: Blackwell.

Coddon, K. S. (1994). "Such Strange Desygns": Madness, Subjectivity in *Hamlet* and Elizabethan Culture. In S. L. Wofford (ed.) *William Shakespeare: "Hamlet"*. Case Studies in Contemporary Criticism. Boston, MA: St. Martin's Press.

Danson, L. (2000). *Shakespeare's Dramatic Genres*. Oxford: Oxford University Press.

Dollimore, J. (1989). *Radical Tragedy: Religion, Ideology and Power in the Drama of Shakespeare and his Contemporaries*. London: Harvester Wheatsheaf.

——(1991). Subversion through Transgression. In D. S. Kastan and P. Stallybrass (eds.) *Staging the Renaissance*. London: Routledge.

Findlay, A. (1999). *A Feminist Perspective on Renaissance Drama*. Oxford: Blackwell.

Frye, R. M. (1984). *The Renaissance "Hamlet": Issues and Responses in 1600*. Princeton, NJ: Princeton University Press.

Howard, J. E. (1999). Shakespeare and Genre. In D. S. Kastan (ed.) *A Companion to Shakespeare*. Oxford: Blackwell.

Howard, J. E. and Rackin, P. (1997). *Engendering a Nation: A Feminist Account of Shakespeare's English Histories*. London: Routledge.

Hunter, G. K. (1982). Tyrant and Martyr: Religious Heroisms in Elizabethan Tragedy. In M. Mack and G. deForest Lord (eds.) *Poetic Traditions of the English Renaissance*. New Haven, CT: Yale University Press.

Kastan, D. S. (ed.) (1999). *A Companion to Shakespeare*. Oxford: Blackwell.

Kastan, D. S. and Stallybrass, P. (eds.) (1991). *Staging the Renaissance: Reinterpretations of Elizabethan and Jacobean Drama*. London: Routledge.

Kinney, A. F. (ed.) (1999). *Renaissance Drama: An Anthology of Plays and Entertainments*. Oxford: Blackwell.

Kott, J. (1964). *Shakespeare Our Contemporary*. London: Methuen.

Loughrey, B. and Taylor, N. (eds.) (1988). *Thomas Middleton: Five Plays*. Harmondsworth: Penguin Books.

McMillin, S. and MacLean, S. (1998). *The Queen's Men and Their Plays*. Cambridge: Cambridge University Press.

Mullaney, S. (1988). *The Place of the Stage: Licence, Play, and Power in Renaissance England*. Chicago, IL: University of Chicago Press.

Neill, M. (1997). *Issues of Death: Mortality and Identity in English Renaissance Tragedy*. Oxford: Clarendon Press.

Patterson, A. (1989). *Shakespeare and the Popular Voice*. Oxford: Blackwell.

Sawday, J. (1995). *The Body Emblazoned: Dissection and the Human Body in Renaissance Culture*. London: Routledge.

Simkin, S. (ed.) (2001). *Revenge Tragedy*. New Casebooks series. Basingstoke: Palgrave.

Sinfield, A. (1992). *Faultlines: Cultural Materialism and the Politics of Dissident Reading*. Oxford: Clarendon Press.

Smith, M. E. (2001). The Theatre and the Scaffold: Death as Spectacle in *The Spanish Tragedy*. In S. Simkin (ed.) *Revenge Tragedy*. Basingstoke: Palgrave.

Steane, J. B. (ed.) (1969). *Christopher Marlowe: The Complete Plays*. Harmondsworth: Penguin Books.

Watson, E. P. (ed.) (1997). *Philip Sidney: Defence of Poesie, Astrophil and Stella and Other Writings*. London: J. M. Dent.

Wells, S. and Taylor, G. (eds.) (1986). *William Shakespeare: The Complete Works*. Oxford: Oxford University Press.

Whigham, F. (1991). Incest and Ideology: *The Duchess of Malfi* (1614). In D. S. Kastan and P. Stallybrass (eds.) *Staging the Renaissance*. London: Routledge.

Wiggins, M. (2000). *Shakespeare and the Drama of his Time*. Oxford: Oxford University Press.

Wiseman, S. J. (2001). *'Tis Pity She's a Whore*: Representing the Incestuous Body. In S. Simkin (ed.) *Revenge Tragedy*. Basingstoke: Palgrave.

3
Minds in Company:
Shakespearean Tragic Emotions
Katherine Rowe

The action of the theater, though modern states esteem it but ludicrous, unless it be satirical and biting, was carefully watched by the ancients, that it might improve mankind in virtue; and indeed many wise men and great philosophers have thought it to the mind as the bow to the fiddle; and certain it is, though a great secret in nature, that the minds of men in company are more open to affections and impressions than when alone.

Francis Bacon, De Augmentis

Several traditions have guided critical discussions of emotion in Shakespearean tragedy. It is conventional for scholars (and scholarly companions) to make some reference to the Aristotelian notion that tragedies purged fear and pity: the relationship between audience and spectacle involved ridding the self of these emotions. Recent discussions of Shakespearean emotion have highlighted the poet's praise of Stoicism, emphasizing the salutary, "cold" control such purging makes possible (Schoenfeldt 1999). The figure of the tyrant, defined by his inability to govern his passions in this cold way, has long been recognized as a vehicle for Stoic arguments in Renaissance tragedy. As George Puttenham and Thomas Elyot explain, tragedies "set forth the doleful falles of infortunate and afflicted Princes" and "the intollerable life of tyrantes" (Puttenham 1970: 41; Elyot 1883, I: 71).

I aim here to overturn these generalizations about the role of emotion in tragedy and in Shakespeare by renewing our attention to the relationship between audience and theatrical performance. More Ciceronian than Aristotelian, tragedies sought to temper emotions, put them to good use and produce them collectively. Shakespeare's interest in tragic emotions is as often anti-Stoic as Stoic, seeking the virtue in the emotional vulnerability that distinguishes early English psychology. Surprisingly, the figure of the tyrant is not always the man overruled by emotions, but the man who – as in the case of Macbeth – transforms himself perversely into someone who can no longer be moved by or move others. Rather than purging the passions,

Shakespearean tragedy seeks to convert and redirect them in virtuous and politically effectual ways.

Modern readers of Renaissance texts face several methodological hurdles when they interpret expressions of emotion. First the indissolubility of subject matter and affect poses significant challenges for scholars interested in the way headline emotions such as pity, grief, and fear were understood to work in a playgoing audience. In practical as well as generic terms, of course, dramatic action and the emotions that action solicits were indistiguishable. "A Tragedy treats of exilements, murders, matters of grief " Thomas Blount (1969) glosses. If we seek individual impressions – the music of the theatre playing on a single mind, as Bacon describes it in 1622 – generic expectations can take us only so far (Bacon 1869, I: 519, V: 316). Translating Bacon's description, Andrew Gurr explains the problem. Plays

> could appeal to sensationalism at one level, and an audience might voice a majority view as the most overt reaction. Between the appeal to sensation, though, and the more thoughtful responses is a chasm which swallows the best attempts to register the possible range between mass and individual reactions. (Gurr 1996: 116)

Eyewitness reports of plays tend to be conventional, Gurr reminds us. They reflect the normative emotions associated with different kinds of plot as much as particular responses to specific performances (ibid: 115). Such reports are performances of feeling, as scripted by shared cultural assumptions as the passions played on stage. Gurr's impasse stems from the wish for a different kind of access to emotional knowledge. When we read descriptions of Shakespearean passions – or the confessions of a Catholic recusant, or Samuel Pepys's diary – we do not learn authoritatively from the inside what early modern subjects felt. Yet as critics have observed, the appeal of these formalized experiences – in Shakespearean tragedy in particular – has seemed precisely to be the inward access they offer.[1]

Few negotiate the challenges of performance history more thoughtfully than Gurr. Yet the chasm he describes here involves a critical bias towards emotions known from the inside that should be reassessed. Gurr emphasizes the incommensurability of "mass emotion" (Bacon's "minds of men in company") and the responses of individual playgoers in their full, occasional, and nuanced variation. Even if we knew that playgoers felt compassion as advertised – when they learned of the "pittiefull murther" of Richard III's "innocent nephewes" in 1597, for example – the generic association between pity and tragedy gives us little leverage to distinguish "majority views" from "individual reactions." Every playgoer had feelings. Yet the ones that matter to us are by definition elusive: individual, internal, and transitory.

This is an orthodoxy we can productively complicate by attending to the historicity of emotion: by thinking in historical terms about what it means to know what someone feels and why we now privilege that knowledge as inside knowledge. We might start by exploring the degree to which Gurr's scene of reception matches what we know about early modern affects and their work. Like other Shakespeareans, Gurr inherits ideas about emotion from different strains of sixteenth- and seventeenth-century thought. First, he assumes that primary (apparently common) "sensations" are assessed by secondary, "thoughtful" cognition. Versions of this idea were transmitted with the medical model of the passions offered by the Greek physician Galen, influential in English physiology until the end of the seventeenth century. In this respect, the experience of playgoing implied in Gurr's passage – in which information passes through the senses to the faculties of thought – appears consistent with the classical psychology inherited by Shakespeare and his contemporaries. What Bacon calls "affections and impressions" were understood as bodily movements of animal spirits, communicating between the higher internal faculties (judgment, memory, and will) and the external, animal faculties of the senses. In his compendium of medical authority, *Microcosmographia*, Helkiah Crooke defines spirit as "a subtile and thinne body always moouable, engendred of blood and vapour, and the vehicle or carriage of the Faculties of the soule" (Crooke 1615: 173–4). These animated spirits move the will to act, as Thomas Wright explains in *The Passions of the Minde in Generall* (1604): by "the sensual motion of our appetitive faculty, through imagination of some good or ill thing" (Wright 1986: 8).

The fact that passions were themselves material actions or causes was a paradox specialists such as Crooke and Wright easily resolved – by reminding readers of the bodily basis by which all mental functions (psychological, cognitive, spiritual) pressed on and altered each other. The earliest sense of our term "emotion" reflects this material bias, denoting any movement, agitation, or excitation in or through a physical environment (*OED*). In the environment of the body, passions alter and respond to alterations in blood, phlegm, choler (yellow bile), and melancholy (black bile), the fluids in which Galenic medicine localized psychological functions (Park 1988: 469). The brain, heart, and liver distributed these fluids through three sorts of vessels, "veines, arteries, and sinewes [nerves]" (Crooke 1615: 825). Within this network, Gail Kern Paster observes, "blood, spirit and sensation become nearly indistinguishable in action and properties. 'Blood' becomes related integrally to 'sense,' and blood vessels become, in effect, sites of production and dissemination for the lower reaches of somatic consciousness" (Paster 1997: 113). Early modern passions theorists typically framed this process as an administrative scene within the polis of the body:

> To our imagination commeth by sense or memorie, some object to be known, convenient or discovenient to Nature . . . presently the purer spirits, flocke from the brayne, by certaine secret channels to the heart, where they pitch at the dore, signifying what an object was presented, convenient or discovenient for it. The heart immediately bendeth, either to prosecute it, or to eschew it: and the better to effect that affection, draweth other humours to helpe him, and so in pleasure concurre great store of pure spirits; in paine and sadnesse, much melancholy blood . . . (Wright 1986: 45)

When Lady Macbeth calls on spirits to "make thick" her blood, stopping up "th' access and passage" through which "compunctious visitings of nature" negotiate between "purpose" and "effect," she conjures a similar scene of internal messengers, interrupted in their administrative work (1.5.43–5). Her "compunctious visitings" suggest both sensory perceptions that press on affects and the affects themselves – here the tragic passion of "remorse," or pity. The very ambiguity of causes points to the material consciousness she describes, in which passions are both responses (compunction) and actions (visitings).

Perhaps the most persistent challenge of this material psychology, for modern readers, is the fact that passions are understood as environmental factors, moving through a porous body. Emotions are meaningful for early modern subjects to the extent that they function as "transactions" between the body and the world (Floyd-Wilson 2003). Passions constitute one of the six "non-natural" elements of Galenic physiology (Siraisi 1990: 101). Like air, diet, exercise, elimination, and sleep, they destabilize but also regulate the body's dynamic balance of cold and hot, wet and dry humors. Such alterations might be salubrious or pernicious, depending on the current temper of a given body. The early modern synonyms for passion reflect these alternatives. As Wright explains,

> They are called *Passions*, (although indeed they be acts of the sensitive power, or facultie of our soule . . .) because when these affections are stirring in our minds, they alter the humors of our bodies, causing some passion or alteration in them. They are called *perturbations*, for that (as afterward shall be declared) they trouble wonderfully the soule, corrupting the judgement and seducing the will, inducing (for the most part) to vice, and commonly withdrawing from vertue, and therefore some cal them *maladies*, or sores of the soule. They bee also named *affections*, because the soul by them, either affecteth some good, or for the affection of some good, detesteth some ill. (Wright 1986: 8; my emphasis)

Conventional wisdom held that different combinations of humors explained different emotional tendencies. "According to the disposition of the heart, humors and body, divers sorts of persons be subject to divers sorts of passions, and the same passion affecteth divers persons in divers manners" (ibid: 37). Phlegmatic persons are difficult to anger and slow to please; the internal heat and dryness of choleric men inflames them "at every trifle"; "goodfellows" of a sanguine complexion are "soone angrie, soone friended"; melancholy men, like iron, are very hard to inflame but "afterward, with extreme difficulty reconciled" (ibid).

Several points bear emphasizing in relation to these commonplaces. Early modern Galenic thought naturalized social relations in the body, Paster reminds us, anchoring its hierarchies of gender, ethnicity, age, and estate in organic differences of heat and humidity. "As with everything else in nature, states of consciousness and cognitive awareness were ranked in terms of cold/hot, moist/dry. Waking consciousness was thought to be a hotter and drier state than sleep; rationality was less cold and clammy than irrationality" (Paster 1998: 419). Reason and clear-headedness thus belonged to the hotter, drier humors of men. Yet their warmer, quicker spirits might also dispose them to courage or (away from reason) to anger. In other words, though the physical properties that anchored social hierarchies were deeply essentialized, they were also radically labile: prone to alter and lapse from the temperate mean of civility. Moreover, the degree to which environmental forces like the passions might influence a body, either positively or negatively, also varied according to kind. Mary Floyd-Wilson explains the disadvantage this represented to the English. Along with other northerners they were affectively inconstant and uncivil, by classical tradition (Floyd-Wilson 2003). Wright worries about this in his preface to *The Passions of the Minde*, lamenting the lack of affective policy displayed by "theese Northerne Climates." Savvier, climatically temperate "Spaniards and Italians goe before us, for commonly they can better conceale their own Passions, and discover others, than we" (Wright 1986: lxiii). The geohumoral logic Wright rehearses here positioned the English in a particularly anxious relation to their native humors, as Floyd-Wilson argues. For to correct their labile affections meant estranging themselves from kind, potentially losing the "virtue" of their native impressibility (Floyd-Wilson 2003). Passions, then, were a matter of kind. That matter might be habituated to emotional excess or moderation by social and physical intervention: education, worldly experience, seeing a play, reading a sermon, taking different air, drinking more beer, letting blood. Yet these affective disciplines held significantly different meanings depending on the person who adopted them.

For these reasons, humoral self-experience is typically understood in comparative terms, as a relation to prior or normative states. The early modern experience of strong passions is one of self-alteration: being moved measurably "besides" oneself, as Levinus Lemnius describes it in *The Secret Miracles of Nature*, rather than as we phrase it now, to "have" feelings (Lemnius 1658: 73–4). To return to Gurr's impasse in this context, we can begin to see discontinuities between this psychological materialism and the implicitly dualist way in which Gurr's scene of reception allies "thoughtful" responses with "individual reactions." Individual reactions are evidenced not as movements through or between subjects, but as actions within a consciousness that stands at some Cartesian distance from its sensory and social environment. In this dualist model emotions occur idiopathically, in the separate phenomenological realm of the individual body. Catherine Lutz describes the paradox that underlies Gurr's impasse as a broadly Western phenomenon (Lutz 1990: 69). But it is also a specifically historical paradox, as my invocation of Descartes is meant to suggest. The imperative to know emotions from the inside gains some of its present urgency in the early modern period, as a legacy of late seventeenth-century cognitive and political theory. Writers such as Descartes and Locke reimagined the body as "a solid container, only rarely breached, in principle autonomous from culture and environment, tampered with only by diseases and experts" (Sutton 1998: 41). They revised Galenic models of emotion (at least in theory), refashioning the more volatile, porous Galenic body into an arena of self-possession, volition, and executive control (ibid: 166; Taylor 1989: 159). What Sutton calls "voluntary cognitive propriety" sustains a backward accounting of affective life, providing for the "sameness of self through time" required of contractarian subjects (Locke 1975: 335). Calvinist theories of salvation required a similar forensic examination of spiritual life, as a warrant of personal commitment. Thus we might read the vogue for recusant confessions in this period as part of a wider discursive shift that puts an increased premium on the continuity of self-experience (Macdonald 1992; Taylor 1989: 185). Modern, liberal thought conceives of passions that can perform and warrant this forensic inwardness, and thus ascribes them in proprietary terms: Othello's jealousy, Hamlet's melancholy, Lady Macbeth's hysteria.

Our commonplace concepts of emotion, in other words, are historical composites that reflect the vocabularies, psychology, and social work of emotion in different periods. Their composite nature suggests a different set of cautions about how we read early modern passions. Absent the context of humoral self-experience, for example, we may miss the biomedical logic that explains changes of affect. A familiar example might be the way in which Puck's botanical interventions in *A Midsummer Night's Dream* often strike our undergraduates as false explanations for altered love. Plant magic is a logical way to correct the course of true love in a culture accustomed to titrating affections through diet. But it is at odds with the politics of autonomous consciousness and affective choice that figure so largely in post-Lockean liberal culture. What registers as potentially false or unsatisfying in Shakespearean emotions, in other words, is not only a matter of the different vocabulary and phenomenology of early modern passions. That phenomenology entails what anthropologist Anna Wierzbicka calls different "emotion scripts": the often unspoken social meanings conveyed in affective exchanges. A successful cross-cultural analysis of affect, Wierzbicka argues, will attend to "attitudes towards feelings, different communications strategies asso-ciated with feelings, and different norms governing the handling of feelings (one's own and other people's)" that underpin different scripts (Wierzbicka 1994: 189).

For modern readers, early modern texts display a mixture of familiar and strange attitudes towards feelings, reflecting the historically composite nature of the emotion concepts we bring to our reading. The value of attempting to name the familiar and strange, in a comparatist way, is not somehow to discipline oneself into a humoral self-experience.[2] We can, rather, begin to draw out the interests that shape different emotion routines, keeping their continuous but uneven historical development in mind. For example, Wierzbicka describes a dominant American norm for emotions – the norm of friendliness – that we might connect suggestively to early modern con-cerns. The norm of friendliness involves a social script ("I feel something good toward everyone") expressed through cheerful compliments ("you look great"). This empha-sis on "good feelings," Wierzbicka concludes, reflects the pressures of middle-class mobility: where "one autonomous individual had to deal with other autonomous indi-viduals in situations where one's self-esteem and prospects depended on one's ability to impress and negotiate" (Wierzbicka 1994: 186).

Widening Wierzbicka's comparatist frame, we might connect the routine of "good feelings" to a longer history of credit, noting a similar emphasis on interpersonal impressions in early English writings on debt. Craig Muldrew describes emotions as the currency of the emerging credit economy. In turn-of-the-century England, social and economic success depended on a reputation for reliability, constancy, and attachments that survive over time (Muldrew 1998: 3, 209). In this context the practice of seeking counsel testifies to passions that can sustain overlapping circles of credit. Wright, for one, strongly endorses counsel as part of the civil regime of moderating passions. "It is good also to have a wise & discreet friend, to admonish us of our passions" (Wright 1986: 79). The emotion scripts involved in seeking friendly advice this way might be parsed as follows: "my good feelings are constant" (and will continue to enforce my sense of obligation in the future) and "my good feelings are open to others" (and may therefore be known, verified, and managed according to our mutual needs).[3] Early modern drama is preoccupied by the mismatch between these demands for affective continuity and the essential inconstancy of humoral passions, so prone to alter with environment and occasion (Rowe 2002).

Emotion scripts rarely come in single or unitary force. "My feelings are constant" and "my feelings are open to counsel" are cases in point. The demands for emotional constancy and openness in a culture of overlapping debt are significantly different from the requirements of the patronage economy simultaneously in force in this period (ibid). In a credit economy, knowledge of emotional temper circulates among a relatively level community of intimate creditors (the wise friends one seeks out for moderating advice). In a patronage economy, emotional knowledge properly flows in one direction, from subordinate to superior. As Wright explains,

> Superiors may learn to conjecture the affections of their subjects mindes, by a silent speech pronounced in their very countenances; . . . by this we may know the cause, why children, and especially women, cannot abide to looke in their fathers, masters, or betters faces, because, even nature it self seemeth to teach them, that thorow their eyes they see their hearts. (Wright 1986: 29)

By contrast, emotional *conformity* flows in the other direction. Subordinates learn to conform their passions to their superiors' in what Paster calls the humoral "right of way" accorded those of higher estate (Paster 2003). Still, subordinates have significant leverage in this top-down transaction. They are charged with mitigating the erring passions of their superiors with countervailing affects and advice. Superiors are distinguished by their relative receptiveness to such counsel from below. Early conduct books stress the importance of this interchange, framing emotions as the moral medium of negotiation.[4] Wright's guide stresses the effort involved as courtiers, civil gentlemen, and servants navigate circles where even "Noblemen by birth" are so "appassionate in affections that their company [is] to most men intolerable" (Wright 1986: 6). We should hear an echo here of Elyot's definition of the intolerable passions that preoccupy Renaissance tragedy from *Cambyses* to John Webster.

Across these various writings the intersubjective flow of passions is the subject of ongoing debate and conflicting wisdom. The costs and benefits of being open to the passions of others appear radically different — even within the work of a single writer — depending on the parties involved and the ideological investments at stake. As we have seen, Wright's sense of the appropriate flow of emotional knowledge changes depending on the relationship in question: patronage or credit, hierarchical or unhierarchical. Dramatic expressions of passion are similarly dynamic, invested with interests and anxieties that vary with social context. In what follows I outline a few of the emotion scripts common to early modern conduct books, passions theory, and the theatre, concentrating on variations in one Renaissance investment traditional to tragedy: the education of kings. George Puttenham sums up the classical roots of this topos in his genealogy of English kinds. The ancient "Tragical Poets" aimed to educate a royal audience:

> The bad and illawdable parts of all estates and degrees were taxed by the Poets in one sort or another, and those of great Princes by Tragedie in especial . . . to th' intent that such exemplifying (as it were) of their blames and adversities . . . might worke for a secret reprehension to others that were alive, living in the same or like abuses. (Puttenham 1970: 50)

Proverbially, the "abuses" of tyrants result from their inconstant affections. As Rebecca Bushnell has shown, inconstancy belonged to tyranny by a syllogism common to Renaissance tragedy and passions theory: inconstant passions tyrannize over reason; those whose passions tyrannize reason cannot govern themselves; those who cannot govern themselves cannot govern others reasonably (Bushnell 1990: 21–2). To the extent that tragic affects were thought to redress such inconstant passions by exemplifying them, it was by virtue of their orderly and conventional emergence on stage. Puttenham's description sustains this conjecture: the royal audience comes to emotional knowledge through the perception of established convention. Theatrical "abuses" provide an external standard for comparison. Recognizing "like abuses," the auditor comes to experience his passions as needing reform. Wright popularizes this principle as a daily "remedy to know thy selfe" by comparison with the affective performances of others (Wright 1986: 79).

The possibility of such "secret reprehension" through conventional matter is the central subject of the passionate exchanges in *Macbeth*. The play's spectacle of tyrannical passions and its interest in the education of kings have been well described. Yet the material phenomenology that makes such reprehension possible has been less explored. We therefore tend to miss Shakespeare's contrarian spin on the proverbial association of tyranny with inconstant humors. As in Wright, the traffic of Shakespearean emotions reflects different investments depending on the context. The sonnets may emphasize a neo-Stoic line of argument, as Michael Schoenfeldt has argued. The tragic affects of *Macbeth*, by contrast, play out an anti-Stoic line of thought.[5] They dramatize a salutary kind of emotional openness – one that sustains the possibility of corrective education both up and down the vertical hierarchy of humors. Macbeth's tyranny, surprisingly, turns out not to be a function of inconstant passions but of passions too sternly disciplined. This dramatic argument outlines several features of the early modern traffic in passions: the Ciceronian phenomenology of theatrical affects; their intersubjectivity; the strategic divisions of emotional labor that distinguish passionate subjects.

Rhetorical Regimens and Intersubjective Passions

A. C. Bradley observed that *Macbeth* "has little pathos except of the sternest kind" (Bradley 1955: 309). In the material psychology of the period this would be a truism. Sternness was understood both as a stance towards passion and as an affective quality itself. As Schoenfeldt points out, Renaissance selves were differentiated by their capacity to moderate their passions; a stony imperviousness to alteration testified to powerful self-control (Schoenfeldt 1999: 17). Yet stern control is far from unequivocally positive. Passionate alterations were not understood as "invariably harmful" (ibid). They were also critical tools of civil persuasion and salutary change. On the Shakespearean stage the matter of emotional control is rarely separated from the imperative to solicit passions for ethical purposes.

The Macbeths achieve their sternness through mutual persuasion – pouring spirits in the ear, as Lady Macbeth phrases it. These scenes of intimate counsel reflect the critical role of rhetoric in early modern passions discourse, both as an ethical resource and as a practical regime. For anti-Stoic humanists from Petrarch to Francis Bacon, rhetoric speaks to the whole-body experience of passion. A loose translation of Aristotelian catharsis as a process of ridding the self of emotion misses the complexity of this whole-body phenomenology. Shakespearean tragedy and English passions discourse more generally emphasized the careful solicitation of passions, "because one passion often cureth another: so here the passion of feare may expell the passion of anger, lust, or what else soeuer, either to the passionates evill, or any disorder in the Common-weale" (Wright 1986: 100). Classical paradigms for tragedy come filtered through humoral phenomenology. Philip Sidney's familiar account of tragic emotions in the *Defense of Poesy* is a case in point, sounding as Galenic as it does Aristotelian. Tragedy "openeth the greatest wounds, and showeth forth the ulcers that are covered with tissue; that maketh kings fear to be tyrants, and tyrants manifest their tyrannical humors; that with stirring the affects of admiration and commiseration teacheth the uncertainty of this world" (Sidney 1970: 29).

Explaining this salutary process, English passions theorists cite an array of classical authorities, with Cicero's *De natura deorum* looming large in their concern to distinguish true sensations from false ones (Cicero 1933: 15). Aristotle put emotions at the center of political life, to be sure (Staines 2003). Yet for writers advocating the industrious use of passions such as fear, Cicero provided the practical advice.[6] Richard Strier cites Petrarch's opinion on the matter as representative. While Aristotle teaches virtue, he is "slow in rousing the mind." Authorities such as Cicero, who understand the phenomenology of passionate persuasion, "stamp and drive deep in the heart the sharpest and most ardent stings of speech, by which the lazy are startled, the ailing are kindled, and the sleepy aroused, the sick healed" (Petrarch 1948: 103–4; Strier

2003). Aristotle's relative lack of interest in the affections, in fact, mystifies English writers interested in the civil uses of passion (Bacon 1869, III: 40, VII: 219–20; Reynolds 1971: 42). What Aristotle unaccountably neglects is the bodily temper of moral experience. What stings the heart stings throughout the body, Wright stresses: "And not onely, as I said, the heart draweth [the humors], but also the same soul that informeth the heart residing in other parts, sendeth the humours unto the heart, to performe their service . . . in like maner as when we feele hunger . . . the same soule which informeth the stomack, resideth in the hands, eyes, and mouth" (Wright 1986: 45–6).

The same whole-body epistemology led Bacon, in the *Advancement of Learning*, to call for a systematic study of Ciceronian *actio*, the techniques of performance. The art that combines reason, voice, and gesture gives the best leverage on sensitive motions and moral affect. "For the Lineaments of the body do disclose the disposition and inclination of the mind in general; but the Motions of the countenance and parts do not only so, but do further disclose the present humour and state of the mind and will" (Bacon 1869, VI: 238). Texts such as John Bulwer's *Chirologia . . . Chironomia* (1644) set out to answer this call. The degree to which early modern plays pursue a similar anatomy of *actio* remains relatively unexplored in current scholarship. But it would be easy to read *Macbeth* in this context, as a kind of glossary and archive of affective action. Line after line calls attention to the play of emotion on the players' faces, cataloging the forensic symptoms of horror and fear. Here's Lennox describing Ross, as he arrives from battle: "what haste looks through his eyes! So should he look / That seems to speak things strange" (1.2.46–7). "Look how our partner's rapt," Banquo observes to us aside, as Macbeth ponders the first prophecy. The witches gloss Macbeth's astonishment at the parade of kings, and Macbeth himself comments on his changing countenance continuously. "You make me strange / Even to the disposition that I owe, / When now I think you can behold such sights / And keep the natural ruby of your cheeks, / When mine is blanched with fear" (3.4.111–15). When the Scottish Doctor diagnoses Lady Macbeth's "perturbations," he diagnoses what the Gentleman calls her "accustom'd action," observing "look how she rubs her hands" (5.1.26–7).

The ambiguous causality of the phrase "accustom'd action" is suggestive. Lady Macbeth's action discovers her perturbations for the audience. It also makes the habituation of passions to action part of the spectacle. Bulwer describes the rhetorical gesture she performs as a sign of the *attempt* to establish innocence through performance:

Gestus XI: *Innocentiam ostendo*
   To imitate the posture of washing the hands by rubbing the back of one in the hollow of the other with a kind of detersive motion is a gesture sometimes used by those who would profess their innocency and declare they have no hand in that foul business . . . And it was practiced by Pilate when he would have transferred from himself unto the Jews the guilt of our Savior's blood. (Bulwer 1974: 40; Roach 1993: 37)

In this context we may read Lady Macbeth's hand-rubbing as continuous with her earlier emotional disciplines: an attempt to regulate her humors through actions that declare her innocence to herself. The extent of her perturbation testifies to her lack of success. But the scene also suggests the degree to which the habituation that suits action to affect was understood to work in reverse. Cognitive and emotional states conform to deliberate disciplines. Rhetoric provides the key principles for such affective "industry": what Edward Reynolds calls the hard social and personal work involved in conforming one's affects to a desired temper. "Our desires ought not to bee faint and sluggish, but industrious and painefull . . . True desires as they are right in regard of their object, so are they laborious in respect of their motion" (Reynolds 1971: 1995–6). Recent scholarship has made us more familiar with the early modern celebration of this labor – in the discourses of spiritual commitment and civil self-fashioning – than with the anxiety that emerges in Shakespearean scenes such as this (Schoenfeldt 1999; Shuger 1988).

Missing the self-disciplinary labor of *actio* and its verbal counterpart, *vociferatio*, modern readers sometimes mistake formally wrought accounts of early modern passion for dispassion. Schoenfeldt observes this tendency in the commentary on the sonnets, where the young man's "unmooved" and cold temper often strikes modern critics as a lack of feeling. In the humoral discourse that saturates the sequence, he argues, it would be likelier to signify "the victory of unruffled reason" over inconstant, amorous heat (Schoenfeldt 1999: 88). A similar misreading of the conventions for restraining grief informs Lawrence Stone's notorious assessment of the English Renaissance as a culture in which affections were less "warm" and the costs of personal loss felt less strongly than now (Stone 1977: 221). The difficulty seems especially acute in the context of tragedy, where post-Romantic expectations of spontaneously overflowing feeling often skew our assessment of formalized grief. So modern readers have historically struggled with Marcus' Petrarchan lament in *Titus Andronicus*, finding it a poor expression of feeling, inadequate to his loss and Lavinia's hurt.

Renaissance writers, too, registered the way in which humoral passions could be incommensurate with rhetorical composure. However, they understood the attempt at control itself as an index of intense feeling. The Third Queen in *The Two Noble Kinsmen* makes this point with bitter humoral puns:

> O, my petition was
> Set down in ice, which by hot grief uncandied
> Melts into drops; so sorrow, wanting form
> Is pressed with deeper matter. (1.1.106–9)

Her icy rhetoric should be suited to melancholy (a cold, dry humor). Yet her grief is so pressing and vehement ("hot") that the "deeper matter" of affect deconstructs its conventional forms. Here and in Marcus' lament a Renaissance audience would understand the attempt at rhetorical control as an index of distress and also a device for moderating it. Experts as diverse as Henry Peacham, Sir Thomas Elyot, and Richard Mulcaster prescribed verbal exercises as a means of tempering the passions, for

> *vociferatio* . . . encreaseth, cleanseth, strengtheneth and fineth, the naturall heat . . . for that by mouing the vocall instrumentes the inward moysture consumeth and wasteth, as it doeth appeare by that thicke and grosse vapour, which proceedeth out of his mouth that speaketh alowd, and other congealed excrementes resting of olde in other passages, which this exercise expelled from the inward partes. (Mulcaster 1581: 55–6)

Wright's advice for moderating grief is itself scripted by rhetorical convention. Offering the hypothetical example of a woman "who hath lost her onely sonne in wars," Wright describes a rhetorical regimen of good counsel. The regime follows the familiar conventions of elegy:

> shew her, that death apprehendeth all men sooner or later; it is a tribute must bee paid; this world yeeldeth nothing but miserie; happier are they that depart from it . . . his death was glorious, for his Countrey, for his Prince, the which among valiant Captaines, and noble mindes, that alwayes beene prized aboue tenne thousand liues. (Wright 1986: 52)

And so on.

The passionate oxymorons of Petrarchan lyric – "hot grief," "burning ice" – serve a similar purpose. They display the caloric alterations wrought by love, but their formal antitheses also serve for therapy. Such displays of rhetorical self-command have their own myth of origins in the Renaissance, Cicero's prehistoric "orator civilizer" (Rebhorn 1978: 23). Where once "men wandered at large in the fields like animals and lived on wild fare," the orator brought "every useful and honourable occupation . . . [and] transformed them into a kind and gentle folk" (Cicero 1949: 5).

The rhetorical regimens described here sustain a radically intersubjective model of emotional experience, in which passions circulate through and between feeling subjects. This is particularly clear in the case of the Third Queen's grief. She solicits Theseus' help by a kind of affective contagion, inducing sympathetic alterations not just in him but in the whole onstage audience. Her "hot grief" "beats so ardently upon" Emilia that it makes "a counter-reflect 'gainst" Theseus' heart. The responsive affect, of course, is pity, into which state the circulating heat "warms" his heart, "though it were made of stone" (1.1.126–9). Such caloric "sympathies" were defined as the "unity, agreements of the spirites, humors and members" in the body (Jones 1574: 29). These sympathies occurred between bodies as well as within them. Thus a playgoing audience that recognized the topos of "weeping queens" would have understood conformation of their own humors as the logical extension of the emotion script.[7] The active spirits in a player's body were understood to move an auditor's mind by a kind of classical *enargeia*, passing through the eyes and ears to excite similar physical motions.[8] "Action," Wright explains,

universally is a naturall or artificiall moderation, qualification, modification, or composition of the voice, countenance, and gesture of body proceeding from some passion, and
apt to stir up the like, for it seemeth that the soule plaieth upon these three parts, as a
musitian upon three strings, & according to his striking so they sound. (Wright 1986:
176)

Passions sound as they move through the material soul:

for the passion in the perswader seemeth to me, to resemble the wind a trumpeter
bloweth in at one end of the trumpet, & in what maner it proceedeth from him, so it
issueth forth at the other end, & commeth to our eares: & as it is qualified, so it worketh
in us. (Ibid: 174)

Bacon's description of theatrical affections working on the "minds of men in company"
like a bow on a fiddle invokes these commonplace musical similes. Like music, Bacon
suggests, the emotions within a playgoer's mind resonate in the minds of nearby playgoers. In the rhetorical idiom of contemporary passions theory such theatrical circulation of affections models passionate communication more generally. All compassion
is inherently theatrical, Nicolas Coeffeteau observes in *A Table of Humane Passions*,
moving us most when "our eyes are spectators" (Coeffeteau 1621: 374).[9] Such theatrical circulation had potentially powerful therapeutic effects, especially for grief. The
grieving mind "doth receive (as it were) some lightnesse and comfort, when it finds
it selfe generative unto others, and produces sympathie in them"; the heaviest "inter-
nall torment" is "reflexive upon it selfe" and not "any whit transient, to work commiseration in any spectator" (Reynolds 1971: 54–5). Of course theatrical affections,
like other occasional causes, might turn "the Bias of mens Desires . . . contrary to the
standing temper and complexion of the Body" (ibid: 11–12). This is one reason why
English antitheatrical polemicists found the alterations brought on by theatrical passions so radically self-estranging.

To return to *Macbeth*, the possibilities of Ciceronian persuasion seem to be precisely
what is at stake in the play's numerous scenes of sympathetic spectation. Shakespeare
repeatedly recalls our attention from traumatic scenery – offstage horrors such as
the "New Gorgon" of Duncan's dead body, the apparition of Banquo's ghost – to
the reactions of an onstage audience. When Macduff returns from Duncan's bedchamber crying horror, the affective work involved in spectation plays out at some
length. The spectacle of Duncan's body destroys sight, he tells us. Nevertheless it
requires to be internalized and communicated. So as he raises the alarm, Macduff calls
for reaction:

> Up, up, and see
> The great doom's image! Malcolm! Banquo!
> As from your graves rise up, and walk like sprites,
> To countenance this horror! (2.3.77–80)

Here, Macduff describes the humoral sympathy required of good actors and expected of spectators in the period: conforming affect and expression. The oxymoron "countenance this horror" suggests the complexity of this process. Accept horror in order to abjure it: behold it, conform your feelings to it, reflect it in your aspect, reflect on it morally, give it moral expression. Among the affects the thanes might catch, horror communicates especially swiftly and legibly. "Horrors" (from the Latin for "roughness") are surface symptoms, such as shivering or bristling hair, that reflect the perturbed motions of animal spirits the way a rugged landscape or ruffled water reflects the weather (*OED* n. 2 a, b). In fear, as Reynolds explains, the spirits rush from the extremities to the heart, causing a constellation of symptoms: from starting, paleness, immobility, to suspension of thought (Reynolds 1971: 297). By such motions of spirit the witches' prophecies "unfix" Macbeth's hair and make his "seated heart knock" at his ribs (1.3.135–6).

The intensity of the "New Gorgon" scene derives in part from the diversity of persons through whom the horrifying prospect passes. The offstage audience doesn't see the murdered king; but we hear his body being seen. Emotional knowledge emerges in this process not as a primary, self-possessed experience but as one filtered and deferred. Lady Macbeth first describes Duncan murdered. Yet she does so in anticipation, through the mediating image of her father that fills the moment of Duncan's offstage death. "Had he not resembled / My father as he slept, I had done't" (2.2.12–13). Later, Macduff calls the lords to Duncan's chamber to "see, and then speak yourselves" (2.3.73). Then, as if in response, Macbeth conjures the deathbed with extraordinary rhetorical poise, using it as an emotional pretext for killing the guards:

> Here lay Duncan,
> His silver skin laced with his golden blood,
> And his gashed stabs looked like a breach in nature
> For ruin's wasteful entrance. (2.3.111–14)

To the degree that Macbeth recognizes the "breach in nature" he describes, his apparent horror is surely genuine. To the degree that he marshals that recognition tactically, it is also artificial. Read in the post-Lockean context of a possessive inner life, Macbeth's equivocal passions pose a problem of authenticity: is this horror truly his own? Read in a humoral context, they raise a different set of anxieties: does this horror set him apart rather than attach him? To what degree does his response estrange him from the emotional routines of kind – in this case, from being powerfully moved, in company, by the horror he perceives? English passions theorists repeatedly remind their readers that one cannot move companions to a passion one does not feel oneself. In such persuasive exchanges, fear has a particularly powerful, cohesive reach.[10] As Reynolds writes in 1640, on the eve of civil war, "men in a fright and amazement, looke one another in the face; one mans countenance, as it were, asking counsell of another" (Reynolds 1971: 283). Macduff's call to "countenance" horror as shared internal motions defines the community of thanes in this way. Yet Macbeth's attempts at stoic discipline are so self-alienating that even his horror appears perversely individual and inward rather than social.

Such intersubjective exchanges posed theoretical and practical challenges, whether in Wright's "Courts, Fields, and Senates" or in the theatre. Too much impressibility led to excessively labile, perturbed passions of the kind that tyrannize over reason. It was the work of a civil subject (or playgoer) to moderate circulating passions industriously, applying his judgment to the difficult task of evaluating the "true sensations . . . associated with false ones so closely resembling them" (Cicero 1933: 15). Wright cautions the judicious auditor against being overswayed by rhetorical action (Wright 1986: 98–9). The *locus classicus* of this concern is Seneca's *De clementia*, which offered the categorical line against spontaneous compassion and framed it in effeminate terms (Seneca 1985, I: 439). We can see this principle at work in Shakespeare, moderating the affective reach of his weeping queens, as Theseus cautions Emilia against thoughtless compassion: "You are a right woman, sister: you have pity, / But want the understanding where to use it" (3.6.214–16). For Renaissance anti-Stoics, as for Theseus, Senecan misogyny works strategically to displace anxieties about excessive openness and to recuperate it in a civil and masculine form. In this way, as we have seen, the destabilizing "hot grief" that unglues the Third Queen reappears as more moderate "warmth" in Theseus' heart. Similar displacements script the ethical antitheses in *Macbeth* – courage and fearfulness, sternness and impressibility, firmness of purpose and inconstancy – as they play out differently in different characters.

Divisions of Emotional Labor

Divisions of emotional labor are critical to what we call the dramatic "arcs" of Shakespearean characters. The scripts for pity in *Macbeth*, for example, play out according to the gender of the character suffering or resisting the passion. Macbeth and Lady Macbeth appear to follow the same, self-imposed regime of sternness as they pursue their political ambitions. As the plan for Duncan's murder develops, both undertake to short-circuit the economy of affections, imagining actions that proceed without wit's oversight, independent of passion's informing response. Yet Macbeth's immunity to horror is the gradual result of self-discipline. First he proposes to break the cognitive connection between what he plans to do and the fears his plans elicit:

> . . . Stars, hide your fires,
> Let not light see my black and deep desires;
> The eye wink at the hand; yet let that be
> Which the eye fears, when it is done, to see. (1.4.50–3)

Here and elsewhere in the play his diction is marked by metonymic compression and displacement. The eye fears, light sees not desires, and so on. His conceit is to circumvent the emotional delivery system that connects perception, understanding, and action – a sleight of hand in which sensory evidence slips past overseeing wit and moral judgment. Desire moves the body to act; yet the motions of desire remain internally undetectable. In this way, as he understands it, "Strange things I have in head, that will to hand, / They must be acted, ere they may be scanne'd" (3.4.138–9). By reducing the robust economy that connects senses, passions, thought, and action he arrives, eventually, at the fiat: "be it thought and done" (4.1.149). Immunity to fear is a natural quality of a seasoned warrior, consistent with the manly fortitude he displays in his fight with Macdonwald. But Macbeth achieves a more extreme form of Stoic control by the end of the play, through a dietary discipline in which he sups "full of horrors," inuring himself to fearful prospects that should keep him pale.

The reactions Macbeth has lost by the end of the play – "the taste of fears," rising hair, a sudden start (5.5.9–13) – epitomize what he gives up in this process: the capacity to alter in response to his senses and know informing passion. Lady Macbeth calls this Stoicism manly. But the play stresses its cost, particularly the social leverage the passions provide. Properly directed fear has salutary effects; "feare expelleth sin," Wright notes briskly (Wright 1986: 17). But the passion must be felt for such effects to be gained. Impressibility is a prerequisite for activating the good counsel of wit, for moving the passions of others, and directing them to virtuous service. "Passions are not only, not wholy to be extinguished (as the Stoicks seemed to affirme) but sometimes to be moved, & stirred up for the service of vertue" (ibid). What Macbeth loses in his perverse Stoicism, paradoxically, is this capacity to move himself and others for salutary purposes, forging a kind of affective *comitatus*. This turns out to be a significant political liability. Macbeth's bloody, bold resoluteness isolates him from every social bond that might supply countervailing emotion: from friends and spouse, from the community of counselors at supper, and from the army that will not fight with him. "Honor, love, obedience, troops of friends," he acknowledges, "I must not look to have" (5.3.25–6).

Lady Macbeth sets out to short-circuit her own passions along similar lines. Yet the psychobiological consequences of her attempt are notably different. For Lady Macbeth, as we have seen, blocking remorse depends on being filled "top-full" with cruelty and thickening her blood. In a female body, already thought to be overproductive of fluids, such clogging entails a higher psychosomatic cost: the later "perturbations" (loss of reason, a consciousness closer to sleep than waking) are consistent with a mind oppressed by its humors (Paster 1998: 419). My point is not to diagnose Lady Macbeth's pathology here, but to observe an argument against Stoic eradication of passions that develops differently in Macbeth's plot and Lady Macbeth's.[11] His bloody sternness emerges slowly, through systematic labor. Her sternness is offered in vexed terms from the start, in part because the norm of impressible feminine humors should incline her to compassion. As Wright concludes, "the tenderness" of female complexion moves women more to compassion and pity, "they surpasse men also in pitie and devotion," and are less prone to incontinence "for lacke of heate" (Wright 1986: 40). Lemnius offers a darker spin on female complexion, against which

Lady Macbeth's transformation might also be measured. The softness of women's flesh, saturated throughout by excessive humors, makes them "subject to all passions and perturbations . . . a woman enraged, is besides her selfe, and hath not power over her self, so that she cannot rule her passions, or bridle her disturbed affections, or stand against them with force of reason and judgement" (Lemnius 1658: 73–4). Lady Macbeth's flash of sympathetic pity at the moment of Duncan's murder strengthens the comparison between such ordinary, labile female passions and the self-discipline that can contemplate a child murdered at the breast. Such moments of imaginative sympathy, which measure emotional control against an imagined personal loss, invoke the classical humanist debates about *apathia*. Cicero's *Tusculan Disputations* cites the familiar scenario (the death of a child) as an established test for apathy (Cicero 1945, III: xxiv; also discussed in Strier 2003). Wright, as we saw, uses a similar hypothetical situation to explain how to manage excessive grief. The particular force of this topos in *Macbeth* – and its anti-Stoic bias – depends on its delivery through a gendered consciousness that in normative terms would be habituated to pity.

The point here is not only that Lady Macbeth's perturbed reason works as a counterpoint to Macbeth's political isolation. Her disorder also displaces anxiety about the potentially detrimental consequences of passionate impressibility, by associating its costs (disordered reason) with the labile extremes of femininity. Recuperating impressibility in this way, Shakespeare affirms the leverage that Renaissance anti-Stoics found in emotional transactions: the good offices of education and counsel perverted by the Macbeths' Stoic practice. In this way, Lady Macbeth's sleepwalking scene offers a dramatic counterpoint to the encounter between Macduff and Malcolm that directly precedes it, in 4.3. There, in the English scene, Shakespeare takes up the problem of impressibility directly, invoking the conventional association of labile passions and tyranny. As Malcolm tests Macduff by claiming a variety of vices, Macduff recognizes the topos:

> Boundless intemperance
> In nature is a tyranny; it hath been
> Th'untimely emptying of the happy throne,
> And fall of many kings. (4.3.66–9)

The incontinent desires Malcolm claims in this scene invoke the specter that haunts anti-Stoic passions theory: the especially close relationship between the senses and the passions. In terms of emotional discipline, Malcolm's "ill-compos'd affections," wholly bound up in sensual drives, would seem the effeminate opposite of Macbeth's painfully wrought sternness. Malcolm deflects some of the force of this association when he retracts his "taints and blames," starting with the extraordinary claim that he is "yet / Unknown to woman" (4.3.125–6). His judicious performance shows up especially well in comparison to Lady Macbeth's wandering reason. Yet Malcolm's performance turns out to be less invested in containing or accommodating passions – the problem that Macduff at first responds to – than in soliciting and governing them. As the scene progresses Shakespeare explores the proper circulation of knowledge about the passions and the affective strategies involved in civil education. Knowledge of the passions flows here, as Wright recommends, from Macduff to Malcolm. Governance of the passions flows in reverse, top down. Moreover, Malcolm's disciplined performance of a tyrant provides the standard of abuse against which to measure his future receptiveness. His cautious dissembling emerges as a judicious ability to sway and be swayed through good counsel, in the tradition of advice to princes (Mapstone 1998: 178–80; Fowler 2000: 91–2). As he comforts Macduff, Malcolm promises "even now / I put myself to thy direction . . . What I am truly / Is thine, and my poor country's, to command" (4.3.121–2, 131–2).

Beyond testing Macduff and showing Malcolm to be a savvier ruler than his father, of course, the English scene demonstrates the Ciceronian procedures of passionate governance. Malcolm's success in playing the stock tyrant depends on Macduff's responsive horror as his audience. When Ross enters with the news of Macduff's murdered family, the instruction continues in a different register, as Malcolm coaches Macduff into his grief. Macduff's gruff initial response keeps open the possibility that he either lacks family feeling (as his wife accuses) or could pass the Stoic test for *apathia*. Malcolm solicits Macduff's grief by stages, framing it instrumentally with a figure borrowed from Cicero. "Be this the whetstone of your sword, let grief / Convert to anger; blunt not the heart, enrage it" (4.3.228–9).[12] Only when Macduff achieves the rhetorical poise that signifies grief felt but mastered – as in Marcus' lament in *Titus Andronicus* – can the scene close:

> O, I could play the woman with mine eyes,
> And braggart with my tongue! But, gentle heavens,
> Cut short all intermission. Front to front
> Bring thou this fiend of Scotland and myself;
> Within my sword's length set him . . . (4.3.230–4)

"This [tune] goes manly," Malcolm responds with satisfaction. "Come go we to the King, our power is ready" (4.3.235–6).

Topical Emotions

To return to the impasse described so powerfully by Andrew Gurr, what constitutes Macduff's "thoughtful" response to horrifying events is not the exclusive product of internal processes but the work of minds in company. Thoughtfulness, in this context, means the salutary reception of impressions and guidance, both of which direct powerful passions such as grief toward a shared, civil norm. In the public theatre the gap between a normative response to a pitiful prospect and the notoriously various, even intransigent reactions of English playgoers opens precisely the opportunity for affective industry that anti-Stoic humanists looked for. As Steven Mullaney observes, the popular stage served the period not only as a dominant metaphor for emotional exchange, but also "as a forum for the representation, solicitation, shaping, and enacting of affect in various forms, for both the reflection and . . . the reformation of emotions and their economies" (Mullaney 1996: 244).

The Shakespearean investments in the English scene follow the same anxious logic Floyd-Wilson finds in Wright, recuperating impressibility as a courtly virtue. Malcolm's repeated references to the English court reinforce a connection between this salutary solicitation of emotion and Englishness. The flow of passionate impressions in this scene offers conservative reassurance, as we watch Macduff conform his affects to the adept direction of his prospective monarch. Yet the odd, topical interpolation that splits the scene – the interruption of the English Doctor – suggests that the politics of the new Stuart court may vex this top-down script. The interpolation also suggests a partial motive for Shakespeare's cautionary vision of destructive control. James's counselors and the sovereign himself represent a mixed ethnic heritage of barbarian and civil, raising questions about the sources of counsel at court and the native receptiveness of the monarch. Early English ethnographers describe the Scots as stubbornly barbaric, resistant to education and civil reform (Braunmuller 1997: 38). The underlying logic for these claims was humoral, as Floyd-Wilson (1998: 198) has shown. The native intractability of Scottish temper, amply testified by Scotland's long internal struggles, presented a significant obstacle to the project of union: the integration of separate legal, educational, and religious systems so urgent to James I, but flagging in 1606. Debating this problem, contemporary politicians produced a tripartite account of Scottishness. As he advises Prince Henry on how to manage Scotland, for example, James details a plan for integration that reflects the different regions of the country and the different ways they take to education. The former "borders" will soon become the civil midlands of a unified Britain. Mainland highlanders are barbaric and independent, but some civility intermixed makes them educable. A third group, those that "dwelleth in the Iles, and are alluterly barbares, without any sort or shew of civilitie," can only be handled by aggressive colonization (James I 1994: 24–5). The same strategic divisions show up in the union debates of the next decade. A. R. Braunmuller cites the example of Sir Christopher Piggott, sent to the Tower for enjoining the House of Commons not to "join murderers, thieves, and the roguish Scots with the well-deserving Scots." In terms that echo Holinshed's version of the historical past, Piggott goes on to observe that such "roguish Scots" "have not suffered above two kings to die in their beds, these 200 years" (Braunmuller 1997: 13). James was publicly negotiating the reputations of thieving borderers and murderous highlanders (with whom he had his own difficult history) as late as 1610.[13]

Shakespeare's account of national passions in *Macbeth* follows similar strategic divisions, as Braunmuller observes. Though Macbeth first defeats Macdonald's mixed forces, from the "western iles," he soon assumes both their rebellious plot and the stern cruelty celebrated by early historiographers. In contrast, Midland Scots like Macduff and Malcolm respond immediately to fearful knowledge. Their impressibility is continually associated with the Anglo-Scottish alliance – to the extent that the play endorses tactics such as flight and desertion, that in other contexts would appear cowardly or treasonous. Malcolm and Donaldbain worry that they cannot summon the emotions Macduff calls for when he discovers their father's murder. They flee in a flurry of antitheatrical excuses. "Let's not consort with them; / To show an unfelt sorrow is an office / Which the false man does easy. I'll to England" (2.3.135–7). Yet the play ultimately endorses both their flight and the theatrical governance of emotion they scorn here. Ross and Angus repeatedly remind us that their flight represents the better part of valor and preserves Scotland's future. And in England, Malcolm's antitheatricality itself reverses course. England is a stage for very good theatre, where he proves a much better player than Macbeth, as we have seen.

Shakespeare adds a final twist to these issues in the closing scene, where he modulates Malcolm's success in governing the passions of others. In 5.9 Old Siward and Malcolm reprise the topos of a father grieving the death of his son. Whether Siward grieves properly has been an open question for critics. We see a different problem, however, if we shift our attention from inward grief to emotional exchange: from feelings as such, to the attitudes towards feelings in this scene. Siward seems to reject Malcolm's guidance. Malcolm corrects Siward as he did Macduff: "He's worth more sorrow, / And that I'll spend for him." Yet Siward sticks gruffly to his position: "He's worth no more" (5.9.17–18). If we follow the ethnic logic of these parallel scenes – the grief of a Scots father vs. the grief of an English one – we might find a subtle partisan claim. Siward's apparent coldness suggests the neo-Stoic superiority of the English nobleman. Yet the partisan claim here is less neo-Stoic than it appears. The exchange rehearses the familiar, elegiac conventions for mastering grief, in terms that echo Wright's prescription for managing excessive grief. To see this it is worth reading the scene in full.

Act 5, scene 9 begins with Malcolm's concern for missing comrades and Siward's gruff assessment that some loss is necessary for such a great gain. Ross again delivers the critical news: young Siward died honorably in battle. "Then he is dead?" Siward asks. Ross confirms this and warns against excessive grief: "Your cause of sorrow / Must not be measured by his worth, for then / It hath no end" (5.9.9–11). Siward checks again that the death was honorable and then consigns his son to a better fight:

> Why then, God's soldier be he.
> Had I as many sons as I have hairs
> I would not wish them to a fairer death;
> And so his knell is knolled. (5.9.13–16)

Reading, as Wierzbicka reminds us, for communication strategies, we can hear the familiar topoi of elegy here – he's God's soldier, his death was honorable (many are not) – that communicate a struggle to master strong grief. We do not have to endorse this military ethos to recognize the solace it seeks. That conclusion might lend us to the norms governing the handling of feelings at play in this scene. When Malcolm extends the conversation, offering emotional guidance as he did with Macduff, Siward redirects the younger man, affirming his own capacity to turn his feelings to constructive ends: "He's worth no more. / They say he parted well and paid his score, / so God be with him. Here comes newer comfort" (5.9.17–19).

The significance of Malcolm's intervention is slightly different here than in 4.3, a difference that returns us to the problem of Anglo-Scottish union. The classic Stoic test plays out as a three-way exchange: between a Scottish thane (Ross) and an English noble (Siward is Earl of Northumberland), with the emotions of the prospective monarch located somewhere in between. The political positions dramatized here bear on the problem of access at the new court. To what degree is James's temper impressible and to whom? To what degree are royal passions symptomatic or predictive of the possibilities of union? The play addresses these questions directly in the interpolated passage that splits 4.3, the reported scene of Edward's Royal Touch. The passions transacted in this ritual, as reported by Malcolm, explain Malcolm's offer to "spend" "more sorrow" for Siward's son.

As in the "New Gorgon" scene, the burden of this interpolated passage is the reaction of an audience (Malcolm) rather than the spectacle itself. Explaining the ritual to Macduff, Malcolm reports Edward's cure of his scrofulous petitioners in graphic detail:

> strangely visited people,
> All swoll'n and ulcerous, pitiful to the eye,
> The mere despair of surgery, he cures,
> Hanging a golden stamp about their necks,
> Put on with holy prayers; and 'tis spoken
> To the succeeding royalty he leaves
> The healing benediction. (4.3.150–6)

This report measures the affective responses conjured in the scene – disgust, pity, despair – against Edward's apparently unruffled "grace" (4.3.159). Edward's "miraculous work" (4.3.147) may be a royal legacy, but as Marc Bloch makes clear, James's own repugnance for the ritual was an open secret. Bloch repeats an eyewitness account of James's first ceremony of touching, in 1603, that plays out the crucial matters of influence and access at stake in the performance. As the eyewitness describes it, James goes through the ritual reluctantly. He is led by his English counselors but unable to begin without debunking the event. "During the whole of [his preamble]," the observer adds, "it was noticeable that the king several times looked towards the Scottish ministers by his side, as though expecting some sign of approval, since he had previously discussed the matter with them" (Bloch 1989: 188). Bloch's informant records divided national affiliations that play out in James's public control of disbelief and disgust. The import of the scene for the eyewitness, of course, is how well James takes counsel and from whom. Read in this context, Malcolm's eyewitness account of Edward's ritual invokes the open secret of James's disgust. It also offers a corrective vision of the ritual, giving royal access to multiple audiences. Indeed,

Shakespeare qualifies royal access – including theatrical access to Edward's grace and its salutary affects in a witness such as Malcolm – as an English legacy. It is not only English to take counsel well, but also advisable to take English counsel.

Shakespeare finesses this partisan line by making the normative royal passions Malcolm describes (Edward's lack of disgust) exceptional. Edward's "grace" evokes the condition of saints such as Catherine of Siena, whose self-disciplines sustained an extraordinary openness and intimacy with bodily decay – welcoming what repulsed all others in *imitatio Christi*.[14] What Malcolm's report anglicizes, in sum, is Edward's transformative openness. Edward's gracious passions reorder the affects of witnesses, who like Malcolm may come to contemplate scrofulous ulcers with pity rather than aversion. Malcolm's intervention with Siward confirms Edward's radical accessibility. Where Malcolm offers Macduff emotional direction, he offers Siward affective largesse: the capacity to "spend" more emotion in *imitatio* Edward. The scene of emotion that matters here is not, finally, the inward motions that fill Edward, but their counter-reflect at court and outside it. That sympathetic reflection may reach as far, the passage suggests, as Malcolm's Scotland or James's England. The most pressing testimony of these tragic affects is less their inwardness than their contagious reach.

NOTES

My thinking on this topic evolved in collaboration with Mary Floyd-Wilson and Gail Kern Paster. The introduction to our forthcoming volume, *Reading the Early Modern Passions: Essays in the Cultural History of Emotion* (University of Pennsylvania Press, 2003) will extend some of the arguments outlined here. Several essays in this volume (cited below) explore the contours of English anti-Stoicism, as does Floyd-Wilson's discussion of *Othello* (Floyd-Wilson 2002).

1   The question of "inwardness" has generated several approaches in recent histories of the self. Katherine Maus (1995) explores the discourses of interiority in legal, political, and religious writings. She ascribes early modern subjectivity to an historically grounded discontinuity between deep inner life and surface show. This account parallels Charles Taylor's (1989) picture of the "disengaged" subject of late seventeenth-century political philosophy. Mary Floyd-Wilson, Katherine Park, Gail Kern Paster, Michael Schoenfeldt, and others have emphasized the inextricability of psychological states, bodily conditions, and social identity in the early modern period. With William Ian Miller, I assume that the perception of a "deep inner life" is common to many cultures but that the meaning of this experience is construed historically, in very different ways (Miller 1995). My interest, like that of Lorraine Daston (1994), is in the shifting epistemology of seventeenth-century English emotions. The changing ways in which emotions are known, in this period, register the mutual accommodations of physiological and social theory. Emotions, *pace* Paster, are performances that materialize social facts (Paster 1998: 440).

2   Recent work in neuropsychology reopens the prospect of bodily alteration through affective discipline. See, for example, Damasio (1994) and Hochschild (1983).

3   On the importance of communal verification, see also Shapin (1994).

4   See Strier (1988) on ethical disobedience.

5   Floyd-Wilson (2002) suggests that this bias may be more typical of Shakespearean drama than the neo-Stoicism Schoenfeldt describes.

6   Stephen Halliwell cautions against overemphasizing the influence of the *Poetics*. "Not only was it regularly interpreted alongside, and in the light of, Horace's *Ars Poetica*, in such a way as to dilute

many of its own distinctive ideas into a kind of homogenized rhetorical classicism; but there was constant, if unsystematic, reference and comparison to other classical sources (Plato, Cicero, Quintilian, as well as classical poets, Latin much more often than Greek) whose interests and aims were not always consistent with Aristotle's" (Halliwell 1992: 413).

7   See George Farquhar's *The Inconstant*, 4.3: "Cry then, handsomely; cry like a queen in a tragedy."

8   On *enargeia* in the Renaissance theatre, see Roach (1993: ch. 1, esp. pp. 24–5, 30). The phrase "active spirits" is from Thomas Heywood's *Apology for Actors* (Heywood 1841: 45).

9   On the "sanctified Contagion" of compassion in the early public sphere, see Staines (2003).

10   Suspicious of the cognitively disabling affect of fear, English anti-Stoics also find it a salutary passion. Reynolds testifies to the positive uses of fear in war and politics (Reynolds 1971: 299). Both Wright and Reynolds describe communities forged through fear, citing biblical and historical examples (Reynolds 1971: 12; Wright 1986: 274–7).

11   For comprehensive diagnoses of humoral passions in Shakespeare, see Campbell (1930) and Babb (1951). For scholarship that reads early psychological categories in terms of their cultural history, see Daston (1994), Leinwand (1999), and Macdonald (1992).

12   The commonplace about sharpened passion comes from the *Disputations*. As Wright notes: "Cicero, in *4.Tusculan*, calleth anger, *cotem*, the whetstone of fortitude" (Wright 1986: 16). Reynolds elaborates: "Anger, Zeale, Shame, Griefe, Love," as whetstones on which "true fortitude sharpneth its sword" (Reynolds 1971: 59).

13   In 1607, discussing naturalization, James describes the borders as a "Navel or Umbilick" of the unified nation (James I 1994: 169). In 1610, on standardizing common law, James cites the murderous highlanders as an obstacle to universal legal codes (ibid: 185).

14   For an alternative account of Catherine of Siena's self-control, see Miller (1997: 158).

References and Further Reading

Babb, L. (1951). *The Elizabeth Malady: A Study of Melancholia in English Literature from 1580 to 1642*. East Lansing: Michigan State College Press.

Bacon, F. (1869). *The Works of Francis Bacon*, ed. J. Spedding, R. L. Ellis, and D. D. Heath. New York.

Bloch, M. (1989). *The Royal Touch: Sacred Monarchy and Scrofula in England and France*, trans. E. J. E. Anderson. New York: Dorset Press.

Blount, T. (1969) [1656]. *Glossographia*, s.v. "Tragedie." Menston, UK: Scolar Press.

Bradley, A. C. (1955) [1904]. *Shakespearean Tragedy: Hamlet, Othello, King Lear, Macbeth*. New York: Meridian Books.

Braunmuller, A. R. (1997). Introduction. In W. Shakespeare, *The Tragedy of Macbeth*. Cambridge: Cambridge University Press.

Bulwer, J. (1974) [1644]. *Chirologia: or the naturall language of the hand; Chironomia: or, the art of manuall rhetorique*, ed. J. W. Cleary, foreword by D. Potter. Carbondale: Southern Illinois University Press.

Bushnell, R. (1990). *Tragedies of Tyrants: Political Thought and Theater in the English Renaissance*. Ithaca, NY: Cornell University Press.

Campbell, L. B. (1930). *Shakespeare's Tragic Heroes, Slaves of Passion*. Cambridge: Cambridge University Press.

Cicero (1933). *De natura deorum: Academica*, trans. H. Rackham. London: W. Heinemann; New York: G. P. Putnam's Sons.

——(1945). *Tusculan Disputations*, 2nd edn., trans. J. E. King. Cambridge, MA: Harvard University Press.

——(1949). *De inventione*, trans. H. M. Hubbell. Cambridge, MA: Harvard University Press.

Coeffeteau, N. (1621). *A Table of Humane Passions with Their Causes and Effects*, trans. E. Grimston. London: Printed by Nicholas Okes.

Crooke, H. (1615). *Microcosmographia: A Description of the Body of Man*. London: W. Jaggard.

Damasio, A. R. (1994). *Descartes' Error: Emotion, Reason, and the Human Brain*. New York: G. P. Putnam.

Daston, L. (1994). Fortuna and the Passions. In T. Kavanagh (ed.) *Chance, Culture and the Literary Text*. Ann Arbor: University of Michigan Press, 25–47.

Elias, N. (1978). *The Civilizing Process*. vol. 1, trans. E. Jephcott. New York: Urizen Books.

Elyot, T. (1883) [1531]. *The boke named The gouernour*, 2 vols., ed. H. Croft. London: Kegan Paul, Trench.

Floyd-Wilson, M. (1998). Temperature, Temperance, and Racial Difference in Ben Jonson's *The Masque of Blackness*. *English Literary Renaissance*, 28, 2, 183–209.

——(2002). Othello, Passion, and Race. In P. Beidler and G. L. Taylor (eds.) *Writing Race Across the Atlantic World, 1492–1763*. New York: Palgrave.

——(2003). *English Ethnicity and Race in Early Modern Drama*. Cambridge: Cambridge University Press.

Fowler, E. (2000). The Rhetoric of Policial Forms: Social Persons and the Criterion of Fit in Colonial Law, *Macbeth* and the *Irish Masque at Court*. In A. Boesky and M. T. Crane (eds.) *Form and Reform in Renaissance England: Essays in Honor of Barbara Kiefer Lewalski*. Newark: University of Delaware Press, 70–104.

Gurr, A. (1996). *Playgoing in Shakespeare's London*, 2nd edn. Cambridge: Cambridge University Press.

Hadfield, G. (1992). Descartes' Physiology and Its Relation to Its Psychology. In J. Cottingham (ed.) *The Cambridge Companion to Descartes*. Cambridge: Cambridge University Press, 333–70.

Halliwell, S. (1992). *The Poetics* and its Interpreters. In A. O. Rorty (ed.) *Essays on the Poetics*. Princeton, NJ: Princeton University Press.

Heywood, T. (1841) [1612]. *Apology for Actors*. London: Shakespeare Society.

Hochschild, A. R. (1983). *The Managed Heart: Commercialization of Human Feeling*. Berkeley: University of California Press.

James I. (1994). *King James VI and I: Political Writings*, ed. J. P. Sommerville. Cambridge: Cambridge University Press.

James, S. (1997). *Passion and Action: The Emotions in Seventeenth-Century Philosophy*. Oxford: Clarendon Press; New York: Oxford University Press.

Jones, J. (1574). *A briefe, excellent, and profitable discourse, of the naturall beginning of all growing and liuing things, heate, generation, effects of the spirits, gouernment, vse and abuse of phisicke, preseruation, &c*. London.

Leinwand, T. (1999). *Theatre, Finance, and Society in Early Modern England*. Cambridge: Cambridge University Press.

Lemnius, L. (1658). *The Secret Miracles of Nature*. London.

Locke, J. (1975) [1690]. *An Essay Concerning Human Understanding*, ed. P. H. Nidditch. Oxford: Clarendon Press.

Lutz, C. (1990). Engendered Emotion: Gender, Power, and the Rhetoric of Emotional Control in American Discourse, In C. Lutz and L. Abu-Lughod (eds.) *Language and the Politics of Emotion*. Cambridge: Cambridge University Press.

Macdonald, M. (1992). The Fearefull Estate of Francis Spira: Narrative, Identity, and Emotion in Early Modern England. *Journal of British Studies*, 31, 32–61.

Mapstone, S. (1998). Shakespeare and Scottish Kingship: A Case History. In S. Mapstone and J. Wood (eds.) *The Rose and the Thistle: Essays on the Culture of Late Medieval and Renaissance Scotland*. East Lothian: Tuchivell Press, 158–89.

Maus, K. E. (1995). *Inwardness and Theater in the English Renaissance*. Chicago, IL: University of Chicago Press.

Miller, W. I. (1995). Deep Inner Lives, Individualism, and People of Honour. *History of Political Thought*, 16, 190–207.

——(1997). *The Anatomy of Disgust*. Cambridge, MA: Harvard University Press.

Mulcaster, R. (1581). *Positions wherin those primitive circumstances be examined, which are necessarie for the training vp of children*. London.

Muldrew, C. (1998). *The Economy of Obligation: The Culture of Credit and Social Relations in Early Modern England.* New York: St. Martin's Press.

Mullaney, S. (1996). Mourning and Misogyny: *Hamlet, The Revenger's Tragedy*, and the Final Progress of Elizabeth I, 1600–1607. In R. Newman (ed.) *Centuries' Ends, Narrative Means.* Stanford, CA: Stanford University Press, 238–60.

Park, K. (1988). The Organic Soul. In C. B. Schmitt et al. (eds.) *The Cambridge History of Renaissance Philosophy.* Cambridge: Cambridge University Press, 464–84.

Paster, G. K. (1997). Nervous Tension: Networks of Blood and Spirit in the Early Modern Body. In D. Hillman and C. Mazzio (eds.) *The Body in Parts: Fantasies of Corporeality in Early Modern Europe.* New York: Routledge, 107–25.

——(1998). The Unbearable Coldness of Female Being: Women's Imperfection and the Humoral Economy. *English Literary Renaissance*, 28, 416–40.

——(2003). The Humor of It. In R. Dutton and J. Howard (eds.) *A Companion to Shakespeare's Works, Vol. 3: The Comedies.* Oxford: Blackwell.

Petrarch, F. (1948). On His Own Ignorance and That of Many Others, trans. H. Nachod. In E. Cassirer, P. O. Kristeller, and J. H. Randall, Jr. (eds.) *The Renaissance Philosophy of Man.* Chicago, IL: University of Chicago Press.

Puttenham, G. (1970). *The Arte of English Poesie.* Kent, OH: Kent State University Press.

Rebhorn, W. A. (1978). *Courtly Performances: Masking and Festivity in Castiglione's Book of the Courtier.* Detroit, MI: Wayne State University Press.

Reynolds, E. (1971) [1640]. *A Treatise of the Passions and Faculties of the Soule of Man*, ed. M. L. Wiley. Gainesville, FL: Scholars' Facsimiles and Reprints.

Roach, J. (1993). *The Player's Passion: Studies in the Science of Acting.* Ann Arbor: University of Michigan Press.

Rowe, K. (1999). *Dead Hands: Fictions of Agency, Renaissance to Modern.* Stanford, CA: Stanford University Press.

——(2002). Memory and Revision in Chapman's Bussy Plays. *Renaissance Drama*, 31, 112–35.

Schoenfeldt, M. C. (1999). *Bodies and Selves in Early Modern England: Physiology and Inwardness in Spenser, Shakespeare, Herbert, and Milton.* Cambridge: Cambridge University Press.

Seneca (1985). *De clementia.* In J. W. Basore (trans.) *Seneca: Moral Essays*, 3 vols. Cambridge, MA: Harvard University Press.

Shapin, S. (1994). *The Social History of Truth: Civility and Science in Seventeenth-Century England.* Chicago, IL: University of Chicago Press.

Shuger, D. (1988). *Sacred Rhetoric: The Christian Grand Style in the English Renaissance.* Princeton, NJ: Princeton University Press.

Sidney, P. (1970) [1595]. *Defense of Poesy*, ed. L. Soens. Lincoln: University of Nebraska Press.

Siraisi, N. G. (1990). *Medieval and Early Renaissance Medicine: An Introduction to Knowledge and Practice.* Chicago. IL: University of Chicago Press.

Staines, J. (2003). Reason, Passion, and Compassion in the Early Modern Public Sphere. In M. Floyd-Wilson, G. K. Paster, and K. Rowe (eds.) *Reading the Early Modern Passions: Essays in the Cultural History of Emotion.* Philadelphia: University of Pennsylvania Press.

Stone, L. (1977). The Growth of Affective Individualism. In *The Family, Sex and Marriage in England, 1500–1800.* New York: Harper and Row.

Strier, R. (1988). Faithful Servants: Shakespeare's Praise of Disobedience. In H. Dubrow (ed.) *The Historical Renaissance: New Essays on Tudor and Stuart Literature and Culture.* Chicago, IL: Chicago University Press, 104–33.

——(2003). Against the Rule of Reason: Praise of Passion from Petrarch to Luther to Shakespeare to Herbert. In M. Floyd-Wilson, G. K. Paster, and K, Rowe (eds.) *Reading the Early Modern Passions: Essays in the Cultural History of Emotion.* Philadelphia: University of Pennsylvania Press.

Sutton, J. (1998). *Philosophy and Memory Traces: Descartes to Connectionism*. Cambridge: Cambridge University Press.

Taylor, C. (1989). *Sources of the Self: The Making of the Modern Identity*. Cambridge, MA: Harvard University Press.

Wierzbicka, A. (1994). Emotion, Language, and Cultural Scripts. In S. Kitayama and H. R. Marcus (eds.) *Emotion and Culture: Empirical Studies of Mutual Influence*. Washington, DC: American Psychological Association, 133–95.

Wright, T. (1986) [1601]. *The Passions of the Mind in General*, ed. W. W. Newbold. New York: Garland.

4
The Divided Tragic Hero
Catherine Belsey

Body Parts

"Then let them anatomize Regan," exclaims mad Lear in Gloucester's outhouse; "see what breeds about her heart. Is there any cause in nature that makes these hard hearts?" (*King Lear*, 3.6.73–5).[1] We are so accustomed to hearts in their modern, every-day metaphorical usage, and so aware of figurative anatomies of wit, abuses, or melancholy in Shakespeare's own period, that it would be easy to miss what was probably the first association of these lines for Shakespeare's original audience. Lear is condemning his daughter to the practice of dissection carried out in the contemporary anatomy theatres. With his fellow outcasts, the Fool, Poor Tom, and his servant Caius, as his fellow judges, he has proposed to arraign Goneril and "another whose warped looks proclaim / What store her heart is made on" (3.6.52–3). Evidently, his daughters have now been found guilty and condemned to death. The next logical stage in this fantasy of vengeance is to subject Regan's corpse to the further indignity due to a handful of felons every year. She is to be stripped of the rich clothes that proclaim her royal status, exposed to the common gaze, and dismembered in the interests of medical science, to see whether there is any condition or disease that can be held accountable for hardness of the heart.

The anatomists made visible those areas normally concealed from view: their central concern was the internal organs. It is conceivable that familiarity with their practices added a certain frisson to the fable of the revolt of the body's members against the belly, as Menenius tells it in *Coriolanus* (1.1.95–162); it is more than likely that the spread of anatomical knowledge explains the apparent intelligibility of his account of the relationship between the blood, heart, brain, nerves, and veins, all features that were put on display in the flayed bodies depicted in illustrations to anatomy text-books (134–7).[2] Elsewhere, however, Shakespeare's tragedies also invest the outward parts of the body with a degree of autonomy we again all too easily naturalize as figurative. It is true that in *Lear* itself Gloucester's eyes are emblematic: the moment he loses them, he begins to "see" his error (3.7.87–91); in a grotesque recognition of the illicit conception in darkness of the bastard Edmund (5.3.170–1), Lear calls Gloucester "blind Cupid" (4.6.134). But it is as physical body parts that each "vile jelly" shockingly loses its luster on stage (3.7.82–3), leaving their owner, the empty sockets anointed with flax and egg whites, to "smell / His way to Dover" (93–4).

A person, these plays imply, is in a strong sense of the term *divisible*. *Titus Andronicus* stages a somber festival of dismemberment that begins when Lucius demands a prisoner from among the conquered army of the Goths. The victim is to be hewn in pieces on his own funeral pyre (1.1.100, 132). "See," Lucius urges, when the ritual is accomplished, "how we have performed / Our Roman rites: Alarbus' limbs are lopped / And entrails feed the sacrificing fire" (145–7). It is not clear from their history that the Romans ever treated human beings in any such way, but in the action of the play this sacrificial mutilation directly inaugurates a sequence of bodily severances, leading up to the preparation of the Thyestean banquet where the Empress will devour her children's heads.

When Bassianus with heavy irony taunts Alarbus' adulterous mother with her resemblance to Diana, goddess of chastity, Tamora at once turns the comparison back on him, rehearsing the fate of Actaeon as it is recounted in the *Metamorphoses* (*Titus*, 2.2.57–65). The young huntsman accidentally caught sight of the naked goddess, who in revenge turned him into a stag. Actaeon became the quarry of his own hounds and was torn apart by them. In Ovid's graphic account, two of the dogs sink their teeth into his back, then another seizes his shoulder; finally the whole pack tear at his body until he dies (3.232–52). Elizabethan schoolboys, who learned their Latin grammar from the *Metamorphoses*, must have relished this story.

Tamora's threat is by no means empty, although in practice the victim will be Lavinia, not Bassianus. As Chiron and Demetrius drag off the bride to rape her on her husband's lifeless "trunk" (*Titus*, 2.2.130), Tamora reminds her sons of their brother's fate. "Therefore away with her and use her as you will: / The worse to her, the better loved of me" (166–7). Her words do not, however, adequately prepare the audience for the interpretation Chiron and Demetrius will put on them. The Goths outdo another familiar Ovidian narrative, this time the story of Philomel, whose brother-in-law raped her and then cut out her tongue so that she could not accuse him. But Philomel wove a tapestry that told her story and revealed the identity of the villain (Ovid 1977: 6.438–586). When Lavinia reappears, she has neither tongue nor hands. The horrified response of her uncle Marcus echoes the vocabulary of the sacrifice that initiated the whole succession of severed limbs and organs: "Speak, gentle niece, what stern ungentle hands / Hath lopped and hewed and made thy body bare / Of her two branches" (*Titus*, 2.3.16–18). But as Chiron and Demetrius have glee-fully established, she is no longer able to speak – or write, or wash her hands, or even hang herself (2.3.3–10).

Aaron's offer to save his sons' lives in exchange for Titus' hand begins another pattern of symmetrical crimes and punishments. The Emperor's contemptuous return of the amputated hand with their heads represents a moment of decision: the

Andronici now swear to be avenged. Despatching the only one of his children who remains whole to raise an army against Rome, Titus busily lines up the remainder of the family in grotesque preparation:

> The vow is made. Come, brother, take a head,
> And in this hand the other will I bear.
> And, Lavinia, thou shalt be employed:
> Bear thou my hand, sweet wench, between thy teeth. (3.1.280–3)

His vengeance, when it is completed, involves butchering Chiron and Demetrius to make out of their blood and bonemeal pastry cases for their heads.

Our own popular culture has learnt to accommodate violent death. In that respect the films of Martin Scorsese or Quentin Tarantino can match the early modern stage horror for horror, and indeed Julie Taymor's excellent film version of *Titus* (2000) alludes to the work of both, while creating a spectacle that also goes beyond either. But cinema specializes in death itself. It is hard to think of many current entertainments that stress, with Shakespeare's tragedies, the identity of the human organism as a precarious assembly of body parts and, in consequence, easily susceptible to their loss. The Western culture of our own period makes *person* and *individual* virtually synonymous. As the etymology of *individual* suggests, our everyday language tends to take for granted the indivisibility of human beings. We know, of course, that mutilation is both possible and appalling, but we do not stage it on anything like an early modern scale. If Jack the Ripper is still remembered a century after he stopped dissecting London prostitutes, that may well be precisely because his crime was so exceptional. Alive or dead, our human bodies now more commonly come in one piece.

Titus Andronicus would be an extraordinary play in any period, though it is worth remembering that Hieronimo had already bitten out his own tongue on stage in Thomas Kyd's *Spanish Tragedy* (1586–90?), that hands are lopped off, also on stage, in the anonymous *Selimus* (1592?), and that a severed hand would play a macabre part in the action of John Webster's *The Duchess of Malfi* as late as 1613–14. Meanwhile, outside the theatre, amputation, as well as public drawing and quartering, were regarded as legitimate forms of judicial punishment. (For this reason, I disagree with Francis Barker when, in an otherwise excellent essay, he argues that *Titus occludes* the actual violence practiced by the early modern state (Barker 1993: 143–206).) These repeated displays of the body in pieces bear witness to a conception of the human being as a tenuous and temporary conjunction of components that remain perpetually vulnerable to dispersal or disintegration.

Faculties

Moreover, the physical capacities implied by limbs and organs are similarly liable to dissociation from each other. Shakespeare was not to repeat the success of *Titus* in detail, but a whole subsidiary drama of eyes and hands at the level of the vocabulary in *Macbeth*, though it is not played out literally, seems to me, nevertheless, more than metaphorical. "Stars, hide your fires!", the hero exclaims:

> Let not light see my black and deep desires;
> The eye wink at the hand; yet let that be,
> Which the eye fears, when it is done, to see. (1.4.51–3)

Divided impulses promote an imagined corporeal division between the hand's deed and the eye's awareness, as if one faculty could be ignorant of the action carried out by another. After Duncan's murder Macbeth's hands appear so bright with blood that they blind him: "Ha! They pluck out mine eyes" (2.2.58). Ironically, Macbeth coopts the biblical imperative virtuously to "pluck out" one offending eye rather than be cast into hell with two (Matthew 18: 9) on behalf of a damning unwillingness to recognize the evil implications of his own action. Later he will reiterate this projected separation of seeing from doing: "Strange things I have in head, that will to hand, / Which must be acted ere they may be scann'd" (3.4.138–9).

At the climactic moment of this sequence of allusions, eye and bloodstained hand are attributed to the macrocosm itself:

> Come, seeing Night,
> Scarf up the tender eye of pitiful Day,
> And with thy bloody and invisible hand,
> Cancel, and tear to pieces, that great bond
> Which keeps me pale! (3.2.46–50)

Darkness, stitching up the eye of day like a falcon's, the blood on its hand unseen in consequence, is to blindfold pity, and in the process erase the bond that keeps Macbeth fearful. What is this bond? The contract which represents the lease on life that Banquo and Fleance hold, which makes Macbeth fear for the succession? Perhaps. But also, surely, the bond that binds human beings to one another, "human kindness" (1.5.17), or humankind-ness, the kinship between human beings that made the still innocent Macbeth of act 1 claim, "I dare do all that may become a man; / Who dares do more, is none" (1.7.46–7). And beyond both, perhaps, the contractual bond that for the duration of this life joins the disseverable faculties of each human being into a "single state of man" (1.3.140), and vindicates the fear of deliberate, knowing murder.

In order to carry out the crime of regicide Macbeth does his best to dismantle this single state, separate it into its component elements in a more than figurative sense, and in the process close off awareness of what he is doing. But the separation cannot be sustained. Try as he might to "bend up / Each corporal agent" (1.7.80–1) to the deed, he finds in practice that his power to see exercises an agency independent of his will. A succession of vivid spectacles presents itself before his eyes, reaffirming the handiwork that he so longs to forget. Even before the murder of Duncan, a spectral dagger appears to his sight, "The handle toward my hand" (2.1.34). Later the vision of Banquo's bloodstained ghost will bring him to what seems the verge of madness: "Pr'ythee, see there! Behold! look! lo!" (3.4.67–8), until at last the witches' "show" (4.1.107–10) reveals that his crimes have been for nothing, for "Banquo's issue" (3.1.64), who parade before what the text repeatedly insists is his horrified *gaze*:

> Thou art too like the spirit of Banquo: down!
> Thy crown does sear mine eye-balls: – and thy hair,
> Thou other gold-bound brow, is like the first: –
> A third is like the former: – filthy hags!
> Why do you show me this? – A fourth? – Start, eyes!
> What! will the line stretch out to th' crack of doom?
> Another yet? – A seventh? – I'll see no more: –
> And yet the eighth appears, who bears a glass,
> Which shows me many more; and some I see,
> That two-fold balls and treble sceptres carry.
> Horrible sight! – Now, I see, 'tis true;
> For the blood-bolter'd Banquo smiles upon me,
> And points at them for his. (4.1.112–24)

Macbeth turns his back on loyalty to his king and then to his comrade-in-arms, the allegiances of a soldier, surrendering instead to "black and deep desires." By this means he empowers the instruments of darkness, who exploit the faculty of sight he longs to subdue. The hero of Duncan's regime becomes at the moment of the witches' final spectacle a committed tyrant in his own. From now on, oppression will be carried out without pause for thought: "The very firstlings of my heart shall be / The firstlings of my hand," "But no more sights!" (4.1.147–8, 155). There is no gratification in this, however: the purpose is only to defer damnation until the latest possible moment. In the interim, since Macbeth has once again prematurely cancelled the bond that integrates his faculties, he experiences power as insubstantial (5.3.24–8) and monarchy as mere theatre, noisy but vacuous (5.5.24–8).

Elsewhere the plays make clear that what is temporarily held together eventually disintegrates in the normal course of things. Indeed, the process of ageing is understood as the progressive loss of faculties, until the old man sinks into oblivion, "Sans teeth, sans eyes, sans taste, sans everything" (*As You Like It*, 2.7.160). Though the Romans in the play look back wistfully to the days when its hero was a great soldier, *Antony and Cleopatra* begins with his "dotage" (lust, but also, in the context, decline) (1.1.1) and goes on to chart the stages by which the grizzled general, "lated in the world" (3.11.3), is challenged and supplanted by the youthful Caesar. As Antony begins to lose battles, authority "melts" from him (3.13.95) and the god Hercules, embodiment of heroic masculinity, "leaves" him (4.3.21–2) to the sound of strange music. On dark evenings, Antony explains to Eros, you can see the clouds change shape and dissolve: "That which is now a horse, even with a thought / The rack dislimns and makes it indistinct / As water is in water" (4.14.9–11). The spelling in the modern edition emphasizes the comparison with the sky that will form the basis of Antony's analogy: in the same way, "Here I am Antony, / Yet cannot hold this visible shape" (13–14). The "rack" (cloud formation), he says, "dislimns" (undefines itself, loses its shape). But the Folio text gives "dislimes," which does not specify interpretation quite so sharply, and an early modern audience might also have heard "the wrack [wreck] dis-limbs," as the protagonist records the dissolution of the capabilities that combine to constitute his identity.

I have listed so many instances, and dwelt on some of them in such detail, with a view to stressing the eccentricity, from the point of view of a culture that predominantly equates identity with consciousness, of the early modern perception of what it is to be a person. It is always possible, of course, to insist that the cases I have cited owe their oddity to what is no more than a way of putting it, the vivid imagery Shakespeare is renowned for, which is reducible, in the end, to our own understanding of personality. But the cumulative effect of these examples seems to me to indicate a historical difference that goes beyond a mere trick of style.

When, a generation after Shakespeare's death, René Descartes specified for the Enlightenment the one truth that it was not possible to doubt, he established a distinction between what "I" am and my body that has entered into the commonsense beliefs of the West. He concluded, he says,

> that I was a substance, of which the whole essence or nature consists in thinking, and which, in order to exist, needs no place and depends on no material thing; so that this "I", that is to say the mind, by which I am what I am, is entirely distinct from the body . . . and moreover, that even if the body were not, it would not cease to be all that it is. (Descartes 1968: 54)

While cultures are complex and often contradictory, there is clear evidence that the dualism by which Descartes relegated the body to this subsidiary status still prevails in our own modern or postmodern moment. The widespread success in the 1990s of Judith Butler's repeated affirmation that culture *produces* the materiality of the body was one instance of the continuing prevalence of idealism in serious places (Butler 1990, 1993).

We do indeed display, shape, decorate, and discipline our bodies, pierce them, reconstruct them surgically and subject them to regimes of diet and exercise, as if they were objects to be controlled by our "selves" and brought into line with our cultural norms. We do not, on the other hand, practice judicial amputation, disembowelling, or quartering; we do not dissect bodies for public entertainment and instruction. On the contrary, we commonly find such corporeal punishments shocking – "primitive," "barbaric," "medieval" – and the idea of public dissection scandalous. For many years after its initial success on the early modern stage, *Titus Andronicus* was regarded as too horrifying to perform. The strength of our revulsion against dismemberment, however, may testify to an unconscious anxiety concerning the relegated body, a fear that in pain or mutilation it might show itself capable of exercising determinations idealism has no place for.

Qualities

In a world that takes the supernatural seriously, nature, and in particular human nature, occupies a place in the structure that is both distinct from and continuous with the regions of heaven and hell. The entire action of *Macbeth*, for example, is conducted in the shadow of the Last Judgment. Appalled by the discovery of Duncan's murder, Macduff summons the sleepers from their beds:

> up, up, and see
> The great doom's image! – Malcolm! Banquo!
> As from your graves rise up, and walk like sprites,
> To countenance this horror! (2.3.76–9)

He accurately evokes the Doom paintings that conventionally decorated the space above the chancel arch in English parish churches, until the Reformation demanded that they be whitewashed over. There was one at Stratford-upon-Avon. Naked figures of the dead would push up their gravestones and clamber out towards St. Michael, who would weigh their souls in the balance with their sins. On the right hand of God, who sat enthroned above, the redeemed would make their way past St. Peter to heaven. The damned, meanwhile, trooped down to hell, with demons snapping at their heels, to face punishments often graphically appropriate to their particular sins. Earlier in the same scene of *Macbeth* the castle's "devil-porter" has already admitted some of them in fantasy, before letting Macduff himself and Lenox into the castle.

Macduff's cry is like a trumpet, perhaps the last trump, Lady Macbeth notices (2.3.80). We have heard this trumpet earlier in the play, in the more kaleidoscopic – indeed, more apocalyptic – realization of the end of the world, as it is staged before the murder in Macbeth's own thought. At Doomsday Duncan's virtues, he acknowledges,

> Will plead like angels, trumpet-tongu'd, against
> The deep damnation of his taking-off;
> And Pity, like a naked, new-born babe,
> Striding the blast, or heaven's Cherubins, hors'd
> Upon the sightless couriers of the air,
> Shall blow the horrid deed in every eye,
> That tears shall drown the wind. (1.7.19–25)

If Macbeth conflates Judgment with the turmoil of the last days as the scriptures imagined them, Othello combines this with the images of hell made familiar by the wall-paintings:

> Whip me, ye devils,
> From the possession of this heavenly sight!
> Blow me about in winds, roast me in sulphur,
> Wash me in steep-down gulfs of liquid fire! (5.2.275–8)

The Roman plays make strenuous efforts to avoid anachronism, but damnation forms a reference point for the figures in *Hamlet*, from Laertes, who dares it (4.5.133), to the hero, who does his best to avoid it but is eager to inflict it on Claudius (3.3.94–5). And where exactly does the Ghost come from? He himself is evasive (1.5.13–16), but Hamlet has had his suspicions from the beginning (1.4.40–1; 2.2.594–5).

The soul that lived in expectation of Judgment was as subject to division as the body, torn in the first instance between good and evil, but in the tradition of the psychomachia, accustomed to see itself dispersed across a range of subtly differentiated virtues and vices, externalized personifications of moral qualities contending for dominance. By the time Shakespeare began writing, two centuries of moral plays had presented any number of versions of this contest by way of popular entertainment and instruction. If in 1587 Christopher Marlowe repudiated as the "jigging veins of rhyming mother wits" the fourteeners characteristic of the moral interludes that were the staple of the stage in his childhood and Shakespeare's (*1 Tamburlaine*, 1.1.1), he showed, nevertheless, how effectively he could rewrite the tradition in the blank verse of *Doctor Faustus* (1592?). The moral plays, staged by small companies of traveling players, provided the main form of dramatic entertainment in the intervals between the performances at fixed times of year in specific towns of the great mystery cycles. These predominantly allegorical dramas commonly showed a representative human hero coaxed by virtuous abstractions on the one hand, and disarmingly comic but dangerous vices on the other, to choose a destiny which would become irrevocable at the moment of death. The status of the virtues and vices was to some degree ambiguous. Though the vices often behaved like petty criminals, chancers and contemporary ne'er-do-wells, their true, demonic nature would emerge on those occasions when the Devil came on at the end to claim them as his own. The virtues, sometimes characterized as ministers of the church, were at other times more evidently not of this world. Marlowe represented both good and evil as angels.

In this respect, then, the previous dramatic tradition depicted human beings as sites of struggle between forces that existed outside and beyond them, but took up residence with them or within them, once they had succeeded in securing their allegiance. Thereafter, these qualities made their presence felt in the acts and utterances of the protagonist. The heroes of the moral plays were thus seen as agents of their own choices, but little more. Their dispositions, insofar as these existed at all, were externalized in the form of figures whose origins and loyalties were supernatural, whether divine or demonic. The inner world of the hero was thus understood to be the local and transitory habitation of the cosmic conflict that would continue until Doomsday.

The prevalence of allegory in early modern culture at large is evident in court masques and pageantry, in monumental sculpture and the popularity of emblems, as well, of course, as in Spenser's epic *Faerie Queene*. Not surprisingly, the allegorical tradition of personification is everywhere apparent as an element of Shakespeare's vocabulary: "Ingratitude, thou marble-hearted fiend," exclaims King Lear (1.4.251); "this fell sergeant, Death, / Is strict in his arrest," Hamlet complains (5.2.341–2). To Macbeth in the small hours of a starless night,

> Nature seems dead, and wicked dreams abuse
> The curtain'd sleep: Witchcraft celebrates
> Pale Hecate's off 'rings; and wither'd Murther,
> Alarum'd by his sentinel, the wolf,
> Whose howl's his watch, thus with his stealthy pace,
> With Tarquin's ravishing strides, towards his design
> Moves like a ghost. (2.1.50–6)

His own "thought" of murder seems to him like a revolution in his "state" (1.3.139–40), just as for Brutus the idea of Caesar's assassination is experienced as a nightmare in which

> The genius and the mortal instruments
> Are then in council, and the state of man,
> Like to a little kingdom, suffers then
> The nature of an insurrection. (*Julius Caesar*, 2.1.66–9)

But it is perhaps above all the specific tradition of the moral plays that survives, at least residually, in Shakespeare's depiction of psychological qualities. *The Interlude of Vice*, John Pikeryng's play, printed in 1567 when Shakespeare was three, shows an Elizabethan Vice called Revenge inciting the Greek hero, Horestes, to vengeance against his mother, Clytemnestra, for the murder of his father. Tamora presents herself to Titus as the personification of Revenge, and he feeds her delusion that he is mad enough to believe her by joining in with the masquerade to name her sons Rape and Murder (5.2.40–5). We might be tempted to see this episode as a repudiation of the crude allegorical techniques of the old drama in favor of a more sophisticated psychology. Surely, only a lunatic would believe in the manifestation of a personified abstraction: even Titus doesn't (142), although it is not clear at this stage that he is fully in his right mind. And yet the issue is complicated by an earlier episode in the play, the moral turning point, when the Andronici lose hope of justice. Titus stages this moment in the vocabulary of psychic warfare, repudiating the incapacitating misery that inhibits action, and choosing in its place an allegorical quest for vengeance:

> Besides, this sorrow is an enemy
> And would usurp upon my watery eyes
> And make them blind with tributary tears.
> Then which way shall I find Revenge's cave? (3.1.268–71)

Moreover, it is when he promises to "embrace" Tamora/Revenge (5.2.67–9) that he conceives the plan for the cannibalistic banquet which exceeds in ingenuity and horror any one of the series of revenges by which Tamora has herself repaid the initial sacri-fice of Alarbus. In other words, Tamora both is and is not Revenge; Titus does and does not embrace what she is; and the tradition of the psychomachia is at once invoked and relegated at the climactic moments of the play.

In other instances it is as if the personifications survive without their abstract names. Iago is undoubtedly a direct descendant of the stage Vice, charming, deceiv-ing, and ensnaring Othello into incurring his own damnation, and ensuring by unapologetic and witty asides to the audience a degree of collusion on our part with the tragic process. Edmund is evidently another: insouciant, seductive, and utterly unscrupulous, at least until the moment of his unpredicted repentance at the end of the play, in a pattern which suddenly evokes the human protagonist in the moral plays, rather than the Vice. Bernard Spivack's *Shakespeare and the Allegory of Evil* (1958) might perhaps have been carried away by its own enthusiasm for finding unrecon-structed Vices everywhere, but its main case surely remains irresistible.

Alan Dessen, who brings a formidable scholarly knowledge to bear on the case for our recognition in early modern drama of vestiges of the previous tradition, con-cludes, "both chronologically and, I suspect, in subtler ways as well, Shakespeare was closer to the moral plays than we are to him" (Dessen 1986: 166). "Come not between the dragon and his wrath," commands Lear, momentarily isolating his own anger from himself (1.1.123). Kent has tried to do exactly that, like the traditional Good Angel, intervening between the hero and the Vice. And like the Good Angel, Kent persists: "whilst I can vent clamour from my throat / I'll tell thee thou dost evil" (1.1.166–7). The protagonist responds in the traditional way, by dismiss-ing him. Kent is banished, but in line with the earlier virtues, he remains in atten-dance, waiting for the moment when the hero will seek his help. Later in the same play, an anonymous servant comes momentarily between Cornwall and Gloucester's second eye, but he does not survive to be recalled. Horatio tries physically to prevent Hamlet from following the Ghost: "Be rul'd," he begs (1.5.81), in vain. "O step between her and her fighting soul," the Ghost will later urge Hamlet, who is evi-dently not addressing his mother with sufficient conviction (3.4.113).

Miniature invocations of the psychomachia occur at the level of vocabulary throughout the plays. "Let not my worser spirit tempt me again," implores Gloucester of Poor Tom, who is guiding him in exactly the manner of a stage virtue (*King Lear*, 4.6.214). "Patience and sorrow strove / Who should express her goodliest," a Gentleman reports of Cordelia (4.3.16–17). The divisions that inhabit subjectivity and determine action are given in advance by their inscription in a vocabulary of psychic warfare.

R. B.'s play, *Apius and Virginia*, printed in 1575, dramatizes the division of the tragic hero visually, while he himself defines the process in soliloquy: "But out I am wounded, how am I devided? / Two states of my life, from me are now glided" (1911: lines 501–2). The stage direction requires Conscience and Justice to "come out of him" at this moment, though quite what the audience would see is not clear at this distance of time. "Beat at this gate that let thy folly in / And thy dear judgement out," Lear instructs himself (1.4.263–4). "To hell allegiance! Vows to the blackest devil," cries Laertes, "Conscience and grace, to the profoundest pit! I dare damnation" (*Hamlet*, 4.5.131–3).

The allegorical manner of defining human qualities evidently offers Shakespeare a rich seam of imagery, but more than that, it also represents his protagonists as the meeting point of characteristics that preexist and, indeed, survive them. The conscience and grace Laertes repudiates do not in any sense originate with him. They "belong" to him only to the degree that they are borrowed from virtue itself – and can be returned by an act of will. The qualities of individual figures are thus not seen as idiosyncratic. On the contrary, they are infinitely generalizable, available to anyone.

Moreover, these transferable characteristics are seen to be inscribed in language; they make their appearance precisely as meanings made palpable. Personification allegory invests the signifier with a materiality that throws into relief the degree to which what we see as psychological properties are alternatively identifiable as the meanings cultures strive to inhabit. By embracing Revenge, Titus takes up a position in a network of meanings that minutely differentiates revenge from justice (4.1.128); in damning conscience, Laertes, who by this declaration makes himself a revenger, is specifying the moral implications of human vengeance. More than merely a way of putting it, a trick, again, of style, the heritage of the psychomachia permits Shakespearean tragedy to judge the feelings it also dramatizes. And in the process of measuring in this way, it also depersonalizes them, locates them in the culture at large, indicating the degree to which to be human is to inhabit the meanings already in circulation.

Words equivocate: that is their nature. Meaning does not pose before us as pure and fixed intelligibility. There are no concepts independent of language, no meanings that are not supplanted, relegated, or, as Jacques Derrida would say, deferred by the signifier itself (Derrida 1973). By the time Laertes casts conscience aside to become a revenger, Hamlet has already struggled with the relationship, which is to say the difference, between conscience and revenge, and he will go on to reconsider the relationship between conscience and killing Claudius, when it seems that revenge is no longer the issue (5.2.62–70). Macbeth, meanwhile, is entrapped by the very personification the play allots him. "Valour's minion" (1.2.19), a man of blood, like his stand-in on the stage, the "bleeding Captain" (1.2.1 and s.d.), he is repeatedly "valiant" in these early scenes (1.2.24; 1.4.54), and in consequence, "Nothing afeard" of what he himself makes, "Strange images [pictures, statues] of death" (1.3.96–7). But when Lady Macbeth chastizes him with the "valour" of her tongue (1.5.27) he divorces the blood and the images of death from loyalty, to redefine "manhood" in line with her understanding of the term. This definition proves, in the event, to be empty, rendering his life "a tale / Told by an idiot . . . / Signifying nothing" (5.5.26–8).

The Subject

If this view of Shakespeare's tragic heroes, corporeally and psychologically divisible, their disseverable bodies impelled and motivated by both their own conflicting demands and the contested, shifting cultural meanings they struggle to inhabit, is apparent to us now, in a way that it was not, say, to the Victorians, who preferred to perceive them as novelistic "characters," this may be because the portrait as I have described it bears an uncanny resemblance to the understanding of what it is to be human given by poststructuralist theory, and by the psychoanalysis of Jacques Lacan in particular. Lacan, too, sees human beings as the uneasy conjunction of a vulnerable organism and a subjectivity brought into being from outside itself, composed of meanings that, while they remain irretrievably Other, are all we have to live by. Lacanian subjects are agents of their own actions; they make choices and live their lives; and they are in that sense analagous to the grammatical subject of a sentence, the figure that performs the verb. But they do so in relation to irresistible drives on the one hand and, on the other, to the discipline defined by language and culture, imposed from elsewhere, a tissue of prohibitions that forbid the gratification of these drives. They are thus at the same time also subjected beings, doubly *subjects* – in an exploitation of the ambiguity that resides at the heart of language.

The subject, then, is what signifies, and it is so-named from grammar. It is in that sense the author of initiatives. But the subject is not a person, still less a consciousness. On the contrary, it is that speaking construct which is divided from the inextricable real of the organism, in submission to the threat of symbolic castration, the "no" of the symbolic order. In the subject consciousness is redoubled, in consequence of this alienation, with an unconscious, the residue of the lost real, that "speaks" in the interstices of what we think we say. It follows from this account, though Lacan's own interests are not in this issue, that the subject speaks – or is spoken for – from a range of positions, perhaps inconsistent, possibly contradictory, certainly discontinuous. No indivisible core of "character," no stable center, keeps these positions in line with each other. The subject is not, therefore, an individual in the etymological sense of that term, but an assembly of meanings, tenuously held together.

Of course, it is not really uncanny at all that there should be a resemblance between Shakespeare's tragic heroes and Lacanian human beings. We read from the present, and on the basis of the knowledges we take for granted. How else can we make sense of texts, especially texts as complex and subtle as Shakespearean tragedy? But if I have quoted extensively, possibly to the point of exhausting the reader's attention, it is in the hope of making the parallels stick, or demonstrating that my affirmation of an analogy is not fashionably capricious, the effect of a willful anachronism.

In that respect it is crucial to emphasize, of course, that there are also radical historical differences between the psychomachia and psychoanalysis. The first inhabits a fundamentally religious universe; the second is irretrievably secular. The first invests concepts with material capabilities; the second takes concepts, if they can be said to exist at all, to be the effect of language. More locally, Lacan is not much interested in conscious ethical choices at the level of the virtues, duties, and obligations he dismissively names "the goods" (see especially Lacan 1992: 302–25). These can be identified as all those calls on us for self-sacrifice: "Private goods, family goods, domestic goods, other goods that solicit us, the goods of our trade or our profession, the goods of the city, etc." (p. 303).[3] At the same time, if Shakespeare's plays seem now and then to acknowledge unconscious motivations, they certainly do not call them that.

What links the tragedies with psychoanalysis, however, is, to my mind, the effect of history itself. Shakespeare was writing a generation before Descartes was to conflate identity with consciousness at the expense of the body, while Lacan, writing in the light of the psychoanalytic insistence on the interaction – in both the drive and the symptom – between psychic processes and the organism, inaugurated his career with a declaration of hostility to "any philosophy directly issuing from the *Cogito*" (Lacan 1977: 1). Located one each side of modernity, these two understandings of what it is to be a person can thus perhaps illuminate each other, and justify the practice of borrowing for discussion of early modern drama a term drawn from a distinctively postmodern knowledge.

Subject or Character?

Not everyone agrees, of course. The Victorian novelistic notion of what D. H. Lawrence called "the old stable *ego* – of the character" (Lawrence 1962: 282), as individuality or idiosyncrasy, retains a strong hold. In spite of the modernist rejection of this model, it remains pervasive in popular culture: soap opera would be unintelligible without it; Hollywood trades in it. Actors commonly define their roles in terms of character, and teachers may also find this the easiest way into a drama which is now in so many ways alien to their pupils. Academic Shakespeareans, too, are often unwilling to let go of the critical vocabularies they grew up with. Perhaps they long to find at the end of their inquiries the unified individual as the origin of meaning and action. A. C. Bradley's position represents the acme of this humanist view: tragic heroes are the agents of their own downfall, and they fail because of the kinds of people they essentially are. Individual human beings, in other words, are the sole, untrammeled source of the choices they make, and thus entirely responsible for the consequences, including the tragic outcome of their own lives.

Are those who approach Shakespearean tragedy from the point of view of character wrong? Not necessarily. However much the tragedies may draw on the tradition of the psychomachia, they are not moral plays. Instead, they invest their protagonists with personal names, and place them in a plausible fictional world, broadly located in time and space. If Shakespeare's plays refer back to the previous allegorical dramatic tradition, they also point forward towards the mimetic representational techniques of the novel, though not, perhaps, with quite the singlemindedness the nineteenth century insisted on discovering in them.

There are anticipations of unified "character" in the texts of the plays. "Yet do I fear thy nature," Lady Macbeth reflects. "It is too full of the milk of human kindness." And she goes on, somewhat in the manner of a school report: "Thou wouldst be great; / Art not without ambition, but without / The illness should attend it . . ." (1.5.16–20). Lear, Regan observes, "hath ever but slenderly known himself" (1.1.294–5). Edmund finds Gloucester "credulous," Edgar "noble" (1.2.177). Hamlet castigates himself with his own cowardice (unjustly, as it turns out). Enobarbus famously "characterizes" Cleopatra in the sense in which the period itself would have understood the term, that is to say, he invests her with what Monticelso in Webster's *The White Devil* calls the "character" of a whore (3.2.80):

> Age cannot wither her, nor custom stale
> Her infinite variety. Other women cloy
> The appetites they feed, but she makes hungry
> Where most she satisfies. (*Antony and Cleopatra*, 2.2.245–8)

There are few individualizing insights here, however. The accounts are remarkably generalized, inclined to ethical evaluation rather than psychological analysis, precisely in the tradition of the moral plays.

Besides, there are any number of counter-examples, instances of radical instability and discontinuity which denote division rather than unity. Among the most glaring, Desdemona speaks in the first half of the play from the position of a calm, dignified, self-possessed wife, able to defend her choice eloquently in public; in the second, she becomes, as the plot seems to necessitate, bewildered, timid, ineffectual and, most striking of all, suddenly afraid to tell the truth (3.4.55–103). Within the space of two scenes Antony moves from unconditional love for Cleopatra and contempt for the empire (1.1.34–5) to a determination that he will break from her and resume his Roman obligations (1.2.135–7). Moreover, he will not keep this resolution either. Meanwhile, in a single prayer Claudius oscillates between sin and repentance, for all the world like any morality protagonist (*Hamlet*, 3.3.36–71). Not that these discontinuities are implausible. On the contrary. But they point to an understanding of what it is to be human that is perhaps not best explained by the stabilizing and unifying idea of character.

The Soliloquy

How, then, did critics so consistently manage to find satisfaction in such explanation for upwards of two centuries? The single device that does most to support the idea of character, especially in the tragedies, is the deliberative soliloquy. Unlike monologues addressed to the audience, soliloquies are the special property of the heroes, and show them communing above all with themselves. They put before us a single figure revealing, as it seems in private, the most personal, the most intimate thought processes, and these apparently give the audience access to what, above all, the heroes truly *are*. The soliloquies are not designed to impress, persuade, or delude an interlocutor; they simply display a consciousness, which for a Cartesian world means an identity, at work.

But these utterances can also be read as internalizing and explicitly psychologizing precisely what a generation earlier would have been externalized in personification allegory (Belsey 1973). They are intelligible, in other words, as dramatizations of successive and often conflicting subject positions which are not necessarily held together by a single, stable ego. (It would be an interesting exercise, though perhaps one beyond the scope of this essay, to compare Shakespeare's tragic soliloquies with Browning's dramatic monologues. I suspect that Browning's would score higher in terms of the revelation of consistent character.)

As an example, we might consider the most famous of them all. Suppose, for the sake of argument, we think of Hamlet's "To be, or not to be" speech (3.1.56–88) as an internalized dialogue between the personified abstractions Resolution and Conscience. The project, as Hamlet sets it up, is to determine which is "nobler": to endure what fortune brings, or take arms against these troubles and put an end to them – in both senses of that term. No revenger ever lives to tell the tale; no Renaissance prince can honorably (nobly) kill the king and get away with it. But to die, Resolution urges, is nothing: to sleep, no more than that, and in the process, to be done with the miseries of this life. And yet, Conscience interjects, there may be dreams in that sleep, something after death which inhibits the kind of action that might incur damnation (regicide, say). The fear of that result, an unknown destiny after death, makes us bear the troubles fortune brings here and now, rather than rush towards others that might be worse.

Apius undergoes a similar ethical struggle. In his case, as Conscience and Justice come out of him, they speak, he records, to warn him of the consequences of his decision, which include "fier eternall." But the Vice insists, "Why these are but thoughts, man?" (lines 508–9), and Apius seizes the courage to rape Virginia. (For other examples, see Belsey 1979.) Hamlet, by contrast, opts, logically enough, for Conscience, which makes us all "cowards," afraid of hell, "And thus the native hue of resolution / Is sicklied o'er with the pale cast of thought." Divided between two conflicting imperatives, pale Conscience and the red-faced desire for vengeance, Hamlet defers action.

There are, it must be conceded at once, certain ellipses here. Hamlet does not spell it all out for the audience in this soliloquy. He does not discuss the common fate of revengers; he does not (though the play does, repeatedly) distinguish between the crime of revenge and the legitimacy of justice; and he does not mention the special hellishness of regicide. I have supplied what he leaves out.

Nor, however, does he once use the word "I" in the course of the debate. The nineteenth century supplied *this* deficiency instead, placing at the heart of the speech a suicidal hero, unified as too sensitive, too thoughtful, too effeminate and, in the end, too "sickly" to be capable of decisive action (Belsey 2002). There are problems here too. Nothing in the text of the speech itself appears particularly effeminate or sickly. It is not always clear which of the options, suffering or opposing troubles, is equated with suicide. Moreover, self-inflicted death in Shakespeare as a way of evading action is never "nobler." Suicide can be right in a Roman setting, as Horatio indicates (5.2.345–7), but only after the battle has been fought and lost, not as an alternative to beginning it.

In the absence of a developed science of psychology, the nineteenth century practiced psychological analysis on fictional figures. Bradley diagnosed melancholia as Hamlet's clinical condition. But in our own period, case histories are two-a-penny. Perhaps we look for a different kind of interest? If so, a debate about the nature of right ethical and political action in certain specific circumstances might appeal to us more.

Bradley or Lacan?

In other words, where the text is not decisive, perhaps the worth of an interpretation depends on what it can do? As an analyst of character in the tragedies, Bradley remains, in my view, unsurpassed. His book, a set of ten lectures, was first published in 1904, in the last years of the Victorian novel, when the understanding of human individuality was a passion and emotional literacy was to be acquired by the study of fiction. His readings are intelligent, informed, and exceptionally textual.

Bradley finds *King Lear* a puzzle. It has been seen as Shakespeare's most magnificent work, and yet on the stage it is not a success; it is, he affirms, "Shakespeare's greatest achievement," but it is not "his best play" (Bradley 1905: 199). How can this be? The fact is, Bradley concludes, that the characters are a bit thin. "Considered simply as psychological studies few of them, surely, are of the highest interest" (p. 215).

As it happens, Bradley has already demonstrated precisely this in his defense of the opening scene, which others, he says, have found improbable or absurd. It is not absurd, he maintains, "though it must be pronounced dramatically faulty in so far as it discloses the true position of affairs only to an attention more alert than can be expected in a theatrical audience" (p. 205). The opening scene, in other words, requires us to interpret the ellipses, to fill in what is missing. Bradley does this novelistically: he explains the motives of the hero. Lear never intended to live with anyone but Cordelia (1.1.124–5); the division of the kingdom had been settled in advance; and the speeches of his daughters were intended to be no more than a performance, "a mere form, devised as a childish scheme to gratify his love of absolute power and his hunger for assurances of devotion. And this scheme is perfectly in character" (Bradley 1905: 204). Moreover, it is not entirely Lear's fault that the plan goes wrong, and this too is attributable to character, this time Cordelia's. "We may even say that the main cause of its failure was not that Goneril and Regan were exceptionally hypocritical, but that Cordelia was exceptionally sincere and unbending" (p. 204).

There is something disappointing about this reading of the opening of a tragedy on the scale of *Lear*. That a childish and needy old man should encounter a loving but inflexible daughter seems more pathetic than tragic. What makes Bradley a great critic is that he knows this. Character belongs on the stage, he assumes, but *King Lear* is better read than seen. Only then does it reveal its true grandeur, "the half-realized suggestions of vast universal powers working in the world of individual fates and passions" (p. 202). It is as if the audience were witnessing a conflict between good and evil, not specific characters, he says. The dramatis personae divide into two distinct groups, with love on one side and hate on the other, almost as if these were the driving forces of the universe (p. 215). Moreover, we seem to trace in the play "the tendency of imagination to analyse and abstract, to decompose human nature into its constituent factors" (p. 216). And this tendency is, of course, allegorical, Bradley tells us, and one that Shakespeare was familiar with from Spenser and the morality plays (pp. 216–17).

Is it possible that Bradley was not only a good literary historian, as this attribution demonstrates, but also a Lacanian *avant la lettre*? Probably not, on reflection, but it might be worth conjecturing what Lacan would have made of *King Lear*. In fact, he mentions it briefly in the context of a detailed analysis of *Antigone*. The Sophoclean protagonist is driven to bury her brother by an unwritten law that conflicts with the law of the land, as the result of an imperative that has its roots in the real of the organism, and pushes the signifying subject towards the outer limits of language. Polynices was a traitor. Fully aware that the consequence will be her own death, Antigone has to bury him nevertheless, not because of his moral worth, not for the sake of "the goods," but for a reason she cannot name, except to say that he was her brother. Like Oedipus, therefore, Antigone knowingly crosses over from the world defined by the symbolic order of language and culture into the zone of dispossession and death, and dies unreconciled with society's values (Lacan 1992: 241–87).[4]

Lear, Lacan says, undertakes that same crossing over into the zone of death, but "in a derisory form." "The old fool believes he is lovable" and "hands over the service of the goods to his daughters" (p. 305). But he thinks he can enjoy himself in that zone, because he can trust to the words and social obligations that belong to the symbolic order; in short, "he doesn't understand a thing," but he "makes the ocean and the earth echo" because he has tried and failed to cross into the zone of death with general approval (p. 310). What might Lacan have made of the opening scene?

Possibly (and who would have the effrontery to speak for Lacan?), in the first instance that the old fool does not know what words mean. He proposes to divest himself "of rule, / Interest of territory, cares of state" (1.1.49–50), and at the same time retain "The name and all th' addition to a king" (137). What is a king? The ruler, precisely, of a territory, whose ability to command depends on consent. And consent is in the last analysis backed by the corresponding ability to enforce his instructions, on the basis of the patronage and military service the territory in question enables him to maintain. Interest, territory, and cares are inseparable from kingship. Lear wants to hold onto his identity as king, as if the identity of a king were separable from the office.

Kingship belongs to what Lacan calls the symbolic order, the order of language and culture; of social relations, as supported, where appropriate, by the possession of material property. Kingship, we might want to say, is quintessentially symbolic. At the same time, the old fool tries to conflate kingship with love, and while supposing that his identity as king can be maintained outside the symbolic order that gives it meaning, paradoxically imagines that love can be rendered symbolic, *spoken* in elaborate speeches, and socially rewarded with land and property. The love between a child and a parent, however, must be something like the relationship between siblings, the effect of an imperative that has its roots in the organism, a "bond," as Cordelia calls it, both a link and a contract, that pushes the signifying subject towards silence (1.1.93, 62). Not understanding a thing, however, Lear promptly divests himself of parenthood as well (114–15).

It cannot be done. But whether or not he learns from his errors in the course of the play, this strange opening scene, in some ways more like folktale than tragedy, surely stages for the audience not merely a confrontation between an infantile father and a stubborn daughter, but the impasse that occurs when the hero tries to bring together the contradictory components of a human being intelligible, on the one hand, as a signifying subject and, on the other, by virtue of that same signifying subjectivity, forever divided from gratification in the inextricable but unattainable real. Cordelia cannot give him what he wants, because it is beyond the symbolic – and he cannot reward it symbolically with property. There is, it will turn out, no realm of pure love, not even in prison, and nowhere that living human beings can be truly "unaccommodated," "the thing itself" (3.4.104–5).

Shakespeare and Plutarch

Plutarch was a brilliant storyteller. He was also a great gossip. He liked to be clear about the characters whose lives he was narrating: he wanted to take into account their patterns of thought in the process of explaining what happened to them. Plutarch's version of history confirms to a high degree Bradley's reading of Shakespearean tragedy, as showing that "the calamities and catastrophe follow inevitably from the deeds of men, and that the main source of these deeds is character" (Bradley 1905: 7).

Shakespeare must have learnt something about unifying his fictional figures as characters from his reading of Plutarch. Certainly, it is in the Roman plays that the dramatis personae most commonly talk about each other, especially in order to determine who and what these others essentially are. The Romans talk about Antony; Enobarbus talks endlessly about Cleopatra; Cassius talks about Julius Caesar, leading Brutus to do the same; Mark Antony talks about Caesar to the citizens, with devastating effect; and everyone talks about Coriolanus.

Who is Coriolanus? Plutarch characterizes him right at the beginning of his biography:

> this *Martius* naturall wit and great harte dyd marvelously sturre up his corage, to doe and attempt notable actes. But on the other side for lacke of education, he was so chollericke and impacient, that he would yeld to no living creature: which made him churlishe, uncivill, and altogether unfit for any mans conversation. Yet men marveling much at his constancy, that he was never overcome with pleasure, nor money, and howe he would endure easely all manner of paynes & travailles: thereupon they well liked and commended his stowtnes and temperancie. But for all that, they could not be acquainted with him, as one cittizen useth to be with another in the cittie. His behaviour was so unpleasaunt to them, by reason of a certaine insolent and sterne manner he had, which bicause it was to lordly, was disliked. (Shakespeare 1976: 314)

Though there are paradoxes here, as there are in the story (the Romans reward him, admire him, and banish him), they are reconciled in this portrait of a brave, austere, unrelenting figure who has no social graces. Plutarch will go on to show him as a political autocrat, a terrifying warrior, passionate and willful, caring only for honor and contemptuous of riches. Moreover, all these features can be explained by his upbringing. His father died, leaving his mother to educate him. As a result, he was always anxious to make her proud of him, but he lacked the civilizing effect of a proper (classical) education.

Much of this reappears in Shakespeare, and continues to take the form of third-person accounts, though in dialogue, which has the effect of enhancing the paradoxes. A consecutive account of the play scene-by-scene would reveal the amount of time the other characters spend trying to make sense of the enigmatic hero. After his exit in the first scene, the Tribunes begin: "Was ever man so proud as is this Martius?" (1.1.251). They discuss his facial expressions, his taunts, his reputation, his position in the army. Aufidius mentions how the Romans hate him in the following scene, and in the third Volumnia describes his upbringing. He is then on stage until 1.10, when the Volscians talk about him. "He's the devil," in the view of one soldier (16). "Bolder, though not so subtle," Aufidius rejoins, almost as succinctly (17). In the first scene of act 2 the tribunes discuss him with Menenius; and then Menenius discusses him with Volumnia, Valeria, and Virgilia. In the following scene two officers decide he's a worthy man, if it weren't for his pride. Coriolanus then refuses to stay and hear his triumphs narrated to the senate, so Cominius recounts them in his absence. In 2.3 he stands for election, while the citizens talk about him. It would be tedious to unfold the remainder of this pattern, which continues until he joins Aufidius in Antium. Here the Volscian servants try again to pluck out the heart of his mystery in exchanges that parody what has gone before:

> *Second Serv.* Nay, I knew by his face that there was something in him. He had, sir, a kind of face, methought – I cannot tell how to term it.
> *First Serv.* He had so, looking as it were – would I were hanged, but I thought there was more in him than I could think. (4.5.157–62)

Ironically, however, none of this protracted and repetitive analysis seems to have a great deal of bearing on the climactic scene of the play, and the critical moment of the tragedy. The banished hero has formed a new network of alliances with the Volscians, and successive embassies from Rome fail to persuade him to relent, despite his comradeship with Cominius and his love for his surrogate father, Menenius (5.3.10, 12), until he recognizes in the approach of his mother, wife, and child the reaffirmation of a "bond" of kinship (25, 37). This is what destroys him.

It would be tempting to call this bond nature, as Coriolanus himself does (5.3.25, 33). But there is also something more complex here, registered, according to the Folio stage direction, by a silence that resembles, perhaps, the silence of Cordelia. It has to do with the physiological tie between mother and son (Kahn 1997: 148–9). At the same time, there is little of warmth or benevolence in it, and nothing of reconciliation. Coriolanus will not return to Rome, to his family and his former social relationships, but will remain with Aufidius, in full awareness of the consequences. The gods do not smile, but jeer. The event, indeed, is "unnatural," and doubly so: a mother kneels to a son; but she does so in a cause that must incur his death:

> (*Holds her by the hand silent.*) O mother, mother!
> What have you done? Behold, the heavens do ope,
> The gods look down, and this unnatural scene
> They laugh at. O my mother, mother! O!
> You have won a happy victory to Rome;
> But for your son, believe it, O, believe it,
> Most dangerously you have with him prevail'd,
> If not most mortal to him. But let it come. (5.3.183–9)

In a succession of repetitions, as well as the "O"s in which the most eloquent of playwrights commonly indicates an encounter with the limits of language, Coriolanus moves knowingly into the zone of death, alone and dispossessed. The "bond" represents an imperative that cannot be resisted. It stands for nothing nameable, the contract and the link that binds living human beings, as organisms-in-culture, to the real from which, at the same time, as signifying subjects, they must also remain forever divided.

Desire

In the gap between the little human animal on the one hand and, on the other, the subject of and to the alienating symbolic order that it becomes, Lacan locates desire. This is not necessarily sexual, but constitutes a radical discontent, a structural dissatisfaction and a quest for objects that are sutured into place in the subject's own culture, and therefore in history and, indeed, biography.

What makes Shakespeare's heroes tragic is surely the grand scale and the unconditional quality of their desire, regardless of whether the specific objects they name deserve it or account for it. "Let Rome in Tiber melt" (*Antony and Cleopatra*, 1.1.34); "When I love thee not / Chaos is come again" (*Othello*, 3.3.91–2); "like an eagle in a dove-cote, I / Flutter'd your Volscians in Corioles" (*Coriolanus*, 5.6.114–15). These desiring, uncompromising figures storm and rage, make the earth and ocean echo, when they cannot have what they want. And what they want is in each case beyond "the goods," beyond moral obligation, duty, or self-denial. They are restrained, if at all, not by the prohibitions of the symbolic order, but by something deeper, a contractual bond, which represents nothing nameable, but ties together – to constitute for a time the desiring human being itself – readily separable body parts, faculties, meanings, and discontents, in what Cleopatra calls "the knot intrinsicate / Of life" (5.2.303–4).

The divisibility of the subject, and beyond this the divisibility of the human being, was not unique to early modern drama, but it was, perhaps, uniquely perceptible at that moment, thanks to the period's understanding of what it was to be human. It was also uniquely stageable in terms of the intersection at the time of two theatrical vocabularies, one looking forward to the sovereign, choosing individual of modernity, and the other still able to draw on an earlier model of what dramatic choice might be.

NOTES

1   All Shakespeare references are to the Arden editions. I have listed the plays individually under "Shakespeare" in the bibliography.
2   For an account of the science of anatomy in the period see Sawday (1995).
3   Perhaps surprisingly, Lacan was interested in the Last Judgment, at least as a structural point of view, a position from which to ask the "ethical" question, "Have you acted in conformity with the desire that is in you?" (Lacan 1992: 314).
4   In Paris the "zone" was the intermediary space between the city and its suburbs, a virtual wasteland created by the demolition of the city wall at the end of the nineteenth century. "Officially uninhabited, the zone in fact became a kind of giant shantytown encircling central Paris" (Lyotard 1997: 17, n. 1).

REFERENCES AND FURTHER READING

Armstrong, P. (2001). *Shakespeare in Psychoanalysis*. London: Routledge.
Barker, F. (1993). *The Culture of Violence*. Manchester: Manchester University Press.
Belsey, C. (1973). Senecan Vacillation and Elizabethan Deliberation: Influence or Confluence? *Renaissance Drama*, n.s. 6, 65–88.
——(1979). The Case of Hamlet's Conscience. *Studies in Philology*, 76, 127–48.
——(2002). "Was Hamlet a Man or a Woman?" The Prince in the Graveyard, 1800–1920. In A. Kinney (ed.) *Hamlet: New Critical Essays*. New York: Routledge, 135–58.
Bradley, A. C. (1905). *Shakespearean Tragedy*. London: Macmillan.
Butler, J. (1990). *Gender Trouble: Feminism and the Subversion of Identity*. New York: Routledge.

——(1993). *Bodies That Matter: On the Discursive Limits of Sex.* New York: Routledge.

Derrida, J. (1973). *"Differance", "Speech and Phenomena" and Other Essays on Husserl's Theory of Signs*, trans. D. B. Allison. Evanston, IL: Northwestern University Press, 129–60.

Descartes, R. (1968). *Discourse on Method and the Meditations*, trans. F. E. Sutcliffe. Harmondsworth: Penguin Books.

Dessen, A. C. (1986). *Shakespeare and the Late Moral Plays.* Lincoln: University of Nebraska Press.

Fineman, J. (1991). The Structure of Allegorical Desire. In *The Subjectivity Effect in Western Literary Tradition: Essays Toward the Release of Shakespeare's Will.* Cambridge, MA: MIT Press, 3–31.

Kahn, C. (1997). *Roman Shakespeare: Warriors, Wounds and Women.* London: Routledge.

Lacan, J. (1977). *Ecrits: A Selection*, trans. A. Sheridan. London: Tavistock.

——(1992). *The Ethics of Psychoanalysis (Seminar 7)*, trans. D. Porter. London: Routledge.

Lawrence, D. H. (1962). *Collected Letters*, ed. H. T. Moore. London: Heinemann.

Lyotard, J.-F. (1997). *Postmodern Fables*, trans. G. Van Den Abbeele. Minneapolis: University of Minnesota Press.

Marlowe, C. (1981). *Tamburlaine the Great*, ed. J. S. Cunningham. Manchester: Manchester University Press.

Ovid (1977). *Metamorphoses 1–8*, trans. F. J. Miller. Cambridge, MA: Harvard University Press.

Pikeryng, J. (1962). *The Interlude of Vice (Horestes)*, ed. D. Seltzer. Oxford: Oxford University Press.

R. B. (1911). *Apius and Virginia*, ed. R. B. McKerrow. London: Malone Society.

Sawday, J. (1995). *The Body Emblazoned: Dissection and the Human Body in Renaissance Culture.* London: Routledge.

Shakespeare, W. (1962). *Macbeth*, ed. K. Muir. London: Methuen.

——(1975). *As You Like It*, ed. A. Latham. London: Methuen.

——(1976). *Coriolanus*, ed. P. Brockbank. London: Methuen.

——(1982). *Hamlet*, ed. H. Jenkins. London: Methuen.

——(1995a). *Antony and Cleopatra*, ed. J. Wilders. London: Routledge.

——(1995b). *Titus Andronicus*, ed. J. Bate. London: Routledge.

——(1997a). *Othello*, ed. E. A. J. Honigmann. London: Thomas Nelson.

——(1997b). *King Lear*, ed. R. A. Foakes. London: Thomas Nelson.

——(1998). *Julius Caesar*, ed. D. Daniell. London: Thomas Nelson.

Sophocles (1947). *The Theban Plays*, trans. E. F. Watling. Harmondsworth: Penguin Books.

Spivack, B. (1958). *Shakespeare and the Allegory of Evil.* New York: Columbia University Press.

Webster, J. (1996). *The White Devil*, ed. C. Luckyj. London: A. and C. Black.

5

Disjointed Times and Half-Remembered Truths in Shakespearean Tragedy

Philippa Berry

I

The cultural epoch in which Shakespeare wrote has for nearly two hundred years been identified by scholars as "the Renaissance." Currently, however, it is undergoing a subtle shift of identity, following its redescription as the "early modern" period. So Leah S. Marcus has argued that:

> We are moving away from interpreting the period as a time of re-naissance, cultural rebirth, the awakening of an earlier era conceived of as (in some sense) classic; we are coming to view the period more in terms of elements repeated thereafter, those features of the age that appear to us precursors of our own twentieth century, the modern, the postmodern. (Marcus 1992: 41–63)

In fact, both new and old labels suggest the future-oriented concerns of the epoch in question; however, while the label "early modern" appears to position the cultural changes which occurred in Europe between the fifteenth and seventeenth centuries as a point of origin – as the beginning of a new and "modern" era – the concept of "Renaissance" implies a rather more complex, Janus-faced, and uneasy relationship between this epoch and the linear unfolding of time. For of course the word "Renaissance" identifies this moment of cultural change not simply as a beginning, but rather as a *rebirth* or *renewal* of culture: as a process, then, which is in some respect mimetic, or commemorative, of an earlier historical epoch – or rather more problematically, of several earlier epochs. In the contemporary effacing of this idea of "Renaissance," therefore, we should be reminded of the ways in which significant cultural change can produce damaging aporias within its new paradigms of knowledge, as each rememorizing of the past is informed by a selective forgetting – or disjointing – of whatever details do not fit the new interpretive narrative. My argument in this essay is that Shakespearean tragedy articulates a comparable kind of awareness, as it explores the paradoxical temporality of tragic experience, and attributes to the tragic protagonist a powerful, but painfully incomplete, aporetic relationship to a past or history which is configured as a site of a powerful yet only partially accessible knowledge.

I want to take as my starting point, then, the hypothesis that an identification of Shakespeare's tragedies as *both* Renaissance *and* early modern texts can usefully serve to remind us that these plays are peculiarly troubled by the question of temporal difference. For what is frequently read by critics as the tragedies' proleptic or prophetic encoding of a modern sensibility – in an anticipation of modernity *avant la lettre*, as it were – is also peculiarly implicated in a recurrent turning backwards in time, sometimes to a recent, but most frequently to a distant historical or even prehistorical past. One effect of this seeming hesitation between a still dimly imagined future and a rapidly receding past is that it is peculiarly hard to determine the temporality of the tragic subjectivity which is staged in these plays. What is indisputable is that most of Shakespeare's tragedies exhibit an acute awareness of the rapid processes of historical change, which they frequently configure as producing an almost violent discontinuity of or within time, a disjunction equivalent to Hamlet's trope of a time that is "out of joint": "The time is out of joint. O cursed spite / That ever I was born to set it right" (1.5.189–90).

Occurring as it does immediately after his supernatural conversation with the ghost, Hamlet's evocation of a disjointed time appears to identify his vivid sense of a contemporary mutilation of former conceptions of temporal unity or integrity with the heavy burden of a tragic knowledge that is itself "out of joint," since it is disjointed from his own time or historical epoch. In one sense, the especial knowledge which Hamlet will both reveal and conceal in the play (as a satirical malcontent or revenger figure who is also shown to be much more than these limited dramatic roles) is not dissimilar, in its opposition to the usurped and implicitly unsanctified authority of Claudius and his court, from the secret "intelligence" of the spy or Catholic recusant. The act of resistance or treason committed by the Jesuit priest was motivated by a spiritual agenda, and it is similarly a supernatural vision that dissevers Hamlet's former relationship to linear and secular time, when he encounters the spectral figure of his father. In accordance with Catholic (but not Protestant) visions of the Christian afterlife, the ghost is apparently experiencing an otherworldly, purgatorial version of "doing time" or completing a prison sentence, for Old Hamlet declares that he is "Doomed for a certain term to walk the night, / And for the day confined to fast in fires / Till the foul crimes done in my days of nature / Are burnt and purged away" (1.5.10–13). But of eternity – the unmeasured, joyous timing of paradise held to be experienced by Christian souls who have been saved or have passed through Purgatory – the royal apparition can tell his son nothing.

After Hamlet has spoken with his father's ghost, he interprets his filial obligation of revenge as being equivalent to a heroic rectification of the disordered or dismembered time of the Danish court. Yet, in different ways, all of the tragedies attest to the impossibility of such a Herculean task. It is still customary to speak of Shakespeare's tragic protagonists as tragic heroes. Yet Hamlet discovers, rather sooner than do the other male protagonists of Shakespearean tragedy, such as Antony, Coriolanus, Othello, and Lear, that he must live and act, as best he can, in a post-heroic world, where even the memory of heroic masculinity is now questionable. Hamlet begins the play by stressing his difference from the paradigmatic hero-figure of Hercules, to whom his martial father is indirectly compared when he declares that Claudius is "no more like my father / Than I to Hercules" (1.2.152–3). But the ghost's subsequent revelation of his purgatorial punishment abruptly undermines the memorial authority of the Danish or Viking-like heroism attributed to Old Hamlet in accounts of his single combat with Fortinbras of Norway; the implication is not simply that transforming, heroic modes of action are now things of the past, but rather that Hamlet is being required to reimagine or reconceptualize Denmark's putatively heroic past in order to understand its disjointed present. Indeed, as tragedies like *Lear*, *Othello*, and *Antony and Cleopatra* also place classical heroism under erasure in different ways (to use a Heideggerian formulation), their various evocations of a prehistorical or primordial mode of temporality appear to identify this vanished origin, not with the imagined plenitude of a lost heroic subject, but instead with a distinctly different form of subjectivity: one that is not exclusively either masculine or feminine, and is distinguished more by a paradoxical or riddling knowledge than by a capacity for action.

These tragedies imply, then, that the legendary purity or simplicity of heroic masculine action is no longer a realistic narrative in a historical world. Yet in the void or aporia which is the newly discovered impossibility of heroic action, the tragic protagonist who either is not primarily defined by action, or who personifies the highly compromised and contradictory character of a post-"heroic" action, repeatedly articulates or encounters peculiarly enigmatic insights. These are perceptions that appear, like the culture of the Renaissance or early modern period itself, to be both new and old: novel and immediate, yet simultaneously inspired by and embedded in earlier cultural paradigms.

For in spite of their painful sense of the temporal remoteness of a quasi-mythic past, the tragedies incorporate numerous fragmentary allusions to archaic or aboriginal forms of knowledge that are not equivalent to any system of empirical or rational truths, but which instead approximate to the "riddling" half-truths common to myth and folktale. This ahistorical mode of apprehension and knowing is articulated most vividly and memorably by Hamlet and Ophelia, by the Fool, Edgar, and the mad Lear, by the "weyard" sisters in *Macbeth*, and in *Antony and Cleopatra* by several characters: the soothsayer, Enobarbus, and finally the tragic lovers themselves. In the specific case of *Macbeth*, however, it is striking that the riddling prophetic knowledge which the witches provide leads to evil precisely because, unlike Banquo, Macbeth decides to realize it in action.

It is important to remember in this connection, as I have already observed, that a deliberate backwards glance towards the example(s) of classical antiquity was integral to the cultural and intellectual project of the Renaissance (and to Renaissance humanism in particular). But what is often overlooked in accounts of this Renaissance preoccupation with ancient cultures is its implicitly tragic conception of the archaic past as a disjointed collection of fragments that can never be completely reassembled. In his translation into English of Plutarch's *Moralia*, published in 1603, Philemon Holland observes that:

> The wisedome and learning of the Aegyptians hath bene much recommended unto us by ancient writers, and not without good cause; considering that Aegypt hath bene the source and fountaine from whence have flowed into the world arts and liberall sciences, as a man may gather by the testimony of the first Poets and philosophers that ever were. But time, which consumeth all things, hath bereft us of the knowledge of such wisdome: or if there remaine still with us any thing at all, it is but in fragments and peeces scattered heere and there. (Plutarch 1603: 1286)

This sense of the fragmentary but still potent wisdom of the remote past was vividly expressed in the riddles, enigmas, emblems, and hieroglyphs beloved by many Renaissance writers, from Erasmus and Rabelais to Nashe and Shakespeare. Yet the frequently painful awareness felt during the Renaissance, of the incompleteness of its empirical knowledge of the past, was also compensated for by the celebration of a distinctly different model of memory in the work of several Renaissance scholars and philosophers. Following Plato, these thinkers defined the most elevated kind of memory as an act that was primarily moral, philosophical, and spiritual, concerned not so much with the recovery of empirical facts about past cultures, but instead, much more importantly, with the recollection of the "native and original notions" of the soul.

When, in his *Advancement of Learning* (1605), Sir Francis Bacon compliments James I of England and VI of Scotland on the centrality accorded to memory in his kingly intelligence, Bacon argues that the highest form of recollection, called *anamnesis* by Plato, will produce a near-divine expansion of human intelligence:

> your Majesty were the best instance to make a man of Plato's opinion, that all knowledge is but remembrance, and that the mind of man by nature knoweth all things, and hath but her own native and original notions (which by the strangeness and darkness of this tabernacle of the body are sequestered) again revived and restored . . . (Bacon 1674, I: 2)

The model of knowledge described here by Bacon was derived from diverse classical sources, including several Platonic texts, and most notably from Plato's *Meno* (a text already known in the Middle Ages). In the *Meno*, Socrates, having only just admitted the weakness of his short-term memory (or his memory of facts), expounds the *significance of learning as anamnesis* by relating it to the Pythagorean doctrine of reincarnation:

> Seeing then that the soul is immortal and has been born many times, and has beheld all things both in this world and in the nether realms, she has acquired knowledge of

all and everything, so that it is no wonder that she *should be able* to recollect all that she knew before about virtue *and other things*. For as all nature is akin, and the soul has learned all things, there is no reason why we should not, *by remembering but one single thing* – an act which men call learning – discover everything else, if we have courage and faint not in the search; since, it would seem, research and learning are wholly recollection. (Plato 1967: 81 B-D, 303; emphasis added)

There is actually an odd shift of emphasis in this passage, as what seems to be an allusion to the mystical Pythagorean practice of memory exercises – exercises designed to recover soul-knowledge – is followed by a highly pragmatic and discursive approach to the search for truth; for the technique that Socrates recommends in order to accomplish *anamnesis* is Platonic dialectic or reasoned debate (Vernant 1983: ch. 3). This makes it quite clear, I think, that the goal of Platonic *anamnesis* was the acquisition of moral and philosophical, not empirical, truths. Yet by the late classical period the seeming paradox which is emphasized here, that the memory of "but one single thing" can lead to a full recollection, not of a narrow empirical knowledge, but instead of "the truth of all things that are" (86B), had become central to a very different intellectual methodology, in the form of the arts of memory. First developed for specifically rhetorical purposes, the arts of memory were reformulated in the sixteenth century in accordance with the Platonic notion of soul-memory, most famously by the philosopher Giordano Bruno. The central assumption informing these mnemonic arts was that the extraordinary was a crucial aid to memory; thus the classical rhetorician Quintilian had observed:

When we see in everyday life things that are petty, ordinary, and banal, we generally fail to remember them, because the mind is not being stirred by anything novel or marvellous. But if we see or hear something exceptionally base, dishonourable, unusual, great, unbelievable, or ridiculous, that we are likely to remember for a long time. (Quintilian, *Ad Herennium*, III, xxii)

You will note that one implication of these remarks by Quintilian is that the riddle must have a particular mnemonic force, by virtue both of its ridiculousness and its strangeness.

II

With the exception of *Romeo and Juliet* and *Othello*, all of Shakespeare's tragedies dramatize different versions of a seemingly barbaric, "antique" but also "antic," past: a past that is almost prehistorical in its perceived remoteness. These plays situate a tragic sensibility which we may rather too casually want to identify as "modern" (or early modern) within the following archaic locations: a Denmark that is seemingly situated on the historical cusp between paganism and Christianity; eleventh-century Scotland; ancient Celtic Britain; and ancient Greece, Egypt, and Rome. But the

tragedies also use specific devices to allude to a still more remote past, almost forgotten, than that in which their plays are set. So when the soldier Barnardo describes
the ghost of Old Hamlet as a "portentous figure," the royal apparition is implied to
have an especially powerful mnemonic significance for those who, as they gather on
the battlements of Elsinore in the first act of the play, are implicitly alienated from a
new historical epoch. The ghostly or uncanny presence of the disguised Edgar in *Lear*,
of the soothsayer in *Antony and Cleopatra*, and of the "weyard" sisters in *Macbeth*, all
produce somewhat similar effects; for while the soothsayer and the witches speak of
the future, their "strange intelligence" (*Macbeth*, 1.3.76) or uncanny knowledge of
"nature's infinite book of secrecy" (*Antony and Cleopatra*, 1.2.9) is disturbing precisely
because, like the witches themselves, it seems both "withered" and "wild" – implicitly archaic or aboriginal in character.

   If, therefore, we interpret his words in the context of this far-reaching Renaissance
preoccupation with memory, the ghost's repeated injunction to Hamlet – "Remember me" – should be heard not simply as an appeal for filial piety. For in the specter's
assertion that "duller shouldst thou be than the fat weed / That rots itself in ease on
Lethe's wharf / Wouldst thou not stir in this" (1.5.32–4), he is appealing indirectly
to that spiritual faculty of recollection which classical tradition associated with the
transmigrating soul, and which was supposedly eradicated before rebirth when the
soul drank from the underworld river of forgetfulness, Lethe. Hamlet's impassioned
response certainly suggests that his father's spectral image is impelling him beyond
the memory of that heroic action associated with the already limited and limiting
figure of the dead father as hero, and into an unfamiliar and more generalized process
of "remembrance," akin to that of Platonic *anamnesis* or recollection. For the prince
commits himself to a bizarre reordering of memory that also, paradoxically, necessi-
tates a forgetting of "baser matter" or more superficial forms of knowledge:

> Remember thee?
> Ay, thou poor ghost, whiles memory holds a seat
> In this distracted globe. Remember thee?
> Yea, from the table of my memory
> I'll wipe away all trivial fond records,
> All saws of books, all forms, all pressures past,
> That youth and observation copied there,
> And thy commandment all alone shall live
> Within the book and volume of my brain
> Unmixed with baser matter. Yes, yes by heaven. (1.5.95–104)

   It is this heightened and purified faculty of memory, seemingly, that produces
Hamlet's "madness," in which what is articulated by the mad prince is not substan-
tive knowledge as such, but rather a peculiarly riddling style of wit that expresses a
subtle understanding of the corruption he sees around him. The dark riddles and puns
used by Hamlet parallel those used by the bizarre folkloric and fool-like figure who

was himself behind the cunning revenger of the play's medieval source text: the
Amleth of the *Gesta Danorum* by Saxo Grammaticus (Hansen 1983). For Saxo's story
of Amleth was itself a literary reformulation of pre-Christian, Norse, and Icelandic
oral legend or folktale. And certainly the riddle was a common feature not just of biblical and ancient Greek cultures, but also of early North European cultures; it was
very widely used in Old English, for example, in both oral and literary contexts.
Hence, when Hamlet tells Rosencrantz and Guildenstern that "Denmark's a prison,"
and asks them "Will you play upon this pipe?" (3.2.341–2); or when he declares to
Claudius, enigmatically, that his "fare" is "the chameleon's dish. I eat the air, promise
crammed. You cannot feed capons so" (3.2.93–4), he is expressing an enigmatic
wisdom which the Danish setting of the play invites us, by implication, to derive
from North European saga and folktale. Indeed, his witty remark to Polonius that
"yourself, sir, shall grow as old as I am — if like a crab you could go backward"
(2.2.203–4) plays on a seemingly impossible turning backwards of time that he
implies has made him figuratively older than Polonius — at least in wisdom. A similar
inversion of conventional assumptions about the place and destiny of the human is at
work in Hamlet's declaration to Claudius that the decaying corpse of Polonius is "at
supper" (4.3.17), where he is not eating, but being eaten — by worms.

Hamlet comments obliquely on events at court in equally riddling snatches of the
old ballads in which many legendary tales were preserved, such as the ballad about
Jephthah, the judge of Israel who foolishly (like Polonius) sacrificed his daughter, or
the famous story of Damon and Pythias, to whom, after *The Mousetrap*, he compares
his friendship with Horatio. And a few scenes later, enigmatic fragments of ballad
will also punctuate the mad utterances of Ophelia, who imitates or echoes Hamlet by
invoking the obscure insights of folktale and popular lore to comment on the amoral-
ity of the court. In folktale, intricate patterns of parallelism and difference create multiple links between numerous characters and plot motifs. So Ophelia will cryptically
observe: "They say the owl was a baker's daughter. Lord, we know what we are, but
know not what we may be" (4.5.42–3); and a scene later: "It is the false steward that
stole his master's daughter," at which Laertes exclaims: "This nothing's more than
matter" (4.6.170–2). In these allusions the oblique parallelism between recent events
and fragments of a fictionalized past may not strike us as important. But in the oral
tradition of storytelling from which both folktale and riddle derive, the perception
of resemblances between two apparently different stories was of vital significance,
enabling both the storyteller and audience to comprehend the moral meaning of particular actions and events, and also to predict their consequences.

According to Boswell and Reaver (1962), the riddle encodes a higher level of cultural complexity than the proverb, since while the proverb is declarative and obvious,
the riddle is esoteric and implicitly interrogative, in its appeal to the mental acuity and
agility of the addressee. At the court of Elsinore, however, both Hamlet's and Ophelia's
riddles appear to elude total comprehension, in spite of dark forebodings about their
import expressed by both Claudius and Laertes. Just a few lines before the entry of
the Danish court to witness the fateful duel between Hamlet and Laertes, Hamlet

ironically sums up to Horatio his failure to discover any riddle-solvers in Elsinore, when he dismisses the foolishness of Osric, the grotesquely fashionable courtier:

> Thus has he – and many more of the same bevy that I know the drossy age dotes on – only got the tune of the time, and out of an habit of encounter, a kind of yeasty collection, which carries them through and through the most fanned and winnowed opinions; and do but blow them to their trial, the bubbles are out. (5.2.184–91)

In his entry on riddles in the *Dictionary of Folklore*, Charles Potter observes that riddling was "anciently and primitively employed at times of crisis or on occasions when the fate of someone or even a whole tribe hung in the balance" (Potter 1949–50, II: 940). The almost total isolation of Hamlet the riddler within the Danish court, coupled with the strange resumption, during his absence in England, of his distinctive riddling activity by his former mistress, creates the cumulative impression of a hopelessly corrupt society. Rosencrantz finally says to Hamlet, "I understand you not, my lord" (4.2.21); the court's failure to solve either the prince's or Ophelia's verbal puzzles confirms that it is ineluctably headed towards self-destruction.

Some five years after he created his riddling Danish anti-hero, Shakespeare revisited and reexamined the complex relationship between an archaic and "antic" temporality and the tragic knowledge encoded in riddles and enigmas. Riddling is of central importance in *Macbeth*, *King Lear*, and *Antony and Cleopatra* – the three tragedies which he is now thought to have written in quite rapid succession around 1606. (Shakespeare's interest in the device at this particular historical moment may also be attributed, at least in part, to the ambiguous role played by Jesuitical equivocation in the trial of Catholics associated with the Gunpowder Plot, especially Father Garnet.) As an interpreter of enigmas, we may see Macbeth as tragically literal, even proleptically "modern," in his response to the cryptic utterances of the witches. For his determination to fulfill part of their prophecy himself shows that he is ignorant of the ancient premise that fate itself accomplishes the working out of prophecy – in spite of human agency. Indeed, Shakespeare's witches mark a deep temporal fissure within his "Scottish" play, which transplants James I of England's highly contemporary concern with witchcraft to eleventh-century Scotland but also looks much further back, to the three "weyard sisters" or goddesses of fate called the Norns in Old English and Norse mythology. Just as the Norns ruled over the past, present, and future of human life, so the "weyard sisters" that encounter Macbeth and Banquo on the heath have a threefold association with time: with the "future" reign of James, with the play's present – the historical Scotland of Duncan and Macbeth – but also with the virtually prehistorical, pre-Christian beliefs of which the "weyard sisters" are a cultural remnant. It is precisely because he does not understand the archaic cultural context of their utterances – because he hears them in another time, as it were – that Macbeth converts the witches into evil accessories to his crime of regicide. This is another tragic environment where a quasi-mythic or legendary mode of heroic action is demonstrated to be tragically compromised and misguided from the very start of the play, as represented by the two (equally treacherous) Thanes of Cawdor. Macbeth's career is distinguished by a deepening temporal dislocation, in a greedy orientation towards a promised future which betokens a radical failure to understand and value either the present or the past. At the end of the play some of the imaginary proportions of a seemingly polluted heroism are briefly restored by the advent, not of Malcolm, but of Macduff: the man not born of woman who is accompanied to Dunsinane by the landscape of myth – a moving wood. Yet it is the cryptic utterances of the witches that have prepared for Macduff's martial triumph; like the fall of Macbeth, therefore, his heroic act of deposition is implied to have been previously encoded within this primordial language of riddle and enigma.

When the "Scottish" play is considered in relation to the high status accorded to riddling in other tragedies, however, Macbeth as the failed or corrupted hero seems to be most significantly flawed by his failure to practice the art of riddling himself. But in the radical void of meaning that is the storm-tossed heath of *King Lear*, a similarly enigmatic language to that used by both *Hamlet* and the "weyard sisters" elicits a subtly different response, as the prophetic jests and riddles of the Fool begin to be understood and imitated by both Edgar and Lear in the harsh and desolate landscape of the heath. The cryptic utterances of Poor Tom are seemingly half-understood by Edgar's now demented godfather, King Lear, who refers to him as a "noble philosopher." This sibylline style of communication was plausibly intended by Shakespeare to resemble that of the ancient Gallic peoples and their Druid priests, of whom Diodorus Siculus had commented that "when they meet together, they converse with few words and in riddles, hinting darkly at things for the most part, and using one word when they mean another" (Diodorus Siculus 1961, III: v, 31, 1). But like the Fool, Hamlet, and Ophelia, Edgar as Poor Tom uses traditional song as well as riddling or sibylline utterance; thus he reenters the hovel with Lear chanting lines from a well-known cycle of folktales: *"Child Rowland to the dark tower came, / His word was still Fie, foh and fum, / I smell the blood of a British man"* (3.4.179–81). From the perspective of folklore and legend, the implication seems to be that any "heroic" form of leadership or kingship must be preceded by and founded upon an understanding and appropriate use of this enigmatic language.

Yet it seems that the acquisition of such riddling skills depends once again upon a painful form of temporal dislocation. For the radical void of meaning that is the storm-tossed heath of *King Lear* is also a kind of temporal void, as the legendary yet quasi-historical past in which this British or Celtic British play is set (given its indebtedness to Geoffrey of Monmouth's *History of the Kings of Britain*) appears suddenly to recede before an evocation of man's most primitive origins, associated both with the heath and with the flooded hovel where Edgar is sheltering. As Lear and the Fool move towards the hovel, this vivid sense of temporal disjointedness, or being out of time, is given verbal form by the Fool's riddling "prophecy" of two radically different futures: one, when "the realm of Albion [shall] / Come to great confusion," another, when virtue is pervasive "And bawds and whores do churches build" (3.2.90–1). The Fool concludes that "This prophecy Merlin shall make, for I live before his time" (3.2.95). Thus, here also, time appears to become multifaceted as it exceeds the linear perspective of tragedy.

In a characteristically cryptic but also highly suggestive formulation, Jacques Derrida has remarked that "At the origin there was the ruin. At the origin the ruin happens, it is what happens first, to the origin" (Derrida 1990: 69). On one level, of course, Derrida's words stress the impossibility of recovering a precise knowledge or memory of any privileged site of beginning. But they also hint at a more subtle, paradoxical connection between *lethe* as forgetfulness – the ruination of conventional forms of memory – and the obscure ways in which fragmentary remnants of primordial or archaic time continue mysteriously to signify or speak to us. As you will recall, in order to remember what the ghost has told him, Hamlet asserts that he has first to forget everything else. And in *Antony and Cleopatra* the erotic and sensual pleasures of Egypt are represented as inspiring a "leth'd dullness" in both lovers – a stupor of sexual and temporal forgetfulness as it were, that appears also, mysteriously, to facilitate a quasi-Platonic form of recollection. Whereas Antony's brain fumes with the effects of Egyptian liquor, and his military responsibilities are "prorogued" in Alexandria by sleep and "feeding" – "even till a leth'd dullness" – Cleopatra also experiences the mutability of their love as inducing an effect of forgetfulness, as she identifies Antony himself with oblivion in which her own distinct identity's consumed: "O, my oblivion is a very Antony, / And I am all forgotten" (1.3.90–1). Later, Cleopatra desires to drink mandragora "That I may sleep out this great gap of time / My Antony is away" (1.5.5–6). This forgetfulness of their historical, temporal selves – which is also, by implication, a forgetting of historical time – is certainly seen as the cause of the lovers' tragedy. But it should not, I think, be read as unequivocally negative in a play that is extremely suspicious of the limitations of a narrowly historical form of memory.

For, of course, Ancient Egypt was an especially potent memory-site for those many Renaissance thinkers, writers, and artists who wanted to create fragmentary memorializations of antique cultures. Moreover, Egypt was seen as especially compelling, yet also especially ambivalent, because of its much greater antiquity than either Greece or Rome. Several factors contributed to this status, including the supposedly Egyptian origin of the writings of Hermes Trismegistus, venerated by Renaissance Neoplatonists, and the growing interest of Renaissance emblem-collectors in Egyptian hieroglyphics. In late Renaissance England the first two books of Herodotus' *Histories*, which were much concerned with Egypt's customs and antiquity, were translated into English in 1584; Pliny's *Natural History*, with its allusions to Egypt's "boast and glorie antiquitie," followed in 1601; while Plutarch's *De Iside et Osiride* appeared in Philemon Holland's translation of *The Morals* in 1603.

In act 2 scene 7 Shakespeare dramatizes a lavish feast held for the Roman Triumvirate – Caesar, Antony, and Lepidus and their men – on the barge of their enemy, Pompey the Younger. The stage is full of Romans, with not an Egyptian in sight. Yet military conflicts, political mistrust, and the risk of betrayal have been temporarily suspended in obedience to the time-honored laws of hospitality. And it is at this pivotal moment in the play, as what begins as a Roman feast somehow becomes

Egyptian, or "Alexandrian," and as two very different temporalities and cultures briefly merge, that the peculiar interrelationship of the Egyptian "lethe" with a riddling or "antic" behavior that is seemingly charged with unusual archaic significance is most vividly suggested.

The scene begins with Pompey's servants riddling about Lepidus, the weakest member of the Roman Triumvirate. One of them observes that "To be called into a huge sphere [of power], and not to be seen to move in't [in other words, not to act] are the holes where eyes should be, which pitifully disaster the cheeks." The implication of this riddle is that the triadic Roman power structure is fatally flawed by the inadequacy of Lepidus to his task, with the likely result (soon to be realized) of a crisis of cosmological proportions, as the two powerful Triumvirs, Antony and Octavius Caesar, battle for supremacy. But this prescient first riddle about Rome is followed by the scene's extended exposition of Egypt as a virtually indecipherable enigma. The difficulty Egypt poses to its would-be interpreters is encapsulated in Antony's riddling reply to Lepidus' drunken query about the Egyptian crocodile:

> It is shap'd, sir, like itself, and is as broad as it hath breadth: it is just so high as it is, and moves with it own organs. It lives by that which nourisheth it, and the elements once out of it, it transmigrates. (2.7.41–4)

Antony's "description" reveals precisely nothing in empirical terms about the appearance of this "strange serpent," but it does tell us one thing that could certainly not be proven – that the crocodile "transmigrates" into other forms upon death. Perhaps the implication here is that some kernel of Egyptian wisdom can survive even its cultural decay. And in the dance with which the scene ends, as Antony declares "Come, let's all take hands / Till that the conquering wine hath steep'd our sense / In soft and delicate Lethe" (2.7.105–6), this concern with enigmas is extended to encompass a brief yet riddling "transmigration" of Roman heroic identity, through a purportedly Egyptian ritual to Bacchus/Dionysus (identified by Plutarch with Osiris, Egyptian god of the underworld and consort of Isis), as rhythmic movement is substituted for heroic action, and not the dancer but the earth is felt to move:

> Come, thou monarch of the vine,
> Plumpy Bacchus with pink eyne!
> In thy fats our cares be drowned,
> With thy grapes our hairs be crown'd.
>> Cup us till the world go round
>> Cup us till the world go round. (2.7.111–16)

Caesar, who is sternly critical of the self-oblivion that is produced by the dance, as well as by excess of drink, remarks that the Romans' complexions have been darkened by the wine – "You see we have burnt our cheeks" – and he exits declaring that "the wild disguise hath almost / Antick'd us all" (2.7.122–3). But his words additionally suggest that the "antic" folly of this drunken obliviousness (whose disruption or disjointing of conventional ideas of historical time is imaged, according to Gilberto Sacerdoti (1990), by the still radical (Copernican) conception of the moving earth) may indeed be allied with a momentary effect of *anamnesis*.

Writing of the archaic origins of dance, the Greek author Lucian, who was much admired in the Renaissance, claims that "Dance came into being contemporaneously with the primal origin of the Universe, making her appearance together with Love – the Love that is age-old" (Lucian 1962, V: 7, 220–1). Lucian asserts that "not a single ancient mystery-cult can be found that is without dancing . . . those who let out the mysteries in conversation are commonly said to dance them out" (ibid: 15, 228–9). Hence he stresses that dance is crucially related to the power of memory:

> Before all else . . . it behoves her [Dance] to enjoy the favour of Mnemosyne and her daughter Polyhymnia, and she endeavours to remember everything; like Calchas in Homer, the dancer must know "what is, and what shall be, and was of old" . . . Beginning with Chaos and the primeval origin of the world, he must know everything, *down to the story of Cleopatra the Egyptian.* (Ibid: 37, 246–9; emphasis added)

In Shakespeare's "Egyptian Bacchanals" the racial, cultural, and temporal differences separating Rome and Egypt are briefly extinguished, as the Romans experience a state of joyful unity in the nonrational, enigmatic meaningfulness of the dance. The scene is therefore implied to offer us, the audience, a disjointed glimpse of an antique form of knowledge that is also "antic," both in its riddling and obscure character and in its forgetfulness or disruption of existing cultural and temporal concepts. But the extent to which the riddle or enigma is central to Egypt's archaic identity is made most explicit in the riddling death of Cleopatra, whose perplexingly Sphinx-like character suggests that Egypt itself, although conquered, will continue to elude the mastery of heroic action – or at least any heroic effort to decode or forcefully appropriate these secrets. Her death leaves behind a barely discernible trail of signs – simply a small vent of blood on the dead queen's body, and a trace of slime on a fig leaf – for the Romans to decipher. In this tragedy, therefore, after Cleopatra's "monument" has received the dissolving heroic identity of Antony, the remains of a fragmented and almost effaced archaic origin are finally invested with a distinctive feminine character. At the same time, the last scene of *Antony and Cleopatra* also directs our attention to the existence of a subtle yet highly significant pattern within Shakespeare's configuration of the self-concealing character of tragic knowledge. For like and yet unlike the Roman soldiers – who may solve the empirical riddle of Cleopatra's death but who cannot, it is implied, understand the more abstract riddle or mystery of Egypt – it is essential that we do not perfectly comprehend the riddles which are posed by Shakespearean tragedy. Indeed, it is precisely the cryptic and self-concealing character of these riddles which ensures that the reader or spectator will continue to meditate upon these half-remembered truths.

REFERENCES AND FURTHER READING

Bacon, F. (1674) [1605]. *Of the Advancement and Proficiencie of Learning*, trans. G. Wats. London.

Boswell, G. and Reaver, J. R. (1962). *Fundamentals of Folk Literature*. Oosterhout: Anthropological Publications.

Derrida, J. (1990). *Mémoires d'aveugle. L'autoportrait et autres ruines*. Paris: Louvre, Editions de la réunion des musées nationaux.

Diodorus Siculus (1961). Trans. C. H. Oldfather, 12 vols. London: Heinemann.

Hansen, W. F. (1983). *Saxo Grammaticus and the Life of Hamlet: A Translation, History and Commentary*. Lincoln: University of Nebraska Press.

Lucian (1962). The Dance. In *Lucian*, 8 vols., trans. A. M. Harman. London: Heinemann.

Marcus, L. S. (1992). Renaissance/Early Modern Studies. In S. Greenblatt and G. Gunn (eds.) *Redrawing the Boundaries: The Transformation of English and American Literary Studies*. New York: Modern Language Association of America.

Plato (1967). *Meno*. In *Plato*, 12 vols., trans. W. R. M. Lamb. London: Heinemann.

Plutarch (1603). *Moralia*, trans. P. Holland. London.

Potter, C. (1949–50). Riddles. In M. Leach (ed.) *Funk and Wagnalls Standard Dictionary of Folklore*. New York: Funk and Wagnalls.

Sacerdoti, G. (1990). *Nuovo Cielo, Nuova Terra: la rivelazione copernicana di "Antonio e Cleopatra" di Shakespeare*. Bologna: Il Mulino.

Shakespeare, W. (1951). *Macbeth*, ed. K. Muir. London: Methuen.

——(1954). *Antony and Cleopatra*, ed. M. R. Ridley. London: Methuen.

——(1972). *King Lear*, ed. K. Muir. London: Methuen.

——(1982). *Hamlet*, ed. H. Jenkins. London: Methuen.

Vernant, J.-P. (1983). Mythical Aspects of Memory. In *Myth and Thought Among the Greeks*. London: Routledge.

6
Reading Shakespeare's Tragedies of Love: *Romeo and Juliet*, *Othello*, and *Antony and Cleopatra* in Early Modern England

Sasha Roberts

By the turn of the seventeenth century Shakespeare was perhaps primarily regarded as a writer on romantic and erotic love. In 1598, for instance, Francis Meres concluded that Shakespeare was one of "the most passionate among us to bewaile and bemoane the perplexities of Love" in *Palladis Tamia. Or Wits Treasury* (1598: 284); two years later the skeptical press-corrector Judicio in *The First Return of Parnassus*, a comedy performed at Cambridge University, lamented that Shakespeare could not be contented with a "grauer subject" than "loues foolish lazy languishment" (ll. 301–4). Shakespeare's "bestselling" work (at least in terms of reprints) during his lifetime was his narrative poem *Venus and Adonis* (1593) depicting Venus' frustrated erotic trysts with the coy Adonis – which swiftly earned him the dubious reputation of being a witty purveyor of bawdy gear. Furthermore, in *Romeo and Juliet* – one of his most frequently cited plays in the early modern period – Shakespeare turned a genre that had traditionally been associated with politics and history to the throes of passion. Today, the death of young lovers has become a naturalized choice for a tragedy but in 1594–6, when *Romeo and Juliet* was probably written, tragedy typically focused upon the fall of political figures such as kings, princes, or generals (consider Shakespeare's more conventional tragic heroes: Hamlet, Othello, King Lear, Macbeth). As Harry Levin (1993) notes, Shakespeare's contemporaries "would have been surprised, and possibly shocked, at seeing lovers taken so seriously. Legend, it had been heretofore taken for granted, was the proper matter for serious drama; romance was the stuff of the comic stage" (p. 45).

For the purposes of this volume *Romeo and Juliet*, *Othello*, and *Antony and Cleopatra* have been grouped together as Shakespeare's "tragedies of love," but to what extent did early modern readers respond to these plays as tragedies of love? How did seventeenth-century readers *use* these plays? Despite the extraordinary investment of research into Shakespeare little attention has been paid to how his works were *read* in early modern England; far more is known of Shakespeare's companies, competitors, stationers, and theatrical audiences than his readers. In part this reflects an emphasis in Shakespeare and Renaissance literary studies on texts as sites of production rather than reception; New Historicism in particular, by privileging the cultural moment of a text's production, has been charged with neglect of the reader.[1] But if we are seriously interested in historicizing early modern literature then we cannot afford to ignore the history of how it was read in early modern England; how books were transmitted, used, and regarded by their contemporaries and subsequent generations. Readers may be the final link in the chain of literary production, but they are also its most vital.

In fact the testimony of early modern readers of *Romeo and Juliet*, *Othello*, and *Antony and Cleopatra* is often surprising, unpredictable, and at odds with the issues we find so compelling today in Shakespeare's works. In this chapter I want to explore how these tragedies functioned as *moral* commentary. It has become commonplace in modern Shakespeare studies to uphold the contentious and ambivalent nature of Shakespearean drama; to assume that Shakespearean drama tends to unsettle the very idea that we can arrive at any moral certainty, particularly since the figures and institutions of moral authority in Shakespearean drama are repeatedly shown to be conflicted or compromised. Thus Franklin Dickey's *Not Wisely But Too Well* (a quote from *Othello*) – which contends that these plays pursue a moralizing, even didactic, agenda by showing the tragic outcome of "excessive or misdirected love" – has long come under attack as overly reductive.[2] To be sure, the potential for Shakespeare's tragedies to operate as critique is no chimera of the heady 1980s: precisely because Shakespeare's plays are so open-ended and multifaceted, available for reinterpretation by subsequent generations of readers, performers, and audiences, they can be put to an infinite variety of interpretations. However, the thrust of Dickey's (1957) argument that Shakespeare's tragedies of love operated *for early modern readers* "as exemplum . . . as examples of how not to behave" (p. 156) should not, I think, be dismissed out of hand as redundant thinking. Whilst I would not agree with Dickey that Shakespeare's plays present straightforward answers to the ethical questions they pose, it remains the case that for many early modern readers of Shakespeare moral instruction, even certitude, was precisely what his plays offered.

At one level reading an early modern play for moral instruction entails reading it as narrative – following the outcomes of actions, the effects of character, the consequences of social, cultural, and political ideas and institutions. To read, for instance, warnings against rash behavior in *Romeo and Juliet*, jealousy in *Othello*, or adultery in *Antony and Cleopatra*, requires engagement with the plays' plots. However, while some early modern readers responded to the narrative or character coordinates of Shakespeare's plays others ignored them entirely, instead gathering moral instruction from *sententiae* extracted from the plays – pithy comments and observations, often with a philosophical, moralizing, or didactic edge, that could be applied to general circumstances (as when Iago's hypocritical advice to beware the green-eyed monster of jealousy was deployed without irony as well-meaning advice). Shakespeare's early modern readers, then, read both along *and* against the narratives of his works; thus if we are to read Shakespeare historically, we need to have the critical agility to move beyond the habit – so engrained in our practice as to be second nature – of reading plays not only for the stories they tell but for their partial effects and applications.

Early Modern Responses to *Romeo and Juliet*, *Othello*, and *Antony and Cleopatra*

The status of English drama was far from secure in the early seventeenth century. Not only was the institution of the theatre subject to periodic attack for its licentiousness, subversive role-playing, and social impropriety (witnessed, for instance, in the antitheatrical diatribes of Philip Stubbes and William Prynne), but also vernacular drama – as opposed to the classics of ancient Greece and Rome – had yet to achieve critical respectability, remaining tainted by the fact of its ephemeral performance before an apparently indiscriminate and socially diverse audience. Thus the anonymous address "To the Reader" in the First Quarto of *Troilus and Cressida* (1609) promises that the play was "Neuer stal'd with the Stage, neuer clapper-clawd with the palmes of the uulgar," remaining unsullied by the "smoaky breath of the multitude"; instead it appeals to a discriminating readership able to appreciate "dexteritie, and power of witte" (sig. A2). Moreover, in the context of a humanist curriculum of classics, rhetoric, history, and theology, vernacular fiction (especially drama, romance, and love poetry) was repeatedly trivialized as "light" literature of merely recreational value. Hence it was associated with supposedly weaker readers, especially women – as Richard Brome put it in "Verses upon Aglaura" (ca. 1656). "Ladies . . . never look! But in a Poem or in a Play-book" – and banished as "idle bookes, & riffe-raffes" from Thomas Bodley's library at Oxford.[3]

Thus to be regarded as a writer principally on love, as Shakespeare was by 1600, was no guarantee of critical respectability. In the anonymous *The First Part of the Returne from Parnassus* (ca. 1598), the first play in the *Parnassus* trilogy performed at Cambridge University ca. 1598–1601, for instance, Shakespeare is repeatedly cited as the preferred reading matter of the idle courtier Gullio – a "gull" and "knowne foole" who ridiculously fashions himself as "a scholler" (ll. 835, 1412, 1133). Boasting to a sharp-witted poet under his patronage, Ingenioso, about how he courted his mistress, Gullio recites his seduction set-piece – an "enthusiasticall oration" drawn from *Romeo and Juliet* and the opening stanzas of *Venus and Adonis*:

> *Ingenioso.* I feare this speach thats a comminge will breede a deadly disease in my ears.
> *Gullio.* Pardon, faire lady, thoughe sicke thoughted Gullio maks a maine vnto thee, & like a bould faced sutore gins to woo thee.

Ingenioso. We shall have nothinge but pure Shakspeare and shreds of poetrie that he hath gathered at the theators.

Gullio. Pardon mee moy mistressa, ast am a gentleman the moone in comparison of thy bright hue a meere slutt, Anthonies Cleopatra a blacke browde milkmaide, Hellen a dowdie.

Ingenioso. Marke, Romeo and Iuliet: O monstrous theft, I thinke he will runn throughe a whole booke of Samuell Daniells. (ll. 981–94)

Taking Venus' role of a "bould faced sutore," Gullio garbles Mercutio's lines from *Romeo and Juliet* in what appears to be an inaccurate memorial reconstruction of the play: "Laura to his lady was a kitchen wench (marry, she had a better love to berhyme her). Dido a dowdy, Cleopatra a gipsy, Helen and Hero hildings and harlots . . ." (2.4.34–6). The *First Return from Parnassus* shows *Romeo and Juliet* and *Venus and Adonis* to be the recreational, middlebrow reading of an "ass," a "base carle clothed in a saittin sute" and the "scorne of all good wittes" (ll. 1441–55); likewise Marston's satire 10 of the frivolous Luscus in *The Scourge of Villanie* (1598) deploys the same motif of Shakespeare as lowbrow reading matter:

> I set thy lips abroach, from whence doth flow
> Naught but pure *Iuliat* and *Romio* . . .
> Now I have him, that nere of ought did speake
> But when of plays or Plaiers he did treate.
> H'ath made a common-place booke out of plaies.
> . . .
>   speakes he not movingly,
> From out some new pathetique Tragedy?
> He writes, he railes, he iests, he courts what not,
> And all from out his huge long scraped stock
> Of well-penn'd playes. (sig. H3v)

Instead of filling his common-place book (in this context probably a manuscript notebook) with the serious stuff of humanist learning, Luscus consumes only recreational literature; as in the *Parnassus* plays, Marston's satiric speaker characterizes plays, and *Romeo and Juliet* in particular, as the lightweight reading of a dim-witted gentleman.

But the stigmatization of light literature did not, of course, stop readers from reading it. Far from it; the newly emerging vernacular literatures of pleasure and entertainment in the late sixteenth and early seventeenth centuries were avidly read by men and women alike. Although gentlemen's libraries were (as far as one can risk generalizing) predominantly utilitarian in the seventeenth century, they often yield rich holdings in light literature, especially plays, romances, novellas, and miscellanies; indeed, many gentlemen's libraries were far more extensive in these genres than those of women. Thus T. A. Birrell argues that "plays were read as the most accessible form of fiction" by gentlemen, while romances – a genre so frequently associated with indulgent women readers – can also be found in large numbers in gentlemen's libraries (Sir Robert Gordon of Gordonstoun, for instance, owned more than sixty French romances).[4] Ironically, when *Romeo and Juliet* was finally accepted onto the shelves of the Bodleian Library in the seventeenth century, it was so frequently thumbed by (male) students that it soon had to be replaced.

As one of Shakespeare's most popular plays, *Romeo and Juliet* attracted considerable attention in early modern England – ranging from John Weever's 1594 praise for Shakespeare's characters (*Romeo-Richard*) that "burn in love," to the acerbic remarks of Marston; from Leonard Digges's admiration of Shakespeare's depiction of the "Passions of *Juliet*, and her *Romeo*" in the First Folio of 1623, to Samuel Pepys's distaste for the play in performance in 1661–2 ("a play of itself the worst that ever I heard in my life").[5] But there is little sense in any of these passing comments that Romeo and Juliet are vindicated in their passion. It has become standard in criticism and performance that Shakespeare's *Romeo and Juliet* represents an ideal and an endorsement of romantic love. Dympna Callaghan has subtly refined this view by arguing that *Romeo and Juliet* promotes the *ideology* of romantic love by presenting Juliet's desire as "benign and unthreatening" and validating Romeo and Juliet's marriage; in so doing, the play makes marriage and the nuclear family – the "bourgeois family form" advocated by early modern Protestant treatises on companionate marriage – "the social destination of desire" (Callaghan 1994: 62, 88). But the play works rather to complicate, question, and problematize Romeo and Juliet's marriage. As I have argued elsewhere, Juliet's exceptionally young age (thirteen), the rashness of the couple's contract and marriage within two days – "too rash, too unadvised, too sudden" (2.2.118) – and their depiction as melancholic, immature, and "hot" Italians (3.1.4) cast doubt upon the appropriateness and advisability of their actions, even as their plight and romance evokes sympathy (Roberts 1998). Far from following the accepted conventions of Protestant bourgeois marriage, Romeo and Juliet's marriage is inherently controversial because it is clandestine: covert, secret, furtive, unauthorized, illicit. Thus in Brooke's *Romeus* the keynote of the lovers' marriage is not romantic love but scandal and shame:

> to this ende (good Reader) is this tragicall matter written, to describe unto thee a coople of unfortunate lovers, thralling themselves to unhonest desire, neglecting the authoritie and advise of parents and frendes, conferring their principall counsels with dronken gossyppes, and superstitious friers (the naturally fitte instruments of unchastitie) attemptyng all adventures of perull, for thattanyng of their wished lust, usyng auriculer confession (the key of whoredome, and treason) for furtherance of theyr purpose, *abusyng the honorable name of lawefull mariage, to cloke the shame of stolne contractes*, finially, by all meanes of unhonest lyfe, hastyng to most unhappye deathe. (Emphasis added)[6]

To be sure, Shakespeare presents a more complex account of filial duty than Brooke, but *Romeo and Juliet* does not skirt the controversy of a clandestine marriage: hence the Friar's anxious request that the heavens "chide us not" (2.6.2), and Juliet's misgivings that the Friar "should be dishonoured" by secretly marrying her to Romeo (4.3.26).

Further, Juliet breaches orthodox codes of ideal femininity – in Richard Brathwaite's *The English Gentlewoman* (1631), for instance, the model gentlewoman should be "never yet acquainted with a passionate *ah me*, nor a careless folding of her arms, as if the thought of a prevailing lover had wrought in her thoughts some violent distemper."[7] Juliet's opening words in the orchard scene, however, are precisely "Ay me!" (2.2.23–4) – a contemporary cliché for indulgent passion which Mercutio mocks in his parody "Cry but 'Ay me!'" (2.2.10) – while her "desperate" behavior in threatening suicide (see 4.1.69 and 5.3.263–4) manifests the "violent distemper" Brathwaite warned women against. Moreover, Juliet is shown to be sexually forward: she enthusiastically allows Romeo to kiss her within minutes of their first meeting ("I should have been more strange"; 2.2.98–102), while in her epithalamion anticipating her wedding night (3.2.1–31) she is "impatient" (3.2.30) to lose her "maidenhead," comparing her with an unrestrained ("unmanned") falcon whose wings flutter wildly ("bate") and looking forward to her own sexual pleasure "when I shall die" (the line has curiously been emended by some editors, perhaps reticent about Juliet's precocious sexuality, to Q4's "when *he* shall die"). As Mary Bly (1996) suggests, an Elizabethan audience would be sure to grasp the sexual double-meaning of "die" as orgasm: its addition to Q2 *Romeo and Juliet* testifies to Shakespeare's interest in the erotic nature of Juliet's passion, while its excision from Q1 points, Bly argues, "to the fact that Juliet's expression of erotic desire represented a breach of cultural expectation" (p. 105). Romeo, meanwhile, is repeatedly characterized as "effeminate" (3.1.105): "Thy tears are womanish, thy wild acts denote / The unreasonable fury of a beast. / Unseemly woman in a seeming man" rebukes the Friar (3.3.108–22; see also 3.3.143–5); stop "weeping and blubb'ring. / Stand up, stand up, stand, and you be a man; / For Juliet's sake, for her sake, rise and stand" orders the Nurse (3.3.85–9). By contrast, Brooke's Romeus suffers no such indignity.

Attempts to recuperate Romeo and Juliet as romantic heroes or ideals have been made by appealing to their rapid maturity, but the play continues to stress Romeo and Juliet's continued rashness, lack of control, and immaturity, and tragically bears out the Friar's warning: "violent delights have violent ends . . . Therefore love moderately" (Friar Lawrence, 2.6.9–14; lines that do not appear in Q1). In the final scene Romeo speaks of his "savage-wild" intentions "More fierce and more inexorable far / Than empty tigers or the roaring sea," threatens to tear Balthasar "joint by joint" (5.3.35–9), and describes himself to Paris as a "madman" (5.3.67) – hardly a picture of controlled maturity. Friar Lawrence describes Juliet's first proposal of suicide as "desperate" (4.1.69), and in the final scene explains that Juliet was "too desperate" to leave the tomb, and in this state of mind "did violence on herself" (5.3.263–4). Although suicide was acknowledged as an act of stoicism in the context of ancient Greece and Rome, most early modern commentators regarded suicide in contemporary culture as a desperate, violent act that ran against God's will (consider Hamlet's qualms over suicide, and the argument over whether Ophelia should be buried in consecrated ground).

Thus for Robert Burton in the second edition of *The Anatomy of Melancholy* (1624), *Romeo and Juliet* speaks loud and clear of the tormented violence of *amor insanus* (p. 426). In a section headed "Prognostickes of Loue Melancholy" (Pt. 3, sec. 2, mem. 4), Burton argues that:

> Hee that runnes headlong from the top of a rocke, is not in so bad a case, as hee that falls into this gulfe of Loue. For hence, saith *Platina, comes Repentance, Dotage, they loose themselues, their wits, and make shipwracke of their fortunes altogether*, Madnesse, to make away themselues & others, violent death . . . [Yet] it is so well knowne in euery village, how many haue either died for loue or voluntary made away themselues, that I need not much labor to proue it. (Ibid: 426–7; original italics)

Arguing that the love-melancholic will "commonly make away themselues," Burton cites the examples of "*Dido, Pyramus* and *Thisbe, Medea, Coresus and* Callyrhoe, *Theagines* the Philosopher, & many Myriades besides" before citing the closing couplet of *Romeo and Juliet*:

> Who euer heard a story of more woe,
> Then that of *Iuliet* and her *Romeo*. (p. 427)[8]

There is no sense in Burton's citation of the play that Romeo and Juliet's passion is to be admired; instead Burton treats it as a disorder that, in leading to the desperate violence of suicide, becomes the occasion for lament. In so doing Burton reads *Romeo and Juliet* as a tragedy of love-melancholy with a moral attached: beware the rage of intemperate love.

Like *Romeo and Juliet*, *Antony and Cleopatra* was coopted in the period as a lesson in how not to love. It is not hard to see why: both Antony and Cleopatra are presented in the play as compromised, flawed characters. This is not to deny the play's investigation of social mores and institutions – the poverty of Roman diplomatic marriage, the imperatives of military imperialism, the conflicted relationship between East and West, for instance – but to understand that the play is also fascinated by personality and celebrity. As a serial adulterer Antony has few redeeming features, and his cavalier treatment first of Fulvia then Octavia is surely not condoned by the play. Rather, "th'adulterous Antony, most large / In his abhominations" (Maecenas, 3.6.95–6) is shown to be a calculating hypocrite; his declaration of fidelity to Octavia – "If I lose mine honour, / I lose myself; better I were not yours / Than yours so branchless" (3.4.22–4) – is rendered worthless by his previous admission that "though I make this marriage for my peace, / th' East my pleasure lies" (2.3.38–9). But marital peace and adulterous pleasure cannot coexist: one of the insights of *Antony and Cleopatra* is that there is no transcendent world for the extramarital affair. The adulterous lovers may enjoy their play-time of drinking, dressing up, and sex, but their hours of recreation are not infinite and the ties of marriage are not escapable – except, perhaps, in death. Antony and Cleopatra may romanticize their love for each other, but does the play?

Certainly Antony and Cleopatra enjoy brief moments of intimacy and affection, but the descriptions of romantic love that they offer each other are more often than not retrospective or spoken in the absence of the other; indeed, the apotheosis of their expressions of love comes only at the most final absence of them all, death: "Where souls do couch on flowers we'll hand in hand / And with our sprightly port make the ghosts gaze" (Antony, 4.14.52–3); "Methinks I hear / Antony call . . . Husband, I come! /Now to that name my courage prove my title!" (5.2.282–7). While the gestures Antony and Cleopatra offer each other in death may be loaded with pathos, in life increasingly acrimonious argument remains their chief mode of exchange: "You'll heat my blood. No more" (Antony, 1.3.81); "I found you as a morsel, cold upon / Dead Caesar's trencher" (Antony, 3.13.121–2); "the greatest spot / Of all thy sex; most monster-like be shown / For poor'st diminutives" (Antony, 4.11.36–7; see also 1.3.7–12). Of course dissension does not preclude love; Antony and Cleopatra's argumentative relationship can be read, like that of Beatrice and Benedick in *Much Ado About Nothing*, as a signal of their absorption in each other. Yet *Antony and Cleopatra* inhabits a very different world from the temperate gardens of *Much Ado*: in *Antony and Cleopatra* we are not only in the exotic, heady lands of North Africa but, more importantly, in the realm of tragedy. There is no wronged wife waiting in the wings in *Much Ado*, and no marriage to look forward to in act 5 of *Antony and Cleopatra*.

Further, despite their grand gestures, Antony and Cleopatra's desire for each other is more often defined in terms of "pleasure" and "sport" than romantic love (see 1.1.47–8, 1.2.131–3, 1.4.30–2, and 2.4.38–9), while other characters in the play – including Antony's chief follower, Enobarbus – describe Antony and Cleopatra's affair in terms of lust not love: "The ne'er-lust-wearied Antony" (Pompey, 2.1.39); "the unlawful issue that their lust / Since then hath made between them" (Caesar, 3.6.7–8); "The itch of his affection" (Enobarbus, 3.13.7; see also 1.1,10, 1.4.17, 1.4.57, and 2.1.22). Above all, Antony's "dotage" (1.1.1) for Cleopatra is portrayed as destructive, sending him on a doomed path of emasculation and humiliation. Although Antony at times proclaims their love as mutual ("The nobleness of life / Is to do thus, when such a mutual pair / And such a twain can do't"; 1.1.37–9), Cleopatra remains the dominant partner as Antony has to acknowledge: "These strong Egyptian fetters I must break / Or lose myself in dotage" (1.2.122–3; see also 3.10.20–9 and 3.11.15). This is in keeping with Plutarch's account of Antony and Cleopatra in *The Parallel Lives of the Greeks and the Romans*, Shakespeare's source for the play, which stresses Antony's submission to the women in his life: "so Cleopatra was to give Fulvia thanks for that she had taught Antonius this obedience to women, that learned so well to be at their commandment."[9] As "a doting mallard" (3.10.20), Antony's manhood is stripped from him both figuratively and literally: thus Caesar remarks, he "is not more manlike / Than Cleopatra, nor the Queen of Ptolemy / More womanly than he"

(Caesar, 1.4.5–7); Cleopatra removes "his sword Philippan," wearing it herself and dressing Antony in her "tires and mantles" (2.5.21–3), and in battle Canidius laments "our leader's led / And we are women's men" (Canidius, 3.7.68–9; see also 3.7.13–15). Keenly aware of his own path of self-destruction – "I / Have lost my way for ever . . . Indeed I have lost command" (3.11.4–23); "Authority melts from me" (3.13.95) – Antony is finally subjected to a series of humiliations: Eros and his guards refuse to kill him (4.14.97–111), he fails to kill himself ("I have done my work ill"; 4.14.106), and – emblematic of "the miserable change now at my end" (4.15.53) – he is ignominiously, almost farcically, hauled up to Cleopatra's monument ("Here's sport indeed! How heavy weighs my lord!", 4.15.31–8).

By contrast Cleopatra dies with a dignity "fitting for a princess / Descended of so many royal kings" (Charmian, 5.2.325–6). But this is one of the few moments in which Cleopatra's composure and independent spirit is actually displayed in the play: while it has been argued that she is one of Shakespeare's most independent heroines – a woman who not only rules effectively over her subjects but, through Antony, increases her territories – by comparison with Juliet and Desdemona, Cleopatra is shown to be emotionally dependent, constantly requiring reassurance. And the play makes clear her exotic and, in the context of contemporary orthodox morality, promiscuous sexual history: "He ploughed her, and she cropped" (Agrippa, 2.2.238); "Triple-turned whore!" (Antony, 4.12.13); "a right gipsy" (Antony, 4.12.28). The presentation of Cleopatra as, at best, a problematic heroine in Shakespeare's play becomes even clearer in comparison to its predecessors with which it shares several verbal echoes: Mary Sidney, Countess of Pembroke's *Antonius* (1592), an adaptation of Robert Garnier's *Marc Antoine* (1578), and Samuel Daniel's *Cleopatra* (1594), designed as a companion piece to Sidney's *Antonius*. In Sidney's play Cleopatra is almost wholly sympathetic: a woman who commands respect in her stoicism, and whose suicide is motivated simply by her wish to be reunited in death with Antony (rather as Chaucer coopted Cleopatra as an example of romantic fidelity in *The Legend of Good Women*). As Eve Rachelle Sanders suggests, "her *Antonius* introduced to the canon of published English literature a female anti-example recast in positive terms as a stage heroine."[10] Daniel's *Cleopatra*, which opens after the death of Antony, constructs a more complex Cleopatra who is driven to suicide not only because she wants to join Antony, but also because of the ignominy of appearing in Caesar's triumph and to redeem her infamous past. Although the Chorus of Daniel's play delivers a moralizing commentary condemning Cleopatra's "luxurie" and the vanity and pride of human desires, as John Wilders puts it, Daniel's Cleopatra "has none of the vulgarity of Shakespeare's heroine" (in Shakespeare 1995b: 63). While Shakespeare may have borrowed from Daniel Cleopatra's various motives for suicide and her stoic dignity in death from Sidney, Shakespeare shows us a Cleopatra who is capable of vanity (see especially 3.3.11–40), pettiness, selfishness, dissimulation, and manipulation.

By this I do not mean to trivialize Cleopatra, deny her subversive appeal or the fraught dynamics of race and sexuality in the play (which have been examined effectively elsewhere), but rather to rehearse how Antony and Cleopatra could be readily coopted into a moralizing agenda. Consider, for instance, Brathwaite's commentary on their affair in *The English Gentlewoman* (1631). In a chapter on "Fancy" aiming to "discover those incendiaries or forments of this inordinate passion, or intoxicating poyson" (p. 138), Richard Brathwaite warns of the false security our fancy – imagination in the throes of passion – may give:

> Loves enteruiew betwixt *Cleopatra* and *Marke Anthony*, promised to it selfe as much secure freedome as fading fancy could tender; yet the last Scene clozed all those Comicke passages with a Tragicke conclusion. (p. 197)

Given Brathwaite's allusion to "Comicke passages" this would seem to be a reference to Shakespeare's play; the Countess of Pembroke's and Daniel's plays do not allow much scope for comedy, functioning more as a series of set-pieces in the mode of Senecan tragedy. In so doing Brathwaite reads *Antony and Cleopatra* in moralizing terms as a demonstration of the delusions of passion and the terrible consequences of heedlessly following one's passions. Of course, Brathwaite (and conduct literature more widely) is not representative of early modern cultural values; rather, his is the conservative voice shouting against the winds of change – particularly with regard to the status and behavior of women. But if we are to *historicize* Shakespeare's works, and early modern literature more widely, we have to take such voices into account.

Similarly, in the 1660s John Dryden commended "the excellency of the moral" told by *Antony and Cleopatra*, "for the chief persons represented were famous patterns of *unlawful love*; and their end accordingly was unfortunate" (my italics); hence in *All For Love*, Dryden's adaptation of Shakespeare's play, the theme of adultery is given prominence and pathos with scenes dwelling on Antony's rejected wife Octavia and children.[11] Dryden's views were not idiosyncratic in the period; as early as 1616 Robert Anton can be found lamenting the "immodest" habits of women playgoers gadding to the public playhouses where "shall they see the *uices* of the *times*, / *Orestes* incest, *Cleopatres* crimes" (p. 46). Given that Shakespeare's play was perhaps the best known on Cleopatra in the period, Anton here seems to respond to *Antony and Cleopatra* as a document in sexual crime – specifically, one presumes, the crime of adultery.

This makes it all the more intriguing that in the first sustained piece of criticism on Shakespeare, Margaret Cavendish's *Sociable Letter* (1664), Cavendish appears to coopt Cleopatra as a typical woman:

> . . . one would think that [Shakespeare] had been Metamorphosed from a Man to a Woman, for who could Describe *Cleopatra* Better than he hath done, and many other Females of his own Creating, as *Nan Page*, Mrs. *Page*, Mrs. *Ford*, the Doctors Maid, *Bettrice* [Beatrice], Mrs. *Quickly*, *Doll Tearsheet*, and others, too many to Relate? and in his Tragick Vein, he Presents Passions so naturally, and Misfortunes so Probably, as he Pierces the Souls of his Readers with such a True Sense and Feeling thereof, that it Forces Tears through their Eyes. (Cavendish 1997: 13)

One wonders what essentially female traits Cavendish had in mind when proposing Shakespeare presented her so intuitively and "naturally": Cleopatra's coquetishness, capriciousness, and vanity – or her quick-wittedness and humor? The list Cavendish here provides of Shakespeare's noteworthy female characters centers upon women who are forceful speakers and assertive in their relations with men; as such, she would seem to regard Cleopatra as representative of women's capacity to speak out and for themselves. Certainly this would seem plausible from a woman who was herself outspoken in her views on the status and education of women: in *Philosophical and Physical Opinions* (1655), for instance, she objected to women being "kept like Birds in Cages, to Hop up and down in our Homes, not Suffer'd to fly abroad," and in 1662 issued a polemic against the restrictions and prejudices reducing women to inferiority and powerlessness in *Orations of Divers Sorts* (1662).[12]

Cavendish's early praise for Shakespeare's naturalism, especially in depicting "Passions," proved a common theme of other late seventeenth-century accounts of *Antony and Cleopatra*. Dryden, for instance, remarked that "*Tully* ne'r spoke as [Shakespeare] makes *Anthony*," while Thomas Shadwell praised Charles Sedley's *Antony and Cleopatra . . . A Play after Shakspere* (1677) and Shakespeare's original as tragedies "wherein *Romans* are made to speak and do like *Romans*."[13] Nahum Tate expanded the point, claiming that in Shakespeare's Roman plays "the Persons, the Passages, the Manners, the Circumstances, the Ceremonies, all are Roman," before commending Shakespeare's "absolute Command of the Passions, and Mastery in distinguishing of Characters":

> You find his *Anthony* in all the Defects and Excellencies of his Mind, a Souldier, a Reveller, Amorous, sometimes Rash, sometimes Considerate, with all the various Emotions of his Mind . . . [Shakespeare] was a most diligent Spie upon Nature, trac'd her through her darkest Recesses, pictur'd her in her just Proportion and Colours . . .[14]

A manuscript volume of miscellaneous extracts from ten Shakespeare plays, transcribed in a neat italic hand and compiled in the late seventeenth century, likewise opens with praise for Shakespeare's naturalism:

> Shakespears Descriptions are stronger and more natural than any of ye other Poets, who generally described with too strict and learned a manner, and often not to be understood by those that are unacquainted with ye fiction of Poetry. (British Library Lansdowne 1185, fol. 2)

Each play is dealt with as a separate unit in the volume as though the compiler was working through a Folio of Shakespeare's plays, and extracts are organized under headings. When gathering quotations from *Antony and Cleopatra* the compiler appears to have had an interest in plot – incorporating quotations under such headings as "Anthonys shame and generosity after ye battle" (fol. 31v), "Anthony persuading his freed man to kill him" (fol. 34), and "Cleop. Dying" (fol. 35v) – and character, especially Antony's. While the compiler includes the occasional quotation commending Antony – such as "Of Anthony's military hardiness" ("At thy heel / Did famine follow . . . Was born so like a souldier, that thy Cheeke / So much as lankd not"; fol. 28) – their attention was drawn to extracts illustrating Antony's dissolute lifestyle gathered under such headings as "Of Anthony's blushing" (fol. 26v), "Of Anthony's Effeminacy," "His untimely Negligence" (fol. 27v), "Ever comforting himself with drinking" (fol. 33v), while "A Fine construction of Anthonys humour" cites Cleopatra's dismissal of his "well divided disposition" (fol. 28v). In this respect the compiler's headings echo Dryden's view of the play as a tale of unlawful love and Tate's attention to Antony's "Defects." The compiler also drew general observations from the play, one of the most intriguing coming under the heading "Of Love," in which Antony's remarks on living for the pleasurable moment (1.1.45–8) are turned into a wider philosophical dilemma on putting love before conflict:

> The problem of Life
> Is to do this:
> [Now] for ye l[o]ue of love and her soft hours
> Lets not confound [&] Sinne with Conference harsh
> There's not a minute of our lives should stretch
> Without some pleasure – (fol. 26v)

The compiler adapts the text here to suit their own purposes, substituting Shakespeare's "Lets not confound the time with conference harsh" with the more emphatic "Lets not confound *{&} Sinne* with Conference harsh" (my italics) – "Sinne" perhaps evoking a Christian message of striving towards peace. Thus the compiler is able to deploy the lines of morally culpable characters in a Shakespearean tragedy to moralizing ends.

While contemporary responses to *Romeo and Juliet* and *Antony and Cleopatra* apportion responsibility, sometimes blame, for the tragic turn of events to their female protagonists, Desdemona emerges as less culpable in contemporary commentary than Juliet or Cleopatra: she is the object of sympathy, not disapproval. This is intriguing given recent critical analysis of Desdemona as an outspoken figure who, in defending her right to determine her own marriage partner, challenges patriarchal authority: as she exclaims in the opening act, "My downright violence and storm of fortunes / May trumpet to the world" (1.3.244–5). The First Quarto of *The Tragoedy of Othello. The Moore of Venice* (1622), however, paints a subtly different picture of Desdemona's choice of Othello as a husband to the First Folio text. Absent from Q1 are a cluster of derogatory allusions to Othello's race, such as Iago's mocking description of Othello as his "Moorship" (1.1.33; the equivalent line in Q1 reads his "Worship"; p. 42), Roderigo's speech that Desdemona "hath made a gross revolt," doing Brabantio "bold and saucy wrongs" in "tying" herself "To the gross clasps of a lascivious Moor" (1.1.120–36), and Brabantio's accusations against Othello practicing witchcraft on Desdemona in order to seduce her: "thou hast practised on her with foul charms, / Abused her delicate youth . . ." (1.2.72–7; see also 1.2.65, 1.3.91, and 1.3.168). The consequence, as Nevill Coghill has suggested, is that F1 makes more of the supposed unnaturalness of Desdemona's choice of Othello as a partner.[15] Since Emilia's biting speech on the maltreatment of wives by their husbands ("But I do think it is their husbands' faults / If wives do fall . . . The ills we do, their ills instruct us so"; 4.3.82–99) is also omitted from Q1, the impression of women revolting against their fathers and husbands in *Othello* becomes more pronounced in F1.

Of course, like Juliet, Desdemona's ethnicity might have counted against her: uncontrolled sexual passion, often attributed to the hot climate, was considered an Italian characteristic; a stereotype intensified by the sensational accounts of Italian debauchery that proliferated in the period. Roger Ascham, for instance, reported that on a nine-day visit to Venice he saw "more libertie to sinne than ever I heard tell of in our noble Citie of London in nine yeare" (*The Scholemaster*, 1570; quoted by Levith 1989: 6). Thus Iago connects female promiscuity with Italian ethnicity:

> I know our country disposition well:
> In Venice they do let God see the pranks
> They dare not show their husbands. Their best conscience
> Is not to leave't undone, but keep't unknown. (3.3.203–6)

The dirt sticks: when Othello directly accuses Desdemona of being "a strumpet" (4.2.81) he remarks "I took you for that cunning whore of Venice" (4.2.88). Of course Iago's specific accusations against Desdemona are unfounded; my point is rather that for an early modern audience Desdemona's forthright expressions of desire (albeit within the bounds of marriage) *may* have evoked a milieu of Venetian indulgence, making her an intriguing, if ultimately pitiable, spectacle of Italian passion. Indeed, we have to remember that all the attendant characters in *Othello* are, with the notable exception of Othello, Italian. Perhaps then what is constructed in the play is a society in which all are subject to excess – Iago to professional and sexual jealousy that "Doth like a poisonous mineral gnaw my inwards" (2.1.278), Emilia to bitterness, Cassio (despite his attempt to steer an even course) to drink and whoring, Roderigo to ambition. This would be in keeping with the vogue for tragedies set in Italy that combined a heady mix of passion, lust, murder, corruption, and innocence, such as Marston's *Antonio and Mellida* (ca. 1599), Tourneur and Middleton's *The Revenger's Tragedy*, Webster's *The White Devil* and *The Duchess of Malfi*, and Ford's *'Tis Pity She's a Whore*. If we read *Othello* in the context of these works rather than in the context of Shakespeare's *oeuvre*, its depiction of a tumultuous foreign cultural order that infects domestic relations becomes clearer. The play's subtitle after all, by which it was often referred to throughout the seventeenth century, signals not simply Othello's race but the play's Italian milieu: "The Moore of *Venice*" (my italics).

For all the declamatory remarks against Italy, however, early modern readings of *Othello* have little to say about race and ethnicity; pathos is the order of the day. When *Othello* was performed by the King's Men touring at Oxford in 1610, Desdemona's

deathbed was close enough to the audience for them to be moved by the facial "countenance" of the boy actor playing Desdemona – as one member of the audience, Henry
Jackson, reported:

> not only by their speech but also by their deeds [the actors] drew tears. – But indeed
> Desdemona, killed by her husband, although she always acted the matter very well, in
> her death moved us still more greatly; when lying in bed she implored the pity of those
> watching with her countenance alone.[16]

Jackson's comment reveals how audiences were, as Andrew Gurr (1992) suggests,
sometimes "highly responsive in sentiment," moved to tears by performances (p. 226);
a phenomenon that persisted into the Restoration judging by Samuel Pepys's account
of how "a very pretty lady that sat by me, called out, to see Desdemona smothered"
(October 11, 1660).[17] Intriguingly, Jackson makes no reference to Othello's race,
though it is hard to gauge what his "silence" on Othello's color might mean. However,
Jackson's use of pronouns indicates how the illusion of the boy actor as woman could
be so convincing that Jackson treats the boy actor as though he were female (or alternatively, that the practice of boy actors playing women was so conventional as not to
be worthy of comment in the context of a play which makes no explicit allusion to
crossdressing): "*she* always acted the matter very well . . . *she* implored the pity of those
watching with *her* countenance" (my italics).

By comparison with *Romeo and Juliet* few allusions to *Othello* before the Restoration
have survived. A fascinating exception, however, is the ca. 1640s manuscript
notebook of Abraham Wright (1611–90), an Anglican divine, entitled "Excerpta
Quaedem per A. W. Adolecsentem" (British Library Add MS 22608). Crammed full
of excerpts from some twenty-nine plays by the likes of Jonson, Beaumont and
Fletcher, Webster, Shirley, and Davenant, Wright's notebook serves as a compendium
of early mid-seventeenth century drama and an example of Caroline dramatic taste:
Wright had a penchant for tragicomedy, and in his brief summaries of the plays he
especially admired intricate and varied plots, strong characterization, and figurative
language. He noted only two Shakespeare plays (a useful reminder of Shakespeare's
diminishing popularity in the context of Caroline taste), *Othello* and *Hamlet*, which he
concluded was

> But an indifferent play, ye lines but meane: and in nothing like Othello. Hamlet is an
> indifferent good part for a madman. And ye scene in ye beginning of ye 5 act betweene
> Hamlet and ye graudemaker a good scene but since betterd in ye iealous louers. (fol.
> 85v)

Wright was much more effusive, however, about *Othello*:

> A uery good play both for lines and plot, but especially ye plot. Iago for a rogue and
> Othello for a iealous husband 2 parts well pend. Act: 3 hye scene beetwixt Iago and

Othello, and ye I sce: of ye 4 Act beetween ye same shew admirably ye uillanous humour of Iago when hee p[er]suades Othello to his iealousy. (fol. 84v)

While modern criticism tends to stress the complexity of Shakespeare's characterization, Wright responds to the play in terms of its portrayal of character-types: stock figures within a dramatic tradition, not individuated personalities with specific axes (whether psychological, political, or cultural) to grind. Thus he is silent on the issue of Othello's race, regarding him as "a iealous husband"; similarly, he finds in Iago a well-penned part for a stage villain or "rogue." In so doing the dynamics of tragic responsibility arguably become simpler: in Wright's analysis, *Othello* can be summed up as the story of a husband persuaded into jealousy by the "uillanous humour" of the stage villain.

Wright's attention to the "plot" of *Othello* bears out T. A. Birrell's remarks that seventeenth-century gentlemen read plays as the most accessible form of fiction. But how did Wright make use of the "lines" of *Othello*? Preceding his general remarks on the plot of *Othello*, Wright copied out some sixty-seven extracts from the play organized under act numbers (suggesting that he was working from the First or Second Folio, since the First Quarto of *Othello* has few act divisions). He altered the phrasing of many of the extracts; for instance, Iago's "Even now, now, very now, an old black ram / Is tupping your white ewe" becomes "A ramme is said to tupp ye ewe. And a horse to couer a mare" (fol. 83v), completely removing the racial slur from the line. Some extracts he marked with a cross, a standard marginal notation in the period to indicate lines of specific importance to a reader, as Comenius explained: "[a student] readeth *Books*, which being within his reach, he layeth open upon *a Desk* and picketh all the best things out of them into his own *Manual*, or marketh them in them with a dash, or *a little star*, in the *Margent*."[18] In fact Wright noted that "those [passages] yt are markd thus + either here or in my books are not phrases but expression and lines" (fol. 69) – apparently distinguishing between paraphrases adapted for his own use and direct quotation of "expressions and lines." Even so, many of the "expressions and lines" that Wright crossed he also emended: thus "One that excels the quirks of blazoning pens" (2.1.63) is altered to "A virgin yt farre excells ye quirkes of blasoning pens . . ." (fol. 83v).

It was act 5 – particularly the final scene – that seemed to hold most interest for Wright. He marked some ten lines spoken by Othello on the verge of killing Desdemona and after realizing his tragic mistake; lines that bear witness to Othello's tenderness for his wife and heighten the awful pathos of the scene – including the stage direction "(kisses her)" that precedes Othello's line "a balmy breath, yt doth allmost pleade / justice herself to breathe her" (an adaptation of 5.2.1 6–17). The longest quotation included by Wright in this section, with several crosses against it, is Othello's final speech in which he asks to be remembered as "one, yt loued not wisely, but too well: / of one not easily iealous, but beeing / wrought, [per]plext in ye extreame: of one whose hand / like ye base Indian thew a pearle away" (5.2.344–7; fol. 84v). If the occurrence of marked quotations is anything to go by, apparently the most powerful episode in the play for Wright was the final scene with its tragic culmination of Desdemona's innocence, Othello's gullibility, and the doomed love between them. Pathos, sympathy, regret, and repentance: these seem to be the qualities that Wright most valued when transcribing the play into his notebook. And while Wright passed literary judgment on the plays he read his notebook evidently functioned as a sourcebook: as Arthur Kirsch (1968–9) suggests, he was using plays "as rhetorical primers for his own sermons" (p. 260).

In the second half of the seventeenth century *Othello* was both one of the most popular of Shakespeare's plays on the Restoration stage – such that Thomas Rymer (now known for his dismissal of *Othello* as the tragedy of a handkerchief) could remark that of "all the tragedies on our English stage, *Othello* is said to bear the bell away" – and singled out for its vulgar language and graphic sexual imagination.[19] In a generic "letter to a friend upon his marriage" in Thomas Blount's *Academie of Eloquence. Containing a Compleat English Rhetorique* (1654), for instance, one H.T. professes distaste at Iago's image of marital sex – "the Beast with two backs, which the knavish *Shakespear* speaks of" – while thirty years later in her preface to *The Luckey Chance* (1687), Aphra Behn cited "The *Moor* of *Venice*" as one of several "Celebrated Plays" that "in many places" contains "Indecencys . . . yet are never taken Notice of, because a Man writ them."[20] Allusions to *Othello* in the period also continued to stress the play's capacity to arouse pity. Thus in "The Play-House. A Satyr" (1689), Robert Gould heaped praise upon Shakespeare in an unusually detailed account of reading the play:

> Whene'r I *Hamlet*, or *Othello* read,
> *My Hair* starts up, and my *Nerues* shrink with dread:
> *Pity* and *fear* raise my concern still higher,
> Till, betwixt both, I'm ready to expire!
> When cursed *Iago*, cruelly, I see
> Work up the *noble Moore* to Jealousie,
> How counningly the Villain weaves his sin,
> And how the other takes the poison in;
> . . .
> When these and other such-like Scenes I scan,
> 'Tis then, great Soul, I think thee [Shakespeare] more than Man! (Gould 1688–9: 176–7)

If Gould's rhetoric is to be believed, his experience of reading *Othello* – and the pathos aroused by the play – was positively visceral. For Gould, as for Wright forty years earlier, Iago seems to bear greatest responsibility for the tragedy as a "Villain" who cruelly works on the otherwise "noble" Othello. Similarly, Gould makes no explicit allusion to Othello's race – although perhaps the word "*Moore*" sufficed in itself as a marker of difference or prejudice?

Gould's admiration of the pity provoked by *Othello* appears, however, to be confined to the play's tragic hero, since earlier in the poem he is scathing of Desdemona. Indeed, the satiric speaker of Gould's "Satyr" appears to have conflicting views on the merits of Shakespeare and *Othello* more particularly: thus he defends contemporary plays (such as Aphra Behn's *"The Emp'rour of the Moon"*) over the otherwise praise-worthy Shakespeare, Jonson, and Fletcher: "They were so modest they were always dull; / For what is *Desdemona* but a Fool?" (p. 173). By comparison with contemporary drama in which "the Suffrage of both Sexes wins" (p. 174), Shakespeare's characterization of the pliant and gullible Desdemona seems scarcely credible; Gould's (ironical?) description of her as a mere "fool" suggests that her submission to Othello and ultimately to her death made little sense within Gould's milieu of an urbane, metropolitan elite in which women were supposedly increasingly vocal and gave as good as they got.

Gould's dismissal of Desdemona was not shared, however, by Dryden – who regarded her instead as a compelling figure bearing witness to Shakespeare's "Universal mind, which comprehended all Characters and Passions": *"Shakespear* taught *Fletcher* to write love; and *Juliet*, and *Desdemona*, are Originals."[21] And shortly after Gould's *Poems* hit the press William Walsh can be found citing Desdemona as a figure of sympathy in *A Dialogue Concerning Women, Being a Defence of the Sex* (1691). Opening with a preface by Dryden that commends Walsh as women's "new Champion" at a time "wherein I find more Heroines than Heroes" (sig. A4), Walsh's defense proceeds as a dialogue between *Philogynes*, "a Woman-lover," and *Misogynes*, "a Woman-hater," overheard as they take a walk in St. James's Park (p. 6). After countering Misogynes' remarks about women's inconstancy and commending the learning of "our *English* Poetesses" (p. 95), Philogynes argues against defaming a woman until one has "very full satisfaction of the Matter of Fact first":

> let him not go upon dubious Grounds, nor jealous Surmises; let him not believe the Vanity of some, nor the Malice of others; let him consider the Stories of *Bradamante* in *Ariosto*, of *Aurestilla* in *Consalo de Cepdes*, of *Othello* in *Shakespear*, and let him see how far Jealousie may seem reasonable, whilst nevertheless the person of whom they are Jealous may be innocent. (p. 119)

For Walsh, *Othello* serves as a warning against "Jealousie," even when it may "seem reasonable"; the tragedy serves a moral purpose.

Thus *Romeo and Juliet, Antony and Cleopatra*, and *Othello* were readily coopted by early modern readers into a moralizing agenda. I am not proposing that this agenda should be ours today or was shared by every reader in the period; here I have sought to *rehearse* rather than *promote* moralizing readings of the plays. But to find in literature the pithy moral that could be applied more widely was nonetheless a fundamental mode of reading in the sixteenth and seventeenth centuries. This is a way of reading which stands wholly at odds, however, with recent attempts to historicize Shakespearean drama as a complex expression of critique and subversion. By this I do not mean that such attempts are misjudged, but rather that if we are to nuance our historicization of early modern literature then we should take into account the testimony, albeit fragmented, of its first readers who repeatedly discovered conservative moral codes in the plays. In the theatre, of course, early modern drama may have worked quite differently. More widely, how we construct meaning in literary texts is bound up in the questions we want to ask of them. My point is that it is vitally important to be clear about the tacit assumptions that lie behind our own critical procedures; about *where* we invest meaning in literary texts: in ourselves as critics?; in authors?; in the historical circumstances or cultural contexts of a text's production?; in a text's reception?; in its readers, its audiences? What piques my curiosity here is not how to read Shakespeare's plays today — the conventional role of a literary critic — but how they were read and transmitted in early modern England.

Commonplacing Shakespeare's Tragedies of Love

Shakespeare's tragedies were not only disseminated as playtexts in quarto or folio; they were also deployed as commonplaces — extracts or marked passages of text grouped or titled under general headings or *common places* for ease of reference, used for their wider application as sententiae, exempla, illustrations, or reflections upon a general argument or theme (*OED* 1, 3, 4). Commonplacing was was not only fundamental to humanist educational practices but, as Mary Thomas Crane (1993) has argued, the key modes of commonplacing — gathering and framing texts — were also "basic discursive practices . . . constitutive of social, economic, political, and literary discourse" at large (pp. 3–4). In the case of Shakespeare's tragedies, it often meant the antithesis of reading for plot or character. Divorced from the playtexts the "Observations" that were plucked from characters' mouths were given a different texture and meaning, no longer bearing the marks or ironies of plot or character; instead they functioned like a Choral voice — detached and supposedly impartial. The morality that the compilers of early modern printed commonplace books discover in *Romeo and Juliet*, *Othello*, and *Antony and Cleopatra* works not in terms of narrative outcomes (as in the remarks of Burton or Brathwaite) but at the local level of the line. As such they cease to operate as "tragedies of love" but as a sourcebook of commentary on a plethora of topics.

In the 1590s a spate of printed commonplace books appeared, emulating the habits of readers in manuscript. They have often been dismissed by modern critics and editors as inaccurate and misleading compilations of bowdlerized verse, but this is to misunderstand the nature of commonplacing and to underestimate the place of the printed commonplace book in the transmission of early modern literature — particularly among a socially inclusive readership composed, argues Mary Thomas Crane (1993), of "common readers," artisans and citizens, urban merchants, and the ambitious lesser gentry (p. 181). Two stationers in particular, John Bodenham and Nicholas Ling (who went on to print the First Quarto of *Lear*), carved out a profitable niche in this literary marketplace; after joining forces on *Wits Commonwealth* (which ran to three editions in its first year of publication, 1597), Meres's *Palladis Tamia. Or Wits Treasury* (1598), and *Wits Theater of the Little World* (1599), in 1600 they separately published *England's Parnassus. The choysest Flowers of our Moderne Poets, with their Poetical comparisons* and *Belvedere. Or the Garden of Muses.* The prefatory rhetoric of these volumes dispels any charge of peddling light literature; thus Robert Allott commends the "Learning" and "wisdoms in these writings" in *England's Parnassus* (sig. A4); Bodenham claims that *Belvedere* compiles "many singular mens workes; and the worth of them all hauing been so especially approoued" (sig. A3), while one A.M. (possibly Anthony Munday) describes Bodenham, "the first causer and collectour" of *Belvedere*, as "Arts lover, Learnings friend" (sig. A7). Such descriptions serve a rhetorical function, of course: to present the volume to the prospective reader as a "great affaire" (A.M.), a worthy and worthwhile expenditure. Nonetheless, the rhetoric of the prefatory matter of *Belvedere* and *England's Parnassus* is a far cry from the rhetoric of contemporary commentary and satire on reading light literature.

In *England's Parnassus* and *Belvedere* new contexts and meanings were created for Shakespeare's works. *England's Parnassus*, compiled by Robert Allott and printed by Nicholas Ling, aspires to offer its readers a superlative source of contemporary literary achievement, compiling some 2,000 literary extracts under general subject headings; although Allott pays attention to the decorums of authorship in the volume, providing attributions (sometimes erroneous) for most extracts, he does not attempt to locate the textual origins of those extracts. The majority of Shakespearean extracts in *England's Parnassus* are culled from *Venus and Adonis* and *Lucrece* (indicative of their currency in the emerging Shakespearean canon at the turn of the seventeenth century); of the five Shakespeare plays incorporated in the volume (*Love's Labour's Lost, 1 Henry IV, Richard II, Richard III,* and *Romeo and Juliet*), *Romeo and Juliet* is the most heavily represented, signaling the play's popularity, or perhaps utility, in the period. Nearly half of the twelve extracts from *Romeo and Juliet* appear under the heading "Love" – but intriguingly, little of the idealizing language of love that infuses *Romeo and Juliet* makes its way into the section (with the possible exception of the pithy image of Love going "toward Love, as schoole-boyes from their bookes"; 2.2.156–7; p. 182). Instead Allott was drawn to Romeo's glib Petrarchan clichés on the pains of loving Rosaline which, divorced from the narrative of the play, no longer read as a foil to his love for Juliet but as genuine warnings on the "madness" and "chaos" that love can bring – "Love is a smoke made with the fume of sighs . . . a madness most discreet, / A choking gall, and a preserving sweet" (Romeo, 1.1.181–5; p. 173); "O brawling love . . . Misshapen chaos of well-seeming forms" (Romeo, 1.1.67–72; p. 176) – and Friar Lawrence's sage advice to love moderately and heed the insubstantiality ("vanity") of earthly happiness: "The sweetest honey / Is loathsome in his own deliciousness . . . Therefore love moderately, long love doth so" (Friar Lawrence, 2.6.11–15, a line unique to Q2–4 and F1; p. 185); "A lover may bestride the gossamers . . . And yet not fall, so light is vanity" (2.6.18–20; p. 192). Indeed, since Friar Lawrence's remarks so often lend themselves to aphorism Allott draws more on his remarks than those of any other character in the play: "Care keeps his watch in every old man's eye . . ." (2.3.35–8; p. 24); "Virtue itself turns vice, being misapplied

. . ." (2.3.21–2; p. 291); "Women may fall, when there's no strength in men" (2.3.80; p. 313); "The grey-eyed morn smiles on the frowning night . . ." (2.3.1–4; p. 328).[22] In *England's Parnassus*, then, *Romeo and Juliet* is deployed not as an affecting story of young love but as a source of sententious wisdom; hence it is Friar Lawrence, ready to "pronounce [a] sentence" (2.3.79) at the drop of a hat, who becomes the play's key spokesperson.

Similarly in *Belvedere*, *Romeo and Juliet* is incorporated into pithy aphorisms on a variety of topics: virtue, love, women, good deeds, tears, pain, youth, and age. Bodenham's method of commonplacing is to cull "learned, graue, and wittie sentences," "none exceeding two lines at the vttermost," and run them together as continuous verse; hence all the extracts he includes from Shakespeare's plays are embedded between the lines of other works and remain unattributed. The moralizing couplet Bodenham supplies as an overview for the section "Of Love" – contrasting temperance and duty over headstrong opportunism – speaks directly to the themes of *Romeo and Juliet*: "Loue is a uertue, measur'd by duterous choice, / But not if it be maim'd with wilfull chaunce" (p. 28). Unlike *England's Parnassus*, however, the three quotations Bodenham adapts from the play do not so much reiterate this theme as supply observations on the endurance of love:

> No stonie limits can hold out true loue. [2.2.67]
> What loue can doe, that dare it still attempt. [2.2.68]
> Sweet are those bands that true loue doth combine.
>   Loue goes toward loue like schoole-boyes from their bookes:
>   But loue from loue, to schoole with heauie lookes. [2.2.156–7][23]

While *England's Parnassus* culled *Romeo and Juliet* for warnings against the excesses of love, Bodenham drew elsewhere in the play for moralizing remarks – making extensive use of Friar Lawrence's speeches. Thus he incorporates three couplets from the Friar's speech on the use of plants under the headings "Vertue" ("*Vertue it selfe turnes uice, being mispplyed: / And uice sometimes be action dignified*"; 2.3.21–2; p. 17) and "Of good Deeds" ("*There's nought so uile that on the earth doth liue, / But to the earth some speciall good doth giue*", "*There's nought so good, but strain'd from that faire use: / Reuolts to uice, and stumbles on abuse*"; 2.3.17–18 and 19–20; pp. 178–9).[24] Similarly, the Friar's speech on youth versus age ("Young son, it argues a distempered head / So soon to bid good morrow to thy bed . . ."; 2.3.33–42) is used to supply quotations on "Youth" and "Age," while Bodenham's opening epigraph for "Youth" – that it affects "*speediest spoile, without most wise respect*" (p. 219) – is aptly illustrated by one of the Friar's lines unique to Q1 appended to an unidentified couplet on the shallowness of young men's love:

> *It's often seene, that loue in young men lyes*
> *Not truly in their hearts, but in their eyes.*
> Youths loue is quicke, swifter than swiftest speed.[25]

Further pearls of "learning" are plucked from Friar Lawrence's mouth under the heading "Of Women," a section which opens with the promising couplet that *"Women are equall euery way to men"* (p. 104) but then proceeds with a compendium of largely antifeminist sentiments documenting women's faults. In this context the line Bodenham incorporates from *Romeo and Juliet*, Friar Lawrence's remark that "Women may fall, when there's no strength in men" (2.3.80), reads not, as in the play, as implied criticism of Romeo but contributes to the general theme of women's frailty.

That Robert Allott and John Bodenham found Friar Lawrence's remarks to be by far the most useful in compiling their commonplace books should alert us to the potential significance of his role for early modern readers. Perhaps in part because aphoristic knowledge has become so unappealing for modern readers – variously dismissed as trite, simplistic, or plain dull – Friar Lawrence tends to be regarded with suspicion by modern commentators. True, he conforms in several respects to the contemporary stereotype of the scheming Catholic friar (not least in performing a clandestine marriage), yet *England's Parnassus* and *Belvedere* demonstrate how he could become a voice of moral authority – even its center – when the play was not read as a linear narrative.

The commonplacing of Shakespeare's plays was remarkably persistent throughout the mid-seventeenth century. John Cotgrave's *The English Treasury of Wit and Language, Collected Out of the most, and best of our English Drammatick Poems; Methodically digested into Common Places for Generall use* (1655) is a case in point. Issued by Humphrey Moseley, a prolific publisher of plays in the mid-seventeenth century who was hugely influential in the formation of the canon of English drama in print, Cotgrave makes a spirited defense of vernacular drama on the grounds of its utility:

> the Drammatick Poem seemes to me (and many of my friends, better able to judge then I) to have beene lately too much slighted [by many] who through a stiffe and obstinate prejudice, have (in neglecting things of this nature) lost the benefit of many rich and usefull Observations, not duly considering, or believing, that the Framers of them, were the most fluent [Wits] that this age (or I think any other) ever knew . . . (sig. A2v)

While acknowledging that commonplaced extracts may lose something of their "native vigour or beauty in the transplanting," Cotgrave stresses the "usefulnesse" of the volume in collecting "Observations" from a host of playwrights (including Shakespeare, Beaumont and Fletcher, Middleton, Webster, Tourneur, Jonson, Ford, Chapman, Davenant, Suckling, and Shirley) and organizing them under subject headings: "extractions therefore are the best conservers of knowledge, if not the readiest way to it" (sig. A2v). More often than not, Cotgrave's "extractions" tend towards moralizing *sententiae*. The only extract to be included from *Romeo and Juliet*, for instance, is Friar Lawrence's warning from Q2–4 and F1 against the "violent ends" of "violent delights" – "Therefore love moderately, long love doth so" – incorporated under the telling heading "Of Extreames" (2.6.9–15, p. 98). The two extracts Cotgrave draws from *Antony and Cleopatra* also work as moralizing *sententiae* under the heading "Of

Sin" ("When in our viciousnesse we grow hard . . . we strut to our confusion"; p. 259), and "Of Valour" ("When valour preys on reason, it does eat / The sword it should fight with"; p. 282). Similarly, of the six extracts Cotgrave included from *Othello* the majority offer conventional advice: Cassio's remarks on "good name" included under the heading "Of Credit, Reputation" (p. 63), Othello's comment that devils "do suggest at first with heavenly shews" under the heading "Of Dissimulation, Hypocrisie" (p. 85), Cassio's regret at the "Inordinate Cup" included under "Drunkenness" (p. 85) and Iago's warning against "the green-ey'd monster" of jealousy, predictably incorporated under the heading "Jealousie" (p. 139). Perhaps the most intriguing citation from *Othello* in *The English Treasury* is Emilia's biting speech on the exploitation of women by men – "They are all but stomacks, and we all but food" – included under the heading "Of Man" (pp. 186–7). Since the other quotations in this section speak of the vulnerability and weakness of generic Mankind this "observation" stands out for its critical view of gender relations, while its very presence in the volume suggests that Cotgrave found Emilia's sentiments worthy of serious consideration.

What especially fascinates me about the commonplacing of Shakespearean tragedy are the discrepancies it exposes between early modern modes of reading and our current critical methods and concerns. As Charles Whitney (2000) has argued, early modern responses were "ante-aesthetic, that is, productive, purposeful, and performative," linking literature to the lives and worlds of its readers "rather than referable primarily to an aesthetic dimension" (p. 42). And as useful textual commodities that could be applied to all manner of circumstances, Shakespeare's plays were invariably treated by their readers as a series of parts. While modern literary criticism is so often intent upon elaborating the text as a whole, discovering its overall narratives, meanings, and significances, early modern readers were often drawn to its fragmented local observations. Further, commonplacing tends to work against the assumption that literary and dramatic works are to be judged according to their aesthetic merits. For all their prefatory rhetoric on gathering the "especially approoued" work of "singular" men (*Belvedere*, sig. A3), Shakespeare's tragedies become noteworthy in the printed commonplace book not for their exceptional literary or dramatic qualities, or indeed for the compelling stories they tell, but for their utterly conventional wisdom: in sententious reading *utility* becomes paramount. In so doing the Shakespearean text became malleable in the hands of early modern readers and writers; appropriated, adapted, and emended to suit different applications. As Mary Thomas Crane (1993) has argued, the practice of commonplacing fostered "common ownership of texts and ideas, and a collective model of authorship" that is about "as far from the values reflected in our poetic canon as poetry can get" (pp. 6, 185). Early modern modes of reading thus teach us to question the assumptions we may have about how authorship, literary property (ownership or control over literary texts), and textual authority (authority invested in specific texts, especially those deemed to be authorized by the author) worked in sixteenth- and seventeenth-century England.

By thinking about early modern literary culture as reader-centered rather than author-led we can begin to see its literary artifacts afresh. If this means pausing over claims for the radicalism and subversion of Shakespearean drama, then so be it. By this I emphatically do *not* mean that Shakespeare's plays are inherently conservative, peddling the status quo, unavailable to readers in the period as expressions of critique or dissent – or that in the context of the theatre contemporary drama and its socially diverse audience (including the illiterate) did not question, challenge, or provoke (*Richard II*, after all, was controversial in the midst of the Essex rebellion). Rather, the disjunction between modern critical agendas and early modern reading practices should give us pause for thought. How, if our concern is to historicize literature, do we take into account the very different critical vocabularies of early modern England? What are we to make of the paucity of contemporary commentary deploying the ideological challenges posed by Shakespearean drama versus the (comparative) plenty turning it to more orthodox ends? In other words the testimony of early modern readers demands that we think carefully about our methodologies as historicist critics of literature.

This includes consideration of how we think of playtexts functioning in the period. If, at the level of content, some readers summoned literary works for conventional or conservative agendas, their use of texts often challenges the legacy of *form* that has characterized so much post-Romantic criticism of Shakespeare: an attachment to the (singular) author; textual authority and literary property; the integral playtext (whether quarto or folio); aesthetic criteria and benchmarks for approaching and appreciating his works. Thus even the most hackneyed of morals or *sententiae* drawn from Shakespeare's works can prompt us to rethink how literature works at different historical junctures. Far from closing doors on the possibilities for interpreting literary works in the past, the history of reading and textual transmission throws them and our assumptions about literary culture wide open.

NOTES

1 See, for instance, Dimock (1995: 123).
2 Dickey (1957: 9); for a critique of Dickey's thesis see, for instance, Williamson (1974: 3–5, 222–3).
3 Richard Brome in *Parnassus Biceps*, sig. E5; for Bodley, see Hackel (1997: 120–1).
4 Birrell (1991: 114, 119–20); on playbooks in men's libraries, see also Hackel (1997); on gentlemen reading light literature in early modern England, especially Shakespeare's *Venus and Adonis*, see Roberts (forthcoming).
5 Pepys's *Diary*, cited in *Shakspere Allusion-Book*, vol. 2, p. 90.
6 Cited in Shakespeare (1992: 213–14).
7 Brathwaite, cited in Klein (1992: 237).
8 Some thirty years later Gilbert Swinhoe adapted the same couplet in his *Tragedy of The unhappy Fair Irene* (1658) when, after Daemosthenes kills himself with a dagger to join his lover in death, the assembled cast lament "This is a Spectacle of like Woe / To that of *Juliet*, and her *Romeo*" (p. 30; cited in *Shakspere Allusion-Book*, vol. 2, p. 75).
9 Plutarch, cited in Williamson (1974: 38–9).

10 Sanders (1998: 92; see also p. 66). By contrast in *Salve Deus Rex Judaeorum* Aemilia Lanyer was ambivalent about "Great Cleopatra" as a model of passion: "Shee left her Love in his extremitie, / When greatest need should cause her to combine / Her force with his, to get the Victory: / Her Love was earthly, and thy Love Divine; / Her Love was onely to support her pride" (ll. 1411–15; see also ll. 215–16); see Lanyer (1993). Elizabeth Cary cites Cleopatra as a beauty who "fled" Antony during the battle at Actium, thereby causing his "fall," and Mariam responds to her as an anti-example: "With purest body will I press my tomb, / And with no favours Antony could give": *The Tragedy of Mariam*, 1.2.201–2, in Cary (1994).

11 Dryden, *All For Love*, cited by Norman Sanders in Shakespeare (1993: 39).

12 See Thompson and Roberts (1997: 11).

13 Dryden (attr.), "Prologue to Julius Caesar" in *Covent Garden Drollery* (1672), cited in *Shakspere Allusion-Book*, vol. 2, p. 172; Shadwell, *A True Widow, A Comedy* (1679), cited in *Shakspere Allusion-Book*, vol. 2, p. 252.

14 Nahum Tate, "Address to Edward Taylor," *The Loyal General, a Tragedy* (1680), cited in *Shakspere Allusion-Book*, vol. 2, pp. 266–7.

15 Coghill (1964: 183–7). While Q1's construction of a more forceful Desdemona than we see in F1 may not always be consistent, the differences between the texts are sufficient enough to warrant our careful attention before we draw conclusions about her characterization in the play; see Murphy in Shakespeare (1995c).

16 Cited by Gurr (1992: 226). Jackson's comment was written in Latin and is translated with minor variations in Hankey (1987: 18). On the role of the bed in Shakespearean tragedy, see Roberts (2003).

17 Pepys, cited in *Shakspere Allusion-Book*, vol. 2, p. 89.

18 Comenius, cited in Love (1993: 222).

19 Hence the version of the play prepared for the Smock Alley Theatre, Dublin, excised Othello's visualization of Cassio and Desdemona "naked in bed": "Lie with her? Lie on her? . . ." (4.1.5 and 35). For Rymer, see Sanders in Shakespeare (1993: 39).

20 Thomas Blount, cited in *Shakspere Allusion-Book*, vol. 2, p. 38; Behn (1996, VII: 216 and 441).

21 Dryden, Preface (*The Grounds of Criticism in Tragedy*) to *Troilus and Cressida, or, Truth found too late. A Tragedy, by John Dryden* (1679), cited in *Shakspere Allusion-Book*, vol. 2, pp. 249–50. As David Scott Kastan (2001) points out, critical responses to Shakespeare's plays after the Restoration are often ambivalent, even in the case of Dryden: "Shakespeare's excellence is repeatedly gestured at but finally subordinated to different standards of taste" (p. 85).

22 The most romantic language extracted from *Romeo and Juliet* in *England's Parnassus* is Romeo's description of Juliet – "O she doth teach the torches to burn bright! . . ." (1.5.42–8) – included under the heading "Discriptions of Beautie & personage" (p. 407). Allott also included Lady Capulet's advice to the weeping Juliet, "Some grief shows much of love, / But much of grief shows still some want of wit" under the heading "Grief" (3.5.72–3; p. 124); the Prince's remark, "Mercy but murders, pardoning those that kill" under the heading "Mercie" (3.1.189; p. 207); and Romeo's description of night ("Night's candles are burnt out . . .", 3.5.9–10; p. 327).

23 The same image of Love going towards love "as school boys from their books" was extracted under the heading "The Constancy of Lovers" in the 1640 printed commonplace book *The Academy of Compliments*, p. 141; cited in *Shakspere Allusion-Book*, vol. 1, p. 452.

24 In 1635 John Swan quoted from the same speech by Friar Lawrence ("Oh mickle is the pow'rfull good that lies . . . But to the earth some secret good doth give"), adding four lines of his own, in *Speculum Mundi. Or a glasse representing the face of the world* (cited in *Shakspere Allusion-Book*, vol. 1, p. 399).

25 *Belvedere*, p. 220. This line is unique to Q1 (p. 61), being replaced in Q2–4 and F1 by Friar Lawrence's speech, "These violent delights have violent ends . . . Therefore love moderately" (2.6.9–15). *Belvedere* also includes the lines *"Looke where unbruised youth, with unstuft braines / Doth*

couch his limbes, there golden sleepe remaines" (2.3.37–8) under "Youth" and *"Care keepes his watch in euery old mans eye . . ."* (2.3.35–6) under the heading "Age" (pp. 220 and 222).

REFERENCES AND FURTHER READING

Anton, R. (1616). Fifth Satyr. Of Venus. In *The Philosopher's Satyres*. London.

Behn, A. (1996). *The Works of Aphra Behn, Volume 7: The Plays, 1682–1696*, ed. J. Todd. London: William Pickering.

Belvedere. Or the Garden of Muses (1600). Ed.(?) J. Bodenham. London.

Birrell, T. A. (1991). Reading as Pastime: The Place of Light Literature in Some Gentlemen's Libraries of the 17th Century. In R. Myers and M. Harris (eds.) *The Property of a Gentleman: The Formation, Organisation and Dispersal of the Private Library 1620–1920*. Winchester: St. Paul's Bibliographies, 113–31.

Bly, M. (1996). Bawdy Puns and Lustful Virgins: The Legacy of Juliet's Desire in Comedies of the Early 1600s. *Shakespeare Survey*, 49, 97–109.

Brathwaite, R. (1631). *The English Gentlewoman*. London.

Burton, R. (1624) [1621]. *The Anatomy of Melancholy*. Oxford.

Callaghan, D. (1994). The Ideology of Romantic Love: The Case of *Romeo and Juliet*. In D. Callaghan, L. Helms, and J. Singh (eds.) *The Weyward Sisters: Shakespeare and Feminist Politics*. Oxford: Blackwell, 59–101.

Cary, E. (1994). *The Tragedy of Mariam*. In D. Purkiss (ed.) *Renaissance Women: The Plays of Elizabeth Cary, the Poems of Aemilia Lanyer*. London: William Pickering.

Cavendish, M., Duchess of Newcastle (1997) [1664]. Letter CXXIII in *CCXI Sociable Letters*. In A. Thompson and S. Roberts (eds.) *Women Reading Shakespeare 1660–1900: An Anthology of Criticism*. Manchester: Manchester University Press.

Coghill, N. (1964). *Shakespeare's Professional Skills*. Cambridge: Cambridge University Press.

Cotgrave, J. (1655). *The English Treasury of Wit and Language, Collected Out of the most, and best of our English Drammatick Poems; Methodically digested into Common Places for Generall use*. London.

Crane, M. T. (1993). *Framing Authority: Sayings, Self, and Society in Sixteenth-Century England*. Princeton, NJ: Princeton University Press.

Dickey, F. M. (1957). *Not Wisely But Too Well: Shakespeare's Love Tragedies*. San Marino, CA: Huntington Library.

Dimock, W.-C. (1995) [1991]. Feminism, New Historicism, and the Reader. *American Literature*, 63, 4, 601–22; reprinted in *Readers and Reading*, ed. A. Burnett. London: Longman: 122–31.

England's Parnassus. The choysest Flowers of our Moderne Poets, with their Poetical comparisons (1970) [1600]. Ed.(?) R. Allott. Scolar Press Facsimile. Menston: Scolar Press.

First Part of the Returne from Parnassus, The (1949) [ca. 1600]. In J. B. Leishman (ed.) *The Three Parnassus Plays*. London: Nicholson and Watson.

Gould, R. (1688–9). *Poems Chiefly consisting of Satyrs and Satyrical Epistles*.

Gurr, A. (1992). *The Shakespearean Stage 1574–1642*. Cambridge: Cambridge University Press.

Hackel, H. B. (1997). Rowme of Its Own: Printed Drama in Early Libraries. In J. D. Cox and D. S. Kastan (eds.) *A New History of Early English Drama*. New York: Columbia University Press, 113–30.

Hankey, J. (1987). *Othello*. Plays in Performance Series. Bristol: Bristol Classical Press.

Kastan, D. S. (2001). *Shakespeare and the Book*. Cambridge: Cambridge University Press.

Kirsch, A. C. (1968–9). A Caroline Commentary on the Drama. *Modern Philology*, 66, 256–61.

Klein, J. L. (ed.) (1992). *Daughters, Wives and Widows: Writing by Men about Women and Marriage in England, 1500–1640*. Urbana: University of Illinois Press.

Lanyer, A. (1993). *The Poems of Aemilia Lanyer: Salve Deus Rex Judaeorum*, ed. D. Woods. Oxford: Oxford University Press.

Levin, H. (1993) [1960]. Form and Formality in *Romeo and Juliet*. *Shakespeare Quarterly*, 11, 3–11; reprinted in *Romeo and Juliet: Critical Essays*, ed. J. F. Andrews. London: Garland, 1993.

Levith, M. J. (1989). *Shakespeare's Italian Settings and Plays*. Basingstoke: Macmillan.

Love, H. (1993). *Scribal Publication in Seventeenth Century England*. Oxford: Clarendon Press.

Marston, J. (1598). *Scourge of Villanie*. London.

Masten, J. (1997). *Textual Intercourse: Collaboration, Authorship, and Sexualities*. Cambridge: Cambridge University Press.

Meres, F. (1598). *Palladis Tamia. Wits Treasury, Being the Second Part of Wits Commonwealth*.

Parnassus Biceps. Or Severall Choice Pieces of Poetry, Composed by the best Wits that were in both the Universities before their Disolution (1656). London.

Roberts, S. (1998). *Romeo and Juliet*. Writers and their Work. Plymouth: Northcote House.

——(2003). "Let me the curtains draw": The Dramatic and Symbolic Properties of the Bed in Shakespearean Tragedy. In G. Harris and N. Korda (eds.) *Staged Properties*. Cambridge: Cambridge University Press.

——(forthcoming). *Reading Shakespeare's Poems in Early Modern England*. Basingstoke: Palgrave.

Sanders, E. R. (1998). *Gender and Literacy on Stage in Early Modern England*. Cambridge: Cambridge University Press.

Shakespeare, W. (1609). *The Historie of Troylus and Cressida. As it was acted by the Kings Maiesties seruants at the Globe. Written by William Shakespeare*. London: G. Eld for R. Bonion and H. Walley.

——(1992). *Romeo and Juliet*, ed. G. B. Evans. New Cambridge Shakespeare. Cambridge: Cambridge University Press.

——(1993). *Othello*, ed. N. Sanders. New Cambridge Shakespeare. Cambridge: Cambridge University Press.

——(1995a). *An Excellent Conceited Tragedie of Romeo and Juliet*, ed. C. Watts. Shakespearean Originals. Hemel Hempstead: Prentice-Hall.

——(1995b). *Antony and Cleopatra*, ed. J. Wilders. Arden Shakespeare, third series. London: Routledge.

——(1995c). *The Tragoedie of Othello, the Moore of Venice*, ed. A. Murphy. Shakespearean Originals. Hemel Hempstead: Prentice-Hall.

Shakspere Allusion-Book: A Collection of Allusions to Shakspere from 1591 to 1700 (1932). 2 vols. London: Oxford University Press.

Taylor, G. (1989). *Reinventing Shakespeare: A Cultural History 1642–1986*. New York: Weidenfeld and Nicolson.

Thompson, A. and Roberts, S. (eds.) (1997). *Women Reading Shakespeare, 1600–1900: An Anthology of Criticism*. Manchester: Manchester University Press.

Walsh, W. (1691). *A Dialogue Concerning Women, Being a Defence of the Sex*. London.

Whitney, C. (2000). Ante-aesthetics: Towards a Theory of Early Modern Response. In H. Grady (ed.) *Shakespeare and Modernity*. London: Routledge, 40–60.

Williamson, M. L. (1974). *Infinite Variety: Antony and Cleopatra in Renaissance Drama and Earlier Tradition*. Mystic, CN: Lawrence Verry.

7

Hamlet Productions Starring Beale, Hawke, and Darling From the Perspective of Performance History

Bernice W. Kliman

Identical twin actors, Anthony Meyer and David Meyer, playing Hamlet as well as the ghost in Celestino Coronado's 1976 film, can stand for the multiple possibilities of Hamlet: angel and devil, one or the other or both together, and everything in between. Hamlet has, from the beginning, elicited vehement responses from audiences, readers, actors, and directors. Three recent productions, viewed against the background of performance history, will show that meanings for *Hamlet* have been and must be teased out from between the lines. Simon Russell Beale (directed by John Caird, 2000–1), mature and lovable, is the most recent in a long line of superior Hamlets – kind, intelligent, and better than anyone in the play, better than anyone in the audience. Ethan Hawke (directed by Michael Almereyda, 2000) is a young dropout who rejects his world, which is our world. Peter Darling (directed by Robert Lepage, 1996–7) exploits the playfulness inherent in Shakespeare's art. These disparate productions – the first on stage, the second on film, and the last an amalgam of theatre and video – demonstrate that putting aside distinctions among performance genres allows us to attend to the play's richness.[1]

Why Fifteen Productions can Appear in One Country (Japan) in One Year (1990)[2]

Part of the reason for Hamlet's multiplicity is that Shakespeare endows him with trompe l'oeil verisimilitude. Shakespeare famously rounds out even his minor characters – his evil or stupid characters with redeeming attributes, his "good" characters with peccadillos – but Hamlet is the most complex of his characters. Partly this is true because of the way we learn about him compared to Shakespeare's technique for other tragic protagonists. In other plays the text is more definite, less ambiguous. (Shakespeare introduces the word "ambiguous" for the first and only time in *Hamlet*, TLN 374.)[3] This is not to say that other plays lack ambiguity; every play is capable of multiple interpretations; nor do I claim that there isn't a set of adjectives one might apply to Hamlet to which most would agree: "introspective" and "witty" being two of many. I do claim, though, that *Hamlet* expands the possibilities for interpretation beyond those in any other play. Built into the text of most plays is a range of reactions by other characters as well as the protagonist's actions and soliloquies. It is especially significant that the audience knows the flaws of most tragic characters through both action and reaction. This is not to say that Shakespeare is an Aristotelian: imperfections contribute to characters' wholeness but not necessarily to their downfall. To focus reductively for a moment only on imperfections: protagonists may be solipsistic (Othello, Lear, Antony, Cleopatra, Shylock, Brutus, Richard II), despicable (Richard III, Titus, Macbeth), lacking in self-knowledge (Timon, Lady Macbeth), or muddled (Romeo, Juliet) and combinations thereof. The basic materials are evident in the texts. Hamlet stands apart from the heroes of these tragedies in that his attributes depend, in the absence of firm textual evidence, more than usual on interpretation. Since no one in *Hamlet* speaks of Hamlet (except himself) with anything but respect, his characterization requires interpretation of his relations to the other characters, of his actions, reactions, and failures to act. Levin Schücking (1937), for one, notes that "the expression on the King's face [in the 'Mousetrap' scene] becomes the turning-point of the whole dramatic action" (p. 3). On that actor's expression, then, depends an audience's perception of Hamlet's reaction to the "Mousetrap," and thus of him in total. Supposing Schücking correct, we must agree that no other play depends on an actor's unscripted expression, rather than words, to sharpen the turning point. Not only here but throughout the play, each performance can display expressions, relations, and actions in ways that aggrandize or diminish Hamlet. With so many lacunae, *Hamlet* may be the best worst play in the world; the possibilities for artists, readers, and audience to fill in the gaps are what make it the play most performed and most written about in dramatic literature.

Eighteenth-Century Attitudes

Hamlet has always generated widely divergent opinions. From early on appreciation vied with deprecation; George Steevens in 1773 criticized the development of play and character:

> Shakespeare has been unfortunate in his management of the story of this play, the most striking circumstances of which arise so early in its formation, as not to leave him room for a conclusion suitable to the importance of its beginning. After this last interview with the Ghost, the character of Hamlet has lost all its consequence. (Steevens and Johnson 1773, X: 277, n. 7)

Others had similar reservations. Late in his career, after many successful *Hamlet* productions based on the Robert Wilkes performance editions, which were republished repeatedly in the eighteenth century, David Garrick (1717–79), in 1771, in a letter to Steevens, broached the topic of excess after act 3 and acted upon his idea in his production of 1772, which discarded most of the fourth and fifth acts.[4] Most commentators fail to note that all of Garrick's productions before 1772 had trimmed the text only to the extent that Robert Wilkes had (with some restorations) – but to much the same overall effect as far as concerns Hamlet's dominance. The 1772 text was played near the end of Garrick's career. Its cut of the gravedigger and other of the standard act 4 and 5 scenes has not been widely emulated but is approximated in the early Hallmark television production with Maurice Evans (1953).

Like all early *Hamlets* until William Poel's ensemble production (1900), Garrick's was star-centered (with, often, rather poor actors among the cast); thus, since most of act 4 has little of Hamlet, especially with Fortinbras cut as he was regularly, it was dispensable. The drastic cuts Garrick made in 1772 did not much affect his interpretation of his Hamlet. Commentators praise his characterization in every version for fidelity to nature, gentlemanliness, and nuances of feeling, for rhythm-breaking catches in his speech, for abrupt movement reflecting passion. Like most early players, Garrick believed that personality alone would explain why Hamlet cannot fulfill his beloved father's sacred commission, to kill the usurper; Garrick's answer is quicksilver variations in mood overlaid with a gentle melancholy.

Goethe is among the first to theorize, in psychological terms, Hamlet's failure to avenge his father's death and thus to redeem the play from Steevens's censure, to which he alludes in his novel *Wilhelm Meister's Apprenticeship* (Bk. 4, ch. 15, 151). Goethe, who had begun the novel by 1777 but did not publish it until 1796 (in a revised version), lays out his eponymous hero's and perhaps his own famous interpretation. Since critics usually quote a few words out of context, looking at the interpretation in some detail could be revelatory. Goethe has his characters discuss *Hamlet* in the context of their proposed much altered production of the play, in which Wilhelm will play Hamlet.

> "Just to think clearly about this young man, this son of a prince," Wilhelm went on to say. "Visualize his position, and observe him when he learns that his father's spirit is abroad. Stand by him when, in that terrible night, the venerable ghost appears before his eyes. He is overcome by intense horror, speaks to the spirit, sees it beckon him, follows, and hears – the terrible accusation of his uncle continues to ring in his ears, with its challenge to seek revenge, and that repeated urgent cry: 'Remember me!'"
>
> "And when the ghost has vanished, what do we see standing before us? A young hero thirsting for revenge? A prince by birth, happy to be charged with unseating the usurper of his throne? Not at all! Amazement and sadness descend on this lonely spirit; he becomes bitter at the smiling villains, swears not to forget his departed father, and ends with a heavy sigh: 'The time is out of joint; O cursed spite! That ever I was born to set it right!'"
>
> "In these words, so I believe, lies the key to Hamlet's whole behavior, and it is clear to me what Shakespeare has set out to portray: a heavy deed placed on a soul which is

not adequate to cope with it. And it is in this sense that I find the whole play constructed."

There follows the most famous image, since then endlessly quoted:

An oak tree planted in a precious pot which should only have held delicate flowers. The roots spread out, the vessel is shattered.

Most translators prefer "vase" to the homely "pot" but perhaps the latter better conveys the absence of preciousness in Wilhelm's conception. Wilhelm continues describing Hamlet:

A fine, pure, noble and highly moral person, but devoid of that emotional strength that characterizes a hero, goes to pieces beneath a burden that it can neither support nor cast off. Every obligation is sacred to him, but this one is too heavy. The impossible is demanded of him – not the impossible in any absolute sense, but what is impossible for him. How he twists and turns, trembles, advances and retreats, always being reminded, always reminding himself, and finally almost losing sight of his goal, yet without ever regaining happiness! (Bk. 4, ch. 13, 145–6).

To achieve his conception, Wilhelm restructures the play thoroughly. He found two separate strands in the play, the more important *internal* and the vital but malleable *external*. Wilhelm and the troupe's director, Serlo, thought the Fortinbras episode extremely important because without it the play would be merely a domestic drama, and would lose "the whole stupendous idea that a regal household is destroyed by internal crimes and ineptness" (Bk. 5, ch. 5, 180). But all the separate references to Paris, Wittenberg, ambassadors, and the like had to be collapsed into one unified image. Wilhelm describes the external plot elements as he rearranges them:

After the death of Hamlet senior, the recently conquered Norwegians become restless. The [Danish] governor there sends his son Horatio, an old school friend of Hamlet's and superior in courage and shrewdness to all the others, to Denmark, to press for the readying of the fleet, which is not proceeding apace because of the easy living of the new king. Horatio knew the previous king, having fought under him in his last battles, and had always enjoyed his favor: the first scene with the Ghost will gain by this means.

Wilhelm does not say how an audience will know all this about Horatio; throughout dialogue would have to be added to convey his ideas, but since the novel contains no promptbook, Goethe does not have to do more than generalize. Wilhelm continues:

The new king then gives an audience to Horatio and sends Laertes to Norway with the news that the fleet will soon be landing there, while Horatio is charged with speeding up its preparation. Hamlet's mother, however, will not agree to her son going to sea with Horatio, as Hamlet himself would have wished.

You can easily see how I would link up all the rest. When Hamlet tells Horatio about his stepfather's crime, Horatio advises him to go with him to Norway, gain control of the army and return with it in force. When Hamlet becomes too dangerous for both the king and the queen, they have no easier means of getting rid of him than sending him to join the fleet and instructing Rosencrantz and Guildenstern to keep an eye on him; and when Laertes returns in the meantime, they send him after Hamlet as well, for Laertes is in a murderous temper. The fleet is delayed by unfavorable winds; Hamlet returns. His wandering through the churchyard could perhaps be better motivated. But his encounter with Laertes at the grave of Ophelia is a great moment and absolutely indispensable. The king can then decide that it would be better to rid himself of Hamlet at once. The celebration to mark his departure and his apparent reconciliation with Laertes is carried out with great ceremony, including chivalrous combats in which Hamlet and Laertes fence with each other. I cannot do without the four corpses at the end, no one should be left alive. And since the people now have to elect a new king, Hamlet, as he dies, gives his vote to Horatio. (Bk. 5, ch. 4, 178–9)

Wilhelm's ending for the play may have inspired Horatio's royal demeanor in Olivier's 1948 film. From Wilhelm as well, perhaps Olivier had the notion that Hamlet had to be a blond – but Wilhelm also thought he should be fat, as described by the queen in the last scene (Bk. 5, ch. 6, 185). Wilhelm's interpretation of Hamlet is still influential, always presented as Goethe's view – which of course it may well be. Ironically, the most famous interpretation of the play is based on a fictional, incomplete, and much revised version of the play – not the near-4,000 line text, which of course is seldom acted in full.

Though Wilhelm distinguishes the internal essence from the external conditions as if they run on two separate tracks, his alterations of the latter materially affect one's perception of Hamlet. With the help of his friend Horatio as drawn by Wilhelm, Hamlet could indeed have accomplished more than he does; that he cannot enfeebles him. Turning to Shakespeare's Horatio, we note how passive he is, how unlikely he is to be a helper to Hamlet, and how isolated Shakespeare makes his hero. The burden is his alone.

Goethe's concept may well have been in the air, because two British writers expressed similar ideas. Henry Mackenzie independently had written, in 1780:

The incident of the *Ghost*, which is entirely the poet's own, and not to be found in the Danish legend, not only produces the happiest stage-effect, but is also of the greatest advantage in unfolding the character which is stamped on the young prince at the opening of the play. In the communications of such a visionary being, there is an uncertain kind of belief, and a dark unlimited horror, which are aptly suited to display the wavering purpose and varied emotions of a mind endowed with a delicacy of feeling that often shakes his fortitude, with sensibility that overpowers its strength. (Mackenzie 1780: 236–7)

Mackenzie deserves credit for the first psychological portrait of Hamlet.

Writing in 1788, Thomas Robertson describes a similar Hamlet. To Robertson, Hamlet is a person whose complex range of attributes prevents him from acting as he thought he should (p. 256). To Robertson, Shakespeare's art was to create the character and then to allow him to act as such a character would have behaved:

> . . . [E]xquisite sensibility to virtue and vice, and an extreme gentleness of spirit and sweetness of disposition . . . the most brilliant and cultivated talents, an imagination transcendentally vivid and strong, together with what may be called, rather an *intuition*, than an acquired knowledge of mankind. And . . . a singular gaiety of spirits, which hardly at any after period, the very gloomiest only excepted, seems to have failed him. (Robertson 1790: 254)

He is a

> polished gentleman, a soldier, a scholar and a philosopher . . . At one time, mild, courteous and contemplative; at another animated with the keenest feelings; upon occasions, all wrath and fire; looking down, at all times, as if from a superior orb, upon whatever was little, insincere or base among men . . . Resentment, revenge, eternal indignation, stimulated Hamlet at one moment; at the next, we have mere unbending and recoil of his passions; and not only this, which was transient, but there followed, almost at the same instant, that gentleness which so seldom left him. From this, he could not, at any time, act in cold blood; he could strike only in the fiercest moments of provocation . . . In the general tenor of his mind he could do nothing . . . (Ibid: 255–6)

Though Hamlet constantly chides himself for inaction, Robertson continues, he was not formed to act. His pretended madness suited him and was not designed for his safety.

> . . . [T]he more narrowly we take a view of him, the more we shall always find his sensibility to be, in the first moments, such, as led to instant and mortal action, while his gentleness, like an equal weight on the other side, counteracted its whole force. (Ibid: 260)

Robertson excuses Hamlet's behavior to Ophelia (pp. 257–8), the king at prayer (pp. 260–1), and Rosencrantz and Guildenstern (p. 262); reconciles melancholy and jocularity in Hamlet (p. 259); and concludes that to understand Hamlet we cannot isolate now one trait (sensibility, which, as Robertson defines it, could lead to violent action), now another (gentleness, which resulted only in passivity). "It is the struggle between the two, upon which his conduct hinges" (p. 265).

The views of Goethe, Mackenzie, and Robertson were probably influenced by performances by Garrick and others in the same mold, just as their views influenced subsequent writers and players.

The Nineteenth Century Builds on the Eighteenth

Goethe himself never produced anything like Wilhelm's *Hamlet*, though as artistic director for the State Theatre at Weimar, he might have done so. The script in the novel is sketchy, focusing mainly on Hamlet's reaction to the ghost and Wilhelm's negative feelings about his own father. However, Goethe's sensitive Hamlet, with minor variations, prevailed for years – most luminously via lectures of Schlegel (1808) and Coleridge (1809–19), who thought intellectualization froze Hamlet's power to act. The romantic Hamlet held forth on stage at least through the end of the nineteenth century.

The work of Edwin Booth (1833–93) comes close to embodying Wilhelm's ideal Hamlet – at least the "internal" aspects. Charles Clarke, a young man of fragile health and heightened sensibility, meticulously recorded Booth's intonations, gestures, movements, and minute emotional effects during and after eight performances he saw in 1870, Booth's career peak. Working not only with Clarke's journals (at the Folger Shakespeare Library) but also with promptbooks, reviews, illustrations, and Booth's notebooks and letters, among other accounts, Charles Shattuck describes Booth's performances from 1853 to 1891, with special emphasis on the 1870 production. The idea that killing the king is a holy obligation still holds sway, not only in Clarke's view, but also in Shattuck's. Clarke describes Booth's Hamlet as "a man of first-class intellect and second-class will" (Shattuck 1969: xiv).

> In the catastrophe, when the killing was done, Clarke saw in [Hamlet's] face and action the sorriest bewilderment – no glint of triumph, but doubt, dismay, the beginnings of remorse. Thus, according to Clarke's reading of it, the tragic pattern was firmly conceived, worked out in passion, and sustained to the final curtain. (Ibid)

Booth's Hamlet was "mannerly, meditative, darkly romantic, wise, kindly, fierce for good only, [and] pure" (ibid). Booth saw Hamlet as "not merely a Prince, but a most delicate and exquisitely refined creature – an absolute gentleman," who, while "not effeminate," is "feminine" in sensibility (ibid: xviii). It would have been impossible for his Hamlet to be rude to Polonius – and thus he must say "These tedious old fools" (TLN 1262) only after Polonius has left the stage (Shattuck 1969: 166). Booth did not believe Hamlet loved Ophelia, but his gentle behavior to her and the cuts of the worst of his *double entendres* to her persuaded audiences that he did love her. Shattuck says that Booth wrote more in his notebooks about Hamlet's not loving Ophelia than about any other topic (ibid: xxi–xxii). As a Hamlet in the Booth tradition who disagreed with Booth on this point, Johnston Forbes Robertson expressed his love for Ophelia by kissing a lock of her hair as she wept for him and their lost love (3.1), a gesture that Olivier copied (see photos in Kliman 1988: 252–3).

Clarke recognized that

Booth's Hamlet is not natural. Shakespeare's Hamlet is not natural. Shakespeare's Hamlet is full of art, full of rhetoric, full of versification. Booth's Hamlet is full of art, full of mechanical rhetoric, full of that poetry of way and method which in the actor is akin to the versification of the poet. Both are ideal – too ideal for life. Yet both are full of human nature. (Clarke, quoted in Shattuck 1969: 97)

Unlike Clarke, people often write of Hamlet as if he were a real person and thus fill in the blanks. He is as real to them as if he were a historical person and more real to them than many of the people they meet.

He is so for scholars like Karl Werder, who, arguing in 1859 against Goethe, claims that Hamlet was correct to wait until the whole story could be laid before the people, with proof adequate to justify a king's execution (Werder 1975: 115–16, 210). But he cannot point to lines where Hamlet in soliloquy or in conversation with Horatio expresses such plans. Werder's Hamlet, largely drawn from the white spaces in *Hamlet*, is a splendidly intelligent and restrained hero:

"Killing the King *before* the proof is adduced would be, not killing the guilty, but killing the *proof*; it would be, not the murder of the criminal, but the murder of justice!" Verily, in Hamlet's own words, this would be "hire and salary, not revenge." (Ibid: 17)

But in the absence of lines, it would be an actor's responsibility to express that restraint. Even when Hamlet has the proof he needs, the king's order for his execution in England, which he shows to Horatio (TLN 3527), he has (textually) no plan to use it.

George MacDonald in his fine 1885 edition admits wryly that he speaks of "Hamlet as if he were a real man and not the invention of Shakspere," but he dares anyone to try writing about the character without doing the same (pp. xv–xvi). MacDonald sums up the gentlemanly Hamlet but at the same time notes the deprecatory view:

It seems to me most admirable that Hamlet, being so great, is yet outwardly so like other people: the Poet never obtrudes his greatness. And just because he is modest, confessing weakness and perplexity, small people take him for yet smaller than themselves who never confess anything, and seldom feel anything amiss with them. Such will adduce even Hamlet's disparagement of himself to Ophelia when overwhelmed with a sense of human worthlessness [TLN 1778–83], as proof that he was no hero! They call it weakness that he would not, foolishly and selfishly, make good his succession against the king, regardless of the law of election, and careless of the weal of the kingdom for which he shows himself so anxious even in the throes of death! To my mind he is the grandest hero in fiction – absolutely human – so troubled, yet so true! (p. 277)

To MacDonald, Hamlet's greatness lies in his capacity for weighing right action and for trying to do no wrong, even when urged to it by a powerful image – that of his father. But in his effort to excuse Hamlet for delaying, MacDonald, like Werder, does not (cannot) point to any line of text in which Hamlet, pondering his inaction, reasons that he is justified by considerations of State and Law, Ethics and Morality; both scholars must infer it from the way they imagine Hamlet comports himself.

MacDonald's sneer about "small people" alludes to writers like Frank Marshall, who a few years before had written:

> It seems to me that the principal flaw in Hamlet's character is the want of humility and consequently of faith [–] that humility which is the backbone of enthusiasm, which consists of a complete subordination of one's own prejudices and desires and will to some great purpose, and of a belief, so thorough and unquestioning in the justice of that purpose, as to render any hesitation, in one's efforts to accomplish it, impossible. Had Hamlet possessed this humility he would never have doubted for one moment that the Ghost's charge of vengeance was to be fulfilled at any cost; he would never have thought of the consequences to his body or to his soul; but would have openly slain Claudius, and would have stood before the people with the blood fresh on his hands, indifferent as to their judgment and fearless of their punishment. Such humility does not always lend itself to the accomplishment of great or good ends; the fanatic shares it with the enthusiast, the assassin with the liberator.
>
> [Hamlet's soul has] a yearning desire to be convinced, but its power of conviction [is] hopelessly debilitated. (Marshall 1875: 110)

Marshall's censorious comments remind us that, throughout the play's history, Hamlet has received a fair amount of condemnation for inaction as well as for misguided action.

Others locate in his brooding about the ghost's command Hamlet's excellence as a representation of a superior human being, Shakespeare's subtlety in shaping this character, and the great knot that makes the play work: he is not Laertes, to unhesitatingly commit murder, regicide, and usurpation. In commanding that Hamlet leave his mother to heaven yet cleanse Denmark (never saying how), the ghost assigns a finely tuned Hamlet an impossible task. Whether the character realizes this impossibility or struggles with it unconsciously or is unaware of it is a job for an actor to convey: Hamlet has no lines expressing this dilemma. Shakespeare's character is driven by the plot: Hamlet cannot kill the king until after he kills Polonius, which activates Laertes' revenge – leading directly to the denouement. Productions must work with the given circumstances.

Twentieth-Century Amplifications

John Barrymore in 1922 (New York) and 1925 (London), who in his *Confessions* says he relied on Goethe's explanation (Hapgood 1999: 59–61), continues the tradition of ideal hero. This is not to say that Barrymore's Hamlet is identical to Booth's. The twentieth-century actor brought to his role more passion, more sexuality, than Booth's tender prince could (or would have wished to) muster. Their Hamlets were alike, though, in alert awareness, quick intellect and sensitivity. Barrymore gave the impression that had he been able to direct his energies, he would have been able to outfox the opposition.

Beale, Hawke, and Darling

In recent times, few actors have attempted the romantic approach, but the Hamlet of Simon Russell Beale (2000–1) revivified Goethe's Hamlet, showing brilliantly that an intelligent, sensitive, gentle, and sweet-tempered Hamlet is still a viable possibility that does much to unify and elucidate the play.[5] Beale on the surface is not a heroic figure. Above average in girth and below average in height, he relies on his sensibility and intelligence to create the character. Solid and quiet, Beale moves quickly when occasion demands (getting out of the way of the funeral procession, fencing adroitly), but he is also capable of a focused and generative stillness. One of the finest actors currently on stage, he has range and depth sufficient for the text. He is an actor who can let audiences know what he is thinking, and his thoughts are worth attending to. Through him, the National Theatre production yields perfect clarity (not necessarily the ideal goal for the play) about the character: this Hamlet has no desire to be a king, no urge to be a hero. He wants to do the right thing. He is deeply grieved by his father's death and mother's swift remarriage but incapable of hatred. One admires him because he has a pleasing wit and a serious intellect. One likes him because he is warm-hearted, lovable, and sensitive; he is a better person than most people we know. This is not a popular take on Hamlet these days. Hamlet should be nasty and brutish (but not short), wicked and closer to Iago (like the devilish Coronado twin) than to the eighteenth- and nineteenth-century Romantic Hamlet. Beale knows how to do Iago, having played a definitive one a few years ago, but his Hamlet is sweet and humane, without being a prig. He can become irritated, as he does with Laertes at Ophelia's grave, but he quickly recollects himself. One might multiply adjectives to describe Beale; he is multifaceted and every facet gleams. Many of us have wondered how stocky, fortyish Richard Burbage, Shakespeare's Hamlet, could have played the Dane. Very well, it seems, if he were as superb as stocky, fortyish Beale.

Of course, the National's production is not completely retrograde; it puts to use tricks of setting (packing cases moved around a lot, a bright cyclorama glimpsed at times through the opening in the back wall), lighting (chandeliers that rise and descend), and sound effects. But its main appeal is Beale's Hamlet.

His gestures are small; he uses the space between his outstretched fingers to mime the "little month" since his father died (TLN 331). He suggests his pose of madness by pulling strands of hair to stand up rather than anything more obviously manic. His hair makes for a little throughline: there is a charming moment when near the end of the closet scene he shrugs off his mother (Sara Kestelman) as she tries to smooth his hair and then smooths it himself; it is a teenager's gesture.

Though Beale's vocal range is wide, the production makes him work within the bounds of rationality, loving kindness, bewilderment at the demand of his father (asking him to do what it is impossible for this Hamlet to do), shock at the behavior of his beloved mother, and deep sadness about Ophelia. He does not impose his melancholy on others.

He is the contemplative man who absorbs and wonders. In his mother's closet, Hamlet believes he has killed the king: he is dismayed by the sight of Polonius, who falls excruciatingly slowly and is still alive to hear Hamlet's sad words, "Thou find'st to be too busy is some danger" (TLN 2415). In the graveyard scene he connects viscerally with the blue-collar sexton. Beale shivers to see the skull of someone he had known and loved: it brings home to him the meaning of death as the ghost's visitations and his killing of Polonius had not. The scene is a significant marker on the curve of Beale's performance, a wonderful preparation for "There is speciall prouidence in the fall of a Sparrowe . . . let be" (TLN 3668–73+1).

Caird's inventiveness with the text furthers Beale's interpretation of Hamlet. The king (Peter McEnery) wants Hamlet at Elsinore not to spy on him but to be his father and thus to complete the takeover of his brother's life: "thinke of vs as of a father" (TLN 289) has never been as sincere. He warmly kisses Hamlet on the forehead, hands on his shoulders, just as later the ghost will also put hands on Hamlet. There are no desperate villains in this Denmark, making Hamlet's task all the more difficult. Hamlet's disrespect for his father's spirit in the "Old Mole" sequence has been variously explained away; Caird and Beale suggest it derives from anger at the ghost's (Sylvester Morand's) ranting revelations. The ghost's demand is likely to result in Hamlet's death – as Beale's Hamlet realizes even if the ghost does not.

That the production makes more of Ophelia than most do has a positive effect on our perception of Hamlet. In the first court scene her connectedness to him is lovely as she mourns with him, standing comfortably behind him. Editors, even those whose copytext is the Folio (1623), persist in following the Second Quarto (1604) in omitting Ophelia from the scene. Productions seldom emulate the editions in this respect. With few opportunities for Hamlet and Ophelia to be together, productions take advantage of the opportunity in this scene to show the attachment or lack of it between them – to clarify another ambiguous aspect of the text. After the first court scene Caird provides further opportunities to enhance Ophelia's status. In act 2, scene 2, when told by Polonius about Hamlet's love, the king turns to Ophelia (rather than to Gertrude) to ask "Do you think 'tis this?" (TLN 1181), giving Ophelia presence and dignity. In the nunnery scene she signals with a gesture that her father, whom she says is at home (TLN 1786), is actually present unseen. Hamlet's anger is directed at her father more than at her, though he faults her also for playing a part in this entrapment. After the nunnery scene, realizing that their relationship is over, she reads, then tears, the letters she had tried to return to him, then tenderly places them in her reticule; she will later withdraw these fragments and hand them out as flowers. The relationship between Hamlet and Ophelia is deep and poignant, much of it depending on gestures and blocking rather than on text.

Though Horatio is his special friend whom Hamlet detains to listen to words usually delivered as soliloquies in other productions (at the end of 1.2, 1.5, and 3.2, for example), Hamlet is sweetly genial to all. He is delighted to see Rosencrantz and Guildenstern. Only when Guildenstern starts pressing him about ambition does Hamlet become bewildered and begin to understand them. His disappointment, however, does not deteriorate into bitterness. Like Booth's Hamlet, Beale's would not insult Polonius crudely; when Polonius, as he is leaving, hears "These tedious old fools" and turns back, Hamlet, feigning innocence, indicates with a gesture that it is his book, continuing its attack on old men in general, not he who says that about Polonius in particular.

Textual illuminations through nontextual means like these radiate throughout the play. The queen has been moved by the play-within to rummage in her chests for the painting of her first husband whom she had forgotten till reminded by the player queen's declarations of fidelity. Gertrude kisses his image over and over; later, Hamlet points to that picture and the picture in her locket to compare the two husbands (a fresh solution to the two-picture problem, and a relief from the ubiquitous double lockets of so many productions: Beale's Hamlet does not wear his father's picture in a locket; he is neither father- nor mother-fixated). He can be gentler than most Hamlets to his mother because she has already recognized her faithlessness. Thus Hamlet's "Mousetrap" successfully achieves one of the ghost's great behests, awakening his mother's conscience "to those thornes that in her bosome lodge To prick and sting her" (TLN 772–3). She separates herself from the king, refusing to exit with him at the end of 4.1 and 4.7. Later she will drop her dried wedding bouquet and her veil, which she had also rediscovered in her trunk, into Ophelia's grave, linking herself decisively to the younger woman.

Through thoughtful excisions Caird eliminates textual cruxes that can affect one's perception of Hamlet's stability and intellect. Cutting Hamlet's lines to the First Player about some "dozen or sixteen lines" (TLN 1581–2) that might be added to *The Murder of Gonzago*, Caird makes Hamlet's idea about using the play come freshly at the climax of the soliloquy that ends act 2 (TLN 1644–5). Almost every production cuts at least a third of the text; all should do it as intelligently as Caird did, to further the chosen interpretation.

With a daring transposition, Caird heightens the effect of the play-within: a Hamlet (like Derek Jacobi in the BBC version) could very well destroy the efficacy of his "Mousetrap" by leaping into the action before the play's poisoner has a chance to entrap the king. In Caird's version Gonzago and Baptista sit facing the king and queen on their seats upstage, but the actors also turn to each other to present profiles to the theatre audience – a clever staging, which puts Hamlet downstage, able to observe both the performance and the king. Caird's king rises, mesmerized by Lucianus, and virtually acts out the poisoning, mirroring Lucianus's gestures. Hamlet rocks with nervous energy, watching. When the king pauses, Hamlet jumps forward, prompting him to continue with gestures and words: "He poisons him i'th garden for his estate?" as if to say, "Go on, go on." But the king instead rushes out, then calls for light. One can see why the court might not have caught on to the revelation of murder and at the same time how Hamlet could be convinced. Most productions never explain satisfactorily the failure of the court to notice what so convinces Hamlet.

Caird places the one intermission in 3.2 after Hamlet elicits from Horatio his ambiguous corroboration and before the re-entrance of Rosencrantz and Guildenstern. At the end of this first act Hamlet, sitting upstage in the king's place with Horatio next to him in the queen's place, calls for music (TLN 2167). The musicians sit with backs to the audience where the players had performed. Ophelia, who has remained standing where she had watched the play with Hamlet, now slowly walks across the stage from downstage left to downstage right and off, as Hamlet sits sobbing. The curtain falls. When the curtain rises, there has been a filmic reverse shot: the thrones are now where the musicians had been and vice versa, a visualization of a turning point, or as Samuel Crowl (2001) says, a turn "deeper into the private psyches of the play's central characters" (p. 10). Hamlet knows that all is over now: love, life itself. The "Mousetrap," of course, has put the king on notice that Hamlet knows his secret.

In act 1, scene 4, after threatening his companions with a snatched up sword when they tried to stop him from following the ghost, Beale's Hamlet had sheepishly returned it, recollecting himself: violence is not natural to him. Discounting the ambiguous moment in the prayer scene, this production gives Hamlet an opportunity to kill the king when, after Polonius's death, Claudius confronts him (4.3). Hamlet holds his knife to the king's chest as the latter extends his arms wide, his palms facing outward, calmly daring Hamlet to strike. When he does not, the king turns his right palm upward for the knife, which Hamlet relinquishes. Caird recreates the same picture of Hamlet and the king in the last scene, but this time Hamlet drags the blade of the poisoned foil across the king's extended hand. This is an apt culmination for Beale's Hamlet. If indeed the foil is poisoned, then the king is dead, for the blow itself is certainly not mortal. Hamlet has achieved the ghost's command without betraying his nature. Those who missed his stage Hamlet can listen to Beale's excellent verse speaking on the Arkangel recording (Penguin 1999), but they will find the impact much diminished because most of the effects Beale depends on are supertextual, developed not only on the lines but also in the spaces between words, communicated through enactment on stage.

From being too good to kill, as in Booth and his followers, Hamlets in the 1930s were too sick to kill. Early on, scholars and critics had weighed in on Hamlet's insanity, but few productions found it expedient to portray him as mad. The Freudian theory espoused by Ernest Jones and others, however, led directly to several notable Hamlets, whose Oedipal fixations prevented them from doing what they "should" have done: the father is still "he who must be obeyed." Laurence Olivier's stage (1937) and screen performance (1948) can stand for many in the psychological mold (see Dawson 1995: 110–13). While Freudian scholars sometimes sketch a pathetically neurotic Hamlet, in Olivier's materialization Hamlet was attractive enough to influence followers from the mid- to late-twentieth century. For a sick Hamlet, see Mark Rylance, directed by Ron Daniels in 1988 (Hapgood 1999: 82–5). Rylance, who appears in soiled, striped pajamas, suffers pitiably but evokes no admiration, nor is he meant to.

Olivier, though melancholy, was vigorous and excitable when he felt himself called upon to act suddenly; handsome and muscular, this prince could only have been kept from fulfilling the ghost's command by inner demons. Goethe had called attention to the external, political frame, but many Freudian productions found the Fortinbras elements distracting. The Freudian family drama does not require external forces. While psychological criticism of Hamlet is far from dead, the Freudian interpretation for the most part is finished in performance. Recent productions avoid having Hamlet toss his mother about on the bed as if he means to rape her.

A shift in opinion about Hamlet comes from two directions, one emanating from the text and the other from social and political consciousness. From the beginning of commentary on the play there were always some who doubted that fulfilling the ghost's behest would have been the noblest achievement of Hamlet's life. Textual evidence abounds about the ghost's ambiguous nature. Stephen Greenblatt (2001) underscores in his book-length study of purgatory the difficulty Shakespeare's audience might have had in taking the ghost's "word for a thousand pound" (TLN 2158–9).

It is important to emphasize that the ghost's unreliability as a guide to moral behavior does not explain Hamlet's inaction; he fails (textually) to give voice to its limitations. He can only "express" the idea with the help of the actor playing the ghost. With his "Mousetrap," for example, he proves to his own satisfaction the truth of the ghost's story, but he is apparently (textually) unaware that an accurate ghost may yet be a demonic ghost, not fit to follow. Some, like Eleanor Prosser, who believe that Shakespeare intended a malign ghost, assert that Shakespeare meant audiences to condemn Hamlet for wanting to wreak vengeance (even were he incapable of action), just as we censure virtually every other tragic protagonist for corrupt, immoral, or ineffectual motives and actions – regardless of their grandeur. Prosser (1971) asserts that to achieve the post-Reformation dignified ghost and blemish-free protagonist the text had to be thoroughly expurgated (p. 244). But even full-length productions can manipulate audience response to ghost, Hamlet, action, and inaction (see Trewin 1987).

Productions that introduce ambiguous ghosts can mix Hamlet's despicable and honorable attributes (as does Branagh's 1996 film); or they can complicate the mix if Hamlet knows that he must cleanse the state, whatever the nature of the ghost (Kozinstev's 1964 film). These productions, like all others, work with and between the lines of the text.

The impetus of the anti-Vietnam War movement in the 1960s helped to bring political *Hamlet*s, temporarily, to the fore. The idea that the ghost is unreliable made possible Hamlets in revolt against society. Such productions have been more trenchant outside the West, perhaps, where Aesopian interpretations can move audiences stifled by politically repressive states. In addition to Kozinstev's version, Akira Kurosawa's *The Bad Sleep Well* is a flawed but fascinating early example (1960) of a *Hamlet* used for social commentary.

One of the important twentieth-century stage productions that views Hamlet in a political light is Peter Hall's 1965 Royal Shakespeare Company production with David Warner. Influenced, as Anthony Dawson points out, by the Angry Young Men movement of the 1950s, Hall and Warner created a corrupt world, stuffed with sycophants, and a Hamlet more moved by disgust at political corruption than by love for his father or horror at a single murder (Dawson 1995: 132–46). Hamlet's lassitude is determined by the hopelessness of stopping the smooth bureaucratic machinery of government.

In some ways the late twentieth-century film by Almereyda with Ethan Hawke springs from the same aims that drove Hall's version – release from the gentlemanly Hamlet and an opportunity to comment on society. In its low-budget modesty (shot in super 16 mm for under 2 million dollars, about one-tenth of the budget for Baz Luhrmann's *Romeo + Juliet*), the adaptation, as Almereyda calls it, is a refreshing relief from the glossy pretentiousness of some Shakespeare films. Many planned settings were unavailable to Almereyda – though some of those that remain are splendid, including the Guggenheim Museum, corporate offices, and vast New York City lobbies.[6] The film is reminiscent of Ragnar Lyth's 1984 film, which did much with found locations, such as the derelict Nobel dynamite factory. Each filmmaker makes do with what is available and allows the spectator to fill in the details. And settings were not the only problem; probably the main one was time: more money would have meant more time, more negotiating power with location supervisors, more expert help. But adversity led Almereyda to daring experimentation and gives the film its real-life, impromptu, improvised luster.

Since his original scripts had much more of the *Hamlet* text – and in play order – than does the released film, Almereyda might justifiably have called his film a performance rather than an adaptation, but his scripts all refer diffidently to his work as an adaptation. Never meant to be a definitive *Hamlet*, it is an essay on the play, influenced by Almereyda's considerable knowledge of literature, philosophy, theatre, and film. As released, the film excised much of the text, one-third or more (no more than Booth's stage version), and transposed many scene segments.

This *Hamlet* is about corporate America, about medium-tech and high-tech saturation. Almereyda integrates closed-circuit monitors, faxes, home video equipment, voice mail, Hamlet's raw video scenes in grainy black and white, Ophelia's photography, omnipresent computers, and allusions to major and minor brands, magazines, and stores. The film is about consumerism, from which none of the characters is free. Almereyda engages in aggressive product display, making his film fully complicit in corporate society. This product placement is not an extraneous gesture to glean some extra funding, as some reviewers claimed, but integral to the film. The ghost fades into a Pepsi dispenser; Hamlet ponders "To be or not to be" along the empty aisles of a Blockbuster Store, with every rack blaring "Action" and with bombs blazing on TV monitors; Fortinbras's photo is on the front page of *USA Today* and on the screens of television sets.

An early Almereyda script calls for the ghost (Sam Shepherd), who appears on the balcony of Hamlet's apartment, to walk through the glass; instead of this special effect,

Shepherd opens the door and walks in. The low-tech solution may have been an accident of the budget, but the effect is to humanize the ghost: though Shepherd has charisma and presence, his ghost is not a metaphysical entity; he is dead, but with humanity intact, including a smoking habit. Almereyda (2001: 133) states that his *Hamlet* was influenced by the conception of filmmaker Andrei Tarkovsky, who had expected to stage *Hamlet*. In his diary, Tarkovsky had outlined his plan to humanize the ghost, who, he says,

> walks out perfectly normally, factually, he doesn't vanish in a theatrical way. Altogether the Ghost ought to be the most real, concrete character in the play . . . All the pain is now concentrated in him, all the suffering of the world. He could even have a handkerchief in his hand, and put it to his ear, as if he could still feel the poison there, as if it were still seeping. (Tarkovsky 1993: 381)

Interestingly, the Russian filmmaker thought he could better fulfill his aim with a staged production. Almereyda shows that the aim could also be realized on film. Like Tarkovsky's ghost, Almereyda's, recounting his grievances to Hamlet, holds a handkerchief to his ear, mopping up the oozing poison. Once he has delivered his message to Hamlet, he hangs around looking as if pained by the world's ills.

Humanizing the ghost, which can also be effected in more traditional productions (Caird's blowhard ghost may be a nod in that direction), is one way to explain the play. As a revenant, who carries with him the baggage of his humanity, he is not the grand presence whom Hamlet must obey unquestioningly. In Almereyda's version Hamlet has to make the moral choices without supernatural solicitings. Shepherd's compassionate ghost, with deeply pitying eyes, is a model only and as limited as any human mentor might be. Hamlet glances at him resentfully when he turns up in the closet scene and again near the end of the play (during the early portion of 5.1 when Hamlet is discussing his plans or lack thereof with Horatio). This ghost also seems to have interests beyond those he brought to Hamlet. When Hamlet enters Horatio's apartment (shared with Marcella), the ghost, now a pale shadow unseen by the other characters, is seated at her bedside, tenderly watching her sleep off a cold.

Of course the film's updating clashes with the Shakespearean language: why would a king lead the Denmark Corporation? But considering Kurosawa's *The Bad Sleep Well* and Aki Kaurismäki's 1987 *Hamlet Goes Business*, which are modern-dress adaptations of *Hamlet* in the corporate world that do not use Shakespearean language, I cannot regret the disjunction between image and language in Almereyda's film. The more experienced Shakespeareans in the cast, like Liev Schreiber (Laertes) and Diane Venora (Gertrude), are excellent verse interpreters.[7] The rest of the cast – stellar actors all – are sometimes merely adequate verse speakers, but their awkwardness with the language throws them back into what film does best – that is, revealing, through close-ups of faces, characters' inner thoughts and feelings. In Shakespeare, reaction is as important as speech; not all of *Hamlet* is in the lines even were one to discount my idea of lacunae. For a long time in stage history, the actor playing Hamlet had to play all the roles, had to, in a sense, act the awe and terror that an insufficient actor playing the ghost could not project. In Almereyda's film each player has his or her moment, even Horatio, even his almost silent girlfriend Marcella, to be the significant one, the one the camera idolizes. It is no accident that some of the most highly prized Shakespeare films are, at most, subtitled in rags of Shakespearean verse (Lyth, Kozinstev), or they are altogether without Shakespeare's language (Kurosawa). That such a fine *film* set in contemporary New York City could be made with Shakespeare's language is a small miracle.

The *mise-en-scène* and the film personalities do much of the work, but the protagonist's age also contributes mightily to the film's emotional effect. Though Ethan Hawke was twenty-eight when the film was shot in 1998, he looks much younger. Hamlet is a student, apparently not yet twenty. Many have written and speculated about Shakespeare's intentions for Hamlet's age, but the best guess is that he is a youth at the beginning (young enough to be lectured) and a young man of thirty at the end (though only about two months separate beginning from end). Along with the ghost's humanity, Hamlet's callow youthfulness, his adolescent bewilderment, does much to explain his disgust with his beautiful mother's sexuality (Diana Venora is a stunning Gertrude), and his difficulty stomaching the corporate world of Claudius and Polonius. He would have had similar difficulty while his father was in charge; the life of a CEO is not for him. He is impossible to imagine as a suit. A note in the published screenplay implies that Hamlet's conversation with his father is probably the most intimate they have ever shared: "His father, we might sense, never spoke to him so directly while alive" (Almereyda 2001: 31).

Infantilized by her loving but controlling father, Ophelia is a few years younger than Hamlet (Julia Stiles was seventeen in 1998 and has made a career thus far of playing teenagers). While seated with her against bright windows (for 1.3), Polonius (Bill Murray) lifts her foot to his lap and ties the laces of her sneaker as he warns her against Hamlet (one of the most endearing moments in the film). The camera cuts away from her sullen face before she can respond. Later Polonius brings her balloons and a cake, perhaps to soften his sternness to her. There, catching her kissing Hamlet, who has brought her his poem (TLN 1144–7), Polonius seizes it and drags her to see the king and queen. (For once, Hamlet and the poem match; as portrayed by Hawke, he is as adolescent as it is.) Wounded by her father's betrayal of her, Ophelia's first thoughts of suicide come in this scene (act 2, scene 2): standing at the edge of the executive pool, where the scene takes place, she imagines herself jumping into the water. Stiles's wonderful face displays the truculence common to rebellious teens, but Ophelia lacks the will to rebel. For the nunnery scene Polonius outfits her with a recording device, which Hamlet discovers when he reaches under her shirt while kissing her. She fails him miserably, but Hamlet's video shots of her in quiet poses, reading in some and joyously skating in others, sweeten their relationship.

Twice before the end Hamlet tries to kill Claudius, a young CEO with heroic chin, who is always accompanied in public by his bodyguard (who is absent, however, when Laertes rushes in). Once, just after the fishmonger scene, Hamlet storms Claudius's office with gun outstretched, ready to shoot, but the office is empty. Another time, Hamlet pushes aside Claudius's chauffeur and takes his place (unknown to Claudius). Driving through dark Manhattan streets, Hamlet surreptitiously switches on the intercom and listens as his uncle, crouched on the back seat of his stretch limo, groans his confession and attempts to repent (3.3). Pitying him, Hamlet cannot kill him. Later he uses the gun in his mother's bedroom, shooting through the mirrored doors of the closet, hitting Polonius in the eye. Ingmar Bergman, in his anti-romantic *Hamlet* for the Royal Swedish Theatre in 1987, which, soon after, played at the Brooklyn Academy of Music, also had Polonius killed through his spying eye.[8] It is witty of Almereyda to have closets in the closet scene while retaining the bed for the near throttling of Gertrude. Laertes, shown Hamlet's gun, which had been confiscated as evidence, pockets it and in the grapple of the high-tech fencing match (with digital readouts recording hits), uses it to shoot Hamlet and is in turn shot. Schreiber's Laertes is a sympathetic character, who threatens Hamlet at Ophelia's grave only after Hamlet persists in tormenting him with questions. He shoots Hamlet almost without meaning to. With the same gun, after Laertes and Gertrude are dead, the dying Hamlet shoots Claudius.

Through his images within the text's interstices, Almereyda offers yet another possible version of the play's meaning. Hawke's Hamlet is not heroic; there is no room for heroism in this New York City world. But neither is he ineffectual. He is confused, sad, and sympathetic.

Calling the home of Hamlet's family the Elsinore Hotel is a Luhrmann-like move, and Almereyda ends the film with another; he adopts useful ploys but rejects Luhrmann's outrageous self-indulgence. The conclusion of *Hamlet* has real-life journalist Robert MacNeil, on television, seated beside an on-screen photo captioned "Fortinbras, Denmark's New King." MacNeil intones a few lines from the end of the play, including "This quarry cries on hauock" (3957) and "The sight is dismal" (3961), ending with two lines, creating a couplet, from the play-within: "Our wills and fates doe so contrary runne" (TLN 2079) and "Our thoughts are ours, their ends none of our owne" (TLN 2081). The couplet exonerates Hamlet – and the ghost – by suggesting that intentions and results do not often match. The couplet might be an epigraph for the production itself, which had to compromise so often and yet achieved so much.

Almereyda has metafilmic impulses; his Hamlet frequently works with his video camera and video images; Hamlet's video-within-the-film takes the place of the play-within; Hamlet's last images are of his father and Ophelia as he had captured them on video. Images over and between the words and images within images forge Almereyda's interpretation – augmented of course by the nonverbal elements always added to the text – design, sound effects, nonverbal actions and reactions.

Similarly, for Robert Lepage, metadrama is an important concern. Artistic director of the Montreal-based Ex Machina, Lepage has directed for stage, television, film, and opera. His *Elsinore* connects theatricality, metadrama, celebration of the work of actors, designers, and musicians, and above all, playfulness. With the abandon usually reserved for parody, he ruffles *Hamlet* and invites the audience to join in. Billed as a one-man show, it is actually an intense collaboration among actors (including mime Pierre Bernier), stage designer (Carl Fillion), technicians, video artist (Michel Pétrin), costume designer (Yvan Gaudin), lighting designers (Alaine Lortie, Nancy Mongrain), music composer and performer (Robert Caux), and audience. And it has something to say about *Hamlet.*

In the original, 1996 version, Lepage wrote, directed, and starred – aided by Hamlet's alter ego, played by Bernier. The show experienced some technical difficulties with the Monolith, a machine that rotated into vertical, horizontal, or canted positions to become Hamlet's private room, the court, a rocking ship, the queen's closet, and Ophelia's grave. In its four-hour length Lepage stretched his adaptation beyond the limits of its material. Nancy Copeland, writing about the Ex Machina production in April 1996 in Toronto, while admiring Lepage's virtuosity, faulted him for privileging the production's technology over the play's emotional center. She did not think that Lepage acted well enough to hold the play together.

At the Brooklyn Academy of Music (BAM), British actor Peter Darling embodied the main character, with Bernier again as Hamlet's occasional double (at BAM he was billed also as co-director). By this time in its run, October 1997, the production had acquired temperance to give it smoothness; the revision ran about ninety minutes without an intermission, and the mechanical aspects worked flawlessly. Lepage, in a program note, states that his play is a meditation in Hamlet's mind. Darling, playing all the characters, gave each one a particular stamp: a militaristic, swinish king; a delicate, heart-rending Ophelia; a doddering Polonius; and so on. He could change from Hamlet to Gertrude by draping himself with a brocade garment when speaking her lines; playing the king, he could change to the queen by crossing his legs. With a face that conflates the expressions of Coronado's Meyer twins, Darling can play villains as easily as he can a thought-tormented hero. In a sense, the role of Hamlet incorporating all other roles parallels Garrick's method: by reflecting in his reactions what an insufficient subordinate actor was supposed to be, Garrick could play his associates' as well as his own role.[9] Paradoxically, Darling gives full weight to all the characters.

Lepage in a preperformance lecture at BAM asserted that the last thing he wanted to do was to "solve the play": he wanted to "blow it up," to explode the idea of a definitive version. He thinks that actors should do less acting and more playing. Considering his *Elsinore* a sketch only, a step towards a full production, he could be the director as trickster, playing with language, and creating traps for actors and audience. His work reminds me of Allan Kaprow's; the Happening artist ultimately rejected the idea of audiences for his work and demanded that all participate. Like Almereyda, who distanced his film from Shakespeare by calling it an adaptation, Lepage firmly positioned his play as an offshoot by calling it *Elsinore.* The question (though perhaps not the main one) about an offshoot often is, "Does it illuminate Shakespeare's play?" Looking over the long history of *Hamlet*s in performance, one might counter that all are offshoots in some sense: but that avoids the question. The answer in this case? No particular revelations about the plot, but all sorts of ideas about playing, about the confluence of stage crafts that make up a performance, and about moment-by-moment energy and surprise. Spectacle, music, movement, design, vocal and instrumental sound effects are its point. Seeing it is like watching an orchestra at work under the direction of a superb conductor with a master first violinist and a world class soprano. The aesthetic responses trump the tragic emotions of fear and pity – or whatever the play, in any incarnation, makes an audience feel. Yet many moments are achingly moving, and always Lepage foregrounds the actor's skill and audacity. One exits from the theatre with a joy and hopefulness about performance, thrilled by the actor's agility and flexibility of voice, features, and body.

Lepage's work is not so much *Hamlet* as it is a play about playing Hamlet. In that sense it is reminiscent of Andrzej Wajda's 1989 *Hamlet IV*, which placed the audience backstage beyond the actor's dressing room, observing the actor (Teresa Budziscz-Krzyzanowska) prepare for the arduous task of performing Hamlet, watching her scan the backstage video monitors to see when she has to leave for the "stage," which was sometimes visible beyond curtains upstage of the dressing room. Instead of asking us to lose ourselves in Hamlet's world, productions like Wajda's and Lepage's demand our full attention to the inner mechanism of performance. What is admirable about the Lepage play is the technical brilliance of the entire crew that heightens the focus on Darling's elegant transformations and distinct characterizations. It's a *tour de force*.

The ghost, so important in most productions, is merely an offstage voice (Darling's of course), and an onstage suit of half armor, which appears now and then. His words to Hamlet open the play, from "I am thy father's spirit" (694) to "And gins to pale his uneffectual fire" (775), omitting the ghost's request, "remember me" (776). Moved by his awareness that early texts do not reflect Shakespeare's punctuation, Lepage arranged the script as prose, but retained the capital letters of the lines of verse.[10] While the ghost speaks, Hamlet writhes in his chair, rubbing his head, and finally rouses himself to consider "To be, or not to be" (1710). These transpositions are typical of Lepage's textual manipulations for the shortened version. One might call it a play of shreds and patches, held together by its theatricality.

Minor characters are sometimes offstage voices, with perhaps a hand exposed from behind a screen (Osric, Laertes). Or, like Rosencrantz and Guildenstern for act 2, scene 2, they are real-time video projections, by two cameras, of Darling, appearing with Hamlet. Instant changes in Darling's facial expression, body language, and tones of voice create the three characterizations. Similarly, when Hamlet seeks out Horatio to tell him to help him watch the king during the play, the video projector puts both characters before our eyes. For the fishmonger scene, a film projection makes the whole stage look like a library. Within a window in the machine, we see a ladder and Hamlet's legs, as he slides along to pick his book, his torso hidden by the library wall; Polonius, below, speaks to him. The clever angles keep a casual spectator from seeing the magician's tricks, but nothing is really hidden (or is it?): we note Hamlet's black shirt, one sleeve rolled up, the other down, his two mismatched shoes, beneath Polonius's long robe. So the feet on the ladder must be Bernier's, but then "Hamlet" bends down into visibility and it is Darling. So is Polonius Bernier? The game is part of the fun. Polonius, trying to ingratiate himself with the king and queen at the expense of his daughter, tries to keep his feet while the floor rotates beneath him. Hamlet's poem is projected on the back wall, a giant sheet of parchment with fine script, and Polonius with his stick points to the words far above him.

The stagings and Darling's economic gestures aid the king and queen's performances materially. The king (unnamed in the script) always has a cup in hand or nearby and a grimace on his face. For his first scene, in this play the welcome to Rosencrantz and Guildenstern (TLN 1021), he sits on a throne framed in a playing card, the king of spades. When Darling crosses his leg demurely to be the queen, the frame card is the queen of hearts. Both voices are echoic (duplicitous), a doubling and tripling of sound, the king's grating and dangerous, the queen's sweetly flirtatious. Rubbing her fingers together, she indicates that money will be the king's remembrance (TLN 1045). They address us, the audience, as if we were the two spies. When the king interrogates Hamlet in act 4, scene 3, they sit at a table that each character rotates swiftly to change from one to the other. The king sits with his cup, of course, his leg up on the table. Hamlet leans on the table with his left arm, with playing cards before him. (When he reaches his apotheosis near the end of the play, he holds up an ace of spades.) As the table rotates faster and faster for the stichomythic exchange, the cup lands on Hamlet's side and Darling, stepping out of character, looks at it in mock dismay. Later, when the king plots with Laertes, we spy on the king as if from above (Darling is lying down with his head facing the audience) at a table (actually a vertical slab) on which is Hamlet's letter, a dagger, and of course, the cup. Laertes can be imagined as present in the dim light because we hear his voice.

All of these tricks are fanciful interludes between more emotionally charged moments – Hamlet alone, Hamlet and Ophelia, Hamlet and the queen. The most breathtaking transformation is of Hamlet into Ophelia. Hamlet peers down from the upper level of the Monolith, seeing below a bed with pillow. He leaps down, lifts the sheet to his face and inhales deeply, his eyes closed, feeling Ophelia's presence. Barechested now, he opens bottles of perfume and sniffs until he finds the one that evokes her. With his finger he dabs some on his face, down his chest, and below his belt, eyes closed in ecstatic recollection. Putting on her dress, Darling becomes Ophelia. For the nunnery scene, he can play both of them, just by adjusting the garment, tightly buttoned up for her, pulled down in dishabille for him. Later when she drowns, the queen describes the death (4.7) sitting next to a blue silk stream. Then the actor, after removing the queen's brocade to expose the white lace dress, as Ophelia sings the Valentine's Day song from act 4, scene 5, enters the water. Finally, the blue silk water cannot hold her. She falls slowly through the Monolith, struggling, drowning, pulling the blue silk down with her. All these beautiful moves take much longer to describe than to play (and description can mirror their effect only dimly).

In its dazzling deployment of techniques of stage, screen, and music video *Elsinore* can stand for the interdisciplinarity that has transformed performance in the last few decades. The gaps in *Hamlet* can lead to heroic endeavors to explicate in performance. This shared purpose among the genres means that little is to be gained from sorting out current *Hamlet* productions into film, video, or stage versions. The work of Caird, Almereyda, and Lepage is a response to multiple influences and genres, including literary criticism, bibliographical studies, and philosophy. Their work stands among the rare productions that can sweep out of our heads the preconceived notions we have of Hamlet and the play and marshal us towards the diverse paths productions will take in the future. Though both the literature and performance history are full of explanations by those who think they understand the one, true Hamlet, Coronado had it right, jamming into one production his polar-opposite Hamlets. Fifteen productions can appear in one year in Japan – and countless other productions all over the globe every year – because no one *Hamlet* can satisfy all. Each one tries to respond artfully to this most open of Shakespearean plays.

NOTES

1 Jean Howard (1999) makes a similar point about the inutility of rigid divisions of Shakespeare's works into genre classifications (p. 297).

  Obviously, my essay omits or provides reductive summaries of many of the countless productions of *Hamlet* that have appeared in 400 years. Readers seeking full performance histories will want to consult Dawson (1995), Hapgood (1999), and Rosenberg (1992), among others.

  On Coronado's *Hamlet* see Rothwell (1999: 201–3). For screen credits of Coronado's and other films mentioned, see Rothwell and Melzer (1990); http://imdb.com/; and Kliman (1988), which discusses silent and sound *Hamlet* films through 1984.

2 Murakami lists "no fewer than fifteen productions" in Japan in 1990, not counting revivals. My thanks to Graham Bradshaw for the reference. Also thanks to Toby Bird.

3 Quotations of *Hamlet* are from Kliman (1996). Through-Line-Numbers (TLN) derive from Hinman's First Folio and are used by permission from Norton. Occasionally, I refer instead to standard act and scene numbers.

4 Folger Prompt Ham 6 (a marked-up, 1747 Wilkes text) is Garrick's raw preparation copy rather than a promptbook (see Shattuck 1965: 91–2) for the 1772 performance; the modern edited version (Pedicord and Bergmann 1981) obscures the provisional and problematic elements of Garrick's work in progress (as does the Folger restoration of the preparation copy, which I was fortunate to see in its original condition).

5 My comments on Beale are adapted from my review in *Shakespeare Newsletter*, 51 (spring/summer 2001): 39, 42, 44.

6 I am grateful to Amy Hobby, co-producer of the Almereyda *Hamlet* for Double A Films, who provided several early scripts outlining planned location shots and the full text. Almereyda, in his published script, discusses the impact on the final cut of accidental changes in location and other mishaps (pp. 135–43). For anyone who wants to understand the pitfalls of low-budget filmmaking and the intellectual underpinnings of Almereyda's film, his introduction and director's notes are required reading.

7 Venora and Schreiber played Hamlet at the Public Theater in New York City, she in 1982, directed by Joseph Papp, and he in 1999, directed by André Serban. Schreiber deserves a chance to play Hamlet in a better production.

8 Bergman's stage production borrows significantly from Ragnar Lyth's film. Almereyda's film borrows from Bergman and from Baz Luhrmann. And so it goes.

9   Macready in his journals bemoans regularly the inability of his fellow actors to play their parts appropriately (Macready 1912, I: 95 et passim). Clarke's journal, with its total avoidance of all actors aside from Booth, suggests that Booth's troupe was no better than Garrick's or Macready's.

10   Thanks to the stage manager, Éric Fauque, for a copy of the verbal script (without stage directions), and to Mr. Darling and Mr. Bernier, who spoke to me about the production while it was at BAM. Thanks also to BAM for permission to screen the videotape of the performance at Lincoln Center Performing Arts Library, Theater on Film and Tape (TOFT).

REFERENCES AND FURTHER READING

Almereyda, M. (2001). *William Shakespeare's Hamlet Adapted by Michael Almereyda.* London: Faber and Faber.

Calderwood, J. L. (1971). *Shakespearean Metadrama.* Minneapolis: University of Minnesota Press.

Charney, M. (1988). *Hamlet's Fictions.* New York: Routledge.

Clarke, C. (1870). Ms. journals. Folger Shakespeare Library. (See Shattuck 1965: 108–9)

Coleridge, S. T. (1987). *Lectures 1808–19 on Literature*, ed. R. A. Foakes. Vols. 5.1 and 5.2 (1987) of *Collected Works.* Bollingen Series 75. Princeton, NJ: Princeton University Press, 1969–.

Conklin, P. S. (1968). *A History of Hamlet Criticism: 1601–1821.* New York: Humanities Press.

Copeland, N. (1996). *Elsinore. Shakespeare Bulletin*, p. 27.

Croall, J. (2001). *Hamlet Observed: The National Theatre at Work.* London: National Theatre.

Crowl, S. (2001). *"Hamlet." Shakespeare Bulletin*, 19, 1, 9–10.

Dawson, A. B. (1995). *Hamlet.* Shakespeare in Performance. Manchester: Manchester University Press.

Garrick, D. (1771). Letter to George Steevens. Folger Shakespeare Library Ms. Y.c. 1434 (2).

——(1772). Preparation text for *Hamlet.* Folger Prompt Ham 16. (See Pedicord and Bergmann)

Goethe, J. W. von (1989) [1796]. *Wilhelm Meister's Apprenticeship*, ed. and trans. E. A. Blackall in cooperation with V. Lange. New York: Suhrkamp.

Greenblatt, S. (2001). *Hamlet in Purgatory.* Princeton, NJ: Princeton University Press.

Hapgood, R. (ed.) (1999). *Hamlet, Prince of Denmark.* Shakespeare in Production. Cambridge: Cambridge University Press.

Hinman, C. (ed.) (1968). *The Norton Facsimile: The First Folio of Shakespeare.* New York: Norton; London: Paul Hamlyn.

Howard, J. (1999). Shakespeare and Genre. In D. S. Kastan (ed.) *A Companion to Shakespeare.* Oxford: Blackwell, 297–310.

Jones, E. (1949) [1923]. *Hamlet and Oedipus.* New York: Norton.

Kliman, B. W. (1988). *Hamlet: Film, Television, and Audio Performance.* Rutherford, NJ: Fairleigh Dickinson University Press.

——(ed.) (1996). *The Enfolded Hamlet. Shakespeare Newsletter* Special Issue. April. http://www.global-language.com/enfolded.html.

Lepage, R. (1997). *Elsinore.* Performed by Peter Darling. The Ex Machina production videotaped at the Brooklyn Academy of Music. Majestic Theater. 92 min.

MacDonald, G. (1885). *The Tragedie of Hamlet, Prince of Denmarke: A Study with the Text of the Folio of 1623.* London: George Allen.

Mackenzie, H. (April 18, 1780 and April 22, 1780). Observations on Shakespeare's *Hamlet. The Mirror*, No. 99, 227–37, and No. 100, 393–9; excerpt rpt. Vickers 6: 272–80.

Macready, W. C. (1912). *The Diaries of William Charles Macready, 1833–1851*, 2 vols., ed. W. Toynbee. New York: Putnam's.

Maher, M. Z. (1992). *Modern Hamlets and Their Soliloquies.* Studies in Theatre History and Culture. Iowa City: University of Iowa Press.

Mooney, M. E. (ed.) (1999). *Hamlet: An Annotated Bibliography of Shakespeare Studies 1604–1998*. Pegasus Shakespeare Bibliographies. Asheville: Pegasus, University of North Carolina.

Pedicord, W. and Bergmann, F. L. (eds.) (1981). *"Hamlet." Garrick's Adaptations of Shakespeare, 1759–1773. The Plays of David Garrick*. Carbondale: Southern Illinois University Press, IV: 241–323.

Prosser, E. (1971). *Hamlet and Revenge*, 2nd edn. Stanford, CA: Stanford University Press.

Robertson, T. (1790). An essay on the character of Hamlet, in Shakespeare's tragedy of *Hamlet. Read by Mr. Dalzel, Secretary, July 21*, 1788. *Transactions of the Royal Society of Edinburgh*, 2, 251–67.

Rosenberg, M. (1992). *Masks of Hamlet*. Newark: University of Delaware Press.

Rothwell, K. S. (1999). *A History of Shakespeare on Screen*. Cambridge: Cambridge University Press.

Rothwell, K. and Melzer, A. H. (1990). *Shakespeare on Screen: An International Filmography and Videography*. New York: Neal-Schuman.

Schlegel, A. W. (1846). *Course of Lectures on Dramatic Art and Literature*, trans. J. Black. London.

Schücking, L. L. (1937). *The Meaning of Hamlet*, trans. G. Rawson. London: Oxford University Press.

Shattuck, C. H. (1965). *The Shakespeare Promptbooks: A Descriptive Catalogue*. Urbana: University of Illinois Press.

——(1969). *The Hamlet of Edwin Booth*. Urbana: University of Illinois Press.

Steevens, G. and Johnson, S. (1773). *Hamlet, Prince of Denmark. The Plays of William Shakespeare*. London, vol. 10, 143–353.

Tarkovsky, A. (1993). On *Hamlet. Time Within Time: The Diaries 1970–1986*. London: Verso.

Trewin, J. C. (1987). *Five & Eighty Hamlets*. New York: New Amsterdam.

Vickers, B. (ed.) (1974–81). *Shakespeare: The Critical Heritage*, 6 vols. London: Routledge.

Werder, K. (1975) [1859]. *The Heart of Hamlet's Mystery*, trans. E. Wilder. Intro. W. J. Rolfe. New York: Putnam, 1907. Rpt. Norwood, PA: Norwood Editions, 1975.

[Wilkes, Robert (Hamlet)] (1969). *Hamlet, Prince of Denmark. A Tragedy. As It is now Acted by his Majesty's Servants. Written by William Shakespear*. London: Cornmarket. (Original performance edition published in 1718 with reprints and derivative texts published throughout the eighteenth century.)

8
Text and Tragedy
Graham Holderness

I

Now make your choyse.
The Merchant of Venice (Hinman 1968: TLN 974)

In 1994, introducing the "Early Quartos" section of the New Cambridge Shakespeare, Brian Gibbons correctly stated that "these early quartos are . . . not readily available, though indispensable to advanced students of Shakespeare and of textual bibliography" (Halio 1994: v). The same point had been made more generally as the basis for launching in 1992 the Shakespearean Originals series, which include both quarto and folio (here meaning throughout the First Folio of 1623) texts in its list. In the early 1990s therefore, despite the number and range of Shakespeare editions on the market, there was agreement that general access to modern publications designed to reflect more accurately specific characteristics of the original early modern printed texts was significantly circumscribed.

In August 2001 I was able to walk into a Bloomsbury high-street bookshop and choose, from among a veritable plethora of alternative editions, a number of variant texts of Shakespeare's "great tragedies." Modernized editions of the first quartos of both *Hamlet* (1603) and *King Lear* (1608) were there in the New Cambridge Shakespeare series, as *The First Quarto of Hamlet* (Irace 1998) and *The First Quarto of King Lear* (Halio 1994). Both texts were also there as diplomatic reprints in the Shakespearean Originals series: *The Tragicall Historie of Hamlet Prince of Denmarke* (Holderness and Loughrey 1992a), and *M. William Shake-speare HIS true chronicle historie of the life and death of King Lear and his three daughters* (Holderness 1995).

On the same shelves were paperback texts of the First Folio *Hamlet*, now accessible in a new series from Nick Hern Books, *The Shakespeare Folios: Hamlet* (De Somogyi 2000), as well as in the *Applause First Folio* edition (Freeman 1998). There also was the 1622 Quarto text of *The Tragoedie of Othello, The Moore of Venice* (Murphy

1995). Further choice was offered by the Oxford *Complete Works*, edited by Stanley Wells and Gary Taylor, which was the first collected Shakespeare to print the 1608 and 1623 texts of *King Lear* as two separate plays (Wells et al. 1986). Both texts were represented together in Rene Weis's modernized *King Lear: A Parallel-Text Edition* (Weis 1993).

Many other versions of these individual texts are also of course available to the scholar, in modernized editions, facsimiles, and diplomatic reprints (see the list of references and further reading). But the point of this anecdote is to indicate, from the shelf contents of a high-street bookshop, that the "textual revolution" of the 1980s has genuinely made a difference to the way Shakespeare's playtexts are produced and circulated within contemporary culture. Most of the shelfspace is still occupied by the traditional standard (which here means broadly modernized, collated, emended, and conflated) editions of Shakespeare's tragedies, the Ardens[1] and Penguins and Signets and Riversides. But alongside them there is now ready access to publications that can reveal to their readers something of the real historical genesis, in discrepant and variant textualizations, of plays familiarized for centuries in their conflated editions as *Hamlet*, *Othello*, or *King Lear*.

II

His mind and hand went together.
(Heminge and Condelle 1998: 7)

The palpable presence of these alternative versions serves to highlight just what a very odd phenomenon the standard Shakespeare edition really is. If it is now common knowledge that there are two substantially different texts of *King Lear*, why have we for centuries been content with (and indeed still very largely remain resigned to, if not content) editions that merge them into a hybrid that never existed in early modern culture, a text that is by definition, in David Scott Kastan's words, "different from any that Shakespeare ever intended" (Kastan 1999: 61)?

"Textual theory" has in modern critical parlance largely replaced the more familiar term which for centuries underpinned the editorial production of Shakespeare: "bibliography." Until quite recently regarded as a poor relation of literary criticism, it was the discipline of bibliography that nonetheless provided, often invisibly, the raw materials upon which criticism worked its interpretive operations. The main source for early twentieth-century bibliography was a form of textual analysis that derived in the later nineteenth century from biblical studies, and took as its objective the establishing of texts. Documents were studied, analyzed, compared, and evaluated with a view to fixing the true form of the texts they contained beyond dispute, and thereby settling and securing their meaning. The study of Shakespeare's text became a matter of analyzing the printed records in order to identify and correct inaccuracies that were assumed to have entered those texts through the vagaries of

Elizabethan and Jacobean printing practice and the conditions of theatrical writing. These practices of textual scholarship ("New Bibliography") were formulated in strongly "scientific" terms, and aimed at discovering the physical reality of texts as a basis for positing their meanings. W. W. Greg defined the method of this "New Bibliography" as one that

> Lays stress upon the material processes of book-production, concerning itself primarily with the fortunes of the actual piece of paper on which the texts were written or printed.
>
> Bibliographers have in fact brought criticism down from . . . the heights of aesthetic and philosophical speculation to the concrete familiarities of the theatre, the scrivener's shop, and the printing house. (Greg 1967: 2)

The baffling suggestion that criticism should somehow be detached from aesthetic and philosophical speculation reflects the deep ideological divisions that until relatively recently existed between "criticism" (concerned with interpreting, evaluating, and contextualizing creative works) and bibliography (addressed to the problems of fixing a text upon which criticism could confidently operate). The ultimate objective of New Bibliography's search was not in fact anything concrete or material at all, but something much more speculative, a vanished historical primary source: what Shakespeare wrote. The methodology aimed to identify and correct, in the early printed texts, inaccuracies that could be attributed to Elizabethan printing practices; and to reconstruct, from the fallible evidence of these printed texts, the manuscripts that lay behind them. Applying these principles could produce, it was believed, an edition that approximated as closely as possible to what Shakespeare himself actually wrote, and can be assumed to have wished (if he'd cared) to see published. Shakespeare's "intended" text was assumed by definition to be not exactly (or in some cases not at all) what was to be found in the actual early printed texts themselves, since most scholars had been agreeing since the eighteenth century that these were very unreliable witnesses to the manuscript versions from which they must have derived. The methodology can be found explicitly defined as far back as Nicholas Rowe's edition of 1709:

> I must not pretend to have restor'd this Work to the Exactness of the Author's Original Manuscripts. These are lost, or, at least, are gone beyond any Inquiry I could make; so that there was nothing left, but to compare the several Editions, and give the true Reading as well as I could from thence. This I have endeavour'd to do pretty carefully, and render'd very many places intelligible, that were not so before. (Rowe 1709, I: A2–Av)

Inheriting this responsibility, the New Bibliographic editor's task was conceived as to "strip the veil of print from the text" (Bowers 1966: 869) in order to perceive its underlying reality.

Thus the New Bibliographers consolidated a narrative of textual history in which a stable and coherent authorial text, embodied somewhere in a lost manuscript, was "corrupted" in the process of entering the printed state. The language of textual scholarship became pervaded, partly by virtue of its roots in Augustan high culture, partly perhaps by its proximity to biblical studies, by a morally charged lexicon of corruption and illegitimacy, purification and redemption. To be born into print was necessarily to carry a stigma of corruption. Scholarship could however reconstruct from these perishable materials a form of the text (the modern edition) that would redeem its fallen state and restore it to the condition of perfection it possessed at the point where it left the author's hand. "Editions offer themselves as reconstructions of the play that the author wrote before it suffered the inevitable contamination of playhouse and printshop" (Kastan 1999: 62).

New Bibliography has been, and arguably still remains, the basis of the modern Shakespeare edition. Certainly prior to the 1980s the dominant conception of those early modern texts was the belief that they all stood in similar but differential relation to a lost authorial manuscript. The assumption is that the true text, once embodied in Shakespeare's manuscript, gave rise to the various printed versions that we find in history. Although some texts would be considered closer to the putative authorial manuscript than others – e.g., Q2 *Hamlet* as distinct from Q1 or F – any of them might bear traces of the lost original (this applies even to the so-called "Bad Quartos," which are still generally held to be tertiary sources, deriving not directly from the manuscript but indirectly via a performance version). Editing a play was therefore a matter of choosing which of the available texts, Folio or "Good Quarto," approximated most nearly to the imagined manuscript, using this as "copytext," and then supplementing it by appropriating material from other texts. Where multiple contemporary texts exist (as they do for nineteen plays of the canon) the texts are sorted according to their imputed "authority" and then subjected to a process of conflation and consolidation, whereby a particular copytext is added to or subtracted from to arrive at "the most authoritative possible texts of Shakespeare . . . his own manuscript versions just as he meant them to stand" (Hinman 1968: xi). It is New Bibliography's search for the "manuscript," and a remarkable unanimity about what that manuscript might have contained, that produces relatively uniform and unitary editions out of the multiplicity of original texts from which the modern editions are compiled. A more recent revision of New Bibliography, that of G. Thomas Tanselle, supplies alternative terms but adheres to the basic theory. The single uniform entity (e.g., *King Lear*) is here conceived as the "core" or essence of the "work," and variant texts are assimilated or rejected as they approximate or deviate from that "core." The "work" is an ideal category, of which any individual text can only ever be an imperfect representation. The "real work" can be perceived, like one of Plato's forms, "hovering somehow behind the physical text" (Tanselle 1989: 14–15).

This orthodoxy is gradually losing its hold, though as Barbara Mowatt (1998: 132) comments it still remains the foundational belief of most Shakespeare editing:

The belief of Bowers and the other New Bibliographers remains current orthodoxy among Shakespeare editors, as one can see from the textual introductions to the standard Shakespeare editions, where the editorial rationale is inextricably linked to the editor's view of "the manuscript" seen as lying behind the chosen early printed text.

Mowatt further observes that even the apparently alternative editorial policy, most strongly associated with the Oxford editors, of choosing as copytext the text most closely associated with the theatre (e.g., F1 *Hamlet*, supposed to derive from a promptbook, rather than Q2) still presupposes an authorial manuscript in the form of the promptbook (p. 132). David Scott Kastan points out that recent study of extant promptbooks shows that they contain none of the characteristics attributed to them by editorial speculation (Kastan 1999: 65). To some extent the Oxford Shakespeare enterprise, by its definition of the text as constitutive only of a particular theatrical moment, and in its acceptance of nonauthorial elements (e.g., "*Macbeth* adapted by Thomas Middleton") led the way towards a text- rather than an author-centered editorial focus, and Stanley Wells has certainly expressed a preference for single editions of discrete texts (Wells 1991). "Revision theory" nonetheless remains firmly attached to the authority of the author (see Mowatt 1998: 138; Holderness, Loughrey, and Murphy 1995: 98–100).

Mowatt goes on to demonstrate that this traditional view of the relation between printed text and manuscript is underpinned by a number of fallacies. One is that some texts carry a visible signature of authority marking them as more authentic (i.e., closer to the manuscript) than others, whereas in fact the early modern *Hamlet* text was in the seventeenth century "as problematic as it is today":

> It existed, as it does today, in three printed forms that relate to each other in strange and interesting ways. Each claims to be an authentic text, but none carries any guarantee of authenticity, even though manuscripts of the play were available at the time. (Mowatt 1998: 134)

The other "equally large fallacy" is the belief that manuscript copies, if they existed or were discovered, would solve the problem of stabilizing the texts. Evidence from early modern manuscripts, even holographs written by authors like Middleton or Donne, actually suggests the opposite: that manuscripts were if anything even more unstable, iterable, in continuous alteration, less trustworthy, than printed texts.

> Instead of considering the possibility that each version may represent a printing of one of the many manuscript copies of a play circulating in the early 1620s, editors continue to try to link each version to a particular holograph. I would argue that it is this clinging to illusions about "prompt-books" and "authorial manuscripts" that blinds us to the possibility that there may have been a large flow of manuscript copies of Shakespeare's plays, copies marked by the idiosyncrasies of manuscript transmission, idiosyncrasies that would inevitably have made their way into the printed copies. (Mowatt 1998: 136)

III

> It had bene a thing, we confesse, worthie to haue bene wished, that the Author him-
> selfe had liu'd to haue set forth, and ouerseen his owne writings. (Heminge and
> Condelle 1998: 7)

As the influence of "New Bibliography," at least at the level of textual theory, has
weakened, another important strand of textual scholarship has come into corresponding prominence. The methodology that has come to be known as "the history
of the book" derived initially from *historia litteraria*, the academic study of book-
history, but has been strongly influenced by the French *annales* school of historical
writing, particularly in *L'Apparition du livre* (1958) by Lucien Febvre and Henri-Jean
Martin, which came into English in 1976 as *The Coming of the Book: The Impact of
Printing 1450–1800*. From this work comes the idea of *le rapport livre-societe*, the interrelationship between printed works and the society in which they are produced and
circulated. The significant impact of this school of thought on modern critical studies
can be recognized in the currency of Jerome McGann's influential study *The Textual
Condition* (1991), which displaces the locus of "authority" from the author to society:

> Authority is a social nexus, not a personal possession: and if the authority for specific
> literary works is initiated anew for each work by some specific artists, its initiation takes
> place in a necessary and integral historical environment of great complexity. (McGann
> 1991: 21)

Reversing the traditional view of the author as both producer and guarantor (autho-
rizer) of meanings that are then disseminated by secondary processes of distribution
and exchange, McGann argues that the "social nexus" which collaboratively generates
and produces meaning is the real "author" of the literary text. Clearly this approach
to scholarship is consistent with some significant currents of modern literary theory,
for example the idea formulated by Barthes as "the death of the author," that "to give
a text an Author is to impose a limit on that text, to furnish it with a final signified,
to close the writing" (Barthes 1984: 147). Foucault took this further by arguing that
the concept of the author itself is a strategy of containment, whereby meaning is
limited, divided, and constrained:

> The author does not precede the works; he is a certain functional principle by which,
> in our culture, one limits, excludes and chooses; in short, by which one impedes the free
> circulation, the free manipulation, the free composition, decomposition and recomposi-
> tion of fiction. (Foucault 1984: 119)

While traditional bibliography has pinned textual studies firmly to the traditional
concept of authorship, the "history of the book" has in this way managed to
bring textual theory much closer to modern theoretical criticism. It is increasingly

acknowledged that the Shakespearean drama is best understood as a collaborative cultural activity within which the author played a significant but by no means an isolated part:

> The author certainly is not dead, but every act of writing is now understood to be inevitably compromised and fettered rather than some free and autonomous imaginative activity. An author writes always and only within available conditions of possibility, both imaginative and institutional, and the text is realizable through (and inevitably altered by) the labors of other agents. Increasingly, textual criticism, if not editing itself, has attempted to uncover the full network of agents involved in the production of the text, restoring the literary work to the collaborative economies necessary for its realization and recognizing in the evidence of these collaborations not the causes of the text's deterioration but the enabling circumstances of its actualization, whether on stage or in the printing house. (Kastan 1999: 67)

Barbara Mowatt (1998) aligns the "radical destabilizing of the received Shakespeare text" (p. 138) with directions taken by contemporary criticism:

> Today, many Shakespeareans . . . see the plays as free from the process of filiation and (again to cite Barthes) read them "without the father's signature." They see them as subject not to interpretation but to explosion, dissemination: as woven from a "stenographic plurality of signifiers" of cultural languages. A similar shift in perception, a similar freeing of the text, occurs when critics place Shakespeare's plays among other documents of the period – literary, historical, cultural – viewing them, in Barthes' language, as networks rather than organisms. Immediately the play is heard as separate, distinct voices, each voice making its claim, each fighting for its cultural and gendered place, instead of all being absorbed into the larger single voice that was for so long heard as Shakespeare's own. (Mowatt 1998: 137–8, quoting Barthes 1979)

Hugh Grady has drawn a similar analogy between what he sees as the Oxford Shakespeare's revival of late nineteenth-century textual "disintegration" (the attempt to distinguish Shakespearean from non-Shakespearean elements in the texts) and the "differentiation" of modern cultural studies (Grady 1991); and Jonathan Goldberg notes the same convergence: "post-structuralism and the new textual criticism coincide, historically – and theoretically. Both have called the criterion of authorial intention into question, thereby detaching the sovereign author from texts open to and constituted by a variety of intentions" (Goldberg 1986: 213). It is no coincidence that the gradual consolidation of this position in mainstream criticism has taken place in the context of discussion around the variant Shakespeare texts. Once the massively influential New Bibliographical strategy of editing to emulate Shakespeare's manuscript is exposed for what it is, the traditional Shakespeare "text" again "decomposes" into its constituent components, the original printed editions. At the level of frontline literary commerce this position has become accepted, as we have seen, to the degree symptomatized by the current availability of individual variant texts, by the fact that we now have not *Lear*, *Hamlet*, *Othello*, but *King(s) Lear*, *Prince(s) Hamlet*, and *(Moore) Othello*.

The plurality of accessible modern editions indicates a now much more firmly established understanding that the Quarto and Folio texts of *Hamlet*, *King Lear*, and *Othello* provide valuable primary evidence about how these plays were produced, both as printed works and as texts-for-performance, in the collaborative economy of the Elizabethan and Jacobean theatres. The world of bibliographical and editorial scholarship is gradually coming round to accepting that the various early printed texts of Shakespeare's plays – the so-called "Good" and "Bad" Quartos, and the Folio texts – should be considered as discrete and valid textualizations of artifacts that were never completed or finally stabilized, but continued to change and develop through a process of cultural production. It would not be an exaggeration to say that scholarly opinion has, over the last ten years, gravitated towards the view that every early modern printed text is a snapshot provisionally and temporarily fixing a particular stage in this process.

> We need . . . to rethink Shakespeare in relation to our own new knowledge of collaborative writing, collaborative printing and the historical contingencies of textual production . . . if there is any single object between us and such a project, it is the sense that the value of Shakespeare lies elsewhere, in the inner regions of the text rather than in the practices recorded on its surface . . . the Shakespearean text is thus, like any renaissance book, a provisional state in the circulation of matter. (de Grazia and Stallybrass 1993: 278–9)

This constitutes a huge change in the way that texts are regarded, and as indicated the repercussions of the debate have had large implications for the publishing of Shakespeare texts.

IV

> Originall Copies.
> (Heminge and Condelle 1998: frontispiece)

What then are the main features of this "radically destabilized," thoroughly historicized, theoretically oriented Shakespeare text of the twenty-first century? In order to appreciate the texts as historic cultural productions, one naturally needs first of all to see the variant early printings published, as they are now beginning to be published, as discrete and to some degree independent texts. Once they are present in the debate (and even if the two texts of *Lear* are treated, as they are in "revision theory," as both equally by Shakespeare, and therefore as both belonging to Tanselle's "work"), the results of textual differentiation cannot help but draw attention to the specific historical circumstances of their initial cultural production, and to the fact that many more influences than the controlling direction of an authorial "hand" were involved. In addition, if the plays are to be regarded as the collaborative products of a writing and theatre industry, one needs to see the plays in their historical context, fore-grounded (as they were in the early printings) in front of the author, even to be received "without the father's signature." A play such as *The Taming of A Shrew*, which has never been accepted into the Shakespeare canon, is as valid and interesting a textualization as *The Taming of the Shrew*, the text that appears in the First Folio (see Holderness and Loughrey 1992b). "If the study and presentation of the text are designed to reveal the historically determined and meaningful collaboration of autho-rial and non-authorial intentions, there are no longer grounds on which one version of a text might be thought superior to another" (Kastan 1999: 67).

But more is involved in returning these texts to history and opening them to the illuminations of modern theoretical criticism than restoring their original independence. Where these variant texts are published in modernized form, or even in the partially modernized form of "diplomatic reprint," much of their historical character is necessarily effaced. Modernization in traditional editing entails far more than simply transcribing old spelling into modern orthography. Features of the old texts such as the frequent absence of act and scene divisions; the actual speech-headings used; aspects of grammar, punctuation, and lineation, are all sys-tematically expunged from them in a way that serves to "idealize the activity of authorship, actively seeking to remove it from the conditions of its production" (ibid: 63).

All these characteristics are of course visible if the text is reproduced in photo-graphic facsimile, and a number of influential scholars and critics have argued that it is in this form that the text lends itself most readily to both historical and theoreti-cal interpretation. In the early modern printed text or facsimile reproduction

> ... the features that modernization and emendation smooth away remain stubbornly in place to block the illusion of transparency – the impression that there is some ideal original behind the text ... old type-faces and spellings, irregular line and scene divisions, title pages and other paratextual matters, and textual cruces. Discarded or transformed beyond recognition in standard modern editions, they remain obstinately on the pages of the early texts, insisting upon being looked at, not seen through. Their refusal to yield to modern norms bears witness to the specific history of the texts they make up. (de Grazia and Stallybrass 1993: 257)

This view inevitably points to the facsimile as that form of the text that preserves these examples of linguistic and typographical strangeness, those aspects of the early modern texts that insist on their historical difference. At the same time the facsim-ile makes these historical features available to criticism in ways that the standard modern edition occludes. Renaissance books operated, to use Randall McLeod's term, by a different set of codes from their edited successor texts, and the modern reader needs to interpret such texts on their own terms, by reading and interpreting their own peculiar codes (McLeod 1990: 76). This view is summarized by David Scott Kastan as one in which "the unedited text, even in its manifest error, is the only and fully reliable witness to the complex process of the text's production and to the necessary resistance . . . of its materiality" (Kastan 1999: 67).

V

"the Author being dead, I thought good to take that piece of worke vpon mee" (Thomas Walkley 1622: A2)

So far though these critical and theoretical developments have not had the kind of impact one might have expected on the standard editions themselves. No doubt this is partly to do with the scale of the publishing enterprises involved, which are embedded in relatively massive institutional formations; and partly with the magnitude and longevity of the scholarly labor entailed in editing a play like *Hamlet* or *King Lear*. But there is also in current thinking on these matters a curious circular return to the modernized standard edition. I have quoted a number of influential voices espousing new currents of textual theory. Yet each of them ultimately comes round to an interesting reconciliation with certain key features of the standard modern edition:

If, as we have argued, there is no "original," the later editions cannot be accused of a falling off and away, for there is no fixed point from which such a falling could be measured . . . There is no intrinsic reason not to have a modernized, translated, rewritten "Shakespeare." In an important sense, that is all we can have, because the material signs of early modern quartos and folios will themselves necessarily mean differently when read within new systems of textual production. (de Grazia and Stallybrass 1993: 279)

In truth most of us will for the foreseeable future continue to read Shakespeare's plays and teach them in edited versions, in book form rather than off a computer screen, with spelling and punctuation modernized . . . If we must admit that in actuality there is no fully acceptable way to edit Shakespeare, at least no way to edit without losses that, depending upon one's interests and needs, will at times vitiate the advantages of the text's accessibility in whatever form it is presented, we must also admit that reading an edited text is a remarkably convenient way to engage the play . . . in reality there is no other way to engage the play, for from its very first appearance as printed text it has been edited, mediated by agents other than the author, and intended for the convenience of its readers. (Kastan 1999: 69)

David Scott Kastan is of course a general editor of the Arden Shakespeare. Barbara Mowatt is a general editor of the Folger Shakespeare, and in the essay already extensively quoted goes on to discuss matters of editorial policy:

Once one abandons the notion of the authorial manuscript behind the early printing, one is again and again left with the choice of reproducing, on the one hand, an early printing, with all its faults, and, on the other hand, the editorially, culturally constructed play . . .

What does one do, for example, about the name of Hamlet's mother? . . . Most editors . . . use Q2 as the text on which to base their editions. Yet each edition names Hamlet's mother not as she was named in Q2, but as she was named in the Folio . . . They do so, I suspect, for the same reason that Paul Werstine and I do in the New Folger Hamlet: namely, because it is as Gertrude that she exists and has existed for nearly three hundred years . . . we allow the "Shakespeare" that is culturally constructed to outweigh the Shakespeare that may be reflected in Q2 Hamlet, and name her "Gertrude." (Mowatt 1998: 142)

This example may be a relatively trivial point, but the editorial strategy described indicates a reconciliation with the principles of conflation, the role of the editor being always to make pragmatic choices between alternative readings, rather than to respect consistently the historical integrity of a particular text. In an interesting, though unexamined, semantic shift the quality of "integrity" is displaced from a characterization of the text to a moral responsibility of the editor (ibid: 143).

The arguments that underlie this return to the standard conflated edition are important ones. The early printed texts are "original" historical documents, with dates on them, that can be located in a particular context of cultural production and exchange. But does that mean that they are more authentic records of the meanings generated in the seventeenth century by their publication and performance, and therefore more reliable guarantors of meaning for a historical criticism, than subsequent redactions, revisions, editorial reconstructions?

A number of scholars have correctly observed that even the facsimile gives only partial access to the nature of these texts as they were produced and reproduced in early modern culture. A facsimile edition usually has to choose one from among a range of copies of a particular text that differ from one another as a consequence of the practice of "continuous correction" in the printing house. A single edition cannot show this diversity of copies, although of course variants can be marginally recorded in editorial collation.

Facsimile, for all its obvious ability to reproduce many of the significant visual characteristics of the original texts, performs, in both printed and electronic modes, its own act of idealization. It reifies the particulars of a single copy of the text, producing multiple copies of a textual form that would have been unique. (Kastan 1999: 68)

It is impossible to effect a return to an "original" text, as any reproduction of a text is in some way a mediation (Hawkes 1986: 75). Neither modern printing and publication practices, nor modern methods of decoding a text, can emulate or even imitate early modern book production and reading.

Jonathan Goldberg rightly argues that these texts were already editions, copies not originals (Goldberg 1986: 213):

There never has been, and never can be, an unedited Shakespeare text. Textual criticism and post-structuralism agree therefore: we have no originals, only copies. The historicity of the text means that there is no text itself; it means that the text cannot be fixed in terms of original or final intentions.

Or as Stephen Orgel succinctly puts the same point:

The history of realizations of the text . . . is the history of the text. (Orgel 1988: 14)

Here "realization" can refer to any number of cultural events that participated in the history of a particular Shakespeare text. The 1608 Quarto of *Lear* was one such realization, in printing and publication. So was the Folio text, explicitly of course an edition, with named editors who claimed privileged access to the original manuscripts ("True Originall Copies"). But there were obviously other "realizations" that have not left any comparable traces. There were theatrical performances that can be assumed to have differed from one another in ways that the two texts differ – e.g., Globe performances may have used something like the Folio text, while the recusant players who acted *King Lear* at Gowthwaite Hall in Yorkshire in 1610 used the published Quarto – and probably in other ways as well. Once the texts were in circulation there were possibly acts of individual reading and interpretation that also "realized" the text in individual and incommensurable acts of cultural production. Since the story of King Lear circulated in a number of different versions, in prose and poetry as well as theatrical rendition, the Shakespearean texts and performances were obviously "realizing" something (the "King Lear" myth?) that was being differentially and discrepantly realized within the culture as a whole (see Holderness 1995: 30–5).

In this post-bibliographic textual condition we have no basis for regarding, say, Q1 *Hamlet* as a better or worse, a more or less authentic, text than Q2 or F (and by the same token no basis for regarding F, as Wells and Taylor do, as more authentically theatrical than Q1), since we cannot relate any of them directly to that controlling authority, "the author." Each version is an equally complex, overdetermined cultural product of the collaborative early modern theatre industry. Each may record the active participation of dramatist, actors, theatrical entrepreneurs, prompters, booksellers, compositors in the generation of theatrical and literary significance. Each reflects both authorial and nonauthorial contributions in a synthesis impossible (even, since Homer nodded and Shakespeare couldn't spell, at the basic level of manifest error) to disentangle.

But exactly the same may be said of other "realizations" normally thought of as falling outside the originating moment of cultural production: for example Restoration and eighteenth-century adaptations and rewritings of Shakespeare's plays. Once this direction is pursued, it becomes difficult to object to modern editions of the texts, from the eighteenth-century editors onwards, as not equally representative of historic "realizations" of the text. For if Q1, Q2, and F are no longer in the traditional sense "Shakespeare's," but (to use an equally convenient though less misleading shorthand),

Trundell's, and Roberts's, and Heminge and Condelle's, then in what ways are they different, other than chronologically, from Rowe's, and Pope's, and Warburton's; or even from Dryden's and Nahum Tate's?

> Shakespeare's *King Lear* and Shakespeare's *Hamlet*, as their covers proclaim, turn out to be something less than truth in advertising. They are more properly Alfred Harbage's *King Lear* or Kenneth Muir's, Harold Jenkins's *Hamlet* or Maynard Mack's . . . (Kastan 1999: 61)

Provided that these attributions are properly understood to reflect a quasi-authorial, editorial input into a textualization that is just as historically specific, critically debatable, and theoretically questionable as the early modern published texts, then they become in principle no less valid and valuable "realizations." It's only the dates that differ.

VI

> You've only got one Macbeth.
> (Stoppard 1980: 56)

The variant texts of Shakespeare's tragedies are, then, here to stay. A substantial body of editorial, scholarly, critical, and theatrical commentary has already developed around them, and this will no doubt continue to grow. Isolated among the great tragedies, "in lone splendour hung aloft the night," stands *The Tragedy of Macbeth*, the only one of the four to lack any printed-text evidence prior to the First Folio. Once it is accepted that early Quarto versions like those of *Hamlet* and *King Lear* are not secondary sources, garbled, bastardized, or pirated versions of otherwise potentially recoverable complete and authentic texts, but rather valid and valuable contemporary versions of the plays, a tragedy without at least a Bad Quarto to back it up seems to be at something of a disadvantage.

Furthermore the Folio version of *Macbeth* itself bears some of the characteristics often associated with "Bad Quarto" texts. It is short. Many editors have regarded the Folio text as an abridgement of an earlier, fuller version (see, for example, the Arden and Signet editions). Dover Wilson (1947) thought it was reproduced from a transcript of the author's manuscript which had been largely written down to dictation; and F. G. Fleay speculated that the original manuscript having perished in the Globe fire of 1613, the play must have been reconstructed from memory by the actors (Fleay 1884: 128–44). These fantasies are both interesting variations on the "memorial reconstruction" theory (see also Amneus 1961: 435–40; 1964: 185–90).

Macbeth contains abundant evidence of multiple authorship. Wells and Taylor published the play in the Oxford Shakespeare as "adapted by Thomas Middleton," and many scholars have attempted to identify Middleton's contribution (frequently nominating for example the "Bleeding Captain" scene, 1.2). The Folio *Macbeth* certainly contains cue-lines for songs that were printed in full in later editions and adaptations such as the 1673 Quarto text of Shakespeare's *Macbeth*, and the 1674 adaptation by William Davenant, and that are also to be found in Middleton's play *The Witch* (see Shakespeare 1969, and Davenant 1969).

Macbeth is full of linguistic obscurity and textual cruces. It is characterized by an overt, crowd-pleasing, "mob-accordant" theatricality, visible especially in the witches' song-and-dance routines. It displays confused stage directions (e.g., Macbeth is apparently killed onstage, but his head is produced from off). All these idiosyncrasies have obliged scholars to speculate intensively about the possible alternative versions of *Macbeth* that clearly circulated in Jacobean culture.

It has been argued that the topics of rebellion and regicide were matters too dangerous to present to James, and an earlier composition in the closing years of Elizabeth's reign accordingly proposed, e.g., by Dover Wilson in his 1947 Cambridge edition. Most modern scholarship relates the play via circumstantial evidence (Scottish history, witches, touching for the King's Evil, and equivocation) to the early years of James I's accession, and specifically to the Gunpowder Plot (though, interestingly, A. R. Braunmuller has recently called all these allusions "vague, circumstantial or undatable") (Braunmuller 1997: 6).

It has been proposed that distinct versions of *Macbeth*, any of which might have been captured by a particular printed edition, existed in 1604–5 (played at the Globe as a topical drama); 1606, when it may have been performed before James and King Christian of Denmark at Hampton Court; 1611, when it was witnessed at the Globe by Simon Forman, who left a detailed account of the production (discussed below); and 1623, in the form of the text (which may have been the script used for the 1606 court performance) integrated into the First Folio. Thereafter of course the play continued to change. The Padua promptbook, a marked-up performance copy of the First Folio text, which G. Blakemore Evans dates to around 1625–35, may therefore reflect in its cuts and amendments pre-Restoration stage practice (Blakemore Evans 1960). After the Restoration Sir William Davenant's adaptation (published 1674) seems to have triggered the publication of the 1673 Quarto text of *Macbeth*, which prints in full the Middleton songs only cued in the Folio (Spencer 1961: 16). In one sense *Macbeth* had to wait until this latter moment to acquire its own belated "Bad Quarto."

VII

There is just room for a bolder conjectural criticism of this play than perhaps in any other. (Hunter 1870, II: 152)

Such abundance of evidence about the play's iterability makes the absence of early printed witnesses particularly frustrating. But if we ask the simple question "what did Jacobean audiences actually see at the Globe around 1610 when they went to see a play called *Macbeth*?", a set of answers lies very readily to hand in the form of the substantial and detailed description by doctor and astrologist Simon Forman of the production he saw on April 20, 1610 or 1611.[2]

> In Mackbeth at the glod 1610 the 20 of Aprill [Saturday] ther was to be observed firste howe Mackbeth and Bancko, 2 noble men of Scotland Ridinge thorowe a wod the stode befor them 3 women feiries or Numphes And saluted Mackbeth sayinge of. 3 tyms unto him haille Mackbeth king of Codon for thou shalt be a kinge but shalt beget No kinges &c and then said Bancko What all to macbeth And nothing to me. yes said the nimphes Haille to thee Banko thou shalt beget kinges yet be no kinge And so they departed & cam to the Courte of Scotland to Dunkin king of Scotes and yt was in the dais of Edward the Confessor. And Dunkin bad them both kindly wellcom. And made Mackbeth forth with the Prince of Northumberland. and sent him hom to his own castell and appointed mackbeth to provid for him for he wold Sup with him the next dai at night & did soe. And mackebeth Contrived to kill Dumkin. & and thorowe the persuasion of his wife did that night Murder the kinge in his owne Castell beinge his guest. And ther were many prodigies seen that night & the dai before. And when Mack Beth had murdred the kinge the blod on his hands could not be vashed of by Any means. nor from his wives handes which handled the bloddi daggers in hiding them By which means they became both moch amazed & Affronted. the murder being knowen Dunkins 2 sonns fled the on to England the [other to] Walles to save them selves. they being fled, they were supposed guilty of the murder of their father which was nothinge soe. Then was Mackbeth Crowned kinge and then he for feare of Banko his old Companion that hre should beget kinges but be no kinge him selfe he contrived the death of Banko and caused him to be murdred on his way as he Rode. The next night beinge at supper with his noble men whom he had bid to a feaste to the which also Banco should have com, he began to speake of Noble Banco and wish the he were ther. And as he thus did standing up to derincke a Carouse to him. the ghoste of banco came and sate down in his cheier behind him. And he turninge About to sit down Again sawe the goste of Banco which fronted him so. that he fell into a great passion of fear & fury. utteringe many wordes about his murder by which when they hard that Banco was Murdred they Suspected Mackbet. Then mack dove fled to England to the kinges sonn And soe they Raised an Army And cam into scotland. And at dunstone Anyse overthrue mackbet. In the meantym whille macdovee Was in England mackbet slew mackdoves wife &children. and after in the battelle mackdove slew mackbet.
>
>   Observe Also howe mackbetes quen did Rise in the night in her slep & walke and talked and confessed all & the doctor noted her wordes. (Quoted from Schoenbaum 1969: 7–8)

Of course there is no doubt that this is substantially the play recorded in the 1623 Folio text. But there are interesting discrepancies in Forman's account. Why for instance did he recall seeing Macbeth and Banquo riding through a wood, a sylvan and equestrian effect we would not expect to have been presented on the Globe stage? Why did he record that this happened " firste," since the play's first scene in the Folio text involves the witches alone, and is followed by the scene of the reported battle? Why, given the play's imputed "topicality," did he think the witches were "feiries or Numphes" rather than just witches? At times Forman seems to be recording the play's dialogue with some exactness (e.g., "The next night beinge at supper with his noble men whom he had bid to a feaste to the which also Banco should have com, he began to speake of Noble Banco and wish the he were ther"); yet at other times his recollections vary (e.g., in the witches' addresses to both Macbeth and Banquo) from the wording of the Folio. The notes on hand-washing have been taken to indicate that both Macbeth and Lady Macbeth attempted to cleanse their hands as a piece of stage business, which though intelligible as an account of the Folio's narrative, seems in describing specific action much more literal in its implications than the largely metaphorical language of the text.

Forman's description may also be said to be as interesting for what it omits as for what it contains. His "feiries or Numphes" don't seem to dance or sing, and are not accompanied by Hecate; in fact there is no mention of Macbeth's second meeting with the Witches (the so-called "Cavern Scene," 4.1) at all. The drunken Porter, bearer of the most topical of *Macbeth*'s contemporary allusions, doesn't appear in his account (2.3). The terse phrase "contrived the death of Banko" skips quickly over that part of 3.1 in which Macbeth converses with the murderers; and there also seems to be no equivalent of 4.3, in which Malcolm and Macduff discuss the fate of Scotland.

The most obvious explanation for these discrepancies is to question the accuracy of Forman's description. Some of his visual and verbal recollections seem closer to Holinshed's version of this story than to Shakespeare's, so Forman might have consulted Holinshed before or after attending the theatre and so "contaminated" his recollections. Some of his notes must be simply incorrect: "King of Codon" sounds highly improbable, and it makes no sense for Macbeth to be made Prince of Northumberland. It has been argued that Forman recorded a very partial account since his interest in plays was not primarily aesthetic, and he recorded only what he found illuminating or useful. He may have omitted details that did not interest him. Or he may have arrived late, missed acts 1.1 and 1.2, and gone for a piss during 4.1.

However, what remains unavoidable here is the primary evidence of Forman's record, as that of a man who went to the Globe theatre on Saturday April 20, 1611 to see a production of *Macbeth*, and may even have made some of his notes at the scene (note how he notes the presence on stage of another doctor taking notes of Lady Macbeth's sleepwalking indiscretions: "& the doctor noted her wordes"). Whatever the genesis of his recollections, there can be no disputing that Forman has left for us the documentation of a particular "realization" of the text of *Macbeth*. It is at the very least a record of his experience, his "response" to the play he saw, the "realization" of Macbeth in an eyewitness's perception and memory.

Beyond that, we might conjecture that Forman's account tells us with some degree of accuracy what was actually presented on stage. We may then have access here to a stage version that may in turn adumbrate a textual version of *Macbeth* as it existed, in an unpublished script, in 1611. As such the document is both valid and valuable, standing as it does by proxy for the missing Quarto text that might have given us a variant Macbeth. The bulk of Forman's account agrees with the Folio text, and the divergences could reflect genuine textual differences between the *Macbeth* of 1611 and that printed in 1623. The text of this performance might have represented the earliest version of the play. It might even, if we follow F. G. Fleay's fanciful theory, have been destroyed in the Globe fire of 1613.

One particularly striking feature is the congruence between Forman's omissions and the Padua promptbook. Scholars frequently note how short *Macbeth* is in comparison with the other great tragedies; and yet the Padua promptbook shows us that it was still extensively cut in performance, especially around the Porter scene (2.3), the first interview with the murderers (3.1), the choric commentary of 3.4, and the long Macduff–Malcolm interview of 4.3. The cuts may reflect conventional stage practice, or might even adumbrate a text of *Macbeth* that had never contained these dramatic materials. Such a text could have produced something very like what Forman saw, prior to being padded out, perhaps by Shakespeare himself, possibly by Middleton or another dramatist, maybe for the 1606 court performance, certainly some time before 1623.

Another intriguing parallel is with the summary "Argument" prefaced to the publication of Davenant's adaptation, which seems to have little to do with what follows, yet strikingly concurs with Forman's abstract.

> Duncan, King of the Scots, had two principal men, whom he imployed in all matters of importance, Macbeth and Banquo, those two trauelling together through a Forrest, were met by three Fairy Witches (Weirds the Scots call them) whereof the first making obeysance unto Macbeth saluted him, Thane (a Title unto which that of Earl afterwards succeeded) of Glammis, the second Thane of Cawdor, and the third King of Scotland: This is unequal dealing, saith Banquo, to give my Friend all the Honours, and none unto me: To which one of the Weirds made answer, That he indeed should not be a King, but out of his Loins should come a Race of Kings that should for ever rule the Scots. (Davenant 1969: The Argument)

Forman's manuscript could not have been available to the writer of this preface (Nosworthy 1948: 109). The shared links with Holinshed may point to a common source, and the "Argument" could of course be not so much a summary of the play as a summary of the historical narrative on which it is based. But the possibility remains that both Forman and the author of the 1674 "Argument" might have been reflecting theatrical traditions in the production of *Macbeth* prior to the closure of the theatres. Even Davenant's much-maligned adaptation, Macbeth's belated "Bad Quarto," may have much in common with the text of *Macbeth* as it stood, in one of its many realizations, in 1611.

VIII

What is an author? An editor.
What is an editor? An author.
(Taylor 1995: 240)

We are now in a position where multiple texts of *Hamlet*, *King Lear*, and *Othello* are in general circulation, and their availability is generating both critical debate and theatrical realization. Study of these texts and their interrelationships has helped prompt critics and editors towards the recognition that every text, every edition, is a new rewriting of Shakespeare. This is of course a commonplace of poststructuralist criticism – "Our Shakespeare is our invention: to read him is to write him" (Hawkes 1986: 124) – but a new realization in the world of bibliography.

The presence of variant texts is not of course a *sine qua non* of such reconstructive criticism. Terry Hawkes bases a poststructuralist critique of *Hamlet* on the editorial effacement of Hamlet's last sounds in the Folio text – "O, o, o, o" (Hawkes 1986: 73–91). But Hawkes did not need to invoke textual variance in order to practice a form of criticism that is also a rewriting of Shakespeare. Similarly, the absence of multiple texts for *Macbeth* has never prevented huge divergences in critical reading, theatrical interpretation, and film realization. On the other hand the new focus on alternative texts lends a particular point to speculations which used to be ridiculed – "How many children had Lady Macbeth?" – about the missing texts of *Macbeth*.

My own conviction is that this changed critical and scholarly environment has freed us to attempt new kinds of work on Shakespeare. If every critical reading is a rewriting, and every editorial attempt to establish a text is equally a reconstruction, then are we not free to write our own Shakespeares, using the historical documents left to us as raw materials? While this practice has always been widespread, from the Restoration adaptations to the experiments of modern dramatists such as Stoppard and Berkoff, both New Criticism and New Bibliography have conspired to marginalize them as fringe activities. Are we not however now faced with a realization that the "mainstream" activities of critical interpretation and editorial reconstruction are different only in degree, not in kind, from formal adaptation?[3]

Such activities are commonplace in secondary schools, where Shakespearean text is used very much as raw material for a wide range of quasi-creative learning activities, and where teachers are more likely to engage student interest in *Romeo and Juliet* and *Twelfth Night* via the film *Shakespeare in Love* than through critical interpretation of the text. Is it not now time to develop the creative rewriting of Shakespeare at more advanced levels? Coleridge said of Shakespeare:

You feel him to be an poet inasmuch as for a time he has made you one – an active, creative being. (Quoted in Hawkes 1986: 90)

The time for developing "active, creative" approaches to Shakespeare has never been so near at hand (see, for an example, Holderness 2001).

NOTES

1 Recently, editions have been produced that formally differentiate between source texts, for example by the use of brackets. In the new Arden edition of *King Lear*, edited by R. A. Foakes, the signs of the textual revolution are indelibly inscribed, with every section marked in superscript as originating from Quarto or Folio text.

2 The original of Forman's manuscript is in the Bodleian Library, Oxford, MS Ashmole 208. Transcript quoted from Schoenbaum (1969: 7–8). April 20, 1610 was not a Saturday, but April 20, 1611 was; so scholars have assumed Forman made a common mistake in getting the new year wrong.

3 For a reconstruction of the text of *Macbeth* 1611, see my *Textual Shakespeare: writing and the word* (Hatfield: University of Hertfordshire Press, 2003).

REFERENCES AND FURTHER READING

Amneus, D. A. (1961). A Missing Scene in *Macbeth*. *Journal of English and Germanic Philology*, 60, 435–40.

——(1964). The Cawdor Episode in *Macbeth*. *Journal of English and Germanic Philology*, 63, 185–90.

Barthes, R. (1977). The Death of the Author. In S. Heath (trans.) *Image Music Text*. London: Fontana, 142–8.

——(1979). From Work to Text, trans. J. V. Harari. In J. V. Harari (ed.) *Textual Strategies: Perspectives in Poststructuralist Criticism*. Ithaca, NY: Cornell University Press, 73–81.

——(1984). The Death of the Author. In S. Heath (trans.) *Image Music Text*. London: Flamingo.

Blakemore Evans, G. (1960). *Shakespearean Prompt-books of the Seventeenth Century*, vol. 1, part 2, Text of the Padua *Macbeth*. Charlottesville: Bibliographical Society of the University of Virginia.

Bowers, F. (1966). Textual Criticism. In O. J. Campbell and E. G. Quinn (eds.) *A Shakespeare Encyclopaedia*. London: Methuen, 864–9.

Braunmuller, A. R. (1997). *Macbeth*. New Cambridge Shakespeare. Cambridge: Cambridge University Press.

Davenant, Sir William (1969). *Macbeth (1674)*. Cornmarket Shakespeare Series. London: Cornmarket Press.

de Grazia, M. and Stallybrass, P. (1993). The Materiality of the Shakespearean Text. *Shakespeare Quarterly*, 44, 255–83.

De Somogyi, N. (2000). *The Shakespeare Folios: Hamlet*. London: Nick Hern Books.

Dover Wilson, J. (1947). *Macbeth*. Cambridge: Cambridge University Press.

Febvre, L. and Martin, H.-J. (1990) [1976]. *The Coming of the Book: The Impact of Printing 1450–1800*, trans. D. Gerard. London: Verso.

Fleay, F. G. (1884). Davenant's Macbeth and Shakespeare's Witches. *Anglia*, 7, 128–44.

Foucault, M. (1984). What is an Author? In P. Rabinow (ed.) *The Foucault Reader*. New York: Pantheon, 115–20.

Freeman, N. (ed.) (1998). *Applause First Folio: Hamlet*. Vancouver: Folio Scripts.

Goldberg, J. (1986). Textual Properties. *Shakespeare Quarterly*, 37, 2, 213–17.

Grady, H. (1991). Disintegration and its Reverberations. In J. I. Marsden (ed.), *The Appropriation of Shakespeare: Post-Renaissance Reconstructions of the Works and the Myth*. Hemel Hempstead: Harvester Wheatsheaf, 111–27.

Greg, W. W. (1967). *The Editorial Problem in Shakespeare: A Survey of the Foundations of the Text.* Oxford: Oxford University Press.

Halio, J. L. (ed.) (1992). *The Tragedy of King Lear.* Cambridge: Cambridge University Press.

——(ed.) (1994). *The First Quarto of King Lear.* Cambridge: Cambridge University Press.

Hawkes, T. (1986). *That Shakespeherian Rag.* London: Routledge.

Heminge, J. and Condelle, H. (1998). To the great Variety of Readers. In *Mr William Shakespeares Comedies, Histories and Tragedies: A Facsimile of the First Folio* (1623). London: Routledge.

Hinman, C. (ed.) (1968). *The Norton Facsimile: The First Folio of Shakespeare.* New York: W. W. Norton.

Holderness, G. (ed.) (1995). *M. William Shake-speare HIS true chronicle historie of the life and death of King Lear and his three daughters.* Hemel Hempstead: Harvester Wheatsheaf.

Holderness, G. (2001). *The Prince of Denmark.* Hatfield: University of Hertfordshire Press.

Holderness, G. and Loughrey, B. (eds.) (1992a). *The Tragicall Historie of Hamlet Prince of Denmarke.* Hemel Hempstead: Harvester Wheatsheaf.

——(eds.) (1992b). *The Taming of A Shrew.* Hemel Hempstead: Harvester Wheatsheaf.

Holderness, G., Loughrey, B., and Murphy, A. (1995). "What's the matter?": Shakespeare and Textual Theory. *Textual Practice*, 9, 1, 93–119.

Hunter, J. (1870). *Macbeth.* London: Longman.

Irace, K. O. (ed.) (1998). *The First Quarto of Hamlet.* Cambridge: Cambridge University Press.

Kastan, D. S. (1999). *Shakespeare After Theory.* London: Routledge.

McGann, J. (1991). *The Textual Condition.* Princeton, NJ: Princeton University Press.

McLeod, R. (1990). From Tranceformations in the Text of *Orlando Fvrioso. Library Chronicle of the University of Texas at Austin*, 20, 1/2, 60–85.

Mowatt, B. (1998). The Problem of Shakespeare's Texts. In L. E. Maguire and T. L. Berger (eds.) *Textual Formations and Reformations.* London: Associated University Presses, 131–48.

Murphy, A. (ed.) (1995). *The Tragoedie of Othello, The Moore of Venice.* Hemel Hempstead: Harvester Wheatsheaf.

Nosworthy, J. M. (1948). *Macbeth* at the Globe. *The Library*, 5th series, 2, 108–18.

Orgel, S. (1988). The Authentic Shakespeare. *Representations*, 21, 1–26.

——(1994). Acting Scripts, Performing Texts. In R. McLeod (ed.) *Crisis in Editing: Texts of the English Renaissance.* New York: AMS Press, 252–94.

Rowe, N. (ed.) (1709). *The Works of Mr. William Shakespeare.* London: J. Tonson.

Schoenbaum, S. (1969). *William Shakespeare: Records and Images.* London: Scolar Press.

Shakespeare, W. (1969). *Macbeth (1673).* Cornmarket Shakespeare Series. London: Cornmarket Press.

Spencer, C. (1961). *Davenant's Macbeth from the Yale Manuscript: An Edition, With a Discussion of the Relation of Davenant's Text to Shakespeare's.* New Haven, CT: Yale University Press.

Stoppard, T. (1980). *Dogg's Hamlet, Cahoot's Macbeth.* London: Faber and Faber.

Tanselle, G. T. (1989). *A Rationale of Textual Criticism.* Philadelphia: University of Pennsylvania Press.

Taylor, G. (1995). What is an Author (not)? *Critical Survey*, 7, 3, 241–54.

Walkley, T. (1622). The Stationer to the Reader. In William Shakespeare, *Othello.* London: T. Walkley.

Weis, R. (ed.) (1993). *King Lear: A Parallel-Text Edition.* Harlow: Longman.

Wells, S. (1991). Theatricalizing Shakespeare's Texts. *New Theatre Quarterly*, 26, 184–6.

Wells, S., Taylor, G., Jowett, J., and Montgomery, W. (eds.) (1986a). *William Shakespeare, The Complete Works.* Oxford: Oxford University Press.

——(eds.) (1986b). *William Shakespeare, The Complete Works, Original Spelling Edition.* Oxford: Clarendon Press.

——(1987). *William Shakespeare: A Textual Companion.* Oxford: Oxford University Press.

9

Shakespearean Tragedy and Religious Identity

Richard C. McCoy

When William Shakespeare was born in 1564, his country's religious identity was unsettled and uncertain. About thirty years earlier, Henry VIII had launched a reformation that eventually transformed England, in the words of Patrick Collinson, from one of Europe's "most Catholic countries to one of its least" (Collinson 1988: 75). Nevertheless, as Christopher Haigh explains, this momentous change proceeded slowly and erratically, "by spasmodic fits, uncertain starts, and threats of reversal" (Haigh 1993: 169), since none of the "reformations" undertaken by English rulers was either inevitable or entirely successful. Henry broke with Rome because he needed a divorce, but he remained a staunch theological conservative. Even after he declared himself Supreme Head of the Church he continued to affirm many bedrock Catholic beliefs, making denial of transubstantiation a capital crime, persecuting more zealous reformers, and providing generously in his will for prayers and masses to speed his soul through purgatory. Ironically, the young son he so ardently desired as a successor dismantled these final intercessory arrangements and opened the door to more radical reforms. Shortly after Edward VI succeeded his father in 1547, the Chantries Act put an end to "phantsying opinions of purgatory and masses satisfactory, to be done for them which be departed" (Dickens 1964: 230). A vernacular prayer book was adopted and then revised, eventually eliminating even the name of "what was commonly called the Masse" and abolishing the doctrine of Christ's real presence in the eucharist (ibid: 243). Edward died in 1553, and the changes wrought during his brief reign were reversed by his step-sister, Mary I, known as "Bloody Mary" for her campaign of religious persecution. Her reign was even shorter than Edward's, and her attempt at a counter-reformation was soon thwarted by the accession of Elizabeth I in 1558, who reigned for more than forty years.

All these drastic "alterations of state" made questions of religious identity painfully harrowing for many Tudor subjects (McCoy 2002: ix–x). In a time of *cuius regio, eius religio*, a change of regime demanded a change of religious allegiance, and compliance was sometimes enforced by threats of persecution, torture, and death. Such a death definitively established religious identity, since martyrdom constitutes the ultimate profession of the victim's beliefs and principles: the Greek root of "martyr" means to bear witness. Martyrs on both sides embraced the role of open witness to their inmost convictions. John Foxe immortalized the harrowing ordeals of those persecuted during Mary's reign in his *Acts and Monuments*, better known as the Book of Martyrs, and it became one of the greatest propaganda triumphs of Protestant England. The first of many editions appeared in 1563, the year before Shakespeare's birth, and, by 1570, it could be found in every cathedral church as well as many parishes. One of Mary's most illustrious victims was Hugh Latimer, the Bishop of Worcester. Before he was led to the stake to be burned, he affirmed his faith by proclaiming "there is nothing hid but it shall be opened."[1] Persecution continued under Elizabeth, but the martyrs during her reign were Catholic priests. Edmund Campion was a Jesuit who returned from the Continent on a secret mission to England in 1580. Apprehended the next year, he was tortured on the rack and condemned to death for sedition. On his way to be drawn and quartered, he also accepted his grisly death as the supreme manifestation of his faith by quoting Saint Paul and saying: "We are made a spectacle, or a sight, unto God, unto his angels, and unto men" (Miola 2001: 35). Reformation martyrs were made truly terrifying spectacles. As their sinews burst in the flames and their intestines spilled on the scaffold, their ordeals turned them inside out physically and spiritually.

While undoubtedly moved by such heroics, few of Shakespeare's contemporaries were so ardent or firm in their theological convictions, and religious traditionalism and inertia remained powerful forces. Indeed, many of Elizabeth's subjects remained "habitual Catholics," reluctant to forego old ways of worship and eager to avoid the risks of recusancy (Haigh 1993: 292). Both Catholic and Puritan zealots denounced such characters as weak-willed "church papists," but the Elizabethan church was happy to nurture what its greatest theologian, Richard Hooker, calls "the feeble smoke of conformity" (Walsham 1993: 19). Most probably accepted the common view that "it is safer to doe in religion as most doe" (Duffy 1992: 591). Nevertheless, conformity did not dispel suspicions of those who "can keep their conscience to themselves" (Walsham 1993: 2), and it certainly deepened confusion about questions of religious identity in Shakespeare's time. As Peter Lake explains, England's paradoxical combination of pervasive "*de facto* religious pluralism" and increasingly polarized religious antagonisms "opened up a gap between the inward and the outward, the real inner convictions of a person and his or her outward behavior, a space which, it seemed to many contemporaries, could be exploited for all sorts of dissimulation and pretence by the faithless and the unscrupulous" (Lake 1999: 64). Few of Shakespeare's contemporaries were eager to be "made a spectacle . . . unto God . . . and unto men" and have everything in them revealed.

Queen Elizabeth herself was never keenly interested in probing the gap between inward and outward in order to determine her subjects' religious identity. She began her reign resolved, in the famous words of Francis Bacon, not to "make windows into men's hearts and secret thoughts" (Guy 1988: 296). She imposed a Protestant

religious settlement less radical and more ambiguous than Edward's. Elizabeth suppressed the host's elevation as a form of Catholic idolatry, but her version of The Book
of Common Prayer (1559) omitted the Black Rubric in Edward's 1552 prayer book
denying "any real and essential presence" in the eucharist (Dickens 1964: 243, 280–3).
Such mixed and confusing signals were sometimes part of a deliberate strategy, first
proposed in an anonymous memorandum called the "Device for the Alteration of
Religion" circulated at the beginning of Elizabeth's reign. It warned that many
Marian exiles would be disappointed that "some old ceremonies shall be left still" and
correctly anticipated that many reformers would denounce the Elizabethan settlement
as "a cloaked papistry or a mingle-mangle" (Guy 1988: 259). She was urged to ignore
such criticisms and pursue a cautious and ambiguous compromise, a course she
adhered to for much of her reign. As a result, her religious settlement remained
haunted, in the words of Diarmaid MacCulloch, by the "ghost . . . of an older world
of Catholic authority and devotional practice" (MacCulloch 2001: 6). Moderation and
muddle helped her follow an ecclesiastical *via media*, but religious divisions still intensified. For one thing, Protestant domination of the universities led to greater control
over the clergy and the parishes (Haigh 1993: 270), and "papistical superstitions and
abuses" were gradually suppressed (Duffy 1992: 585). Moreover, the queen's excom-
munication in 1571 and the growing belligerence of Catholic adversaries further
polarized confessional conflicts, and threats of conspiracy, assassination, and invasion
prompted growing paranoia about religious identity. Even so, stricter church discipline still focused on outward conformity rather than internal identity, placing
"emphasis on actions rather than thoughts, public worship rather than private prayer"
(Litzenberger 1998: 152). Elizabeth remained reluctant to "make windows into men's
hearts and secret thoughts."

John Shakespeare, William's father, lived, flourished, and languished through some
of these tumultuous "reformations," and their impact on his religious identity and his
social and financial status is somewhat uncertain. He was presumably baptized in the
old religion and he married during the reign of Mary I. He also prospered for the first
decade of Elizabeth's reign as a successful glover, property-owner, and dealer in farm
products in Stratford-upon-Avon, and he became one of its leading citizens. He served
as an alderman, magistrate, and bailiff or mayor and applied for a coat of arms, a mark
of status and gentility that his son subsequently obtained. His prosperity and social
standing suggests some sort of adjustment to the new Protestant religious settlement.
Members of the town council managed both civic and parish affairs, and John joined
with his fellows in replacing their Catholic curate shortly after Elizabeth's accession
in 1559. By 1561 they found a respectable replacement, John Bretchgirdle, Master
of Arts from Oxford. William was born under this new dispensation and was chris-
tened by Bretchgirdle in 1564. John was also one of those responsible for Protestant
changes to Stratford's chapel, and he helped handle payments "for defacing images in
the chapel," whitewashing frescos, and dismantling the rood screen (Schoenbaum
1977: 54). Eamon Duffy notes that such iconoclasm was "not in most cases the result
of a landslide of Protestant fervour, but of weary obedience to unpopular measures"

(Duffy 1992: 570) enforced by ecclesiastical commissions and visitations, and that may have been the case at Stratford. Certainly some of these changes proceeded at a slower pace. The church did not get rid of its old vestments for more than a decade, and a glazier was not hired until 1571 to replace the chapel's stained glass with clear panes (Schoenbaum 1977: 54). Sacred objects outlawed in Edward's reign had been carefully concealed and retrieved from hiding under Mary, and many parishes remained reluctant to dispose of these venerable (as well as expensive) objects.

However willing or reluctant to get rid of some remnants of the old religion, John Shakespeare evidently remained attached to other traditional beliefs and practices. His will, discovered in 1757 and subsequently lost, conformed to a Counter-Reformation testament composed by Charles Borromeo and distributed by the Jesuits Robert Parsons and Edmund Campion during their secret mission to England in 1580; at some point during his travels, Campion stayed in a house only 12 miles from Stratford (Schoenbaum 1977: 50–1). Copies were distributed to the faithful, and John Shakespeare signed one and hid it in the rafters of his house around 1581 when Campion was martyred. In it, the older Shakespeare asks, among other things, that his friends and family "will vouchsafe to assist and succour me with their holy prayers and satisfactory works, especially with the holy sacrifice of the mass, as being the most effectual means to deliver souls from their torments and pains" in Purgatory (ibid: 47). John Shakespeare prepared his will amidst financial and social misfortunes. He stopped attending council meetings after 1576 for several years and was finally replaced as alderman ten years later. During this same period he incurred significant debts, sold and mortgaged land, and was entangled in expensive lawsuits. In 1592 his prolonged absence from church is recorded and attributed to "fear of process for debt." Some scholars have attributed the older Shakespeare's difficulties to religious persecution during a time of increasing sectarian hostility, concluding that John was a staunch recusant Catholic. Yet procedures against him were not all that rigorous, and he eventually recovered his standing in the community, presumably with the help of his son. A coat of arms was granted in 1596 and he returned to the borough council in 1601, his last year of life. His last will and testament is the strongest evidence of an enduring attachment to Catholicism, but, as Duffy notes, funeral rites and preparations were an area where "feeling remained most conservative" (Duffy 1992: 578). John's will may reflect a search for traditional solace rather than firm theological conviction.

William Shakespeare's religious identity has stirred considerable speculation and debate because the evidence is vague and scanty, lending itself, as E. J. A. Honigmann says, "to diametrically opposed interpretations" (Honigmann 1985: 115). William was probably influenced by pervasive traces of traditional religion in the Elizabethan church as well as his father's own lingering attachment to Catholic beliefs. Shakespeare may have spent time in the countryside before coming to London. Honigmann makes a convincing case that he might have served as a tutor and actor in service to a wealthy Catholic household in Lancashire, and he concludes that William is the "William Shakeshaft" mentioned in the will of a prominent recusant landowner, Alexander Hoghton, who died in 1581 (ibid: 3–4). Peter Milward thinks that Shakespeare's attachment to Catholicism persisted throughout his life and says that his plays treat older religious beliefs and customs with "familiarity and reverence" (Milward 1973: 24). Honigmann, though convinced that Shakespeare's father lived and died a Catholic (Honigmann 1985: 118), still concludes that the son renounced the old faith as it became increasingly untenable, and he sees an ambivalent blend of "lapsed Catholicism" and "anti-Catholic feeling" in the work (pp. 122–3).

Shakespeare's ambivalence towards doctrinal differences has led others to see him as a more skeptical and secular agnostic. Roland Mushat Frye says that he resisted "systematic theology" (Frye 1963: 9) of any sort and "was primarily concerned with the life of man within the secular order" (p. 133). Such a characterization is consistent with John Keats's praise for Shakespeare's "*Negative Capability*, that is when man is capable of being in uncertainties, Mysteries, doubts without any irritable reaching after fact & reason."[2] George Santayana took this perspective to more radical conclusions in an essay entitled "The Absence of Religion in Shakespeare," concluding that Shakespeare "is remarkable among poets for being without a philosophy and without a religion" (quoted in Knapp 2001: 66). Jeffrey Knapp sees Shakespeare's diffidence less as evidence of secularism than of an aversion to sectarian division and fanaticism. Knapp cites the apposite remarks of a moderate Puritan preacher, Richard Sibbes, who says "In some cases peace by *keeping our faith to our selves*, is of more consequence, than the open discovery of some things we take to be true, considering the weakness of man's nature is such that there can hardly be a discovery of any difference in opinion, without some estrangement of affection" (p. 68). Knapp contends that Shakespeare's theatre fosters the charitable accommodation and fellowship promoted by religious moderates and sees more positive affinities between players and preachers overlooked by those emphasizing more familiar antitheatrical prejudices. Whether his motives were more evasively self-protective or evangelically sociable, Shakespeare certainly succeeded in keeping his faith to himself, thereby making it impossible to pin down his religious identity.

Religious identity in Shakespeare's tragedies is a particularly tantalizing question because tragic action often pivots on a dramatic moment of self-recognition and fixed resolve at the climax of terrible suffering. Moreover, the torments endured by his tragic protagonists resemble, in some ways, the ordeals of contemporary martyrs. Noting the parallel in her study of subjectivity in Renaissance theatre, Katharine Eisaman Maus notes that religious persecution and inquisition were designed to secure sure knowledge of the "inward heart" (Maus 1995: 16–17) through "discoveries" and "detections." Early modern drama often puts its protagonists through comparable torments to effect its moments of recognition and insight. In the course of the Reformation, examinations of conscience became increasingly focused and rigorous and could have dire consequences when conducted by external authorities. Yet even when internalized, the anguish occasioned by introspection could still be almost as ruthlessly intense as inquisition by another. Journals kept by devout

Puritans carefully chronicled the daily experience of "the self that suffers and . . . the self that observes, weighs, and tries to understand" (McGiffert 1972: 18) as they struggled to avoid becoming "deceivers of their own souls" (p. 17); although begun as "a means of assurance," such journals also provoked excruciating guilt and terror (p. 19). Many of Shakespeare's protagonists undergo comparable struggles, and their internal anguish frequently exceeds the sufferings imposed by others. As Lear says, the "tempest in my mind / Doth from my senses take all feeling else" (3.4.12–13). At the same time, his daughters' cruelty nearly destroys him, and "his little world of man" (3.1.10) is all but overwhelmed by the "eyeless rage" (8) of the storm. Either way, in Shakespearean tragedy, "characterization" is "achieved, in part," as Debora Shuger suggests, "by representing the self as suffering subject" (Shuger 1996: 57), and suffering defines identity.

Shakespeare's tragic protagonists certainly suffer, and their suffering is, to some degree, influenced by Christian ideas of altruism and sacrifice. Nevertheless, even when their torments resemble those of martyrs, they do not share the martyrs' confidence in the hope of the life to come. Gloucester resolves that "I am tied to the stake and I must stand the course" (3.7.53), but he bitterly complains that his agonies finally have no providential purpose, declaring "As flies to wanton boys, are we to th' Gods; / They kill us for their sport" (4.1.36–7). When he wavers in his resolve, his son, Edgar, encourages him to "Bear free and patient thoughts" (4.6.80) and says, "Men must endure / Their going hence, even as their coming hither" (5.3.9–10). Yet such encouragement does not sustain any faith in divine mercy or redemptive justice. Edgar's own assumption that "The Gods are just" is notoriously mocked by the hideous injustice of the play's end. Endurance in the face of suffering relies on stoic reflexes rather than Christian hope. Macbeth's comparable resolve conflates the courage of a martyr at the stake with the desperate ferocity of a bear bound and baited: "They have tied me to a stake: I cannot fly, / But, bear-like, I must fight the course" (5.7.1–2). Macbeth's courage derives not from faith but from depravity and despair. "I have almost forgot the taste of fears" (5.5.9) because "I have supp'd full with horrors" (5.5.14); for him, life has become "a tale / Told by an idiot, full of sound and fury, / Signifying nothing" (5.5.28). Realizing that all his previous hopes were delusions, fostered by the seductive deceptions of the Weird Sisters, Macbeth now begins "To doubt th' equivocation of the fiend, / That lies like truth" (5.5.43–4).

Equivocation is a pervasive element in all of Shakespeare's tragedies, and its persistence deprives his protagonists' fates of the clarity of martyrdom. References to equivocation in *Macbeth* are, in part, provocatively topical, alluding to contemporary religious conflicts and controversies, notably the Gunpowder Plot of 1605 and the arrest of Father Henry Garnet. The head of the Jesuit mission and the author of a tract defending careful evasions of efforts to pin down and persecute Catholics under oath entitled *A Treatise of Equivocation*, Garnet is presumed to be the butt of the Porter's snide joke about "an equivocator, that could swear in both the scales against either scale; who committed treason enough for God's sake, yet could not equivocate to heaven" (2.3.7–10). When Garnet was apprehended and executed for conspiracy, it was assumed that his equivocations could no longer conceal his true identity. After all, death at the stake was supposed to ensure that "there is nothing hid but it shall be opened." Shakespeare's tragic protagonists undergo comparably terrible ordeals, exposing manifold recesses of the "inward heart," but their identities remain enigmatic even in death. In these tragedies equivocation acquires the broader philosophical significance assigned it by Sir Thomas Browne in *Religio Medici*: "this visible world is but a picture of the invisible, wherein, as in a portrait, things are not truly but in equivocal shapes."[3] This is the cosmic "Sophoclean irony" ascribed to equivocation in *Macbeth* by A. C. Bradley in which words have a "further and ominous sense" hidden from the actors (Bradley 1991: 311–12). All of Shakespeare's tragic protagonists succumb to equivocation of this sort. Hamlet persistently tries to "suit the action to the word, the word to the action" (3.2.17–18), yet he also insists that he has "that within which passes show" and tells Ophelia "You should not have believed me" (3.1.116). Othello believes far more earnestly in the possibility of perfect transparency, proclaiming that "my perfect soul shall manifest me rightly," but he finds himself fatally entangled in deceptions and delusions. In this broader sense, equivocation is a variant of the "*Negative Capability*" that John Keats praises as Shakespeare's supreme attainment, because, as noted above, it permits the persistence of "uncertainties, Mysteries, doubts."[4] Keats sees Shakespeare's tragedies as "a World of pains and troubles" in which man appears, in Lear's words, as "'a poor forked creature' . . . destined to hardships and disquietude of some kind or other." Suffering yields no salvation, but it still has a kind of redemptive value in what Keats calls a "grander system of salvation than the chrystean religion." Indeed, for Keats, it becomes the key factor in a "System of Soul-making" in which souls "acquire identities" through suffering.[5] Yet, however vivid these souls may be, Shakespeare's tragic protagonists lack any clear religious identity. Like their author, they succeed in keeping their conscience to themselves.

Macbeth is entangled in equivocation from the play's beginning. In his first encounter with the Weird Sisters they sow confusion by insisting that "Fair is foul, and foul is fair" (1.1.10). The bizarre, indeterminate appearance of these women with beards also perplexes and unsettles. Macbeth wonders about the origins of those that "look not like th' inhabitant o'th'earth, / And yet are on 't" (1.3.39–40) when "what seem'd corporal, / Melted as breath into the wind" (79–80), and Banquo asks "Are ye fantastical or that indeed / Which outwardly ye show?" (51–2). Their questions are never answered, but these characters do seem to have a power beyond mere witchcraft, tempting Macbeth with a "supernatural soliciting" (129). The impact of their temptations is extraordinary. Macbeth succumbs to "horrible imaginings" and "surmise," concluding that "nothing is / But what is not" (137–41). He is carried away by his imaginings, and Bradley contends persuasively that Macbeth's "imagination is . . . the best of him, something usually deeper and higher than his conscious thoughts" (Bradley 1991: 323). Nevertheless, imagination agitates rather than edifies him, driving him to terrible crimes.

The worst of these is regicide, described as a blasphemous profanation. After Macbeth murders Duncan and the body is discovered, Macduff exclaims: "Most sacrilegious murder hath broke ope / The Lord's anointed temple and stole thence / The life o'th'building" (2.3.63–5). The equation of regicide with sacrilege reflects a persistent belief in the monarch's sanctity, as does the imputation of thaumaturgic powers to the English king. When Duncan's sons flee Scotland they seek protection from Edward the Confessor, whose royal touch enables him to cure those "All swoll'n and ulcerous, pitiful to the eye, / The mere despair of surgery . . . and 'tis spoken / To the succeeding royalty he leaves / The healing benediction" (4.3.152–7). To this "most miraculous work in this good King" (148) is added "a heavenly gift of prophecy, / And sundry blessings hang about his throne / That speak him full of grace" (158–60). As I have argued elsewhere, these traditional attributes of medieval sacred kingship were in some ways amplified by Tudor claims of royal supremacy and Stuart theories of divine right during the English Reformation as "the royal presence acquired some of the awesome sanctity of Christ's real presence in the Eucharist" (McCoy 2002: viii). Macbeth's own exclamation after the discovery of Duncan's corpse reinforces this equation of the real and royal presence by emphasizing the terrible consequences of a royal absence: "Renown and grace is dead. / The wine of life is drawn, and the mere lees / Is left this vault to brag of" (2.3.90–2). The blood shed by the king is seen as the "wine of life," now irretrievably spilt. Macbeth's murderous usurpation of the throne proceeds to pollute the royal sacramental system. When the ghost of Banquo appears at the banquet, Macbeth's guilt prevents him from drinking "to th'general joy o'th'whole table" (3.4.88) and celebrating communion with his noble peers. Even before he kills Duncan, he realizes that "Justice" will force "th'ingredience of our poison'd chalice / To our own lips" (1.7.11–12).

Macbeth's assault on sacred kingship makes equivocation a pervasive condition. Action can no longer be fitted to the word, and his mind is defiled and opaque, making him "strange / Even to the disposition that I owe" (3.4.111–12). Macbeth finds himself unable to comprehend, much less encounter, the consequences of his deeds: "I am afraid to think what I have done, / Look on't again I dare not" (2.2.48–9). Knowledge of his actions precludes self-knowledge: "To know my deed 'twere best not know myself" (71). Haunted by Banquo's ghost, his torments only increase, but he persists in his determination to do things he cannot comprehend: "Strange things I have in head that will to hand / Which must be acted ere they may be scanned" (3.4.138–9). The dissociation of word from action culminates in the ominous rites of the witches' brew; when asked by Macbeth "What is it that you do?" they reply "A deed without a name" (4.1.49).

Macbeth and the Weird Sisters are not the only ones entangled in equivocation. Malcolm, Duncan's heir apparent, proves himself a dubious successor in his equivocal exchange with Macduff. Malcolm initially presents himself as a vulnerable *ingénue* whom someone might "offer up [as] a weak, poor, innocent lamb / t'appease an angry god" (4.3.16–17), but, no sooner does Macduff renounce any intention of harming him, than Malcolm describes himself as a wolf in sheep's clothing prepared to commit heinous crimes, prey upon his country, and "confound / All unity on earth" (100–1). Macduff at first refrains from criticism but eventually balks at

Malcolm's recitation of his iniquities, yielding to Malcolm's own comparison of himself with the reigning tyrant: "Better Macbeth / Than such an one to reign" (66–7). Macduff laments the prospect of another tyrant, but he will not revolt, seeking exile from Scotland as an alternative: "Fare thee well, / These evils thou repeat'st upon thyself / Hath banish'd me from Scotland" (112–14). At this point, Malcolm reveals that his self-defamation was a lie and a test, intended to confirm Macduff's integrity. Now Malcolm is ready to "put myself to thy direction and / Unspeak mine own detraction . . . My first false-speaking / Was this upon myself" (131–2). Macduff finds "Such welcome and unwelcome things at once / . . . hard to reconcile" (139–40). His perplexity in the face of such behavior recalls Macbeth's first line in the play, spoken just before his encounter with the witches: "So foul and fair a day I have not seen" (1.3.36). Disentangling fair from foul and unspeaking false detraction may not prove so easy.

In the last act Macbeth fights to the death against Macduff, refusing to accept the ignominious alternative his opponent offers him just before their last encounter:

> Then yield thee, coward,
> And live to be the show and gaze o'th'time:
> We'll have thee, as our rarer monsters are,
> Painted upon a pole, and underwrit,
> "Here may you see the tyrant." (5.9.23–7)

The mocking portrait Macduff proposes would have made Macbeth into something like the "painted devil" used to frighten "the eye of childhood" (2.2.52–3) described earlier by Lady Macbeth. By taking Macbeth alive, Macduff anticipates advertising him with an emblematic combination of painted *pictura* and "underwrit" *subscriptio*. This lucid union of word and image promises to render equivocation and ambiguity impossible by precisely defining and confining villainy: "Here may you see the tyrant." Macduff defeats Macbeth, killing and decapitating him, and he presents "Th'usurper's cursèd head" (5.9.21) impaled upon his weapon in the last scene. At first, this seems just as complete a victory and just as transparent a spectacle as Macbeth taken alive because the traitor's severed head should have the Manichaean clarity of a "painted devil." But the "Strange things" in that head are no more easily "scann'd" (3.4.138–9) in hindsight than before. Duncan's lament at the play's beginning that "There's no art / To find the mind's construction in the face" (1.4.11–12) still holds true at its conclusion as we gaze upon the face of the dead Macbeth.

In *King Lear* the monarch's fall is self-inflicted. It results in calamitous suffering for everyone, but Lear's miseries are especially terrible, presenting a "sight most pitiful in the meanest wretch, / Past speaking of in a King!" (4.6.198–9). Suffering is still supposed to have redeeming features in this play, and Lear ardently embraces them on the heath and in the hovel. His own pain periodically allows him to recognize and feel compassion for others' sorrows. He asks his loyal fool, "How doest, my boy? Art cold? / I am cold myself," and says that "The art of our necessities is strange, / That can make vile things precious" (3.2.66–9). Lear regrets his previous neglect of "houseless poverty" (3.4.27) and, addressing other rulers, he urges them to recognize the need for a more equal distributive justice: "Take physic, pomp; / Expose thyself to feel what wretches feel" (34–5). His new sympathy for "Poor naked wretches" (29) makes him see Edgar in the dreadful rags of Poor Tom as "the thing itself; unaccommodated man is no more but such a poor, bare, forked animal as thou art" (98–100), and fellow-feeling prompts him to try to strip himself of his own clothes. Gloucester, by contrast, does not recognize his own son at this point and asks slightingly, "What has your grace no better company?" to which Edgar replies, "The Prince of Darkness is a gentleman" (130–1). Once blinded and cast out, the earl is less fastidious about the company he keeps. He now acknowledges that "I stumbled when I saw" (4.1.20), and he gives Poor Tom his purse and asks for help in finding his way. Suffering thus has redeeming features even for the otherwise despairing Gloucester. Immediately after his outburst against the gods' cruelty, he acknowledges the rough justice of his fate:

> Let the superfluous and lust-dieted man,
> That slaves your ordinance, that will not see
> Because he does not feel, feel your power quickly;
> So distribution should undo excess,
> And each man have enough. (4.1.67–71)

Gloucester subsequently confirms that his blindness affords new insight into the ways of the world by forcing him to "see it feelingly" (4.6.145).

Edgar is both a self-conscious exemplar and earnest proponent of the uses of adversity and "fellowship" in suffering (3.6.100). He describes himself as "A most poor man, made tame to fortune's blows; / Who, by the art of known and feeling sorrows, / Am pregnant to good pity" (4.6.216–18). He is also, at least initially, optimistically certain that suffering will prove redemptive and that "The worst returns to laughter" (4.1.6). The sight of his father's abject misery immediately shatters such confidence, but he remains determined to save the older man from despair. Edgar tricks Gloucester into thinking that he has survived his own suicide attempt, assuring him that his "life's a miracle" (4.6.55). The younger man's efforts work up to a point. Gloucester promises to "bear / Affliction till it do cry out itself" (75–6). When his father relapses into "ill thoughts" (5.2.9) after the king's forces are defeated, Edgar urges him not to give up and helps him flee the field. Having thus "sav'd him from despair" (5.3.190), Edgar finally reveals his identity and asks "his blessing" while telling him, "from first to last," the story of his flight and disguise,

> . . . but his flaw'd heart,
> Alack, too weak the conflict to support!
> 'Twixt two extremes of passion, joy and grief,
> Burst smilingly. (5.3.194–8)

It is a poignant but "good" death, in which Gloucester attains something like emotional equilibrium. This sense of a harmonious resolution is sustained by Edgar's concise, symmetrical, almost Euphuistic formulation in which "two extremes of passion, joy and grief" combine in a rhapsodic *discordia concors*.

Cordelia also comes to the rescue of a father who rejected her, and in her efforts to save Lear from despair and further tribulations, she herself embodies a comparable *discordia concors*. Her feelings for her father's sufferings are described accordingly by an anonymous gentleman: "patience and sorrow strove / Who should express her good-liest. You have seen / Sunshine and rain at once; her smiles and tears / Were like, a better way" (4.3.16–19). Lear has a harder time accepting his daughter's help because he knows who she is and what he has done to her, and "his own unkindness, / That stripp'd her from his benediction" stings "His mind so venomously that burning shame / Detains him from Cordelia" (41–6). Fleeing from her soldiers who have come to his aid, Lear encounters Gloucester and Edgar immediately after Edgar has urged his father to "Bear free and patient thoughts" (4.6.80) in the wake of the failed suicide attempt. Edgar is dismayed by the king's deranged ravings, with their "matter and impertinency mix'd; / Reason in madness" (168–9). Nevertheless, near the end of their exchange, Lear becomes somewhat more lucid and repeats Edgar's exhortations, saying "I know thee well enough, thy name is Gloucester. / Thou must be patient," even proposing to "preach to thee" on the theme (171–4). Unfortunately, thoughts of his enemies abruptly reduce him to homicidal rage: "Kill, kill, kill, kill, kill, kill!" (181).

Lear's struggle is more wrenching than Gloucester's, but, when he is finally reunited with Cordelia, their reconciliation achieves a moment of extraordinary harmony. At first he succumbs to despair even deeper than Gloucester's. Upon waking and seeing her, he is convinced that he has died and gone to hell, telling her: "You do me wrong to take me out o' the grave / Thou art a soul in bliss, but I am bound / Upon a wheel of fire, that mine own tears / Do scald like molten lead" (4.7.45–8). Cordelia urges her father to "look upon me, sir, / And hold your hand in benediction o'er me," insisting that "you must not kneel" (57–9). The implicit stage direction in the last phrase recalls a previous encounter with one of his wicked daughters. Earlier in the play Lear had knelt before Regan and sarcastically begged for "raiment, bed, and food" (2.4.149), but there it was a mocking gesture and rebuked as such by his other daughter: "Good sir, no more; these are unsightly tricks" (150). Here these religious postures and the celestial vision they evoke create a scene of such sublimity and pathos that Bradley finds it "almost a profanity to touch" (Bradley 1991: 263). As he begins to get his bearings and to see that the lady before him is not a "spirit" (4.7.49) but rather "my child Cordelia" (71), Lear sees himself as "a very foolish, fond old man" (61) rather than one of the damned. Self-knowledge still combines with self-loathing, and, convinced "you do not love me" because "You have some cause" (74–6), he too asks his child's assistance in suicide, saying he is willing to drink poison at Cordelia's hands. Eventually, he accepts her assistance and asks that she "bear with me. / Pray you now forget and forgive; / I am old and foolish" (84–5). Lear's admission of his folly and plea for forgiveness hold out the possibility of complete redemption. Moreover, Cordelia is herself assigned the role of redeemer by the gentleman who describes her as the "daughter / Who redeems nature from the general curse / Which twain have brought her to" (4.6.199–201).

The description of Cordelia as a redeemer is part of *King Lear's* pervasive but painfully ironic god-talk. Various characters repeatedly invoke the gods to ask for providential justice and divine protection. When both are banished by Lear at the play's beginning, Kent says to Cordelia: "The Gods to their dear shelter take thee, maid" (1.1.183). After returning from exile Cordelia prays for her father's recovery, pleading "O you kind Gods, / Cure this great breach in his abusèd nature!" (4.7.14–15). Once they are reunited, Lear remains euphoric even in defeat, convinced that all their sorrows are behind them. As they are hustled off to prison he assures Cordelia that their losses are really divinely sanctioned gains: "Upon such sacrifices . . . / The Gods themselves throw incense" (5.3.20–1). In confinement, he is certain they "will sing like birds i'th'cage" (9) and blithely "tell old tales, and laugh / At gilded butterflies, and hear poor rogues / Talk of court news" (12–14). Their departure from the "packs and sects of great ones" will allow them to escape fortune's fickle cycle and transcend the world's tribulations, enabling them to "take upon's the mystery of things, / As if we were Gods' spies" (16–18). In his poem "Lapis Lazuli" William Butler Yeats ascribes to Lear a paradoxically tragic cheer, and, in his penultimate scene with Cordelia, Lear exemplifies this "Gaiety transfiguring all that dread." Lear also aspires here to something like "the artifice of eternity" described in Yeats's "Sailing to Byzantium," a transcendent realm more congenial to old men who can be "set upon a golden bough to sing" in perpetuity "of what is past, or passing, or to come."[6] Lear's vision of their future together recalls their profoundly harrowing reunion in the previous act when Cordelia asked him to "look upon me, Sir, / And hold your hand in benediction o'er me. / No, Sir, you must not kneel" (4.6.57–9). In their withdrawal from the world Lear anticipates endlessly reenacting those moving and spontaneous gestures in a series of stylized repetitions: "When thou dost ask me blessing, I'll kneel down / And ask of thee forgiveness" (10–11).

Stylized repetition of powerful emotional gestures is the stock in trade of Shakespeare's theatre. In his influential essay on *King Lear*, Stephen Greenblatt has shown how Shakespeare simultaneously exploits and exposes theatre's power to create consoling illusions through the dramatization of strong emotions, a power that draws on religious beliefs and practices. Edgar's deception of his father is one example of just such a fraudulent "miracle," and Lear's beatific vision of reunion with Cordelia imagines a comparably happy outcome. Yet even as the play arouses "a forlorn hope of an impossible redemption" (Greenblatt 1988: 125), it ultimately refuses to gratify it. Cordelia is hanged, and, almost immediately after Albany prays for her safety – "The Gods defend her" (5.3.254) – Lear enters with her body, howling in grief and despair. If she were alive, he says, "It is a chance which does redeem all sorrows" (265), but, he soon laments, "she's gone for ever!" (269). He later repeats, "Thou'lt come no more, / Never, never, never, never, never!" (306–7), but then he asks those around him to "Look on her, look, her lips, / Look there, Look there!" (309–10). These are his last words, suggesting perhaps a delusional relapse, a desperate hope that her lips move and she still lives. Whatever they mean, they are heartbreaking for all who hear them, and they shatter any possibility of emotional equilibrium.

The play leaves us, in Greenblatt's view, with an "intimation of a fullness that we can savor only in the conviction of its irremediable loss" (Greenblatt 1988: 128). In withholding all hope of redemption, Greenblatt suggests that *King Lear* empties out or "evacuates" its own gestures; he adapts this provocative term from Reformation theology, citing Richard Hooker's analysis of "the evacuation of the Law of Moses" in his *Laws of Ecclesiastical Polity* (p. 126), but, as he acknowledges, Hooker adds that this does not mean "that the very name of Altar, of Priest, of Sacrifice itself, should be banished out of the world. For though God do now hate sacrifice, whether it be heathenish or Jewish, so that we cannot have the same things which they had but with impiety," yet "the words which were do continue: the only difference is, that whereas before they had a literal, they now have a metaphorical use, and are as so many notes of remembrance unto us, that what they did signify in the letter is accomplished in the truth" (p. 191, n. 50). Sacrifice and sacrament retain their truth-value and validity as metaphorical "notes of remembrance." Cordelia's death is indeed the unendurable shock described by Samuel Johnson, and the idea that "the gods themselves throw incense" on her literal sacrifice is appalling. At the same time the sacrifices she makes to move beyond a love "According to my bond; not more nor less" (1.1.92) to an absolute, uncalculating devotion are also moving and edifying. They affirm the value of a love not "mingled with regards that stands / Aloof from the entire point" (1.1.241).

The hatred of sacrifice Hooker attributes to God reflects a deeper cultural ambivalence in the Reformation, according to Debora Shuger. Hooker and other reformers found themselves increasingly revolted by "the appalling sacrificial subtext of the Calvinist subject" and what they recognized as "the violence of the sacred" at the heart of traditional religion (Shuger 1994: 90). John Calvin himself objected to Catholicism's carnal fixation on the real presence of Christ's body and blood in the sacrament. The disturbing cruelty of blood sacrifice is perhaps most apparent in Shakespeare's Roman plays. Their violence may suggest that Shakespeare shares the reformers' revulsion at the perceived primitivism of the Roman church. In *Titus Andronicus* the vanquished Tamora denounces the "cruel irreligious piety" of her son's sacrifice by Titus after battle (1.1.330), and even the Roman commander implicitly concedes the ultimate futility of his own rituals. As he proceeds with the funeral solemnities in the opening scene and places his own son's corpse in the family crypt, he describes the sepulcher as the "sacred receptacle of my joys" which holds "many sons . . . in store / That thou wilt never render to me more!" (92–5). By the play's end, the same sepulcher affords him an honorable burial while desecration and torture befall the bodies of his enemies, but all that he rendered to Rome will never be rendered in return. It is hard to imagine the survivors can ever knit the play's many "broken limbs again into one body" (5.3.71). In *Julius Caesar* Brutus would prefer that he and his fellow conspirators "be sacrificers, not butchers"

(2.1.166), but, since bloodshed is inevitable, he orders everyone to "bathe our hands in Caesar's blood / Up to the elbows" (3.1.107–8) immediately after the assassination. He hopes to redeem this otherwise "savage spectacle" (225) by a scrupulous observation of "all true rites and lawful ceremonies" (243) at the funeral, but Antony uses the sight of those bloody wounds to arouse the populace against them. Stalked by Caesar's ghost, Brutus finds that Rome's emperor is "mighty yet. / Thy spirit walks abroad, and turns our swords / In our own proper entrails" (5.3.93–5), and he and the others fall on their own swords. In *Coriolanus* sacrificial devotion to Rome proves no less pointless or self-destructive. The play's hero fights unflinchingly on Rome's behalf, but he recoils from the custom of soliciting the citizens' votes and voices for the office of consul by displaying his battle scars. The people see themselves putting "our tongues into those wounds" to "speak for them" (2.3.6–7), and this queasy image to Christ-like vulnerability disgusts the proud Coriolanus. At the first sign of resistance he resolves to "pluck out / The multitudinous tongue" (3.1.158–9), and his arrogant fury prompts the tribunes and people to banish him. In exile, Coriolanus presents himself as a human sacrifice to his former enemy, offering either "My throat to thee and to thy ancient malice" (4.5.95) or his service as an ally. After Rome surrenders to their joint forces he refuses to show mercy until his mother, wife, and child "shame him with our knees" (5.3.170). Coriolanus yields but knows that his mother has won "a happy victory to Rome; / But for your son . . . most mortal to him" (187–90). He is swiftly sacrificed to the Volscians' wrath, but while their leader's "rage is gone" (5.6.147), there is little sense of communal solidarity or renewal. Only the deaths of Antony and Cleopatra evoke any hopes of immortality, manifest in Cleopatra's determination to "show the cinders of my spirits / Through th'ashes of my chance" (5.2.169–70).

Othello is set in a cosmopolitan and confusing contemporary world where different racial and religious identities collide. The Moor himself is a Christian convert who remains confident in his own absolute integrity and transparency. Faced with scurrilous accusations, Othello remains calmly convinced that "my perfect soul / Shall manifest me rightly" (1.2.31–2). For him, there can be no "gap between the inward and the outward, the real inner convictions of a person and his or her outward behavior" (Lake 1999: 64). After Desdemona elopes with Othello, her bereaved father is convinced that she could only have been won by "charms / By which the property of youth and maidhood / May be abused" (1.1.172–4). Brabantio formally accuses Othello of "witchcraft" (1.3.64) and other nefarious practices before the Venetian Senate, but when Othello calmly proceeds to describe "what drugs, what charms, / What conjuration and what mighty magic" (93–4) he employed on his beloved, his only means of wooing her turns out to be "the story of my life" (128). Desdemona confirms that no coercive tricks were used to win her love; unforced, her "heart's subdued / Even to the very quality of my lord" (249–50).

Iago is the perfect foil and nemesis to such "a constant, loving, noble nature" (2.1.276). His rank and title as Othello's ensign or standard-bearer are rendered painfully ironic by his duplicity as he detaches sign from signified. He later says, with characteristic disingenuousness, "knowing what I am, I know what she shall be" (4.1.71), but he is, in fact, too cunning and self-aware to succumb to such projection. Othello, by contrast, really does believe, at least initially, that all minds are as transparent as his own. Iago remains inscrutable even when he professes to reveal himself. With Roderigo, he brazenly declares himself a bad servant "Who, trimmed in forms and visages of duty, / Keep yet their hearts attending on themselves" (1.1.50–1). Roderigo still misses the point that confidantes like these betray every master. Iago then ominously warns his dupe that

> . . . when my outward action doth demonstrate
> The native act and figure of my heart
> In compliment extern, 'tis not long after
> But I will wear my heart upon my sleeve
> For daws to peck at. I am not what I am. (1.1.61–5)

Even Iago's soliloquies are baffling exercises in bad faith and improvised conjecture. He says he hates the Moor because others think Othello cuckolded Iago even though such rumors leave him cynically indifferent: "I know not if't be true, / But I, for mere suspicion in that kind, / Will do as if for surety" (1.3.370–2). His lack of any inner conviction enables him to exploit the "gap between the inward and the outward" by thwarting comprehension. Indeed, he exults in the impenetrability of his thoughts. After disparaging "Reputation" as "an idle and most false imposition" (2.3.251) to Cassio, Iago hooks Othello by paying lip service to the irretrievable value of "a good name" (3.3.160) while provoking suspicions of its fraudulence. Exasperated, Othello insists, "By heaven, I'll know thy thoughts." Iago obstinately – and accurately – replies "You cannot, if my heart were in your hand; / Nor shall whilst 'tis in my custody" (166–8). He attributes this same impenetrable secrecy to Desdemona and other Venetian women, equating it with their moral faculty: "their best conscience / Is not to leave't undone, but keep't unknown" (207–8). Regaining its original meaning of inmost thought and privity, "conscience" here connotes furtive inwardness and becomes a devious means of concealing one's own misdeeds. Such remarks are slyly aimed at inflaming suspicions of those who "can keep their conscience to themselves."

Desdemona is just as constant and open as Othello, and she too assumes all women are as honorable as she. She finds it hard to believe that "there be women who do abuse their husbands" by adulterous betrayal (4.3.60), and the accusations he makes against her are almost beyond utterance as well as comprehension. When Othello calls her a "whore" (4.2.93), she finds "I cannot say 'whore.' / It does abhor me now I speak the word" (165–6). Yet despite her manifest integrity, Iago is right to insist that "her honor is an essence that's not seen" (4.1.16). This invisibility is the source of her downfall, enabling Iago to "turn her virtue into pitch, / And out of her own goodness make the net / That shall enmesh them all" (2.3.334–6). Tormented and enthralled by Iago's insinuations, Othello ferociously tells Iago, "be sure thou prove / My love a whore.

Be sure of it. Give me the ocular proof" (3.3.363–5). Iago audaciously parries this demand by proffering a lurid scene too shocking to contemplate: "How, how satis- fied, my lord? / Would you, the supervisor, grossly gape on, / Behold her topped?" (3.3.399–401). That forbidden sight – like her honor – remains unseen. Instead of "ocular proof," Iago provides "imputation and strong circumstance" (411) and the fiendish fluency of his own suggestions. Their compact is confirmed by an exchange of "sacred vows" (464) as Iago proclaims "I am your own forever" (482), reiterating the oath made by Othello in the previous act (3.3.217). Iago's triumph over Othello is consummated when the man of unshaken valor succumbs to a seizure and collapses at his ensign's feet. Before he falls, Othello insists that "It is not words that shakes me thus" (4.1.39–40), but words and the handkerchief are, in fact, the only sources of all his grief.

When he turns on Desdemona, Othello attributes magical powers to the lost hand- kerchief. In the beginning, Othello had dispelled charges of witchcraft with candor and assurance. The straightforward story of his life and noble qualities was enough to subdue Desdemona's heart, and he had no need for "drugs" or "charms" or "mighty magic." Now, his faith shattered, he resorts to more ambiguous and sinister stories, replete with the duplicity and menace of witchcraft. He claims that the handkerchief was obtained by his mother from a gypsy charmer who dyed it with "Mummy, which the skilful / Conserved of maidens' hearts" (3.4.72–3). Mummy was preserved dead flesh from which blood and other liquids were extracted for their supposedly medicinal qualities. The dye's source in "maidens' hearts" carries chilling connota- tions of virgin sacrifice or, at least, a morbid fixation on virgin flesh. Moreover, the claim that the handkerchief allowed his mother to "subdue my father / Entirely to her love" (57–8) gives it the qualities of a powerful fetish. Desdemona reacts to these appalling revelations by exclaiming, "Then would to God I had never seen it" (75). The supposedly blood-stained handkerchief becomes yet another lurid and forbidden sight, perilous to behold, and Othello initially plans to match it with another grisly spectacle, determined that her "bed, lust-stained, shall with lust's blood be spotted" (5.1.37).

When he enters their bedchamber in the last act, Othello struggles to regain decorum and emotional control, now proclaiming "I'll not shed her blood" (5.2.3). His soliloquy unfolds with great ceremonial and rhetorical solemnity while Desdemona sleeps. At first he insists her sin remain unspoken: "Let me not name it to you, you chaste stars" (5.2.2–3). He repeatedly proclaims the sanctity of his inten- tions. "This sorrow's heavenly / It strikes where it doth love" (5.1.21–2). When she awakes, he urges her to pray and repent, saying "I would not kill thy unprepared spirit. / No heavens forfend! I would not kill thy soul" (32–3). When she responds, "That death's unnatural that kills for loving" (45) and struggles against his efforts to smother her, he grows enraged because she forces him to "call what I intend to do / A murder, which I thought a sacrifice" (69–70). As her resistance weakens, he briefly regains his factitious composure and hastily dispatches her, saying: "I that am cruel am yet merciful, / I would not have thee linger in thy pain" (96–7).

His composure is swiftly destroyed when Emilia bursts in to denounce him as a murderer and dupe of her husband. Iago mortally wounds his wife and flees, and Othello is left to gape upon Desdemona. He anticipates a painful reunion at the Last Judgment when "This look of thine will hurl my soul from heaven, / And fiends will snatch at it" (281–2). Iago is captured but, now that his treachery is known, he withdraws into impenetrable silence: "From this time forth I never will speak word" (310). The authorities are characteristically confident that "Torments will ope your lips" (312), but it remains dubious, in his case, that torture could ever open Iago's "inward heart" or reveal his true identity. Othello, by contrast, is more voluble, eager to offer "a word or two before you go" (351). His words are characteristically eloquent but dubious and misleading, combining self-praise and self-denunciation with an appeal to "Speak of me as I am" (351). Having insisted that "naught I did in hate, but all in honour" (301), he maintains that he "loved not wisely but too well" (353). He then describes himself in the third person as either a base "Indian" in the Quarto or "Judean" in the Folio who "threw a pearl away / Richer than all his tribe" (356–7) as well as a "malignant and a turbaned Turk" who "Beat a Venetian and traduced the state" (362–3), associating himself with nearly every pagan or infidel alien of Shakespeare's day. Reverting to the first person, he identifies with the European aggressor who takes "by th'throat the circumcisèd dog" (364) and stabs himself. Yet, despite the violent self-division of his speech and gestures, he reaches again for harmony in the balanced, rhyming reciprocity of his dying words: "I kissed thee ere I killed thee. No way but this. / Killing myself, to die upon a kiss" (368–9). Although Othello fastidiously refrained from shedding her blood, his stabbing brings their last scene together to "a bloody period" (366). Lodovico concludes the play by denouncing Iago with a contradictory exhortation: "Look on the tragic loading of this bed / This is thy work. The object poisons sight. / Let it be hid" (373–5). Despite Othello's efforts to preserve decorum, the play's last scene becomes one last lurid and forbidden sight too terrible to contemplate. As the curtains are drawn on this blood-stained spectacle, Othello's confidence in spiritual transparency is irreparably shattered.

Like the Elizabethan religious settlement, *Hamlet* is haunted by a ghost come from the grave of an older religious world. Hamlet's father claims to arise from a suppressed Catholic purgatory where his "foul crimes . . . / Are burnt and purged away" (1.5.12–13). In the course of the play's many funerals, the consolations of a "sage requiem" (5.1.220) are invoked only to be withdrawn, leaving all the mourners with a sense of "maimèd rites" (202). In some ways *Hamlet* reflects the uncertainty of what constitutes a decent burial in Shakespeare's time. In his account of Reformation funeral rites, Ralph Houlbrooke traces the wrenching transition from intercession to commemoration in the Reformation and concludes that English Protestants had difficulties with both: "after pulling down the structure of inherited observances, [they] failed (partly because of their own divisions) to create a generally accepted way of death thoroughly imbued with their own spirit" (Houlbrooke 1989: 40–2). Finally, there is the play's troubled and equivocal preoccupation with sacred kingship. Shakespeare attributes the claim that "There's such divinity doth hedge a king / That treason can but peep to what it would" (4.5.120–1) to a regicide and usurper, undercutting belief in that divinity. The feelings stirred by the "cease of majesty" (3.3.15) are similarly conflicted by the bad faith of those who express them. When Guildenstern worries about the threat Hamlet poses to Claudius, he attributes his own concern to a "Most holy and religious fear . . . / To keep those many many bodies safe / That live and feed upon your majesty" (8–10). Rosencrantz continues:

> The single and peculiar life is bound
> With all the strength and armour of the mind
> To keep itself from noyance; but much more
> That spirit upon whose weal depends and rests
> The lives of many. The cease of majesty
> Dies not alone, but like a gulf doth draw
> What's near with it. (3.3.11–17)

Each speaker is primarily concerned with his own "single and peculiar life," yet, for all their unctuous hypocrisy, their speeches really do express a "most holy and religious fear." The venerable concept of the king's two bodies informs their notion that the monarch's well-being preserves his subjects' "many many bodies." A legitimate succession entails a kind of sovereign immortality – "the king is dead, long live the king" – as well as ensuring political continuity.[7] At the same time, the royal presence becomes a sacramental real presence as the image of the king as the embodiment of the common "weal" transforms an otherwise revoltingly parasitic image of those who "live and feed upon your majesty" into a form of holy communion.

Unfortunately, in *Hamlet* as in *Macbeth*, the loss of the legitimate king undercuts the equation of the royal presence with the real presence, and a usurper on the throne means that "Something is rotten in the state of Denmark" (1.4.67). Ghosts stalk both Hamlet and Macbeth, but, for Hamlet, the dead king's return excites great hopes as well as fears. When the specter appears again in the closet scene, Hamlet exclaims, "His form and cause conjoined, preaching to stones / Would make them capable" (3.4.117–18). In a realm where so much is "out of joint," such a conjunction sounds like "a consummation / Devoutly to be wished" (3.1.65–6). For Hamlet, his father's return to his mother's bedchamber not only holds out the prospect of an otherwise impossible family reunion; it also arouses hopes of a mystical recombination of the king's two bodies, transforming a royal absence to a real presence. Unfortunately, no such miracle occurs. Gertrude cannot see the ghost, and it vanishes from the play never to reappear. Divisions ramify in this scene and afterwards as Hamlet reverts to his characteristic double-talk and equivocation, telling his mother not to do what "I bid you do" (3.4.165). In his next encounter with Claudius, Hamlet dismisses him as a king who "is a thing . . . of nothing" (4.2.27–9). With his uncle on the throne, a conjunction of the king's two bodies is impossible: "The body is with the King, but the King is not with the body" (26–7).

Hamlet meets his match in "equivocation" in the grave-digger (5.1.127), and he disrupts Ophelia's funeral by fighting with her brother and vowing "to rant as well as thou" (268). As the play nears its end he grows, for a time, more resigned and contemplative. At the beginning of the final scene he tells Horatio how he replaced his own death warrant with "a new commission" (5.2.33) ordering the execution of Rosencrantz and Guildenstern before escaping from the ship, and he explains this expedient by saying, "There's a divinity that shapes our ends / Rough hew them how we may" (5.2.10–11). Later he dismisses his own apprehensions regarding the duel arranged by Claudius with the assurance that "There's a special providence in the fall of a sparrow" (5.2.157–8). Some see evidence of genuine religious feeling, but Harold Goddard scorns such notions of divinity as kin to Iago's "Divinity of Hell" (Goddard 1951: 1.376). Yet, here and elsewhere, Hamlet's sense of himself as heaven's "scourge and minister" (3.4.159) is reinforced by his notorious passivity. As Claudius anticipates, he approaches the fatal show-down in a spirit "Most generous, and free from all contriving" (4.7.104). The poisoned foil and cup that Hamlet forces on Claudius in their climactic battle royal are the king's contrivances, and he is thus "*Hoised with his own petard*" (3.4.185–6). Hamlet's own death assures his triumph in another way. Even as he avenges his father he also supplants the ghost and acquires some of its uncanny powers, twice declaring, "I am dead" (5.2.275 and 280). As he expires, he demands that Horatio "Absent thee from felicity awhile, / And in this harsh world draw thy breath in pain / To tell my story" (5.2.289–91). Horatio tries to oblige, but his eulogy is postponed and his benediction disrupted by the noisy arrival of Fortinbras: "Good night sweet prince, / And flights of angels sing thee to thy rest. – / Why does the drum come hither" (5.2.312–14). Fortinbras promises to hear the report later, but he is first determined to assert his own authority which precedes that conferred by the "dying voice" (308) of his dead rival: "For me, with sorrow I embrace my fortune. / I have some rights of memory in this kingdom, / Which now to claim my vantage doth invite me" (5.2.342–5). Like many survivors, Fortinbras uses "the rights of memory" for his own self-serving purposes. It does not matter. Neither "the rites of war" (343) he orders nor the eulogy Horatio promises would ever constitute an adequate tribute, and each is irrelevant to Hamlet's own "rights of memory." Although Hamlet asks Horatio "To tell my story," the play itself has already done that and it stands as his true memorial. Indeed, *Hamlet* is so effective that it renders the paternal imperative, "Remember me," wholly superfluous. Hamlet has so dominated modern memory that he has acquired a kind of palpable presence. His is not a real presence since he is only a fictional character, but, as Richard Hooker says in the passage cited earlier, words which "have a metaphorical use" can still function as "notes of remembrance." Even when Hamlet meets his end, he will not let us "pluck out the heart of my mystery" (3.2.336) and the "divinity that shapes" his end remains no less mysterious, but his character cannot be forgotten.

NOTES

1   John Foxe (1965) [1843–9], *Acts and Monuments*, 8 vols., ed. G. Townsend (New York: AMS), VII: 549.
2   John Keats (1959), *Selected Poems and Letters*, ed. D. Bush (Boston, MA: Houghton Mifflin), p. 261.
3   Sir Thomas Browne (1963), *Religio Medici*, ed. J. Winny (Cambridge: Cambridge University Press), p. 14.
4   Keats, *Selected Poems*, p. 261.
5   Ibid, pp. 287–9.
6   "Lapis Lazuli" (p. 291) and "Sailing to Byzantium" (pp. 191–2) in *The Collected Poems of W. B. Yeats* (New York: Macmillan, 1966).
7   See Ernst Kantorowicz (1981), *The King's Two Bodies: A Study in Medieval Political Theology* (Princeton, NJ: Princeton University Press). This section draws here and elsewhere on my discussion of *Hamlet* in McCoy (2001, 2002).

REFERENCES AND FURTHER READING

Bradley, A. C. (1991) [1904]. *Shakespearean Tragedy*. London: Penguin Books.
Collinson, P. (1988). Comment on Eamon Duffy's Neale Lecture and the Colloquium. In N. Tyacke (ed.) *England's Long Reformation: 1500–1800*. London: University College Press, 71–86.
Dickens, A. G. (1964). *The English Reformation*. New York: Schocken.
Duffy, E. (1992). *The Stripping of the Altars: Traditional Religion in England, 1400–1580*. New Haven, CT: Yale University Press.
Frye, R. M. (1963). *Shakespeare and Christian Doctrine*. Oxford: Oxford University Press.
Goddard, H. (1960). *The Meaning of Shakespeare*, 2 vols. Chicago, IL: University of Chicago Press.
Greenblatt, S. (1988). *Shakespearean Negotiations: The Circulation of Social Energy in Renaissance England*. Berkeley: University of California Press.
Guy, J. (1988). *Tudor England*. Oxford: Oxford University Press.
Haigh, C. (1993). *English Reformations: Religion, Politics and Society under the Tudors*. Oxford: Clarendon Press.
Honigmann, E. A. J. (1985). *Shakespeare: The "Lost Years."* Manchester: Manchester University Press.
Houlbrooke, R. (1989). *Death, Ritual and Bereavement*. London: Routledge.
Knapp, J. (2001). Jonson, Shakespeare, and the Religion of the Players. *Shakespeare Survey*, 54, 57–70.
Lake, P. (1999). Religious Identities in Shakespeare's England. In D. S. Kastan (ed.) *A Companion to Shakespeare*. Oxford: Blackwell.
Litzenberger, C. (1998). Defining the Church of England: Religious Change in the 1570s. In S. Wabuda and C. Litzenberger (eds.) *Belief and Practice in Reformation England*. Aldershot: Ashgate, 137–53.
McCoy, R. C. (2001). A Wedding and Four Funerals: Conjunction and Commemoration in *Hamlet*. *Shakespeare Survey*, 54, 122–39.
——(2002). *Alterations of State: Sacred Kingship in the English Reformation*. New York: Columbia University Press.
MacCulloch, D. (2001). *The Later Reformation in England, 1547–1603*, 2nd edn. London: Palgrave.
McGiffert, M. (ed.) (1972). *God's Plot: The Paradoxes of Puritan Piety, Being the Autobiography & Journal of Thomas Shepard*. Amherst: University of Massachusetts Press.
Maus, K. E. (1995). *Inwardness and the Theater in the English Renaissance*. Chicago, IL: University of Chicago Press.
Milward, P. (1973). *Shakespeare's Religious Background*. Bloomington: Indiana University Press.

Miola, R. S. (2001). "An Alien People Clutching their Gods"?: Shakespeare's Ancient Religions. *Shakespeare Survey*, 54, 31–45.

Schoenbaum, S. S. (1977). *William Shakespeare: A Compact Documentary Life.* New York: Oxford University Press.

Shuger, D. K. (1994). *The Renaissance Bible: Scholarship, Sacrifice, and Subjectivity.* Berkeley: University of California Press.

——(1996). Subversive Fathers and Suffering Subjects: Shakespeare and Christianity. In D. Hamilton and R. Strier (eds.) *Religion, Literature, and Politics in Post-Reformation England, 1540–1688.* Cambridge: Cambridge University Press, 46–69.

Walsham, A. (1993). *Church Papists: Catholicism, Conformity and Confessional Polemic in Early Modern England.* Woodbridge: Royal Historical Society.

Watson, R. N. (1994). *The Rest Is Silence: Death as Annihilation in the English Renaissance.* Berkeley: University of California Press.

10

Shakespeare's Roman Tragedies

Gordon Braden

Toward the end of the film *Hannibal* (2001), after a Thyestean banquet taken in classically competitive spirit to a new level of refinement – a treacherous official from the Justice Department is led to dine appreciatively not on his offspring but on his own sautéed brain tissue – the title character, played by Anthony Hopkins, must free himself from a tight spot by ("This is really going to hurt") chopping off his own hand with a meat cleaver. This act does not take place in Thomas Harris's novel on which the film is based; it comes into the film as part of a general attempt to make the story's outcome more palatable, but has a pedigree of its own. Hopkins had undergone the same surgery on screen two years earlier, as the title character in *Titus*, Julie Taymor's film of *Titus Andronicus*. It was Taymor's doing to set the scene in a kitchen and use, indeed, a meat cleaver; but the mutilation itself is of course scripted by Shakespeare, as is the conclusion of the story in its own scene of Thyestean vengeance. It is hard not to think that Hopkins's earlier performance as the cannibalistic Dr. Lecter in *The Silence of the Lambs* (1991) was part of what brought him to the role of Titus; that path had already been taken by Brian Cox, who portrayed Harris's character in his first incarnation on film (*Manhunter*, 1986), and then went on to play Titus in Deborah Warner's stage production (1987–8). Both Hopkins and Cox are estimable actors, and I do not think the intertextual commerce here is superficial.

At the very least it allows us to be specific about the access Shakespeare's play has acquired to contemporary taste. Long a puzzle on the Shakespearean roster, it has gradually but steadily become a script that can be read and performed with real conviction; this revaluation has been in process since Peter Brook's production in 1955 (with Laurence Olivier as Titus), and Taymor's film (itself based upon and evidently improving a stage production of her own) brings it to a new level of certainty. The film was not to be sure a theatrical success – ambitions for general distribution faltered and it played only briefly in a few major cities – but it has made its mark on DVD and tape as one of the most intelligent and compelling of a number of Shakespearean films in the last two decades. Its sure-handedness is all the more impressive in view of

Taymor's relative lack of experience with either Shakespeare or moviemaking; the happy result owes something to her finding a Shakespearean text especially appropriate to the manner she brings to it, a deliberately spectacular and witty mix of period styles, from archaic pagan ritual to contemporary video games. (Politicians in one scene speak into the microphone of SPQR-TV.) The Longleat drawing that is our oldest illustration of any Shakespearean performance shows *Titus Andronicus* being staged in Shakespeare's own time with a conspicuous mix of Roman, Elizabethan, and medieval costumes; and if such casualness would have been typical of playhouse practice generally, it also would have been particularly natural for a play of such antic historical confusion. *Titus Andronicus* is, notoriously, set in a Rome of no particular period, with institutions from both the republican and the imperial periods jumbled together according to no obvious system, and with no characters from real history to set anything like a date. This addlement was long attributed to authorial immaturity; but on another line of sight it adds to the play's power, giving its brutalities a sinister feel of timelessness. Taymor exploits that potential beautifully, but also adds another dimension with the decision to do most of the filming in Rome itself and its environs, where she could with minimal travel find most of what she needed, from the ruins of Hadrian's villa to the fascist modernities of EUR. For the living embodiment of both her eclecticism and Shakespeare's is the actual city of Rome itself, where historical strata are less often layered on top of each other than juxtaposed side by side in the open air: a sight which Shakespeare himself would not have experienced but which displayed on the modern screen makes his own derangement of Roman history seem like simple observation of reality.

A comparable event on the academic side of things is Jonathan Bate's remarkable edition in the new Arden series (1995). Defensiveness about the play is here no more than vestigial; Bate assimilates and adds to what is by now a significant body of criticism that treats it with interested respect, and seems freed in the process to give fresh and vigorous attention to some traditional scholarly questions. He makes an excellent case that the seventeenth-century German version of the play preserves a key stage direction for 3.1, and incorporates it into his own text. Lavinia now kisses neither Titus nor Lucius but the severed heads of her dead brothers – an unforgettable moment that once proposed seems right on almost all counts. (Taymor does not stage it this way; I do not know if it has yet been tried.) Bate also argues with new force for what had generally been minority opinions on some other matters: for a late date of composition (1593, with a first performance in early 1594) and for the play's priority to both the ballad and the prose chapbook that provide the only other versions of the story. Larger issues hinge on both points. A date of 1593 would definitively remove the play from the category of Shakespeare's juvenilia, and indeed in Bate's reading of the record would make it "*the* pivotal play in Shakespeare's early career . . . the play in which he draws on the new skills learned in his eighteen-month sabbatical as a non-dramatic poet and paves the way for his later achievements in tragedy" (p. 79). And if the play has no ascertainable main source, it goes on a very short and important list: like *A Midsummer Night's Dream* and *The Tempest*, it gives us a look into what

Shakespeare's narrative imagination was like when it relied primarily on its own resources. That list looks even stranger now than it did before.

None of Bate's specific conclusions are beyond debate, but the general recovery of respect for *Titus Andronicus* seems to me irreversible. It is stimulated in obvious ways by the particular horrors of the century just finished, but it is also in effect a recursion to both the popular and the learned taste of the Renaissance, which venerated Seneca above all other dramatists and frequently defined tragedy in terms of the atrocity of its actions. Having Shakespeare's first play about classical Rome firmly back on the playlist promises to affect discussion of all of them in interesting and historically appropriate ways. M. W. MacCallum in 1910 set a strong precedent by excluding *Titus* from the coverage of a book entitled *Shakespeare's Roman Plays*, and for almost three quarters of a century it could be expected that such a rubric would cover just the triptych *Julius Caesar*, *Antony and Cleopatra*, and *Coriolanus*. It was accordingly of some moment when a book called *Shakespeare's Rome* (by Robert Miola, 1983) pointedly included *Titus*, along with *Lucrece* and *Cymbeline*, in its analysis; books by Michael Platt (1983) and Coppélia Kahn (1997) have dealt with the same list. *Cymbeline* may be too specialized a taste for its inclusion to become a habit, but I think the count of Shakespeare's Roman plays for most future discussion is now securely more than three.

Some of the consequences of a wider view here are explored by Clifford Ronan (1995) in what is surprisingly the first book-length study of the Roman plays, not just of Shakespeare, but of his contemporaries as well. MacCallum's own conception of his topic restricted his attention only to a handful of other plays, some of them continental, that might conceivably have influenced Shakespeare (and briefly to William Alexander's later *Julius Caesar*). Ronan, on the other hand, canvasses "some forty-three" English Roman plays (*Cymbeline* is included) extant from the period 1585–1635. He does not try to be exhaustive in his treatment or even particularly systematic; he organizes his discussion around particular topics, motifs, or images that have caught his eye. What emerges, however, is consistent enough to support some useful generalizations, most of them compressed into the pun in his title: the "Roman" in these plays is both "antique" and "antic," evocative of "the playfulness and garishness of Antiquity" (Ronan 1995: 4) that later ages will do much to remove from the picture. Renaissance authors are in part responding to real features in the classical record (e.g., "the sniggling sadism of Lucan"; p. 5) and in part adding to it from contemporary predilections; many of the new embellishments heighten the sense of the classical Romans as particularly violent and cruel (there is no good evidence that they regularly trod on the heads of their captives during a formal triumph, but this ritual gesture of "insultment" – the word first appearing with this meaning at *Cymbeline*, 3.5.140 – is widespread in Renaissance Roman plays). Ronan's analysis obviously makes *Titus* look less aberrant within this general theatrical practice, but it also highlights the ways in which Shakespeare's later Roman plays also breathe this spirit; e.g., tracing Lucan's "trope of disembowelment of one's native land in civil war" through a number of other playwrights leads Ronan to *Coriolanus*, *Titus*, *King John*,

Richard III, and *Julius Caesar*. The last of these "seems to have been written by a person who has very recently perused or revisited Lucan. Within fewer than sixty lines [5.3.41–96], Shakespeare reemphasizes the idea of 'piercing' the vitals with steel, 'thrusting' it into the 'bowels,' 'bosom,' 'heart,' 'entrails,' and even 'ears'" (pp. 148–9). We are not used to pausing over such language, but there is enough of it to make us look twice once it is pointed out; cumulatively, Ronan's arguments do much to reduce the traditionally perceived distance between Shakespeare's first Roman play and its successors.

Expanding the frame this way, to reveal a strongly negative counterpoint to any idealization of Rome and its civilization, facilitates an appropriately nuanced formulation of the political relevance of the Roman play: "As an age of colonization and empire was launched, England found in Rome a glass where the island could behold its own image simultaneously civilized and barbarous, powerful and hollow" (p. 7). For the most part Ronan leaves it about at that, but he has good reasons for doing so. He glances at some of the suggestions of specific topicality that have been advanced, but recognizes the trickiness of decoding particular political statements: "Even where we can look at governmental records, or glance over the shoulder of a dramatist as he or she adapts sources, it is hard to distinguish truly topical political intent from a mere desire to seem interesting" (p. 50). As far as speculation about the actual political effect of these plays is concerned, his hesitancy is clear-headed and largely unanswerable:

> There was no political party sponsoring the hustling artists of the time, and the political interests that spectators brought to the theater were widely diverse. Audiences contained future regicides like John Bradshaw and the fellow traveler John Milton . . . But they also included the politically passive, the positive supporters of the monarchy, and the trivially curious. Thus almost any popular drama would have in it something of seeming political relevance, or irrelevance, for everyone, according to taste. (p. 51)

Yet such skepticism does not threaten a conviction that the genre participates vitally in the political turbulence of the time: "Rome's goal of tyrannical absolutism and the processes by which it enforced its will were topical subjects . . . easily understood by commoner and monarch alike" (p. 153).

Ronan's perspective can be confirmed in a general way from non-theatrical evidence, though such evidence is surprisingly modest. "There was no history of the Romans in Shakespeare's lifetime comparable (for example) to the *History of Great Britain* by John Speed or the *Generall Historie of the Turkes* by Richard Knolles" (Spenser 1957: 29). What we have are scattered comments in various contexts and compilations of translated excerpts from the ancient historians, followed eventually by complete translations of some of the major classical sources: Plutarch in 1579, Tacitus in 1591 and 1598, Livy in 1600. This evidence is not easily digested into reliable generalizations, and still awaits its comprehensive study. Leeds Barroll (1958) has argued that during the period classical sources are largely assimilated into the medieval schema of the four monarchies foretold by the prophet Daniel; one quite creditable book has been written about Shakespeare's Roman plays from this perspective. A different thesis, the most interesting one currently on the table, has been sketched by G. K. Hunter (1977); focusing on the notably late date of the translations of Tacitus and Livy, he attributes the delay to the way these texts "posed particular difficulties for Tudor writers" by offering, when studied in their entirety, "an overall intepretation of the sweep of Roman history from Romulus to Vespasian . . . in terms of an ethic that denies the official beliefs of the modern world as Tudor historians were given to understand them," implying "that the characteristic virtues of Rome . . . are essentially republican in their social context, and so are set implacably against kingship" (p. 97). The belated availability of this version of Roman history is in turn part of the attempt of an intellectual avant-garde "to catch up with currents of thought that had been around in continental Europe for some time" (p. 103); at a time when the English state began to heighten the rhetoric in favor of monarchical rule, "Tacitus offered an acerbic and disenchanted observation of the gradual strangulation, under the Empire, of all those ethical wonders of Republican Rome" (p. 104). Jonson was a clear member of this avant-garde, and theatrical practice generally catches its glow. Shakespeare was not quite in the group — as Jonson's scorn, especially for *Julius Caesar*, would seem to indicate — but his Roman plays focus on the same oppositions of republican virtue and imperial decay:

> *Titus* shows us Roman integrity, legality, inflexibility, chastity in one fictional family set against the self-indulgence, irresponsibility, lust and tyranny of another fictional group. *Julius Caesar* offers us a more complex mixture of the alternatives than *Titus*, since Julius is no mere tyrant and Brutus is no mere tyrannicide, but the same polarities remain the controlling elements of the conceptual diagram that the play contains. (p. 114)

I think much future work will be moving in a similar direction, but I also think it would be a mistake to announce either the end or the obsolescence of the critical tradition descending from MacCallum, of more or less isolated attention to *Julius Caesar*, *Antony and Cleopatra*, and *Coriolanus*. The traditional grouping of three is by no means an exhausted topic; Geoffrey Miles's (1996) book is a strong enough work to forestall any such conclusion. And heightened attention to Roman plays beyond the old canon will not simply elide the boundaries of that canon; it can also clarify what it is that sets that canon off as something special. Artistic quality is obviously one of the considerations here; but you can think *Titus* a good, even a great play, and still recognize that Shakespeare's later Roman plays represent a very different kind of enterprise. If Bate is right on the matter of sources, in fact, the contrast on that level is one of the most extreme in Shakespeare's career: between one of the few plays for which the story is almost entirely his invention and three plays which are more closely tied to a quite specific source than are any of his others. In North's Plutarch he found not only historical narratives and often quite vividly rendered characters, but also particular language, phrases, sometimes entire passages which he took over verbatim or with minor changes. These borrowings include one of his most famous set-pieces ("The barge she sat in . . ."); so close are they that at one point in *Coriolanus* we can restore from North an entire line inadvertently dropped from the Folio text (2.3.243). Not even Golding's Ovid is used with such extensive intimacy. The nature of that intimacy still rewards study; in the most recent look, Cynthia Marshall (2000) argues that Shakespeare's transformation of Plutarch's narrative into drama involves "the establishment of our culture's prevailing model of character as one that is at once intensely performative and putatively interiorized" (p. 73). The street sometimes runs both ways, as when a recent scholar of Plutarch cites Shakespeare as a useful collaborator: "the concerns of the two writers are often closely similar: so similar, indeed, that comparison with [Shakespeare] continually illuminates [Plutarch's] own narrative and dramatic techniques" (Pelling 1988: 37). At the same time, no other English dramatist demonstrates anything like Shakespeare's interest in Plutarch (though Jonson does make comparable use of Tacitus and other Latin sources for *Catiline* and *Sejanus*). The traditional triptych – Shakespeare's Plutarchan plays – still has good claim to being a special phenomenon worth studying on its own.

MacCallum's book itself is still basic reading on the subject. The details of Shakespeare's use of Plutarch are set out there with a detail and amplitude not available anywhere else, with both the parallels and divergences lucidly and thoroughly analyzed; others have made additions and adjustments, but none of them substantial. The sourcework, moreover, is woven into a larger discussion of the plays themselves that commands respect and has its share of surprises even now. There is no particular attempt at an inclusive thesis. What references there are to the idea of Rome are mostly positive and unremarkable; the advent of empire is seen as right and inevitable, but not transcendently so: "in the process very much has been lost" (MacCallum 1910: 344). The discussion of action and especially character, however, is richly inquisitive and nuanced; MacCallum seems to be staking his own territory when he praises the "purely humane and literary appreciations" of F. A. T. Kreyssig over the "metaphysical lucubrations" and "ponderous commentaries" of other German Shakespeareans (pp. vii–viii), and his own book is a worthy companion to Bradley. To read through it now is to find many of the conflicting positions of twentieth-century criticism already mapped out as possibilities, as well as a savviness about human behavior that is both old-fashioned and fresh:

> [Casca] seems to be one of those alert, precocious natures, clever at the uptake in their youth and full of a promise that is not always fulfilled: Brutus recalls that "he was quick mettle when we went to school" [1.2.296]. Such sprightly youngsters, when they fail, often do so from a certain lack of moral fibre. And so with Casca. He appears before us at first as the most obsequious henchman of Caesar. (p. 286)

Despite his general lack of interest in political issues in the abstract and what he takes to be "Shakespeare's indifference to questions of constitutional theory" (p. 518),

MacCallum has very interesting things to say about the political calculations of characters as they navigate the situations in which they find themselves. The most remarkable example is a sustained and still unsurpassed analysis of the behavior of the tribunes in *Coriolanus* (pp. 532ff.); the discussion is both canny and outraged, with the feel of real politics closely observed: "the means they take to ruin Coriolanus, though not without its astuteness, and similar enough to what is practised every day in parliamentary tactics, is altogether base" (p. 537). It builds to an unexpected and memorable conclusion:

> Yet they are not bad men. They are very like the majority of the citizens of Great and Greater Britain, and no inconsiderable portion of those who govern the Empire and its members. They have a certain amount of principle, shrewdness, and, if the test of misfortune comes, even of proper feeling. They would have made very worthy aldermen of a small municipality. (p. 541)

The tribunes are the rising bourgeoisie, in the root sense of that term.

A half-century later, books by Maurice Charney (1961) and D. A. Traversi (1963) respectively discuss the dramatic function of imagery in the Plutarchan plays and provide a close scene-by-scene commentary on the dramatic action. Charney's book in particular is a fine piece of work and still valuable on particular passages, but neither makes a major attempt at an inclusive thesis. G. Wilson Knight devotes the greater part of *The Imperial Theme* (1931) to the three plays, and fits them into a dithyrambic argument of his own, from *Julius Caesar* – "Love is here the regal, the conquering reality: the murder of Caesar is a gash in the body of Rome, and this gash is healed by love" (p. 63) – to *Antony and Cleopatra*: "we watch love calling man to her bosom; and death, gentle and soft as a nurse's love, drawing the wanderers, life, and last love itself, back to its peace" (p. 324). With the 1970s more aggressively and rigorously argued theories about the Plutarchan grouping begin to present themselves, and three in particular are worth reviewing in some detail.

J. L. Simmons (1973) argues for placing the three plays (*Titus* and *Cymbeline* as well, in a brief epilogue) within the Christian frame advocated by Barroll: Shakespeare's Rome is Augustine's *ciuitas terrena*, as yet ignorant of the true *ciuitas Dei*, but still to be understood from that perspective. It is almost an argument from absence. When Antony speaks of finding out new heaven, new earth, he does quote a biblical text that did not yet exist in the historical time of the play, and as though by accident reminds his audience that his own defeat will bring about the arrival of the Fourth Monarchy; but in general Simmons credits Shakespeare with pointedly avoiding this particular kind of anachronism. Seeing things this way makes possible some confident moral judgments on the characters' behavior, though they are not in fact Simmons's main goal; indeed, on *Antony and Cleopatra* he ends up as indulgent as anyone: "even the member of the audience who approaches it with Christian expectations is forced, finally, to approve the lovers" (p. 163). Simmons's real concern is with analyzing the situation of characters who do indeed have transcendent aspirations but find themselves in a world in which no genuine transcendence is possible or, except as may be said to happen in the last act of *Antony and Cleopatra*, imaginable. Such aspirations can only take the form of deluded ambitions that cannot do anything but fail. *Julius Caesar* is the tragic encounter of two such idealists: "a conflict between the good of Caesar (political order, stability, and glory), flawed by his potential evil, and Brutus's ideal of a world in which no Caesar is necessary, flawed by the nature of man" (p. 86). This model allows some compelling accounts of individual psychology, e.g., of "the ignoble aspect of Caesarism: since the aspirer cannot in reality attain the ideal, he must either accept himself as less or, because that is incompatible with his nature, finally pose as the ideal" (p. 106). The argument fits *Coriolanus* with austere clarity: "The ideals defining Roman virtue may be entirely of the Earthly City, but Coriolanus maintains and defends those ideals in a manner characteristic of one whose devotion is to the Eternal City" (p. 23). In particular, his implacable scorn of worldly praise – a scorn which Shakespeare perceptibly heightened beyond what he found in Plutarch – leads almost logically to a destructive rejection of the city to which he is so passionately devoted. Highminded desires that with the right object could seem wholly admirable become dangerous fanaticism when earthly politics is all there is.

It is possible to reach very similar conclusions without invoking Christianity, as Geoffrey Miles (1996) shows in his study of "constancy," an ethical standard which was quite explicit within the pagan world and received a serious revival in sixteenth-century thought. The first half of his book is a detailed study of the virtue of constancy as it is discussed by an influential series of classical and Renaissance writers (Cicero, Seneca, Lipsius, Montaigne), with particular attention to its role in Stoic philosophy and to its common involvement with metaphors of theatrical performance. From this vantage point he sees Shakespeare's choice of subjects for his Plutarchan plays as the deliberate creation of "a kind of triptych on the theme of constancy." The topic is not quite there in Plutarch himself, who was generally anti-Stoic in his philosophy, but Amyot and North "make it into a central issue by using the words 'constancy' and 'constant' to translate a variety of Greek expressions" (p. 110); and Shakespeare's own mind sorted things out into "an Aristotelian pattern of virtue as a mean between excess and defect: Brutus embodying the virtue of constancy, Antony its defect, inconstancy, and Coriolanus its excess, wilful obstinacy" (p. 111).

Miles does not, to be sure, think that Shakespeare's own judgments are ultimately Aristotelian; they are usually seen as closer to those of the French writer who has the longest single entry in the index. With Antony, the defect is finally something to celebrate: "Antony's ideal is un-Roman and un-Stoic, and is best defined in the words of Montaigne: in a mutable world, he chooses to embrace 'the benefit of inconstancy'" (p. 169). Cleopatra of course goes him one better, with a "triumphant evasion of the choice between constancy and mutability" that "makes the ending of *Antony and Cleopatra* more liberating than those of the other two Roman plays" (p. 188). Even earlier, in *Julius Caesar*, the ideal of constancy "is shown to be a flawed ideal, not humanly attainable, and therefore liable to involve its adherents in continual pretence and self-deception. In Montaigne's formula, it is 'a profitable desire; but likewise absurd'" (p. 135). Even the noblest Roman, the most balanced exemplar of the central Roman virtue, does not escape this absurdity:

> The death of Brutus embodies the complexity of "constancy" in *Julius Caesar*. He simultaneously fulfils the demands of Stoic ethics, remaining "constant as the Northern Star" in the face of defeat and death, and of Roman decorum, maintaining "formal constancy" and playing his part consistently to the end; in both ways he has been "always the same" in life, and will remain so in fame after his death. Both ideals, however, involve the strain of pretending to be what he is not, and concealing and suppressing his human weakness. It is not surprising that Brutus welcomes death. (pp. 147–8)

As in Simmons's book, the most powerful chapter is on *Coriolanus*; Miles indeed professes serious indebtedness to Simmons's reading, which he may be said to reformulate in secular terms, a conflict as it were between essentialist and constructivist assumptions: "The Roman concept of virtue, which for [Coriolanus] has been absolute truth, is for Rome a matter of opinion, a convenient assumption" (p. 156). The category mistake here drives the tragic action: "The Roman ideal of constancy logically leads the hero who pursues it to a point where he becomes no longer human, and, in order to remain consistent with the ideals his society has taught him but has failed to live up to, has to destroy it." In this connection Miles recalls a stunning observation of Kenneth Burke's: if the play's hero "became 'Coriolanus' by sacking Corioles, the name he would forge in the fire of Rome would have to be 'Romanus'" (p. 164).

Paul Cantor (1976) provides the most elaborate attempt so far to read these three plays as a cohesive statement about Roman history. His book is organized as a discussion of *Coriolanus* and *Antony and Cleopatra*, but *Julius Caesar* is always kept in view and is part of the foreconceit: "the three Roman plays form a kind of historical trilogy, dramatizing the rise and fall of the Roman Republic, in a sense the tragedy of Rome itself, in which the Republic is corrupted and eventually destroyed by its very success in conquering the world" (p. 16). The perspective that Cantor attributes to Shakespeare is less that of an outraged moralist than that of a political theorist; Cantor denies MacCallum's claim that Shakespeare is uninterested in such matters, and in particular that he was handicapped by "his inability to understand the ideals of an antique self-governing commonwealth controlled by all its free members as a body" (MacCallum 1910: 518). Quite the contrary, Shakespeare was attracted to the story of Coriolanus in part because it turned on the event that gave the Republic its distinctive constitutional shape: the creation of the tribunate, which made the regime a complicated, even confusing mixture of aristocracy and democracy. That confusion itself has a point; establishing the tribunate is a canny way of both deflecting a potential revolution while rewarding and harnessing the competitive energies of the more talented agitators: "The plebeians demand grain and instead get the right to elect five officers . . . The creation of the tribunate . . . while it does nothing about the demands of the people at large, does appeal to the real movers of the uprising by giving them an office of their own to which they can aspire" (Cantor 1976: 61). The genius of the Republic's success, as Cantor understands it, is its ability to stimulate such aspiration and turn it to account:

> The Republic works on a kind of merit system and, if it must err in one direction, it does so on behalf of the man on the way up in the world . . . Subordinates hope to rise to positions of authority by proving their courage and ability, while commanders must remain alert to opportunities for glory if they are not to be eclipsed by the men who serve under them. (p. 43)

Caesarism, on the other hand, changes things, and we see the consequences in *Antony and Cleopatra*:

> Because in the Empire a commander generally gets credit for his subordinates' accomplishments, the advantage is with those already in power, and the temptation for a commander to rest on his laurels is much greater than it is in the Republic. At the same time, for men trying to make their fortunes in the world, the inducement to perform heroic and glorious deeds for Rome is much less. (p. 44)

With this change comes "the demotion of the whole sphere of the political itself":

> The whole matter of a career in politics inevitably seems less attractive . . . The comparative rigidity of political hierarchy in the Empire works to redirect the energies of men from public to private life. Once the world of politics loses its glory, the world of eros can take on a new glamor. (p. 45)

Hence the love story that seems to swamp all rational political calculation; and though the military victory of Octavius over Antony and Cleopatra is secure, the values that Antony and Cleopatra embody are in many ways the natural product of the new regime:

> The early Roman Empire supplies the hothouse conditions necessary for such exotic flowers as the imperial love of Antony and Cleopatra to flourish. Antony, in evaluating the relative merits of politics and love, is confronted with a particular form of politics that encourages a very special brand of love. (p. 128)

The Roman world will inevitably be seeing more of this.

Cantor develops his thesis almost entirely through evidence from the plays themselves, with an occasional assist from Plutarch (several of the quotations above follow specifically from an adroit juxtaposition of *Coriolanus*, 1.1.252ff. and *Antony and Cleopatra*, 3.1). Cantor deliberately avoids reference to thinking about Roman history elsewhere in Renaissance England; the argument he detects in Shakespeare has some correlation with the *Tacitismo* that Hunter finds in advanced intellectual circles of the time, though it is more detailed than anything we can document elsewhere and also takes some turns of its own. For one thing, the erotic indulgence associated with the onset of the Empire is not merely decadence. Cantor is less romantic than many in his discussion of Antony and Cleopatra – he writes of a "bedrock of nihilism" underlying their passion (p. 166) and thinks their own imperial reign would be cruel and ugly – but he does not deny the celebratory tone with which Shakespeare renders their gorgeously un-Republican way of life; traditional Roman values do indeed repress things that ought not to be repressed. And the Republic itself, as depicted in *Coriolanus*, is a set-up with major internal contradictions that are inseparable from its virtues and make its demise inevitable; the story in question, after all, is of how the city cannot accommodate the purest product of its own system and is almost destroyed as a consequence. In the final analysis both regimes are most notable for their failures:

> Either Rome, Republic or Empire, is potentially tragic in the disparity between human aspirations and the reality they encounter. Ultimately the source of tragedy in Rome can be traced to the fact that the Republic seems to offer men nobility only at the price of wisdom and self-knowledge, while the Empire offers freedom in private life only at the price of a lasting and meaningful public context for nobility. (p. 207)

In structuring his discussion, Cantor expands on a suggestion apparently first made by Geoffrey Bullough, that *Coriolanus* and *Antony and Cleopatra* are in effect programmatic explorations of what came to be called, respectively, the irascibile and the concupiscible parts of the soul. Cantor reverts to the original form of this opposition in Plato's tripartite division of the soul in the *Republic* and the *Phaedrus*; below the rational part are ranked two other parts, τὸ θυμοειδές and τὸ ἐπιθυμητικόν, both irrational but in very different ways. As far as Shakespeare's usage is concerned, Cantor thinks the Platonic terms roughly correlate with "pride" and "appetite"; in his own discussion, he generally calls the third part "eros," and for the the second part he uses the rather awkward "spiritedness," intended as a translation of the Greek *thumos*. No claim is made that Shakespeare read Plato (it is not likely that he did), and the schema runs the risk of looking like an arbitrary importation; I think it is actually one of the most suggestive ideas in Cantor's book, more so than he realized at the time, and I will be returning to it below.

Miola's (1983) book offers the most significant polemics on the need to go beyond the three Plutarchan plays in talking about Shakespeare's Rome, though doing so does not yield a thesis as tightly crafted as those just surveyed, nor until its last act an especially innovative one. Miola is not in fact particularly kind to *Lucrece* and *Titus*: "Romans here, for the most part, are stereotypes, stiff figures of cardboard and paste . . . Both the narrative poem and the early play are exercise pieces" (p. 236). Their value is primarily to set out a rather stark version of Romanitas:

> [Lucrece's] suicide is an exercise of *pietas*, the quintessentially Roman and Vergilian subordination of self to the obligations of family and city. It transforms Lucrece into a

symbol of constancy and honor, thereby winning the fame that to her mind is an acquittal and a glorious reward. (p. 39)

In *Lucrece* this act is fully successful on its own terms, and brings about the city's moral and political regeneration; in subsequent Roman works, however, Shakespeare highlights the problematics of the Roman ethos, especially the ways in which *pietas* is repeatedly ignored or perverted and the obsession with fame leads directly to violence against oneself and others. The first mature product of this endeavor is *Julius Caesar*, which "depicts the city that entangles itself with its strength" (p. 236), with no real solution in evidence. When Shakespeare returns to Rome a decade later in *Antony and Cleopatra*, he is as concerned with non-Roman values as with Roman ones, and eventually gives the latter the edge: "No longer the central focus of our attention, Rome is relegated at the end of the play to the status of its former opponents" (pp. 162–3). *Coriolanus* is a sour return to Rome at its most unappealing and self-destructive, with "precious little of that tragedy which catches the throat, swells the heart, and lifts the spirit, leaving us wise and rich in sorrow" (p. 237). Miola's argument becomes liveliest and most interesting when he moves from this negativity to the countervailing promise in *Cymbeline*, whose Christian overtones he interprets primarily in ethnic terms. "The grand conclusion . . . reconciles the warring factions of the larger, extended Trojan family and thus creates the blessed peace that descends upon all, Briton and Roman alike" – though it is a reconciliation in which one party clearly comes off the better: "British valor triumphs over Roman might, but more importantly, British flexibility and humility overcome Roman constancy and honor" (p. 233). The story of Imogen is the story of Lucrece with a happier outcome, and her chastened husband becomes an exemplar of Roman values transcended:

> Posthumus's intention to "shame the guise o' th' world" by starting a new "fashion" aims directly at overturning the Roman military ethos that encourages destruction of life for fame and glory . . . After vanquishing and disarming Iachimo, he leaves him unharmed, pointedly refusing to exalt himself over the body of an enemy. Posthumus rejects the Roman vanity of personal honor for the exercise of British mercy and compassion. (p. 227)

The most notable feature of Miola's book, however, is its ongoing attention to a number of classical texts whose allusive weight may be felt pressing on all of Shakespeare's Roman works. There has been no lack of such scrutiny in the past, of course, though Plutarch's prominence has tended to attract most of the attention his way; Miola brings a mind unusually well stocked with some of the standard Latin works of Renaissance literacy – especially Ovid and Vergil – and a vigorous willingness to explore the possibilities, particularly as they relate to Shakespeare's commerce with classical mythmaking about Rome and its fate. Miola's eye for his own detections is not especially critical:

The scene in Titus's house recalls the original scene of Procne's revenge and Ovid's description, *pars inde cavis exsultat aenis, / pars veribus stridunt; manant penetralia tabo* [*Metamorphoses*, 6.645–6], "part bubbles in brazen kettles, part sputters on spits; while the whole room drips with gore." This *penetralia* in turn may summon up remembrance of the other Roman *penetralia* where Tarquin raped Lucrece [*Fasti*, 2.787] and, of course, the archetypal Trojan *penetralia* where vengeful Pyrrhus slew Priam and his son [*Aeneid*, 2.508]. Like Pyrrhus and Tarquin, Titus perverts the life-sustaining *penetralia* to a chamber of horrors. (p. 70)

"Like" is itself not worth quarreling with, but the specific linkage here by way of a Latin word that has no particular equivalent in either of the English texts in question is something of a card trick. We have no good reason to think that Shakespeare actually laid eyes on the Latin word; and even if he did, it is not likely that he would have made the association that is not in fact relevant in classical Latin but that clearly hovers over Miola's interest in the matter, the modern leap from architectural *penetralia* to sexual penetration.

On other occasions, though, the bells ring in his head to better effect. One goes off in connection with an *aposiopesis* of Cleopatra's that has been something of a crux: "Something it is I would – / O, my oblivion is a very Antony, / And I am all forgotten" (1.3.89–91). MacCallum devotes an appendix to the question, rejects the theory that Cleopatra declines to announce her pregnancy and favors the notion that she declines to suggest marriage. Pursuing that kind of answer, Miola thinks, is to miss a connection that you would not want to miss: "Shakespeare . . . probably has no one word in mind, but merely wishes to dramatize Cleopatra's love by depicting her confusion. He may well have taken his cue from Vergil's description of Dido in love: *exposcit pendetque iterum narrantis ab ore* [*Aeneid*, 4.79], 'she essays to speak and stops with the word half-spoken.'" Marlowe, unquestionably working from Vergil, has his Dido say something close enough to Shakespeare's wording to inhibit suspicions that Miola is just hearing things (*Dido, Queen of Carthage*, 3.4.26–9); and within this similarity, the difference in the respective contexts has its weight of significance: "The transfer of Dido's initial confusion to Cleopatra's leavetaking reverses the Vergilian progression from loving speechlessness to articulate anger. Shakespeare's Cleopatra progresses from articulate anger to loving speechlessness" (p. 126). We should probably never feel sure that such filiations have been fully explored.

Two recent books offer themselves as representing self-conscious critical movements as they come to deal with these plays. One is a collection edited by Graham Holderness, Bryan Loughrey, and Andrew Murphy (1996), which gathers examples of the "radical new criticism" of the 1980s and early 1990s "produced by those critics who can be said, very broadly speaking, to fall within the New Historicist/Cultural Materialist critical spectrum" (p. 3). The existence of the collection itself points up the absence so far of a thoroughgoing treatment of these plays from this direction; as a prospectus for such a treatment, though, it is disappointing, with even good discussions repeatedly getting off track. In that volume, Terence Hawkes compromises an absorbing account of a 1926 production of *Coriolanus* (in Stratford, on

Shakespeare's birthday, at the time of the General Strike) by tying it to a very sloppy case for retaining F1's "flatter'd" at 5.6.115, rather than F3's "flutter'd," and goes so far – he admits he is being "briefly outrageous" – as to hold up a nineteenth-century performance in which "flutter'd" was memorably performed by William Phelps as "a crucial moment of containment and enlistment. In it, the play is finally and irrevocably recruited to a conservative project in which the claims of single subjectivity are asserted against the collective demands of the state" (p. 164). Presumably, if you want to contest that project and challenge that irrevocability you have to reject the usual emendation; moreover: "It is not insignificant that Phelps's performance was first given in 1848, the year in which Charlotte Brontë wrote *Shirley* and, of course, the year of European revolutions" (pp. 164–5). Before he is done, the transfer of the 1926 performance to a movie theatre (the Shakespeare Memorial Theatre had mysteriously burned down) is making Hawkes think of the advent of talkies the next year with Al Jolson singing "Mammy" in blackface: "another errant protagonist, kneeling at his mother's feet" (p. 167). The drive for polemical brilliance is so impatient it keeps any serious argument from gathering its resources.

The best representative of the collection's announced agenda is Annabel Patterson's excerpted discussion of *Coriolanus* from *Shakespeare and the Popular Voice* (published in 1989). This is the Roman play with the most clearly documentable topicality, a long recognized connection to the Midlands Rising of 1607. Patterson, working through the evidence and carefully analyzing Shakespeare's portrayal of the plebeians, argues that, whatever the play's later attractiveness (Hawkes gives some memorable details) to reactionaries and even fascists, in its own time it shows the power of appeals to classical antiquity to authorize a more democratic politics than might otherwise be imaginable: "ancient history provided precedents for attributing far more power to the common people than seventeenth-century England; and . . . Shakespeare exploited these precedents to the utmost by refusing to let the matter drop" (p. 123). Patterson follows this up with a look at proceedings in parliament in 1610, where a version of Menenius' metaphor of the body becomes a point of contention, to very interesting effect; she finds no particular evidence that the parliamentarians had seen Shakespeare's play or that he was reading their speeches, but she earns the right to say that

> our interpretation of both is richer if we assume a horizontal force field of connections between them, an intertextuality authorized by historical circumstances, and by the intensity of the concerns that revitalized old metaphors and carried them, on the popular circuits, from mouth to mouth and from mind to mind. (p. 126)

Much of what is on display, however, is more on the order of Hawkes's essay. There is a good deal of posturing about being in a movement ("as a cultural materialist I don't believe in common humanity"; Alan Sinfield, p. 50); much energy goes into asserting a sharp break with the critical past, sometimes by cartoonish exaggeration ("Traversi's texts appear virtually to be hermetically sealed, viewed by Traversi entirely within their own terms and held in splendid isolation from their historical context";

the editors, p. 6) or by belligerent misrepresentation (Simmons is slotted by Michael Bristol into a line of "traditional historicism" that makes *Coriolanus* "a theodicy of the absolutist state" (p. 136) – more or less the opposite of Simmons's main point). In the strangest instance of this, the editors include one essay from outside the movement, an excerpt from Miola's chapter on *Cymbeline* (their one real venture beyond the Plutarchan triptych), and deliberately present it as a bad example, the work of a "naive Christian" who "fails to attend to the *imperial* politics which provides the true link between Rome and Britain" (p. 14). The editors also misidentify it as a selection from Cantor's book of the same name.

None of this makes the movement look good. The higher purpose repeatedly invoked is political, the need "to check the tendency . . . to add Shakespearean authority to reactionary discourses" in the contemporary world (Sinfield, p. 59). The contributors often write as if that tendency were a clear and present danger, but they are not very resourceful in describing it for those who do not already see it. Sinfield is amusingly scathing about the use of Shakespeare in an advertisement for the Royal Ordnance Company in *The Armed Forces Journal International* ("We helped protect the Globe in 1588"), and builds to a dire conclusion: "The conferral of cultural authority is a principal role of Shakespeare in our societies: he may be made to underwrite state bellicosity" (p. 49). But Sinfield also mocks the place of a now privatized Royal Ordnance in the present scheme of things – "the weapons business is an uncertain one for a British manufacturing base enfeebled by a decade of Thatcherism and subject to international developments over which it has no influence" (p. 46) – and has no evidence to offer that the really dangerous players in the international arms trade make any use of Shakespeare in their marketing. Sinfield's real target is of course not the arms merchants but his own professional colleagues, whose generally leftwing allegiances (I do not exclude myself here) make them particularly susceptible to bullying on political grounds. Step back a bit and what you see is not a call to practical political action but a strategy of group intimidation within the always competitive world of academic ambition; an important part of the argument is scaring the reader with what it would take to dispute, say, John Drakakis's reading of Thomas Platter's description of his visit to the Globe: "this carefully tailored brand of anti-intellectual prophylactic consumerism demands a kind of passivity that refuses to contemplate, among other things, the popular significance of that unsettling carnivalesque dance that closed the Globe performance of *Julius Caesar*" (p. 41, attacking Boris Ford). Nobody but a "humanities intellectual" (Sinfield's term) would even understand the insult you would be trying to duck by agreeing.

Kahn's (1997) book is a more rewarding look at Shakespeare's Roman works under the rubric of feminist criticism. She trips at the gate with an assertion that the word "patriarchy" itself "comes from Latin," but she is convincing about "the degree to which . . . Romanness is virtually identical with an ideology of masculinity" in almost all theorizing and mythmaking with that concept; it is her contention that Shakespeare "dramatized precisely this linkage and, in doing so, demystified its power." She offers the new work as both a continuation of her earlier book, *Man's Estate* (1981), and a change of direction away from the psychoanalytic: "I am concerned here with the social dimensions of *virtus* – its interdependence with political constructions of the state and the family, and with the intertextuality of Shakespeare and the Latin authors he read" (p. 2). There has of course been a fair amount of recent thinking in this spirit about individual works and characters; Kahn cites it generously and in detail – including some as late as 1995 – and her book is among other things a well documented window onto this chapter in the critical tradition. Kahn's own chapters deal, for the most part, with particular works from the perspective of a particular topic: in *Titus* the "'exchange model' of father–daughter sacrifice" (p. 48), for instance, or in *Coriolanus* the "interaction between mothering and warmaking" (p. 145). These topics tend not to carry over from chapter to chapter, in a way that interferes with any sense of a continuous argument. A postscript on *Cymbeline* attempts some shaping:

> Posthumus's forgiveness of Imogen is . . . a striking departure not only from the intransigence of Claudio, Leontes, and Othello, but from the Roman pattern of placing women in a separate domain while pairing heroes most importantly with their emulous male rivals rather than with women . . . Surely the play works as hard to enable Posthumus to accept "the woman's part" as to foster manly virtue in him. (p. 168)

But there has been little in the previous chapters to suggest a movement in this direction – even, interestingly enough, in the chapter on *Antony* – and *Cymbeline* provides more a point of contrast than a sense of narrative closure.

Kahn summarizes her thesis in terms of "three main foci of Shakespeare's problematic of Roman virtue," linked to the three topics in her subtitle: warriors, wounds, and women. The alliteration does not quite unify this trinity, whose members certainly are not at war with each other, and often cooperate, but also at times function pretty much on their own. The dominant one, and also the most consequential, seems to me the first:

> "Warriors" evokes the central motif of the Greco-Roman heroic tradition – the agon, that "zero-sun game" of rivalry through which the hero wins his name by pitting himself against his likeness or equal in contests of courage and strength. From Achilles and Hector to Antony and Octavius, pairs of evenly matched heroes act out a mixture of admiration, imitation, and domination which the English Renaissance calls emulation . . . Shakespeare's Roman heroes strive to prove themselves men not in relation to women, but against a rival whom they emulate in two senses – by imitating as the mirror-image of an ideal self, and by competing against with the aim of excelling and dominating. Emulation figures and enacts the differences *within* the masculine; thus it fractures a seemingly unified *virtus*. (p. 15)

This development of Eve Sedgwick's theory of male homosocial relations is central in two chapters. Kahn sees the Roman agonistic spirit as responsible for the political situation that we find in *Julius Caesar*:

Instead of holding monarchy, aristocracy and democracy in balance, the republic has fostered the division of the aristocracy into factions and the rise of military superheroes, The republic, in fact, has generated what it was designed to oppose: the concentration of power in one man's hands. (p. 86)

In this regard, Caesar's "insistence on his own superiority to any fellow Roman is only seemingly unrepublican" (p. 88); and indeed, his opponents play the same game, without entirely reckoning what they are up to:

At precisely those points at which [Brutus] fulfills his function as the voice of republican purism . . . he also pursues a not-so-subtle one-upmanship against Cassius . . . In each instance, as many critics have noted, Brutus makes a tactical error. This succession of blunders marks the ideological fault line of *Julius Caesar*, the point at which republican idealism and emulation meet and clash. (p. 95)

This is so exclusively a man's game that Portia, even after proving her masculine *bona fides* by hurting herself, serves as Kahn understands it only the purpose of giving voice to misgivings that her husband can then dismiss as wifely.

Even more remarkably, Kahn deemphasizes the role of the most important woman in any of the Roman plays; *Antony and Cleopatra* is discussed primarily as the story of Antony and Octavius: "Their contest for mastery is at least as important in Shakespeare's play as the love story" (p. 112). In that contest others repeatedly find themselves only temporary players:

The play's rivalrous dyads constantly re-form into trios, then revert to dyads, for third parties give the fractious "brothers" cause to part as much as they also make peace between them . . . Antony has just patched up his quarrel with Caesar and bound himself anew to him as "brother" by marrying Octavia. Precisely at this moment, he feels the itch of emulation again, the urge to match himself against Caesar. (p. 114)

In this long-running game the famous polarity between Rome and Egypt is not so much a profound contrast of values as simply part of the grid:

Antony's attraction to Cleopatra, rather than simply feminizing him in the service of her lust (as the Romans believe), in fact enters into the dynamics of rivalry. His surrenders to her wily charms, combined with her perceived betrayals, impel him to reassert his masculinity and his Roman identity precisely through his emulous bond with Caesar. (p. 116)

His suicide is itself a move in that game, and he is in it right to the end:

By spending his last moments with Cleopatra, Antony, it cannot be denied, attests to his love for her – a love that sets him decisively apart from his Roman comrades . . . But even in her arms, with death upon him, he portrays himself as "a Roman by a Roman / Valiantly vanquished" [4.15.56–7], countering the undertow of her attraction

for him by evoking a reciprocity with Caesar that, even though fatal, insures Romanness. (p. 137)

In her strong development of this theme, Kahn seems to be preparing for her chapter
on *Coriolanus*; it is something of a surprise when that (comparatively short) chapter is
almost wholly devoted to the relations between mother and son, without anything of
importance to say about Coriolanus and Aufidius. As it is, Kahn comes close, within
her more general complex of concerns, to offering her own tightly conceived thesis
about the Plutarchan triptych.

That thesis is worth more comment. Kahn's interest in Roman competitiveness
emerges in connection with her feminist agenda, as an area in which the unstable and
problematic nature of Roman manliness is unusually clear and open to scrutiny; but
other agendas prompt the same interest, and it is useful to widen the field of view
here. Public competitiveness is also the mainspring of Roman republicanism in
Cantor's theory, and a significantly mixed blessing: a source of communal strength
when managed right, but full of inherent dangers and indeed, as for Kahn, the key
to the republic's own demise when the contest finally yields a single winner. The term
"spiritedness" does not make the point clear, but English translations of Plato never
do. The Greek, however, is consistent and specific; the second part of the soul is the
part that is φιλόνικος and φιλότιμος, in love with winning and with receiving τιμή,
prizes in the game of public combat (*Republic* 581B and elsewhere) – the competitive
part of the soul. Postulating an entire part of the soul for this appetite implies that
that appetite is not, in current parlance, a cultural construct; but having it so does
not make it unproblematic. In Plato's model it is a nobler appetite than that of the
third part – for bodily sustenance and physical pleasure – but nevertheless an irrational appetite and destructive when left to its own devices. It needs to be firmly allied
to the rational part of the soul in order for its energy to be put to good use; indeed,
ascertaining what alliances are being formed in the party politics of a particular soul
is an important analytic act. That still seems to me a good way to think about the
matter; among others who have thought so, and have approached some of the most
important questions about their cultural heritage from this angle, is Plutarch:

> For men like Agesilaüs, or Lysander, or Nicias, or Alcibiades could indeed conduct wars
> well, and understood how to be victorious commanders in battles by land and sea, but
> they would not use their successes so as to win legitimate favour and promote the right.
> Indeed, if one excepts the action at Marathon, the sea-fight at Salamis Plataea, Ther-
> mopylae, and the achievements of Cimon at the Eurymedon and about Cyprus, Greece
> has fought all her battles to bring servitude upon herself, and every one of her trophies
> stands as a memorial of her own calamity and disgrace, since she owed her overthrow
> chiefly to the baseness and contentiousness [φιλονεικία] of her leaders. (*Flamininus*, 11.3,
> trans. Perrin)

Plutarch's writing is deeply steeped in Plato, and he refers more than once to the
tripartite model of the soul; two such references, in fact, provide specific authoriza-

tion for Cantor's schematizing of Shakespeare's second and third Plutarchan plays as contrasting studies of *thumos* and *eros* (Plutarch, *Coriolanus*, 15.3 and *Antony*, 36.1). The terminology associated with the Platonic model and with its Aristotelian descendent filters through the *Lives*, particularly that related to the soul's second part; it is key to assessing a personal style that could fuel the military and political achievements that were responsible for Plutarch's interest in writing about these individuals, but that also in his view brought the Hellenic world as a whole to ultimate defeat. The same analytic eye is now turned on the victors in that fight, who have proven themselves more successful at reconciling individual ambition and imperial stability, but have not escaped the underlying problematic. Plutarch views the Romans from an intimate distance, an almost fully assimilated Greek performing his offices within the Roman political structure (and even learning Latin) but also capable of a detachment informed precisely by the course of Greek cultural history. The story of Coriolanus in particular is a warning of what can happen with insufficient education and conditioning: an overindulgence τῷ θυμοειδεῖ καὶ φιλονείκῳ μέρει τῆς ψυχῆς, in the thumoeidic and victory-loving part of the soul, beyond anything on view among the Greeks.

The specificity of language often does not survive the passage through Amyot to North. The phrase from the life of Coriolanus becomes simply "too full of passion and choler" (North 1963, I: 125); when Alexander the Great is described as θυμοειδής (*Alexander*, 4.7), North manages nothing more salient than "hasty" (ibid: 283). These lapses may perhaps be seen as the conceptual vacuum being filled by the new language of constancy which Miles catalogs. Yet Plutarch's own orientation inheres in many of the narrative choices he makes about character and action, and it is not unreasonable to see Shakespeare as responding to them in a version of the spirit in which they were originally made. As Kahn notes, the *Lives* themselves were overtly marketed to their Elizabethan audience as a source of models for emulation, and the otherwise puzzling habit of presenting paired lives makes the very business of biography competitive: "Plutarch implicitly sets up rivalries between Greeks and Romans, setting one against another" (pp. 16–17). She also pauses over Plutarch's description of Julius Caesar as engaged in "no other but an emulation with himself as with another man" (Kahn 1997: 90; North 1963, II: 38) – a passage which Shakespeare does not quote directly but which has seemed to more than one critic to be guiding Shakespeare's conception of that character. I think the full picture here has yet to be drawn. What Cantor and Kahn have come upon is one of the deepest levels of Shakespeare's kinship with Plutarch, and their respective theories are contemporary turns in an almost bimillennial conversation.

REFERENCES AND FURTHER READING

Barroll, J. L. (1958). Shakespeare and Roman History. *Modern Language Review*, 53, 327–43.

Bate, J. (ed.) (1995). *Titus Andronicus*. The Arden Shakespeare. London: Routledge.

Cantor, P. A. (1976). *Shakespeare's Rome: Republic and Empire.* Ithaca, NY: Cornell University Press.

Charney, M. (1961). *Shakespeare's Roman Plays: The Function of Imagery in the Drama.* Cambridge, MA: Harvard University Press.

Holderness, G., Loughrey, B., and Murphy, A. (eds.) (1996). *Shakespeare: The Roman Plays.* Longman Critical Readers. London: Longman.

Hunter G. K. (1977). A Roman Thought: Attitudes to History Exemplified in Shakespeare and Jonson. In B. S. Lee (ed.) *An English Miscellany Presented to W. S. Mackie.* Cape Town: Oxford University Press.

Kahn, C. (1997). *Roman Shakespeare: Warriors, Wounds, and Women.* London: Routledge.

Knight, G. W. (1931). *The Imperial Theme: Further Interpretations of Shakespeare's Tragedies, Including the Roman Plays.* London: Oxford University Press.

Leggatt, A. (1988). *Shakespeare's Political Drama: The History Plays and the Roman Plays.* London: Routledge.

MacCallum, M. W. (1910). *Shakespeare's Roman Plays and their Background.* London: Macmillan.

Marshall, C. (2000). Shakespeare, Crossing the Rubicon. *Shakespeare Survey,* 53, 73–88.

Martindale, C. and Martindale, M. (1990). *Shakespeare and the Uses of Antiquity: An Introductory Essay,* London: Routledge.

Miles, G. B. (1989). How Roman are Shakespeare's "Romans"? *Shakespeare Quarterly,* 40, 257–83.

——(1996). *Shakespeare and the Constant Romans.* Oxford: Clarendon Press.

Miola, R. S. (1983). *Shakespeare's Rome.* Cambridge: Cambridge University Press.

North, Sir Thomas (trans.) (1963). *Selected Lives from the Lives of the Noble Grecians and Romans,* 2 vols., ed. P. Turner. Carbondale: Southern Illinois University Press.

Pelling, C. B. R. (ed.) (1988). *Plutarch: Life of Antony.* Cambridge Greek and Latin Classics. Cambridge: Cambridge University Press.

Platt, M. (1983). *Rome and Romans According to Shakespeare,* revd. edn. Lanham, MD: University Press of America.

Plutarch (1914–26). *Plutarch's Lives,* 11 vols., ed. and trans. B. Perrin. Loeb Classical Library. Cambridge, MA: Harvard University Press.

Ronan, C. (1995). *"Antike Roman": Power Symbology and the Roman Play in Early Modern England, 1585–1635.* Athens, GA: University of Georgia Press.

Shakespeare, W. (1974). *The Riverside Shakespeare,* ed. G. B. Evans et al. Boston, MA: Houghton Mifflin.

Siegel, P. N. (1986). *Shakespeare's English and Roman History Plays: A Marxist Approach.* London: Associated University Presses.

Simmons, J. L. (1973). *Shakespeare's Pagan World: The Roman Tragedies.* Charlottesville: University Press of Virginia.

Spenser, T. J. B. (1957). Shakespeare and the Elizabethan Romans. *Shakespeare Survey,* 10, 27–38.

Thomas, V. (1989). *Shakespeare's Roman Worlds.* London: Routledge.

Traversi, D. (1963). *Shakespeare: The Roman Plays.* Stanford, CA: Stanford University Press.

Velz, J. W. (1978). The Ancient World in Shakespeare: Authenticity or Anachronism? A Retrospect. *Shakespeare Survey,* 31, 1–12.

11

Tragedy and Geography

Jerry Brotton

Meantime we shall express our darker purpose.
Give me a map there. Know that we have divided
In three our kingdom.
King Lear (1.1.34–6)

Lear's famously opaque lines are a good place to begin any discussion of the relation-ship between geography and Shakespearean tragedy. However, Lear's map actually poses more questions than it answers. The physical presence of the map on stage might suggest both a sophisticated understanding of the place of geography and the impor-tance of cartography in the dramatic action of the play. But what is the specific nature of Lear's map? Does its presence suggest a more profound understanding of the geog-raphy of tragedy, or is it simply a convenient stage prop? Would the original use of the map attempt to recreate the historical geography of the play's setting in ancient Britain, or anachronistically deploy a modern, late sixteenth-century map to speak to more contemporary concerns?

The ambivalent status of Lear's map has led modern film and theatre directors to recreate this moment using anything from a giant medieval *mappa mundi* to a hand-held ordnance survey map. It is tempting to use recent developments in the field of cultural geography and the critical theory of space to argue that Lear's map, and Shakespeare's interest in geography, provide a new way of reading the tragedies. Various literary critics of the period have identified an increasingly spatial dimension to sixteenth-century poetry, prose, and drama. Examining literary developments in early modern France, Tom Conley (1996) has explored how "writings are spatially conceived and materially determined; they explore surfaces and volumes in ways that were perhaps unknown prior to the development of print culture and the discovery of the New World" (p. xi). In his analysis of the work of writers including Rabelais and Montaigne, Conley identifies a "drive to locate and implant oneself in a named space" (p. 303) in response to an expanding world picture and the slow, uneven rise of the national sovereign state. Prior to Conley's work, Walter Cohen argued in his classic study *Drama of a Nation: Public Theater in Renaissance England and Spain* (1985), that one abiding dimension of late sixteenth-century popular commercial theatre in England and Spain was its drive towards the enactment and definition of these emerging national spaces. For Cohen, "public theater was a crucial mediator between drama and society" (p. 151). In a culture that possessed few means by which to disseminate mass, standardized images of itself to its subjects, the public theatre possessed a unique ability to dramatize the space of a national "imagined community" (Anderson 1983) for its audience.

The most obvious point to make in any discussion of Shakespeare's geography is the sheer *range* and diversity of his dramatic locations. Rome, Verona, Denmark, Venice, ancient Britain and Scotland are all primary locations for his tragedies, not to mention the journeys within the plays that take us to places as varied as Mantua, Cyprus, Syria, Antium and even, just occasionally, England. The plays also exhibit some highly topical examples of Shakespeare's interest in cartography and contemporary mapmaking. His most famous explicit use of cartography occurs in act 3.2 of *Twelfth Night*, where Maria satirizes Malvolio's comical ability to "smile his face into more lines than is in the new map with the augmentation of the Indies" (3.2.67–8), an explicit reference to Edward Wright's 1599 map of the world. Curiously, a similar cartographic humor occurs in *The Comedy of Errors*: Dromio of Syracuse similarly mocks Nell, as "spherical, like a globe. I could find out countries in her" (3.2.113–14). However, it is important to distinguish between Shakespeare's use of maps and geography with the more integral role that geography plays in the drama of his contemporaries, most noticeably Marlowe. Both parts of *Tamburlaine Parts I and II* draw extensively on the maps and geographical rhetoric to be found in Abraham Ortelius's hugely influential atlas, *Theatrum orbis terrarum* (1570) (Seaton 1964), which, as John Gillies (1994) has already pointed out, is symptomatic of the intimate rhetorical relations between theatre, globe, and atlas (pp. 70–98). However, it would be overstating the case to claim that Shakespeare's drama, and in particular his tragedies, are exclusively structured around contemporary apprehensions of geography and mapping.

In what follows I want to suggest that the tragedies display a growing awareness of the dramatic and rhetorical opportunities afforded by geography in its varied metaphorical possibilities as well as its material manifestation in the shape of maps of the kind that Lear uses to divide his kingdom and launch the tragedy of *King Lear*. From the geographical (and concomitantly historical) imprecision of early tragedies like *Titus Andronicus* and *Romeo and Juliet*, high tragedies such as *King Lear* and *Macbeth* are heavily influenced by the accession of James I, and the pressing political requirement to incorporate the new geographical idea of "Britain" into the dramatic imagination.

Subsequent tragedies like *Othello* represent an increasingly sophisticated representation of the metaphorical and material possibilities of geography in heightening the poetic texture of the language, and increasing the dramatic intensity of the tragic action. This culminates in the epic geography of *Antony and Cleopatra*, where a global panorama draws on wider cultural and political assumptions about the power associated with the geographical gaze. This is not a smooth development towards a comprehensive vision of geography, but a discontinuous borrowing and absorption of various overlapping aspects of geographical discourse, that allows Shakespeare's tragedies to construct a sense of geographical awareness as much as they represent it, through the uniquely popular form of drama itself.

Before expanding on this approach to Shakespearean tragedy, it is necessary to define just what is meant by the term "geography," and its related terms cosmography, chorography, hydrography, and topography. The classic definition of geography that circulated throughout the sixteenth century came from Ptolemy's second-century AD *Geographia*. Ptolemy stated: "Geography is a representation in picture of the whole known world together with the phenomena which are contained therein" (Ptolemy 1991: 25). This is an elegant but notoriously imprecise definition, which encapsulated chorography (the representation of local and regional territory), hydrography (the cartographic representation of the sea and its currents), and topography (the art of surveying and estate management). However, scholars and practitioners working in one or more of these fields often preferred to refer to their practice as cosmography. The term referred to the integrated study of earthly and celestial spheres, and conferred an aura of expertise and mystical power upon those working in what would otherwise appear to be quite basic areas of land measurement and coastal plotting. Throughout the sixteenth century cosmography covered a multitude of geographical practices, whilst always grounding its exploration of the terrestrial world within a larger celestial world picture (Lestringant 1994).

Whilst care needs to be taken when discussing sixteenth-century apprehensions of "geography," it should also be remembered that mapping provided fiction with one of its basic structural terms: plot. Lorna Hutson and William Sherman have both pointed out that in the sixteenth century the term "plot" (often spelt "plat") referred to the plan or scheme of action in literature, as well as a map (Hutson 1993; Sherman 1995). In the 1570s Sir Thomas Smith wrote to Elizabeth concerning the English plantation in Ulster, arguing, "It is high time some conclusion were made, and some plat drawn up to be followed in that enterprise of Ulster" (Andrews 1970). Maps were therefore regarded as rhetorically powerful tools with which to move and shape people and ideas. However, this is also the task of the plot in a literary text – it shapes people's emotions and encourages them to make investments in the text they are reading or performance they are watching. This close connection between the worlds of literature and geography suggests that fiction drew on the spatial and rhetorical dimensions of "plot" in creating emotionally effective poetry and drama. So even before establishing specific examples of Shakespeare's use of geography, it would seem that his "plots" were already imbued with spatial and geographical resonance.

The printing and publication of Shakespeare's sources for many of the tragedies, Belleforest's *Histoires Tragiques* (1576) and Holinshed's *Chronicles* (second edition, 1587), were also symptomatic of a wider late sixteenth-century drive to spatialize the "plot" of historical narration. "Plots" as spatial and narratological devices had already been held up as crucial to the practice of statecraft in Thomas Elyot's hugely influential book on statecraft, *The Boke Named the Governour* (1531). Elyot advised young gentlemen to incorporate maps and geographical material into narrative history as a way of more vividly understanding its action. Elyot encouraged aspiring diplomats and counselors "to behold the old tables of Ptolemy, wherein all the world is painted" (p. 35). Such maps and charts "persuadeth and stirreth the beholder, and sooner instructeth him, than the declaration in writing" (p. 24) of history.

Finally, an important distinction should be made between Shakespeare's use of *cartography* as opposed to *geography*. Cartography refers strictly to the creation of maps and charts, whilst geography deals more generally with the physical and political description of the earth's surface in all its manifestations. Shakespeare's explicit references to maps (see above) are not necessarily related to the geographical place, or ground, upon which his dramatic action takes place. What follows is not an historical geography of Shakespeare's apprehension of locations from Denmark to Venice, but an attempt to grasp how Shakespeare understood geography both practically and metaphorically, and how he incorporated these insights into the tragic process.

In Shakespeare's earliest experiments in tragedy, there is very little sustained engagement with geography either at the level of setting and place, or in terms of language and metaphor. In *Romeo and Juliet* the geographical setting of Verona is little more than an early experiment in the dramatic recreation of Italianate settings, in much the same way that *The Comedy of Errors* absorbs and reproduces the classical geography of Plautine comedy. The geography of the play is primarily domestic, in its focus on the "two households" whose conflict structures the play's action. Romeo's claim that "There is no world without Verona walls" (3.3.17) following news of his banishment is all the more forceful as there is very little sense of a geographical reality beyond Shakespeare's vision of "Verona."

Titus Andronicus offers a more developed engagement with geography, although Shakespeare's first portrayal of late imperial Rome lacks the later geographical expansiveness that structures *Coriolanus* and to an even greater extent *Antony and Cleopatra*. Francis Barker and John Gillies have alluded to the spatial demarcations established within *Titus*, but both see this concern as ethnographic, rather than cartographic (Barker 1993: 143–63; Gillies 1994: 102–12). Gillies argues "the action of the play articulates the ancient tragic myth of barbarian intrusion in which an exemplary city is entered, polluted and violated at the level of an exemplary family" (p. 102). Tamora, Queen of the Goths and Aaron the Moor represent a polluting threat to the boundaries of the "civilized" values of Rome. However, as Gillies suggests, the "barbaric" nature of the political world of Rome, this "wilderness of tigers," is itself rendered unnatural by the actions of Saturninus and ultimately even Titus himself.

The model of society employed here is ethnographic, whose modern theoretical conception is represented as explicitly cartographic. In her classic study of dirt and pollution, *Purity and Danger*, the anthropologist Mary Douglas claimed:

The idea of society is a powerful image. It is potent in its own right to control or to stir men to action. This image has form; it has external boundaries, margins, internal structure. Its outlines contain power to reward conformity and repulse attack. There is energy in its margins and unstructured areas. For symbols of society, any human of experience of structures, margins or boundaries is ready to hand. (Douglas 1979: 114)

The "form" that Douglas accords her model of society is spatial and cartographic. It consists of the "external boundaries, margins" from which the world of *Titus Andronicus* is constituted. Shakespeare reproduces a Roman civic geography with its emphasis on the boundaries of the city, beyond which lie the "margins and unstructured areas" from which emanate Goths and Moors. It is also the location of the "obscure plot," the forest beyond the limits of the city, where the play's most barbaric act takes place, the rape and mutilation of Lavinia. The spatial incorporation of "barbarism" is finally expelled at the end of the play in another metaphorically graphic image of civic geography. Lucius commands that

> My father and Lavinia shall forthwith
> Be closed in our houschold's monument.
> As for that ravenous tiger, Tamora,
> No funeral rite nor man in mourning weed,
> No mournful bell shall ring her burial;
> But throw her forth to beasts and birds to prey. (5.3.192–7)

Titus and Lavinia are reincorporated into the body politic in the "heart" of the city. In contrast, Tamora's polluting body is expelled beyond the limits of the city, into a barbaric no man's land where even her remains are denied the cultural rites of civilization. Here Shakespeare draws on the complex associations between ethnography, anatomy, and geography, which view the city as a living organism (with all the play's associated images of consumption, pollution, violation, dismemberment, and reproduction). The spaces of both city and body are understood through recourse to cartographic metaphors, even though the explicit geography of the wider action of the play remains unspecific.

If there is a shift in Shakespeare's geographical consciousness, it surely happens in the late 1590s, with the completion of the tetralogy of history plays stretching from *Richard II* to *Henry V*. As many critics have observed, all four plays exhibit a compelling sense of imaginative geography and national space (Holderness 1991; Rackin 1990), from Gaunt's "teeming womb of royal kings" in *Richard II* (2.1.51), to the Chorus's imaginative evocation of England and Henry's emotive nationalist rhetoric in *Henry V*. But undoubtedly the most sustained consideration of the power of geography and dramatic impact of maps occurs in *1 Henry IV*, where the rebels Glendower, Mortimer, and Carlisle gather to agree the terms of their rebellion, and in a moment that foreshadows Lear, carve up England on a map that is brought onstage. In act 3.1 the rebels appear onstage, including "Owain Glyndwr [with a map]." The intemperate Hotspur immediately curses, "A plague upon it, I forgot the map" (3.1.5).

Significantly, it is the more calculating Welshman, Glyndwr, who holds the map of England, and assures Hotspur of its presence. Glyndwr again resolves the subsequent bickering by focusing on the map:

> *Glyndwr.* Come, here's the map. Shall we divide our right,
> According to our threefold order ta'en?
> *Mortimer.* The Archdeacon hath divided it
> Into three limits very equally.
> England from Trent to Severn hitherto
> By south and east is to my part assigned;
> All westward – Wales beyond the Severn shore
> And all the fertile land within that bound –
> To Owain Glyndwr; [to *Hotspur*] and, dear coz, to you
> The remnant northward lying off from Trent. (3.1.67–76)

This is a very sophisticated use of the map onstage, with its precise geographical division of the realm into three, from the southeast ("from Trent to Severn"), the west ("Wales beyond the Severn shore"), and the north ("lying off from Trent"). The moment is surely all the more dramatically arresting if the audience can actually *see* the map of England, and the proposed partition along toponymic lines. As Lear's own division of the kingdom generally follows the same regional partition it is tempting to consider that a similar (if not the same) map was used onstage several years later.

The rebels' use of the map in *1 Henry IV* is recognizably chorographic. Ptolemy saw chorography as one dimension of geography, which he argued "differs from chorography in that chorography, selecting certain places from the whole, treats more fully the particulars of each by themselves – even dealing with the smallest conceivable localities, such as harbours, farms, villages, river courses, and such like" (Ptolemy 1991: 25). Throughout the sixteenth century, chorography became one of the basic tools of political and administrative life. As Peter Barber has pointed out in his analysis of Tudor geography, Henry VIII utilized new surveying methods in maps of England's coastal defenses from 1539 onwards, as well as subsequent charts of English possessions in Calais and Boulogne. "Between 1530 and 1550," Barber argues, "maps were enrolled into the service of English government . . . a fully integrated aid in the formulation of policy and an instrument of administration" (Barber 1992: 45). Richard Helgerson has already pointed out the ways in which Lord Burghley used Christopher Saxton's 1579 Survey of England in the political administration and surveillance of the kingdom (Helgerson 1992: 107–47). Helgerson saw the growing use of local, chorographic mapping as providing a challenge to the established, absolutist conception of the kingdom as an extension of the sovereign's body, in favor of a more recognizably modern conception of the nation-state. However, this argument is too simplistic and anachronistic in separating out absolutist and nationalist authority in late Tudor ideology, where both impulses often went hand in hand.

In Shakespeare's drama, despite attempts to argue to the contrary, there is little explicit trace of this tension between absolutism and nationalism in the representation of geography at the local, regional level. For instance, what kind of political dispensation is envisaged in the projected tripartite division of the kingdom between Mortimer, Hotspur, and Glyndwr that takes place in *1 Henry IV*? This is surely no republic, but nor can it be seen as the simple replacement of one absolutist sovereign for another. The other irony that emerges from this scene is that, despite the dramatic rhetoric that recoils at the thought of geographical and political division, it is the threat (and often the success) of partition, division, and invasion that establishes political boundaries and shapes regional and national space. This point is graphically made by one of Elizabethan England's most eloquent proponents of a "British Empire," Dr. John Dee. In his *General and Rare Memorials Pertayning to the Perfecte Arte of Navigation* (1577), Dee argued that national security could be enhanced through the creation of a national navy. Rhetorically, Dee's text constructs a powerful understanding of the space of England through the fear of invasion from the margins. Dee warns against both internal and external threats to the kingdom, and is explicit about the need to provide accurate cartographic representations to counter such a threat:

> And, of these sorte of people they be, which (other whiles) by collour and pretence of coming about their feat of fishing, do subtly and secretly use Sowndings, and Serchings, of our Channells, Deeps, Showles, Banks, or Bars, along the Sea Coasts, and in our Haven Mowthes also, and up in our Creeks, sometimes in our Roads &c. Taking good Marks, for avoiding of the dangers: and also trying good Landings. And (*so, making perfect Chartes of all our Coasts, round about England, and Ireland*) are become (almost) perfecter in them, then the most parte of our Maisters, Lodmen or Pilots. (Dee 1577: 7)

Dee's rhetoric defines the parameters of "England" through the fear of invasion and division. In terms that define the modern discourse of nationhood, the national space is defined as much by the threat of division and erosion as unity and inclusiveness. Dee's strategy finds its perfect cartographic correlation in John Speed's map of England dated 1601. Its title, *The Invasions of England and Ireland with all their Civil Wars Since the Conquest*, offers a spatial history of the formation of the kingdom, whose geographical boundaries are defined through the history of rebellion, conflict, and invasion (both real and projected) (Brotton 1996). Instead of wholeness, the national space is riven with narratives and visual descriptions of alien incursion, which paradoxically strengthen the space of the nation, rather than undermining it.

Dee and Speed suggest just how prevalent this belief in geography and definitions of "England" had become by the beginning of the seventeenth century. Shakespeare picks up on this understanding of the shape of England, and uses it right through his career. In *Richard II* Gaunt defines England as a place "that was wont to conquer others," but which has now "made a shameful conquest of itself" (2.1.65–6). In *Henry V*, as the king prepares for war against France, one of his lords counsels him that

> . . . once the eagle England being in prey,
> To her unguarded nest the weasel Scot
> Comes sneaking, and so sucks her princely egg. (1.2.169–71)

Policing your territorial margins is advisable not only for political expediency and survival, but also as a way of defining the kingdom more generally. Henry learns from the mistakes of both his own father, Henry IV, and Richard II, by policing both Scotland and Ireland, as a way of securing his realm. For Shakespeare's audience, attending to the margins (especially in Ireland) was of crucial importance in defining the national realm. A similar image appears with the representation of Milford Haven in *Cymbeline*. As Leah Marcus has pointed out, Milford Haven is part of the symbolic geography of the Tudor monarchy, the Welsh port where "Henry VII had landed when he came to claim the kingdom in the name of the Tudors" (Marcus 1988: 131). However, the decisive difference between the geographical representations of the History Plays of the 1590s and *Cymbeline* is the remarkable mutation of the rhetoric of "Englishness" into a celebration of "Britishness." There can be little doubt that this shift is closely connected to the accession of King James I (formerly James VI of Scotland) in 1603.

James's cherished political project was an act of union between his Scottish and (newly acquired) English kingdoms. However, in styling himself "King of Great Brittaine" it was unclear where Ireland and Wales fitted into this scheme. Throughout the 1530s Henry VIII had assimilated Wales into the English crown, established direct rule in Ireland, but kept Scotland at political arm's length. However, it was never completely clear what kind of polity this established, and just what constituted "England." Elizabeth cultivated the popular identification of England, but was also happy to let an adviser like Dee develop the idea of a Tudor maritime empire that was resolutely "British" (just to complicate matters even further, Dee was Welsh). As the rhetoric of *Henry V* suggests, England led, whilst the Welsh, Scots, and Irish followed in a descending line of suspicion.

James's accession threw this deeply compromised political situation into further confusion. The king immediately tried to establish Britain as a natural, historically established geographical fact. It was

> . . . the true and ancient Name, which God and Time have imposed upon this Isle, extant and received in Histories, in all Mappes and Cartes, wherein this Isle is described, and in ordinary Letters to Our selfe from divers Forraine Princes . . . and other records of great Antiquitie. (Quoted in Wormald 1996: 152)

James's compromised attempt at nation building is based here on two remarkably modern practices: cartography and international relations. He argues that both confirm the reality of Britain, whilst the "records of great Antiquitie" also give the term an acceptable historical lineage. As the Romans possessed a strong sense of the island as "Britannia," it is no wonder that James rapidly adopted the style of a Roman emperor; the mantle united both his imperial ambitions and the aspiration to rule a united "Great Britain." However, political opposition to his plans for political unification of England and Scotland ensured that union did not take place until 1707.

Nevertheless, the impact upon Shakespeare's drama was significant, and the shift from the earlier celebrations of "Englishness" is striking. Shakespeare's tragedies dramatize the complex, shifting space of "Britain" in the aftermath of James's coronation, from the world of ancient Britain in *King Lear*, to the Scotland of *Macbeth*. They also adopt a far more international and cosmopolitan geography, represented in the Venetian world of *Othello* and the sophisticated imperial world of *Antony and Cleopatra*, which could also be seen as a response to James's far more outward-looking foreign policy. More recently historians such as Jenny Wormald have suggested "in James' reign, the search for clarity over the creation of a British identity . . . is fruitless. It did not exist, because the king did not want it to exist" (Wormald 1996: 170). Whilst James did pursue political accommodation between England and Scotland, he retained a level of ambiguity over unification that allowed him to play different factions off against each other. This ambivalence over the status of "Britain" is a productive tension that is repeatedly dramatized in Shakespeare's subsequent plays, from *King Lear* to *Cymbeline*.

However, it is in the tragedies that Shakespeare most profoundly interrogates these geographical issues, and nowhere more explicitly than in *King Lear*. In the history plays the fear of the division of the kingdom is based upon a collection of rebels who are already represented as outsiders to the body politic. Glyndwr is a Welshman, Hotspur is a northerner, and Mortimer is seen as an outcast due to his marriage to a Welsh-speaking woman (Hawkes 1998). The audience also knows that historically the plot will fail. However, in *King Lear* there are no such guarantees. Even worse, the exclusive decision to divide the kingdom emanates from the very heart of the body politic, the king himself. To this extent, the tragic action of *King Lear* intensifies the political anxiety dramatized in *Henry IV Parts 1 and 2*, and pursues the consequences of what might happen if the division of the kingdom *did* take place. However, under the pressure of James's plans for a united "Britain," the potential division of the kingdom takes on added significance. Lear's projected partition of ancient Britain is based on a tripartite division between Cornwall, Albany, and Cordelia. At first this appears to be a division that reproduces the proposed division between England, Wales, and Scotland in *1 Henry IV*. Cornwall appears to symbolize the Cornish–Welsh fringe, whilst Albany's name is suggestive of the Gaelic term "Albia," which represents both Scotland and England ("Albion"), although by the time that the play was performed it was more recognizably "English" than "Scottish." Shakespeare is self-consciously drawing on ancient *British* geography in his dramatization of partition. The fact that Albany, an enigmatic figure with Anglo-Scottish associations, ultimately survives to rule over the shattered realm of Britain takes on added significance in the light of James I's accession (although Edgar's appropriation of Albany's final words in the Folio text of 1623 would indicate that authorial and editorial belief over who should assume power remained a sensitive and ambiguous issue).

James's attempts to construct a new political map of Britain obviously shape the geography of *Lear*. However, a closer examination of Lear's map suggests that Shakespeare takes his interest in geography in different directions. Lear's map is chorographic in the sense that in its close association with the representatives of Albany, Cornwall, Gloucester, and Kent, the focus remains fixed on the local and the regional. However, in *Lear* the territory represented by the map is given highly specific values. Following Goneril's speech, Lear turns to the map and announces:

> Of all these bounds even from this line to this,
> With shadowy forests and with champaigns riched,
> With plenteous rivers and wide-skirted meads,
> We make thee lady. (1.1.61–4)

The implication here is that the fertile plenitude of Goneril's newly acquired territory is visible on the map itself. This does not accord with the modern, political map of *1 Henry IV*. Instead, the description of Lear's pastoral cartography, complete with forests, plains, rivers, and meadows teeming with abundance sounds more like a medieval *mappa mundi*, with its heavily stylized and oversized representation of the natural world, as well as symbolic buildings and arterial rivers. This scene does not seem to reflect Shakespeare's ignorance of modern developments in cartography. It is instead a deliberately anachronistic description of a residual world picture that is about to be, literally and symbolically, ripped apart, and which is already passing into geographical and political history.

One of the dictums of the new cultural geography is that the map is not the territory, and Lear's actions suggest that Shakespeare had already grasped this insight at the beginning of the seventeenth century. Lear's map is an abstraction; it is only a *representation* of the territory over which he has ruled but never really known. The plenitude of the map is a pastoral fantasy, a mirror of Lear's own absolutist projection, which is also notoriously absent of subject. It is only when Lear finds himself on the heath, and he faces the harsh reality of this cartographic fantasy, that he realizes that "I have ta'en / Too little care of this" (3.4.32–3). The heath is a topographical dead zone, a meaningless area rarely accorded any spatial significance on the kind of maps with which the play begins. Lear has in effect been dropped into the very heart of his map, which represents the very antithesis to the "space, validity and pleasure" (1.1.89) he promised Regan.

Lear's division of the map symbolizes the ultimate dissolution of the kingdom. Most directors and filmmakers now follow Grigori Kozintsev's highly influential 1970 film of the play by showing Lear furiously ripping up the map at the end of the first act. As Francis Barker has observed in his perceptive account of the topography of *Lear* (Barker 1993: 3–31), the play descends into a series of what he calls "decentres" (p. 5), as the play's centralized controlling authorities fall apart, and both the characters and the action disperse across an increasingly hostile landscape. As Lear begins to journey with increasing desperation across increasingly inhospitable territory, Edgar envisages the kingdom as a desolate and dangerous place. It is made up of "low farms, / Poor pelting villages, sheep-cotes and mills" (2.2.174–5) whose inhabitants are prey to the "winds and persecutions of the sky" (2.2.169). The nadir of the storm on the heath finally leads to the convergence of the play's characters upon Dover. As Graham Holderness (1991) has pointed out, Dover is both the vulnerable site of invasion, but also, and precisely because of its vulnerability, one of the most resonant geographical symbols of the kingdom (and future nation-state). However, Dover offers no sense of political recuperation. Instead, it becomes an absurd illusion, where Edgar can pretend he stands with his father overlooking its mighty cliffs, and where Lear's world is finally destroyed by the death of Cordelia. It has often been remarked that Shakespeare throws away any conventional tragic script in writing *King Lear*. There is little doubt that as the play reaches its climax, he has also jettisoned the map as anything other than a vehicle to dramatize the initial disintegration of Lear and his kingdom. We have traveled so far from Lear's original meditation on geography that it almost seems absurd to ask what kind of map could represent "the gored state" (5.3.319) with which the play concludes.

King Lear is Shakespeare's most explicit meditation on the ways in which geography can be utilized to intensify tragic action. It is also definably chorographic in its representation of (an admittedly anachronistic) Britain. Whilst the play goes way beyond the dramatization of the wider changes to the political and national landscape, it is clearly influenced by James I's attempt to unify the realms of England and Scotland. The play's sustained interest in both political geography and cartography can be gauged if compared to *Hamlet*, written just before Elizabeth's death and James's accession. Its geographically specific portrayal of the Danish court of Elsinore and its conflict with Norway appears to deliberately avoid the more contentious political geography of turn-of-the-century Europe. Instead of drawing on the more local and political dimensions of chorography subsequently explored in *Lear*, Shakespeare uses the more abstract tradition of global cosmography of Ortelius, Mercator, and Dee to situate Hamlet's dilemma within a larger cosmic framework. Hamlet's lament for the state of "this distracted globe" (1.5.97) and his disgust at "this goodly frame, the earth . . . this brave o'erhanging firmament, this majestical roof fretted with golden fire" (2.2.298–301), draw their metaphors from the global cosmography of the likes of Ortelius and Mercator. There is an obvious correlation here between the idea of geography as a "theatre" developed by Ortelius. But there is also a dramatic development of the idea of the weight of global geography pressing down on the stoical, heroic figure of Atlas, an idea developed by Mercator in his widely admired *Atlas sive Cosmographicae Meditationes* (1595). Hamlet's humanist apprehension of cosmography and geography equips him with a better understanding of the individual's place in the wider universe, but this only leads to an intensification of his sense of insecurity.

This brief survey of *Hamlet* emphasizes how political geography rarely drives the drama of Shakespeare's plays, but acts as a useful adjunct to the tragic action. However, in *Macbeth* the dramatic is primarily shaped by the changing political geography of early Jacobean England, as James struggled to define it as Britain. The play remains one of Shakespeare's most topical, due to its probable performance before the king in 1606 by the reformed "King's Men," the references to the Gunpowder Plot of 1605, and its dramatization of the life of Banquo, from whom James traced his own line of royal descent. Critical opinion has tended to assume that the play celebrates James's authority for three broad reasons. Firstly, the play's ultimate condemnation of Macbeth and his murder of Duncan, the legitimate sovereign. Secondly, the triumphant portrayal of the inevitable succession of Banquo's royal offspring and their display of the "twofold balls and treble sceptres" (4.1.137) representing Scottish and English political union. Thirdly, the play's portrayal of the witches bore strong affinities with James's own position that had already been developed in his infamous publication, *Daemonologie* (1597). However, as David Norbrook (1987) has persuasively argued, the play's complex historiography and source material offer uncomfortable challenges to James's absolutism.

The geography of the play only adds to its dramatic ambivalence. From the outset the play is riddled with the troubling "open places," the blanks on the map of the realm that Shakespeare had already explored in *King Lear*. However, the gendering of the geography of Scotland becomes increasingly significant as the play progresses. Whilst the monstrous femininity of Lady Macbeth and the witches is seen as destroying the unity of the kingdom, Scotland itself is increasingly represented as a wounded mother. Her only hope of rescue lies in the hands of a Scot living in England, Malcolm:

> I think our country sinks beneath the yoke.
> It weeps, it bleeds, and each new day a gash
> Is added to her wounds. I think withal
> There would be hands uplifted in my right,
> And here from gracious England have I offer
> Of goodly thousands. (4.2.40–5)

Despite Malcolm's subsequent protestations that he is not fit to rule, it is indeed the military support of King Edward the Confessor that allows Malcolm to overthrow Macbeth and retain his crown. However, this is an extremely ambivalent resolution to the play's struggle for power. As the play briefly shuttles back and forth between Scotland and England, it is unclear quite what approach to union this resolution endorses. Is this a harmonious union of England and Scotland, or the annexation of the latter on the part of the former? Perhaps English dominance over Scotland is endorsed as strongly as unified power sharing.

Shakespeare's subsequent tragedies move away from a direct confrontation of the issues of Britishness and political authority raised by James I. Instead, Shakespeare embraces more global and international perspectives, that for a time almost deliberately turn their back on the political realities of early Jacobean life. Their development moves outwards from the chorographic perspective of the earlier histories and tragedies, to embrace a far more global and cosmographic view of what *Coriolanus* calls "a world elsewhere" (3.3.135). This expanding geographical horizon is developed in *Othello*, and reaches its culmination in the global and metaphorical panorama of

Antony and Cleopatra. It is this expansion of Shakespeare's world picture that creates the conditions for the fluid epic voyages and landscapes of the later plays (particularly *Pericles* and *The Tempest*); but that is a topic that goes beyond the limits of this particular volume.

With the recent development of interest in issues of race and empire in Shakespeare's plays, much has already been said about *Othello*'s immersion in the eastern Mediterranean world of Venice, Cyprus, and the shadowy presence of the Ottoman Empire (Vaughan 1996; Vitkus 1997). A key text for discussions of Othello's own identity and his "traveller's history" (1.3.139) is John Pory's 1600 translation of *A Geographical Historie of Africa, Written in Arabicke and Italian by John Leo a More, borne in Granada, and brought up in Barbarie*. Leo's book is a rich source of material on the history, geography, and customs of topics as diverse – but central to the action of *Othello* – as slavery, conversion, marriage, circumcision, Islam, and the complex North African origins of Othello's "Moorish" identity. However, Pory's dedication and address to the reader suggest that the *Historie* had its own highly specific agenda. This was a book that was to be "studied for action" (Grafton and Jardine 1990), to be used as an affective diplomatic handbook in dealing with contemporary issues of trade and politics in a region that had become strategically important for Elizabeth and her statesmen. The contents of the *Historie* were dedicated to "Robert Cecil, Knight, principall Secretarie to her Majestie," to whom Pory points out that "at this time especially I thought they would prove the more acceptable: in that the Marocan ambassadour (whose Kings dominions are heere most amplie and particularly described) hath so lately treated with your Honour" (Pory 1600). Pory envisaged the book as a political briefing on North African matters that would enable Cecil to pursue the growing commercial and diplomatic links between England and North Africa that had developed towards the end of the sixteenth century.

Even more revealing is Pory's address to the reader. In establishing the *Historie*'s intellectual credentials, the address emphasizes its status as both historiography and geography:

> I appeal also to the grand and most judiciall Cosmographer Master John Baptista Ramusius, sometime Secretarie to the state of Venice, who in the *Preface* to his first volume of voyages, so highly commendeth it to learned Fracastoro, and placeth every word in the very forefront of his discourses, as the principal and most praiseworthy of them all. And were renowned Ortelius alive, I would under correction report me to him; whether his map of Barbarie and Biledulgerid, as also in his last *Additament* that of the king-domes of Maroco and Fez, were not particularly and from point to point framed out of this present relation, which he also in two places at the least preffereth farre before all other histories written of Africa. But to leave the testimonies of others, and to come neerer the matter it selfe; like as our prime and peerlesse English Antiquarie master William Camden in his learned *Britannia*, hath exactly described England, Scotland, Ireland, and the isles adjacent (the which by Leander for Italie, by Damianus Goez briefly for Spaine, by Belforest for France, by Munster for upper Germanie, by Guiccardini for the Netherlandes, and by others for other countries hath been performed) so likewise

this our author John Leo in the historie ensuing hath so largely, particularly, and methodically deciphered the countries of Barbarie, Numidia, Libya, the land of Negros and the
hither part of Egypt. (Pory 1600: "To the Reader")

The passage is worth quoting at such length for what it says about the ways in which
so many of Shakespeare's own sources (Camden, Belleforest, etc.) are here seen as part
of a new way of writing history, which contains a heightened sense of geography, space,
and "plot." Narrative history was no longer perceived as a speedy, rhetorically effective tool of political administration. Instead, written accounts were perceived as more
effective, and speedily digestible, when supplemented with maps and geographical
material. The power of cartography as an analytical tool was not lost on Abraham
Ortelius. In his *Theatrum Orbis terrarum* (first published in Antwerp in 1570, and translated into English in 1606), Ortelius famously defined geography as "the eye of
history" (Ortelius 1606: unpaginated). It is precisely this fusion of ocularity and historiography that Shakespeare uses to create the fluid geographical movement and
exotic topography of *Othello*.

It has become a critical commonplace that Iago's improvisational rhetoric inexorably ensnares Othello, who is "little blessed with the soft phrase of peace" (1.3.82).
As he confesses, "Rude am I in my speech" (1.3.81), except at the point at which he
has to defend his relationship with Desdemona. In front of a suspicious Venetian
Seignory, Othello recounts his visits to Brabanzio's house, where he tells "the story of
my life" (1.3.128), from accounts of "the battles, sieges, fortunes / That I have passed"
(129–30), "Of being taken by the insolent foe / And sold to slavery" (136–7), to fantastic stories of "The Anthropophagi, and men whose heads / Do grow beneath their
shoulders" (143–4). Whilst his stories inevitably invite comparisons with the fabu-
lous exotic stories of Marco Polo and Sir John Mandeville, at another level the impact
of Othello's narrative is remarkably similar to the perception of contemporary maps
and geographical treatises of distant lands. Othello's story seduces Brabanzio (and by
implication the eavesdropping Desdemona), but repeated it also captivates the Duke
and his senators: "I think this tale would win my daughter, too" (170). Othello
becomes a living embodiment of the fascinated ambivalence with which maps, travel
narratives, and geographical paraphernalia describing long-distance travel and faraway
places were regarded in early modern England. This attitude is reflected in William
Cunningham's *Cosmographicall Glasse*, published in 1555. Cunningham, a self-styled
cosmographer, wrote of his pleasure in gazing at maps from the safety of

> . . . a warm and pleasant house, without any peril of the raging seas: danger of enemies:
> loss of time: spending of substance: weariness of body, or anguish of mind . . . in which
> we may behold the diversities of countries: natures of people, and innumerable forms of
> beasts, fowls, fishes, trees, fruits, streams and metals. (p. 120)

Like the Venetian Duke, Cunningham was the ultimate armchair geographer.
However, whilst both are captivated by their loyal servants, be they maps or hired,

exotic warriors, anxieties remain. The questions that continue to trouble the Venetians are ones that also permeate anxieties regarding the ultimate veracity of maps and their compilers: where have they come from, what have they experienced in their exotic travels, and how might they have been changed by their encounter with alterity? Here again it is possible to detect Shakespeare drawing on the complex attitudes towards geography (or perhaps more accurately cosmography) and long-distance travel in creating the ambivalent identity of his tragic protagonist, both insider and outsider, apparently indispensable, but ultimately interchangeable with one of many of his "type."

This ambivalence is perceptible in the wider dramatic and geographical action of the play. Unlike prose sources such as Cinthio's *Heccatomithi*, Shakespeare's play dramatically heightens the shift in tone and action between Venice and Cyprus. Up to the end of the first act in Venice, the audience could anticipate a comic resolution to the play's romantic dilemma, along the lines of Shakespeare's other Venetian play, *The Merchant of Venice*. However, as soon as the action moves to Cyprus, the tragic tone is quickly established. Shakespeare also develops the presence of "the general enemy Ottoman" (1.3.49) as a shadowy specter that haunts the play and its repeated fear of turning Turk. As several critics have noted recently (Vitkus 1997), the dramatization of both Cyprus and the Turk has an added resonance within the geopolitical world of the late sixteenth century. Cyprus had fallen to the Turks in 1571, and in act 1.3.21 the First Senator reminds the audience of "the importancy of Cyprus to the Turk." However, the fall of Cyprus also coincided with the establishment of amicable commercial and military relations between Queen Elizabeth and the Ottoman Porte in Istanbul. Elizabeth despatched several commercial and diplomatic envoys to Istanbul, as well as cloth and lead for weaponry, and quickly accepted England's position as a vassal of the Ottoman sultan (Skillitter 1977). Whilst the portrayal of the Turkish threat would have evoked an orthodox response of horror at the fall of one of the furthest eastern outposts of Christendom, it might also have been intended to trigger more uncomfortable anxieties regarding England's own status as potentially "turning Turk" in its friendly relations with the Ottomans.

In shifting the play's action to Cyprus, Shakespeare makes both Othello and Desdemona even more vulnerable to the threat of turning Turk at a liminal point where east and west were in perennial political tension and conflict. As Patricia Parker (1994) has pointed out, Desdemona herself is increasingly exoticized and "blackened" in the second half of the play, until she herself identifies with the "maid called Barbary" (4.3.25). Iago's slander ensures that she herself is represented as having sexually "turned Turk" in her supposed infidelity. Othello, of course, ultimately comes to identify himself as "a malignant and turbaned Turk" (5.2.362) in his final great speech. This has already been anticipated in act 3.3 with his close identification with the geography of the Ottoman Empire, when he rejects Iago's suggestion that he may change his mind in agreeing to murder Desdemona:

> Never Iago. Like to the Pontic Sea,
> Whose icy current and compulsive course
> Ne'er knows retiring ebb, but keeps due on
> To the Propontic and the Hellespont,
> Even so my bloody thoughts with violent pace
> Shall ne'er look back. (3.3.456–61)

Othello offers an extremely detailed account of the flow of the "Pontic Sea," in other words the Black Sea, into the "Propontic," the present-day Sea of Marmara, and onwards into the "Hellespont" (the Dardanelles) and the Aegean Sea. The city that overlooks this confluence was the seat of the Ottoman Empire, Istanbul. Othello's intimate knowledge of Turkish geography further identifies him as gradually turning into a Turk, adumbrating his final extraordinary account of the moment in Ottoman-controlled Aleppo, where he encountered a Turk and "took by th'throat the circumcised dog / And smote him thus" (5.2.364–5). At the moment of identifying himself as a Turk, Othello kills himself. This is a complex moment of tragic self-division that can be read two ways. It can be seen as a moment where Othello finally concedes his "essence" as a demonic, murderous Turk, whose violence and irrationality finally overwhelms him in a religiously scandalous moment of suicide. Or if Othello is granted greater tragic agency, he can be seen as tragically expunging the demonic figure of the Turk from his identity, loyally purging the Venetian body politic of its enemy by sacrificing himself. I would suggest that both readings are given equal validity, precisely because of the ambivalence with which Shakespeare regards the figure of the Turk throughout the play. It is not just Venice which is condemned for its attempt to absorb "an extravagant and wheeling stranger / Of here and everywhere" (1.1.137–8) into the highest echelons of political authority (as is the case with Shylock in *The Merchant of Venice*). By 1603 England had established long-standing relations with both Turkish and Moorish powers, from the early embassies to Istanbul in the 1570s, to the arrival of the Moroccan ambassador in London in 1600. Shakespeare's deployment of the exotic geography of Venice, Cyprus, Aleppo, and the Hellespont creates one of his most mobile pieces of tragic dramatic action; but it also addresses the fear of England itself "turning Turk" through its encounters with such places.

Despite repeated attempts by critics to see a similar parallel between *Antony and Cleopatra* and events in England, I would argue that the play signals another departure in Shakespeare's representation of geography. In its epic sweep and scope *Antony and Cleopatra* is without doubt the most geographically expansive of all Shakespeare's Roman plays. Whilst the focus is predominantly on the opposition between Rome and Egypt, the play delights in extended lists of exotic kingdoms and itineraries, from the plains of Syria (3.1) to Libya, Thrace, and Comagene (3.6.69–75). The map of the play is far more global and epic than Shakespeare's previous high tragedies that focus on relatively anonymous rulers (Hamlet, Lear, Macbeth, Othello) and their domestic conflicts. *Antony and Cleopatra* requires a more ambitious geographical frame because its protagonists and their historical achievements demand it (Parker 1994). Shakespeare's earlier dramatization of *Julius Caesar* lacks the epic sweep of *Antony and Cleopatra*, which fuses Roman history with the interest in the east already developed in *Othello*. The intensely political debate and urban setting of *Julius Caesar* gives way to a much more poetic meditation on desire and imperial grandeur in *Antony and Cleopatra*. Whilst the protagonists of the earlier Roman play remain trapped inside the inexorable logic of political history, both Antony and Cleopatra act and speak the need to transcend their history. One of the ways in which Shakespeare dramatizes this ultimately doomed attempt at transcendence is by drawing on late sixteenth-century global cosmography.

In his brilliant study of the history of the global imagination, *Apollo's Eye: A Cartographic Genealogy of the Earth in the Western Imagination* (2001), Denis Cosgrove points out that "earthbound humans are unable to embrace more than a tiny part of the planetary surface. But in their imagination they can grasp the whole of the earth, as a surface or a solid body, to locate it within infinities of space and to communicate and share images of it" (p. ix). Cosgrove charts the rich association of global imagining through the classical figure of Greek and Roman mythology, Phoebus Apollo, as he drives the sun's chariot above the terrestrial sphere, embracing a "synoptic grasp of a circumnavigated globe" (p. 1). In tracing what he calls "the Apollonian gaze" across history, Cosgrove sees this tradition as encapsulating both individual transcendence and an imperial will to power:

> The Apollonian gaze, which pulls diverse life on earth into a vision of unity, is individualized, a divine and mastering view from a single perspective. That view is at once empowering and visionary, implying ascent from the terrestrial sphere into the zones of planets and stars. The theme of ascent connects the earth to cosmographic spheres, so that rising above the earth in flight is an enduring element of global thought and imagination . . . Alternatively, the Apollonian gaze seizes divine authority for itself, radiating power across the global surface from a sacred centre, locating and projecting human authority imperially towards the ends of the earth. (p. xi)

This movement between individual transcendence and imperial ambition occurs repeatedly throughout *Antony and Cleopatra*. "World" occurs thirty-nine times in the play. Its usage oscillates between a dramatization of the struggle for global and imperial power that defines the relationship between Antony and Octavius Caesar, and the representation of the more intimate world that Antony and Cleopatra attempt to construct in the midst of this larger imperial imagining.

From the outset of the play Philo captures this remarkable telescoping of global images from the public to the private, encapsulated in his cutting remark that Antony is the "triple pillar of the world transformed / Into a strumpet's fool" (1.1.12–13). Antony expands on this parallax geographical perspective in his first great speech, where he announces:

> Let Rome in Tiber melt, and the wide arch
> Of the ranged empire fall. Here is my space.
> Kingdoms are clay. (1.1.35–7)

The language used here has affinities with Cosgrove's vision of the Apollonian gaze, as the collapse of Rome and its imperial architecture is imagined from a godlike perspective, gazing down from afar upon the global panorama. This globalizing dimension of the play's language and action draws heavily on the increasing demand for global geography throughout the sixteenth century. As Cosgrove points out, printed atlases, world landscape painting, and princely map galleries all developed this globalizing perspective in the aftermath of the voyages of Columbus, da Gama, and Magellan, which by the mid-sixteenth century had established a strikingly modern image of the world as globe (Cosgrove 2001: 102–38; Brotton 1999). Global maps and landscapes such as the paintings of Joachim Patinir, Albrecht Altdorfer, and Pieter Brueghel the Elder, as well as Egnazio Danti's map gallery in the Vatican (1577–83) and Abraham Ortelius's printed atlas *Theatrum orbis terrarum* (1570), all portray a global world seen from a godlike or bird's-eye perspective, rising above the terrestrial earth in a movement of individual transcendence. However, this cosmographic tradition is also intimately connected to the assertion of global, imperial power. The ability to record the world from a godlike perspective implies the political conquest and possession of territorial space, or as Cosgrove puts it, "the Apollonian gaze authorized both an individualist, imperial conquest for *Fama* (Fame) and a more structured metaphysics of global order and harmony" (Cosgrove 2001: 123).

Antony and Cleopatra is deeply indebted to this global cosmographic tradition, which consistently shapes the play's rhetoric of imperial power. In act 2.7, when Menas tries to persuade Pompey to murder the triumvirate as they carouse aboard his galley, the image is self-consciously global:

> Thou art, if thou dar'st be, the earthly Jove.
> Whate'er the ocean pales or sky inclips
> Is thine, if thou wilt ha't. (2.7.64–6)

Pompey's refusal to take his opportunity leads to his downfall and the imprisonment of Lepidus, causing Enobarbus to reflect that "Then, world, thou hast a pair of chaps," Antony and Caesar, whose struggle for global domination will see them "grind the one the other" (3.5.12–14). The perspective of the play is consistently Apollonian, as its language invites the audience to assume a bird's-eye perspective in imagining the plains of Syria (3.1), the battle of Actium (3.10), and the sea battle before Alexandria (4.13). It repeatedly draws on imperial iconography from a distant, controlling perspective. Cleopatra imagines Antony from afar as an imperial equestrian statue or portrait medal, "The demi-Atlas of this earth" (2.1.23). Octavius also takes up a suitably cosmographic perspective in his pronouncement before the battle at Alexandria that the "time of universal peace is near," and that "the three-nooked world / Shall bear the olive freely" (4.6.4–6). Octavius confidently predicts that the tripartite world (Europe, Asia, and Africa), divided between Noah's three sons (Japhet, Shem, and Ham), will finally be reunited under his exclusive imperial rule.

However, the language of both Antony and Cleopatra increasingly resists this vision of imperial global ascendancy. From the outset, rather than embracing an elevated cosmographical perspective, Antony seeks to dissipate it. His "space" does not ascend to a position of imperial authority, but instead observes (from a distance) the dissolution and fall of the symbols of imperial Rome. As Octavius closes in on the two lovers, the world begins to take on a more dangerous, elegiac dimension. Following Antony's victorious return from the battlefield in act 4.9, Cleopatra exclaims in relief, "com'st thou smiling / From the world's great snare uncaught?" (4.9.17–18). Lamenting his final humiliation in act 4.15, Antony reflects on his godlike status from another Apollonian perspective: "I, that with my sword / Quartered the world, and o'er green Neptune's back / With ships made cities." Cleopatra develops this image in her famous memorial to Antony that transforms him into the kind of monument from which she herself speaks:

> His legs bestrid the ocean; his reared arm
> Crested the world. His voice was propertied
> As all the tunèd spheres, and that to friends;
> But when he meant to quail and shake the orb,
> He was as rattling thunder . . .
>   Realms and islands were
> As plates dropped from his pocket. (5.2.81–4; 90–1)

Antony's colossal stature is again imagined from an aerial, godlike perspective, that encompasses the oceans and islands across which Antony strides, as well as the "tunèd" celestial spheres that cosmography takes as one of its central subjects. Although both Antony and Cleopatra reject Octavius Caesar's projected world order as "paltry" (5.2.2), they are both more tragically eloquent in describing a poetic geography of transcendence, and viewing the terrestrial world from above and at a distance, that is central to the spatial fantasies of imperial discourse.

In *Antony and Cleopatra* Shakespeare borrows from the world of global cosmography to intensify the dramatic representation of the struggle for imperial dominance between Antony, Cleopatra, and Octavius Caesar. But as Denis Cosgrove has pointed out, cosmographical assertions of global imperial power are usually also associated with individual claims to worldly transcendence. This is partly what both Antony and Cleopatra have developed in their rejection of the trappings of empire, but continued demand for a transcendence of the quotidian reality of the terrestrial world. As well as showing the effects of imperial power upon its actors, the play shows how such power is packaged and presented to its audience. It creates two tragic protagonists who are invariably seen interacting in public and from a distance (it has often been noted that for a pair of lovers they are rarely discovered alone), which is part of the process by which the imperial gaze works, by keeping its audience at a distance, and magnifying the monumental quality of its central protagonists. As a play, it remains notoriously difficult to perform, based on the assumption that it aspires to the condition of poetry rather than drama. Perhaps it is now possible to suggest that what makes the play so difficult to perform is that it aspires to the condition of cosmography, a perspective that can only be imagined, but never staged.

The dramatization of geography in Shakespeare's subsequent Roman play, *Coriolanus* (1608), shifts focus again. Rather than elaborate on a transcendental, Apollonian geography, Shakespeare moves back in time to the early years of the republic to offer a stark representation of the Roman *polis* that has more in common with *Titus Andronicus* than *Antony and Cleopatra*. If *Antony and Cleopatra* looks for poetic and geographical transcendence, *Coriolanus* appears to ruthlessly reject any such possibility in the deeply unsympathetic figure of Caius Martius, a martial hero whose very name is prescribed by political geography.

From the very beginning of the play, Shakespeare dramatizes Rome as an organic body politic in similar terms to those expressed in *Titus Andronicus*. Nevertheless, there is a much deeper sophistication in the representation of the political geography of Rome as both a city and a burgeoning empire at war with its neighbors. In *Titus* the space beyond the city walls is a nebulous "outside," a space that is dramatically hardly ever represented, but simply populated by "aliens" like Goths. *Coriolanus* has a much more developed sense of the space beyond the city, in its dramatization of Caius Martius' campaigns in Corioles and his time in Antium. The scene that connects Coriolanus' defection from Rome and alliance with Aufidius is a particularly resonant representation of geography, "A road between Rome and Antium" (4.3) that echoes the geographical dead zones of the heath in *King Lear*, an "open place" in *Macbeth* (1.1), and the desolate plains of Syria in *Antony and Cleopatra* (3.1). The dramatization of all these desolate places adumbrates the respective downfalls of Coriolanus, Lear, Macbeth, and Antony.

However, by 1608 the geographical and anatomical discourse of the functional body politic was becoming subject to much more searching critique. The dialogic nature of Menenius' debate with the citizens and his fable of the belly (1.1.85–152) that has fascinated materialist critics since Brecht, has its popular roots in the violent agrarian riots that took place throughout the Midlands in 1607 (Patterson 1989: 120–53). If there is little development in Shakespeare's dramatization of geography, it is surely because the play returns to the growing political tensions between crown and city in Jacobean London ca. 1607, and the conflict between absolutist rule and the demand for increasingly popular participation in political decision-making. In the stony *realpolitik* of *Coriolanus*, geography is subsumed within a wider struggle over the relations between country and city and absolutism versus republicanism that would increasingly dominate the landscape of mid-seventeenth century English politics.

This has been a highly selective account of how Shakespeare uses geography in his tragedies, for the simple reason that many of his plays are simply not directly concerned with questions of geography. Shakespeare's immersion in geography and the novel products of cartography and mapmaking produced highly specific but relatively superficial dramatic moments in the comedies and early tragedies. However, the changing political landscape of England, and James I's subsequent development of the discourse of "Britishness" from 1603 onwards, had a decisive impact upon Shakespeare's high tragedies, and his perceptions of geography and its dramatic possibilities. This change is immediately felt in *King Lear*, which starts from a premise grounded in political geography: what happens when a sovereign king decides to divide his kingdom? Here Shakespeare draws directly on a chorographic tradition that has its roots in his earlier use of maps in *1 Henry IV*, but finds even greater resonance in the context of James I's own attempt to unify his diverse kingdoms under the rubric of Britain. Shakespeare then analyzes this problem from a peculiarly Scottish perspective in *Macbeth*, although his conclusions are far from the unqualified celebration of James's rule that many critics have always assumed. Totally distinct from this chorographic dimension of the tragedies is the more exotic geography that connects *Titus Andronicus*, *Othello*, and *Antony and Cleopatra*. Again, all three plays ask different questions, and in the process draw on different dimensions of geography. These include *Titus Andronicus'* interest in the ethnographic dramatization of civic space, *Othello's* attention to the ways in which the political and commercial dimensions of contemporary maps and travel narratives shape relations between east and west, and *Antony and Cleopatra's* fascination with the more global implications of cosmography. There is no coherent line to be drawn through Shakespeare's career in relation to the use of geography. But there is a wonderful irony in the fact that Shakespeare's dramatic geographical representation of locations as diverse as Elsinore, Cawdor, Dover, Venice, and Rome have been more decisive in shaping the imaginative geography of generations of theatregoers than the maps upon which such dramatic creations were based.

References and Further Reading

Anderson, B. (1983). *Imagined Communities*. London: Verso.

Andrews, J. H. (1970). Geography and Government in Elizabethan Ireland. In N. Stephens and R. E. Glasscock (eds.) *Irish Geographical Studies in Honour of E. Estyn Evans*. Belfast: Queen's University Geography Department, 178–91.

Barber, P. (1992). England I: Pageantry, Defense, and Government: Maps at Court to 1550. In D. Buisseret (ed.) *Monarchs, Ministers and Maps*. Chicago: University of Chicago Press, 26–56.

Barker, F. (1993). *The Culture of Violence: Essays on Tragedy and History*. Manchester: Manchester University Press.

Brotton, J. (1996). Mapping the Early Modern Nation: Cartography Along the English Margins. *Paragraph*, 19, 2, 139–55.

——(1999). Terrestrial Globalism: Mapping the Globe in Early Modern Europe. In D. Cosgrove (ed.) *Mappings*. London: Reaktion Books, 71–89.

Cohen, W. (1985). *Drama of a Nation: Public Theater in Renaissance England and Spain*. Ithaca, NY: Cornell University Press.

Conley, T. (1996). *The Self-Made Map: Cartographic Writing in Early Modern France*. Minneapolis: University of Minnesota Press.

Cosgrove, D. (2001). *Apollo's Eye: A Cartographic Genealogy of the Earth in the Western Imagination.* Baltimore, MD: Johns Hopkins University Press.

Cunningham, W. (1555). *A Cosmographicall Glasse.* London.

Dee, J. (1577). *General and Rare Memorials Pertayning to the Perfecte Arte of Navigation.* London.

Douglas, M. (1979). *Purity and Danger.* London: Routledge.

Elyot, T. (1531). *The Boke Named the Governour.* London.

Gillies, J. (1994). *Shakespeare and the Geography of Difference.* Cambridge: Cambridge University Press.

Grafton, A. and Jardine, L. (1990). Studied for Action: How Gabriel Harvey Read his Livy. *Past and Present,* 129, 30–78.

Harley, J. B. (1983). Meaning and Ambiguity in Tudor Cartography. In S. Tyacke (ed.) *English Map-Making 1500–1650.* London: British Library, 22–45.

Hawkes, T. (1998). Bryn Glas. In A. Loomba and M. Orkin (eds.) *Post-Colonial Shakespeares.* London: Routledge, 117–40.

Helgerson, R. (1992). *Forms of Nationhood: The Elizabethan Writing of England.* Chicago, IL: University of Chicago Press.

Holderness, G. (1991). "What ish my nation?": Shakespeare and National Identity. *Textual Practice,* 5, 1, 74–93.

Hutson, L. (1993). Fortunate Travellers: Reading for the Plot in Sixteenth-Century England. *Representations,* 41, 83–103.

Lestringant, F. (1994). *Mapping the Renaissance World.* Cambridge: Polity Press.

Marcus, L. (1988). *Puzzling Shakespeare.* Berkeley: University of California Press.

Mercator, G. (1595). *Atlas sive Cosmographicae Meditationes.* Dusseldorf.

Norbrook, D. (1987). Macbeth and the Politics of Historiography. In K. Sharpe and S. Zwicker (eds.) *Politics of Discourse: The Literature and History of Seventeenth-Century England.* Berkeley: University of California Press, 78–116.

Ortelius, A. (1606). *The Theatre of the Whole World,* trans. W.B. London.

Parker, K. (2000). *Antony and Cleopatra.* London: Northcote House.

Parker, P. (1994). Fantasies of "Race" and "Gender": Africa, *Othello,* and Bringing to Light. In M. Hendricks and P. Parker (eds.) *Women, "Race" and Writing in the Early Modern Period.* London: Routledge, 84–100.

Patterson, A. (1989). *Shakespeare and the Popular Voice.* Oxford: Blackwell.

Pory, J. (ed.) (1600). *A Geographical Historie of Africa, Written in Arabicke and Italian by John Leo a More, borne in Granada, and brought up in Barbarie.* London.

Ptolemy, C. (1991). *The Geography,* ed. E. L. Stevenson. London: Dover Books.

Rackin, P. (1990). *Stages of History: Shakespeare's English Chronicles.* Ithaca, NY: Cornell University Press.

Seaton, E. (1964). Marlowe's Maps. In C. Leech (ed.) *Marlowe: A Collection of Critical Essays.* New York: Prentice-Hall, 36–56.

Sherman, W. (1995). *John Dee: The Politics of Reading and Writing in the English Renaissance.* Amherst: University of Massachusetts Press.

Skillitter, S. (ed.) (1977). *William Harborne and the Trade with Turkey.* Oxford: Oxford University Press.

Vaughan, V. M. (1996). *Othello: A Contextual History.* Cambridge: Cambridge University Press.

Vitkus, D. (1997). Turning Turk in *Othello. Shakespeare Quarterly,* 48, 2, 145–76.

Wormald, J. (1996). James VI, James I and the Identity of Britain. In B. Bradshaw and J. Morrill (eds.) *The British Problem, c.1534–1707.* London: Palgrave, 148–71.

12

Classic Film Versions of Shakespeare's Tragedies: A Mirror for the Times

Kenneth S. Rothwell

Four mid-twentieth-century movies of Shakespeare's tragedies qualify as icons in the pantheon of great cinematic art for reasons of their critical and popular success. The quartet are the Laurence Olivier *Hamlet* (1948), the Peter Brook *King Lear* (1970), the Roman Polanski *Macbeth* (1971), and the Franco Zeffirelli *Romeo and Juliet* (1968). All of course are Anglophone, which raises the specter of bias against meritorious non-Anglophone films such as the Sergei Yutkevich *Othello* (1955), the Akira Kurosawa *Throne of Blood* (1957), and the Grigory Kozintsev *Hamlet* (1964), but in this context it is impossible to give them and others their merited attention. Each of the films was in its day widely publicized; each benefited from a relatively generous budget and major actors; each seriously influenced the way that people, especially the young, came to look at a Shakespeare play; and, most importantly for the purpose of this chapter, each in one way or another carried out intricate negotiations with the intellectual and cultural agendas of the middle of the last century. William Shakespeare did not know about Sigmund Freud, Samuel Beckett, the Manson murder gang, or indeed the 1968 Columbia University student rebellion, but the filmmakers who adapted his plays did and they couldn't help but mirror their own times.

> Hamlet is able to do anything but take vengeance upon the man who did away with his father and has taken his father's place with his mother . . . The loathing which should have driven him to revenge is thus replaced by self-reproach, by conscientious scruples. (Freud 1913)

Laurence Olivier's Academy Award winning black-and-white *Hamlet* (1948) set off a furor among Shakespeare scholars, who were in those days before the invention of videocassettes and DVDs uncomfortable anyway with Shakespeare in moving images. Sometimes the "purists" testily condemned Shakespeare films for doing the same things that would have gone unnoticed on stage; or they assumed that any Shakespeare movie was prima facie a "dumbing down," and part of a conspiracy to usurp the educational establishment's previously unchallenged hegemony. For a voice-over prologue to accompany the Gothic establishing shot of the ghost-haunted battlements of Elsinore, Olivier transposed from act 1, scene 4 a slightly revised version of Hamlet's speech about Claudius's drunken behavior. It begins, of course, with "So oft it chances in particular men / That [through] some vicious mole of nature in them . . ." (1.4.23ff).[1] Taken out of its context as a rebuke to Claudius, it suggests that Hamlet himself has a single tragic flaw, which might account for his notorious delay as an avenger. In case anyone were to miss the point, Olivier embellished it with the fatally reductive dogma: "This is the story of a man who could not make up his mind."

To entire battalions of embattled scholars *Hamlet* is most emphatically *not* a story about a man who could not make up his mind. As long ago as 1875 the German scholar Karl Werder was passionately arguing that there are many sound and ethical reasons for Hamlet's "abulia" in taking revenge on Claudius. Basically, the argument went, the prince could not take his uncle's life without unimpeachable evidence of guilt. In the early twentieth century, however, an offhanded remark by Sigmund Freud about *Hamlet* in *The Interpretation of Dreams* (Freud 1913: 310) undermined Werder's "objectivist" view and opened the way for unbridled subjectivity. Under Freud's Oedipal theory, Hamlet's suppressed desire to sleep with his own mother made it impossible for him to assassinate an uncle who had succeeded where he himself had failed. Hamlet's real motive for delay was thus masked, having been pushed deep into his subconscious and displaced into other areas, such as his stormy relationship with Ophelia. Freud did point out, however, that Hamlet was indecisive *only* when it came to killing Claudius, not in other instances such as in the hasty and improvised dispatch of Rosencrantz and Guildenstern. That way Hamlet could forever hesitate to murder Claudius but in other respects seem to be a strong, decisive figure. Freud in this way made Hamlet over into the guilty creature at his own play.

The movie's release invited strong reactions from traditionalists like John Ashworth, who deplored its replacement of "the drama of Hamlet's life . . . by the drama of what Hamlet might reveal on the couch" (Ashworth 1949: 30). Distinguished scholar Peter Alexander devoted an entire lecture series to pointing out how the film had wrongly privileged Freudianism over Christian humanism (Alexander 1955: 200). In his closely reasoned "Freud and *Hamlet* Again," however, Simon O. Lesser cogently defended the film's Freudian interpretation, falling back on Freud's assertion that it was only when confronted with the major task of killing Claudius that Hamlet hesitated (Lesser 1955: 207–20). Somehow the Freudians had to get around the awkward fact that Hamlet kills without blinking in the bedroom scene when he mistakenly thinks it is the king behind the arras. Hamlet's "Nay, I know not, is it the King?" (3.3.26) faintly suggests that he was in doubt about the identity of the lurker, but Olivier's Hamlet shows no signs of uncertainty.

A major reason that so much has been written about Sigmund Freud and Olivier's *Hamlet* is that Tyrone Guthrie and Laurence Olivier themselves talked so much about it. Guthrie and Olivier had worked out what they thought of as "an original approach to the character" for the Old Vic 1937 production, based largely on Ernest Jones's

Hamlet and Oedipus (1910/49), though earlier in 1922 John Barrymore had already brought an "Oedipal" flavor to *Hamlet* (Hapgood 1999: 61). Kenneth Tynan, however, quotes Olivier as saying, "Yes, that was inspired by Professor Ernest Jones . . . He made a really watertight case about this [the Oedipal complex], and we believed in it thoroughly . . . [in those days] I thought it was the absolute resolution of all the problems concerning Hamlet . . . whether he was man of action, whether he wasn't a man of action." Olivier added: "If there is such a thing as an Oedipus complex . . . it was not entirely absent from the royal court of Denmark" (*New York Times*, August 21, 1966). The Freudian chimera inspired construction of a massive single set, fraught with ominous symbolism, whose bare walls and vacant rooms led to Jack J. Jorgens's inspired labeling of the film as an "Oedipal cinepoem" (Jorgens 1977: 214). Olivier's beliefs in 1937, however, may not have been identical with what he thought a decade later when he actually made the movie. Kenneth Tynan corroborates this conjecture in reporting that Olivier was without a gift for abstract thought and that he was often prone to believing the last thing that he had heard (Tynan 1987: 294).

Fifty years later, in the twenty-first century, the Oedipal theory now seems quaintly old fashioned. While literary scholars like Peter S. Donaldson (1990) still mine it for fascinating insights into Olivier's adolescent phobias, the psychiatrists have jettisoned Freud in favor of biopsychology accompanied with what a major authority describes as a "bewildering array" of pharmaceuticals (Judd 1994: 2401), including such favorites as Prozac and Lithium. As the unkindest cut of all, a neurologist friend recently argued at a cocktail party that dreams are simply "noise," and hence Freud's dream theory is nonsense. Freud's lovely, even comforting, metaphors sound increasingly like the medieval doctrine of humors. It is not so much that Freudian practitioners have completely disappeared, as that prescribing drugs is much less labor intensive than a leisurely session on a padded couch.

Although Freudian theory permeated much of the film, in truth its presence is often more in the breach than in the observance. This is not to say that the film's psychological overtones are nonexistent; it is to say, though, that so much else competes for our attention that to call it simply a "Freudian" treatment is reductive. The portrayal of a suppressed motive that can only be identified by a series of "displacements" is hellishly difficult to transmit to an audience, for it can never be completely mimed or spoken, only inferred. Moreover, despite all the fashionable chatter about Freud in early twentieth-century Bloomsbury and Greenwich Village, this *Hamlet* cannot entirely escape from yet a third specter, the fascination with the Idea of Hamlet, or "Hamletism," that same black-plumed creature who haunted the nineteenth-century stage, a genteel prince who inspired the interpretations of Charles Albert Fechter and Edwin Booth (Hapgood 1999: 30–6). Despite being in his forties, Olivier could still reify Goethe's celebrated sketch in *Wilhelm Meister* (Book V, 1795) of the sensitive soul who is of "a beautiful, pure, noble, and most moral nature, without the strength of nerve which makes the hero, [and who] sinks beneath a burden which it can neither bear nor throw off." His coiffed and mannered Hamlet is closer to Sir Johnston Forbes-Robertson's gentlemanly Victorian model than, for example, Richard

Burton's dynamic histrionics in 1964 on Electronovision. Olivier finally reinvents himself as a warrior when at the end, after gazing down on the carnage left over from the duel with Laertes, and punctuated by William Walton's portentous tremolo strings on the soundtrack, he makes the Great Leap on the terrified Claudius that cost the unfortunate stand-in two teeth (Hapgood 1999: 70).

Forced to choose among a steely avenger, neurotic victim, or sensitive poet, the film's director, not Hamlet, may be the one who "could not make up his mind." There is an uneasy sense of a gap between what the prologue predicts and what actually happens. Self-referentially the director, in attempting to untangle the tangled text, finds himself in the same dilemmas as Hamlet himself. Olivier manages to graft at least three sides of the prince into his film but in getting there, like Hamlet, he sometimes has to kill the wrong people (like Fortinbras who is absent from the movie) or he is as uncertain about Freudian theory as Hamlet is uncertain about the reliability of the ghost, or he eliminates Rosencrantz and Guildenstern to appease the tyranny of film time only to find that none of this gets any closer to plucking out the heart of the mystery. Olivier's clipped, decisive speech also runs against the grain of the image of a hesitant, vacillating person. The very soliloquies that would play up Hamlet's indecisiveness have been cut from the movie, such as his reference in "O, what a rogue and peasant slave am I!" (2.2.550) to his own "weakness and melancholy" (2.2.601), and all of 4.4 with its "How all occasions do inform against me" (4.4.32). At the same time Hamlet can still "drink hot blood" (3.2.390). Lawrence Guntner's (1990) collation of the film's twenty-two scenes with the corresponding elements in Shakespeare's text (pp. 122–5) ferrets out many more such deletions, transpositions, and additions. What has been lost, however, in the absence of a single unified idea of Hamlet has been gained in the hallucinatory spell set by the roving camera.

When the movie's Freudian impulses slip through they come in the displaced guise of intricate parental–child tropes. Although by-play between Laertes (Terence Morgan) and Ophelia (Jean Simmons) during Polonius's (Felix Aylmer) sententious advice has a long stage tradition, it's possible that Olivier's movie in copying silent film strategies endows it with a rarely observed richness in detail. When Polonius says "grapple them [friends] unto thy soul with hoops of steel" (1.3.63), Ophelia mimes the advice by throwing her arms around Laertes's waist; at "beware of entrance to a quarrel" she reaches around and toys with the scabbard of Laertes's dagger; at "rich not gaudy" she outlines the embroidery on the back of her brother's jacket; and at "borrowing dulls the edge of husbandry" she wriggles his purse with her finger. Her gestures in this ambivalent ballet of love, affection, and banter suggest a lightheartedness, an impish playfulness, totally at odds with the melancholy creature of the fourth act singing her sad lays.

In a bedroom encounter that by now has calcified into a stage tradition, the incestuous love between mother and son becomes egregiously apparent. In Hamlet's demonic assault he hurls a bewildered Gertrude to the enormous bed, then with a maniacal look skewers the lurking Polonius. As Hamlet's sword plunges and plunges into the arras, the labial bed drapes and his mother in the background underscore the tension among stepfather, mother, and the powerful springs of hidden sexuality. As Gertrude, actress Eileen Herlie (b. 1920) was in actuality younger than Olivier (b. 1907), which too overtly for notions of Freudian repression reinforced the plausibility of an erotic tension between mother and son, especially the way in which Gertrude resembles a rebuked adolescent as she stares dumbfounded into Hamlet's face. When he hysterically rants about the "rank sweat of an enseamed bed, / Stew'd in corruption, honeying and making love / Over the nasty sty!" (3.4.93), and moves closer and closer to her, they achieve a kind of emotional tumescence. Detumescence follows with the terrifying entrance of the ghost that sends Hamlet to the floor crawling sideways, looking curiously like the crab that "could go backward," which he earlier had described to Polonius (2.2.204).

Ultimately the film will be remembered not for its psychology but for its art. Even the "Souvenir Program" for the world premier "in the presence of the King and Queen at the Odeon Theatre, Leicester Square" (1948: 1) stressed the film's cinematic technique, "the bold use of the camera crane," over any of its ideology. To achieve its dreamlike texture, the movie borrows portraiture from the German expressionists, anticipates Hollywood postwar film noir, and borrows deep focus from Orson Welles's landmark *Citizen Kane* (1941). Examples of portraiture, or what Hollywood called "the Rembrandt effect," appear everywhere in close shot, often with chiaroscuro overtones, as when posed against a dark stone background with his flagrantly dyed blond hair glittering from the refracted light, Olivier resembles a carved statue, or eavesdropping on Claudius's closet speech he hovers like an avenging angel ready to strike. The mere act of his sitting in a chair radiates an aura around him of ineffable grandeur. Ophelia gowned in white is sharply delineated against the dark background as Laertes looks on appalled by her madness. *Tableaux vivants* reminiscent of silent film occur in the depiction of Ophelia's drowning inspired by Sir John Everett Millais's Pre-Raphaelite painting. Film noirish overtones color the establishing shot of the castle with a Gothic mood of foreboding, the body of Hamlet already there so that, as Anthony Davies has pointed out, like Olivier's own *Henry V*, the film begins where it ends (Davies 1988: 45) and takes on the rhythm of a journey. Indeed Olivier apparently conceived the ending first and then used it as a springboard for the entire movie. The interplay between vertical and horizontal space suggests the whirling paradox of a prince who feels at once the claustrophobia of Elsinore and yet could be "a king of infinite space" (2.2.255).

The deep focus cinematography, originally developed by Orson Welles's cameraman, Greg Toland, induces a kinetic, even fluid movement, despite the potential for stasis in a *mise-en-scène* rooted in a sprawling but nevertheless single set.[2] Olivier doesn't just walk; he flows. In a Freudian Valhalla, the interrogating camera peers at the lengthy corridors, the forbidden apertures, the dark doorways, open arches, king-sized bed, where Hamlet can be gazed at beside, near, above, or over Polonius, Ophelia, or Laertes, as the situation calls for high- or low-angle shots to signify empowerment or disempowerment. Hamlet can observe Ophelia approaching from afar across the sprawling semi-theatrical sets. On the castle turret where he delivers his "To be or not to be" soliloquy against a backdrop of a surging sea and crashing waves on the rocks below, the camera actually moves toward the back of his head and then in a very ecstasy of subjectivity even seems to go inside his mind (Alkire 1991: 5). Set designer Carmen Dillon realized that "deep focus photography . . . would demand fastidious care in its sets" and noted the interesting paradox that the result "practically def[ies] outright classification into cinematic or theatrical" categories (Cross 1948: 44). This same consideration led *Hamlet* scholar Dr. Bernice W. Kliman to conclude that "the film is a hybrid form, not a filmed play, not precisely a film, but a film-infused play, or a play-infused film" (Kliman 1988: 23). The stage roots are deep but the constantly moving camera, as it pans, tracks, or perches on a crane over the unified set certifies to the production's cinematic identity. No such flowing narrative could be duplicated on a stage.

After all the excitement of the Mousetrap, the violent death of Polonius, the madness and drowning of Ophelia, the ritualized duel scene with Laertes, and the condign punishment of Claudius, at the close the funeral cortege for Hamlet borne aloft by the four captains exactly reverses the spatial order of the opening shots, which moved downward toward the inferno of Elsinore. Now, to composer William Walton's dirge, the movement goes up, up, past long corridors, past the fetishized chair of Hamlet, through ghostly hallways, up stairs, past the bed chamber with its occult and bloody secrets, toward the turret, the tower, and then emerges against the sky only as a silhouette, a quest for the Paradiso. It's as if this coda, this concession to classical Hollywood protocols for continuity, will bring closure to all our anxieties, but of course it can't. The landscape of *Hamlet* exists only to conceal the volcano underneath. And if it should be discovered that a director, perhaps himself suppressing fears of failure, has felt the same hesitations and doubts as Hamlet, this should be a cause for satisfaction, not embarrassment. This most enigmatic of texts demands that kind of visceral empathy, and if one must vacillate there is no better company to do it in than Hamlet's.

* * *

There is but one truly serious philosophical problem, and that is suicide. (Camus 1955)

As all tragic heroes must suffer, Peter Brook's bleak movie of *King Lear* (1970) explores an old man's unendurable pain when he discovers how "sharper than a serpent's tooth is an ungrateful child" (1.4.288). While Hamlet, perhaps through sloth, delayed in striking out against his enemies and then in Polonius killed the wrong person, Lear fuelled by the sin of wrath struck out in a blind rage, "flying off the handle," so to speak, playing a variation on hot-tempered Titus Andronicus, jealous Leontes, or even impetuous Laertes, and then wrongly picked on Cordelia. In his film Brook used the plight of the aged monarch as metonymy for the modern era and its profound malaise after the *Götterdämmerung* of Hiroshima, so much so that many critics have seen the film as ahistorical, more steeped in "Beckett-time" than in Elizabethan time. Yet to excoriate Brook's work for imposing contemporary pessimism on a Jacobean tragedy, tacitly acknowledging that God is Dead, as it were, is to overlook the very real despair of the Jacobean era when near contemporaries of Shakespeare like a youthful Sir Thomas Browne, steeped in fashionable Neo-Stoicism, could say in his melancholy *Religio Medici* (1642), "For the world I count it not an Inn, but an Hospital; and a place not to live, but to dye in"; or John Donne speaking of the decay of nature in "The First Anniversary" could fret that "new Philosophy calls all in doubt, / The Element of fire is quite put out; . . . / 'Tis all in peeces, all cohaerence gone" (1633).

The black-and-white motion picture in charcoal texture opens with a tableau, a void, with the camera panning over the staring, uncomprehending, sometimes sullen, sometimes baffled, sometimes beseeching faces of the people, without any softening non-diegetic music on the soundtrack, only unbearable silence. Paul Scofield as Lear, unlike a John Gielgud, does not sing the words but growls them. His very first word, "Know," spoken from the hidden depths of his cylindrical, phallic-shaped throne falls on the ears like an ax on oak. Only the monosyllable does not just exhort us to "know" something but it also puns on "No," which turns into a leitmotif for the entire play, as again and again the action unfolds against the backdrop of Cordelia's fatal "Nothing, my lord." "Nothing will come of nothing," replies the old king (1.1.90). Scofield, whose silences are as eloquent as his utterances, embodies the awful power of monarchy even as the demons of encroaching age topple him. Brook frames the film between a map and a mirror. In the beginning, a formidable Lear calls out for a map, "Give me the map there" (1.1.37), as if some kind of surrogate certainty could lead him through a swamp of uncertainty. Brook erases the other end of the frame, however, by omitting the king's request when, after being shocked by Cordelia's death, he calls for a looking glass: "if . . . her breath will mist or stain the stone, / Why then she lives" (5.3.263). The absence of the looking glass seals the film's denial of revelation. The mirror no more than the map can redeem the unrelenting emptiness of the postmodern universe. Let him go from the "rack of this tough world" (5.3.315), says Kent.

Brook's vision of "the horror" underlying the smug facade of bourgeois society rivals in intensity Mr. Kurtz's bleak view of the Belgian Congo in Joseph Conrad's *The Heart of Darkness*. To find a language for such suffering, he even went so far as to enlist Ted Hughes as a scenarist to translate the play into "his own idiom" (Manvell 1971: 137), though even that poet's talents could ultimately not substitute for Shakespeare's powerful language. The draft shooting script, which underwent many revisions before its incarnation on screen, reflects the director's energetic drive to visualize in moving images Shakespeare's verbal pyrotechnics. Goneril (Irene Worth) and Albany (Cyril Cusack) are described as dining together "in [a] discreet, warm, and elegant room," yet outside in the storm are other creatures whose existence is wretched beyond belief. There is poor Edgar (Robert Lloyd), shown by "violently fast tracking shots, over hillocks, swampland, bushes, bracken, trees . . . [He] hides in a ditch . . . runs, slips, tumble[s] down into a pond clogged with mud . . . covered with filth. He stands quivering." Nearby on the heath, the storm grows more and more savage and "the ground cracks open, roots painfully are wrenched on the surface, roofs are carried away, walls burst outwards, great doors fly open, shutters snap their catches, . . . flames mount amongst branches, wells overflow their pitch-black content, out of the gashes and scars in the earth come scorpions, ants, spiders, snakes" (Brook 1968b: 22.71; 27.89).

It seems impossible that any detail capable of supporting an atmosphere that's "cheerless, dark, and deadly" (5.3.291) has been overlooked. Dantesque visions of despair bedevil the spectator's memory long after the movie has been screened. The barren landscape of Jutland gives no hope of brightness or sunshine; in a quotation from Eisenstein the menacing battle axes of Edgar and Edmund (Ian Hogg) are silhouetted against a blank sky; a distraught Goneril, her funereal black skirt drawn tight around her, rocks back and forth to build the terrible momentum needed to dash her head against a rock wall, though of course in the Folio she stabs herself offstage after poisoning Regan.

The visual language approximates the Shakespearean verse that smolders on the page and finally must ignite into apocalypse for lack of adequate signifiers to represent such suffering. As an artist, Brook's general outrage at the state of humankind seems explicable, even though his own comfortable bourgeois background had presumably protected him from feeling what wretches feel, yet even so for Brook it was a voyage on the dark side. The aggressive nihilism that emerged on screen in 1970 did not evolve overnight. There had been the 1962 Stratford production of *King Lear*, which won praise from even the acerbic Kenneth Tynan, who saw the old king as "willfully arrogant, and [deserving of] much of what he gets. Conversely his daughters are not fiends" (*Observer Weekend*, November 11, 1962). Perhaps even more decisive in shaping *King Lear* was Brook's 1967 film of Peter Weiss's *The Persecution and Assassination of Jean-Paul Marat as Performed by the Inmates of the Asylum at Charenton Under the Direction of the Marquis de Sade*. One reviewer famously quipped when asked if he had seen the play that he hadn't seen it but that he had "read the title." Louis Chapin saw it as "a production of dedicated, unstinting unpleasantness," though its "complexity was as brilliant as it was disagreeable" (*Christian Science Monitor*, January 8, 1966). It became a mantra to credit Jan Kott's influential essay "*King Lear* or End Game" (1966) as the prime inspiration for Brook's version *of King Lear*, though Brook has himself vehemently denied that this was the case (Leggatt 1991: 46). Several decades later, he seems justified; it was not simply Kott or Beckett, or even the threat of annihilation by the atomic bomb during the Cuban missile crisis, but the whole unconscious metaphysic of the times created by writers and filmmakers like Albert Camus, Jean-Paul Sartre, Luchino Visconti, and Jean-Luc Godard. All of this set the stage for Brook's own theory that "any empty space may be envisioned as a bare stage" (Brook 1968a). For Brook's film of Shakespeare's tragedy ultimately became a study in bareness, of the essential emptiness of the human condition, indeed of "nothingness," a word that echoes and re-echoes throughout the play itself. Somehow the thought that nothing could ever turn into something had been defeated by the Cold War, or from a left point of view, the Holy War against Communism, which among many other collateral damages squashed the high hopes of the United Nations Charter.

In art this was signaled by Bertolt Brecht's "epic" theatre and especially by Antonin Artaud's theatre of cruelty which, as he told Louis Chapin in an interview, demanded that "the public must atone and suffer as we do on stage in writing and acting" (*Christian Science Monitor*, January 8, 1966). The *Newsweek* critic pronounced anathema, describing Artaud as "a half-mad theologian and high priest of a new religion of drama [who] advocated a drama" that in Artaud's own words "would repudiate the consolations of bourgeois drama in order to shock the spectator into new awareness, through ritual, violence, extreme acts, and shattering taboos" (*Newsweek*, January 10, 1966). A *King Lear* incubated in this milieu would not be a movie for the multiplex but for the art house. It is only a step from Artaud's "cruelty" to Bertolt Brecht's "epic" theatre with its restless probing of alienation, both being steeped in what Arthur Schlesinger, Jr. called "the fashionable commonplaces of the last twenty years": revolution, existentialism, collectivism (*Vogue*, March 1, 1967).

Although often thought of as a stage director, Brook's experience as a movie director went as far back as his undergraduate years at Oxford, when he produced an amateur film, *Sentimental Journey* (1943), while two decades later there was his successful adaptation of William Golding's grim novel *Lord of the Flies* (1963). Many critics underestimated his credentials as a filmmaker, sometimes making him out to be some kind of a pretentious amateur who had been turned loose with a home movie camera. Quite the contrary. Brook simply applied his avant-garde theatrical vision to filmmaking. In his cinema of alienation the audience is required to participate actively rather than to sit back supinely, mesmerized, even lobotomized, by a contrived narrative. Anyone who breaks with the Classical Hollywood Cinema, as described so well by Bordwell, Staiger, and Thompson (1985), can expect a stampede of customers away from the box office. In France this Hollywood assembly line technique captivated the critics, who are said to have loved the American cinema because the films all resembled one another. *King Lear* violates the sacred dogma of seamless continuity, unobtrusive camera work, and bland capitalist ideology. The wintry setting in Jutland, north Denmark, sets up exactly the kind of ironic, sterile universe in harsh black-and-white with deliberately skewed frames that the plight of Lear calls for. It unabashedly flaunts its status as a film by foregrounding its own cinematic tropes, as if in an experimental play the stage were turned inside out by having all the behind-scenes flats, risers, ropes, curtains, costume shops, and switchboards ostentatiously displayed to the audience. In defiance of the Hollywood classical tradition that art must conceal art, Brook never hesitates to draw attention to his camera. The whole New Wave repertory of zoom shots, accelerated motion, reverse angle and over-the-shoulder shots, montage, jump cuts, silent screen titles, eyes-only close-ups, and hand-held cameras comes into play, in a determination to quote from Godard, Welles, and Eisenstein. Brook was not just making a movie about *King Lear*, but also making a movie about making movies.

None of this elegant footwork would be acceptable if it did not somehow usefully redeploy William Shakespeare's tragedy into cinematic idiom, which John Simon beside himself in scorn most emphatically denied, arguing that "the aptly pretentious stage and screen director, Peter Brook . . . misled by that arrogantly inept pseudo-scholar Jan Kott," had produced a "catastrophe and a scandal . . . [an] instant disaster" (*New York Times*, December 19, 1971). Pauline Kael dismissed it less fervently but more concisely in the *New Yorker* (December 11, 1971) with the simple verdict, "I hated it." On the other hand, Frank Kermode thought that Brook had made "the best of all Shakespeare movies" (*New York Review of Books*, May 4, 1972). But the film is not just a representation of the play, but also one commentary among many others on page, stage, or screen. To a degree the film does represent *King Lear*, but it also allows glimpses into its hidden truths, so that it becomes a Book of Revelation about the play. The last part of the fifth act achieves sublimity in its striving to disclose invisible mysteries in visible images. Lear reels and lurches across a sterile countryside cradling the hanged Cordelia (Annelise Gabold) in his arms and howling out his unspeakable pain. After that everything is backlit against a wintry whiteout as the king, who in close-up resembles a grotesque, lumpy, gray death mask kneaded out of children's play dough, vents his anguish over the body of Cordelia. Looking shadowy, ephemeral, Kent (Tom Fleming) asks, "Is this the promis'd end?" (5.3.265) and Edgar asks, "Or image of that horror?" (5.3.266). The relentlessly monochromatic background nearly blinds the audience to the tormented creatures in the foreground. In an emblem of humanity's mute suffering, Lear is for a split second, a few frames, joined by the wraith of an unsmiling Cordelia, reproachful in death as well as in life, as he pathetically says, "My poor fool is hang'd!" (5.3.306). Like Frederick B. Warde in the 1916 Thanhouser silent movie, Scofield then literally drops out of the frame, his head leaning ever backward and backward, leaving finally only a universe of blazing white, evocative of Henry Vaughan's "I saw eternity the other night / Like a great ring of pure and endless light" (1655). None of this is pretentious except insofar as the search for a twentieth-century context to render so great a work as *King Lear* in moving images calls for heroic measures.

* * *

> It [the Manson murder trial] had been the longest murder trial in American history, lasting nine and a half months; the most expensive, costing approximately $1 million; and the most highly publicized; while the jury had been sequestered 225 days, longer than any jury before it. The trial transcript alone ran to 209 volumes, 31,716 pages, approximately eight million words, a mini-library. (Bugliosi 1974: 456)

It is of course the worst kind of violation of the dogmas of the New Criticism, on which I was nurtured, to confuse a work of literary art with the personal life of the author. No less a heresy than the "intentional fallacy" may be at issue. On the other hand, it is virtually impossible to discuss Roman Polanski's superb film of *Macbeth* (1971) without reference to the lurid events surrounding the slaying in Hollywood of his beautiful and pregnant actress wife, Sharon Tate, by a gang of demented young women led by a messianic Charles Manson. It was not possible to watch the savage stabbing of Duncan without suspecting a *roman{polanski}-à-clef* alluding to the murders of Sharon Tate and her friend, Abigail Folger. When the film was then released under the auspices of Hugh Hefner, editor of *Playboy* magazine and inventor of the chic "Playboy lifestyle," a hymn to narcissism, Shakespeare, it would seem, had been merged with trash culture.

It would only "seem" that way because in fact Polanski, using the talents of Kenneth Tynan as a co-scenarist, and even while employing only 40 percent of the Folio text, though apparently making a pact with the devil, never really shortchanged Shakespeare. The film's egregious violence finds precedents in Shakespeare as well as in the Manson murders. Moreover, at a deeper level, it could be placed alongside Brook's *King Lear* as having been spawned by the fashionable interest in Jan Kott's theory of the Grand Mechanism, the idea of history as an implacable and unending power struggle. The difference is that Brook managed to keep his film within the boundaries of genteel (British?) taste; Polanski filmed in Wales but spiritually was in bondage to the hegemonic center of Anglo-American pop culture, down to and including the Third Ear Band's non-diegetic film music. In fact Polanski, without knowing it, was making a revolutionary break with the past in meddling with the hitherto sacred boundaries between high and low culture (Levine 1988; Bristol 1990). His *Macbeth* foreshadowed the century's later hybrids like Derek Jarman's *Tempest* (1980), the Baz Luhrmann *Romeo + Juliet* (1996), and the Michael Almereyda *Hamlet* (2000). The favorite unanswerable question of purists: "Is it Shakespeare?" was soon to give way to the more pragmatic: "Is there any Shakespeare in it?"

There is of course nothing uniquely modern in the linkage of sensational murders with Elizabethan drama. One need only recall the egregious case of *The Lamentable and True Tragedy of M{aster} Arden of Faversham in Kent* (1592), often attributed to Thomas Kyd or William Shakespeare, a dramatization about two real-life "Desperate Ruffians, Black Will and Shakebag," hired by a "Wicked Woman" with "an insatiable Desire of Filthy Lust" to dispose of Mr. Arden, all of it prime fodder for the Elizabethan broadsides, those lively precursors to the Rupert Murdoch tabloids. Somewhat analogously, newspapers throughout the world exploited the Manson case in hysterical headlines, indeed even the staid *New York Times* made it a front-page story. The Los Angeles press intoned: "Manson Guilty, Nixon Declares," "Manson, 3 Girls Sentenced to Die," and "Manson Leaps at Judge, Hurls Threat" (Bugliosi 1974: 340–1). Manson became a poster boy for the sickness of the times, though in some advanced hippie circles he was revered as a martyr to bourgeois complacency. Moreover the satanic themes in Polanski's adaptation of Ira Levin's *Rosemary's Baby* (1968) also reverberated nicely with the cultish Manson killings.

Unperturbed, Polanski denounced as "preposterous" any link between the Tate murder and the film, and his personal experience. "I just had to ignore totally that idiotic implication," he told Joseph Gelmis (*Courier Journal and Times*, December 9, 1973). He complained to journalist Jerry Oster that "the critics don't review the film, they review me" (*New York Sunday News*, June 27, 1976). Brilliant filmmaker as he was, Polanski remained a tortured human being, once, as Kenneth Tynan reported, being characterized cruelly in print as "the original 5-foot Pole you wouldn't touch anyone with" (Tynan 1975: 88). Thorn Mount, a sympathizer, opined that "more than any other philosophic idea, it is the notion of an absurd universe that has shaped the life and creative work of Roman Polanski" (*Interview*, September 1975). Leading film critic Andrew Sarris also rushed to Polanski's defense, arguing that the same people who are trying to "understand" Charles Manson were condemning Polanski "out of hand . . . as if Polanski had been more tainted by the crime against his wife than had Manson himself" (*Village Voice*, March 20, 1978). Unfortunately, even after the uproar over the Manson case had simmered down, Polanski garnered more headlines when he was arrested and accused of raping a 13-year-old aspiring actress (*Time*, March 28, 1977). The gloating by the press over his latest downfall haunted the movie's residual success on VHS in educational circles.

In *Macbeth* Polanski needed to adapt the Shakespearean tragedy that best combined the playwright's poetic and dramatic talent in recording the tale of a Scottish thane who underestimated how high the price was for usurping the throne from a legitimate monarch. The agony of Macbeth as he apprehends the depth of his own corruption leaves him as wretched as a film director under siege from the press. Macbeth's uniqueness lies in being a murderer with an extraordinary gift for language that allows him to comment on his own perfidy. That double status is what allowed Polanski to create a filmed *Macbeth* that is simultaneously beautiful and repellent. The ugliness of soul lies behind the veneer of beauty. The mixture of the "fair" with that which is "foul" ("Fair is foul, and foul is fair, / Hover through the fog and filthy air"; 1.1.11) becomes Polanski's as well as Shakespeare's oxymoronic leitmotif.

The opening sequence of the film serves as brilliant prologue, or dumb show, for what is to follow. The long shot of a lonely beach at sunrise anticipates the Macbeth who will "have supp'd full with horrors" (5.5.13) before he suffers death by beheading at the hands of Macduff. On the deserted beach, two crones and a surprisingly youthful and attractive young woman ("Fair is foul") unload a loathsome collection of clammy junk from a squeaky old cart. The inventory from the cart includes a hangman's noose and a severed arm in the hand of which the women insert a dagger. In close-up, the cackling trio bury the arm in the sand and pour a vial of blood over it. A gull squawks, a talisman of a galaxy of birds' cries to follow, all of which echo Shakespeare's own ornithological obsessions: "Light thickens, and the crow / Makes wing to th' rooky wood" (3.2.50). Fog and mist roll in with superimposed titles fading in and out, while the Third Ear Band provides discordant violin and bagpipe music for the departure of the witches' rickety cart. The soundtrack reverberates with horses' hooves, shouting and screaming, clashing of swords, the whinnying of horses, human wailing, coughing, and moaning, while the superimposed credits continue to roll over the now completely fog-bound battlefield. After the mist dissipates, dead and wounded litter the battlefield. In mid-shot a soldier stops by an injured man lying face down on the ground, yanks at his boot, and the man feebly lifts his head. With two or three whacks of an iron ball on a chain, the soldier shatters the wounded man's spine. The camera moves on to the bleeding sergeant's battle report and then to a bloodied Thane of Cawdor (Vic Abbott), bound and stretched out on a horse-drawn litter.

Ironically, however, all the sordid and grisly events in the director's life could not entirely account for the film's egregious violence. That distinction really belongs to

William Shakespeare, whose Scottish tragedy contains the dozens of images of blood that inspired Polanski's on-screen Guignol. The wouldbe king whose mind is "full of scorpions" confesses to Lady Macbeth that "I am in blood / Stepp'd in so far that, should I wade no more, / Returning were as tedious as go o'er" (3.4.135). And of course the egregious onscreen stabbing of Duncan, which occurs offstage in Shakespeare's play, gains some justification from Lady Macbeth's chilling "Yet who would have thought the old man to have had so much blood in him?" (5.1.39). "Brave Macbeth" himself, a formidable warrior, after the battlefield codes of the day, did not cringe from bloodshed. Confronting an enemy soldier, he "with his brandish'd steel, / Which smok'd with bloody execution, / . . . carv'd out his passage / Till he fac'd the slave; / [and] . . . unseam'd him from the nave to th' chops, / And fix'd his head upon our battlements" (1.2.16ff.).

Separately cataloged, the film's horrors add up to a fearsome blood bath, some being gratuitously embellished but all implied if not spelled out in the Folio text: the killing of the kern in the opening sequence, the hanging of captives, the stabbing of Duncan by Macbeth, the execution of the grooms, the severed head of one of the grooms, the murder of Banquo through an axe in his back, a bear carcass being dragged over bloody floors, the murder of Lady Macduff and her children, the assassination of Seyton by means of a crossbow dart through his head, the slitting of Siward's throat, the interminable duel between Macbeth and MacDuff, and, finally, the beheading of Macbeth by Macduff. In an apotheosis of horror, the subjective camera allows the spectator to see the jeering soldiers as they were reflected in the retina of Macbeth's freshly decapitated head, presumably still in the throes of the death agony.

The violence should not have come as a surprise in view of the source materials. To say this, however, is to overlook the conspiracy of gentility that sacralized Shakespeare's work for decades, persisting well into the twentieth century. Schoolmasters and the Victorian bardolaters were in complete denial about anything in Shakespeare's work that even faintly suggested traffic with low culture. They had apparently forgotten that this was the same man who wrote *Titus Andronicus*, or if they had not forgotten they hastened to prove that the morbid tale of rape, violence, and cannibalism was not really written by Shakespeare at all. No one was better qualified than Polanski to sully this genteel image and reorient it in a twentieth-century context. There was more, too, in the atmosphere besides the antics of Polanski. The assassination of President John F. Kennedy in 1964 had left a miasma of paranoia in its wake in which wild conspiracy theories attached themselves even to the office of the president. Barbara Garson's satiric play *MacBird* opened at the Village Gate in 1967 and made outrageous parallels between the assassination of Kennedy and the murder of Duncan. Lady Macbeth became the paradigm for the ambitious corporate wife. The soil for Polanski's *Macbeth* had been well tilled.

Quite likely it had never occurred to anyone before the *Playboy* production to think of Lord and Lady Macbeth as an attractive young couple at the country club, the popular stereotype hitherto belonging to middle-aged Judith Anderson and Maurice Evans, whose safe but boring Hallmark Greeting Cards *Macbeth* (1954) became a classroom fixture. Even art house patrons in 1948 might have thought of the Macbeths as a bellowing Orson Welles and slightly intimidated Jeanette Nolan. Finch and Annis in their superficial beauty exemplify the witches' mantra that "Fair is foul and foul fair." Who would have thought that the handsome Finch could be "the secret'st man of blood" (3.4.125)? And who could imagine a Lady Macbeth as a *Playboy* centerfold girl doing her sleepwalking in the nude? Unhappily for the panting voyeurs, the scene's erotic quotient is overrated, she seeming more vulnerable than vixenish even in her dishabille.

And yet Polanski hit on exactly the right note in stressing the outwardly attractive but inwardly evil nature of his leading character. In myriad clever ways the movie recycles Shakespeare's verbal images into visual tropes. Macbeth's exposure to the "show of eight Kings" (4.1.12) skirts the Shakespearean theme of the interplay between illusion and reality, suggesting the ambiguous role of these "secret, black, and midnight hags" (4.1.48). Duncan discovers for himself the trickiness of judging men by appearances when he hears the report of Cawdor's death: "There's no art / To find the mind's construction in the face" (1.4.11). In the movie, however, he personally witnesses the brutal execution, which is voyeuristic, even pornographic, in its ritualized sadism. A mesomorphic Cawdor stands on a tower with an obscene iron collar around his thick neck, chains clattering, and moments later, smiling contemptuously, and with unimaginable courage shouting "God save the king!", leaps sickeningly to his death. Especially ironic is the way that Duncan can praise Cawdor's nobility of spirit at the same time that he condemns him to a barbaric death. The illusion/reality topoi continue as Méliès-like trick photography produces the dagger for Macbeth's "Is this a dagger which I see before me" (2.1.33), while the camera pans down to reveal a dagger on the balustrade, but when Macbeth reaches out for it he grasps only air. A bear-baiting brings a gloating expression suggestive of an erotic thrill to Lady Macbeth's lovely face, and ends with the beast fettered to a stone column. The motif anticipates Macbeth's awful realization that he too "bear-like . . . must fight the course" (5.7.2). Noticeably present also is a penchant for having servants wipe up spilled things, like wine, and cover the stains with fresh straw, in yet another manifestation of the obsession to conceal foul with the fair.

Orson Welles's extraordinary ear for sound effects has been widely acclaimed, a talent that was nurtured by extensive radio work, when among other gigs he intoned the portentous words "The shadow knows." For this movie, Polanski can lay claim to equal skills, with an array of sonic aids that do not so much punctuate as participate in the action. Sound energizes images. The clinking when Duncan (Nicholas Selby) lifts Cawdor's chain and medallion from his throat adds a cold metallic flavor of calculation to the king's ruthlessness, especially significant because this same chain and medallion ends up around the neck of Rosse (John Stride). The scheming of Rosse and Seyton (Joel Davis) to succeed Lennox (Andrew Laurence) as chief steward is a subplot in the movie, and mirrors Macbeth's overthrow of Duncan (Rothwell 1983–4). The tinkling medallion chain then carries over into what amounts to a silent movie nested inside the sound movie, which focuses on Rosse, a smirking sociopath, who hovers always obsequiously near Macbeth. Ironically the avant-gardists, Tynan and Polanski, found the inspiration for this exotic interpretation in a Victorian monograph by M. F. Libby, "Some New Notes on Macbeth" (1893).

The accumulation of sound transcends mere randomness and takes on the dimension of a cacophonous symphony, a fit adjunct to the Third Ear Band. There is nearly always something going on. Geese clack, pigs oink, wolfhounds whimper, hens cackle, crows caw, thunder claps, dancers whoop, shutters bang, and so forth, nearly *ad infinitum*. As with Cawdor's chain, each makes a subliminal but decisive impact. An owl hoots and prepares the way for Lady Macbeth's "I heard the owl scream and the crickets cry" (2.2.14), which in turn leads to the knocking at the gate with the drunken lout of a porter who commits a nuisance on the castle wall. The growling dogs and clucking hens demystify Macbeth's medieval castle and expose it as the rural slum it probably was. The sound of splashing water has never sounded more sinister than when it signals the drowning of the two murderers of Banquo in a castle well, pushed down by the obliging Rosse, who also turns out to be the mysterious Third Murderer. These richly varied auralities, insignificant in and of themselves, lend powerful resonance to the envisioning of Shakespeare's tragedy.

At the very end, in reel sixteen actually, Donalbain after the death of Macbeth dismounts from his horse and limps toward the witches' cave as the music changes to crooning and then the crooning back to music. His fresh compact with the witches suggests that the cycle of evil will never end in Scotland and elevates the film to a higher philosophical level, somewhat like the existentialist despair in the Brook *Lear*. Polanski has capitalized on the double nature of Shakespeare's own play, which is both sublime and depraved. In Shakespeare the sublime poetry redeems the depravity; as a filmmaker Polanski must show depravity but redeem it with inspired cinematography. Like Macbeth, he too was confronted with the foul that was fair and fair that was foul, but unlike Macbeth his art redeemed him.

* * *

About the same time [1968], the first rock mass was recorded by a group called the Electric Prunes, and films began . . . to reflect . . . the new life-style. Releases . . . included *The Graduate*, satirizing the get-ahead values of the Establishment . . . the Beatles' escapist cartoon, *Yellow Submarine* . . . (Daniels 1989: 58)

From the scrapheap of the perturbed twentieth century, for his enormously popular film of *Romeo and Juliet* (1968), Franco Zeffirelli capitalized on the rebelliousness of the young against the older generation's bourgeois false consciousness. In Shakespeare's own source for the ancient love-potion story, Arthur Brooke's narrative poem *The Tragicall Historye of Romeus and Juliet* (1562), the young lovers had been partly to blame for their disobedience to authority, but as centuries passed their culpability gradually began to be overshadowed by the tyranny of the older generation. In Leonard Bernstein and Stephen Sondheim's musical adaptation, *West Side Story* (1961), the guilt has almost entirely been absorbed by the parents. By 1968, with the youth revolution blossoming from Columbia University to Paris to Prague to Berkeley, any film of *Romeo and Juliet* was bound to reflect the popular belief that no one over thirty was to be trusted. To reinforce that view Zeffirelli took enormous pains to find just the right loveable teenage actors, Leonard Whiting and Olivia Hussey, for his idealized Romeo and Juliet, who were anything but the kind of sullen adolescents so typical of the age group. To gain even more sympathy for the young people he cast beautiful Natasha Parry as a disdainful Lady Capulet and Paul Hardwick as a remote Lord Capulet. If tragic suffering sometimes wore the borrowed robes of a Hollywood "weepy," the visual and aural artistry was nevertheless unassailable.

Moreover the matrix of oxymorons in Shakespeare's *Romeo and Juliet*, such as "Feather of lead, bright smoke, cold fire, sick health" (1.1.180), which then extend into the play's deepest structure, perfectly fit Franco Zeffirelli's love of paradox. On the one hand, he was committed as a populist in art to entertaining the masses, and, on the other hand, his politics turned him into a fire-eating right-wing senator from Catania. The reconciling of such opposites produces cognitive dissonance in the liberal mind. Zeffirelli may be the Italian version of Charlton Heston, whose love for the gun lobby is only equated by his love for Shakespeare, Shakespeare's Antony in particular, he having heavily invested in his neglected film of *Antony and Cleopatra* (1972). Zeffirelli's radical unpredictability perhaps stems from the influence of his mentor, Luchino Visconti, who despised bourgeois conformity and advocated communism while at the same time living a life of aristocratic grandeur. From Visconti, Zeffirelli learned about the importance of meticulous attention to small details, such as the precious objets d'art scattered throughout the home of Baptista Minola in *The Taming of the Shrew* (1966). The way that Visconti combined neo-realism with bravura operatic effects in his famous epic about Italian peasantry, *La Terra Trema/The Earth Trembles* (1948), also presumably shaped Zeffirelli's use of hand-held cameras in the grubby street fighting of Verona and of conventional cinematography in the majestic ballroom scenes at the Capulet villa.

Zeffirelli's film opens with the charismatic Laurence Olivier reciting the prologue in voice-over (as in *Hamlet*), while in the establishing shot a camera pans over Verona, moves right across a river, over the ancient city, pauses, where the sun hovers shrouded in mist, then zooms toward the sun until nothing remains in the frame but the sun. With a sure eye for visualizing the verbal in Shakespeare, Zeffirelli has singled out the sun, which is in itself a star, as a central icon for the tale of "star-cross'd lovers." Freed from the spatial restraints of the stage, the bustling Verona marketplace appears in long shot and the camera closes in on the swaggering minions of the Capulets, whose codpieces wordlessly stand in for the opening scene's coarse phallic jokes, e.g., Sampson's swaggering "Me they shall feel while I am able to stand" (1.1.2). Like the hoods in *West Side Story*, they strut past heaped stalls of fresh melons, oranges, peppers, and onions, themselves suggestive of heat and passion and fertility. Zeffirelli himself told Gordon Gow how he came to the difficult conclusion that the "beauty of the poetry in Shakespeare is not what matters – there must be something else in him that makes him great" (Gow 1973: 23). This is a film ever in quest of that elusive quality.

John McEnery's reading of Mercutio's Queen Mab speech provides a paradigm for the ingenuity of the entire film. The "mercurial" character of Mercutio implicit in his name is embodied in an amazing frenzy of manic-depressive behavior. The emotional voltage surges out of him as he speaks of "cutting foreign throats, / Of breaches, ambuscadoes, Spanish blades" (1.4.83) until, his anguish palpable, Romeo breaks in anxiously to say "Peace, peace, Mercutio, peace! / Thou talk'st of nothing" (1.4.95). McEnery and Zeffirelli, one or the other or both, have electrified a speech that too often has been read as a sterile elocutionary exercise.

Not that Zeffirelli's movie remains somber at all. His recent staging of *La Traviata* at the Metropolitan Opera (2001) with its gleaming chandeliers and ornate furnishings and banks and banks of flowers and multilevel rooms and swirling costumes reflects the same love for sensuous extravagance that he brought to *Romeo and Juliet*. In Nino Rota, Zeffirelli found a peerless composer of film music, his theme for Francis Ford Coppola's *The Godfather* being one among many acclaimed achievements. In Albert Cirillo's view, Rota's score provides "sonic coloring and punctuation to the color photography itself" (Cirillo 1971: 225) and works multiple variations on themes from festival and liturgical sequences. The leitmotif comes from the vocalization by Sistine Chapel soloist Bruno Filippini in the Capulet ballroom scene of "What Is a Youth," with lyrics by Eugene Walter, which subsequently became a popular radio hit. The variations on a theme, ranging from lighthearted to somber, mirror the two-part division of the film itself, which moves from the comic to the tragic, a division more apparent in England than in America because of the interval for refreshments in British movie houses after the wedding scene. Part two, it will be recalled, begins ominously with Mercutio's ubiquitous handkerchief now proleptically covering his face like a shroud.

The musical/operatic motifs support the film as in the Capulet ballroom scene, the aubade scene, and climactically in the tomb scene. In the Capulet ballroom the call for the "wild Morisco," a Moorish dance reminiscent of Flamenco mentioned in *2 Henry VI* (3.1.365), sets up a visual trope for the isolation of the young lovers from the adults. Romeo (Leonard Whiting) at first remains on the rim, peering anxiously through his visor at the beautiful Olivia Hussey, Zeffirelli's 15-year-old leading lady, whose selection for the role by Zeffirelli involved fierce competition among 350 aspirants. The two concentric rings of dancers moving in opposite directions reflect the play's internal tensions among a variety of opposites. As the circling intensifies, the subjective camera takes the spectator deeper and deeper into the experience, so that there is empathy with the confusion of Romeo and Juliet. As several critics have noted, the circular dance becomes a Dance of Love, the circle motif then being appropriated to Freudian ends and restated in the mosaic tiles on the floor of the church where the wedding is solemnized. In contrast with the heightened festivity of the ballroom scene, the Dance of Death (when a raucous crowd encircles the embattled Tybalt and Romeo), recorded with a hand-held camera and enlivened by guttural sound effects, flaunts its primal neo-realism.

In search of authenticity, Zeffirelli in fact ransacked his beloved northern Italy for plausible locations evocative of the Renaissance. Since modern Verona is now a bustling industrial city, a Romanesque church in San Pietro provided the site for the wedding of the young lovers; the stately Piccolomini Palace in Pienza served as the Capulet home; the Umbrian town of Gubbio became the site of the street fights; and most important of all the Palazzo Borghese in Artena just south of Rome provided the fabled balcony and garden below for the play's most celebrated scene, though the main square of Verona was constructed on the back lot of Rome's Cinecittà studios ("Handbook" 1968: 9)

Zeffirelli weaves an intricate network of figures into a moving tapestry that gathers together the play's recurring motifs. As James Lake (1990) has observed, in the aubade and tomb scenes, Zeffirelli translates key images of lips, kisses, and hands into haunting icons emblematic of the young lovers. The fleeting nudity in Juliet's bedchamber tests the limits of the emerging tolerance for overt sexuality on screen, opening with an old-fashioned tableau of a Juliet chastely covered with a sheet and a Romeo face down with legs asprawl. In a reverse-angle close-up, Romeo slowly awakens to Rota's dulcet score and smiles at the sleeping Juliet. Then Juliet awakens, tucks the sheet up under her chin, and watches as Romeo clumsily attempts to pull on his breeches. Later, in the tomb scene, she will exactly echo this bit of business, only then she will be tugging at a shroud, not a bed sheet. After he half-dresses she sleepily murmurs, "Yond light is not day-light" (3.5.12) as she holds out her arms and he leaps back on to the bed crying "Let me be ta'en" (3.5.17). "It is the lark," she says (3.5.27). The words have dictated movement as well as melody to make the film both balletic and operatic, all of it choreographed to the pace and rhythms of Rota's ineffable score.

The tomb scene again returns to the pervasive motif of the lovers' touching hands and lips, which is noticeable in the balcony scene, and again in the sonnet sequence at the Capulet ball ("For saints have hands that pilgrims' hands do touch"; 1.5.99). The tomb scene parodies the farewell at dawn, except that now the bridegroom is not Romeo but Death. In a tableau perilously close to necrophilia, surrounded by festering corpses, Romeo again kisses Juliet on the lips as he did in the aubade. Then he takes out the vial of poison and as he raises it to his lips does not say, as Shakespeare would have it, "Thus with a kiss I die" (5.3.120) but instead "Here's to my love." In close-up Romeo grasps Juliet's left hand, which had been crossed with her right hand on her breast. As he falls, he drags Juliet's hand down until it rests next to her waistline. After the distraught friar's arrival, the first sign of Juliet's awakening occurs to tremolo strings with a close-up of her repositioned hand beginning to stir. The continuity for this moment has, however, been carefully manufactured by Romeo's "accidental" placement of the hand by her side. The close shot of her hand stirring and gradually coming alive resembles the famous episode in James Whale's classic horror film *Frankenstein* (1931), starring Boris Karloff, when after the crackling and flashing of ludicrous high-voltage equipment the monster's hand in tight close-up suddenly stirs, and an ecstatic and relieved Dr. Henry Frankenstein cries out "It's alive!", though it would be strange if Zeffirelli consciously quoted this trope!

Juliet's hand moves toward the shroud, picks at it, and in a movement analogous to the handling of the bed sheet in the aubade scene, she tucks it up under her chin. To the poignancy of "What is a Youth" as sung at the Capulet ball, Juliet picks up the empty poison vial by Romeo's body, and as the melody swells to a crescendo, she sobs, smothers Romeo's face with kisses, and in an obvious Freudian displacement thrusts his dagger, "O happy dagger" (5.3.169), into her breast. A freeze-frame unites the lovers in perpetuity, with Juliet's head neatly tucked next to Romeo's, almost like the golden statues that their parents with a sure Midas touch plan to commission after their children's double suicide. Death has become her bridegroom, as Capulet says to a distraught Paris after the discovery of her apparently lifeless body: "O son, the night before thy wedding-day / Hath Death lain with thy wife . . . / Death is my son-in-law, Death is my heir" (4.5.35ff.).

In daring to fuse art and sentimentality, Zeffirelli followed the Italian tradition that has produced wonderfully sensuous operas like Puccini's *Madame Butterfly* and Verdi's *La Traviata* and thereby enticed millions into movie theatres to watch Shakespeare. His *Romeo and Juliet* was unrivaled in popularity until Baz Luhrmann's 1996 version, but by then youth had been completely liberated from adult disapproval, indeed adults had themselves come under heavy disapproval, and Shakespeare's tragedy emerged in the vibrant but coarse new idiom of hip-hop, MTV culture. By now, in the twenty-first century, the guilt has unequivocally been passed from the younger to the older generation.

Tragedy calls for a sense of the sublime that, as this essay has implied, was notably absent in the twentieth century. Consequently, the metaphysic behind the quartet of tragedies discussed here coalesced around the shards of the century's experiences, the modish chitchat about Freud and Beckett, the vagaries of pop culture, the great uprising of the rebels without a cause, and a pervasive sense of anomie. It had been a long road from Virginia Woolf's comfy Elizabethan Lumber Room to the twentieth-century's faceless suburban shopping malls. For filmmakers in an ironic age, to adapt Shakespeare's major tragedies was therefore inevitably to add a modernist hue to their Elizabethan colors. The result has not been so much to devalue Shakespeare as to demonstrate again the labyrinthine ways in which his work negotiates with unexpected discourses. The great gift of the twentieth century has been the technology to record Shakespearean performance on screen for posterity as a supplement to his work on page and stage.

NOTES

1   This and subsequent Shakespeare quotations are from G. B. Evans et al. (1974) *The Riverside Shakespeare*. Boston, MA: Houghton Mifflin.
2   It is possible that Olivier's acrobatic camera was also inspired by George More O'Ferrall's ambitious tracking shots in a 1947 BBC *Hamlet*. See Barry (1954: 146).

FILMOGRAPHY

Hamlet UK, 1948. Two Cities Films. Dir. Laurence Olivier. Sd/b&w. 152 mins. With Laurence Olivier (Hamlet), Jean Simmons (Ophelia), Eileen Herlie (Gertrude).

King Lear UK/Denmark, 1970. Filmways (London), Athene/Laterna Films (Copenhagen). Dir. Peter
    Brook. Sd/b&w. 137 mins. With Paul Scofield (King Lear), Irene Worth (Goneril), Jack MacGowran
    (Fool), AnneLise Gabold (Cordelia).
Macbeth UK, 1971. Playboy Productions/Caliban Films. Dir. Roman Polanski. Sd/col. 140 mins. With
    Jon Finch (Macbeth), Francesca Annis (Lady Macbeth).
Romeo and Juliet Italy/UK, 1968. B.H.E./Verona Productions/Dino de Laurentiis Cinematografica. Dir.
    Franco Zeffirelli. Sd/col. 139 mins. With Leonard Whiting (Romeo), Olivia Hussey (Juliet), Michael
    York (Tybalt).

REFERENCES AND FURTHER READING

Alexander, P. (1955). *Hamlet Father and Son.* The Lord Northcliffe Lectures, University College, London,
    1953. Oxford: Clarendon Press.
Alkire, N. L. (1991). Subliminal Masks in Olivier's *Hamlet. Shakespeare on Film Newsletter,* 16, 1 (Dec.),
    5.
Ashworth, J. (1949). Olivier, Freud, and Hamlet. *The Atlantic,* 183 (May), 30–3.
Barry, M. (1954). Shakespeare on Television. *BBC Quarterly,* 9, 3 (autumn), 143–9.
Bordwell, D., Staiger, J., and Thompson, K. (1985). *The Classical Hollywood Cinema: Film Style and Mode
    of Production to 1960.* New York: Columbia University Press.
Bristol, M. (1990). *Shakespeare's America, America's Shakespeare.* New York: Routledge.
Brook, P. (1968a). *The Empty Space.* New York: Avon Books.
——(1968b). *King Lear:* Draft shooting script. Microfilm in Folger Shakespeare Library. Sept 9/Dec. 5.
Bugliosi, V., with Gentry, C. (1974). *Helter Skelter: The True Story of the Manson Murders.* New York:
    W. W. Norton.
Camus, A. (1955). An Absurd Reasoning. In *The Myth of Sisyphus and Other Essays,* trans. J. O'Brien.
    New York: Vintage Books, 1–48.
Cirillo, A. (1971). The Art of Franco Zeffirelli and Shakespeare's *Romeo and Juliet.* In *Film and Literature:
    Contrasts in Media.* Scranton, PA: Chandler, 205–27.
Cross, B. (ed.) (1948). *The Film Hamlet: A Record of Its Production.* New York: Saturn Press.
Daniels, R. V. (1989). *Year of the Heroic Guerilla: World Revolution and Counterrevolution in 1968.* New
    York: Basic Books.
Davies, A. (1988). *Filming Shakespeare's Plays: The Adaptations of Laurence Olivier, Orson Welles, Peter Brook
    and Akira Kurosawa.* Cambridge: Cambridge University Press.
Donaldson, P. S. (1990). *Shakespearean Films/Shakespearean Directors.* Boston, MA: Unwin Hyman.
Freud, S. (1913; 1931; 1938). *The Interpretation of Dreams.* In A. A. Brill (ed.) *The Basic Writings of Sigmund
    Freud.* New York: Modern Library, 181–468.
Gow, G. (1973). Versatility: Franco Zeffirelli in an Interview with Gordon Gow. *Films and Filming,* 19,
    7 (April), 20–6.
Guntner, L. (1990). *Mikrokosmos Kunst: "Hamlet"* (1948). In W. Faulstich and H. Korte (eds.) *Fischer
    Filmgeschichte,* vol. 3. Frankfurt am Main: Fischer Taschenbuch Verlag.
"Handbook" (1968). The Franco Zeffirelli Production of *Romeo and Juliet.* Paramount Pictures Corp.,
    unpublished.
Hapgood, R. (ed.) (1999). *Hamlet Prince of Denmark.* Cambridge: Cambridge University Press.
Heston, C. (1995). *In the Arena: An Autobiography.* New York: Simon and Schuster.
Jones, E. (1995) [1949]. *Hamlet and Oedipus.* New York: Anchor Books.
Jorgens, J. J. (1977). *Shakespeare on Film.* Bloomington: Indiana University Press.
Judd, L. L. et al. (1994). Mental Disorders. In *Harrison's Principles of Internal Medicine,* vol. 2, 13th edn.
    New York: McGraw Hill.

Kliman, B. W. (1988). *"Hamlet." Film, Television, and Audio Performance*. London: Associated University Presses.

Kott, J. (1966). *King Lear* or End Game, trans. B. Taborski. In *Shakespeare Our Contemporary*. New York: Anchor Books, 127–68.

Lake, J. (1990). Hands in Zeffirelli's *Rom*. *Shakespeare on Film Newsletter*, 15, 1 (Dec.), 4.

Leggatt, A. (1991). *"King Lear." Shakespeare in Performance*. Manchester: Manchester University Press.

Lesser, S. O. (1955). Freud and *Hamlet* Again. *The American Imago*, 12, 207–20.

Levine, L. (1988). *Highbrow/Lowbrow: The Emergence of Cultural Hierarchy in America*. Cambridge, MA: Harvard University Press.

Manvell, R. (1979) [1971]. *Shakespeare and the Film*, 2nd Printing 1979. Cranbury, NJ: A. S. Barnes.

Rothwell, K. S. (1983–4). Roman Polanski's *Macbeth*: The "Privileging" of Ross. *The CEA Critic*, 46, 1 & 2, 50–5.

Souvenir Program [*Hamlet*] (1948). Odeon Theatre. Leicester Square, 1.

Tynan, Kathleen (1987). *The Life of Kenneth Tynan*. New York: William Morrow.

Tynan, Kenneth (1975). *The Sound of Two Hands Clapping*. London: Jonathan Cape.

Werder, K. (1875). *Vorlesungen über Shakespeare's Hamlet*. Trans. in *"Hamlet:" A New Variorum Edition*, ed. H. H. Furness, pp. 354–71. Rpt. 1877; New York: Dover Publications, vol. 2, 1963.

Zeffirelli, F. (1986). *Autobiography: The Autobiography of Franco Zeffirelli*. New York: Weidenfeld and Nicolson.

13

Contemporary Film Versions
of the Tragedies

Mark Thornton Burnett

Over the course of the 1990s, new film versions of Shakespeare's tragedies carved out for themselves an unprecedented place in the social imaginary. Stimulated, no doubt, by the inspirational example of Kenneth Branagh's *Henry V* (1989), directors and producers turned with a reinvigorated verve to the best known of the Bard's works, offering up a plethora of art-house and multiplex-oriented cinematic readings. This represented a distinctive break with the previous two decades in which, several note-worthy examples notwithstanding, Shakespeare's status as a filmic icon had commenced a slow but steady decline. It might also be true to say that this period was marked by the last stages of an attitude towards Shakespeare that promoted the sacrosanct qualities of the textual original and ideals of fidelity of adaptation. With the end of the twentieth century, however, and in the wake of advances in critical debate, films such as Oliver Parker's *Othello* (1995), Baz Luhrmann's *William Shakespeare's Romeo + Juliet* (1996), Kenneth Branagh's *Hamlet* (1996), Julie Taymor's *Titus* (1999), and Michael Almereyda's *Hamlet* (2000) broke fresh ground, moving away from theatricality, transporting the dramatist into exciting visual settings, casting rhetoric as image, and forming resonant connections with contemporary popular and mass culture.

On these contemporary film versions of the tragedies this essay concentrates, arguing that, in taking leave from the cultures of their times, they establish fruitful points of contact between expectations about Shakespeare and the experiences of the cinemagoer of modernity. Only two of the films under discussion – Branagh's *Hamlet* and Taymor's *Titus* – have their origins in a theatrical production, while all of them are rooted with a peculiar urgency in filmic visual and performative idioms, in, to cite Branagh, "story-telling in other kinds of genres . . . the ways in which popular cinema tells its stories" (Wray and Burnett 2000: 167). A film such as Taymor's *Titus*, for instance, displays a sensitive indebtedness both to Ridley Scott's *Gladiator* (2000) and to Larry and Andy Wachowski's *The Matrix* (1999) in order to activate the play for the present historical juncture. The result is not so much a Shakespeare representative of, in Denise Albanese's words, "stable literary (and, by extension, ideological) values currently under siege" (Albanese 2001: 207). Rather, the dramatist has, through film adaptation, become a more plural and open-ended entity, a shifting terrain that is open to reinvention from a number of competing quarters. The cinematic Shakespeare, in fact, inhabits a distinctively postmodern guise, since the films collapse artistic categories, favor stylistic promiscuity, and indulge in playfulness in the same moment as they seem to pay homage to an entrenched cultural lineage.

In this connection it is worth reminding ourselves of the wealth of Shakespeare-related versions of the tragedies that emerged during the 1990s, films such as William Reilly's *Men of Respect* (1990), based on *Macbeth*, Branagh's *In the Bleak Midwinter* (1995), a communal theatrical parable with an eye cocked towards *Hamlet*, and Lloyd Kaufman's *Tromeo & Juliet* (1996), the teasing title of which is self-explanatory. If nothing else, this body of work demonstrates how far the parameters of Shakespearean interpretation have moved. Because of the quasi-irreverent mockery of Shakespeare in the filmic parodies, notions of tragedy are interrogated, kitsch claims dominance, and linguistic comprehensiveness cedes place to the soundbite. Although these films are not directly discussed in this essay, they form an alliance with more easily identifiable adaptations in revealing a Shakespeare groomed for recent developments in consumption, taste, and even late capitalist modes of global communication. Like the Shakespearean spin-off, contemporary versions of the tragedies contemplate the burdens of textuality and meditate self-consciously upon their own existence. At the same time, they push at the boundaries of the Shakespearean, feeding from their immediate contexts and from each other in generically variegated, visually arresting, technically versatile, and media-fashioned realizations of the dramatic originals.

Oliver Parker's *Othello* discovers its absorption in a range of other genres at a particularly obvious level, for the film was marketed at its release as a species of "erotic thriller." Building on the precedent set by Paul Verhoeven's *Basic Instinct* (1992), Parker's film invests at the same moment in playing out to the full the tensions of the intrigue and reifying for spectatorly involvement the bodies of the main protagonists. Crucially, the production visits upon Laurence Fishburne, the first African-American actor to have taken the role of Othello in a general release film, a racial–sexual charge. The *mise-en-scène* returns repeatedly to images of black and white colors conjoined, never more evocatively than in the scene in which a black man in a gondola turns to the camera as he puts on a white mask: the gesture serves a dual purpose, both establishing a milieu of deceit and looking forward to the theatricality of Othello's self-presentation. As Deborah Cartmell puts it, "the image disturbingly [makes] . . . the suggestion that, in marrying a white woman, Othello is playing at being white himself" (Cartmell 2000: 76).

Growing out of the film's mobilization of color are its reflections upon alterity. Not only is Othello branded as other through the cinematography; Desdemona, too, played by Irene Jacob, is untypical of her Venetian environment. With her slightly accented Swiss vowels, she, like Othello, appears something of a "wheeling stranger" (1.1.137).

A sense of difference is also underscored in the film's predilection for underlining the points of view of the central players. An audience is repeatedly privy to a gaze that betrays the erotic expectations of the story's triumvirate. As Desdemona dances at her marriage feast and, outside, a pair of lovers copulates on a haycart, Othello is seen watching her performance: by positioning his gaze against such a backdrop, the film both anticipates the consummation and sets the scene for the protagonist's sexually skewed construction of his wife's behavior. But it is on Othello, rather than Desdemona, that the camera's gaze dwells most longingly. In particular, his form is fetishized when, over Desdemona's shoulder, he is glimpsed removing his clothes; through such representational procedures, Othello, "bare-chested or . . . clad in a billowy, white shirt," is, as Lisa S. Starks observes, " 'frozen' as a screen spectacle" (Starks 1997: 73). Nor is Iago absent as a participant from this visual dynamic. He looks at Othello with loathing and possessiveness, suggesting a tense dependency of homoerotic identification and psychological contempt. The result, then, is a competition for the command of the filmic frame, a struggle for visual control. Matching the play's involvement in types of ocular evidence, eyes in the film become the instruments of both interpretation and authority.

If eyes in *Othello* are imbued with importance, so, as well, are properties that communicate a sense both of the characters' developing conditions and of crises to come. Filmed in Venice and at the medieval castle near Lake Bracciano, north of Rome, the film selects from these locales a variety of features as part of a metacommentary on the narrative. For example, near the beginning, Roderigo (Michael Maloney) watches an amorous Othello and Desdemona through a grille. In this scene the structure of the latticework serves not only to implicate Roderigo in a culture of voyeurism but also to introduce the motif of the cage, the metaphorical destination to which Othello, in his enslaved condition, will gravitate. Thus, when Iago (Kenneth Branagh) speaks of Othello being "enfettered to" Desdemona's "love" (2.3.319), the suggestion makes a logistical sense, a visual manifestation of the concept of imprisonment having already been put into play. To unyielding materials such as bars the film adds more flexible and insubstantial objects such as diaphanous drapes, floating handkerchiefs, and water. At once, it would appear as if there is no immediate danger here; however, these elements are also mobilized to meet a familiarly ensnaring purpose. Hence, the watery Venetian landscape of the film's start is returned to at the close when the bodies of Othello and Desdemona are tipped from a boat into the open sea: the shift back to a maritime location implies that the precariousness of Othello's mortality has been a constant, that his end is inscribed in his beginning, and that he will be claimed/caged by the natural environment he earlier commanded. As a whole, therefore, the film's multiple properties would seem to answer to a proleptic imperative. One double-edged example suffices to illustrate this: after the victory against the Turks, an effigy of a Turk is thrown unceremoniously on a Cyprian bonfire. On the one hand, the stuffed figure operates as a prelude to the protagonist's own recollections, at his death, of smiting a "malignant and a turbanned Turk" (5.2.362), reinforcing other preparations for Othello's demise. On the other hand, the burning Turk represents a version of Othello himself, as he writhes in the flames of jealousy that Iago has created. Indeed, with the finale approaching, Othello is increasingly associated with a gathering conflagration. "Fire and brimstone!" (4.1.226), he exclaims, as he processes to his horrific task, the presence of fires and torches in the background acting as an apt correlative for his damnable trajectory. By lacing his film with anticipatory commodities in this manner, Parker forces the narrative to take on a particularly urgent pace. Othello is elaborated less as a free agent than as a type foreordained by his environs and his servants: before he has even had an opportunity to resist, it seems, his fate is decreed.

In the increase of momentum in the concluding moments an audience is encouraged to confront, once again, the catastrophic contribution of Iago to the action. Arguably with a greater expertise than the general, the ancient excels in manipulating the gaze, quickly setting himself up as *Othello*'s resident director. He is the only character permitted directly to address the camera, and, as he confesses that "I am not what I am" (1.1.65), his blank features appear as the page onto which a spectator's speculations might be projected. A series of vignettes testifies to Iago's manipulative abilities. With the first, he contemplates the reflection of Cassio (Nathaniel Parker) and Desdemona in the blade of his knife, the implication being that he will unpeel the couple, and present them as naked in Othello's eyes, just as he peels his piece of fruit. The second vignette pushes further Iago's camera-loving flirtations, since he reaches forward to blacken its lens. Patricia Dorval writes that the "soot [Iago] spreads over the 'eye' of the camera . . . suggests . . . that the characters are overly blind" (Dorval 2000: 8). Attractive as it is, such an argument stops short of taking account of the ways in which Iago racializes the camera, making it the witness of his own manufactured inferno, the dark cage into which Othello will fall. The vignettes culminate in a third interpolation, which discovers Iago brushing two chess pieces, a white queen and a black king, into a well. Clearly, the focus on these symbols of racially opposed royalty extends the film's dialogue with black and white coloring into a different register. Simultaneously, however, it consolidates Iago's place as narrative engineer: predicting his demolition of Othello and Desdemona, he takes upon himself the proleptic dimensions of the film's forward-looking properties. It is ironic, of course, that it should be Branagh who plays a directorial Iago. To an extent, *Othello* trades upon the extra-filmic reputation of the actor/*auteur*, fostering a diegetic relationship between the cinematic *créateur* and the dramatic manipulator, between an Irish Shakespearean interloper and a fictive Spanish ensign never entirely at home in Venetian society.

Nowhere are Iago's directorial abilities better demonstrated than in the seduction, which runs over several locations and activities. It opens with a militaristic stave-fight training exercise; it modulates to a scene of communal washing; and it proceeds to a conversational interlude in the castle's garrison. In so doing, the montage draws attention to issues of contest, competition, begriming, dirt, and vulnerability, all of which crucially underpin Iago's subsequent onslaught. Once installed in the arsenal, Othello and Iago prepare their weaponry; again, the scene's resources are thematically exploited, with the blades connoting phallic frets and the gun-holders evoking a prison's incarcerating doors and windows. Typical, too, is the way in which the camera's gaze becomes giddy when Othello imagines Cassio and Desdemona together: the protagonist is incapable of stabilizing either his world's visual paraphernalia or the unnerving potential of his ensign's language. The latter suggestion, in particular, is reinforced via a close two-shot of Iago's mouth next to Othello's ear, which supports both the play's construction of aural intercourse and the film's elaboration of an ancient himself entangled in homoeroticism. The seduction concludes in the castle's cellars, which, appropriately, serve also as its gaol. A symbolically loaded sequence is here initiated: Othello walks past the prisoners; he sits down among them; he is directed to his own solitary cell. The process of his enslavement to Iago, the film insists, is complete. A now recognizable freeze-frame of a black hand on a white hand rounds off the movement, but, at this point, it betokens the collapse of the old union and the rise of Othello and Iago's erotic confederacy.

In the very final moments the film's prevailing motifs and readings come together in strikingly inventive conjunctions. Panning outwards to disclose the lattice-like design of the bedhead, the camera focuses on the form of the unconscious Desdemona: even she, it seems, has fallen victim to incarcerating forces. "Nay, stare not, masters. It is true indeed" (5.2.195), Othello instructs the assembed throng, pointing to the bed and gaining a measure of autonomy in that he at last assumes for himself visual control. Part of that new-found confidence permits Othello to take his own life, a moment which the film presents self-consciously: as Laurence Olivier had done before him in the 1965 film version of the play, Fishburne plays Othello removing a necklace to strangle himself. In view of Parker's distinctively metaphorical realizations, however, the suicidal action moves beyond repetition to suggest that Othello has, all along, been carrying the imprisoning garrotte of his own mortality. The protagonist having engineered his extinction, Iago climbs on the bed to join the company of its "tragic loading" (5.2.373): the closing image wonderfully concatenates the major considerations – a vital interplay between fetishized bodies, competition for the gaze, homoerotic attraction, black and white pairings, and an intrigue concluded.

Othello owes a measure of its inspiration to the "erotic thriller"; by contrast, Baz Luhrmann's *William Shakespeare's Romeo + Juliet* is thoroughly immersed in a substantial repertoire of filmic genres, to the extent that Shakespeare's claim on the original appears severely compromised. A review published at the time of its release, for example, argued that the film "doesn't . . . adapt the play as kick in its front door, pee on its living-room carpet, evict its tenants, burn the joint down and hold a drug-crazed rave among the smouldering iambs" (Jackson 1997). Certainly, *William Shakespeare's Romeo + Juliet* is highly responsive to the seemingly desacralizing tendencies of late twentieth-century youth culture. These are in evidence in the ways in which a frenetic media industry is constructed as holding sway over the course of the narrative. A television screen is privileged throughout as a conduit of information; headlines of Shakespearean snippets are flashed before the viewer; shots of helicopters, flames, and general mayhem evoke the breakneck *reportage* of popular news programs;

and magazines spiral towards us as commentaries on the "ancient grudge" (Luhrmann 1997: 2). Culminatively, this explosive cocktail of communicative vehicles has the effect of suggesting the plurality of means whereby late capitalism creates and manages its systems of production; at a deeper level the film's heady media mixture points to a culture profoundly infiltrated by consumerism. "Capulet" and "Montague" are inscribed on the sides of corporate skyscrapers as brand names; guns carry personalized designer insignia (such as "Sword 9MM"); and fashionable soft drinks are marketed as emotional ideals ("L'Amour" appears on a billboard in the familiar script of "Coca-Cola"). The Shakespearean love story, it seems, is no more than an excuse for putting into accelerated circulation the symbols of a commercially besotted modernity.

To maintain that *William Shakespeare's Romeo + Juliet* is merely decanonizing, however, is to do the film a disservice, for Luhrmann's stated aim is to preserve the achievement of a "rambunctious, sexy, violent, entertaining storyteller" (Luhrmann 1997: i) in a more recognizable idiom. The director, accordingly, enlists a scintillating array of cinematic techniques in his quest to interpret a Bard understood more as a would-be filmmaker than an actual playmaker. Unsteady, hand-held camerawork keeps the viewer in a state of excited agitation, as does, in James N. Loehlin's words, "staccato editing . . . [a] pop music score . . . slam zooms . . . swish pans . . . changing film speeds, jump cuts and lush, unnatural saturation of colour" (Loehlin 2000: 123). A comparable spectrum of generic borrowings adds to the amalgam, lending the film a synthetic brio, an all-encompassing cultural flavor and a vertiginously allusive appeal. Not only is the opening scene of the Capulet and Montague servants at war styled in the manner of a spaghetti western; related sections of the film also exploit variously the iconography of "Busby Berkeley musicals . . . Ken Russell's or Fellini's surreal spectaculars . . . contemporary action spectacles . . . [and] music video" (Hodgdon 1999: 90). Part of the pleasure of the film, then, becomes recognizing its knowing references, so that to experience Shakespeare is simultaneously to become conscious of the multiple mechanisms whereby he has been mediated. Connected to the film's broad generic compass is its extensive use of locations. Both Mexico City and Veracruz are utilized to suggest, alternately, Los Angeles, Miami, and Venice Beach; indeed, in a slyly Shakespearean reworking, Verona Beach masquerades as the equivalent of California's infamous coastal boardwalk. Shakespeare is still in evidence in all of this, then, even if it is at times difficult to attend to his language amidst the welter of other instruments that insist upon his continuing relevance.

Given the interest of *William Shakespeare's Romeo + Juliet* in revivifying older constructions of the dramatist's street gangs, it is perhaps not surprising that the film should also view its conceits through an ethnic lens. Thus the Capulet family and its dependants are represented as Hispanic, while the rival Montague grouping has an Anglo-Saxon affiliation. Both factions are elaborated as subscribing to an exaggeratedly masculinist code of ethics, as when Tybalt (John Leguizamo) accuses Mercutio (Harold Perrineau) of effeminizing homoerotic conduct: "thou consortest with Romeo" (Luhrmann 1997: 98). Overall, however, the director's ethnic apportioning emerges either as problematically inconsistent or as inappropriately traditionalist. One experiences discomfort, for instance, in being forced to acknowledge that Mercutio, played by a black actor, bears the brunt of the film's homoerotic subtext. By the same token, both Romeo (Leonardo DiCaprio) and Juliet (Claire Danes) speak in a linguistic register that is divorced from any easily identifiable ethnic attachment; further, their pale skin tones place the two protagonists above their racially freighted surroundings and suggest a correlation between whiteness and unadulterated romanticism. Luhrmann may strive to produce a multicultural Shakespeare, but his methods are, at times, in danger of reinforcing precisely those myths of elitism from which his film wishes ostensibly to escape.

Taking energy both from its ethnic detailing and its consumerist ethos is the film's deployment of religious images and icons. Both Catholic and kitsch, these appear at one and the same time as traditional symbols, fashion accessories, Latinate insignia, and postmodern designer labels. On Romeo's shirt is pictured a heart pierced by an arrow, an image which links him to emblems occurring elsewhere of a bleeding heart. The effect is to discover Romeo as a type of devotee of romantic martyrdom; as such, he seems an entirely suitable match for Juliet, surrounded, as she is, by similarly rit-ualistic objects, such as crosses and rings. At once, of course, such visual realizations of the established church insert the protagonists yet more fully into a late capitalist representational modality. At another level, however, by reading Romeo and Juliet through familiar signs of piety, the film seizes upon a metaphorical counterpart for the play's use of cosmic and divine rhetoric. Thus Juliet's request for "gentle night" to "cut [Romeo] out in little stars" to make "fine" the "face of heaven" (Luhrmann 1997: 107) gains an added emphasis from the outfit in which she is attired, a Botticelli-like angel costume with gossamer wings. Similarly, Romeo's anticipation of "Some consequence yet hanging in the stars" (ibid: 43) finds a visual partner in spliced-in scenes of a church aisle lined with flaming crosses and candles; it is only towards the end of the film that we realize that these represent premonitions of the lovers' end, of their mutually suicidal extinction in the city cathedral. Both in terms of their linguistic expressions and their stylistic characteristics, Romeo and Juliet appear very much, therefore, as the "star-crossed lovers" (ibid: 13) of the prologue, a pair defined and doomed by the paradoxically spiritual materialism of their world.

More generally in the film, phrases are privileged in ways that both draw atten-tion to the original and showcase the virtuosity of the translation. Interestingly, more often than not, these jokily reinvented citations from Shakespeare come not from *Romeo and Juliet* but from other plays in the canon. The line "retailed to posterity," for instance, emblazoned on the side of a Montague building, recalls an identical expression (3.1.77) in *Richard III*; the advertisement for an armchair, which resem-bles "such stuff / As dreams are made on" (4.1.156–7), is modeled on Prospero's farewell to his profession in *The Tempest*; and the "Post-Post-Haste Dispatch" (1.3.46) service that fails to communicate with Romeo in Mantua has obviously consulted *Othello* in order to arrive at its name. What these appropriations of various familiar and non-familiar adages suggest is the extent to which Shakespeare is imagined as a guarantor of quality; even as he seems subsumed by market forces, the dramatist is represented rising above it to perpetuate superior values of industry, art, and craft. As such, *William Shakespeare's Romeo + Juliet* implies that Shakespeare has fallen prey to postmodern tendencies. For, in the same moment that he agitates to enshrine the dramatist's classical reputation, Luhrmann is obliged to acknowledge Shakespeare's susceptibility to fragmentation and pastiche. Like Romeo, Shakespeare is cut out into little pieces, stars of wisdom that can be distributed at will.

During the extended ball scene Shakespeare is raided again; rather than a verbal *bricolage*, however, this time the film favors a visual jigsaw of stereotypical memories and allusions. Each character is dressed in such a way as to evoke the specter of a famous Shakespearean personage. Accordingly, Capulet (Paul Sorvino) is festooned in Roman robes (the implication of a tyrannically imperial Julius Caesar is abundantly clear), while Lady Capulet (Diane Venora), wearing a black Egyptian wig, appears as Miami's answer to Cleopatra (the former's suicidal pill-popping is implicitly equated with the latter's deadly entertainment of the asp). Perhaps the closest Shakespearean analogue is suggested at Mercutio's dramatic entrance; cross-dressed in make-up, a white headpiece, heels, and a spangly brassière, he functions as a figurative enactment not only of Queen Mab but also of the hallucination and excess with which she is associated. Once again, these scenes push at Shakespeare's signifying status, the point being that the dramatist's greatest tragic personalities have been hollowed out by post-modernism, transmogrified into style not substance, appearance rather than essence. Yet costuming is not confined only to a Shakespearean realm of reference. Dave Paris (Paul Rudd), for instance, impersonates an astronaut (he is thereby interpellated in a masculinist discourse of the twentieth-century space race), in contrast to Romeo, who has donned the armor of a medieval knight, a garb that ties him to a less aggressive older dispensation and to chivalric romance.

Indeed, both Romeo and Juliet are throughout linked to more traditional tech-nologies (part of a cinematic drive to see them as timeless lovers) and are filmed from a characteristically personalized perspective. One might not wonder, then, at those moments which disclose Romeo scribbling in a notebook (writing is his medium as much as television) or posturing beneath the arch of a former cinema (the outdated stage exhibits a greater interest than the more recent movie industry). Together, more-over, the protagonists inhabit a communally metaphorical realm of water: Juliet con-templates Romeo through the sides of a fishtank, and Romeo splashes about in the glare of a spotlighted swimming pool. As the lovers are drawn to this natural element, so does the film naturalize their own mutual attraction. Finally distinguishing Luhrmann's slant on the lovers is the slow pace of their shared scenes. Deceleration and pauses mark the presence of Romeo and Juliet on screen; there is a greater use of soft focus and close-up; and more leisurely scores are heard, whether these take the form of Des'ree's "Kissing You" or the "Liebestod" from Richard Wagner's opera *Tristan und Isolde*. By reining in montage and music, Lurhmann successfully central-izes the plight of the lovers. He also prepares the cinematic ground for the slowest sequence of all, the joint suicide amidst the burning icons that become yet another signature of the couple's individualized identities.

In the closing moments, however, the film withdraws from too close an alliance with its dominant figures, depersonalizing the lovers and subjecting them to scrutiny from a bewildering range of investigators. It is thus in a type of loss of privacy that the tragedy of Romeo and Juliet is seen to inhere. Although a rehearsal of the prevailing images of their experience is conducted from the lovers' standpoint, other constructions soon intervene to dilute the sensation of intimacy. A high-angle glimpse of the deceased pair spreadeagled on a bier is replicated in a similarly shot-from-above view of bagged bodies being inserted into an ambulance: miming the perspective enjoyed from the summit of the statues of Christ and Madonna, Luhrmann seems at pains to summon an illusion of quasi-divine authority, an inscrutable judgment on events, even a Shakespearean assessment of his film's proceedings. The difficulty of accessing a unitary interpretive position is compounded by the grainy anonymity of the pseudo-footage of the grieving Capulet and Montague families, which makes available for universal consumption a scene of domestic grief. It is further exacerbated via the epilogue: presented as the final news item in an anchorwoman's summary, the narrative of the "star-crossed lovers" becomes itself a media product robbed of particularity. Shakespeare, the film suggests, while still the authenticator of values, is now the splintered source of unfeeling representation, the blank face of a TV screen and the non-committal voice of the public domain.

Like Luhrmann, Kenneth Branagh seeks through his *Hamlet* to fix Shakespeare in a roughly contemporaneous timeframe, situating the play at the end of the nineteenth century and exploiting the colorful imagery of familiar epic films. This enables him to banish the spell of Olivier's somber black-and-white *Hamlet* (1948) and the notion that Shakespeare partakes only of a fusty theatrical tradition. To cite Branagh, "We want this *Hamlet* to be a big, big treat . . . The Ghost is going to be a lot scarier than some faintly benign old sort walking on stage in a white shirt. It ain't gonna be three-and-a-half hours of talking heads" (Arnold 1996). As Branagh's language suggests, *Hamlet* is conceived of as a vehicle for mass entertainment, a production that answers to the numerous generic requirements of a modern-taste public.

Perhaps the most arresting element of the film is Branagh's performance as Hamlet, played in such a way as to bring out the dimensions of a tortured psyche. Thus, from a grieving son lurking in the shadows, Branagh moves to an explosive "man of action" in the later scenes, a knowing impersonator of madness and a theatrically dynamic presence. While Branagh clearly points up a personality-based reading of Shakespeare's play, the film is arguably more dominated by its political resonances. For this *Hamlet* constructs Denmark as a militaristic state. In the opening scenes there are glimpses of preparations for war; Hamlet marches past an arsenal on his way to encounter the ghost; and displays of fencing practice punctuate the narrative, foreshadowing the catastrophic conclusion. Nor is this merely an extraneous interpretation. Branagh takes his cue from the specific orientation of Shakespeare's text in a persuasive reconsideration of the material bases on which Elsinore's preeminence is founded.

It is part of the flexibility of the film's representational scheme that Branagh also develops the Fortinbras subplot, which is so often omitted. Frequent use is made of parallel montage, whereby the scene cuts between unfolding wrangles at Elsinore and the relentless advance of Fortinbras's army. At one point, newspaper headlines are deployed to highlight the threat of the Norwegian commander, played with an icy implacability by Rufus Sewell. As the film progresses it would seem as if there is every justification for the nervousness of the sentry who patrols the castle's gates.

The innovativeness of such devices can be apprehended no less forcibly in set design and staging procedures. Joel Fineman's work on fratricide and cuckoldry has established the importance of *Hamlet*'s "doubling" structures and mirrored arrangements (Fineman 1980: 70–109). Branagh's *Hamlet* fits well with this assessment, since its interior scenes take place in a hall lined with windows and mirrored doors. In such a setting Hamlet is forced to confront reflections of himself, such as Claudius (Derek Jacobi), who, with his blonde hair and clipped beard, bears an uncanny resemblance to Branagh's Dane. The points of contact between the characters are also incestuously underlined when Hamlet pushes Ophelia (Kate Winslet) against one of the hall's mirrors, not realizing that Claudius and Polonius are hidden behind it. Branagh himself has observed that the set was intended to suggest "a vain world . . . looking in on itself . . . that seems confident and open but conceals corruption" (LoMonico 1996: 6). It is a bold and current view, one for which there is ample textual support. Once again, Branagh is keen to place a visual slant upon the concerns of the text, and this imperative is ably demonstrated in the presentation of court, which, as it contemplates its own self-image, faces only an inevitable decline.

To the broad brushstrokes of the design can be added the nuanced local effects. As the versatility of the film is exhibited in its overall montage, so is it also discovered in a spectrum of denser scenic details and correspondences. First, several fresh areas of meaning come into play in images of domestic intimacy. After an assignation with a prostitute, Polonius (Richard Briers) dresses himself to tutor Reynaldo (Gerard Depardieu) in the arts of surveillance, which makes an intriguing link with the following scene where Ophelia describes Hamlet's appearance before her "with his doublet all unbraced" (2.1.79). As she recovers upon her father's bed it is implied that Ophelia has been abused by Hamlet and will be prostituted by her brothel-frequenting father. Second, the depth of scenic business reinforces the narrative continuum and creates surprising poetic points of contact. Claudius and Laertes (Michael Maloney) quaff brandy together as they plot Hamlet's downfall. Their conspiratorial drinking is immediately enhanced by the description of Ophelia's drowning and, subsequently, by the gravedigger's observation that a tanner's hide "will keep out water . . . and your water is a sore decayer of your whoreson dead body" (5.1.157–9). Through such networks of liquid allusion, visual stimuli in the film enrich the play's textual constitution, exposing reductive, consuming systems in which a woman's innocence is at the mercy of paternalistic hypocrisy.

Characteristic of both the general representational strategies and the local coloring is the productively roving camerawork. Often, the camera prowls around groups of characters; "in constant motion," as Samuel Crowl observes, it "tracks, pans, cranes, zooms in and out, flashes back and circles" (Crowl 2000: 232). When Claudius and Polonius agree to spy on the prince, they are circled by the camera, as is Hamlet on confronting his mother in her "closet." This resonant deployment of point of view has several implications. At once, it adds to the sense of a court dominated by tawdry secrets and political espionage. In the same moment, it sharpens an awareness of the ever increasing danger of Fortinbras's army, a force which will eventually encircle the castle itself. The closer Fortinbras draws, the more exactly does he seem to represent the eye that subjects all of Elsinore to an uncompromising, comprehensive scrutiny.

It is perhaps after the "Intermission" that the film displays to their best advantage its innumerable merits. Clearly apparent in *Hamlet*'s latter stages is the shrunken character of the court: only a handful of attendants are present at Ophelia's funeral, a stark contrast with the swelling numbers flocking to enjoy the play-within-the-play and a register of Claudius's waning control. When the climax arrives, Fortinbras's troops crash through the state hall's windows and mirrored doors, a timely lesson for a court that has been incapable of recognizing its own fragile illusions. Hamlet is given a soldier's funeral, a move which identifies him with Fortinbras, the commander whose superior military prowess allows him to declare himself the state's inheritor.

But Branagh's *Hamlet* goes beyond a simple dichotomy between military technology and political supremacy. In many respects it probes subsidiary levels of meaning, which lie outside the merely filmic and textual relationship. Above all, this *Hamlet* intertextually contemplates its connections to a host of other texts and histories. Faithful to the 1623 First Folio version of the play, the film is suitably bookish, and a favorite retreat for Hamlet is his book-lined cell. Branagh, it seems, is concerned to establish himself as a leading Shakespearean by stressing the decision to realize the entire play, an unparalleled endeavor. To this end he is aided by many seasoned veterans of the Shakespearean scene. There is more than a passing intertextuality involved in casting Derek Jacobi as Claudius, for the actor played Hamlet in 1979 at the Old Vic, took the part in a BBC version of the play in 1980, and directed Branagh in the role for the 1988 Renaissance Theatre Company production (Branagh 1996: vi–vii, 175). If Jacobi is Branagh's filmic father, then Branagh is Jacobi's theatrical son, the descendant of a metaphorical parent who both throws into relief and authenticates the younger actor's colonization of hallowed terrain. A legitimating imperative would also appear to lie behind the casting of John Gielgud (Priam) and Judi Dench (Hecuba) in non-speaking appearances, and an intertextual dimension is certainly detectable in Charlton Heston's cameo role as the Player King. By drawing upon the pooled resources of Stratford-upon-Avon dignitaries and Hollywood "epic" legends,

Branagh sets himself up as another epic filmmaker, as a bardic interpreter with impeccable credentials.

Nor does the film's intertextuality end with casting implications. Part of the grandeur of the film depends upon the numerous exterior views of Blenheim Palace (Elsinore), which is shot in a widescreen 70 mm format. From this architectural landscape a number of intertextual resonances can be inferred. Following the defeat of the French at Blenheim in 1704, the palace was constructed for the Duke of Marlborough as thanks for a landmark victory. Sir Winston Churchill was born at Blenheim in 1874, and members of the family still live there. With these contexts in mind, one might argue that Branagh's *Hamlet* finally operates as synecdoche for historical conflicts between England and France, between England and Germany, and even between the English royal family and a more powerful political entity. The film is too multivalent to be strait-jacketed within a simple allegory, however, and is equally interested in provoking contrary contextual readings. At the close, the imposing statue of Hamlet Senior is toppled to the ground, and any spectator attuned to the collapse of the communist countries in the 1990s will not miss the parallel. Branagh's *Hamlet* is an eloquent disquisition on the perils of theatrical, aristocratic, and royal authority; it is also a covert celebration of the plebeian forces that contest the ownership of power and privilege.

Using the film to entertain such considerations did not come to Branagh without a struggle, for in the activities surrounding its production is inscribed a nervousness about the play's status as an enshrined monument. Just before *Hamlet*, Branagh had worked on *In the Bleak Midwinter*, a film whose fantasy scenario of a spectacularly successful production enabled him to address anxieties about the relevance of Shakespeare's play to the postmodern era. No less importantly, *In the Bleak Midwinter* offered Branagh an opportunity autobiographically to negotiate the implications of his grand plan to stage *Hamlet* as a big-budget extravaganza. Certainly, in projects prior to *Hamlet*, the vexed position of the drama as a millennium masterwork seems to have been an issue. Even before it was released, Branagh published an annotated screenplay of the film's making. What is striking about the notes is the alternating between a number of seemingly incompatible positions. References to Goethe (Branagh 1996: viii) sit alongside a commentary that smacks of a more demotic approach: Claudius is described as being in "Norman Schwarzkopf mode" (ibid: 12), the players put on a "good gig" (p. 67), and Hamlet and Laertes resemble "two graduates of the Robocop academy" (p. 163). On the screenplay's release some reviewers took exception to this populist perspective. One notice objected to Branagh's "low interjections," the "boorish" participation of "a rather louche character . . . from *Eastenders*" (S. 1996). But such criticism ignores, I think, the necessarily shifting markers that both cut across and characterize Branagh as a Shakespearean interpreter. As an end-of-the-century artist, Branagh is constituted by straddling "high art" and "popular culture" at one and the same time, precisely because these distinctions no longer hold as indicators of traditional social arrangements. Partly thanks to Branagh, Shakespeare has been reclaimed as a figure whose work reaches beyond a narrow constituency, and film is an essential element in that process. The more recent Bard is an amalgam of inter-penetrating cinematic, televisual, and musical vernacular influences, and out of that melting-pot is born Branagh's multi-voiced mindset. As Branagh has reinvented Shakespeare to suit his own filmic aspirations, so has he himself been shaped by the emergence of Shakespeare as a commodity, a commerical icon, and a locus for ideological warfare.

As Branagh's screenplay entries make clear, he conceives of *Hamlet* as offering an indirect commentary on late twentieth-century political realities. In this regard, he looks forward to Julie Taymor, a director first attracted to *Titus Andronicus* for its thinly veiled modern pertinence. According to her, the play speaks to audiences that "feed daily on tabloid sex scandals, teenage gang rape, high school gun sprees and the private details of a celebrity murder trial" at "a time when racism, ethnic cleansing and genocide have almost ceased to shock by being so commonplace and seemingly inevitable" (De Luca and Lindroth 2000: 28). As part of her mission to build a bridge between the horrors of modernity and a filmed version of the bloodiest of Shakespeare's Roman tragedies, Taymor, like Branagh, makes herself receptive to all manner of influ-ences – the movie productions mentioned at the start, the rabble-rousing documen-taries of Leni Riefenstahl, the visionary decadence of Luchino Visconti, and her own experience of directing the play off-Broadway in 1994 for Theatre for a New Audience. The result is a richly textured filmic statement humming with theatrical ingenuity, Italianate grandeur, propagandistic connotation, and uncomfortably recent historical echoes.

That connection between old and modern horrors is neatly inaugurated. The scene of the Boy (Osheen Jones) at play in a kitchen unfolds via a layering of two filmic realities: artificial sounds of war are drowned out by actual explosions and gunfire; toy robots cede place to soldiers moving in robotic unison; chips and tomato sauce anticipate an image of just-eviscerated entrails steaming in a dish. Although seemingly different, the worlds of the film, it is suggested, are worryingly similar in their belligerent tastes and predilections. By pointing up such parallels the director introduces the key components of her *mise-en-scène*. The blurring of timeframes high-lights the fact that there is no chronology; in Taymor's own words, "I wanted to . . . create a singular period that juxtaposed elements of ancient, barbaric ritual with familiar, contemporary attitude and style" (Blumenthal and Taymor 1999: 219). Hence, the iconography of *Titus* is invariably universalizing rather than particular, with images of convertibles, Mussolini's black shirts, and his EUR Building consort-ing with shots of the ruined Villa Adriana and scenes of Titus processing in a horse-drawn chariot. Following in the footsteps of Luhrmann, Taymor prioritizes a postmodern merging of temporality and an eclectic mix of styles and registers. Central to an understanding of the film's *mélange* is the Boy's perspective; it is through his eyes that we witness the tragedy, as he consistently matches the power of Titus with the fecundity of his own imaginative processes. Strikingly, the Boy only becomes a character in his own right (Young Lucius) when he enters the action to kill a fly. Here, as elsewhere in the film, a range of types of violence is foregrounded, part of an imperative securely to lodge the play's implications in a modern audience's consciousness.

Pursuing this agenda, the film is notable for the overwhelmingly visual interpretation it places on personality and language. Dress is vital in these respects and, as we witness the decline of Titus (Anthony Hopkins), the cinematography emphasizes his costuming's sequential hues, from dark battle attire and black mourning robes to baggy grey sweater and white cook's outfit. Once again, it is not a discrete period invoked in this trajectory but a manner or a character pose. Over the film in its entirety, furthermore, a strictly controlled palette of colors is mobilized: only red, white, blue, and black generally feature, the effect of which is to lend the narrative a singular concentration and coherence. As the colors encourage a critical focus, so, too, do the visual realizations of particular verbal expressions. Thus, when Tamora (Jessica Lange) describes herself as a "loving nurse" (Taymor 2000: 51), the camera dwells on her golden breast-plate in a maternal reinforcement of her claim. Similarly, in the scene where Titus speaks of being surrounded by a "wilderness of sea" (ibid: 100), a viewer's attention is directed to his environment, a suitably rainy and waterlogged field dotted with disconnected imperial relics. To appreciate the appearance of *Titus*, then, is to become aware of the ways in which rhetoric, tone, and plot movement work together in a powerfully premeditated cinematic harmony.

True to her postmodern credentials, however, Taymor does not rest merely with what is provided by the play alone. In the vein of Branagh and Parker, the director fills out and clarifies the stylistic hints of the drama, although her method is unique in privileging the so-called PAN or Penny Arcade Nightmare insert. Four of these surreal sequences appear in the film and they crystallize, variously, grief for the deaths of Alarbus and Mutius, outrage at the rape of Lavinia, despair at the murders of Martius and Quintus, and confusion about the spectacle of Murder, Rape and Revenge. The PANs hence constitute a haiku-like interior landscape of conscience, shock, and guilt, a supplementary emotional space. At the same time, they impress as an integral part of the narrative, for, in keeping with the escalating horror of the action, they come to seem not entirely divorced from a filmic reality that is itself a species of nightmare. Nor are the PANs at odds with the play's metaphorical investments. It is entirely apposite, for instance, that the emblem of a raped Lavinia (Laura Fraser), who appears as a pedestalized Marilyn Monroe figure, should be accompanied by glimpses of leaping tigers, creatures crucial to Titus' vision of a "wilderness of tigers" (Taymor 2000: 98). A comparably considered image is spotlighted in the final PAN, which reveals Tamora attired as Revenge: wearing a crown of daggers reminiscent of the headgear of the Statue of Liberty and blindfolded in the manner of Justice, she is pictured with cones for hands and a tube attached to her breast that provides Murder/Demetrius (Matthew Rhys) with smoky nourishment. The unsettling composition trades upon the concern with limbs, both actual and artificial, and also upon the suggestion of a suffocating or parodic maternity. Their more bizarre dimensions notwithstanding, the PANs are thus deeply rooted in the explorations and implications of the original play.

It is with varieties of maternity, in fact, that *Titus* would seem to expend much of its imaginative energy. Notably, Tamora is discovered as using sexual power to whip up a quasi-incestuous frenzy in her sons; by the same token, the film constructs her as exercising a physical influence over the increasingly foppish and dependent Saturninus (Alan Cumming): "be ruled by me" (Taymor 2000: 62), she instructs him, and soon afterwards he is cradling at her breast. Such maternal manipulations are, however, simultaneously undermined. This is suggested both in the deflation of the large-breasted siren that floats in the pool of Saturninus' palace (the blow-up figure is penetrated, appropriately enough, by Titus' arrows) and in the circulation of a vulgarized image of a she-wolf. The mythical mother of Rome, the creature reflects unfavorably Tamora's own animality and is hijacked to foster a squalid consumerism: even Young Lucius bears a vulpine emblem on the back of his T-shirt. With the exception of Titus, who is seen to be sexually jealous of his daughter's suitor, fathers in the film would appear to fare rather better. One finds that the clown (Dario D'Ambrosi), for instance, who presides over the PAN of the sideshow wagon exhibiting the floating heads of Titus' sons, also plays the soldier-savior of the Boy, rescuing him from carnage on two occasions. And, performed by Harry Lennix, Aaron is represented as a unifying agent of both paternal and maternal energies, providing, in his relations with his son, unambiguous forms of sustenance. By functioning in this manner, Aaron assumes a destabilizing authority, usurping the more entrenched positions of Titus and Tamora and unhinging, in his blackness, the Roman/Gothic ethnic systems on which the film is focused. In this connection it is striking that, among a sea of corpses, Aaron remains alive at the film's close, humbled in words but still defiant in steely facial deportment.

Given the film's fascination with modalities of parenting, it is perhaps not surprising that it should concentrate, too, on bodily signs and images. In particular, *Titus* enlists the physical form, whether in an actual or a figurative manifestation, as an active participant in the narrative, a thematically articulate instrument. Expressive in these respects is the scene in which a beleaguered Titus addresses Saturninus from outside the EUR: the general's environs are littered with a giant stone hand and foot and collapsed columns, apt ciphers of masculine disempowerment and of the bodily desecration to come. When Lavinia's rape is realized, it is conducted off-screen and stylistically, since the viewer's only experience of the crime is the spectacle of the post-deflowered body of the victim. Even here, however, parts and properties are richly communicative: the tree stump on which Lavinia stands echoes the shattered pillars of before, as do the stick-like false hands which project from her arms. More generally in the film, the import of the rape of Lavinia is conveyed via close shots of bloody mouths. It is significant, for instance, that all of Titus' enemies (at least, all those who have been involved in his daughter's defilement) die in an orally grotesque fashion. Once she has ingested her sons' remains, Tamora is sick and vomits blood; blood similarly drips from the gagged mouths of Chiron and Demetrius; Aaron sports a bloody mouth when he is assaulted; and Saturninus chokes on a spoon and his own blood during the cannibalistic banquet. Matching the film's symbolic dovetailing of mouths, tongues, blood, and writing, these moments function to encourage in the audience an acute sensitivity to a painterly design. But they also serve to keep the gravity and implications of Lavinia's rape before us: reminders of the abuses practiced upon her continually intrude, and the agents of her violation are made to suffer similar fates to her own.

By opening out the spectator to the mouth's significance, Taymor brings to the fore a related concern – the crucial role of consumption and appetite. It is at the concluding feast, of course, that eating enjoys a particular focus, aided and abetted, no doubt, by intertextual echoes of Hopkins's earlier performance as Hannibal Lecter in Jonathan Demme's *Silence of the Lambs* (1991). Where the feast connotes gluttony and excess, its aftermath, the formal meting out of punishments, suggests starvation and denial. If Aaron must die a famished death, however, his son, it is implied, will gain a plenteous inheritance. Taymor has spoken of her invented ending in terms of "fruition . . . cleansing . . . forgiveness . . . and hope" (De Luca and Lindroth 2000: 29) and, certainly, as the Boy takes up the black child to walk out of the colosseum into a new dawn, maternal provision, the knitting together of bodies and constituencies, and ethnic reparation are implied. The Boy, who entered the arena in the context of a toy war, leaves it having overruled a larger conflict; in so doing, he becomes himself a type of savior and an alternative to the film's multiple parents. This, interestingly, is not a blood bond but an artificial family unit erected on an adoptive basis. As in Steven Spielberg's *E.T.* (1982), filial disobedience is given a positive twist, and fate remains in children's hands. Its reconstructive ambitions and evocations notwithstanding, the ending simultaneously leaves troubling questions unanswered. Richard Burt describes the conclusion as "the reinstallation . . . of a Fascist romanticization of the child" (Burt 2001: 83), and reactionary tendencies are not difficult to detect. The Boy's bland white suit, for instance, eclipses the exciting distinctiveness of Aaron's blackness, while the appropriation of the black baby smacks of uncomfortable archetypes of the "white man's burden." Although the swelling birdsong of the soundtrack would seem to point to the rescue/presence of all children, moreover, the lack of aural specificity once again erases difference. Taymor seems to aspire in *Titus* for a conclusion that approximates to a Luhrmannesque multiculturalism, but, like that director, she falls short of realizing it persuasively. Despite the film's innumerable felicities, *Titus*'s contemporary investments do not resolve its own internal contradictions.

Of all of the films of the tragedies produced in the 1990s, it is perhaps Michael Almereyda's *Hamlet* that most convincingly refracts the forms and effects of modernity. Shakespeare's play is read as an expression of the corporate anonymity of the urban predicament; Elsinore is figured as the Denmark Corporation; and the New York scene is stamped with the global signs of a late capitalist mindset. The film thus furnishes for its audience a vision of human interaction and individuality distorted by, and in thrall to, familiarly repressive institutional arrangements. But Almereyda does not allow this dystopian perspective to rest unchallenged, since he also foregrounds images of counter-movements and acts of filmmaking, both of which allow Hamlet briefly to achieve a tragically subversive integrity.

Almereyda's *Hamlet* declares its engagement with market forces throughout. The film abounds in logos and advertisements, with the prominence of "Key Food" and "Panasonic" functioning to indicate a moment defined by the need for product placement. Even non-commercial objects are implicated, such as when Hamlet's love-letter to Ophelia is packaged in a plastic specimen bag for royal probing. By privileging manifestations of the corporate world, Almereyda's *Hamlet* stresses not so much personal costs, however, as issues of general consequence. Thus when the Ghost (Sam Shepard) appears before Hamlet, a TV monitor in the background reveals images of oilfields burning. On the one hand, these work as a filmic equivalent to the "fires" in which Shakespeare's sulfurous spirit is obliged to "fast" (Almereyda 2000: 30); on the other, they activate recollections of the Gulf War, a global conflict precipitated by a dispute over one of capitalism's most precious commodities. Similarly, when the ghost disappears into the "Pepsi One Calorie" dispensing machine, more than a brand name joke seems intended. The implication is that Hamlet's father is consumed by the very energies that, as President of the Denmark Corporation, he had earlier commanded.

For Almereyda, the most potent visualization of corporate modernity is found in the reflected surface. His *Hamlet* is awash with plateglass, mirrors, and screens, as when Hamlet (Ethan Hawke) contemplates his own self-image in the revolving drums of the laundrette. These hard interiors and exteriors suggest that communing with the self is directly related to the breakdown of organic social communities; the rigidity of the film's glass surfaces incarnates the unfeeling quality of its human relations. In this connection architectural glass goes hand-in-hand with camera glass, with the specular economy that marks out identity as a transparent property. The dimwitted confidence of Polonius (Bill Murray) that Hamlet is "Still harping on my daughter" (Almereyda 2000: 44) is addressed to a closed-circuit television in a move that associates the spying politician with a culture of surveillance. It is grimly appropriate, then, that the one occasion on which a surface is shattered is at Polonius's death: he is shot in the eye through a mirror, an appositely ironic punishment.

What Almereyda presents for spectatorly involvement, in short, is a corporate jail. Adopting metaphors of incarceration, the director elaborates glass constructions, video store aisles, and coiling civic spaces as so many caged environments. In Hamlet's own words, "Denmark is a prison" (ibid: xi). Both the motif of the prison and the film's late capitalist signifiers come together in technology, in the variety of communicative equipment at the present historical juncture. Almereyda's Manhattan landscape is overwhelmed by listening devices, laptops, cellphones, and recording instruments. As pertinent instances one can cite the bugging of Ophelia (Julia Stiles) with a wiretap or the duel between Hamlet and Laertes (Liev Schreiber) in which every move is tabulated on an electronic score counter. In this scene, as in others, characters are themselves regarded as counters to be reckoned up and calculated: they constitute the inmates of the technological panopticon.

A multivalent postmodern phenomenon, technology, as Almereyda understands it, damages the communicative process. For example, such is the availability of substitutes for one-on-one conversation in *Hamlet* that language fragments and exchanges become discontinuous. Hamlet's "Get thee to a nunnery" (ibid: 64) speech is divided up between a direct address and a message on Ophelia's answering machine. More disturbingly, *Hamlet* suggests that language is no longer the property of the individual subject: it can be taken over by technology and ventriloquized. A suggestion of such linguistic dispossession occurs when a Vietnamese guru explains on video his relational concept of "inter-be" (ibid: 37). Initial impressions suggest that this screen inset anticipates Hamlet's "To be or not to be" (ibid: 41) dilemma. In retrospect, however, it is clear that the monk's cogitations only serve to underscore Hamlet's distance from any sense of communal interaction. At an intertextual level, moreover, the protagonist is robbed of the exclusive ownership of Shakespeare's most celebrated intellectual deliberation: the famous speech, in this multinational universe, has been both ethnically pluralized and philosophically transformed by the new media establishment.

But this is not to suggest that Hamlet is overwhelmed by technology completely. Rather, he is constructed as simultaneously drawn to, and divorced from, the accelerated revolutions of his generation, never more so than when we see him patrolling the aisles of the Blockbuster video store. In this scene an evocative contemporary context is enlisted intriguingly to illuminate the eventual delivery of Hamlet's "To be or not to be" speech: the "Action Movie" placards operate not only as finely tuned articulations of a protagonist who is himself losing "the name of action" (ibid: 52), but also as instances of a masculinity in crisis. Hamlet's intellectual impasse is that he is uniquely unable to master "consummation" or "resolution" (ibid: 50, 52), unlike the ghostly rock musician who revenges himself on urban hoodlums in Tim Pope's conflagration-obsessed *The Crow: City of Angels* (1996), the climax of which unfolds on an overhead monitor.

Locked in an ambiguated relation with the cinema of modernity, Hamlet, as his escape-route, decides upon becoming a filmmaker himself. Throughout, he scripts a personal screenplay and either fast-forwards or rewinds on his "pixelvision" video diary the traces of a lived experience. Thus it is that Almereyda's camera dwells repeatedly on Hamlet's eyes, as if reminding us of the film's internal *auteur*. In addition to screening moments from his own history, Hamlet mobilizes seemingly unconnected filmic sequences involving an appetitive cartoon dragon and a stealth bomber from the recent Bosnian crisis. In a discussion of postmodernism and popular culture, Angela McRobbie observes that "the ransacking and recycling of culture, and the direct invocation to other texts and other images, can create a vibrant critique rather than an inward-looking, second-hand aesthetic" (McRobbie 1986: 57). These dissident potentialities are what we are invited to recognize, I think, in Hamlet's broken-backed directorial undertakings, and it is in his film-within-a-film that the protagonist's critical method comes to the fore.

In his version of *The Mousetrap* allusive motifs and passages articulate Hamlet's abrasive confrontation with contemporary ideologies. The film-within-a-film opens with footage from the 1950s of an idyllic family at leisure: because this is presented as a *home* movie, the implication is that the Elsinore of the millennium can provide no equivalent example of a functional familial unit. Among other amputated extracts, *The Mousetrap* also yields up a section from an army training film (a militaristic Denmark Corporation, it is suggested, has produced similarly faceless recruits) and a scene from Gerard Damiano's infamous porn production of 1972, *Deep Throat*. The film, one might argue, is used intertextually, since it sparked off a crisis in the culture of censorship, which resulted in a landmark court decision to allow explicit sexuality to reach a national audience. Its brevity notwithstanding, the *Deep Throat* vignette helps to bolster the realization of Hamlet as straining at the bounds of per-missiveness, testing out what is and is not representationally possible within corpo-rate parameters. The result is a briefly empowered Hamlet, as the similar lettering that accompanies the credits for *The Mousetrap* and for *Hamlet* itself indicates. The film-within-a-film, it is implied, has permitted the protagonist, if only momen-tarily, to assume for himself a secure *auteurship*, to graduate into the ranks of real-life directors.

The critical edge displayed in *The Mousetrap* forms an alliance with numerous related sites of transgressive energy in *Hamlet*. First, visual flashes of Che Guevara and Malcolm X work to implicate the protagonist in revolutionary discourses and to estab-lish him in the part of a liberating yet doom-laden savior. Secondly, networks of political implication are extended as the relationship between Hamlet and Horatio unfolds. Not only is Horatio (Karl Geary) revealed as a collector of the works of Vladimir Mayakovsky, the ill-fated Soviet communist poet; he also boasts a Dublin accent. Indeed, as the film progresses, it is Ireland (a map of Ireland is prominently posted) that seems to be reified over and above Manhattan/Denmark into a viable alternative. In a not entirely smooth parallel, Almereyda ties Wittenberg, the six-teenth-century breeding-ground for radical religion, with Dublin, the twentieth-century seat of radical politics. By implication, therefore, Hamlet becomes a displaced spokesperson for a history of spiritual strife and national struggle. Whether these scraps of counter-movements amount to a coherent philosophy is questionable. Alan Sinfield has remarked that "through . . . sharing . . . one may learn to inhabit plausi-ble oppositional preoccupations and forms – ways of relating to others and hence develop a plausible oppositonal selfhood" (Sinfield 1992: 37). In *Hamlet*, however, there is no sense of a shared agenda because its representatives survive merely in partial allusions and memories. The film's political heroes, moreover, speak to a past narrative that has already been concluded. Hamlet's role models, with whom he is connected but imperfectly, are outdated; consequently, even as it strives to gesture to new possibilities, the film demonstrates the impossibility of genuine resistance at the postmodern moment.

Whatever political negativity is permitted to circulate in *Hamlet* is, however, transcended by the film's finale. In death, Hamlet is pictured reviewing in a speeded-up montage the events of his life. Through the act of revenge the protagonist is able to script the story that he inaugurated with the film-within-a-film. There is no need for iconic equivalents now that Hamlet has found in himself and in his autobiography a personalized role model. Yet, as occurs so often in this film, spectators are prevented from remaining with a straightforward perspective. For the montage we witness is a *mélange* of Hamlet's point-of-view shots and Almereyda's more obviously directorial interventions, so that the end moments register a tension between *auteurs*, an irresolution in filmic authority. This suggestion of bifurcated points of identification continues into the closing sequence, which reveals a newscaster reading out a patchwork of the play's moralities. As the camera fades to focus on the autocue, it is implied that images have at last ceded place to words. No less powerfully, the shot makes clear that one filmmaker has been superseded by another: Hamlet, the director *manqué*, is debilitated, like Luhrmann's Romeo and Juliet, by a larger technology, one characterized by the surface of a media affairs program. If, on the one hand, the language of *Hamlet* is restored, it is, on the other, pushed out by the typical machinery of corporate modernity.

Earlier parts of this essay have indicated the ways in which the Shakespearean filmic tragedies of the last decade variously responded to, appropriated, and reworked the cinematic cultures of their time. It might also be salutary to remember, however, that, in the process, these enactments of the plays form part of a conversation with previous realizations of the Bard on screen. For every Shakespearean film adaptation reveals a nostalgic tendency, a desire to update the past in the idiom of the present. We might not wonder, then, at how many of the films examined here begin, like Olivier's *Hamlet*, with the elaboration of an imaginative template, as if attempting to enter into and perpetuate an older tradition on celluloid. Also, at a level of specific detail, the filmed tragedies of the 1990s take ideas and impetus from a gallery of precursors: Parker cribs the scene of the hilt-gazing Iago from Sergei Yutkevitch's *Othello* (1955); Branagh lifts his bleached Hamletian hair from Olivier; and Taymor finds inspiration for her PANs in the burning books of Peter Greenaway's *Prospero's Books* (1991). At once, such borrowings would appear to constitute strategies whereby Shakespearean ghosts are put in place. But they simultaneously suggest that cinema has, in some senses, become an alternative source of Shakespearean authority. Merely to copy the existing model is to pay Bardic homage. Imitation thus becomes another means whereby Shakespeare can be venerated. In this respect, it is striking that both Branagh and Hawke, who appear deeply immersed in the legacy of other Hamlets on film, at times subscribe to arguably conservative constructions of the tragedy. For Branagh, this took the form of refusing to cut Shakespeare's text; for Hawke, acting out the protagonist's part on the stage of the Globe Theatre in London was deemed a necessary pre-production experience.

Perhaps more arresting than their allusions backwards, however, are the filmic tragedies' references sideways. A distinctive feature is the extent to which these films absorb energy not only from contemporary spin-offs but also from themselves, thereby becoming a tightly knit, cross-fertilizing cinematic unit. Examples of the former phenomenon would include the equation between food, cannibalism, and contamination investigated in both *Tromeo and Juliet* and *Titus*, and the "wicked queen" trajectory traced by Jessica Lange (only after having played Goneril/Ginny Cook Smith in Jocelyn Moorhouse's *A Thousand Acres* (1997) could she move to Tamora with impunity). Instances of the latter might extend to Luhrmann and Taymor's joint interest in Gothic thuggery and body-bagging, Lurhmann and Almereyda's attraction to late capitalist imagery, and Almereyda's own rivalrous relationship with Branagh, who seems to cast on the director an Olivier-like shadow. It is not accidental, I think, that Almereyda's film stands as an anti-epic *Hamlet*, closed and gray rather than colorful and open, and presented on 16 mm rather than 70 mm film stock. Thus, when we consider the unique virtues of the filmic tragedies (their shared visual restlessness, use of properties, and play with alterity and difference), it is also helpful to reflect upon the ways in which Shakespearean cinema has become a clearly identifiable product, a self-generating body of work funded and sustained by its own internal momentum.

As a result of these kinds of cultural interchange, "Shakespeare" appears more than ever as an unfixed prompt for multivalent association. Matching the spread of films is a comparably wide-ranging Shakespeare, who is neither hidebound nor canonically isolated. Cinema, it might be suggested, has begun to sound the death-knell of the Bard's entrenched status and, even if his influence is courted, the filmic tragedies also acknowledge Shakespeare's new guise as a name, an image, a textual trace, a collocation of signifiers. Above all, the Shakespeare that emerged from the 1990s is an intertextual creation, a focus for competing interpretations of the world and for increasingly polemical interventions in its structures and processes. As such, the Shakespeare and film partnership carries in its wake an unavoidably political aesthetic. More than ever, the tragedies are reflecting back upon the contested events of the late twentieth century, whether these be the trial of O. J. Simpson (Parker's *Othello* invites numerous comparisons with the self-constructions of the American sportsman) or the crisis in Kosovo (Taymor's *Titus*, which touches upon ethnic genocide, was filmed at the Colosseum in Pula, Croatia). Contemporary film versions of the tragedies are indeeed contemporary, since they commemorate both their own stories and additional narratives that gravitate to, and are nuanced by, the Shakespearean affiliation.

REFERENCES AND FURTHER READING

Albanese, D. (2001). The Shakespeare Film and the Americanization of Culture. In J. E. Howard and S. C. Shershow (eds.) *Marxist Shakespeares*. London: Routledge, 206–26.
Almereyda, M. (2000). *William Shakespeare's "Hamlet": A Screenplay Adaptation*. London: Faber and Faber.
Arnold, G. (1996). Branagh Breathes New Life into Classics. *Insight on the News*, January 15, 36–7.
Blumenthal, E. and Taymor, J. (1999). *Julie Taymor: Playing with Fire*. New York: Abrams.

Branagh, K. (1996). *"Hamlet" by William Shakespeare: Screenplay, Introduction and Film Diary*. London: Chatto and Windus.

Burt, R. (2001). Shakespeare and the Holocaust: Julie Taymor's *Titus* is Beautiful, Or Shakesploi Meets (the) Camp. *Colby Quarterly*, 37, 78–106.

Burt, R. and Boose, L. A. (eds.) (1997). *Shakespeare, the Movie: Popularizing the Plays on Film, TV, and Video*. London: Routledge.

Cartmell, D. (2000). *Interpreting Shakespeare on Screen*. Basingstoke: Macmillan.

Crowl, S. (2000). Flamboyant Realist: Kenneth Branagh. In R. Jackson (ed.) *The Cambridge Companion to Shakespeare on Film*. Cambridge: Cambridge University Press, 222–38.

De Luca, M. and Lindroth, M. (2000). Mayhem, Madness, Method: An Interview With Julie Taymor. *Cineaste*, 25, 3, 28–31.

Dorval, P. (2000). Shakespeare on Screen: Threshold Aesthetics in Oliver Parker's *Othello*. *Early Modern Literary Studies*, 6, 1–11.

Fineman, J. (1980). Fratricide and Cuckoldry: Shakespeare's Doubles. In M. M. Schwartz and C. Kahn (eds.) *Representing Shakespeare: New Psychoanalytic Essays*. Baltimore, MD: Johns Hopkins University Press.

Hodgdon, B. (1999). *William Shakespeare's "Romeo + Juliet"*: Everything's Nice in America? *Shakespeare Survey*, 52, 88–98.

Jackson, K. (1997). Film. *Independent on Sunday*, March 30, 15.

Loehlin, J. N. (2000). "These violent delights have violent ends": Baz Luhrmann's Millennial Shakespeare. In M. T. Burnett and R. Wray (eds.) *Shakespeare, Film, Fin de Siècle*. Basingstoke: Macmillan, 121–36.

LoMonico, M. (1996). Branagh's *Hamlet* – Power and Opulence. *Shakespeare*, 1, 1, 6–7.

Luhrmann, B. (1997). *William Shakespeare's "Romeo + Juliet": The Contemporary Film, The Classic Play*. London: Hodder Headline.

McRobbie, A. (1986). Postmodernism and Popular Culture. In L. Appignanesi (ed.) *Postmodernism: ICA Documents 5*. London: ICA, 54–7.

Rothwell, K. S. (1999). *A History of Shakespeare on Screen: A Century of Film and Television*. Cambridge: Cambridge University Press.

S., D. (1996). N. B. *The Times Literary Supplement*, November 22, 16.

Shakespeare, W. (1997). *The Norton Shakespeare*, ed. S. Greenblatt, W. Cohen, J. E. Howard, and K. E. Maus. New York: W. W. Norton.

Sinfield, A. (1992). *Faultlines: Cultural Materialism and the Politics of Dissident Reading*. Oxford: Clarendon Press.

Starks, L. S. (1997). The Veiled (Hot)Bed of Race and Desire: Parker's *Othello* and the Stereotype as Screen Fetish. *Post Script*, 17, 64–78.

Taymor, J. (2000). *"Titus": The Illustrated Screenplay, Adapted from the Play by William Shakespeare*. New York: Newmarket Press.

Wray, R. and Burnett, M. T. (2000). From the Horse's Mouth: Branagh on The Bard. In M. T. Burnett and R. Wray (eds.) *Shakespeare, Film, Fin de Siècle*. Basingstoke: Macmillan, 165–78.

14
Titus Andronicus: A Time for Race and Revenge
Ian Smith

> I started thinking in terms of time rather than space.
>
> Petrarch, "The Ascent of Mount Ventoux"

Titus Andronicus's reputation for excessive violence is singularly matched by its overt use of classical references and the playwright's manifest attention to language. *Titus*'s superlative dramaturgy, both its fierce acts and florid language, might be mistaken for "the brashness and bravura of a younger poet, showing off both his knowledge of classical authors and his mastery of a crowd-pleasing popular genre" (Kahn 1997: 46). However, Coppélia Kahn contends, "this most self-consciously textual of all Shakespearean plays doesn't appropriate, imitate, allude to, and parody a host of classical authors merely to elicit plaudits for its author's learning and virtuosity" (p. 47). While loudly advertising its Renaissance humanist pedigree, the play's classicism is uniquely joined to brutal excesses. Violence and language or literature: this is the play's compelling conjunction that requires exploration. Renaissance humanism cannot be pigeonholed as a philosophical doctrine; rather, it is a set of philological and professional practices having in common "a scholarly, literary, and educational ideal based on the study of classical antiquity" (Kristeller 1962: 22). "The Renaissance 'rediscovery' of the classics," Charles Nauert (1995) adds, "was not so much a real rediscovery as a habit of viewing the classics in a new historical perspective" (p. 21). What *Titus* invites us to consider, therefore, is how, under the rubric of "Renaissance," we practice and perpetuate violence.

I

Titus's sensational effects have commanded critical attention, but the play's dramaturgy balances significant silences against the clamor of horrible deeds. Aaron remains quiet for the entire first act even though he is on stage for a long time; Sempronius, Titus' kinsman, appears but never talks; and Aaron's baby is obviously a non-speaking role. Against a background of linguistic hyperbole, silent figures are quietly etched in bold relief, and Aaron's child assumes special import. The usefulness of the term "Renaissance," meaning "originally a rebirth of letters and arts," has been much debated recently, but Jonathan Hart (1996) reminds us "that those living at the time thought they were involved in such a rebirth in the arts and used the word" (p. 1). That "Rabelais, Veronica Franco, Cervantes, and Mary Sidney all considered themselves as harbingers of a truly modern age" provides a measure of critical justification (ibid). Vasari's well-known formulation of *rinascita* or rebirth emphasizes further the Renaissance's anthropomorphic metaphor. The arts, "like human bodies, have their birth, their growth, their growing old, and their death; they will now be able to recognize more easily the progress of her second birth and of that very perfection whereto she has risen again in our times" (Vasari 1996: 46). Bacon (1990) asserts that "allegorical poetry excels all the others," in that "allegorical poetry is history with its type, which represents intellectual things to the senses" (pp. 63, 62). Thus the term "Renaissance" is additionally useful if it helps us identify and interpret the motifs of births in texts as being related to the intellectual and aesthetic questions raised by the complex process of literary imitation, borrowing, resistance, and appropriation from an estranged classical past. This is the thrust of Thomas Greene's (1982) claim when he writes that the myth of rebirth "can also be applied microcosmically at the level of the individual text, as a basis for interpretation and assessment" (p. 30). A seemingly benign idea takes on renewed interest when we apply this premise to Aaron's black child in *Titus*.

Rabelais provides an instructive comparative gloss. Writing to his son at school in Paris, Gargantua observes that, despite his scholarly assiduity, his education falls short of the intellectual opportunities available to Pantagruel's generation: "Indeed the times were still dark, and mankind was perpetually reminded of the miseries and disasters wrought by those Goths who destroyed all sound scholarship." In a panegyric befitting the Renaissance, however, Gargantua exults: "Now every method of teaching has been restored, and the study of languages has been revived . . . The whole world is full of learned men, of very erudite tutors, and of extensive libraries, and it is my opinion that neither in the time of Plato, of Cicero, nor of Papinian were there such facilities for study as one finds today" (Rabelais 1955: 194). Present achievements aggravate Gargantua's awareness of anachronism, but propagation blunts the angst of temporal alienation that, in Greene's memorable phrase, is "the solitude of history" (Greene 1982: 8). "I shall not now account myself to be absolutely dying," he tells his son, "but to be passing from one place to another, since in you, and by you, I shall remain in visible form in the world," ransoming the past and appropriating a rich intellectual future (Rabelais 1955: 193). The birth of a son, "seminal propagation," is a pregnant trope for Renaissance recuperation (p. 193). Rabelais, like Vasari, underscores the anthropomorphic reality behind the robust metaphor of "Renaissance," and he illustrates how easily birth and generation narratives serve the metaliterary purpose of reflecting on the exegetic, aesthetic, and canonical questions raised by the practice of intense exchange with the past.

In *Titus* Aaron's child is dramaturgically construed as both natural son and literary text, thereby overdetermining the need to locate the play in this context of "Renaissance" figurations of progeny. In a bold transcription, therefore, of what are usually race-neutral images of generation, Shakespeare gives us Aaron's son who, in spectacular fashion, will, indeed, "remain in visible form here in the world." The boy's visibility betrays readily his paternity, and, like Gargantua, Aaron revels in the identity and renewal of generation: "Look how the black slave smiles upon the father, / As who should say, 'Old lad, I am thine own'" (4.2.120–1).[1] He is his father's redemptive hold on the future, and, more importantly, Shakespeare's provocative sign of "rebirth" and intellectual recuperation.[2] But visibility also means death, as from the moment of his birth the boy is threatened with execution, an allegorical motif that can be profitably read in the context of Petrarch's innovative contribution to the construction of Renaissance humanism and his role in literary history.

Petrarch is usually regarded as pioneering the tripartite schema of history and an emergent "historical consciousness" (Nauert 1995: 20): the perfection of Roman antiquity; the decline of his contemporary age; and the promise of a renewed age to come. From this we get the divisions that literary historians have used: Classical, Medieval and Renaissance. Book 9 of his *Africa* documents his dream of future glory: "My life is destined to be spent 'midst storms / and turmoil. But if you, as is my wish / and ardent hope, shall live on after me, / a more propitious age will come again: / this Lethan stupor surely can't endure / forever. Our posterity, perchance, / when the dark clouds are lifted, may enjoy / once more the radiance the ancients knew" (ll. 634–9). "History," in Petrarch's view, "betrayed a rupture, whereas medieval historiography tended to stress continuities" (Greene 1982: 30). Our modern investment in historicist criticism is, arguably, indebted to Petrarch's propositions on temporal estrangement that allowed him to see "more clearly than his predecessors how the individual traits of a given society at a given moment form a distinctive constellation" (ibid: 29).

Yet another "rupture" of sorts remains deeply embedded in Petrarch's text and intellectual program. Written in celebration of Roman imperial expansion over North Africa and other parts of the Mediterranean at the close of the Second Punic, or Hannibalic, War (218–201 BC), *Africa* yearns for a rebirth of antiquity and its politically motivated racial attitudes. Book 1 makes this evident: "I shall not chronicle events still fresh / of recent times; 'tis rather my intent / to utterly destroy the cursed race / of Africa and curb their power's excess" (ll. 74–6). That is, through literary intervention Petrarch will match Scipio's military aggression against Africa with the intellectual warfare of racialist propaganda. Africa's subjection will become an exemplum for the future, for "she'll teach other lands / to bear the Roman yoke" (2: 157–8). The fall of Rome notwithstanding, ushering in Petrarch's "medieval" age, he rails against a future that would countenance the political and cultural ascendancy of Africa and her Spanish provinces: "'ah, who can bear / to think that mankind's dregs, the base and vile survivors of our sword, shall come to reign?'" (2: 362–4).

Thus the Petrarchan notion of historical consciousness does not stand alone; it emerges with a constitutive racial consciousness. Importantly, the idea of discrete, asymmetrically arranged historical periods corresponds to a view of separate and subordinate races. In addition, Petrarch's impatient dismissal of his "medieval" time, more starkly enunciated in his "Letter to Posterity" – "I always disliked our own age" (Petrarch 1985: 3) – is designed so that the future "Renaissance" might live. Similarly, the eradication of Africa is the political and ideological basis for the triumph of European subjectivity. In Petrarch then, the practice of classical veneration, an instrumental feature of Renaissance humanism, reveals a disturbing "educational ideal" grounded in racial marginalization and contempt. The revenge plot of *Titus*, therefore, dramatizes the Petrarchan prejudices outlined here. Yet, in a play where death and murderous execution reign in excess, Shakespeare's emphatic resistance to the absolute, brutal logic of revenge in saving Aaron's son constitutes a crucial aporia that amounts to an apologia.

II

Positioning the audience as a reader who interrogates culture and history is the logical extension of the play's own insistent representation of its characters as inveterate readers engaged in the corollary practices of writing and interpretation. In the aftermath of Lavinia's assault, Titus offers: "Lavinia, go with me; / I'll to thy closet, and go read with thee" (3.2.81–2) and later proposes to his daughter that "thou art deeper read and better skilled; / Come and take choice of all my library / And so beguile thy sorrow" (4.1.33–5). As Titus perceives his world unravel around him, he lies prostrate to implore the tribunes unsuccessfully on behalf of his son: "in the dust I write / My heart's deep languor and my soul's sad tears" (3.1.12–13). On the verge of entrapping Tamora in his plot, Titus resorts again to writing: "See here in bloody lines I have set down, / And what is written shall be executed" (5.2.14–15), and with lurid faithfulness to literature, he destroys Tamora, the parent eating her own children, inspired from Seneca's *Thyestes*. At the play's bloody climax Titus resorts most shockingly to the principle of legitimizing action by way of the learned analogue. He kills Lavinia because she had been "enforced, stained, and deflowered," following the historical "pattern, precedent, and lively warrant" of Virginius as recorded in Livy and, more specifically, Florus (5.3.38, 43).

In Titus' Rome, everything is done, literally, by the book. The received intellectual tradition functions as a cultural Bible, a script that is followed fatally to the letter. "This emphasis on writing," states Grace Starry West (1982), "directs our attention again to the relationship between word and deed in the play, but within a particular context: the effect of 'Roman letters,' that is, Roman literature, the written wisdom of the ancients, on the characters' actions" (pp. 68–9). The profuse references to Ovid, Seneca, Virgil, Cicero, and Horace that mirror, translate, and encode the bloody action of the play only confirm the literary *mentalité* found in Titus as culturally pervasive. In one sense Shakespeare underscores the centrality of literature to life in a way that champions a metatheatrical defense of drama's relevance to society in his time. However, as the play's self-conscious literariness announces its metatheatricality, Shakespeare argues a role for his vernacular theatre in questioning and resisting the bookish, patriarchal conformity for which Titus stands. What we witness among the Andronici led by their patriarch Titus is the tyranny of tradition and an unquestioning allegiance to an orthodox humanist intellectual heritage. Such a rigid code of adherence produces a reflex, uncritical validation of a literary canon. From the beginning of the play Titus blindly subscribes to the custom of primogeniture in electing Saturninus, rashly kills Mutius for challenging misdirected parental authority, and unthinkingly sacrifices Alarbus on the altar of religious ritual – acts which anticipate the lineal logic of Lavinia's patterned death. Shakespeare thus lays the foundation for exploring and exposing the relation of the murderous acts of filicide to the destructive pattern and power of literary filiation. West suggests that Shakespeare draws a connection "between Roman education – the source of all the bookish allusions – and the disintegration of the magnificent city which produced that education" (p. 65). Shakespeare is not simply looking back at the failure of Roman education and its role in the collapse of empire, as West argues (pp. 76–7). He is equally, if not more, concerned with literary history and interrogating the practice of the authorizing "pattern," the reception, use, and shaping influence of the texts that informed the humanist tradition in his time, the canonical texts of the "Renaissance."

If dramatic hyperbole has become the featured target of *Titus* criticism, Shakespeare has used overstatement to emphasize a crucial point. In the play, contemporary events find their justification in a preexisting model or "pattern" supplied in literature, and Romans, like us, make choices about their lives based on their education, the conduit for their informing ideology. Shakespeare presents us with a distorted version of a cultural truism, forcing a conscious apprehension of the unchecked prescriptive power of education in a literate culture and of the texts that map and encode our behavior. The culture's authorizing texts explain and justify the play's spectacular display of physical brutality. At the same time they serve as the appropriate signifiers for the intellectual violence that derives from an unquestioning capitulation to the authority of a literary canon. As a result, physical violence parallels the destructive quotidian and critical praxis generated by unthinking acceptance of a received tradition. When the linguistic turn in literary theory had its salutary impact on *Titus* criticism, several commentators noted a gap between language and action in the play and declared the play to be about the "failures of language" (Hiles 1995: 233).[3] In an important sense, however, the play dramatizes just the opposite set of relations: word is too predictive of horrifying deed, the canon of literary texts dictates indiscriminate, intellectual surrender, and literary history becomes a prejudicial concept that sanctions violence in the form of ideological naivety.

In addition to the intellectually imprisoning impact of the literary tradition, the play also points to another serious effect: the exclusionary intent deriving from the tradition's male-authorizing fictions. Here the central event is Lavinia's overdetermined Ovidian inscription as the Roman Philomel. Titus recognizes the literary analogue as an eerie redaction of the events that befall Lavinia at the hands of the fraternal rapists: "Ay, such a place there is where we did hunt – / O had we never, never hunted there! – / Patterned by that the poet here describes" (4.1.55–7). In this world, however, it appears that the men – including the otherwise contentious grouping of Titus, Chiron, and Demetrius – are the agents who enact the patterned histories, while Lavinia suffers the fate of the doubly silenced sign when she is murdered in her final history-fulfilling role as Virginius' daughter. Douglas Green interprets what must be the most puzzling, yet in some ways most predictable, moment in this masculinist ethos, Titus' killing and silencing of Lavinia. "Indeed, Lavinia's speech – or any uncurtailed mode of signification on her part," he writes, "could expose to the public (and to the audience) her subjection to the arbitrary wills of men . . . For Lavinia to speak now would undermine the play's design – the reconstitution of patriarchy under Lucius" (Green 1989: 323). This observation is properly understood in the wider revisionist context of feminist interventions in Shakespearean tragedy by effectively decentering and "displacing not only the locus of masculine subjectivity but also its implicit claim to universal significance" (Sprengnether 1996: 1).

Thus in *Titus* Shakespeare examines the notion of a received intellectual tradition, the humanist texts of the Renaissance, and observes two key factors: conformity to canonical texts breeds hegemony while fostering a repressive hostility to other rival texts or traditions. He critiques a reactionary notion of literary history in the Renaissance as embroiled in a conservative collusion with the untrammeled dictates of the past and resisting alternative texts and perspectives. One view of the text-based notion of Renaissance humanism pursues precisely an analogical project of resemblance and conformity to the past, "the effacing of temporal and geographical remoteness in the name of a universally apprehensible language, like classical Latin" (Albanese 1996: 33). Such an epistemological trajectory "shows how its collapsing of the distinction between past and present does ideological work in reproducing familiar structures of domination" (ibid). Shakespeare, however, creates a rupture by placing this corroborative literary typology under scrutiny and would seem, like Jonson, to "awake antiquity, call former times into question" (Jonson 1953: 55). "The Andronici are the bearers of the language of the fathers," writes Mary Fawcett (1983), and "should the raped daughter survive after her rape were known, she might become a competing text, she might even supplant Livy" (p. 269). *Titus* situates itself squarely in this humanist debate about history and revises the master–servant prescriptions that are inevitably replicated as its informing ideology. The ancients "opened the gates and made the way that went before us," Jonson maintains, "but as guides, not commanders: *non domini nostri, sed duces fuere* (Jonson 1953: 55). The play shares the anti-authoritarian, supplanting, Jonsonian attitude that, in Shakespeare's case, radicalizes humanist prescription by exposing the repressive thesis concerning not only gender, but also race, in the figure of the silent black baby.

III

The birth of the empress Tamora and Aaron's son effectively throws Rome's imperial succession into a crisis, restating the play's opening conflict between fraternal political rivals in specifically racial terms. From the moment of his birth, the baby's visible difference assumes iconic and racial force. The Nurse describes him: "A joyless, dismal, black, and sorrowful issue. / Here is the babe as loathsome as a toad / Amongst the fair-faced breeders of our clime" (4.2.66–8). Targeted for execution by his brothers, Chiron and Demetrius, after being surrendered by his own mother, the black infant is, however, vigorously guarded by his father, Aaron the Moor: "He dies upon my scimitar's sharp point / That touches this, my first-born son and heir" (4.2.91–2).

Aaron's defense of his son has garnered the only positive reaction among most critics who dismiss the Moor as a particularly perverse villain in an altogether bad play that sensationalizes violence. However, concerning this issue of paternal protection, Bertrand Evans (1979) concludes that "Rome is reduced to the gratuitous practices of one wicked wretch who is not even a Roman, but a Moor, and all of whose fierceness dissolves in his bizarre concern for a spectacular but essentially irrelevant black baby" (p. 21). Analyzing the play's use of the "birth motif – a symbol of new life in certain of Shakespeare's romances," Douglas Parker (1987) submits that *Titus* "gives us no reason to place any hope in the next generation" (pp. 487, 493). He contends that Aaron's son "is of less value for the play as a person than as a symbol of the perpetuation of evil that the play has dramatized. And like the evil – symbolized by the child's color – he has been born both in the presence of grotesque deaths and at the expense of other legitimate relationships" (p. 493). Trenchant declarations of the black baby's human and dramatic irrelevance, balanced against conjectures about denied mythic patterns of generational survival and futurity, remain enmeshed in old, narrowly conceived critical formulations of *Titus* as an overachieved revenge tragedy. Critical disdain aside, the black baby is supremely important.

By construing the baby as text through a series of centrally related theatrical images, Shakespeare directs our attention to the play's engagement with humanist rhetoric. "Words are embodied and disembodied throughout" the play, remarks Fawcett (1983: 263); Kolin (1995) presses the point further: "if words become flesh then the reverse is also true. Flesh itself in *Titus* is often transformed into, or re-emblematized back to, word/text that must be read as any printed source" (p. 250). Act 4 opens memorably with young Lucius fleeing from Lavinia *"with his books under his arms"* (4.1.0) and forms a direct visual analogue to the following scene where the same character reappears *"with a bundle of weapons, and verses writ upon them"* (4.2.0). Aaron alone understands Titus' menacing intent in sending these "weapons wrapped about with lines / That wound, beyond their feeling, to the quick" (4.2.27–8): *"Integer vitae, scelerisque purus, / Non eget Mauri iaculis, nec acru"* (4.2.19–20). Cited twice in Lily's grammar, *Brevissima Institutio*, the Horatian epigram concludes that the man of upright, pure character renounces the Moor and the latter's weapons – javelins and arrows (Baldwin 1944, I: 579). Having evidently passed into the basic educational lore of the Elizabethan schoolboy, the Horatian maxim identifies the wrapped weapons as metonyms for the play's reviled Moor, Aaron.

Thus the stage direction *"Enter Nurse with a blackamoor child"* (4.2.51) extends the chain of visual signifiers, and Aaron's didascalic question, "What dost thou wrap and fumble in thy arms?" (4.2.58), declares the black baby wrapped, evidently, in some cloth. The structural motif of encasement links the newborn to the books enfolded in young Lucius' arms as well as confirms the baby's Moorish filiation to the racially coded weapons enveloped in the Horatian text. Like the Horatian scroll, the cloth that covers the baby throws into sharp relief his "stamp" and "seal" of blackness (4.2.69) as the corporal inscription that renders the baby a voluble text most people want silenced and eradicated. Literally wrapped in his own blackness, then, the baby stands in dramatic contrast to his brothers, whose own chromal inscription Aaron derides: "Ye white-limed walls, ye alehouse painted signs!" (4.2.98). In an important sense, therefore, the baby is doubly wrapped, an emphatic sign of its conjunctive place in the suite of images.

Behind this complex figure of the inscribed body wrapped in cloth lies the Elizabethan rhetorical commonplace that equates linguistic eloquence with apparel that dresses up an idea. In a play so overtly indebted to the humanist investment in classical scholarship, it comes as no surprise that rhetoric, the centerpiece of the sixteenth-century English humanist curriculum, should occupy Shakespeare's attention. Brian Vickers (1981) has scrupulously demonstrated that in the lower schools and the universities in England *elocutio* occupied an advanced and not an "elementary" place in the curriculum (p. 125). In addition, rhetoricians like Sherry, Webbe, and Puttenham, whether adhering to the Ciceronian or Ramist bias, whether Catholic or Protestant, all assert the central place of eloquence "for mastering the details of language in order to master the audience's feelings" (ibid: 125–6). Thus having fully established the intersection of the black baby-as-text and the clothing or wrapping motif, Shakespeare creates a provocative *visual* representation of a widespread epitome of rhetoric. Jonson (1953) offers a typical formulation: "A man should so deliver himself to the nature of the subject whereof he speaks that his hearers may take knowledge of his discipline with some delight, and so apparel fair and good matter that the studious elegancy be not defrauded" (p. 47).

Shakespeare shatters the routine contiguity of cloth and language in rhetorical discourse to reveal a muted third term, skin or the racialized body, which, in a white culture, only becomes visible and articulate when it signifies difference. In a memorable passage from *The Arte of English Poesie* Puttenham presents gender and class as integers of the rhetorical body when he compares "the great Madames of honour" without their wealthy garb to language without figural ornamentation.[4] Similarly, Erasmus observes that those who have not mastered the art of fine speaking appear "no less ridiculous . . . than a beggar who has not got even one garment that he can decently put on, but keeps changing his clothes and coming out in public draped with different sets of rags" (p. 306). It is in Shakespeare, however, that we find the body–language–clothing nexus definitively indexed to race. Since rhetoric is joined, literally, to the materials of culture, especially bodies and cloth, Shakespeare's racial tropology extends and makes explicit rhetoric's materialist investments. By exploring this graphic intersection of skin, text, and cloth, Shakespeare declares the social body the implicit subject of the pervasive Renaissance interest in language arts and suggests further that rhetoric becomes a critical locus for anchoring racial theory and inquiry.

Sir John Cheke's letter, written in 1557 but published with Thomas Hoby's translation of *The Courtier* in 1561, redeploys the rhetoric-clothing conjunction in a way that elaborates the discursive *topos* of the black baby-text in *Titus*.

> I am of this opinion that our own tung shold be written cleane and pure, unmixt and unmangeled with borrowing of other tunges, wherein if we take not heed by tijm, ever borrowing and never payeng, she shall be fain to keep her house as bankrupt. For then doth our tung naturallie and praisablie utter her meaning, when she bouroweth no counterfeitness of other tunges to attire her self withal. (Cheke 1929: 7)

In the mid-sixteenth century the rise of the English vernacular from under the shadow of Latin, Greek, and contemporary European languages charts the emergence of English nationalism, and Cheke's comments derive from a debate that displaced current nationalist obsessions under Elizabeth onto the plane of literary poetics.[5] Cheke supports a vibrant English nationalism linked to a self-sustained financial and cultural economy by arguing against the borrowing of foreign words to "attire" the English language. Ironically, notorious expenditures on foreign fashion, documented by writers like Andrew Boorde (1981: 116–17) and William Harrison (1968: 145–8), inform Cheke's call for an English body plainly dressed in English cloth as the material intertext of English literary evolution. Intensifying as the century grew to a close, the concern over intrusive foreign words exploded in the acrimonious Nashe–Harvey correspondence between 1592–7 over inkhorn or foreign terms. More temperate assertions can be found in Camden's *Remains Concerning Britain* (1605), while sentiments against foreign borrowing preoccupied lexicographers, from Robert Cawdrey's pioneering *A Table Alphabeticall* (1604) until late into the seventeenth century in Elisha Coles's *An English Dictionary* (1676). Linguistic purity as a precondition of national integrity supplies an early modern context for understanding *Titus*'s threat of expulsion of the alien baby-text from the insular ideal of Rome and its linguistic, literary ethos. *Titus* suggests that in Renaissance England, foreign words, like the foreign, Moorish baby, compromise the "attire" and fashioning of a literary and national identity. The anxiety over invading foreign words thus encodes a very real cultural preoccupation: the xenophobic impulse that shaped English nationalism and gave rise to a racialist aesthetics.

Shakespeare's intercalation of text and body in the figural baby institutes a tropology where the rhetorical and the social interpenetrate to produce an exigent cultural poetics. When Albert Tricomi (1995), in his landmark essay, proposes that the violent literalization of metaphors is the distinguishing feature of *Titus*, he calls attention to the startling way cerebral concatenation makes a disturbing purchase on plangent reality. Shakespeare abandons the decorum of euphemistic similitude between tenor and vehicle to radically assert identity, thereby truncating the distance between literary figuration and social enactment. Shakespeare's tropology manifests its unique character to the degree that it expressly collates vehicle and tenor, text and baby, intellectual construct and social reality. Conceptualizing the text as a person and social subject, Shakespeare affirms that rhetorical and aesthetic theories do not circulate independent of the cultural matrix in which they are produced. Conceptualizing the text as a *black* person, Shakespeare insists in *Titus* that rhetorical and aesthetic choices are contingent on cultural practice in a way that forces us to recognize the play's discursive relation to the racialist aesthetics found in the quintessential Renaissance model: Petrarch. Intradramatically, the conventional ethic of revenge tragedy demands the punishment of Aaron, the retributive murder of Tamora, and the collateral destruction of these barbarians' progeny, the baby. According to the revenge trajectory this social eradication of the black child-text is consistent with the Petrarchan literary ideal: the expulsion of Africa from the domain of aesthetics and literary history. The physical violence in *Titus* is only a spectacular precursor to the intellectual violence that attends Renaissance constructions of Africa. In Shakespeare's hands revenge tragedy becomes a singularly compelling genre that expresses the violent assaults made on Africa in the creation of an English Renaissance intellectual tradition.

IV

Shakespeare's focus on rhetorical eloquence by way of the child must not, then, be narrowly misconstrued as an obsession with the minutiae of style, although his manipulation of the figures, like any other writer in the period, is evident everywhere in his *oeuvre* (Joseph 1966; Blake 1989). Cicero signaled the inevitable union of rhetoric to literature in his *De oratore*: "The poet, indeed, is closely allied to the orator, being somewhat more restricted in number, but the freer in the choice of words, yet in many kinds of ornament his ally and almost his equal" (I.16.70). And when Aristotle's *Poetics* made its appearance in the Renaissance, first in Giorgio Valla's Latin translation of 1498 and then definitively, for the period, in Alessandro de Pazzi's 1536 Greek–Latin edition, "it too was absorbed by a rhetorical culture and reinterpreted to fit" (Vickers 1988: 718). *Titus*, then, with its recapitulation of classical sources, its evident poetic ornamentation and, especially, its emblematic evocation of rhetoric in the figure of the baby, bears the pronounced signs of "literature" in sixteenth-century terms – and in Shakespeare's case, *theatrical literature*.

Theatrical literature capitalizes on the spoken and written modalities of rhetoric where dramatic text and oratory are conjoined in theatrical performance as "delivery." However, "delivery," as a pointed pun in the play, is also inseparable from both the baby and the historical figure of Cornelia. To Aaron's demand that the Nurse identify the wrapped object in her arms, she replies: "Our empress' shame and stately Rome's disgrace, / She is delivered, lords, she is delivered" (4.2.61–2), creating yet another verbal link to the wrapped weapons motif when at the opening of 4.2 Chiron announces young Lucius' entry: "here's the son of Lucius; / He hath some message to deliver us" (ll. 1–2). Aaron's baby arrives in the world, the Nurse clarifies further, "delivered" by "Cornelia the midwife" (4.2.141–2). Delivered children, delivered messages: one act is coterminous with the other, natural birth being allied to rhetorical generation and the birth of ideas – the conceptual paradigm of the "Renaissance." Like the visual recurrence of wrapped figures, the repeated word "delivery" in relation to the baby also evokes *pronunciatio* or "delivery," the last of the five canons inherited from classical rhetoric in the Renaissance.[6] Although the figures of style or eloquence dominated the field of literary or text-based rhetoric, it was in the theatre that "delivery" flourished and found a natural early modern home.

That the only other witnesses to the birth are, naturally, the mother and the generically named Nurse, indicates Shakespeare's deliberate attention to the details of nomenclature and "delivery." Earlier in the play when Titus describes Lavinia's relationship to young Lucius, Shakespeare cites the carefully coded historical intertext for reading the delivery of Aaron's child: "Ah, boy, Cornelia never with more care / Read to her sons than she hath read to thee / Sweet poetry and Tully's *Orator*" (4.1.12–14). A revered Roman matron of the second century BC, the widow of Tiberius Sempronius Gracchus, Cornelia achieved fame through her extraordinary devotion to the education of her two sons, Tiberius and Gaius, when imperial "prosperity and its accompanying materialistic emphases" defined the political climate of the late republic (Boren 1968: 35). Imperial success had led to increasing wealth, ostentatious display, the erosion of the middle class, and an ever widening gap between the rich and the poor arising from aristocratic and senatorial abuse of public lands. From Sir Thomas North's translation of Plutarch's *Lives* of 1579, the details of this celebrated widow's impact on her sons, whose controversial land reforms excited senatorial factionalism, were available to Shakespeare's generation. Of twelve children, her two surviving sons, the Gracchi, "she so carefully brought up, that they being become more civil, and better conditioned, than any other Romans in their time: every man judged, that education prevailed more in them, than nature" (North 1921: 164).

In Plutarch's estimation "the worthiest act Tiberius did was the law Agraria, which he brought in for dividing of the lands of the commonwealth amongst the poor citizens" (North 1921: 209). The precipitating event in 133 BC concerned lands accruing to the empire as ransom that were reserved for "the poor citizens that had no lands" (p. 169). However, exorbitant yearly rentals drove the poor off these public lands that were then illegally incorporated by the landed aristocrats. As a tribune of the plebs, Tiberius proposed legislation, relatively cautious at first but growing increasingly bold in proportion to the conservative backlash, in favor of protecting the poor from the "covetousness of the rich men" and curtailing "so great injustice and avarice" (pp. 170, 171). Gaius' basic reforms, including stabilized grain prices under the *lex frumentaria*, addressed the general economic hardship faced by the poor, "who lived in perpetual danger of famine" (Boak and Sinnigen 1965: 182). Further, as tribune, Gaius championed the full citizenship rights of those brought under Roman imperial power and ascribed the ambiguous status as "Latins," a point raised at least three times in the *Lives*: "he gave all the Latins the freedom of Rome to give their voices in choosing of magistrates as freely as the natural Romans" (North 1921: 195; also 191, 194). Being granted "Latin" status only exacerbated the otherness of these near-Romans who, under the preexisting law, were never fully politically integrated. Over a period of years the Sempronian reforms sparked divisions among the ruling oligarchy, pitching the conservative Optimates against the Populares, spurred riots in which both brothers were murdered, and launched the era of the revolution in Roman history that would bring the republic to an end.[7] Doubtless, the motivation behind much of the factional machinations, on both sides, was inspired by political ambition and driven by insidious materialism. Still, the Gracchi carved out a place for themselves as defenders of the people, but within ten years of their deaths their progressive legislation was nullified as eroded republican rule reverted to corrupt senatorial conservatism (ibid: 206).

Delivery, then, in Shakespeare, evokes far more than natural birth, even as it keeps alive the idea of "Renaissance." Through this image Shakespeare propounds, again, the connection between rhetoric, literature, intellectual formation, and political commitment – in short, the connection between literature and life. So influential was Cornelia's instruction in "rhetoric and Greek Stoic philosophy" that historians have speculated on the causal connection between "the liberal influences of the Greek education" from which the Gracchi benefited and agrarian reforms they pursued (Boak and Sinnigen 1965: 176–7). Brian Vickers (1989) points out that "Renaissance readers did not regard literary works as autotelic; indeed the concept that any work of art could be self-ended, without a function in human life, would have been foreign" (p. 715). The classical concerns over land and the exploitation of the poor requiring Sempronian reform echo the economic and social transformations of the enclosure movements in sixteenth-century England (Roseberry 1991: 28–34). Enclosures saw the increased landownership of a few, the decline in arable lands, the resulting depopulation of the rural areas, and the rise in dislocated laborers in urban London who, as vagrants and masterless men, came under severe public scrutiny (Weimann 1978: 161–9; Howard 1994: 23–32). Puritan and bourgeois antitheatrical polemic centered on these unemployed workers, identifying them as the idle patrons of the playhouses who also resided in the nefarious suburban regions where the theatres were located (Gurr 1996: 54–5). Collectively repealed in 1593, the government's laws to protect against enclosure and the decrease in arable lands would no longer contain the protocapitalist enterprise of engrossment (Williams 1979: 180–5). Similarly, the commercial theatre found itself embroiled in a puritanical, moral debate that was a smokescreen for the entrepreneurial and economic threat that it posed to some of its critics. "Beneath all the arguments about [the theatre's] morality," Jean Howard (1994) argues, "lurked the urgent question of who would control the implicit power of this institution" (p. 5).

The theatre's power resided precisely in its ability to "deliver" a "message" whose transmission and reception, despite whatever censorship mechanism might be in place, could never be determined or contained in the dialogic presentation of performance – what Louis Montrose (1996) calls the "cross-purposes of playing" (pp. 99–105). The performativity of theatre provided a perfect instance to observe rhetoric's pragmatic effects, and the politics of antitheatricality meant that, like the black baby, the public theatre's survival was at stake. For Shakespeare the young playwright of *Titus*, the threatened baby translates well the author's anxieties of performance and success, of productivity and acceptance. For Shakespeare the practicing playwright, evoking theatrical literature by way of the black baby elaborates a metatheatrical function that exceeds autotelic formalism. In postulating not just literature but a *black theatrical literature*, Shakespeare asks us to consider the fate of dramatic scripts and performance in the theatre's always controversial and contested environment. *Black* in the English Renaissance context does not obviously construe author ethnicity but a socially specific author function. *Black* is a term of denigration, marking the theatre and its performances as barbarous, threatening, and dangerous as Aaron and the collective progeny of Africa. Where Howard (1994) suggests "that the antitheatrical discourse eventually emerged as an all-purpose language of stigmatization and delegitimation" (p. 6), it is worth adding that blackness, connoted in Africa, assumed an even more comprehensive role as the critical super-category. Read metatheatrically, the black child-as-text reveals how the theatre as a marginal institution is conceptually allied to Africa in Shakespeare's elucidation of discourse contamination. Indeed, for Shakespeare, theatre is inseparable from life, and his own work played a significant role in reforming social and aesthetic attitudes towards this plebian institution and the prevalent notions of Africa and blackness, while promoting a self-consciously racialized idea of "Renaissance."

V

Shakespeare's insistence on the birth and survival of the son of the stereotypical arch-villain, Aaron, is especially noteworthy in a world of relentless murders. According to the logic of a more conventional, moralistic revenge tragedy, the nominal villain and his offspring would probably both suffer the fate of death. This is certainly Lucius' view: "First hang the child, that he may see it sprawl, / A sight to vex the father's soul," until Aaron manages to strike a hard-won, successful bargain for the child's life (5.1.51–2). In two major scenes, therefore, Shakespeare makes the point that extreme efforts are taken to ensure Aaron's child will live, thereby demanding that we attend to the baby's third and final appearance (5.3.118) and understand his place in the emergent world order. Marcus' restorative claim at the conclusion of the tragedy requires us to theorize a very different sense of an ending that must include the black birth: "O let me teach you how to knit again / This scattered corn into one mutual sheaf, / These broken limbs again into one body" (5.3.69–71).

The dramatic function of the baby in *Titus*, which compels the audience to look beyond the formal closure of the text, parallels a technique Shakespeare employs elsewhere. *Hamlet* and *Othello*, for example, both conclude in similar ways: in addition to the recuperative convention of newly instituted rule, both plays require that the heroes' stories be told – again. Hamlet's famous request to Horatio: "Absent thee from felicity awhile, / And in this harsh world draw thy breath in pain / To tell my story" (5.2.349–51), is matched by Othello's appeal: "When you shall these unlucky deeds relate, / Speak of me as I am" (5.2.351–2). Such metanarrative endings postulate, in theory, an endless retelling. In these plays the audience is imaginatively projected into a future space to contemplate the life stories just told, only to replay the drama once again when the narrative arrives at the retelling point. The plays never really end, and the imagined retellings, interestingly, constitute their own narrative pattern of death and rebirth. In each instance the hero's request for narrative retelling is an anxious attempt to reread history, to revise misperceptions and produce a life narrative whose clear meaning seems always compromised by the grudging complexities of "this harsh world." In *Titus* the baby, as a son of the empress and, in theory, a future political contender, is paired with young Lucius as eventual rivals in a way that returns us to the opening of the play, to retell the story of political competition but with a distinct racial emphasis. Thus *Titus*, like *Hamlet* and *Othello*, is constructed to suggest suspended closure predicated on projected narrative retelling that defamiliarizes the stories told and removes them "from the automatism of perception" to induce critical reflection (Shklovsky 1965: 13). In Shakespeare's hands, narrative retelling aims to "make objects 'unfamiliar,' to make forms difficult" (ibid: 12) and in the process transforms aesthetic contemplation into social and political awareness to realize an effect which Brecht, in his admiration of the vigorous forces of the Elizabethan theatre, would call his "epic" theatre (Brecht 1957: 70–1).

In *Titus* Shakespeare takes this elicited critical reflection one step further. The very idea of a Roman future where a black outsider reigns as emperor is inimical to the play's version of *romanitas*. In a revenge tragedy such a projected future would be the ultimate revenge: the Roman state becomes its political and cultural Other. Historical studies of revenge tragedy have long focused on the "ethical dilemma" of the Renaissance audience, arguing the fine points of audience response to private revenge when existing canon and ecclesiastical law appeared to ban such action on the part of English citizens (Campbell 1931; Bowers 1940; Prosser 1971). However, as Robert Ornstein (1965) has pointed out, Jacobean dramatists themselves are not preoccupied with that particular debate: "the crucial issue in revenge tragedy is not, 'Shall there be private vengeance or recourse to law?' but 'Shall one take action in an evil world or retreat into Stoic resignation?'" A crucial, related issue for dramatists, therefore, is that "they grapple with the question of how virtuous action can be taken in an evil world when that action itself must be devious, politic, or tainted with evil" (ibid: 23). J. W. Lever (1971) makes a similar point: "Through personal wrongs the [revenge] play dramatizes the general corruption of the state, and confronts the hero with the imperative necessity to act, even at the price of his own moral contamination" (pp. 12–13).

The Elizabethan–Roman world of *Titus*, however, is not purely the scene of moral disquisition. In this early revenge tragedy Shakespeare transmutes the incipient threat of the revenger's personal "moral contamination" into the dramatic irony of an entire society's racial, that is black, "contamination." First published in 1594, *Titus* appeared at a time when the black presence in England, starting with the arrival of the five black slaves in 1555, had grown, especially since the 1570s. The increasing numbers of blacks eventually prompted the royal warrant of 1596 to deport "blackmoores brought into this realme, of which kinde of people there are allready here to manie" (Fryer 1984: 10). "The existence of both free and enslaved Africans," writes James Walvin (1972), "seemed to contemporaries to exacerbate a problem which plagued the whole nation in the last years of the old Queen's reign: poverty and hunger" (p. 61). Slumping economic conditions in the 1590s, therefore, aggravated by already pervasive negative stereotypes concerning blackness itself, African bestiality, and Africans' supposed cursed religious ancestry in Ham, justified the exploitative expulsion order: "that those kinde of people should be sent forth of the lande" (Fryer 1984: 10).[8] Thus the play's embedded proleptic narrative that envisions black rule as a metonym for racial mixing is grounded in a pressing social reality. The "epic" vision that proceeds from the play's narrative retelling requires the *audience* to perform the final act of revenge: to imagine a denigrated – in its etymological sense – racialized, Roman empire that has been turned into the Other it resisted. The irony is doubled when the performance of revenge extends outward into the social sphere of the English economic and racial order. Tragedy in *Titus* is not simply about physical death, despite the play's reputation for gore, but articulates the socially irreversible racial transformation of a nation embodied as white in its royal iconography.

VI

In a still more urgent sense for modern readers and audiences, Shakespeare requires an imaginative, reformed investigation into a notion of the "Renaissance" that has very troubling investments in racial marginalization and repression. Nauert (1995) writes that the "critical challenge to conventional wisdom always lurked within Renaissance humanism. The rank and file of humanists may have been conformist nonentities. Nevertheless, the critical potential was always there" (p. 215). In *Titus* Shakespeare enters into the critical humanist spirit (the revisionist and "epic" spirit of "revenge" as defined above) and asks that we take full account of the racial construction of a philological and literary practice that has real social consequences. Petrarch's Renaissance is exclusionary and suppresses Africa, while Shakespeare has made it a point to revise this idea to include blackness. Where Petrarch announces his cultural ideal in the figure of Scipio, Africa's conqueror, Shakespeare's reforming vision is enabled by an equally noteworthy choice: Cornelia. The gender difference in classical models is, of course, striking, and one senses in Shakespeare's choice the complementary, though not commensurate, relation between gender and race. What makes Shakespeare's selection of Cornelia particularly striking in the context of Petrarch is her lineage. She was not only the mother of the Gracchi, a role for which she achieved fame. For Shakespeare, Cornelia's other family relations are resonant: she was, in fact, the daughter of Scipio Africanus – Petrarch's hero. Thus these silent figures of the baby, Cornelia, and even the non-speaking Sempronius – not, coincidentally the *nomen* or clan name of the Gracchi – form a network of intertexts that enters into critical dialogue with the Renaissance construct idealized in Petrarch.

In *Titus* Shakespeare invites us to continue inquiring into the role and place of race in "Renaissance" studies. The revolution toward historicist approaches has been a salutary advance in the last twenty years, yet one fears that the still overwhelming attitude is to produce work that remains unaware of or vaguely indifferent to the racial demands of the texts we read. The ethics of our critical and cultural practices are at stake, and our responses subject to scrutiny. The challenge is ever important to submit canonical figures to closer investigation, given the status we accord them, while not failing to admit or to take into account the equally necessary task of dealing with the racial implications of our literary history thus constituted. *Titus Andronicus* asks that along with the legacy of historical consciousness we interrogate the emergence of a racial consciousness in Renaissance humanist practice and literary production. In the terms of the play's full generic and performative import, Shakespeare suggests, in short, that we engage the dialectical critique of revenge.

NOTES

1   All *Titus* references are taken from the Cambridge edition. All other Shakespeare references are from the *Complete Works*.

2   Aaron is not my focus in this essay, but I resist throughout the overwhelming critical tendency to indict Aaron as merely a villain. As I have argued elsewhere, Shakespeare challenges us to rethink Aaron's behavior in light of the character's biblical association with racial slavery, oppression, and liberation. See Smith (1997).

3   Since the 1970s, several important articles have, in a poststructuralist fashion, focused on language in the play. Peter Sacks (1982) perceives an "allegorical rhetoric that is felt to be divided from its referents" (p. 587), and Gillian Kendall (1989) notes that "violence is done to language through the distance between word and thing, between metaphor and what it represents" (p. 299). Like many who focus on Marcus' verbose reaction to the sight of the mutilated Lavinia, Ettin (1970) declares that "we must find the language aesthetically and morally inadequate" (p. 339). S. Clark Hulse (1979) finds that characters have to resort to gestures, a sure sign of a decayed, ineffectual language (pp. 107–8).

4   Having initiated the comparison of the great ladies who "want their courtly habillements or at leastwise such other apparell as custome and ciuilitie haue ordained to couer their naked bodies,"

Puttenham concludes: "Euen so cannot our vulgar Poesie shew it selfe either gallant or gorgious, if any lymme be left naked and bare and not clad in his kindly clothes and colours" (pp. 150–1).

5   Helgerson (1992) gives a solid account of this aesthetics of nationalism; see especially pp. 1–40.

6   Traditionally, the five parts of rhetoric are: invention, arrangement, style or eloquence, memory, and delivery. See Lanham (1991: 164–80).

7   For a detailed account of the period of the Revolution, see Boak and Sinnigen (1965: 174–206).

8   See Semple (1987: 34–5) and Walvin (1972: 61–3). Another deportation order followed in 1601. Fryer (1984) points out that both expulsion orders had a cynical material motive: "This was an astute piece of business, which must have saved the queen a lot of money. The black people concerned were being used as payment for the return of 89 English prisoners" (pp. 11–12).

REFERENCES AND FURTHER READING

Albanese, D. (1996). Making it New: Humanism, Colonialism, and the Gendered Body in Early Modern Culture. In V. Traub, M. L. Kaplan, and D. Callaghan (eds.) *Feminist Readings of Early Modern Culture: Emerging Subjects.* Cambridge: Cambridge University Press.

Bacon, F. (1900). *Advancement of Learning and Novum Organum.* New York: Colonial Press.

Baldwin, T. W. (1944). *William Shakespeare's Small Latine and Lesse Greeke.* Urbana: University of Illinois Press.

Blake, N. F. (1989). *The Language of Shakespeare.* London: Macmillan.

Boak, E. R. and Sinnigen, W. G. (1965). *A History of Rome to AD 565.* New York: Macmillan.

Boorde, A. (1981). *The First Boke of the Introduction of Knowledge,* ed. F. J. Furnival. Millwood, NY: Kraus Reprint.

Boren, H. C. (1968). *The Gracchi.* New York: Twayne.

Bowers, F. T. (1940). *Elizabethan Revenge Tragedy, 1587–1642.* Princeton, NJ: Princeton University Press.

Brecht, B. (1957). *Brecht on Theatre: The Development of an Aesthetic,* trans. and ed. J. Willett. New York: Hill and Wang.

Campbell, L. B. (1931). Theories of Revenge in Renaissance England. *Modern Philology,* 28, 281–96.

Cheke, J. (1929). Letter. In *The Book of the Courtier,* by Baldassare Castiglione, trans. T. Hoby. New York: Dutton.

Erasmus, D. (1978). *Collected Works of Erasmus,* vol. 24, ed. C. R. Thompson. Toronto: University of Toronto Press.

Ettin, A. V. (1970). Shakespeare's First Roman Tragedy. *English Literary History,* 37, 325–41.

Evans, B. (1979). *Shakespeare's Tragic Practice.* Oxford: Clarendon Press.

Fawcett, M. L. (1983). Arms/Words/Tears: Language and the Body in *Titus Andronicus. English Literary History,* 50, 261–77.

Fryer, P. (1984). *Staying Power: The History of Black People in Britain.* London: Pluto Press.

Green, D. E. (1989). Interpreting "her martyr'd signs": Gender and Tragedy in *Titus Andronicus. Shakespeare Quarterly,* 40, 317–26.

Greene, T. M. (1982). *The Light in Troy: Imitation and Discovery in Renaissance Poetry.* New Haven, CT: Yale University Press.

Gurr, A. (1996). *Playgoing in Shakespeare's London,* 2nd edn. Cambridge: Cambridge University Press.

Harrison, W. (1968). *The Description of England,* ed. G. Edelen. Washington, DC: Folger Shakespeare Library.

Hart, J. (1996). Reading the Renaissance: An Introduction. In J. Hart (ed.) *Reading the Renaissance: Culture, Poetics, and Drama.* New York: Garland.

Helgerson, R. (1992). *Forms of Nationhood: The Elizabethan Writing of England.* Chicago, IL: University of Chicago Press.

Hiles, J. (1995). A Margin for Error: Rhetorical Context in *Titus Andronicus*. In P. C. Kolin (ed.) *Titus Andronicus: Critical Essays*. New York: Garland.

Howard, J. E. (1994). *The Stage and Social Struggle in Early Modern England*. New York: Routledge.

Hulse, S. C. (1979). Wresting the Alphabet: Oratory and Action in *Titus Andronicus*. *Criticism*, 21, 106–18.

Jonson, B. (1953). *Timber or Discoveries*, ed. R. S. Walker. Syracuse, NY: Syracuse University Press.

Jordan, W. (1968). *White Over Black: American Attitudes Toward the Negro, 1550–1812*. Chapel Hill: University of North Carolina Press.

Joseph, M. (1966). *Shakespeare's Use of the Arts of Language*. New York: Hafner.

Kahn, C. (1997). *Roman Shakespeare: Warriors, Wounds, and Women*. London: Routledge.

Kendall, G. M. (1989). "Lend me thine hand": Metaphor and Mayhem in *Titus Andronicus*. *Shakespeare Quarterly*, 40, 299–316.

Kolin, P. (1995). Performing Texts in *Titus Andronicus*. In P. Kolin (ed.) *Titus Andronicus: Critical Essays*. New York: Garland.

Kristeller, P. O. (1962). Studies on Renaissance Humanism During the Last Twenty Years. *Studies in the Renaissance*, 9, 7–30.

Lanham, R. A. (1991). *A Handlist of Rhetorical Terms*, 2nd edn. Berkeley: University of California Press.

Lever, J. W. (1971). *The Tragedy of State: A Study of Jacobean Drama*. London: Methuen.

Metz, G. H. (1996). *Shakespeare's Earliest Tragedy: Studies in "Titus Andronicus."* Madison, NJ: Fairleigh Dickinson University Press.

Montrose, L. (1996). *The Purpose of Playing: Shakespeare and the Cultural Politics of the Elizabethan Theater*. Chicago, IL: University of Chicago Press.

Nauert, C. G., Jr. (1995). *Humanism and the Culture of Renaissance Europe*. Cambridge: Cambridge University Press.

North, T. (1921). *Plutarch's Lives: A Selection*, ed. P. Giles. Cambridge: Cambridge University Press.

Ornstein, R. (1965). *The Moral Vision of Jacobean Tragedy*. Madison: University of Wisconsin Press.

Parker, D. (1987). Shakespeare's Use of Comic Conventions in *Titus Andronicus*. *University of Toronto Quarterly*, 56, 486–97.

Petrarch, P. (1977). *Africa*, trans. T. G. Bergin and A. S. Wilson. New Haven, CT: Yale University Press.

——(1985). *Selections from the "Canzoniere" and Other Works*, trans. and ed. M. Musa. Oxford: Oxford University Press.

Prosser, E. (1971). *Hamlet and Revenge*, 2nd edn. Stanford, CA: Stanford University Press.

Puttenham, G. (1869). *The Arte of English Poesie*, ed. E. Arber. London: Alex Murray.

Rabelais, F. (1955). *Gargantua and Pantagruel*. London: Penguin Books.

Roseberry, W. (1991). Potatoes, Sacks, and Enclosures in Early Modern England. In J. O'Brien and W. Roseberry (eds.) *Golden Ages, Dark Ages: Imagining the Past in Anthropology and History*. Berkeley: University of California Press.

Sacks, P. (1982). Where Words Prevail Not: Grief, Revenge, and Language in Kyd and Shakespeare. *English Literary History*, 49, 576–601.

Semple, H. (1987). Shakespeare and Race. *Shakespeare in South Africa*, 1, 30–8.

Shakespeare, W. (1992). *The Complete Works*, 4th edn., ed. D. Bevington. New York: HarperCollins.

——(1994). *Titus Andronicus*, ed. A. Hughes. Cambridge: Cambridge University Press.

Shklovsky, V. (1965). Art as Technique. In *Russian Formalist Criticism: Four Essays*, trans. and ed. L. T. Lemon and M. J. Reis. Lincoln: University of Nebraska Press.

Smith, I. (1997). Those "slippery customers": Rethinking Race in *Titus Andronicus. Journal of Theatre and Drama*, 3, 45–58.

Sprengnether, M. (1996). Introduction: The Gendered Subject of Shakespearean Tragedy. In S. N. Garner and M. Sprengnether (eds.) *Shakespearean Tragedy and Gender*. Bloomington: Indiana University Press.

Tricomi, A. H. (1995). The Aesthetics of Mutilation in *Titus Andronicus*. In M. Rose (ed.) *Shakespeare's Early Tragedies: A Collection of Critical Essays*. Englewood Cliffs, NJ: Prentice-Hall.

Vasari, G. (1996). *Lives of the Painters, Sculptors and Architects*, trans. G. du C. de Vere, vol. 1. New York: Knopf.

Vickers, B. (1981). Rhetorical and Anti-Rhetorical Tropes: On Writing the History of *Elocutio*. *Comparative Criticism*, 3, 105–32.

——(1988). Rhetoric and Poetics. In C. B. Schmitt and Q. Skinner (eds.) *The Cambridge History of Renaissance Philosophy*. Cambridge: Cambridge University Press.

Walvin, J. (1972). *The Black Presence: A Documentary History of the Negro in England, 1555–1860*. New York: Schocken Books.

Weimann, R. (1978). *Shakespeare and the Popular Tradition in the Theater*. Baltimore, MD: Johns Hopkins University Press.

West, G. S. (1982). Going by the Book: Classical Allusions in Shakespeare's *Titus Andronicus*. *Studies in Philology*, 79, 62–77.

Williams, P. (1979). *The Tudor Regime*. Oxford: Clarendon Press.

15

"There is no world without Verona walls": The City in *Romeo and Juliet*

Naomi Conn Liebler

There is beyonde the Alps, a towne of auncient fame
Whose bright renoune yet shineth cleare, Verona men it name,
Bylt in an happy time, bylt on a fertile soyle,
Maynteined by the heavenly fetes, and by the townish toyle.
The fruitfull hilles above, the pleasant vales belowe,
The silver streame with chanell depe, that through the towne doth flow,
The store of springes that serve for use, and eke for ease
And other moe commodities which profite may and please,
Eke many certaine signes of thinges betyde of olde,
To fyll the hongry eyes of those that curiously beholde
Doe make this towne to be preferde above the rest
Of Lumbard townes, or at the least compared with the best.
                    Arthur Brooke, *The Tragicall Historye of Romeus and Juliet*

If we apply the bare outlines of Aristotle's famous criterion for tragedy – "the representation of an action that is serious, complete, and of a certain magnitude" (Aristotle 1987: 37) – to *Romeo and Juliet*, we might think the play a failure in the genre, or a comedy whose more satisfying apotheosis emerged in *A Midsummer Night's Dream*.[1] It has seemed so to a number of critics. Susan Snyder observed that the "action" of *Romeo and Juliet* carries, from the outset, many of the hallmarks of a good Shakespearean comedy, "set in a broader social context, so that the marriage promises not only private satisfaction but renewed social unity . . . The feud functions in *Romeo* very much as the various legal restraints do in Shakespearean comedy" (Snyder 1979: 59); the play "becomes, rather than is, tragic" (p. 57). For Michael Neill, the action of the play resembles "a romantic tragicomedy on a stage hung with funeral blacks . . . to match the oxymoronic patterns of the play's rhetoric and design" (Neill 1997: 283); Ralph Berry labels the play "half comedy, half tragedy" (Berry 1988: 38). It is easy enough to see why they might think so: "action" *per se* is not very much in evidence in *Romeo and Juliet*. Nothing much actually happens there: words are exchanged, but except for the skirmishes between the servants of the Montague and Capulet house-holds, the duel that kills Tybalt and Mercutio, and of course the final double suicide, *Romeo and Juliet* seems more a play about things that *don't* happen. Potentially life-saving words are not said, such as those from the Nurse, Friar Laurence, or Romeo and Juliet themselves, announcing Juliet's marriage to Romeo, that would have can-celled Capulet's plan to marry his daughter to County Paris and precluded the pro-tagonists' deaths, or Romeo's announcement of his marriage to Juliet that might have prevented Tybalt's attack. Perhaps even more significantly, important words about to be spoken are not heard, as when both the Nurse and Juliet do attempt to speak to her parents in 3.5, presumably to announce the marriage, and are silenced, or when the ineffectual Prince tries to address his "rebellious subjects" after the opening scene's skirmish: "Will they not hear?" (1.1.79).[2] Evidently he is speaking to himself, because it takes another twenty-one lines for him to get their cooperation. Important messages are misdelivered: the invitation to the Capulet ball falls into the hands of Romeo's cohort, or undelivered: Friar John's message to Romeo in Mantua is aborted because of the very real "plague" that ultimately, though indirectly, destroys both houses.

We do not find in *Romeo and Juliet* the complex dilemma or soliloquy-debated deci-sion to act that mark, for example, *Julius Caesar, Hamlet, Othello*, or *Macbeth*. In fact, the principal physical actions seen at the start of the play seem almost incidental, if not actually accidental. Some are played for laughs: the "washing blows" of two packs of servants whose combat skills are normally deployed only against laundry,[3] and "old" fathers (so identified by Gibbons (1980) at 1.1.72 and 74 s.d.) wielding swords instead of crutches. Mercutio and Tybalt are accidental casualties of the crucial street fight in the center of the play: the only intended victim is Romeo, who survives; the double suicide at the end is, of course, a mistake. These instances of hamartia are engaged by representations of all the social groups in the play: household servants and their masters, boys on the loose, and finally, the titular protagonists. The "action[s] . . . of a certain magnitude" that matter in this play are verbal actions/non-actions: Friar Laurence marries Romeo and Juliet (though we do not actually see this), the Capulets silence their daughter along with her Nurse, both of whom tried to "speak a word" (3.5.160–202) to explain why Juliet cannot marry Paris; the Prince rescinds the promised death sentence on Romeo for "disturb[ing] our streets again" (1.1.96). These verbal "actions" all lead, one way or another, to the play's tragic conclusion, but they are not, strictly speaking, "actions" in the usual sense of the term. If "three civil brawls bred of an airy word" (1.1.87) can unleash the destruction of a city, could accidents – washing blows, street brawls, misinformed suicides, and especially misspoken/ unspoken words – have been the kinds of "action . . . of a certain magnitude" that Aristotle had in mind?

Perhaps they could have been, if we shift Aristotle's emphasis to ask not what con-stitutes action but what constitutes magnitude. Harriett Hawkins suggested that,

> as chaos theory demonstrates, and as has long been obvious in ordinary life (as in comic
> as well as tragic art) very small, morally neutral, individual effects – a chance encounter,

an undelivered letter (as in *Romeo and Juliet*), or an inadvertent dropping of a handkerchief, or someone else's otherwise insignificant inability to tolerate alcohol (as in *Othello*)
– can exponentially compound with other effects and give rise to disproportionate
impacts. (Hawkins 1995: 16).

Hawkins made a strong case for reading a play such as *Romeo and Juliet* as a new, non-
Aristotelian kind of tragedy that represents actions occurring randomly and
thus beyond the control and influence of human beings: new because even the Greeks
or Seneca, staging tragedies that reflected a pagan cosmology, resisted such a
paradigm. For the ancients, someone was always to blame – or to praise; as I have
written elsewhere, tragedy posits a hero who is also a scapegoat, and hamartia is
usually a deliberate, if misconstructed, "missing of the mark" (Liebler 1995: 20–2,
37–9, 41–4).

Despite its tremendous appeal, however, Hawkins's notion of random causality in
Romeo and Juliet too easily exonerates and exculpates the basic civic and social structures of the community contained within "Verona walls," outside of which, as Romeo
says, "there is no world" (3.3.17). As Raymond Williams reminded us, "the relation
between tragedy and order is dynamic. The tragic action is rooted in a disorder, which
indeed, at a particular stage, can seem to have its own stability. But the whole body
of real forces is engaged by the action, often in such a way that the underlying disorder becomes apparent and terrible in overtly tragic ways" (Williams 1966: 66). For
Williams, tragic action inheres in a continuum of actions, where periods of instability are preceded and followed by periods of stability. In this he shares Walter
Benjamin's view that tragedy always implies a future beyond the end of the fifth act,
or, in Benjamin's terms, the victim/hero is sacrificed to "the, as yet unborn, national
community," and the represented action is one "in which new aspects of the life
of the nation become manifest" (Benjamin 1998: 110). Moreover, "violence and
disorder are institutions as well as acts" (Williams 1966: 66); the city or the state
embodies the "institutions" of violence and disorder, and provides the ideal matrix
for the operation of this dynamic. Shakespeare's Verona is just such a city, and just
such a matrix for the violence and disorder, alternately contained and released in an
oscillation that might well continue, as I will suggest below, beyond the scope of the
play, that constitute the real conditions of civic life. The city both is and is identified
by the institutions of violence and disorder that are part of its underlying structure.
In this regard the heroic sacrifice "is designed not only to bring about the restoration
but above all the undermining of an ancient body of law in the linguistic constitution of the renewed community" (Benjamin 1998: 117).

Romeo and Juliet performs an indictment of the civic institutions and structures of
authority represented in the play, shifting the focus off the protagonists who serve as
the agents for that performance, and on to the collective city for which they stand,
and to which, like Shakespeare's later model citizens Coriolanus and Timon, they are
sacrificed. Their micro-function dissolves into the macro-structure that contains them,
evident in the play's last lines, the recycled, persistent contest between the two houses
that confronts us in the play's opening scenes, enclosed within "Verona walls." Walls,

too, are literally structures of authority, erected, sustained, and defended by the institutions and their human representatives that define or make up "the city." Like the
Althusserian "State Apparatuses," both ideological and repressive (Althusser 1971:
144–5), they are the physical and figurative manifestations of a city's identity, the
visible inscription by which it knows itself.

The idea(l) of the walled city, self-contained and carefully managed, and of its
microcosmic analogue, the family compound (similarly walled, self-contained, and
carefully managed), occurs widely throughout late medieval and early modern
writings, and has been well documented. One recent historian observes that "Nowhere
was this ordered society more eagerly portrayed than in the towns" (Cowan
1998: 170); urban writers were themselves heavily invested in promulgating and
protecting a collective vision of the enclosed and clearly defined city-space as the
best of all possible worlds, but "just as the best laid plans for impressive palaces
constructed along well-organized streets intersecting in geometrically perfect squares
were disturbed by the persistence of older, disordered street patterns nearby,
those who believed in an ordered urban society were constantly aware of the threats
to their vision and of the need to keep them under control" (ibid). Cowan wisely
demurs regarding various popular modes of historicizing early modern cities, citing
the view that urban order was always under constant threat from resident disruptive
forces, the alternate view that urban collectivities represented sets of shared cultural
and social values enabling a normative equilibrium, and a further view that "portrays
urban violence as a symptom of a society at war with itself" (p. 172) – all
as reductively determined, implying a single static model of early modern urban
organizations.

The temptation to collapse various urban models is great, but happily unnecessary.
As Gail Kern Paster offered in her now-classic study, the early modern city was as
much an idea as a locus. The city, she observed, "is a product of reason, a function
of mind . . . [It] will appear as an ideal mode of social organization, or at least as a
benevolent consequence of human aspiration" (Paster 1985: 2). Though she did not
discuss *Romeo and Juliet* or Verona in particular, Paster discerned two dominant paradigms of the Renaissance *urbs* that are very helpful in this context: "the city as a visionary embodiment of ideal community . . . or the city as a predatory trap, founded in
fratricide and shadowed by conflict . . . Not surprisingly, therefore, the conventions
of urban literature reveal an openness to antithetical statement, an affinity for paradox"
(p. 3). Shakespeare's primary source for the play, Brooke's *Tragicall Historye*, in the epigraph at the beginning of this essay, introduces Verona as a utopian ideal, an urban
idyll, the best of all possible worlds, "or at the least compared with the best." In
Shakespeare's version, Verona is already a failed *civitas*, and by the end of the play, a
dying *urbs*, its entire younger generation gone. Whatever ordering principles of city
planning and management or ideals of polity might have informed its establishment,
by the time of the play's action (or non-action), those principles and the practices of
orderly government that should have sustained them have already been radically
effaced by the intramural tensions that define Verona.

In this regard we might see some congruence between Shakespeare's London and his imagined Verona: both were cities desperately struggling to control their unruly populations: historians note, for example, a number of disturbances in London in 1595, largely the work of apprentices protesting the high price of fish and butter, and resulting in a doubling of the watch and increased patrols of the streets by provost marshals (Cowan 1998: 180–1). The failure of the play's Prince Escalus to follow this real-life model by tightening controls over either the servants or the principals of the two noble houses, his neglect of basic machiavellian tenets of "Princely" authority, ends with the death of the city. The "sentence of your moved prince" is just that, literally: a sentence, a syntax of words, and has less impact on his "rebellious subjects, enemies to peace" than the "airy word" that bred the previous "three civil brawls" and "thrice disturb'd the quiet of our streets" (1.1.79–89), and perverted the apparatuses of urban order to "mistemper'd weapons" and "neighbour-stained steer" forged originally to defend against external enemies. He can threaten "pain of torture" (84) and "pain of death" (101), but as we see, or hear, in 3.1 after the deaths of Tybalt and Mercutio, he fails to enforce his own sentence, converting it to Romeo's banishment, which he himself calls merely "a fine" (3.1.192), and which, as the play's sequent events play out, "but murders, pardoning those that kill" (3.1.199).

We get in this play no legible map of an orderly city, no guided tour of its venues, no mention of contiguous loci: none of the "walks, /. . . private arbors and new-planted orchards, / On this side Tiber" (3.2.247–9) that help us to "picture" *Julius Caesar*'s Rome, nothing like the Rialto cited as the primary business district in *The Merchant of Venice* (1.3.19, 38, 107; 3.1.1), no sense that our context in the play is any kind of cohesive community,[4] or even the much admired model of a city that Renaissance humanists learned from Vitruvius via Leon Battista Alberti's *De Rei Aedificatoria*, calling for "the disposition of the streets, squares, and public edifices, their being laid out and contrived beautifully and conveniently; for without order, there can be nothing handsome, convenient, or pleasing," or as he goes on to say, safe (quoted in Cowan 1998: 142). Shakespeare's Verona may be understood as a general *locale*, but we are never given, in the play, a clear sense of *locus*.

From the first line of the Chorus's Prologue, we hear of separateness – "two house-holds" – whose differences seem arbitrary insofar as they are "both alike in dignity," and whose architecture is manifested in separate but equal walled estates. Indeed, we hear much about walls – and about walls within walls – as the play progresses: those surrounding Verona enclosing those surrounding the Capulet household, which perhaps (though this is not made clear) in turn enclose the Capulet tomb: decreasing circles of enclosure and isolation progressively squeeze any vestigial sense of communal space to the size of Queen Mab's "empty hazelnut" (1.4.59) or Hamlet's nutshell (2.2.254). Juliet's weaning, we are told by the Nurse, coincided with an earthquake that shook the dovehouse wall (1.3.33). Both the marriage of the protagonists and the death-propelled plan that separates them begin within Friar Laurence's cell, a presumably small enclosure, like Juliet's chamber within the house that sits within the walled garden. Early in the play we hear from his father that Romeo, like some forlorn

vampire, runs from daylight and hides in his room (1.1.135–8); Lady Capulet, mis-
taking her daughter's grief over Romeo's banishment for grief over Tybalt's death,
tells Paris that she is "mew'd up in her heaviness" (3.4.11). In *The Poetics of Space*
Gaston Bachelard defines domestic space as, first of all, *bounded* space; situated anti-
thetically to the "space of hatred and combat," it is a safe space that "concentrates
being within limits that protect" (Bachelard 1969: xxxii). But the walls-within-walls
in this play only enclose an illusion of safety; windows and doors – like those in *Othello*
or *Merchant* – give access to the dangers of the surrounding city.

In *Richard II*, written around the same time as *Romeo and Juliet*, the dying Gaunt
poignantly notes that walls are meant to protect what is enclosed by excluding external dangers; the "silver sea" serves England, he says, "in the office of a wall, / Or as
[a] moat defensive to a house" (2.1.47–8); in Richard's time, protective urban walls
still functioned enough for this line to resonate, among Shakespeare's audiences, as a
nostalgic *ubi sunt*. Up to the early sixteenth century, "the town wall had been one of
the most important signs of the town. As a physical barrier, it was intended to protect
townspeople from all kinds of external dangers, military attack, unwanted visitors,
disease, even the unseen dangers of the night" (Cowan 1998: 138), though of course
they were useless in protecting those within from each other. In *Romeo and Juliet* walls
are deployed to quite different effects: as separators, as signifiers of social status, as
when Capulet's Gregory says he will "take the wall of any man or maid of Montague's"
(1.1.12), and then, on next thought, as an assist to gestures of power; he "will push
Montague's men from the wall, and thrust his maids to the wall" (17–18). Thus the
first mention of Verona's interior boundaries is given in the distracting context of a
macho challenge followed by a bawdy jest about an act of sexual violence against the
"maids" of a specific house: the sexual is immediately framed in terms of the political. These intra-city "walls" serve not as protecting structures but as sites of confrontation and attack.[5] Similarly, at 2.1.5, Romeo eludes his friends by leaping over
"this orchard wall."[6] The dangerous signification of "wall" intensifies in the next scene
when Juliet questions Romeo's appearance in (perhaps) this same orchard: "How
cam'st thou hither, tell me, and wherefore? / The orchard walls are high and hard to
climb, / And the place death, considering who thou art, / If any of my kinsmen find
thee here" (2.2.62–5), and Romeo refers to the structures as "stony limits" that
"cannot hold love out" (67), but also cannot *let* it out.

When the danger inheres within its walls, as it does in Verona, the ideal of the
city is already compromised, perverted from its original purposes like the "mistemper'd weapons" turned against neighbors. We see the city's agonistic struggle to
survive, and we see it fail. Little fortresses – "two households" – have already sub-
divided the Great Ideal of the polis. Verona is a city of traceable ghettos[7] marked by
the colors of Capulet and Montague: it is no wonder that innumerable modern and
postmodern performances of the play, from *West Side Story* to Baz Luhrmann's 1996
film, have imagined the play in the setting of urban turfs, where the liminal spaces
between compounds are, as in the play itself, susceptible to gang warfare.

Does Verona stand for Shakespeare's London? Probably not, and not least because both the model and the inception of each respective city is different. Indeed, the urban planning that marked the notable Italian city-states did not happen in England "for 300 years before the Restoration . . . The real English inventions are the suburb, the garden city and the suburban lawn" (Pelling 2000: 154). Although London was "a relatively bounded community, largely defined by its walls and the jurisdiction of the mayor and aldermen" (Griffiths and Jenner 2000: 2), its walls were arguably the most permeable of urban enclosures, so much so that its "extramural parishes . . . were as large as any other city in the British Isles" (ibid: 2); even William Harrison's *Description of England* distinguishes London uniquely in his list of parishes and market towns by the designation "London, within the walls and without" (Harrison 1994: 219). London's operation as an urban center was increasingly swollen by accretions of a population that tended to expand with cyclical infusions of needed workers following decimation by plague outbreaks (which in itself might account for the rise of city comedy as a response to the explosive energy of London's engorgement). In contrast to Shakespeare's shrinking Verona, London saw a "rapid growth in size and population drawn from elsewhere in England" in the course of the sixteenth century alone (Paster 1985: 6). Paster further notes that Shakespeare was apparently much less interested than Jonson or Middleton in the particulars of life in his adopted city, instead "constructing a life built around the antitheses, city and country" (ibid: 7). "City" and "country" are in this sense abstractions; Shakespeare's Verona is an idea of a city, an "anywhere" that happens to have been given a named Italian locus in the Boaistuau/Painter/Brooke sources.

Far from "standing" for expansive London whose bulging populous center radiated outward to suburbs, Shakespeare's Verona implodes, collapsing "city" and "community" into "two households" and progressively smaller walled enclosures. The Verona of Shakespeare's source(s), or indeed any similarly designed urban center evincing a deliberate structure, serves to point a different kind of antithesis from the one Paster identifies: in this case the contrast is not between city and country but between an ordered urban *habitus* (to use Bourdieu's term), a point to which I shall return, and the shambles of such a city when the structures of order and authority fail. Shakespeare's Verona is not London; it is not even the historical Verona. It manifests the archetypal cities that Augustine identified as foundational: Cain's City of Enoch, Romulus' Rome – cities established by fratricides (Paster 1985: 10). For Augustine, the earthly city, "which is nothing but a number of people bound together by some tie of fellowship" (Augustine 1972: 608), instantiates a choice to live by human predilection rather than by divine precept;[8] thus it embeds *ab initio* two of the hallmarks of Aristotelian tragedy: dilemma and hamartia. "Appearances of the city in literature . . . tend to be marked either by ambivalence or by a rhetorical vehemence that conceals deep social uneasiness. Great cities are founded by those who have murdered their brothers, probably *because* they have murdered their brothers: aspiration is compensation, shadowed forever by guilt" (Paster 1985: 11).

Although there is no mention in the play of precedent *brudermord*, there is a compelling imbrication of that foundational paradigm in the threads of kinship that inform the play, which we hear about unmistakably in the Prince's sorrowful confession at the end that he, too, has "lost a brace of kinsmen" (5.3.294). We hear it even more directly, however metaphorically, in Capulet's line immediately following the Prince's: "O brother Montague, give me thy hand" (5.3.295), a gesture that is as pathetic as it is empty: too little, too late, and pointless given the feud's cost to both the families' and the city's future. Of course "brother" is figurative rather than literal here, but what does that matter? Kinship is an affect as much as it is a fact of relationship. If Augustine's caveats about the fratricidal origins of secular cities (noted likewise by Girard 1977: 4, 61; 1978: 164, 197; see also Quinones 1991) have merit, then the Verona of this play replicates its mythical (biblical and Roman) antecedents; it can do little or nothing to avoid its destiny and, in solid Aristotelian terms, its tragedy: Aristotle identified kin-killing as what "must be sought" for tragic action (Aristotle 1987: 46). The Prologue's citation of "star-cross'd lovers" bleeds out to encompass not only the eponymous adolescents but also their families, their extended households, their entire community. Prince Escalus is left to grieve but ironically not to rebuild. A devastated Rome founded by fratricide can, at the end of *Titus Andronicus* (which immediately preceded *Romeo and Juliet* in Shakespeare's tragic canon), imagine a new beginning, as Marcus exhorts its remnants to "let me teach you how to knit again / This scattered corn into one mutual sheaf, / These broken limbs again into one body" (5.3.70–2). *Romeo and Juliet's* Verona does not allow even that fantasy of renewal: except for Benvolio, its entire younger generation is gone – and in the 1597 Q1, "yong Benvolio is deceased too" (K3r). "[The] wiping out of the younger generation is complete" (Dessen 1995: 113); the final tableau is "a veritable Slaughter of the Innocents" (Harcourt 1999: 47). The Nurse's Susan "is with God" (1.3.19); Capulet reminds Paris that Juliet is his only remaining child: "Earth hath swallowed all my hopes but she" (1.2.14); in this play we have a repeated emphasis on dead children. Like *Titus*, *Romeo and Juliet* gives us a community on the verge of extinction, although in the earlier play there is at least a gesture towards regeneration. In tragedy, Ares always beats Eros. In *Romeo and Juliet* "regeneration" is heavily ironized in the grieving fathers' promises to erect two golden statues, inorganic metal fetishes that stand for the lost children. Compounding the irony is the exchange between these two bereaved almost-kinsmen. Busy at the end out-bidding each other for fitting monuments, they will separate the effigies of their respective children, who died entwined in each other's bodies, by placing them side-by-side: "As rich shall Romeo's by his lady's lie" (5.3.301), says Capulet, one breath after asking for (but perhaps not receiving?) his "brother" Montague's hand in place of his "daughter's jointure" (5.3.295–6). Separation, isolation, juxtaposition, side-by-sideness instead of oneness, prevail even in death over the (here impossible) union of marriage and its (here thwarted) promise of regeneration.[9]

More obviously than in any other Shakespearean tragedy, *Romeo and Juliet* foregrounds the community's culpability, though to a certain extent the word "community" is misleading. If Verona constitutes a community, that constitution is already fragmented and reduced to "two households" whose "new mutiny" (Prologue 3) rereleases the "plague a' both . . . houses" (3.1.91, 99, 106), and spreads contamination "Where civil blood makes civil hands unclean" (Prologue 4). "Plague" is never in Shakespeare an idle figure of speech. It signals all the uncontrolled virulence of an epidemic, evident in the Prince's inability to stop it (like Richard II's in the jousting debacle), for which he suffers, along with the Montagues and Capulets, a "lost . . . brace of kinsmen. All are punish'd" (5.3.295). At the same time, "plague" is more than a metaphor. There is a real outbreak in Verona that quarantines the city and prevents Friar Laurence's all-important message about Juliet's fake "death" from reaching Romeo in Mantua. As Friar John reports:

> Going to find a barefoot brother out,
> One of our order, to associate me,
> *Here in this city* visiting the sick,
> And finding him, the searchers of the town,
> Suspecting that we both were in a house
> Where the infectious pestilence did reign,
> Seal'd up the doors and would not let us forth,
> So that my speed to Mantua there was stay'd.
> (5.2.5–12; emphasis added)[10]

Romeo must leave for Mantua "before the Watch be set / Or by the break of day disguis'd from hence" (3.3.166–7); open passage from the city is forbidden. This plague outbreak quite literally informs Romeo's plaintive

> Heaven is here
> Where Juliet lives, and every cat and dog
> And little mouse, every unworthy thing,
> Live here in heaven and may look on her,
> But Romeo may not. More validity,
> More honorable state, more courtship lives
> In carrion flies than Romeo . . . (3.3.29–35)

The association of plague with small mammals is confirmed earlier in Mercutio's dying words: "A plague a' both your houses! 'Zounds, a dog, a rat, a mouse, a cat, to scratch a man to death!" (3.1. 99–101). The language in both passages reminds us that during plague outbreaks the freedom of the city belongs only to strays, vermin, and carrion flies. We are further reminded that plague was in fact carried by fleas in turn hosted by "every cat and dog / And little mouse." Although such epidemiology was not demonstrably known in Shakespeare's day (Barroll 1991: 92–6),[11] the connection now seems inescapable. Arguably less compelling because it was a common enough epithet, the staccato repetition of "dog" in reference to the men of the Montague house with which the Capulet servant Samson peppers the opening scene (1.1.8, 11) sets at least

an auditory stage for the later iterations of canine hosts as carriers of "plague on . . .
houses." Most likely written and performed between 1594 and 1596 (Gibbons 1980:
31), *Romeo and Juliet* almost immediately followed a massive plague outbreak in
London in 1593.[12] Of all the plague eruptions during Shakespeare's early years, "none
was wholly comparable to the violence of the pestilence that struck as Shakespeare's
dramatic writing career was beginning . . . In one year at least 15,000 persons of a
London population of 123,000 died – more than 12 percent" (Barroll 1991: 74). Aside
from the very real impact of city-wide mortality on Shakespeare's audience, such decimation leaves a profound after-effect on the collective psychology of the survivors.
The medical historian Margaret Pelling suggests that persistent anxiety about plague
was a more powerful affect than the actual outbreak might have been:

> [It] is plague as epidemic which has been accommodated [by general and literary his-
> torians]; the social consequences of endemic disease, like the mind sets produced by a
> constant threat of disease, have proved more elusive. The "urban penalty" – excess mor-
> tality – is well established on an aggregate basis, but we have little idea of what it meant
> for those most concerned. (Pelling 2000: 160)[13]

Her implicit interrogation of plague's "meaning" reminds us of Antonin Artaud's
more abstract analogy of plague and theatre, both of which constitute "a formidable
call to the forces that impel the mind by example to the source of its conflicts" and
"the revelation, the bringing forth, the exteriorization of a depth of latent cruelty by
means of which all the perverse possibilities of the mind, whether of an individual or
a people, are localized" (Artaud 1958: 30; see also Liebler 1995: 47–8). Ian Munro
suggests what plague signified to the City of London specifically:

> As the quintessential urban malady, plague is a spatial disease; it refigures the lived and
> symbolic space of the city, altering and transforming the urban aspect. At the same time,
> its resonances are temporal, recalling and recycling a long historical and literary tradi-
> tion of urban dissolution. The plague city is always plural: London under plague is
> haunted by Florence, Rome, Jerusalem, Athens, Thebes, the cities of the plain. (Munro
> 2000: 242–3)

It is also haunted by Verona. Brooke mentions plague only once, and very explicitly
as an outbreak within the house of the Franciscan whose company Friar John seeks for
the journey to Mantua. In this matter Shakespeare follows his source to the letter, but
spreads the disease as an idea that neither quarantine nor walls can contain or control.
The "presence of plague mirrors a crisis of urban meaning catalyzed by London's explosive population growth," and further recalls Artaud's notion that "the effects of the
disease *are* the disease" (Munro 2000: 244, 246). Thus, whether we read *Romeo and
Juliet*'s numerous references to plague as literal or metaphoric makes little difference
to the perception of a deadly anxiety whose inflection as the "plague o' both your
houses," the violence of the feud and its tragic results, seems to have been inevitable.

There is nothing about this inevitability that suggests the generic failure of the play as a tragedy. I have argued elsewhere that hamartia, the hallmark of tragedy, is the attempt – by the represented community as much as by the protagonist(s) in a play – to do the right thing in a context or circumstances that will not allow the right thing to be done (Liebler 1995: 42–4). Hamartia is specifically an act of misrecognition. On this view, it is important to suggest just what it is that is "misrecognized" in *Romeo and Juliet*. Among other things, the literal presence of plague in Verona seems to be effaced, noted only in Friar John's lines quoted above. The city is, as modern jargon has it, "in denial"; it has displaced any recognition of a real biological threat to its survival and focused inward, onto an "ancient grudge" whose source, exactly like that of the plague, is never identified. Aligned with this displacement is a repeated emphasis on the neighboring city of Mantua to which Romeo is banished. Verona is mentioned in the dialogue of the play eleven times; Mantua gets thirteen notices. What does this mean? Mantua is not only the place of Romeo's banishment; it is plague-free, and would in another context be considered a place of safety. Mantua, the locale of the apothecary's dwelling, has strict laws against disseminating poison, as Romeo acknowledges (5.1.51) and the poor apothecary unnecessarily reminds him (5.1.66–7); poverty and its consequent criminal acts (5.1.69–74) may threaten that city (Chris Fitter argues that this was the dominant situation in London around the time of the play: Fitter 2000: 160), but there they are interdicted, prevented, or punished. Mantua was also, we learn from the Nurse early on, where the Capulet parents had been (on what business or holiday we are not told) during Juliet's weaning and Verona's earthquake (1.3.28), and where the Capulets still have friends, one of whom Lady Capulet hopes to solicit to kill Romeo in revenge for Tybalt's death (3.5.88–91). Mantua is, then, whatever Verona is not; it is a city where the rule of law still has some strength: in Brooke, the apothecary is hanged (l. 2993). In contrast, in both Shakespeare and Brooke, Verona's prince arbitrarily commutes his original threat of a death sentence, and defers judgment – "Some shall be pardon'd, and some punish'd" (5.3.307) – to an extradramatic "future" time. Mantua is a place where plague is not allowed to enter, and where, like Lysander's widow-aunt's house "remote seven leagues" from Athens in *Romeo and Juliet*'s counter-play *A Midsummer Night's Dream* (1.1.157–9), a displaced lover might have found safety were he not already carrying his city's death in his blood, and a young couple might have fulfilled a Friar's scheme: "that very night / Shall Romeo bear thee hence to Mantua / And this shall free thee from this present shame" (4.1.116–18).

If Verona is neither Mantua nor London, it must be a dream of a city turned to a nightmare, like the happy visions of "ladies' lips, who straight on kisses dream, / Which oft the angry Mab with blisters plagues" (1.4.74–5), perverted to duress – or to herpes simplex – in Mercutio's cynical formulation. In this way, too, Verona bears on its collective body the mark of plague – Mercutio's speech narrates the most inward, isolated, chambered visions that when carried to the waking world turn to ashes. Romeo likewise has a dream (1.4.50): his, unrevealed, may be (as Gibbons suggests in a gloss on this line) of "Some consequence yet hanging in the stars" that shall "expire the term / Of a despised life clos'd in my breast / By some forfeit of untimely death" (1.4.107–11). Significantly, such chambering mirrors the measures taken by urban authorities during plague outbreaks in London. The usual prophylaxis for containing plague in the city was "boarding up the houses with the plague victims inside, left to die in total isolation from community, the door of the house marked with a cross that identified nothing but the illness" (Munro 2000: 258), thereby stripping the infected of all connection with anyone but fellow victims. In the play this is of course exactly what prevents Friar John's delivery of the life-saving letter to Romeo in Mantua. It is also a way of describing the isolated but similarly infected "two households" that are all we know of Verona. The life of the city contracts Mercutio's loaded curse, "A plague o' both your houses," to a two-word epithet: plague-house. "Plague" is thus a doubly inflected signifier: it is at once what kills the city and what *is* the city.

Like any good tragic protagonist, Verona commits suicide, kills itself by the failure of its own immune system, here figured in the weakened hierarchical structures of authority that cannot or will not look after their own collective best interests. These structures are the *habitus* Bourdieu defined in *The Logic of Practice* as

> systems of durable, transposable, dispositions, structured structures predisposed to function as structuring structures, that is, as principles which generate and organize practices and representations that can be objectively adapted to their outcomes without presupposing a conscious aiming at ends or an express mastery of the operations necessary in order to attain them. Objectively "regulated" and "regular" without being in any way the product of obedience to rules, they can be collectively orchestrated without being the product of the organizing action of a conductor. (Bourdieu 1990: 53)

I might add, without being remediable by a single conductor: even Prince Escalus is victim as much as cause of the city's collective collapse. Bourdieu's definition, it seems to me, can serve as a workable definition of a city or community through which we get a fairly accurate picture of what happens in Shakespeare's Verona. In an earlier version of that definition, he identified "the habitus" as "history turned into nature, i.e., denied as such" (Bourdieu 1977: 78), naturalized to "the way things are," inscribed as inevitable because of what he fortuitously calls "genesis amnesia" (p. 79), or,

> the product of the work of inculcation and appropriation necessary in order for those products of collective history, the objective structures (e.g. of language, economy, etc.) to succeed in reproducing themselves more or less completely, in the form of durable dispositions, in the organisms (which one can, if one wishes, call individuals) lastingly subjected to the same conditionings, and hence placed in the same material conditions of existence. (Ibid: 85)

This is exactly the operation of the "three civil brawls bred of an airy word" which hangs as a motto over the city of Verona in the play. As nearly every critic of this play has noticed, no one in Verona seems to remember or care what that "airy word" was that started the feud between the two houses. It doesn't matter anyway; it has become accepted as the inevitable and incurable condition of life in Shakespeare's Verona, constituted by and constitutive of the city's *habitus*. "It is because subjects do not, strictly speaking, know what they are doing that what they do has more meaning than they know" (Bourdieu 1977: 79). The subjects in this case are not, or not only, the Capulets and Montagues, at least not in the strict sense of the two nuclear families exclusively. As we have seen, the family is what we would now call "extended": its servants, its retainers, the Prince who is related to both Mercutio and Paris, are all implicated in this larger *famiglia*. Again Bourdieu supplies a useful frame for understanding these complex extensions: "'interpersonal' relations are never, except in appearance, *individual-to-individual* relationships and . . . the truth of the interaction is never entirely contained in the interaction" (Bourdieu 1977: 81). It is thus impossible, or at least impractical, to think of the play's action as an isolated moment or set of moments; we are told often enough in the play that this feud, this plague, has been going on time out of mind, and because the city (the Prince and the principal families) can do nothing or say nothing to alter its trajectory, plague/feud wins, contained and at the same time uncontained within city walls, and the city dies.

In this play whose "actions" are mostly words, language is also a structure of authority. Writing about New York City, with an opening focus on "Seeing Manhattan from the 110th floor of the World Trade Center . . . A city composed of paroxysmal places in monumental reliefs" (de Certeau 1984: 91) that in 2002 seems ironic if not indeed macabre, Michel de Certeau offers what might serve as an analysis of Verona's fragility:

> The language of power is itself "urbanizing," but the city is left prey to contradictory movements that counter-balance and combine themselves outside the reach of panoptic power. The city becomes the dominant theme in political legends, but it is no longer a field of programmed and regulated operations. Beneath the discourses that ideologize the city, the ruses and combinations of powers that have no readable identity proliferate; without points where one can take hold of them, without rational transparency, they are impossible to administer. (Ibid: 95)

The failure of "the language of power" in the play, through the silencing of the Nurse, Juliet, and Friar John who might have spoken or delivered trajectory-shifting words, the ineffectual because unenforced "sentence" of the Prince, are all part of Verona's *habitus*, its endemic condition of existence and operation, which is simultaneously the condition of its demise. In the ideal city, structures of authority and what Derrida calls, in *Acts of Literature*, "a system of marks," would "deny, while taking note of it, non-coincidence, the separation of monads, the disconnection of experiences, the multiplicity of worlds, . . . or the irremediable detour of a letter" (Derrida, quoted in Murray 1997: 95). Verona, the collective protagonist of the tragedy called *Romeo and Juliet*, misses all those marks.

NOTES

1   I am grateful to Bernice Kliman for suggesting to me the play's urban focus.

2   Quotations from *Romeo and Juliet* follow Brian Gibbons's Arden edition (1980). All others follow *The Riverside Shakespeare*, ed. G. B. Evans (1974).

3   Gibbons glosses "remember thy washing blow" (1.1.60) as "swashing," citing Golding's translation of Ovid's *Metamorphoses* (1567) and Stanyhurst's *Aeneis* (1582) for support, although only Q4 gives "swashing" and Q1 omits the line altogether. Jill Levenson also reads "washing" as "swashing," or "fencing strokes that slash with great force, coarse preliminaries to Tybalt's style of dueling" (Levenson 1995: 90), citing the *OED* (ppl. a. 2). But the *OED* refers to *Romeo and Juliet* as evidence for this meaning, and lists the meaning as "obscure." It therefore seems to me that reading "washing" as "swashing" may be an editorial back-formation. Conversely, the *OED* gives several instances of "washing-bat or washing beetle, a wooden bat used to beat or pound clothes in the process of washing." In several early texts – e.g., Skelton's *Merie Tales* (1566), Richard Harvey's *Plaine Percivall, the Peace-Maker of England* (1590, p. 33), Fletcher's *The Woman's Prize* (1625, 2.5), and his *Wild Goose Chase* (1621, 5.4.36–8) – a "washing-blow" is delivered, in each case, with a laundry implement (mis)used as a battering device. Thus it makes more sense, in my view, to read "washing" literally, for its imputation that servants wielding swords in streets are out of their normal sphere of activity and not specifically trained in the arts of fencing.

4   Ralph Berry's brief discussion of the play emphasizes its frequent gestures toward conciliation, notably in Capulet's willingness to admit Romeo to the party, and in the guest-list itself, which includes Mercutio and "a fair cross-section of Veronese society . . . Verona, everywhere one touches it, is a close-knit and stable community, for all its brawls" (Berry 1988: 38–9).

5   On the play's performance of "the dilemma of masculinity" with particular reference to "walls," see Applebaum (1997); see also Kahn (1981).

6   Capell thought this was the wall surrounding the Capulet orchard. See Gibbons's gloss on the line (1980: 123 n. 5).

7   The *OED*, 2nd edn. (1989) lists the familiar meaning of "ghetto" – "The quarter in a city, chiefly in Italy, to which the Jews were restricted," as its first entry, with the earliest recorded English instance of the word found in Coryat's *Crudities* (1611). Within the second meaning, however, are terms more pertinent to this study: "2. transf. and fig. . . . an area, etc., occupied by an isolated group; an isolated or segregated group, community, or area." The etymology of the word is uncertain.

8   "[The] earthly city was created by self-love reaching the point of contempt for God, the Heavenly City by the love of God carried as far as contempt of self. In fact, the earthly city glories in itself, the Heavenly City glories in the Lord. The former looks for glory from men . . . the lust for domination lords it over its princes as over the nations it subjugates . . . Consequently, in the earthly city its wise men who live by men's standards have pursued the goods of the body or of their own mind, or of both" (Augustine 1972: 593).

9   For a provocatively Derridean reading of "impossibility" in this play, see Murray (1997: 78–98). On doubling and difference in this last scene, see especially p. 94.

10 Ian Munro notes an association between plague and monasteries that seems particularly resonant in regard to this passage: in 1607, "the Recorder of London mentions four large houses (most likely former monastic properties) converted into tenements that together housed eight thousand people; in one house alone eight hundred had died during the 1603 plague" (Munro 2000: 251).

11 Doubtless because the scope of his study is restricted, as the book's subtitle indicates, to "The Stuart Years," Barroll does not mention *Romeo and Juliet*. Where he does refer to Shakespeare's Elizabethan plays, he does so only in regard to early Jacobean court revivals, from which list *Romeo and Juliet* is absent.

12 The conjunction of likely composition date and massive plague outbreak in London is barely noted in critical discussions of the play; Gibbons, quoting Foakes's Arden edition of *The Comedy of Errors*, notes it only in passing in a comment on the likely proximity of the *Comedy*'s date to that of the tragedy (Gibbons 1980: 28). In an essay on contemporary topicality in *Romeo and Juliet*, Chris Fitter cites "the escalating [...] fear of dearth between 1594 and 1597, and the [...]5) as key evidence of the play's political refer-[...]k of plague that nearly – if only temporarily – [...] the same volume, on plague in early modern [...]t.

[...]an mortality" was "a penalty borne mostly by [...]may further bear on our reading of child death

[...]THER READING

[...]aratuses (Notes Towards an Investigation). In
[...]r. New York: Monthly Review Press, 127–86.
[...]Pressures of Masculinity in *Romeo and Juliet*.

[...]ommentary, trans. and ed. S. Halliwell. Chapel

[...]. Richards. New York: Grove.
[...]agans, trans. H. Bettenson. London: Penguin

[...]Boston, MA: Beacon Press.
[...]eater: The Stuart Years. Ithaca, NY: Cornell

[...]akis and N. C. Liebler (eds.) *Tragedy*. London:

[...]hlands, NJ: Humanities Press International.
[...]R. Nice. Cambridge: Cambridge University

[...]CA: Stanford University Press.
[...]nd Juliet. In G. Bullough (ed.) *Narrative and*
[...]bia University Press, I: 284–363.
[...]old.
[...]trans. S. Randall. Berkeley: University of

[...]Theatrical Vocabulary. In J. L. Halio (ed.)
[...]pretation. Newark: University of Delaware

[...]MA: Houghton Mifflin.
[...]us their men": *Romeo and Juliet*, Dearth, and
[...]–83.
[...]re. London: Methuen.
[...]Baltimore, MD: Johns Hopkins University
Press.
——(1978). *"To Double Business Bound": Essays on Literature, Mimesis, and Anthropology*. Baltimore, MD: Johns Hopkins University Press.

Griffiths, P. and Jenner, M. S. R. (eds.) (2000). *Londinopolis: Essays in the Cultural and Social History of Early Modern London*. Manchester: Manchester University Press.

Harcourt, J. B. (1999). "Children of Divers Kind": A Reading of *Romeo and Juliet*. In S. Orgel and S. Keilen (eds.) *Shakespeare and Gender*. New York: Garland, 135–47.

Harrison, W. (1994) [1587]. *The Description of England*, ed. G. Edelen. New York: Dover.

Hawkins, H. (1995). *Strange Attractors: Literature, Culture, and Chaos Theory*. New York and Hemel Hempstead: Prentice-Hall/Harvester Wheatsheaf.

Kahn, C. (1981). *Man's Estate: Masculine Identity in Shakespeare*. Berkeley: University of California Press, 82–103.

Levenson, J. L. (1995). "Alla stoccado carries it away": Codes of Violence in *Romeo and Juliet*. In J. L. Halio (ed.) *Shakespeare's Romeo and Juliet: Texts, Contexts, and Interpretation*. Newark: University of Delaware Press, 83–96.

Levenson, J. L. and Gaines, B. (eds.) (2000). *Romeo and Juliet 1597*. Malone Society Reprints, 163. Oxford: Oxford University Press.

Liebler, N. C. (1995). *Shakespeare's Festive Tragedy: The Ritual Foundations of Genre*. London: Routledge.

Munro, I. (2000). The City and Its Double: Plague Time in Early Modern London. *English Literary Renaissance*, 30, 2, 241–61.

Murray, T. (1997). *Drama Trauma: Specters of Race and Sexuality in Performance, Video, and Art*. London: Routledge.

Neill, M. (1997). *Issues of Death: Mortality and Identity in English Renaissance Tragedy*. Oxford: Clarendon Press.

Paster, G. K. (1985). *The Idea of the City in the Age of Shakespeare*. Athens: University of Georgia Press.

Pelling, M. (2000). Skirting the City? Disease, Social Change and Divided Households in the Seventeenth Century. In P. Griffiths and M. S. R. Jenner (eds.) *Londinopolis*. Manchester: Manchester University Press, 154–75.

Quinones, R. J. (1991). *The Changes of Cain: Violence and the Lost Brother in Cain and Abel Literature*. Princeton, NJ: Princeton University Press.

Snyder, S. (1979). *The Comic Matrix of Shakespeare's Tragedies*. Princeton, NJ: Princeton University Press.

Williams, R. (1966). *Modern Tragedy*. Stanford, CA: Stanford University Press.

16

"He that thou knowest thine": Friendship and Service in *Hamlet*

Michael Neill

When, at the beginning of *Hamlet*, Horatio and Marcellus follow Barnardo onto the battlements of Elsinore, they are met by a repetition of the famous challenge with which their comrade opened the scene: "Who is there?" (1.1.15). This is the question that, in Maynard Mack's well-known formulation, establishes the "interrogative mood" of the tragedy (Mack 1952; cf. Levin 1959); and, as numerous critics have observed, it can be read as a metaphor for the play's elaborate interrogation of identity, an interrogation that, at the psychological level, centers on the Prince's claim to have "that within which passes show" (1.2.88).[1] It is, however, worth paying more attention to the literal context, including the new watchmen's response to the sentry's challenge, which, not surprisingly, directs attention to the social and political concerns of the play, rather than to the inward "mysteries" boasted by its protagonist. When the challenge is repeated, it issues, as it should, from the duty-sentry, rather than his nervous replacement; and the response seems routine: "Friends to this ground," Horatio answers. "And liegemen," adds Marcellus, "to the Dane." On the face of it, both replies simply paraphrase Barnardo's slightly more oblique "Long live the king!" (l. 3). Each man identifies himself through a formal assertion of allegiance; for what matters most here, naturally enough, is not individual selfhood but group loyalty.

On closer inspection, however, their formulaic utterances turn out to be significantly nuanced: Barnardo's subsequent reference to "the king that's dead" (l. 48) serves as a reminder that "Long live the King!" traditionally completed the solemn announcement that "The King is dead" with a consolatory equivocation on the fiction of monarchical immortality – so that the "who?" of the watchmen's challenge touches fleetingly on royal identity and authority even as it seeks to "unfold" the immediate agents of that authority. In this context Marcellus's identification of the King simply as "the Dane" can appear carefully unspecific – a more tactful version of Hubert's ironic evasion in *King John*, when he proclaims his loyalty to "The King of England, when we know the King" (*King John*, 2.1.363); while Horatio's declaration of allegiance to "this ground" – to the land of Denmark, as opposed to the person of the King – sounds even more circumspect.[2] But if the two men are linked in this way, their choice of epithets to describe themselves – "friends" and "liegemen" – suggests a slight, but potentially important, difference in the way they construct their relation to the state. The strong trochaic counterpointing of "friends" emphasizes the key term of a pair whose local meanings appear almost interchangeable, but which will become increasingly divergent as the action of the play unfolds. "Friend," in fact, is a word under significant social pressure in this period – as indeed is the whole vocabulary of feudal "service" to which "liegemen" belongs[3] – and thinking about those pressures and the ways in which they are reflected in *Hamlet* can illuminate aspects of the tragedy that might otherwise seem unremarkable.[4]

The hierarchical arrangement of human relationships in the dispensation of universal service, which early moderns inherited from the feudal system, meant that "friend" and "servant" could be virtually synonymous – hence the condescending usage exemplified in Claudius's welcome to his returning ambassadors as "my good *friends*!" (2.2.62), or in the soothing style of his command to Rosencrantz and Guildenstern ("*Friends* both, go join you with some further aid"; 4.1.34), and even more obviously in Hamlet's addressing Polonius as "friend" (2.2.203). But humanist writers, elaborating ideas derived from the classical moral philosophy of Plato, Aristotle, and Cicero, had popularized a very different notion of friendship which set it in opposition to service: if service was constrained, deferential, and governed by reciprocal but unequal sets of duties and interests, friendship was freely given, disinterested, and governed only by altruistic good will. Thus conceived, friendship was an important instrument in the humanist program for shaping a new kind of civil subject, whose place in the social order would be determined as much by a personal network of affective ties as by the traditional obligations of allegiance and kinship.[5] At the very beginning of his section on friendship in the *Nicomachean Ethics* (Books VIII–IX) Aristotle had argued that "friendship would seem to hold cities together;"[6] and for writers like Montaigne and Bacon, it was the supreme expression of the sociable instinct that Aristotle had described as distinguishing human beings from all other creatures. "There is nothing to which Nature hath more addressed us than to societie," writes Montaigne. "And *Aristotle* saith, *that perfect Lawgivers have had more regardfull care of friendship than of justice.*"[7] Bacon opens his essay "Of Friendship" by quoting the most famous passage in the *Politics*: "*whosoever is delighted in solitude is either a wild beast or a god*"; and he goes on to gloss this aphorism as an illustration of his topic: "whosoever in the frame of his nature and affections, is unfit for *friendship*, he taketh it of the beast, and not from humanity."[8]

Since it constitutes the very foundation of the *polis*, friendship is thus a social and political virtue, even if, as Bacon remarks, it is a "word which is received between private men" (Bacon 1906: 81). Yet in relation to the fiercely hierarchical ordering of early modern society, it could also appear anomalous, since, as Aristotle had repeatedly insisted, "friendship is said to be equality" and "equality is friendship" (*Nicomachean Ethics*, viii, 5, 1157b; ix, 7, 1168b; Pakaluk 1991: 37, 61).[9] Friendship must "involve equality, since both friends get the same and wish the same for each other" – a similarity reflecting the profound mutual identification according to which each partner was recognised as the other's "second self": "The excellent person is related to his friend in the same way that he is related to himself, since a friend is another himself" (viii.6, 1158b; ix, 9, 1170b; Pakaluk 1991: 38, 65).[10]

Seen from this perspective, friendship can appear to be a fundamentally anti-hierarchical form of association: indeed, insofar as Aristotle's idea of the *polis* is of a *koinonia* (community or association) of equal citizens joined in "concord" by the bonds of political amity, friendship may even be thought of as a virtue with a pronounced republican bias.[11] It is, I think, no coincidence that Montaigne should begin and end his disquisition "Of Friendship" with reflections on the political writing of his beloved La Boètie – in particular, the essay "in honour of liberty and against tyranny" which (he claims) formed the initial "medium" of the intense intimacy that the essay celebrates. A similar imaginative link between friendship and republican idealism is apparent in Shakespeare's tragedy of tyrannicide, *Julius Caesar*, where the conspiracy to restore Roman "liberty" is conceived as an alliance of "gentle friends" (2.1.171), at whose center is the intense affective bond between Brutus and Cassius; and this link becomes even more explicit in the Restoration conspiracy drama *Venice Preserved* (1682), where the embrace of friendship becomes the symbol of that "liberty" and allegiance to the "common good" which the conspirators hold up against the "tyranny" of the Venetian oligarchy:[12]

> Once more embrace, my friends – we'll all embrace –
> United thus, we are the mighty engine
> Must twist this rooted empire from its basis! (2.3.41–3)

The social equality assumed by classical ideals of friendship conflicted, of course, with the insistence by theorists of service that servants were bound to their masters by an "undissoluble bond of assured friendship" (I.M. 1968: 114–50);[13] and the tension between these opposing constructions of domestic relationships is vividly illustrated in a text like Angel Day's *The English Secretary* (1599). Day is at pains to argue that the peculiarly intimate nature of the secretary's office, as the living repository of his master's most private secrets, renders him "in one condition as a *seruant* . . . [but] in a second respect as a *Friend*" (Day 1967: 104). However, Day concedes, "there can be no Friend where an inequalitie remaineth, [because t]wixt the partie commaunded and him that commaundeth, there is no societie, and therefore no *Friendship* where resteth a *Superioritie*" (p. 111); and so he has to demonstrate that the "*simpathie* of affections" between master and secretary, combined with the "friendlie *Fidelitie* . . . voluntarily embraced" by the latter, links them in a "friendlie knot of love" that is capable of overcoming mere "inequality of estate" with a superior "equalitie of affections" (pp. 112–14). But the contorted and ultimately circular nature of Day's argument indicates the felt difficulty of reconciling the two roles.

The egalitarian bias of true friendship meant that it was, as Bacon observed, virtually unobtainable for princes (no matter how intensely they might desire it) because it demanded an equality inimical to their authority:

> It is a strange thing to observe, how high a rate, great kings and monarchs, do set upon this fruit of *friendship* . . . so great as they purchase it, many times, at the hazard of their own safety, and greatness. For princes, in regard of the distance of their fortune, from that of their subjects and servants, cannot gather this *fruit*; except (to make themselves capable thereof) they raise some persons, to be as it were companions, and almost equals to themselves, which many times sorteth to inconvenience . . . And we see plainly, that this hath been done, not by weak and passionate *princes* only, but by the wisest, and most politic that ever reigned; who have oftentimes joined to themselves, some of their servants; whom . . . themselves have called *friends*. (Bacon 1906: 81)

So in Marlowe's *Edward II* the King begins his disastrous reign by summoning his minion Gaveston to "share the kingdom with thy dearest friend" (1.1.2), identifying himself, in the language of classical friendship, as "Thy friend, thy self, another Gaveston" (1.1.142), and insisting upon the "equal" condition that the favorite can claim by virtue of his innate "worth" (1.1.160–1).

It is just the problematic shift that occurs when "servants" are "called *friends*" which Shakespeare traces in his sonnet sequence, where the role of the speaker oscillates painfully between "servant," "vassal," "bondsman," "slave," and "friend," while the "fair friend" himself is also acknowledged "master" and "sovereign." The shift became problematic precisely at the point where humanist theory had begun to prise apart the old identification (signaled in the title of Bacon's first essay on the subject) of "followers and friends"; for the fictive equality now attributed to intense affective relationships between sovereign and vassal, or between master and servant, was inevitably compromised by a disproportion of actual power and authority, which uncomfortably exposed the element of interest underlying all friendships. The breach of hierarchy involved in such "disorderly intimacy," Mario DiGangi and Alan Bray have argued, was easily read as unnatural, tainting it with imputations of sodomy (DiGangi 1997; Bray 1994).

Among the "inconveniences" that Bacon saw as resulting from the elevation of servant-friends were the envy and contempt they were liable to attract – as in Shakespeare's *Richard II* or Marlowe's *Edward II*, where the king's closest intimates are denounced as mere minions and flatterers, creatures of corrupt interest. "The modern languages," as Bacon puts it, "give unto such persons, the name of *favourites* or *privadoes*; as if it were matter of grace or conversation" (Bacon 1906: 81). But true friendship, he insists, amounts to something much more than this, which is why the mighty are driven to secure it, even though, as his various exempla illustrate, it is almost always "at the hazard of their own safety, and greatness." Even the "felicity" guaranteed by princes' enjoyment of power is felt to be "but as an half piece, except they mought have a friend to make it entire" (ibid: 82); while the great value of friends is signaled by "the Roman name [which] attaineth the true use, and cause thereof; naming them *partcipes curarum* [sharers of cares]; for it is that, which tieth the knot" (p. 81).[14]

Bacon's essay puts a particularly strong emphasis upon this therapeutic quality – upon what he calls "the comfort of *friendship*," its capacity to lift the burdens of loneliness that attach to greatness:

> this communicating of a man's self to his *friend* works two contrary effects; for it redoubleth *joys*, and cutteth *griefs* in half. For there is no man, that imparteth his *joys* to his *friend*, but he *joyeth* more; and no man, that imparteth his *griefs* to his *friend* but he *grieveth* less. (p. 83)

Those, he insists "that want *friends* to open themselves unto, are cannibals of their own *heart*" (p. 83). In a similar vein, Rosencrantz urges Hamlet to seek relief from the prison of his own melancholy by confiding the secrets of his heart: "You do surely bar the door to your own liberty if you deny your griefs to your friend" (3.2.367). But, of course, Rosencrantz's desire to "open" the barred door of Hamlet's "unknown afflict[ion]" is profoundly compromised by his role as the king's intelligencer; and in the court world, as its most celebrated commentator had warned, such guileless self-exposure as Rosencrantz counsels always exposes one to perilous deception. Thus, in the second book of *The Courtier*, Castiglione has Peter Bembo advise his audience

> never to put . . . trust in any person in the worlde, nor to give him selfe for a pray to friende how deare and Loving soever he were, that without stoppe a man should make him partaker of all his thoughts, as he would his owne selfe: because there are in our minds so many dennes and corners, that it is unpossible for the wit of man to know the dissimulations that lye lurking in them. (Castiglione 1928: 119)

The habit of courtly suspicion encouraged by Bembo is what binds even the ingenuous Ophelia to keep her brother's confidences "locked" in her memory, delivering the key to him; just as it inspires Polonius's warnings to Laertes: "give thy thoughts no tongue . . . Give every man thine ear, but few thy tongue" (1.2.65, 74). Polonius, of all people, who later instructs that creature of prey Reynaldo (the Fox) how confidences may be used to entrap his own son (2.1.7–75), should understand the perils of intimacy; for he himself is one of those false confidants, "officious" men "in great favour," against whom Bacon warns in "Of followers and friends": "a kind of followers which are dangerous, being indeed espials; which enquire into the secrets of the house, and bear tales of them to others" (Bacon 1906: 146). No one, however, is better placed to appreciate the force of Bembo's warning than that cynosure of courtiers' eyes, Prince Hamlet (3.1.165) – the man whose exposure to the hostile stare of authority makes him feel "too much in the sun" (1.2.69), and who taunts his enemy by boasting his impenetrable possession of "that within which passes show" (1.2.88).

The self-consuming isolation of rank and power – emphasized by the devious nature of Rosencrantz's lure to confession – is one of the recurrent themes of Shakespeare's histories and tragedies, while the values of friendship typically belong to the private world of the comedy and romance. In plays from *The Two Gentlemen of Verona* to *The Two Noble Kinsmen* the obligations of same-sex bonding are more absolute than any other; in the histories, by contrast, friendship is sacrificed to the requirements of state. Thus in the second Henriad – whose hero constantly speaks the language of the "heart," but only as an instrument of policy – when the king's "best friend" Falstaff (*Henry V*, 4.7.38) seeks to enter the realm of politics, he must be humiliated, driven out, and then killed. But Henry's consciousness is nevertheless haunted by the "heart's ease . . . that private men enjoy" (4.1.236–7);[15] and in *Richard II*, the tragedy of usurpation and regicide that begins the whole tetralogy, there comes an eloquent moment when the king is overwhelmed by a need for the emotional consolations of true friendship. At Barclowlie Castle, deserted by his most powerful supporters, Richard II symbolically renounces the "respect, / Tradition, form, and ceremonious duty" belonging to his rank, and acknowledges the frailties of "flesh and blood": "I live with bread like you, feel want, / Taste grief, need *friends*: subjected thus, / How can you say to me I am a king?" (*Richard II*, 3.2.171–7).

From one point of view, of course, the "friends" of which Richard stands in need are simply the political and military supporters – the former "liegemen" – whose successive desertions have been the subject of the scene; and it is in this broad social sense that the term has been used up to this point in the play: "friends" are simply allies, followers, "servants" (in the still inclusive meaning of that term), members of a faction, those who are defined – as in the challenge "friend or foe?" – in opposition to "enemies." Such are the "powerful friends" (2.2.55) whom Ross, Beaumond, and Willoughby have taken to Bolingbroke, for example, or the "good friends" whom Bolingbroke promises to reward (2.3.47), or the king's "friends" who, as Salisbury tells him, "are fled to wait upon thy foes" (2.4.23). But the pathos of Richard's speech makes it plain that what he now experiences is something more personal than a failure of allegiance: the need for friends is characterized as a simple human craving, commensurable with hunger, want, and grief. Yet the impossibility of that yearning has been exposed in advance by the repeated denunciations of the king's alleged favorites, Bushy, Bagot, and Greene, as "caterpillars of the commonwealth" (2.3.165), parasites whose "pernicious lives" and "sinful hours" have ostensibly "made a divorce" between Richard and his queen, and "broke the possession of a royal bed" (3.1.4, 11–13). For a prince there can be no friendship untainted by corruptions of interest. Thus, as the Player King reminds the Danish court in *Hamlet*, the vulnerability of the great consists precisely in their inability to command (or even recognize) a love that is not in thrall to the vagaries of *fortuna*: "hitherto doth love on fortune tend,[16] / For who not needs shall never lack a friend" (3.2.216–17).

What Richard faces, then, is one of those recurrent crises, typical of Shakespeare's treatment of kingship, in which the predicament of the king's body politic leaves him suddenly exposed to the vulnerabiities of his body natural; and it is the need for personal friendship, of the kind advocated in humanist doctrine, that more poignantly than anything reveals this frailty. It is a sign of the "subjected" condition that shows the king as no different from his own political "subjects," whilst simultaneously identifying him as a "subject" in the emergent Cartesian sense of that complex word[17] – one whose selfhood is invested as much in the intense subjectivity we associate with Hamlet as with the formal "trappings" of public identity, and with all that Henry V ruefully understands by that "idol, Ceremony" (*Henry V*, 4.1.240).

By the time we reach Richard's great speech of defiance in act 3, scene 3, when he is confronted by Bolingbroke's forces at Flint, the king's confessed want of "friends" has resumed a purely public reference:

> And we are barren and bereft of friends,
> Yet know my master, God omnipotent,
> Is mustering in the clouds on our behalf
> Armies of pestilence . . . (3.3.84–7)

"Friends" here stands for "armies" of supporters or followers, its counterpointing with "my master" suggesting a virtual equivalence with "servants"; but the private, affective sense of the term will return at the end of the play. In act 5 Bolingbroke suborns Exton to the act of regicide, in language that corrupts "friend" to a synonym for the basest kind of servant: "Have I no *friend* will rid me of this living fear?"; and Exton's response justifies his complicity by appealing to a formal opposition between friend and foe that allows for no middle term: "I am the king's *friend*, and will rid his *foe*" (5.4.2, 11). However, this characteristically machiavellian setting of "the word itself against the word" (5.3.122) is designed to contrast with Richard's touching elevation of a mere servant to the status of friend: when his former Groom of the Stable risks his life to bring consolation to his imprisoned master, Richard hails him as his "gentle friend" (5.5.81). The emotional gap between this rhetorical gentling of the Groom's condition and the Lear-like mock with which Richard answered his first deferential greeting ("Hail, royal prince!" "Thanks, noble peer!": l. 67) is bridged by the Groom's parable of Barbary – the horse which (unlike its former keeper, but like so many of Richard's political "friends") has willingly subjected itself to the service of a new master.[18] But the tone and meaning of the whole encounter has already been shaped by the offstage music whose sound moves Richard to pronounce "blessing on his heart that gives it me" at the very moment of the Groom's entry. These harmonies give voice to those values of the "heart" that are silenced by the Groom's exit ("What my tongue dares not, that my heart shall say"; 5.5.97), for they are, as Richard says, "a sign of love; and love to Richard / Is a strange brooch in this all-hating world" (5.5.64–6). The rich jewel that ornaments the king's end is this unexpected and unfettered expression of love from a mere bondsman. Such love – which Richard reciprocates when he urges the Groom's flight from the murderers ("if you love me, 'tis time thou wert away"; l. 96) – is a "strange" thing, however, not just because its hazarding of the self is foreign to a world where almost every action has been governed by interest, but also because it is recognizably alien to Richard's royal condition – a touch of nature ironically made possible only by the unnatural fact of his own unkinging.[19]

The paradoxical frailty that greatness discovers through its need for friendship is once again foregrounded in *Hamlet*. In *The Murder of Gonzago* the Player King is made to utter a lengthy philosophical disquisition on the inconstancy of human resolve (3.2.209–38) – a speech whose obvious relation to the prince's own predicament invites us to read the play-within-the-play as something more than a mere engine of plot. Indeed the way in which the Player King seems to echo Hamlet's most self-lacerating obsessions makes it tempting to identify the passage with the "speech of some dozen or sixteen lines" that the prince promised to "set down and insert" in the First Player's part (2.2.566–9). In a fashion that clearly reflects on Gertrude's betrayal of her dead husband, Gonzago moralizes upon the vulnerability of human affection to the freaks of "slender accident" (l. 222), and proposes to debate the familiar "question" as to whether "love" or "fortune" can claim the victory in their ancient strife:

> For 'tis a question left us yet to prove
> Whether love lead fortune, or else fortune love.

Somewhat unexpectedly, however, he goes on to answer himself not by weighing the relative strength of *eros* and *fortuna*, but by offering a series of sententious reflections on the precarious condition of friendship:

> The great man down, you mark his favourite flies;
> The poor, advanced, makes friends of enemies.
> And hitherto doth love on fortune tend,
> For who not needs shall never lack a friend,
> And who in want a hollow friend doth try
> Directly seasons him his enemy. (3.2.225–32)

Insofar as they attract any comment, these lines tend to be dismissed as a verbose digression, parodying the inflated copiousness of the old-fashioned tragedies on which "The Murder of Gonzago" is modeled. But we have only to reflect on the prominence which the plot gives to Hamlet's relationship with Horatio, Rosencrantz, and Guildenstern, and even with Laertes,[20] to become aware that friendship is an issue of some importance in the play; and the Player King's lines turn out to paraphrase a classical text to which Renaissance writers invariably returned when they wished to explore the centrality of friendship as a social virtue – Cicero's *De amicitia*.[21]

If the isolation of greatness renders love, for Richard, a "strange" thing, Hamlet's double isolation, as both royal heir and alienated malcontent, results in an even more profound estrangement from a world that is itself marked, from the very beginning, as "strange" and "unnatural" (1.1.75; 1.2.232; 1.5.31, 34, 185–6). Ironically, this is a world that puts considerable rhetorical stress on the name of friendship. On the public level, Hamlet's mother urges him to "look like a friend on Denmark" (1.2.71), the equivocation on "Denmark" equating the affective bond between uncle and nephew with loyalty to the state itself: to be a "friend to this ground" is to be a liegeman to *this* Dane. Claudius likes to describe his councilors as "our wisest *friends*" (4.1.34); but he presides over a court in which the obligations of friendship are habitually compromised by the demands of service, and where both become guises of policy and instruments of surveillance. He flatters Polonius with the rhetoric of classical friendship, as though the old man were a part of himself – the heart of Denmark; but his organic metaphors betray the client status of the royal servant: "The *head* is not more native to the *heart*, / The *hand* more native to the *mouth*, / Than is the throne of Denmark to thy father" (1.2.48–50). Livery, we might recall, observing the relation of hand and mouth, originally denoted the master's obligation to provide his servants with food (Neill 2000: 23).

The domestic world represented by Polonius's household is characterized by a similarly ambiguous relationship between the reiterated claims of obedience and the demands of affection. Friendship is, of course, a principal theme of the "precepts" that Polonius seeks to engrave in his son's memory:

> Be thou familiar, but by no means vulgar.
> Those *friends* thou hast, and their adoption tried,
> Grapple them unto thy soul with hoops of steel,
> But do not dull thy palm with entertainment
> Of each new-hatched, unfledged courage . . .
> Give every man thine ear, but few thy voice . . .
> Neither a borrower nor a lender be,
> For loan oft loses both itself and *friend* . . . (1.3.68–82)

Like Claudius, the old man invokes the intimate bonds of classical friendship ("Grapple them unto thy soul"), but "entertainment" – the same word that Hamlet will use to define his relationship both with his schoolfellows, Rosencrantz and Guildenstern, and with his liveried clients, the Players (2.2.398) – is tellingly ambiguous, since it can refer either to the welcome and hospitality accorded to friends, or to the taking and maintaining of servants (*OED* n. 2a, 11 a–b). It is a reminder of the uncomfortably porous boundary between affective and servile relationships in this world – an overlap that is equally apparent in Laertes's own characterization of Hamlet's love for Ophelia in terms of an "inward service" that is rendered dangerously "wide" by the prince's paradoxical "subjection" to his own birth (1.3.16–21).

The labile distinction between friendship and service is something of which Hamlet appears edgily conscious from the start: when Horatio, at their first encounter, offers himself as "your poor *servant* ever" (1.2.168), the prince at once corrects him, stressing the equality that derives from their common past as "fellow-student[s]" at Wittenberg: "Sir, my good *friend*. I'll change that name with you" (ll.184, 169); and

he makes the same correction at the end of the scene when he responds to the proffer
of "duty" from Horatio and his companions by insisting upon "Your *loves*, as mine to
you" (ll. 275–6). Likewise Hamlet's pleas for secrecy after his encounter with the ghost
are couched in an earnest appeal not to duty but to the obligations of friendship:

> And now, *good friends*,
> As you are *friends*, scholars, and soldiers,
> Swear by my sword
> Never to speak of this that you have seen . . .
> Once more remove, *good friends* . . .
>   So, gentlemen,
> With all my *love* I do commend me to you
> And what so poor a man as Hamlet is
> May do t'express his *love and friending* to you
> God willing shall not lack. Let us go in together . . .
> Nay, come, let's go together. (1.5.155–212)

Setting aside its obvious defensive motive, Hamlet's insistence upon secrecy, echoing
Polonius's association of friendship with careful government of the "tongue" and
"voice" (1.3.65, 74), clearly constitutes a kind of test – reminding us that (as Mario
DiGangi puts it) "as a symbol and support of orderly intimacy between men, secrecy
grounds the Renaissance discourse of friendship: in Jeremy Taylor's resonant phrase,
'secrecy is the chastity of friendship'" (DiGangi 1997: 82).[22]

   The significance of the swearing episode for an understanding of the play's treatment of friendship is, however, as much gestural as rhetorical, structured as it is
around two symbolically contrived actions, the swearing on Hamlet's sword, and
the carefully orchestrated exit "together." The first of these is modeled on a famous
republican moment, when Lucius Junius Brutus bound his fellow conspirators to the
destruction of the Roman royal house by making them swear on the "fatal knife" he
had plucked from Lucretia's ravished corpse. Widely represented in Renaissance art,
the episode is described at the end of Shakespeare's own *Rape of Lucrece*, and reenacted
in Heywood's play of the same name.[23] It is also carefully imitated in scenes from
at least two later tragedies – the anonymous *Revenger's Tragedy* (1.3) and Marston's
Antonio's Revenge (4.2), both demonstrably influenced by *Hamlet* – where a group of
revengers affirm allegiance to one another as they swear to join in retribution against
a tyrant. In *Hamlet* the visual echo is even more compelling because the Brutus story,
in which the hero conceals his hostility to the Tarquins behind a mask of stupidity,
provides such an obvious analogue for Hamlet's device of pretended madness.[24] What
results, however, is an oddly disjunctive version of the original rite, since in place of
the victim's corpse, which serves the other revengers like an irreligious relic prompting them to revenge, there is only the disembodied voice of the ghost adjuring Horatio
and his companions to "swear." Moreover, the oath enjoined by the protagonist
(though sworn upon a blade that Hamlet will later associate with suicide, liberty, and
revenge)[25] is not to active conspiracy, but to silence and inaction; so that the entire

gestus seems structured around absence and negation. Yet the ritual of swearing upon a sword, on which Hamlet, echoed by the ghost, insists no fewer than four times (ll. 165, 167–8, 175–6, 179–82), is so fraught with recollections of the Brutus scene that it constantly tempts the viewer to expect a climactic swearing of revenge – to the point where Marcellus protests "We have sworn . . . already" (l. 66), while even Horatio (as if puzzled by the reiterated demands for mere secrecy unallied to action) asks Hamlet to "propose the oath," only to be baffled by a further repetition of the injunction "never to speak of this that you have seen" (l. 173).

One effect of the barrier of evasion that this odd breach of convention erects between Hamlet and his companions is to place an even more striking theatrical emphasis on his reiterated request that they "go together" at the end of the scene (ll. 208, 212). The prince's "Nay, come" draws attention to an implicit stage direction through which he waives the rules of precedence that expressed subordination through the act of physically "following" one's master. What is envisaged here is probably best indicated by the more elaborate directions that accompany Marston's reworking of the scene in *Antonio's Revenge*: when the usurped prince of that play swears his companions to vengeance, he adjures them to enact their mutual resolution in an iconic expression of the equal bonds of friendship – an emblematic enactment of the same "friendlie knot of love" celebrated by Angel Day:

> [*Antonio.*] We must be stiff and steady in resolve.
> Let's thus our hands, our hearts, our arms involve.
> > *They wreathe their arms.*
> *Pandulpho.* Now swear we by this Gordian knot of love . . .
> We'll sit as heavy on Piero's heart
> As Aetna doth on groaning Pelorus.
> *Antonio.* Thanks, good old man. We'll cast at royal chance
> Let's think a plot; then pell-mell vengeance!
> > *Exeunt, their arms wreathed.* (4.2.109–18)

Marston's tragedy is so self-consciously modeled on *Hamlet* that it seems likely that his "Gordian knot of love" repeats the physical enactment of "love and friending" that he had witnessed in the performance of Shakespeare's play.[26] The difference is that, in Shakespeare's original, Hamlet's conspicuous refusal even to confide in his fellows, much less solicit their collaboration in vengeance, ironizes the rhetoric and gestures of friendship on which the scene's political meaning should depend – thereby emphasizing the prince's isolation even as it ostensibly denies it. Within the play it contrasts sharply with the later embrace that seals the pact of revenge between Laertes and Claudius – "To his [i.e., Polonius's] good *friends* thus wide I'll ope my arms, / And, like the kind life-rend'ring pelican, / Repast them with my blood" (4.5.167–9) – an embrace that licenses the king's ingratiating appeal to Laertes in the dialect of classical friendship with which he once flattered Polonius himself: "you must put me in your *heart* for *friend*" (4.7.2).

The contradictory dramatic impulses of the oath-taking scene realize in an intense way the tensions in Hamlet himself between the poles of emotional loneliness and ingrained suspicion that define his isolated condition – an isolation that, in the case of a prince, is ironically proportionate with his power to command service. With this in mind, it is possible to see how, from the very beginning, the action of the tragedy has been constructed around an almost schematic set of variations upon the motifs of service, heterosexual love, and homosocial friendship. The early scenes with Horatio and his fellow watchmen in act 1 are set against those involving the covert watchers, Reynaldo, Rosencrantz, and Guildenstern, in act 2 – parallels that illustrate how in the court world to *serve* is always to *observe*: so the servile Reynaldo is instructed to "observe" Laertes (2.1.79), while Hamlet, himself "the observed of all observers" in more senses than Ophelia intends (3.1.168), commands Horatio to "observe" his uncle's "seeming" (3.2.85–92).[27] By the same token the duties of service repeatedly turn both love and friendship to instruments of espionage: so Polonius orders Reynaldo to employ the "indirections" of false good fellowship in his observation of Laertes (2.1.79, 73), while the king instructs Rosencrantz and Guildenstern to exploit their long intimacy with Hamlet ("being of so young days brought up with him / And sith so neighbored to his youth and havior") to "glean" and "sift" the truth of his nephew's "transformation" (2.2.4–16, 61). But whereas Reynaldo is defined from the beginning of the scene as Polonius's "man," a liveried servant with little option but to do his master's bidding, Hamlet's former schoolfellows willingly subordinate the bonds of friendship to their own self-interest, betraying the bond of secrecy: yielding to the king's confessed need to "use" them, they offer "to lay [their] service freely at [his] feet" (2.2.26–34) in a conscious act of submission that mirrors the submissiveness of Ophelia when she consents to become Polonius's decoy and informer.

Yet service is also precisely what Hamlet's former friends profess to offer the prince when they greet him on their first encounter with the deferential language appropriate to royal retainers ("My honored lord," "Most dear lord"; 2.2.240–1). Hamlet, by contrast, seems to insist that theirs is a more equal relationship, repeatedly saluting them as "excellent good friends," "good friends," and "dear friends" (2.2.242, 259, 294, 572), and once again stressing (as he had done to Horatio) the social disjunction between friendship and service. When Rosencrantz and Guildenstern offer to "wait upon him," he insists:

> I will not sort you with the rest of my *servants*, for, to speak to you like an honest man,
> I am most dreadfully *attended*. (ll. 287–9)

This last phrase is often taken as a punning allusion to the ghost; but since "attended" can mean "watched over," "guarded," and "listened to" as well as "waited upon," its more immediate reference is to the corrupted service that we already know to be exemplified in Rosencrantz and Guildenstern themselves. And because all service is ultimately owed to the king, the only dependable obligations to which Hamlet can appeal are those which lie outside its hierarchy of duties. The challenge which follows, issued in the name of "the beaten way of *friendship*" (l. 290), "the rights of our *fellowship* ... [and] the obligation of our ever preserved *love*" (ll. 290, 306–8), is simply for these two to identify themselves with one role or the other, the bondage of service or the liberty of friendship: "dear *friends* ... Were you not sent for? Is it your own inclining? Is it a free visitation?" (ll. 294–6).

Rosencrantz's characteristically evasive response is to flatter the prince with the promise of more service – this time from the Players: "We coted them on the way, and hither are they coming to offer you *service*" (ll. 341–2). These are not just any traveling troupe, it seems, but "*the* Players ... those that you were wont to take such delight in, the tragedians of the city" – a group apparently so well known to Hamlet that they might plausibly claim the title of the Prince's Men. Hamlet, however, condescends to greet them not as mere servile followers but with all the ostensible marks of friendship – preparing for this amicable extravagance with a disingenuous apology to Rosencrantz and Guildenstern, "lest my extent to the players ... should more appear like entertainment than yours" (2.2.396–8). "Entertainment" here is poised (even more uneasily than in Polonius's advice to Laertes) between employment and amiable hospitality, leaving the actual status attributed to players and courtiers equally ambiguous. The prince greets the actors with the same phrase he used a few moments earlier to his former schoolfellows – "good friends" (l. 445) – whilst the First Player is singled out for specially affectionate attention as his "old friend" (ll. 447, 563). They are to be used, Hamlet informs Polonius, not like servants, "according to their *desert*" (ll. 553–4) – that is to say, by the measure of their service[28] – but with the unquestioning generosity due to friends. The same speech makes it clear, however, that these gestures merely mimic the egalitarian idiom of true friendship, belonging in reality to a condescending theatre of princely "bounty"; and part of the point of Hamlet's exaggeratedly magnanimous "entertainment to the players" is to confuse those histrionic practitioners of friendship, Rosencrantz and Guildenstern, about his real feelings towards them.

There is an elegant symmetry between this scene, in which Hamlet exploits the uncertainty of the distinction between friendship and service, and his second encounter with the players at the beginning of 3.2, where his instructions on acting, delivered with all the authority of a master, are juxtaposed with his profession of friendship to Horatio. Once again Horatio deferentially offers to place himself "at [the prince's] service" (3.2.55); and once again the prince responds in language that redefines their relationship as a "conversation"[29] of equals, slipping for the first time into the intimate second person address ("*thou* art e'en as just a man"; l. 56), and identifying Horatio as the "second self" of classical friendship: "Since my dear soul was mistress of her choice / And could of men distinguish, her election / Hath sealed thee for herself" (ll. 67–9). The unexpected gendering of Hamlet's soul underscores the implied contrast between the perfected constancy of masculine friendship, and the "frailty" he attributes to the love of women, notably his mistress, Ophelia. Horatio's inferiority of rank, the prince asserts, far from being the dangerous obstruction identified by theorists of friendship, simply guarantees his own disinterestedness ("For what advancement may I hope from thee / That no revenue hast but thy good spirits / To feed and clothe thee"; ll. 60–2); while Horatio's ingenuousness is already demonstrated by his capacity to receive "Fortune's buffets and rewards . . . with equal thanks (ll. 70–1). By contrast, the "thrift" that "*follow*[s] fawning," its "candied tongue lick[ing] absurd pomp" (ll. 64–6), perfectly describes the servile habit of Claudius's followers, creatures like the sycophantic Osric, who "did comply . . . with the dug before he sucked" (5.2.201–2), or the pliable Rosencrantz and Guildenstern, whose love, Hamlet believes, is like the queen's or Ophelia's, enslaved to fortune for the same reasons that "purpose is . . . slave to memory" (3.2.211).

The Player King's disquisition on false friendship is a reminder that the Mousetrap is designed not just to "catch the conscience of the King" and to probe the degree of Gertrude's complicity, but to expose the disloyalty of those "hollow friends" whom the prince's "want" has turned to enemies – this, after all, is the point of Hamlet's savage banter with Rosencrantz and Guildenstern at the end of the performance. His complex quibbling on "play" and "instrument," in response to Guildenstern's continued assertion of "duty" and "love," taunts the pair as hypocrite-actors who serve Claudius much as the players serve Hamlet himself – instruments of policy and creatures of fiction whose "touch" is "as easy as lying" (3.2.380–402). When he greets his schoolfellows next it will no longer be as "friends" but as the abject ciphers of royal authority: two of those "*officers* that do the king best *service* in the end" (4.2.16–17). In a contemptuous figure that renders their compliance little different from the "variable *service*" commanded by those "emperor[s] for diet," the "politic worms" of the graveyard – "two dishes but to one table" (4.3.23–7) – Hamlet warns them that the king "keeps them like . . . an apple in the corner of his jaw, first mouthed, to be last swallowed" (4.2.17–19). When they have indeed been swallowed, accidental victims of the murderous service to which they have (however ignorantly) given themselves, Hamlet denies remorse in a line that scornfully conflates their former professions of love with the most degraded servility: "Why, man, they did *make love* to this *employment*" (5.2.64).[30]

The play may leave us, as it evidently leaves Horatio (5.2.63), in doubt about the justice of this brutal condemnation – just as it raises doubts about Hamlet's callousness towards others who profess to care for him, Ophelia, Gertrude, and even Polonius.[31] Nevertheless, the prince's testing and renunciation of these false friends is set against his increasing intimacy with Horatio, apparent even in the affectionate subscription of the letter delivered by the Sailor in 4.6 ("He that thou knowest thine"; 4.6.30), and famously displayed in their final exchange, where, in a last appeal to the obligations of friendship, he beseeches Horatio to remain behind as custodian of his history: "If ever thou didst *hold me in thy heart*, / Absent thee from felicity awhile / And in this harsh world draw thy breath in pain / To tell my story" (5.2.381–4). The Latinate "felicity," carefully chosen to chime with Horatio's claim to be "more an antique Roman than a Dane" (l. 374), surely stands here for something more than just the stoical embrace of death – much less for some vague promise of eternal bliss.

The happiness for which Horatio yearns is like that which Titinius claims at the end of *Julius Caesar*, where suicide is the extreme and irrefutable affirmation of friendship: "this is a Roman's part, / Come, *Cassius' sword* and find *Titinius' heart*" (5.3.89–90). In a quibble that seeks to quieten the play's obsessive anxieties about the histrionics of action, Horatio asserts that to be an antique (or antic) Roman, is to know how to play the part of second self to the point of annihilation. His gesture, affirming the "indissoluble [love]" of "perfect friendship" that Castiglione insists can "endure until death" (Castiglione 1928: 120), contrasts as brutally as possible with the frozen indifference of Claudius's servants to the king's last desperate appeal, "O, yet defend me, *friends*!" (l. 355).

But for all its rhetoric of equality and the intense emotion Hamlet invests in it, royal friendship remains a painfully one-sided thing: Hamlet may garland Horatio with the pronouns of intimacy, "thee" and "thou," but Horatio can never use the same intimate voice to the prince, as even the dying Laertes dares to do (ll. 344–7, 362–3); Hamlet for him is always the politely addressed "you" or "my lord," except for the one touchingly risked moment when the prince is already dead: "Good night, sweet prince, / And flights of angels sing *thee* to *thy* rest" (ll. 397–8). It is part of the play's cruelty (or Hamlet's egotism), moreover, that Horatio is not allowed to proceed to the extremity of sentimental consolation promised by suicide: where Hamlet now claims for himself the "silence" he once enjoined on Horatio and his friends, Horatio is commanded to "speak." He is translated from the role of secretary, the second self appointed to be the privy-closet of his master's confidences, to that of chronicler, faithfully retailing to a "yet [still] unknowing world" that uninstructive narrative of "plots and errors" (5.1.421, 440) behind which the play's innermost "secrets" remain stubbornly occluded.

NOTES

1   All citations from *Hamlet* are to the New Folger Library edition, ed. Barbara A. Mowat and Paul Werstine (1997); other Shakespeare plays are cited from *The Norton Shakespeare*, gen. ed. Stephen Greenblatt (1997) et al. Unless otherwise indicated the emphases throughout are my own.

2   For an illuminating account of the processes by which the land emerged as a focus of loyalty alternative to the monarch in the early modern period, see Helgerson (1992: 105–47).

3   For an account of changing ideas in this period, and the strains to which the old idea of universal service was subject, see Neill (2000: 13–48).

4   A significant index to the shifting connotations of service and friendship in the early modern period is the use of both "servant" and "friend" as euphemistic synonyms for "lover" or "mistress." The former, which belongs to the ritualized language of chivalric love, is traced by *OED* to the mid-fourteenth century, while the latter (apart from a possible example in Caxton, ca. 1490) seems to date from the late sixteenth century. Both usages were available to Shakespeare, but the overwhelming preponderance of examples come from his early comedy, *The Two Gentlemen of Verona* (e.g., 2.4.100–18), while examples of the latter are more common in later plays. The erotic sense of "servant" seems to have been largely obsolete by the 1670s, while that of "friend" survived for

another century. In each case the governing model of relationships between men supplies a kind of ironic template for heterosexual relationships.

5   On the place of classical friendship in the program of humanist education, see Hutson (1994: 2–4, 60–2).

6   Aristotle, *Nicomachean Ethics*, viii, i, 1155a; cited from Pakaluk (1991: 30). All citations from Aristotle are to this edition.

7   I, xxvii, "Of Friendship, p. 196. All citations from Montaigne are to the Everyman edition of Florio's translation (1965).

8   Essay XXVII, "Of Friendship", p. 80. Except where otherwise indicated, all citations are from the Everyman edition (1906); its text is based on the 1625 edition for which Bacon entirely rewrote the Friendship essay. The 1612 version expressed a similar notion of the social importance of friendship in rather different and much less elaborate terms: "There is no greater Desert or wildernesse then to bee without true friendes. For without Friendship, society is but meeting" (D4). The evolution of Bacon's ideas on friendship from the 1597 essay "Of followers and friends" to the 1625 version of the friendship essay shows a distinct progression from a machiavellian reworking of feudal ideas (in which calculated self-interest takes the place of the retainer's loyalty as the governing principle of such alliances) towards a humanist idealization of equal friendship as a source of mutual comfort.

9   In the 1597 edition of the *Essays* Bacon had challenged the orthodox view, effectively limiting friendship to patronage relationships by maintaining that "There is little friendship in the worlde, and least of all betweene equals, which was wont to bee magnified. That that is, is betweene superiour and inferiour, whose fortunes may comprehend the one the other" ("Of followers and friends," p. 5). By 1612, however, he is insisting that "the higher one goeth, the fewer true Friends hee shall haue" (sig. D4v), and by 1625 (while continuing to include a substantially unaltered "Of followers and friends") implicitly acknowledges that true friendship necessarily involves an assumption of equality (p. 81).

10 The idea of the friend as a second self is further elaborated in Cicero's *De amicitia*, as well as in the standard Renaissance essays on friendship – see, for example, Montaigne, "Of Friendship," pp. 203, 205, where the "mutuall agreement" of friends results from their "being no other than one soule in two bodies, according to the fit definition of Aristotle . . . The secret that I have sworne not to reveale to another, I may without perjurie impart it unto him, who is no other but my selfe." Cf. Bacon, p. 86. In Marlowe's *The Jew of Malta* this idea of friendship is parodied in Barabas's flattery of his slave Ithamore, whom he calls "my love . . . thy master's life, / My trusty servant, nay my second self . . . no servant, but my friend" (3.4.14–15, 42) – only for his protestations to be undercut by Ithamore's blunt reminder of the real material basis of their relationship: "Pay me my wages, for my work is done" (l. 116). Barabas's expressed need for friends, but inability to construe friendship as anything more than a matter of calculated "advantage" (5.2.35–40, 111–16), helps to ensure his ultimate destruction. All citations from Marlowe are to *Dr Faustus and Other Plays*, ed. David Bevington and Michael Rasmussen (Marlowe 1995).

11 The political dimension of friendship discourse, with its stress on equality, is explored by Laurie Shannon (2002), who argues that "friendship models configure an image of political consent, offering a counterpoint to prevailing types of polity" (p. 8) and an "alternative to the subordination without limits attempted by the tyrannical ruler" (p. 56). However, Shannon downplays any suggestion that the utopian community-of-two imagined in friendship literature could serve as a model for anything beyond itself: "neither democratic nor republican – and not even directly civic – sixteenth-century friendship does not bespeak larger social or national formations in microcosm, as it would do later in rhetorics surrounding modern democracies . . . [it] offers no compartment or affect to be generalized beyond the pair, no pattern to link all political subjects to *one another*" (p. 18). While this may be true of most representations of friendship, with their emphasis on its ideal equality as something "between private men" (in Bacon's phrase), the collisions between

private and public worlds that characterize tragic action frequently exploit its potential as a site of resistance to tyranny. Despite our disagreement on this point, I regret that I did not have access to Shannon's important book until this essay was already in press.

12 In Restoration comedy the case of Maskwell in Congreve's *Double Dealer* offers an interesting comparison. Maskwell, described in the dramatis personae as "pretended friend" to the romantic hero, Mellefont, but identified by his lover, Lady Touchwood, as being "in the nature of a servant" (1.2.46–7) exploits the still porous boundary between upper servants and friends in order to advance his leveling ambitions in Lord Touchwood's crumbling patriarchy. When he professes to be "bound by duty and gratitude . . . to be ever your lordship's servant," Touchwood insists "you are my friend" (4.4.20–2). Thus the "doubleness" of his dealing contains a subdued play on Montaigne's idea of friendship as a "doubling" of the self (Florio 1965: 205).

13 The hypocritical Luke Frugal appeals to this same ideal of service in *The City Madam*, when he says of his apprentices "What's mine is theirs. They are my friends, not servants" (4.1.38).

14 Plutarch's widely quoted and imitated essay in the Moralia, "How to Tell a Flatterer from a Friend," explores the problem of false friendship to which the great are especially vulnerable. In *Othello*, Iago uses a devious form of flattery to promote himself from servant to "friend" (3.3.385). Cf. Evans (2001).

15 This rhetorical emphasis on the values of the heart, in a world ruthlessly governed by the calculations of the head, is one of the more striking rhetorical features of *Henry V* – from the Hostess's announcement that "the King hath killed [Falstaff's] heart" (2.1.88) to Henry's declaration that "a good heart, Kate, is the sun and the moon" (5.2.162–3).

16 The verb "tend," though normally printed without an apostrophe, was strictly an abbreviation of "attend": in the Player King's allegory, Love is imagined as the *servant* of Fortune.

17 *OED* gives 1682 as the earliest clear use of *subject* in this sense.

18 The metaphoric link between horse and groom is intensified by the subdued word-play in "gentle," since "gentling" a stallion like Barbary would have been part of the Groom's office. Richard's gentling of the Groom is the moral antithesis of that moment in *Henry V* when the king hyperbolically promises every one of his "dear friends," the common soldiers at Agincourt, that "this day shall gentle his condition" (3.1.1, 4.3.63) – once dead, however, they are quickly relegated to the obscurity of their original condition ("None else of name," 4.8.99).

19 Here (as elsewhere) Shakespeare's play seems to be responding to the machiavellian cynicism that characterizes Marlowe's analysis of power in *Edward II*. In both plays the king's enemies stigmatize the king's affection for his favorites with imputations of sodomy; but in Edward's case not even his surrender of the crown and public resolve to "forget myself" (5.1.111) are enough to render the comfort of disinterested friendship accessible to the king. Instead, the consuming need for intimacy that has driven Edward to confuse the boundaries of service and friendship is grotesquely punished in his murder by Mortimer's servant Lightborn – a murder which, as DiGangi (1997: 114) observes, takes the form of a vicious parody of sodomitical rape.

20 In the Q text Hamlet's claim always to have "loved" Laertes (5.1.309) and to regard him as a "brother" (5.2.258) may seem emptily rhetorical; but in the Folio, which shows signs of significant authorial revision, the apology to Laertes is given a powerful emotional charge by the confession to Horatio that his opponent's cause provides "the portraiture" of his own (5.2.88) – making of Laertes another "second self."

21 The passage is worth quoting at some length: "where shall we find those who do not put office . . . high place and power, above friendship, so that when the former advantages are placed before them on one side and the latter on the other they will not much prefer the former? For feeble is the struggle of human nature against power . . . Therefore, true friendships are very hard to find among those whose time is spent in office . . . For where can you find a man so high-minded as to prefer his friend's advancement to his own? And, passing by material considerations . . . how grievous and how hard to most persons does association in another's misfortunes appear! Nor is it easy

to find men who will go down to calamity's depths for a friend. Ennius, however, is right when he says when Fortune's fickle the faithful friend is found [*amicus certus in re incerta cernitur*] . . . most men . . . either hold a friend of little value when their own affairs are prosperous, or they abandon him when things are adverse" (*De amicitia*, xvii, 63–6; Cicero 1927: 173–5).

22   As Richard Dutton reminds me, Hamlet's "friends, scholars, and soldiers" chimes tellingly with Ophelia's later characterization of Hamlet: "The courtier's, soldier's, scholar's, eye, tongue, sword" (3.2.165). In Ophelia's gallery of social types the "courtier" with his coldly observing "eye" takes the place of the "friend."

23   The scene would be staged again after the Restoration in Nathaniel Lee's *Lucius Junius Brutus*, where, however (in keeping with the late seventeenth-century questioning of patriarchal pieties), the political issues are played out less as a struggle between service and friendship, than as a contest between the authority of fathers and the demands of erotic love.

24   Brutus' shadowy presence in Shakespeare's play is signaled by Polonius's unwise reference to his namesake, the later republican conspirator, Marcus Brutus (3.2.109–12), where his "Brutus killed me" is usually taken to be a self-referential allusion to Shakespeare's own *Julius Caesar*, in which the actor now playing Hamlet (Richard Burbage) had previously killed the actor now playing Polonius (then cast as Caesar). In Shakespeare's play Cassius is able to draw Brutus into the republican conspiracy by playing on his friend's adulation for his ancestor, Lucius Junius Brutus.

25   See 3.1.83–4, where the suicide's "bare bodkin" offers the prince release (*quietus*) from psychological enslavement (the "fardels" of a "weary life"), and 3.3.79–93, 3.4.29, and 5.2.352, where a sword becomes the instrument of revenge.

26   Marston had already made use of the same gesture in the symmetrically equivalent scene of *Antonio and Mellida* where Antonio's entry *"wreathed together"* with his father Andrugio shows them "enfolded" against the "united force of chapfall'n death" and "all the venomed stings of misery" (4.2.0–4); but the language of that scene itself seems generally indebted to *Hamlet* – which, moreover, included the first use of "chapfallen" (a neologism from Gerard's *Herbal* (1598) according to *OED*) to describe the gaping jaw of a death's head. The same knot of friendship is displayed in the conspirators' embrace from *Venice Preserved* (2.3), cited above. For conclusive evidence that both Marston plays are dependent on *Hamlet* (rather than vice versa as was once supposed), see Neill and Jackson (1998).

27   On espionage and surveillance in the play, see my *"Hamlet*: A Modern Perspective" in Mowat and Werstine (1997: 307–26).

28   The close conceptual link between "desert" and "service" is illustrated by their common etymological link to Old French *{de}servir* and ultimately to Latin *servus*.

29   "Conversation" here means both "social intercourse" and "intimacy" (*OED* n. 1–2).

30   Significantly, "employment" (a word whose meanings were poised somewhere between "old-fashioned service" and the paid work for which it now stands) seems to have been a coinage of Shakespeare's own (*OED* 1a–b, 2a). The odd erotic suggestiveness of "make love" comes close to branding Rosencrantz and Guildenstern's service with the stigma of sodomitical corruption, which (as Bray 1994 and DiGangi 1997 show) was habitually linked to the disorderly intimacy of royal favorites. In the context of their attempts to expose Hamlet's secrets it resonates with the metaphors in Jeremy Taylor's denunciation of such betrayals as "the adulteries of [friendship, which] dissolve the Union [and] are the proper causes of divorce" (*The Measures and Offices of Friendship*, 1662; cited from DiGangi 1997: 181, n. 55).

31   Furthermore, Graham Bradshaw reminds me, despite Hamlet's parade of affection to the Players, "he shows no trace of concern at whatever might happen to [them] when he has both used them and ruined their performance." The trouble experienced by Shakespeare's company in 1601 when their performance of *Richard II* was similarly used by the Essex conspirators amply illustrates the dangers to which the prince was exposing his "good friends."

REFERENCES AND FURTHER READING

Bacon, F. (1906). *Essays*, intro. O. Smeaton. London: J. M. Dent.

Bray, A. (1994). Homosexuality and the Signs of Male Friendship in Elizabethan England. In J. Goldberg (ed.) *Queering the Renaissance*. Durham, NC: Duke University Press, 40–61.

Burnett, M. and Manning, J. (eds.) (1994). *New Essays on Hamlet*. New York: AMS Press.

Calderwood, J. L. (1983). *To Be and Not To Be: Negation and Metadrama in "Hamlet."* New York: Columbia University Press.

Castiglione, B. (1928). *The Book of the Courtier*, trans. Sir Thomas Hoby, intro. W. H. D. Rouse. London: J. M. Dent.

Cicero, M. T. (1927). *De senectute, De amicitia, De divinatione*, trans W. A. Falconer. Loeb Classical Library. London: William Heinemann.

Congreve, W. (1981). *The Double Dealer*, ed. J. Ross. London: Ernest Benn.

Day, A. (1967). *The English Secretary*. Gainesville, FL: Scholars Facsimiles and Reprints.

DiGangi, M. (1997). *The Homoerotics of Early Modern Drama*. Cambridge: Cambridge University Press.

Evans, R. C. (2001). Flattery in Shakespeare's *Othello*: The Relevance of Plutarch and Sir Thomas Elyot. *Comparative Drama*, 35, 1–41.

Florio, J. (trans.) (1965). *Montaigne's Essays*, 3 vols., intro. L. C. Harmer. London: J. M. Dent.

Frye, R. M. (1984). *The Renaissance Hamlet: Issues and Responses in 1600*. Princeton, NJ: Princeton University Press.

Greenblatt, S. (gen. ed.) (1997). *The Norton Shakespeare*. New York: W. W. Norton.

——(2001). *Hamlet in Purgatory*. Princeton, NJ: Princeton University Press.

Helgerson, R. (1992). *Forms of Nationhood: The Elizabethan Writing of England*. Chicago, IL: University of Chicago Press.

Hutson, L. (1994). *The Usurer's Daughter: Male Friendship and Fictions of Women in Sixteenth-Century England*. London: Routledge.

I.M. (1968) [1598]. *A Health to the Gentlemanly profession of Seruingmen: or, The Seruingmans Comfort*. In *Inedited Tracts: Illustrating the manners, opinions, and occupations of Englishmen during the sixteenth and seventeenth centuries*. Roxburghe Library.

Jackson, M. P. and Neill, M. (eds.) (1986). *The Selected Plays of John Marston*. Cambridge: Cambridge University Press.

Kerrigan, J. (1996). *Revenge Tragedy*. Oxford: Oxford University Press.

Kerrigan, W. (1994). *Hamlet's Perfection*. Baltimore, MD: Johns Hopkins University Press.

Kott, J. (1964). Hamlet in the Mid-Century. In *Shakespeare Our Contemporary*. London: Methuen.

Levin, H. (1959). *The Question of Hamlet*. New York: Oxford University Press.

Mack, M. (1952). The World of *Hamlet*. *Yale Review*, 41, 502–23.

Marlowe, C. (1995). *Dr Faustus and Other Plays*, ed. D. Bevington and M. Rasmussen. Oxford: Oxford University Press.

Massinger, P. (1964). *The City Madam*, ed. C. Hoy. London: Edward Arnold.

Mercer, P. (1987). *Hamlet and the Acting of Revenge*. London: Macmillan.

Mowat, B. A. and Werstine, P. (eds.) (1997). *Hamlet*. New Folger Library edition. New York: Washington Square Press.

Neill, M. (1997). *Issues of Death: Mortality and Identity in English Renaissance Tragedy*. Oxford: Oxford University Press.

——(2000). *Putting History to the Question: Power, Politics, and Society in English Renaissance Drama*. New York: Columbia University Press.

Neill, M. and Jackson, M. P. (1998). Morphew, Leprosy, and the Date of Marston's *Antonio and Mellida*. *Notes and Queries*, n. s., 45, 358–60.

Otway, T. (1969). *Venice Preserved*, ed. M. Kelsall. London: Edward Arnold.

Pakaluk, M. (1991). *Philosophers on Friendship*. Indianapolis, IN: Hackett Publishing.

Shannon, L. (2002). *Sovereign Amity: Figures of Friendship in Shakespearean Contexts*. Chicago, IL: University of Chicago Press.

States, B. O. (1992). *Hamlet and the Concept of Character*. Baltimore, MD: Johns Hopkins University Press.

Weitz, M. (1964). *Hamlet and the Philosophy of Literary Criticism*. London: Faber and Faber.

17

Julius Caesar

Rebecca W. Bushnell

While few Shakespeareans might be willing to admit it, *Julius Caesar* long maintained its prominence in the canon because it is the easy tragedy. The play was featured in the American high school curriculum for decades chiefly for its brevity and simple vocabulary (see Spevack 1988: 2). But the play was also easy to teach for what it lacks: sexual jokes and racial controversy. The play excites few titters from the back of the classroom, and it does not raise controversial issues. Of course, *Julius Caesar* has also attracted students and theatregoers for what it does stage: well-developed male characters, suspense, and explicit violence, including a spectacular assassination and several bloody suicides (Ripley 1980: 1). However, that I know of no high school that still teaches *Julius Caesar* suggests that the play may be losing its primacy for some of the same reasons that made it popular: when teachers now seek "relevant" literature, even the appeal of *Julius Caesar*'s violence fades next to that of *Romeo and Juliet*'s sex and gang wars or the racial and gender politics of *Othello* and *The Merchant of Venice*.

Julius Caesar's critical fortunes have always been mixed. Eighteenth- and nineteenth-century critics deplored what they saw as the play's formal inadequacies: a loose structure, multiple protagonists, and an anticlimactic ending. Twentieth-century critics were the first to come to the play's defense, arguing for the brilliance of its characterizations and its "organic unity" (Ripley 1980: 1–7). However, this formal redemption has not saved the play from a decline in interest in the last two decades, when Shakespearean scholarship moved away from studies of image, theme, and character to explorations of political and social issues. In a period of burgeoning Shakespeare scholarship, interest in *Julius Caesar* has remained flat, while the amount of work on *Titus Andronicus* and *Coriolanus* has increased significantly (the number of studies of *Titus* listed in the *Modern Language Association On-Line Bibliography* almost doubled from the decade of 1970–80 to 1990–2000). The amount of criticism on the Roman plays may never reach that devoted to the major tragedies (*Hamlet* scholarship continues to grow at a staggering rate, with 870 items listed by the *MLA Bibliography* for 1990–2000), but the Roman plays now also lag behind the histories (for example, according to the *MLA Bibliography* 179 pieces of scholarship on *Henry V* were published in 1990–2000, as compared with 130 on *Julius Caesar*), and behind most of the comedies (*Twelfth Night* attracted 147 dissertations, books, and essays in the same period).

This stagnation in *Julius Caesar* scholarship may at first appear inexplicable, since *Julius Caesar* was long considered an exemplary "political" tragedy and recent criticism has been all about politics. Günter Walch has noted the oddity that "*Julius Caesar*, even though it has been referred to as a play about revolution, has yet to play a major role in any recent national or international discussion of the stage or in literary criticism" (Walch 1998: 220–1). But when for Shakespeare critics politics became something other than classical republicanism or early modern theories of monarchy, the play's currency began to fade.

One sign of the change was the publication of Jonathan Dollimore and Alan Sinfield's *Political Shakespeare* in 1985. There "political" criticism signified attention to "the marginalized and the subordinate of Elizabethan and Jacobean culture" (p. 6) as well as "the operations of power" (p. 3), and, implicitly, a widening range of "political" relationships and situations. In the ensuing years Shakespeare criticism with "politics" or "political" in the title proliferated. In the summer of 2001 an *MLA On-Line Bibliography* search with the descriptors "Shakespeare" and "politics" (beginning in 1981) generated 434 items. Items dating before 1985 tend to address "matters of state" in the Roman plays and the histories; after 1985, books and essays as often discuss the "politics" of spectacle, sexuality, desire, the body, and madness, and in plays such as *Twelfth Night*, *As You Like It*, and *A Midsummer Night's Dream*. *Julius Caesar*'s "politics" of honor, republican values, and tyrannicide may have lost their appeal in such a critical new world.

Scholarship on *Julius Caesar* seems to have lost its way in the wake of the profound changes in the field since the early 1980s, and it is time to think about its future in the context of a new political criticism that recognizes the play's concern with matters of state, yet does not merely revive the old pieties. This essay reviews strategies of "political" reading of *Julius Caesar* practiced in the past two decades, which are notable for their contradictions. Thus recognizing the play's tendency to generate conflicting political interpretations, I argue that we accept this as the character of its politics. What the eighteenth- and nineteenth-century critics saw as the play's weaknesses – its fragmentation, anachronisms, and discontinuities – match this political incoherence, and contribute to the play's uncanny power to undermine any ideological certainty.

For this reason, this essay will not offer a coherent "reading" of the play, but instead will highlight its disparate political rhetoric, vocabulary, and ideologies. In resisting any pressure to read *Julius Caesar* as a seamless action and single political statement, we can attend instead to the significant *discontinuity* of its politics: its fractured nature as an urban drama and a drama of state, a play of republican values and Tudor morality, and a play of two places – Rome and London. As Barbara J. Bono has observed, the instability in *Julius Caesar*'s Roman setting reproduces "the shifting political and economic alliances under the English Tudor dynasty, where the London-based court sought to undermine the privileges of the hereditary feudal nobility while finding itself in increasing uneasy alliances with the urban classes" (Bono 1994: 454). The eclecticism of early modern English theatrical style, and in particular the style of the Roman play, was the ideal vehicle for representing that Tudor world, where the institutions, traditions, and languages of court, city, and regions coexisted and often conflicted, and political and social identities changed rapidly. The political resonance of *Julius Caesar* emanates from these conditions of transformation and contradiction.

Whose Politics?

In recent years we have come to see the political world of early modern England as a vibrant, dispersed, and self-contradictory arena, engaging Anglican and Puritan churchmen and courtiers, women and men, commoners and the citizens of London, as well as kings and queens. When looking at the operations and language of the government and the court, scholars have opened our eyes to the conflicts *within* legal, ecclesiastical, and court policy and discourse, breaking up the image of an official orthodoxy. They have also helped us to see politics operating at regional and local levels, as well as in the contested territory of the New World. The return to topicality also deepened our sense of the complexity of Tudor and Stuart England. For Leah Marcus, when she practices "local reading," "a 'local' Shakespeare is a figure of massive instability, a contradiction in terms, a puzzle which keeps coming undone," because of the ideological instability characteristic of "local" politics and "events, gossip, personalities" in city, country, and court (Marcus 1988: xii; see also Wilson 1993: ch. 1).

We now thus speak of histories and not just one history of early modern England, where, in Richard Helgerson's words, writers across the nation, "belonged to different discursive communities and, as a result, wrote England differently" (Helgerson 1992: 5). Critics may argue over whose side Shakespeare took – that of court or city, king or commoner – but the point lies in the differences, not just among writers, but also embedded in a single text. Jean Howard makes the crucial point that

> plays for the public stage were not, by and large, overtly homiletic, committed to the straightforward promulgation of dogma. Frequently composed by several hands and cobbling together a variety of discursive and narrative conventions, the drama often accommodated ideologically incompatible elements within a single text. Rather than as signs of aesthetic failures, these incompatibilities can be read as traces of ideological struggle, of differences within the sense-making machinery of culture. (Howard 1994: 7)

Such ideological "incompatibilities" exist not only at the level of event or character in early modern plays, but at the level of language itself: such was the nature of political discourse in this time of change (Bushnell 1990: ix–xiv). In his many studies of early modern political thought, John Pocock has powerfully demonstrated the ways in which political texts were composed in multiple "languages" and idioms. In these texts, we find social and political languages evolving, as "a plurality of specialized languages, each carrying its own biases as to the definition and distribution of authority . . . converg[e] to form a highly complex language, in which many paradigmatic structures exist simultaneously, debate goes on between them [and] individual terms and concepts migrate from one structure to another, altering some of their implications and retaining others" (Pocock 1971: 22). It is at this level of "political" action and meaning in *Julius Caesar* that this essay will ultimately dwell. The play itself tells us that words and names are all important – even lethal – in the realm of politics: Cinna the poet is killed for his name, and the central question of the play is what to name Caesar – tyrant, king, martyr, friend. Much scholarship has focused on the function of words and the names in the play, and their dangerous ambiguity in a disintegrating polity (see, for example, Foakes 1954; Burckhardt 1961; Bushnell 1990: 146–9). This multiplicity of the play's language corresponds to the layers of its political ideologies and the rapid changes and discontinuities in political discourse in late sixteenth-century England.

Looking for Politics in *Julius Caesar*

As do the other Roman plays, *Julius Caesar* poses the problem of reading through two moments in time and space – republican Rome, and England in the 1590s. In its own time such a doubleness effectively "decentered" the present, when Tudor London sought its own image in the mirror of Rome's politics (Burt 1991: 122). Clifford Ronan has described this kind of spatial and temporal disjunction, surfacing in anachronism and ideological conflict, as defining the style of the English Roman play. In early modern England, Rome was visible in its survival in ruins and fragments, both monumental and textual (Ronan 1995: 37). But while these fragments memorialized Rome's power, they also symbolized its decay, and the sign of Rome in early modern Europe was the fragment that imperfectly recalled the whole. *Julius Caesar* epitomizes that notion of Rome, when it stages Rome falling into ruins through faction, violence, and civil war, a fracturing that occurs on every level, in action, form, and language.

Despite (or perhaps because of) this sense of imminent ruin, political readings of *Julius Caesar* have characteristically sought to extract its single political "essence" or idea: whether it is to be a play about religion, republicanism, monarchy, urban politics, or aristocratic factionalism. The play itself may invite us to do so when the characters themselves invoke political abstractions as a guide to action. So, for one reader, the play may become a statement about republican values (Bathory 1996), while for another it evokes the ideals of the Platonic republic (Parker 1993) or draws on the ethics of tyrannicide (Miola 1985). Another critical strategy imitates the play's characters in seeking to define the classical "idea of Rome." Robert Miola identifies Rome as "the central protagonist of the play" (Miola 1983: 76), when he sees Shakespeare using the "symbolic geography" of a Rome divided by the Tiber to create an image of a city split by civil war, exposing flaws in human judgment and the contradictions of heroism (p. 113). Similarly, Gail Kern Paster follows the idea of Rome as a city, where "the social mandate for heroic self-sacrifice collides with the heroic mandate for self-realization conceived in civic terms" (Paster 1985: 58).

But what city is portrayed in *Julius Caesar*, and whose city is it? For Dennis Kezar, the city's location is the Globe Theatre: when, in the play's opening scene, "we find a remarkably individuated cobbler able to pun with the best of Shakespeare's English tradesmen," "the Tribunes alternately seem like London aldermen policing sumptuary laws and Puritan anti-theatricalists censuring the license, social confusion, and spectacle of the public theater" (Kezar 1998: 44–5). René Girard (1993) views the blood of sacrifice in this play as Roman blood – and the blood of all human sacrificial rituals, but for Richard Wilson, this blood is that which ran from the butcher's stands into the streets of Eastcheap, so that "Brutus corresponds to those puritan city fathers of Shakespeare's London who campaigned not only to close the playhouses, but also to force Eastcheap's butchers to kill cattle out of sight of customers" (Wilson 1996: 26). According to Wayne Rebhorn, however, *Julius Caesar*'s Rome is England's court, and belongs to its combative aristocrats, when he argues that the play reflects a pattern of aristocratic competition or "emulation" in late sixteenth-century England (Rebhorn 1990: 81).

And, indeed, it may be all of these, for the very shifting ground of the play itself allows audience and reader to change or adapt their understanding of its places and political actions, from the intimate scenes set in Brutus' home to the very different "public" crowd scenes. The former scenes suggest that this is a play concerned with aristocratic honor and factional conflict, whereas the latter evoke the streets of London and its restless mobs. Similarly, at some points in the play the discourse of politics sounds very English, with talk of kings, crowns, and commons, whereas, at other points, the political world is very clearly inhabited by senators, patricians, tribunes, and plebeians. Several scholars have explored the anachronisms in the play's religious vocabulary, with its references to rites, pulpits, and ceremonies that had strong contemporary associations (Rose 1992; Kaula 1981). But other of *Julius Caesar*'s political terms, if unfolded, would reveal similar multiple meanings, linked to the incommensurate nature of the Roman and Tudor worlds and the shifting ground of political discourse in the early modern period. The rest of this essay bears down on those moments of the play where England and Rome seem most to clash, in order to focus on the political differences that surface in its language.

Tyrant and King

One of the most explosive words in the play is "tyrant," juxtaposed with the name of "king." The question of tyranny is at the heart of Casca's and Cassius' tense conversation in which they are testing each other's position on Caesar. Cassius' commentary on the night's prodigies point to an unnamed man "prodigious grown," who could be the monster that aroused them. Casca broods that indeed "the senators tomorrow / Mean to establish Caesar as a king; / And he shall wear his crown by sea and land, / In every place save here in Italy." Cassius' response interprets this statement as an implicit declaration of Caesar as a tyrant, when he calls upon the gods who "tyrants do defeat," declaring he knows how to free himself, by suicide, from "that part of tyranny that I do bear." When Casca agrees, Cassius once again shifts the ground, demanding "why should Caesar be a tyrant then: / Poor man, I know he would not be a wolf, / But that he sees the Roman are but sheep; / He were no lion, were not Roman hinds?" (1.3.71–106). It can be argued that the central question of the play is whether Caesar is in fact a "tyrant" and how this is related to the idea of his being named a "king." After stabbing Caesar the conspirators are quick to shout that by this act "Tyranny is dead!" (3.1.78), and after Brutus' speech after the assassination, one of the plebeians is very ready to assent that "This Caesar was a tyrant" (3.2.69). But only a few lines later the plebeians revert to the praise of him as "noble Caesar" and "royal Caesar" (3.2.243–4).

In these moments the play brings to the surface two related issues vigorously debated in early modern political thought: the distinction between kings and tyrants and the justification of tyrannicide. I have argued elsewhere that *Julius Caesar* uses the concept and "name" of tyranny in a contradictory fashion, when it shows the characters self-consciously manipulating conflicting definitions of "tyrant" and "king," characterizing Caesar as a beast or monster while they also call him a tyrant for coveting divine power (Bushnell 1990: 143–4). Early modern British writers and political thinkers spent a great deal of time constructing the difference between the king and the tyrant, even when they recognized that etymology, history, and theory undermined that distinction (ibid: ch. 2). In his *Education of the Christian Prince* Erasmus insisted on the difference, stating that "only those who govern the state not for themselves but for the good of the state itself, deserve the title 'prince.' His title means nothing in the case of one who rules to suit himself, and measures everything to his own convenience: he is no prince, but a tyrant. There is no more honorable title than 'prince' and no terms more detested and accursed than 'tyrant'" (Erasmus 1968: 160–1). Yet political discourse of the period also suggested that a "king" could slide all too easily into a "tyrant": Thomas Smith wrote in his *De republica anglorum* that, since from the first all kings were called "tyrannis" and all ruled absolutely, because they "did for the most part abuse in the same . . . that kind of administration and the maner also, at the first not evil, hath taken the signification and definition of the vice of the abusers, so that now both in Greeke, Latine and English, a tyrant is counted he, who is an evill king and who hath no regard for the wealth of the people" (Smith 1982: 55). Defining the nature of the "tyrant," and arguing the question of whether a tyrant is one who rules unjustly or illegitimately, became an important task, insofar as arguments about who was a tyrant and what should be done about him or her always returned to this problem of naming (see Bushnell 1990; Miola 1985).

Julius Caesar destabilizes this debate by evoking the context of the political values and vocabulary of late republican Rome. In the Roman republic the word *rex* was almost synonymous with *tyrannis*: both were words that the republican Romans hated – and that they knew how to use in political propaganda (Dunkle 1967; Wirszubski 1968: 71). An audience at the Globe at the turn of century would have recognized the arguments against Caesar as a tyrant, while they may not have agreed on the justification for tyrannicide (see Skinner 1978: chs. 7–9). What would have appeared more difficult to grasp was the conspirators' insistence that Caesar should be feared because he wants to be *king*. Caesar was legally declared "dictator" in 48 BCE, an act meant to give him extraordinary power in a time of crisis. In 44 BCE he became what Plutarch calls "perpetual dictator," and as Plutarch judges, "this was a plaine tyranny" (Plutarch, "Life of Julius Caesar," ch. LVII, p. 92). However, as Plutarch relates, "the chiefest cause that made [Caesar] mortally hated was the covetous desire he had to be called king, which first gave the people just cause, and next his secret enemies, honest colour to bear him ill will" (ch. LX, p. 94). Plutarch comments further on the irony that what was really hateful was Caesar's coveting of the symbols of royalty: he scoffed that it was "a wonderful thing that [the people of Rome] suffered all things subjects should do by commandement of their kings; yet they could not abide the name of king, detesting it as the utter destruction of their liberty" (Plutarch, "Life of Marcus Antonius," ch. XII, p. 164).

In thus displacing the scene of tyrannicide to a late republican setting, where the words "king" and "tyrant" had both connected and radically different meanings and political values, *Julius Caesar* could further destabilize the conventions of early modern political thinking about the "natural" differences between kings and tyrants, and with that, the appropriate political response to political ambition. Robert Miola notes the complex characterizations of both Caesar and the conspirators: "In *Julius Caesar* no trustworthy source of sovereignty arises to direct Rome; there is only the politics of the marketplace, a confusing cacophony of claims and counterclaims. In this world, the origins of civil government and sovereignty lie in the possession of power, pure, simple and amoral" (Miola 1985: 288). But the play also brings into direct conflict a Roman world where all claims to be king were suspect and a Tudor one where it was dangerous to inquire too closely into monarchical privilege.

Liberty

When Caesar has been assassinated, and Cinna's first words are "Liberty! Freedom! Tyranny is dead!", Casca quickly proclaims: "Some to the common pulpits and cry out, / Liberty, freedom and enfranchisement." Brutus calls on his co-conspirators to bathe their hands in Caesar's blood, and "Then walk we forth, even to the marketplace, / And waving our red weapons o'er our heads, / Let's all cry 'Peace, freedom, and liberty'." They are to be remembered, says Casca, as "the men that gave their country liberty" (3.1.78–118). The cry for liberty here seems to come as a natural consequence of the overthrow of tyranny.

Liberty: this is a word that falls on modern ears with a familiarity bred by three centuries of revolutions that have used the call to liberty as a rallying cry. But what would that word have meant at the Globe Theatre at the end of the sixteenth century? Certainly it would have signified the opposite of bondage or captivity, the personal state of being free to move at will and being free of ownership by another person (*OED*). For a sixteenth-century English man or woman, of course, the state of being in "bondage" was more of a metaphor or legal term than a reality (see Smith 1982: 135–42, on the question of the status of "bondage" in his time), so the idea of freedom to act at will would have been foremost in people's minds. As such, the notion of liberty could also bear an unfavorable connotation, as in the phrase "taking liberties" or going beyond what is proper or allowed. Examples of both meanings surface in close quarters in *The Comedy of Errors*, that play so rife with images of "bonds," good and bad. When Adriana chafes at her husband's neglect, Luciana defends the principle that "A man is the master of his liberty." But when Adriana then questions why women should not have equal liberty, Luciana warns that "headstrong liberty is lash'd with woe" (2.1.1–15). And so indeed, in just the previous few lines, Antipholus of Syracuse has nervously noted that in Ephesus you will find "disguised cheaters, prating mountebankes, / And many such-like liberties of sin" (1.2.111–12).

Liberty was also defined in spatial terms, as a "freedom" granted within boundaries: so, for example, in *Measure for Measure*, it is said that Barnadine "hath evermore had the liberty of the prison" (4.2.156). Following Steven Mullaney, scholars of the early modern English stage have remembered that the Globe itself was located in Southwark, or in one of London's "liberties," which were exempt from the jurisdiction of municipal authorities. Many recent readers of Shakespeare have eagerly expanded on the contradictions inherent in this definition of liberty, where a "liberty" was a circumscribed place of "license," an authorized space for the containment of forbidden pleasures and criminal activity (see Wilson 1993: 48).

If we judge merely from Shakespearean usage, less common was the use of the term liberty in a political context, as "exemption or freedom from arbitrary, despotic, or autocratic rule or control" (*OED*). It is notable that Shakespeare almost always uses the word liberty in conjunction with personal liberty, i.e., for individuals, except in *Julius Caesar*, where he speaks of Rome's liberty. In the world of Elizabethan political thought, the notion of the "liberty of the subject" was as complex as – and related to – the concept of resistance to tyranny and to the monarch's power. Among the six traditions of political resistance, all with "distinct vocabularies, conventions, styles of argumentation, and intended audiences," Donald Kelley has identified as many notions of liberty: "classical" resistance referred to "Roman formulas of self-defense and popular sovereignty," "the communal" form recalled the "hard-won 'liberties,' religious as well as secular, of the medieval communes," and "ecclesiastical" resistance defended the "spiritual *libertas ecclesiae*." In Protestant political discourse the concept was similarly fraught with ambiguity. As Kelley writes, "there was an obverse, symmetrical ambivalence to the notion of 'liberty', which referred alternately to the *libertas christiana* idealized by Luther and to the arrogant human freedom – whether the 'free will' of which Luther was so contemptuous or the political license of which he was so suspicious" (Kelley 1990: 7–8; on Luther's "liberty of conscience" see Allen 1951: 20). All these ideas were to emerge in the next century's explosive conflict over the defense of the "liberty of the subject" (see Sommerville 1986: ch. 5).

Shakespeare would have found the word "liberty" in North's translation of Plutarch, in the account of the conspirators' meeting before the assassination. When Brutus says he will not be present when Caesar will be named king by the Senate, Cassius asks what he will do if he is sent for: " 'For myself then,' said Brutus, 'I mean not to hold my peace, but to withstand him and rather die than lose my liberty.' Cassius being bold, and taking hold of this word: 'Why,' quoth he, 'what Roman is he alive that will suffer thee to die for thy liberty' " (Plutarch, "Life of Brutus," ch. X, p. 113). In "The Life of Julius Caesar" it is also said that, after the assassination,

> Brutus and his confederates on the other side, being yet hot with this murther they had committed, having their swords drawn in their hands, came all in a troop together out of the Senate, and went into the market-place, not as men that made countenance to fly, but otherwise boldly holding up their heads like men of courage, and called to the people to defend their liberty. (Ch. 44, pp. 101)

Not surprisingly, liberty or *libertas* was defined differently in the republican Rome where Brutus is said to have spoken these words. First, *libertas* was understood as meaningful only in the context of Roman law. It was identified with rights granted by Roman citizenship, and as such, it was not to be confused with *licentia*, a confusion that the English term liberty allowed. In a political language in which the deliberate and rational exercise of positive rights granted by law defined *libertas*, *libertas* necessarily excluded *licentia* (see Wirszubski 1968: 7). Further, as a political condition, *libertas* was not possible in the state of monarchy: in Charles Wirszubski's words, in the context of Roman republicanism,

> the opposite of *libertas* is *regnum*, which, if used in its proper sense, invariably implies absolute monarchy. The relationship between king and people is considered to be analogous to the relation between master and slaves. Consequently Monarchy is called *dominatio*; and subjection to monarchy *servitus*. Freedom enjoyed by the State negatively means absence of *dominatio*, just as freedom enjoyed by an individual negatively means absence of *dominium*. (Ibid: 5).

So it is in these terms that the late republican Roman characters of the play can speak of becoming "bondmen" and losing their liberty if Caesar is to be named a king by the Senate. But that statement really would not have made sense in the context of early modern England (unless you remember that every English man was in a sense in "bond" to the crown, and his land was in "fee" to a higher lord and to the king – see Smith 1982: 138–9).

The moment that *Julius Caesar* depicts, the last gasp of republican Rome, was a time in which the traditional notion of liberty had come to lose much of its power. Patricians, senators, and plebeians were not unified under the law's definition of their *libertas*, and the value of *libertas* was endangered in a state torn apart by internal conflict. The patricians and senators were more concerned with sustaining their own honor and dignity than the values of republicanism, and *libertas* meant little to the plebeians oppressed by war and disorder (see Wirszubski 1968: 95). The gap in *Julius Caesar* between the intrigues of the patrician "heroes" and the actions of the people may be just one marker of this breakdown, adapted from Plutarch's history.

In borrowing the word "liberty" from its context in North's translation of Plutarch, Shakespeare reproduces for his audience a "foreign" definition of the word: a "liberty" that was precluded by monarchy, and possible only within the positive laws of republican Rome (while in its Roman context it was also changing its meaning in new political circumstances). In this sense it exists in the play as a sign of an alien political ideology that was itself unstable. Shakespeare's audience would have also heard "liberty" in their own way. It would have resonated in the urban vocabulary of London, with all of its associations with the "liberties" of Southwark. In the conspirators' cry for "liberty," too, the audience may have understood the call for freedom from tyranny, especially with its echoes of the "liberty of conscience," but they would have also sensed the negative connotation of lawlessness lurking, indeed, close to the surface. Thus "liberty" would have had a dangerous ambiguity in this particular time and place.

Plebeians and Commoners

Commentators on *Julius Caesar* tend to agree that it does not present a favorable view of Rome's people, who are fickle in their allegiance to their leaders and easily roused to violence. But they do not concur as to who these people are. The plebeians of Rome? London's urban mob? Or the audience of Shakespeare's theatre? And what did they signify in the context of early modern English ideas of the status and political role of the "people"?

The confusion is invited by the playtext itself when the stage directions use different names for these people. The opening stage directions identify "certain Commoners" who pass over the stage, whom Flavius and Marullus call "mechanical" when they chastise them for walking "upon a labouring day without the sign / Of your profession" (1.1.3–5). In 1.2.264 the people of Rome are referred to as the "common herd." In his funeral oration over the body of Caesar, Antony calls them the "commons," who will dip their napkins in Caesar's blood upon hearing of Caesar's love for them (3.2.130).

However, the stage directions for 3.2 announce: "Enter Brutus and goes into the pulpit, and Cassius, with the plebeians." And the speech prefixes in this scene read "Pleb," as is the case in the following scene (where the stage directions have announced

"Enter Cinna the poet and after him the Plebeians"). The reader thus registers the fact that "plebeians" and not "commoners" listen to the funeral oration and later riot in the streets and murder Cinna. The commoners of the opening scene are relatively tame holidaymakers, the kind of witty craftsmen familiar from English city comedies like *The Shoemaker's Holiday* (see Dorsch 1955: 5). When they reappear as "plebeians" they lack such signs of "local color" and appear far less passive. They expect an audience and "satisfaction" from the men who murdered Caesar, and then, at Antony's instigation, they erupt into violence.

The difference in the stage directions and speech prefixes would have been imperceptible to the play's audience, but someone did insert them for the reader of the Folio text. We cannot solve the question of authorial intent (i.e., who wrote the speech prefixes), but we can ask what it might have meant for someone to put them there. What did "commons" or "commoners" – terms that do appear in the actors' speeches – mean to a contemporary audience? Were the terms "commons" and "plebeians" merely synonymous for a person of low rank, or did they suggest something different?

In England at the turn of the sixteenth century and into the seventeenth century the words "commoners" or "commons" could signify members of a community (and implicitly a city or town) "having civic rights," burgesses or citizens who were not aldermen or sheriffs (*OED*). Thus, in his *Boke Named the Governour* (1531), Thomas Elyot could write: "In the citie of London and other cities, they that be none aldermen, or sheriffes be called communers" (Elyot 1937: 1). More broadly, "commoner" or "commons" could mean anyone below the rank of peer (as in the "House of Commons"). The term "commons" thus had a social significance, identifying one not noble and possibly connoting "low" or "base." But it also had a political meaning, especially in an urban context, implying the possession of certain responsibilities and rights.

The question of the political status of the "commons" was indeed a vexed one at the time. In his *De republica anglorum* Thomas Smith indicated that the kind of men represented by *Julius Caesar's* "commoners," that is, the carpenter and the cobbler who speak in the opening scene, would have had no political voice. They appear to belong to the category that Smith calls "the fourth sort of men which doe not rule":

> The fourth sort or classe amongst us, is of those which the olde Romans called *capite censij proletariaij* or *operae*, day labourers, poore husbandmen, yea marchantes or retailers which have no free lande, copiholders, all artificers, as Taylers, Shoemakers, Carpenters, Brickemakers, Bricklayers, Mason, & c. They have no voice nor authoritie in our commonwealth and no account is made of them but onelie to be ruled, not to rule other, and yet they be not altogether neglected [since he recognizes that in cities and villages, because of the absence of yeomen, they may hold some offices and serve at inquests]. (Smith 1982: 76–7; see also Palliser 1983: 390–1, on the relationship between Smith's work and William Harrison's *Description of England*)

In this categorization Smith opposes this group to burgesses and citizens and to yeomen, freemen who are not gentlemen but who "have a certain preheminence and more estimation than laborers and artificers" (Smith 1982: 74).

Elsewhere in his treatise, however, Smith lumps together yeomen and artificers in opposition to laborers, when he says that (in Dewar's edition) "we in England divide our men commonly into foure sortes, gentlemen, citizen and burgesses, yeoman artificers, and laborers." Just to make things more complicated, the 1583 edition in fact makes the division into "gentlemen, citizens and yeoman artificers, and laborers" (Smith 1982: 65). This alternative order would imply that *Julius Caesar*'s carpenter and cobbler were *not* among the "fourth sort" who had no political voice at all, but that they had some (unspecified) rights. (One must, of course, remember to separate the idea of the political rights of commons from the question of who had the franchise, which was still limited to males with property of 40 shillings freehold: see Patterson 1989: 2–3). As D. M. Palliser has commented, this kind of categorization in general ends up ignoring "local and regional" variation and presenting an oversimplified view in which "the powerful and wealthy few are distinguished very carefully and the many are lumped together at the end as 'the forth and last sort of people'" (Palliser 1983: 72).

When the discourse of social divisions and political rights was thus uncertain, the use of the term "commons" would have been neither neutral nor unambiguous. Its connotations were further complicated by its associations with the notion of the "commons" as land, the farming land at stake in the ongoing wars over enclosure. In her discussion of the representation of the "common people" in the context of the rural uprising of the sixteenth century, Annabel Patterson notes how the "commons" involvement with the issue of enclosure might be connected with the concept of "common" or "natural inheritance" of land (Patterson 1989: 43). In his funeral oration Antony indeed alludes to this when he tells the people that in his will Caesar has given them "his private arbours and new-planted orchards" for their "common pleasures" (3.2.236–46). The "commons" of *Julius Caesar* may thus represent a distinctly urban set of commoners, resembling the mobs that began to play a role in English politics toward the end of the sixteenth century (see Wilson 1993: 25–6), but in their name they also carry the burden of representing the English commons at large, who, however officially disfranchised, were endowed with recognized rights and responsibilities and who had already become politicized over the matter of enclosure.

In contrast, the word "plebeian" must have had little of the contemporary resonance of "commons." The term appears to have entered into English in the sixteenth century through the translation of Roman history, as a formation from the Latin "plebs." English writers did tend to define the term by analogy to their own class and political system. In his strenuous effort to prove that a "respublica" and "commonweale" does not signify rule by the common people, as contrary to "order," Thomas Elyot contended that "Plebs in englisshe is called the communaltie, which signifieth only the multitude, wherin be contayned the base & vulgare inhabitantes, nat auanced to any honour or dignite: . . . that Plebs in latine is in englisshe communaltie: & Plebeii be communers. Plebs in latin & cominers in englisshe be wordes only made for the discrepance of degrees: wherof procedeth ordre" (Elyot 1937: 1). Thomas Smith also saw the political divisions of Rome and England as parallel in terms of their "orders," but put it quite differently: "When the Romanes did write *senatus populusque Romanus*, they seemed to make but two orders, that is, of the Senate and people of Rome, and so in the name of the people they contained *equites* and *plebem*: so when we in England do say the Lordes and the commons, the knights, the knights esquires, and other gentlemen, with citizens, burgeses and yeoman be accompted to make the commons" (Smith 1982: 68). Smith was also aware of the *difference* between the Roman *plebs* and the English commons, when he wrote elsewhere of the conflicts "among the Romans of *Patritij* and *plebei*, thone striving with thother for a long time, those that were *patricij* many years excluding those that were *plebei* from bearing rule, till at last all magistrates were made common among them" (p. 65). That is, Smith recognized that by the third century BCE the plebeians had in fact achieved a kind of political equity with the patricians, by creating their own political order with its own assemblies, offices, and officials in the form of the tribunes, who played an important role in Rome's republican "mixed polity" (see Erskine-Hill 1996: 142; also Hammond and Scullard 1970: 845), which differed significantly from the political organization of Tudor England.

That Shakespeare knew this aspect of Roman history is shown by *Coriolanus*, his one sustained dramatization of republican politics and the relationship among plebeians, tribunes, and patricians. In this later play Shakespeare's plebeians are more than just an urban mob: they have a voice in Rome and a role in the naming of the consul (see Erskine-Hill 1996: 143–4). As Annabel Patterson has described them, the plebeians or "citizens" in *Coriolanus* do have voices: the play "allows the people to speak for themselves as a political entity, with legitimate grievances, and with a considerable degree of political self-consciousness" (Patterson 1989: 127). Both Erskine-Hill and Patterson, who want to take Shakespeare seriously as a student of republicanism, scrupulously avoid discussing the commons in *Julius Caesar*. In so doing, however, they cannot see that the "plebeians" of *Julius Caesar* do also stand in that play as the sign of a people that "will be satisfied" (3.2.1), with an aura of the plebeians of republican Rome.

The dissonance signaled by the different labels of "commons" and "plebeians" in speeches, stage directions, and speech prefixes does reflect a significant discontinuity in the representation of *Julius Caesar*'s "crowd," and, on a deeper level, an inconsistency in contemporary English ideas of the people's role in political life. Shakespeare's "common" voices – the cobbler, the carpenter, and the "plebeians" – may all be embraced by the term "commons," which in Shakespeare's time conveyed at once the possession of some civic rights and responsibilities, yet at the same time a lack of status or positive political role. The play itself, in turn, figures these "commons" inconsistently. They are cheerful, more or less respectable members of the city, wishing to celebrate Caesar's return, but quickly silenced by their own representatives. They are also the "tag-rag people" (1.2.258) or "rabblement" (1.2.244), who, in Casca's account, throw up their "sweaty nightcaps" at Caesar's public refusal of the crown, thus naively signaling their appreciation of republican sentiments. But in 3.2 they are also the people who must be appeased and whose response to the assassination must be managed. The "plebeians" say that they "will be satisfied" (3.2.1): they require an audience and Brutus must "render" to them the "public reasons" of Caesar's death (3.2.7). It is only in the hands of Antony that they are transformed from the apparently rational political actors at the opening of 3.2, who will compare the "reasons" of Brutus and Cassius, into a raging and murderous mob. This incoherence in the staging of *Julius Caesar's* "commoners" thus raises critical questions about the people's proper role in city and the state, as measured against the values of both England and republican Rome – questions to which Shakespeare would return eight years later, when he wrote *Coriolanus*.

Country and Commonwealth

The actions of commoners and noblemen, patricians and plebeians, take place indeed in a "Rome" which is a city on the Tiber, a "country," and a "commonwealth." All three constructs of the play's political arena are evoked at the end of Brutus' speech to the people, when he introduces Marc Antony entering with the body of Caesar:

> Here comes his body, mourn'd by Marc Antony, who, though he had no hand in his
> death, shall receive the benefit of his dying, a place in the commonwealth, as which of
> you shall not? With this, I depart, that, as I slew my best lover for the good of Rome,
> I have the same dagger for myself, when it shall please my country to need my death.
> (3.2.41–5)

While the word "Rome" functions as a kind of talisman in the play, and the terms "country" and "countrymen" are repeated frequently, this is the only time we hear the word "commonwealth," a word that (along with its cognate "commonweal") had a distinctly different connotation from "country."

Both to cheer themselves and to advance their cause, the conspirators naturally represent themselves as acting for their "country": they want to be the men that "gave their country liberty" (3.1.118). When Brutus defends his actions to the Roman people, he claims that he did what he did for his love of Rome, for "who here is so vile that he will not love his country?" (3.2.33). The younger Cato's final desperate cry on the battlefield of Philippi for himself and when impersonating Brutus is that "I am a foe to tyrants, and my country's friend" (5.4.5–7). The term "countrymen" occurs in *Julius Caesar* more frequently than in any other Shakespeare play (while "country" appears most often – 27 times – in *Coriolanus*). We remember the word "countrymen" most vividly from its uses in act 3, scene 2, where Brutus and then Antony call upon their "friends, Romans and countrymen" to hear them. Brutus uses the word three times in addressing the plebeians, and Antony four times, interchanging it with the affectionate term of "friend." Given the word's use in this context of public rhetoric and pleading, and knowing that Antony uses it cynically, we tend to hear "country" and "countrymen" as words tinged with patriotic fervor, but they are also contaminated by Antony's hypocrisy.

Like liberty, country and countrymen are such familiar words that we rarely stop to ask what they might mean. In Shakespeare's time country could still mean simply "a tract or district having more or less definite limits in relation to human occupation"; that is, one could talk about "the country" of a landowner or a county. But it had also come to signify the territory of land identified with an independent state, or a single race, language, or people, or by extension, one's native land (OED). The shift in meaning was certainly visible in the first half of the sixteenth century in Thomas Starkey's A Dialogue between Reginald Pole and Thomas Lupset where, as Thomas Meyer notes, "in contrast to the more usual meaning of district or county, Starkey used the word to apply to the whole of England" (Meyer 1989: 121). Country and country-men thus implied a shared identity and attachment to a place, and their increasing usage in this way matched a growing sense of England as a country united by language and race.

A commonwealth, however, is something different: a political construct much debated in the sixteenth century. While the notions of commonwealth and country overlapped in the sixteenth century, insofar as both terms signified a state or body politic, a commonwealth was, as The Oxford English Dictionary puts it, "especially viewed as a body in which the whole people have a voice or an interest." The debate about the meaning of the commonwealth was particularly intense at the beginning of the sixteenth century, when men such as Thomas More, Thomas Starkey, and Robert Crowley debated the nature of "the very and true commonweal," a concept rooted in medieval ideas of social duty, cooperation, and the common good (Allen 1951: 3; see also Skinner 1978: 221–8). In the latter part of the century Thomas Smith used the term to embrace all forms of government, including monarchy, oligarchy, and democracy, but he also defined it in a way that emphasized the "common," as "a society or common doing of a multitude of free men collected together and united by common accord and covenauntes among themselves, for the conservation of themselves as well in peace and in warre" (Smith 1982: 57). Not surprisingly, in Shakespeare, the word appears most often in 2 Henry VI, in connection with the members of the "commons" and their complaints, both in act 1, scene 3 and in act 4 (where George Bevis boasts that "Jack Cade the clothier means to dress the commonwealth, and turn it, and set a new nap on it" (4.2.5–6)). It was left for the dissenters of the seventeenth century to reappropriate the word as a synonym for a republic or a democracy, but it had never lost that odor of the "common."

We can probably account for the occurrence of the word in Brutus' speech by looking at Plutarch's telling of the aftermath of the assassination in "The Life of Marcus Antonius." There it is said that after the assassination in the Senate, Antony

preferred a law that all things past should be forgotten, and that they should appoint provinces unto Cassius and Brutus: the which the Senate confirmed and further ordained that they should cancel none of Caesar's laws. Thus went Antonius out of the Senate more praised and better esteemed than ever man was, because it seemed to every man that he had cut off all occasion of civil wars and that he had showed himself a marvellous wise governour of the commonwealth, for the appeasing of these matters of so great weight and importance. (Plutarch, "Life of Marcus Antonius," ch. XIV, p. 165)

It is significant, then, that the phrase emerges out of a context in which the Roman republic was seen to work effectively for common good. It is also ironic, since in fact Antony is about to do precisely the opposite thing, in fomenting civil war. The word stands in the text, jostling with "country" and "Rome," as a trace of an understanding of Roman republican values and English dreams of a "very and true commonweal." It is a trace of a world in which people and the patricians work for the "common weal," but a world almost obliterated by irrationality and factionalism.

Julius Caesar is thus a play in which we can see English politics in action, not through the representation of the acts of kings or queens but, rather, in the conflict and evolution of political values, embedded in language, character, and event. What is most fascinating about the play is how, in its evocation of the political culture of republican Rome, it embeds new forms of political discourse and political action, which drew on the languages of the past and transformed them in the coming decades in England. Liberty, tyranny, commonwealth, and commons: these became the watchwords of a new political age at mid-century. This is not to say that *Julius Caesar* itself is either a radical or even a prophetic play in its depiction of tyrannicide and the failure of the conspiracy that brought Caesar down. Its events and action are too contradictory to offer a clear moral lesson on either side of the case. It does, however, carry the marks of the political fractures – and openness – of its historical moment. Such a way of reading *Julius Caesar* may not restore it to favor in the high school curriculum (this may be a lost cause), but it can let us see it, not as a classical monument or a tired classic, but as a dynamic political text that gives us a glimpse of the English commonwealth in debate and on the move.

NOTE

All citations of Shakespeare plays refer to *The Riverside Shakespeare*, ed. G. B. Evans. Boston, MA: Houghton Mifflin, 1974.

REFERENCES AND FURTHER READING

Allen, J. W. (1951). *A History of Political Thought in the Sixteenth Century*. London: Methuen.

Bathory, D. (1996). "With himself at war": Shakespeare's Roman Hero and the Republican Tradition. In J. Alulis and V. Sullivan (eds.) *Shakespeare's Political Pageant: Essays in Literature and Politics*. Lanham, MD: Rowman and Littlefield, 237–61.

Bono, B. J. (1994). The Birth of Tragedy: Tragic Action in *Julius Caesar*. *English Literary Renaissance*, 24, 449–70.

Burckhardt, S. (1961). The King's Language: Shakespeare's Drama of Social Discovery. *Antioch Review*, 21, 369–87.

Burt, R. A. (1991). "A dangerous Rome": Shakespeare's *Julius Caesar* and the Discursive Determinism of Cultural Politics. In M.-R. Logan and P. L. Rudnytsky (eds.) *Contending Kingdoms: Historical, Psychological and Feminist Approaches to the Literature of Sixteenth-Century England and France*. Detroit, MI: Wayne State University Press, 109–27.

Bushnell, R. W. (1990). *Tragedies of Tyrants: Political Thought and Theater in the English Renaissance*. Ithaca, NY: Cornell University Press.

Dollimore, J. and Sinfield, A. (eds.) (1985). *Political Shakespeare: New Essays in Cultural Materialism*. Ithaca, NY: Cornell University Press.

Dorsch, T. S. (ed.) (1955). *Julius Caesar*. London: Methuen.

Dunkle, J. R. (1967). The Greek Tyrant and Roman Political Invective of the Late Republic. *Transactions of the American Philological Association*, 98, 151–71.

Elyot, T. (1937) [1531]. *The Boke Named the Governour*. London: J. M. Dent.

Erasmus, D. (1968). *Education of the Christian Prince*, trans. L. K. Born. New York: W. W. Norton.

Erskine-Hill, H. (1996). *Poetry and the Realm of Politics: Shakespeare to Dryden*: Oxford: Clarendon Press.

Foakes, R. A. (1954). An Approach to *Julius Caesar*. *Shakespeare Quarterly*, 4, 259–70.

Girard, R. (1993). Collective Violence and Sacrifice in Shakespeare's *Julius Caesar*. In P. Lopate and E. Coleman (eds.) *The Ordering Mirror: Readers and Contexts*. New York: Fordham University Press, 221–42.

Hammond, N. G. L. and Scullard, H. H. (1970). *Oxford Classical Dictionary*. Oxford: Clarendon Press.

Helgerson, R. (1992). *Forms of Nationhood: The Elizabethan Writing of England*. Chicago, IL: University of Chicago Press.

Howard, J. E. (1994). *The Stage and Social Struggle in Early Modern England*. London: Routledge.

Kaula, D. (1981). "Let us be sacrificers". Religious Motifs in *Julius Caesar*. *Shakespeare Studies*, 14, 197–214.

Kelley, D. R. (1990). Ideas of Resistance before Elizabeth. In G. J. Schochet (ed.) *Law, Literature, and the Settlement of Regimes*. Washington, DC: Folger Shakespeare Library, 5–28.

Kezar, D. (1998). *Julius Caesar* and the Properties of Shakespeare's Globe. *English Literary Renaissance*, 28, 18–46.

Marcus, L. S. (1988). *Puzzling Shakespeare: Local Reading and Its Discontents*. Berkeley: University of California Press.

Meyer, T. (1989). *Thomas Starkey and the Commonweal: Humanist Politics and Religion in the Reign of Henry VIII*. Cambridge: Cambridge University Press.

Miola, R. S. (1983). *Shakespeare's Rome*. Cambridge: Cambridge University Press.

——(1985). *Julius Caesar* and the Tyrannicide Debate. *Renaissance Quarterly*, 38, 271–89.

Palliser, D. M. (1983). *The Age of Elizabeth: England under the Late Tudors, 1547–1603*. London: Longman.

Parker, B. L. (1993). "A thing unfirm": Plato's Republic and *Shakespeare's Julius Caesar*. *Shakespeare Quarterly*, 44, 30–43.

Paster, G. K. (1985). *The Idea of the City in the Age of Shakespeare*. Athens, GA: University of Georgia Press.

Patterson, A. (1989). *Shakespeare and the Popular Voice*. Oxford: Blackwell.

Plutarch (1579). *Lives of the Noble Grecians and Romanes*, trans. T. North. London.

Pocock, J. (1971). *Politics, Language and Time: Essays on Political Thought and History*. New York: Atheneum.

Rebhorn, W. (1990). The Crisis of the Aristocracy in *Julius Caesar*. *Renaissance Quarterly*, 43, 75–111.

Ripley, J. (1980). *Julius Caesar on Stage in England and America, 1599–1973*. Cambridge: Cambridge University Press.

Ronan, C. (1995). *"Antike Roman": Power Symbology and the Roman Play in Early Modern England, 1585–1635*. Athens, GA: University of Georgia Press.

Rose, M. (1992). Conjuring Caesar: Ceremony, History, and Authority in 1599. In L. Woodbridge and E. Berry (eds.) *True Rites and Maimed Rites: Ritual and Anti-Ritual in Shakespeare and His Age.* Chicago: University of Illinois Press, 256–69.

Skeat, W. W. (ed.) (1875). *Shakespeare's Plutarch: being a Selection from the Lives in North's Plutarch which Illustrate Shakespeare's plays.* London: Macmillan.

Skinner, Q. (1978). *The Foundations of Modern Political Thought, Vol. 2: The Age of Reformation.* Cambridge: Cambridge University Press.

Smith, T. (1982). *De republica anglorum*, ed. M. Dewar. Cambridge: Cambridge University Press.

Sommerville, J. P. (1986). *Politics and Ideology in England, 1603–1640.* London: Longman.

Spevack, M. (ed.) (1988). *Julius Caesar.* Cambridge: Cambridge University Press.

Walch, G. (1998). The Historical Subject as Roman Actor and Agent of History: Interrogative Dramatic Structure in *Julius Caesar.* In J. L. Halio and H. Richmond (eds.) *Shakespearean Illuminations: Essays in Honor of Marvin Rosenberg.* Newark: University of Delaware Press.

Wilson, R. (1993). *Will Power: Essays on Shakespearean Authority.* New York: Harvester Wheatsheaf.

——(1996). A Brute Part: Julius Caesar and the Rites of Violence. *Cahiers Elisabéthains*, 50, 19–32.

Wirszubski, C. (1968). *Libertas as a Political Idea at Rome During the Late Republic and Early Principate.* Cambridge: Cambridge University Press.

18

Othello and the Problem
of Blackness

Kim F. Hall

Last summer, I arrived in Heathrow airport from Central Asia, dehydrated and bleary eyed – only thinking of reaching a shower and a soft bed. It just so happened that, while my mind was a thousand miles away, the customs agent prematurely put me to work by asking me about *Othello* and race:

> "What brings you to London?"
>   "I am here to do research on Shakespeare's *Othello*."
>   "Well let me ask you something. Othello's a Moor, right? And a Moor is not really black, is he then? He would have been an Arab and not black at all."

I froze for just an instant. While it's a question that I encounter all the time, for a split second I thought, what if I give the "wrong" answer – or worse – a muddled answer? Would that reveal me as a fraud, someone who doesn't really "know" Shakespeare? Trying to sound professorial and knowledgeable, rather than dazed and anxious, I explained that knowing that Othello is a "Moor" doesn't really give us a clear idea what he is, since "Moor" stood for a variety of peoples in the early modern world. Clearly not satisfied, the agent handed back my passport and wished me a good trip. I was not satisfied either. Although my answer was "right," it did not address the more crucial questions – why is Othello's appearance still such a problem? What actually does the speaker want to know when asking whether (or insisting that) Othello was a Moor?

I say that this conversation was about Othello and "race" (rather than saying that it is about Othello and "Moors" or Othello and "blackface") because "race is a concept which signifies and symbolizes social conflicts and interests by referring to different types of human bodies" (Omi and Winant 1994: 55). The question is often based on an assumption that Othello's physical appearance – in this case his color – shapes how the play helps us interpret the world. Although I cannot read the custom agent's mind, I do believe that, at heart, the question doubts the connection of this representation of a "black" man to the peoples of the African Diaspora, people who have had to bear the economic and symbolic weight of historical regimes of enforced labor and contemporary discrimination.[1] To say that Othello was not meant to be conceived of as "black" is to liberate the reader from considering that history in reading, viewing, or performing the play and to liberate Shakespeare from possible charges of racism.

My answer will seem obvious to some and dubious to others: Othello's blackness is symbolically crucial to the play and thus the character was meant to be portrayed with a black skin. However, even when Othello is not portrayed as black, the play is always about race, albeit not in the ways that we think of it now. In this essay I will track the "social conflicts and interests" that arise in conversations about Othello's color in critical conversations since the seventeenth century. As commentators attempt to discern whether Othello should be associated more with North or sub-Saharan Africans, one can see considerations of *Othello* increasingly driven by the categories and theories associated with modern racism. Furthermore, critics and observers of the theatre habitually intermingle the question of color with formalist questions about the quality of the tragedy.

American intellectual W. E. B. DuBois, who famously declared in *The Souls of Black Folk* that "the problem of the twentieth century is the problem of the color-line" (DuBois 1996: 107), begins that work with the more subtle proposal that all of his interactions with whites are inflected by the unasked question: "How does it feel to be a problem?" (p. 101). DuBois maintains that his "race," his difference, disrupts the daily interactions and collective contacts that constitute social life, making it impossible for him to be fully one with the world – to be considered fully human. In critical history Othello's color becomes a directly asked dilemma, one that mirrors the unspoken problem posed by the presence of diasporic Africans in England and America. In DuBois's analysis the presence of an "American Negro" unhappily comments on the highest ideals of American democracy. Similarly, in Anglo-American criticism, Othello's blackness is said to undermine the highest values that come to be associated with Shakespeare in critical and popular consciousness – transcendence, aesthetic guidance, and purity. I propose that questions of tragic form and color are related phenomena that address fears driven by Western associations of blackness with sexuality, emotion, and, significantly, Christian concepts of sin and evil.

Actually, the "problem" of Othello's color is relatively recent in the play's history. For two centuries white English actors used considerable labor to blacken their skins, seemingly without a thought as to whether it conformed to Shakespeare's conception of the play or to more abstract ideals of theatrical propriety.[2] However, in 1814 Drury Lane actor Edmund Kean inaugurated what has come to be known as the "Bronze Age" of *Othello*: maintaining that it was a "gross error to make Othello either black or negro" (Hawkins 1869: 221; see also Kaul 1996: 7ff.), Kean played him as a "tawny" Arab and in an extraordinarily passionate manner described by *Blackwood's* as "the most terrific exhibition of human passion that has been witnessed on the human stage" (quoted in Rosenberg 1961: 62; Honigman 1997: 94). More specific reasons for Kean's innovation are not clear from the theatrical record. Kean played several "exotic" seemingly Arab characters earlier in his career and these performances may have given him the idea for his Othello (Cowhig: 135). More important, Kean's *Othello* was on the boards at the beginning of the Abolitionist movement in England. Ruth Cowhig persuasively argues that Kean may have picked up an unease with Othello's blackness in audiences who were already reading blackness with the demeaning depictions that accompanied exploitation of slaves (p. 134).

What is a Moor? What is a Negro?

But is it necessary that the Moor should be as *black* as a native of Guiney? (*Public Advertiser*, 1787)

Attempts to resolve the question of Othello's blackness by "fixing" the geographical origins – and therefore the identity – of Othello will not clarify Renaissance understandings of the term "Moor." Many critics have traced the multifaceted and at times inconsistent connotations of "Moor" (see Bartels 1977: 61–2; Barthelemy 1987: 5–12; D'Amico 1991; Neill 2000: 269–74; Vaughan 1994: 56–8) and it is generally recognized that "Moor" is a term of complex indeterminacy that generally marks geographic and religious difference in ways that make the Moor a profound Other to Christian Europe. While sharing the common connotations of "alien" or "foreigner," the word "can mean . . . non-black Muslim, black Christian, or black Muslim" (Barthelemy 1987: 7). With these overlapping registers of race, region, and religion, the term's links to the darker-skinned peoples of Africa can therefore be quite confusing. Indeed, there are cases in which English authors deliberately used "Moor" to refer to wide regions of Africa, thereby compounding the ambiguity attached to the term (ibid: 12–17). Unlike "Moor," "Negro" is more specific, almost always referring to African peoples and associating them with blackness and a certain physical type (see Bartels 1977). While scholars of later centuries would assume (or argue for) a strict dichotomy between the two, Moors could also be and often were referred to as "Negroes." As a result, earlier critical discussions of Othello's origins revolve around the attempt to solidify differences between "Moors" and "Negroes," with Moors seen as having lighter skins (and European values) and "Negroes" read through blackness and barbarism.[3]

Given the polyvalence of the term, the color of a given literary Moor can only be deduced from its context. The word, like many others, gains meaning through collateral terms. Often, darker-skinned Africans are referred to as "Blackmoors." For example, in a description of John Lok's voyage to Guinea, the narrator expounds,

It is to be understood, that the people which now inhabit the regions of the coast of Guinea, and the middle parts of Africa, as Libya the inner, and Nubia, with divers other great & large regions about the same, were in old time called Aethiopes and Nigritae, which we now call Moores, Moorens, or Negroes, a people of beastly living, without a God, lawe, religion or common wealth. (Barne 1903–5: 167)

The English version of Leo Africanus's *Geographical Historie of Africa* (1600) refers to the biblical explanation for blackness: "For all the Negros or blacke Moores take their descent from *Chus*, the sonne of *Cham*, who was the son of *Noe*" (p. 791).[4] The links of Moors with blackness and/or Islam were so profound that a "Moor" not associated with them would have to mark his difference from his linguistic cohorts. As Anthony Barthelemy (1987) argues, "If a stage Moor, therefore, was other than Muslim or black, he had to identify himself as such by denying his kinship with his kind" (p. 17).

Allied with the problem of definition is the question of how many early modern people would have actually seen a Moor – either a "black moor" or a Muslim. For complicated reasons having to do with the relationship of Muslims and Blacks to the state, this question defies a definitive answer.[5] For years it has been assumed, as Edward Said does, that the Elizabethan experience of Muslims, at least, was merely textual. More recent and detailed work bolsters Nabil Matar's (1999) argument that "throughout the Elizabethan and Stuart periods Britons had extensive interaction with Turks and Moors" (p. 17). Othello, a well traveled "stranger / Of here and everywhere" (1.1.133–4), sits squarely within the play's mobilization of discourses of blackness and fears of Islam, making him "a hybrid who might be associated with a whole set of related terms – *Moor, Turk, Ottomite, Saracen, Mahometan, Egyptian, Judean, Indian* – all constructed in opposition to Christian faith and virtue" (Vitkus 1997: 161). So, too, the play features the ambivalent or contradictory cultural attitudes towards Moors: the cultures marked by the term could be "admired and reviled at almost the same time" (D'Amico 1991: 4). Michael Neill (2000) suggests that even the putative visibility of the Moor's "aggressive Otherness" was a source of doubt and concern given the term's indeterminacy (p. 272). It would seem that, rather than trying to pin down Othello to a specific geographic location, Shakespeare took advantage of the rich and at times disturbing network of allusions associated with "Moor."

Othello so often becomes a vehicle for articulating an era's racial concerns that it becomes difficult to draw out what is inherent in the play. In the late eighteenth century Othello criticism tends to dwell on the putative differences between "Moors" and "Negroes," creating racialized geographies or ethnographies of Moors in ways that put them in at times tortuous odds with the language of the play. For example, in supporting Kean's change of Othello's color, his nineteenth-century biographer, F. W. Hawkins, readily acknowledges both the character's origins in blackface and the language of color that runs throughout the play; however, he uses a clearly motivated historical geography to ignore that evidence: "Although in the tragedy Othello is called an 'old black ram,' and described with a minuteness which leaves no doubt that Shakespeare intended him to be black, there is no reason to suppose that the Moors were darker than the generality of Spaniards, who indeed are half Moors, and compared with the Venetians he would even then be black" (Hawkins 1869: 22).

Let us look at an early – and rather notorious – controversy over the use of a black "Moor" as the hero of *Othello*. In 1693 critic Thomas Rymer published *A Short View of Tragedy*, an energetic and literal-minded attack on Shakespeare and Renaissance tragedy that derides it as lacking the requisite decorum, and ignoring the classical rules of art. Among other things, he complains, "the Words and Action are seldom akin, generally are inconsistent, at cross purposes, embarrass and destroy each other" (Vickers 1974–81, II: 25). Rymer's rather shocking attack becomes widely read, perhaps because "his literal application of Neo-Classical principles" was an embarrassment to those who agreed with the principles, yet loved Shakespeare (ibid: 3). Such critics were thus forced to defend Shakespeare's plays as brilliant exceptions to these rules or to suggest that the rules were too narrow to encompass Shakespeare's genius. A number of neoclassical critics, Dryden among them, rose to the challenge, claiming that Rymer's "borrow'd Rules blind him to Shakespeare's insights into human nature" (ibid: 302).

For Rymer, probability and common sense are important yardsticks by which tragedy must be measured: he finds Othello almost obscenely lacking in these qualities (Rymer 1956: 17–19). The racial intermarriage and issues of class and character are central to the many improbabilities that he finds in the play. His complaint that Shakespeare violates precepts of noble character by creating characters who act contrary to nature moves rather quickly from an analysis of manners to commentary on the racial climate of Venice/Europe (and by extension, England): "He bestows a name upon his *Moor*, and styles him *the Moor of Venice*: a Note of pre-eminence which neither History nor Heraldry can allow him" (p. 87). For Rymer, Othello's color puts him at odds with his reputed status in the play:

> The Character of that State is to employ strangers in their Wars. But shall a Poet thence fancy that they will set a Negro to be their General, or trust a *Moor* to defend them against the *Turk*? With us a *Black-amoor* might rise to be a Trumpeter: but *Shakespeare* would not have him less than a Lieutenant-General. (p. 91)

Rymer bases this judgment on an improbability from his own era: since a black man could not rise to a position of importance in his own world, the audience cannot be expected to believe it of Shakespeare's play-world. This judgment of *Othello* could be read solely as a statement about class and social position, except that it coincides with an equally negative view of Iago who does not act as a noble soldier. Here, Rymer argues, "He is no Blackamoor Soldier, so we may be sure he should be like other Soldiers of our acquaintance" (p. 93). His assertion that Iago as a white, English soldier could not act with such villainy, throws into relief the assumed negative judgments of the characters of Blacks. Thus character and class conflate to make Othello a walking oxymoron – a noble Moor – who is an improbable husband for a noble lady. Indeed, Desdemona's desire for Othello makes her, in Rymer's eyes, too common for the viewer to be moved by her fate. When she asks, "O God, Iago, / what shall I do to win my Lord again?" (4.2.151), Rymer replies, "No Woman bred out of a Pig-stye cou'd talk

so meanly" (p. 131). The marriage and their mutual desire disrupts the proper alignment of class, race, and decorum, degrading them both and draining the play of its
ability to elicit the requisite responses to tragedy.

The most extended response to Rymer comes from editor–dramatist–critic Charles
Gildon, who in his "Some Reflections on Mr. Rymer's Short View of Tragedy and an
Attempt at a Vindication of Shakespeare . . ." (1694), reasons that "it gives sufficient
ground to our Poet to suppose a _Moor_ employ'd by 'em as well as a _German_; that is,
a _Christian Moor_, as _Othello_ is represented by our Poet, for from such a _Moor_ there cou'd
be no just fear of treachery in favour of the _Mahometans_" (Gildon 1974: 72). Gildon
clearly takes seriously Rymer's implicit claims that the racial climate of England
makes the play improbable and argues that, rather than being bound by social truth,
the playwright should rise above it and offer the audience a moral lesson:

> 'Tis granted, a _Negro_ here does seldom rise above a Trumpeter, nor often perhaps higher
> at _Venice_. But that proceeds from the Vice of Mankind, which is the Poet's Duty, as he
> informs us, to correct, and to represent things as they should be, not as they are. Now
> 'tis certain, there is no reason in the nature of things why a _Negro_ of equal birth and
> merit should not be on an equal bottom with a _German_, _Hollander_, _French-man_, _& c._ The
> Poet, therefore, ought to show justice to Nations as well as Persons, and set them to
> rights, which the common course of things confounds. The Poet has therefore well
> chosen a polite People to cast off this customary Barbarity of confining Nations, without
> regard to their Virtue and Merits, to slavery and contempt for the meer Accident of
> their Complexion. (p. 74)

Even though Gildon shares Rymer's negative views of Blacks (elsewhere he disparag-
ingly condemns Rymer's judgment, offering that he has less poetic taste than the
"Blackamoor . . . in the Western Plantations": p. 69), he discusses Rymer's actual criticism within the context of Atlantic slavery, offering an oblique critique of race-based
slavery in his suggestion that the poet has a duty to "correct" the "Barbarity of confining nations . . . to slavery and contempt."

It is useful to note here that both critics assume that Shakespeare meant to have
Othello performed as a dark-skinned African. Even in finding the characters offensive
and ridiculous, Rymer attributes the choice to Shakespeare's faulty artistic judgment;
that is, the choice is wrong, but it is Shakespeare's choice nonetheless. Moreover, both
writings show the conceptual flux that surrounds the term "Moor" – a semantic "indis-
tinction" that was common (if more indistinct) in Shakespeare's day. Othello is alternatively a "Moor," a "Blackamoor," and a "Negro." We can also see a new element
that will long endure in the history of _Othello_: a concrete connection of blackness with
slavery. England at this point is already a slave-trading power; both critics agree that
that economic and political reality can impinge on the ability of the audience to
connect with the character and feel the pathos of the tragedy.

Samuel Taylor Coleridge produced some of the most influential criticism of
Shakespeare and _Othello_, in large part creating the romanticized Shakespeare of

universal genius that lingers in the Shakespeare industry.[6] In doing so he did for literary readings of *Othello* what Edmund Kean did for dramatic renderings of Othello: he makes a bronze Othello the best vehicle for engaging the audience's sympathy and identification. While embarked on a general project of defending Shakespeare from the neoclassical tradition of criticism, he assumes that only a bronze Othello can fulfill the highest requirements of tragedy:

> Even if we supposed this an uninterrupted tradition of the theatre, and that Shakespeare himself, from want of scenes and the experience that nothing could be made too *marked* for the nerves of the audience – would this prove aught concerning his own intentions as a poet for all ages? Can we suppose him so utterly ignorant as to make a barbarous *negro* plead for royal birth? Were Negroes then known but as slaves? on the contrary were not the Moors the warriors, etc.? (Foakes 1989: 112)[7]

In a striking difference from Rymer's assumption of Shakespeare's bad judgment, Coleridge imposes a clear distinction between Moor and Negro, insisting that Shakespeare would never make the mistake of asking an audience to believe in a noble Negro. An oxymoronic "royal Moor" would not only unacceptably hint at Shakespeare's ignorance of cultural distinctions, it would also detract from his status as universal genius, "a poet for all ages," unhindered by time, place, religion, or race. Here and elsewhere, Coleridge indicates that Othello's blackness interferes with the concerns of art: form, feeling, and the struggle of human will.

Othello's "race" becomes a matter for or barometer of aesthetic judgment – the critics' as well as Shakespeare's. Law Professor Patricia Williams points out that excising overtly racialized language does not remove the power of racism. Other discourses and sentiments can have the structural force of racism, often taking the place of more overtly vicious language. In her discussion of the controversy over integrating the famous Rockettes of the Radio City Music Hall in New York she ponders how viewing the very presence of blackness as an interruption of the order of things has serious social consequences for the black individual:

> An issue that is far more difficult to deal with than the simple omission of those words that signify racism – is the very perception that introducing blacks to a lineup will make it ugly ("unaesthetic"), imbalanced ("nonuniform"), and sloppy ("imprecise"). The ghostly power of this perception will limit everything the sole black dancer does – it will not matter how precise she is in feet and fact, since her presence alone will be constructed as imprecise, it is her inherency that is unpleasant, conspicuous, unbalancing. (Williams 1991: 117)

A similar sense of black "inherency" and conspicuousness haunts the Coleridge comment that a black Othello would be too "marked" – too visible, too present – for his presumably white audience. Indeed, the problem of a conspicuously black Othello continues to be presented as an aesthetic question – albeit one with racial effects.

Efforts at containment through investigation of Othello's color are inevitably tax-onomizing and racializing activities.[8] The criticism that follows obviously partakes of the discourse that most people think of when we refer to "race": that is, a "scientific racism" that attempts to classify peoples into categories based on the idea that indi-viduals represent qualities of his/her type or species and, more important, that there are permanent differences in abilities that co-relate to biological differences and char-acteristics. This methodology follows the principle of natural history that all of nature can be classified according to a design determinable by scientific observation and dis-covery.[9] Early modern writers did not organize nationalities or physical types into the strict and hierarchical categories that are associated with modern race thinking. There was no system of types or species and, equally important, no rigid sense of permanent categories which classify peoples by color and other physical features. Human differ-ences are for Renaissance writers fluid, multiform, and complex, marked not simply by color, but by a host of differences including language, clothing, eating habits, and adornments of body (Hall 1999); but as early modern Europe increasingly ties its for-tunes to the East and the Americas and enters new economic and social relations, these theories of difference become a significant means by which England articulates its sense of place in the world. Older discursive and symbolic forms mutate and are remade as they address new political and economic structures.

One link between later racial formations and the older, more fluid notions typical of the Renaissance is the desire to resolve questions of affinity. Etienne Balibar argues that, at its heart, "race" is about community, kinship, and the transmission of these connections through time: "The symbolic kernel of the idea of race (and of its demo-graphic and cultural equivalents) is the schema of genealogy, that is, quite simply the idea that the filiation of individuals transmits from generation to generation a sub-stance both biological and spiritual and thereby inscribes them in a temporal com-munity known as 'kinship'" (Balibar 2002). More simply, Tessie Liu (1995) suggests that "racial thinking developed historically out of the reasoning people did about the solidarities they held closest to their hearts" (p. 565).[10] Within this schema the ques-tion "Moor or Negro?" can be seen as interrogating place and kinship. In many of these armchair ethnographies the racial project is to frame Othello's "difference" so as to make Othello a tragic hero that the critic (and his presumed audience) can iden-tify with and thus be moved by. Othello has to be made different enough to accom-modate the play's clear emphasis on "belonging and estrangement" (Neill 2000: 207), yet similar enough for an empathy that can lead to self-discovery.

Unfortunately, as Atlantic slave trading and colonial incursions in Europe and America harden negative attitudes towards African-descended peoples, it becomes impossible for critics to see a black Othello as fully human. A black "Noble Moor" becomes an increasingly untenable oxymoron, a "problem" in DuBois's terms that becomes "solved" through claims of affinity and increasingly rigid notions of dif-ference. A Dr. Elits (Stillé 1887) reveals what is at stake in such discussions when he insists, not only that Othello is a "Moor," but that his characteristics are "Caucasian":

Othello was a Moor, not a negro. The monuments of Egypt, from the earliest periods of its history, prove that Negroes have always possessed the same mental and physical characteristics as at the present day. The Moors were not, like them, natives of Africa, but were of Oriental origin. They were in large part Arabians, and *formed one of the channels through which the science and art of the East reached Europe.* They conquered, and for a long time occupied, a large part of Spain, and in literature and art have left imperishable monuments in that country. *Whether Shakespeare fully comprehended the distinction between Moor and Negro may be doubtful*, but it is certain that *all of the characteristics of Othello are those of the Caucasian race.* (Ibid: 15, 16; final emphasis added).

As with other commentators, one is struck here by the enormous effort the author puts into making Othello, not simply a Moor, but a Moor who is Caucasian – that is, like him. Although he rather perplexingly suggests that "Negroes" both do and do not have civilization (they built the pyramids, but have not changed or progressed since that ancient past), in Elits's cosmography, "Negroes" remain stuck in a monumentally frozen past, while "Moors" are active, civilized, and conquering.

Aligned with his insistence on Othello the character's "Moorishness" is a declaration of the purity of the play itself. Elits begins his discussion of the play insisting that Desdemona and Othello's love is removed from sensual desire:

In no other pair of lovers created by Shakespeare do we observe such absolute subordination of the material passion to the nobler traits of love . . . No hint of sensuality is to be found either in the conversations of the lovers themselves, or in the Duke's address, or even in Brabantio's denunciation. It is only out of the foul and devilish soul of Iago and his consorts that such suggestions can spring. (pp. 13–14)

The removal of sensuality from the play is common in nineteenth-century criticism and is often accompanied by banishing Othello's blackness. Underlying the question of Othello's race is an indirect claim that a black Othello is "too common" or "too material" to allow the viewer to feel the pathos of tragedy, a point I will return to later.

In attempting to explain (or explain away) Othello's blackness and to remove a perceived taint of emotion and sensuality from the play, Elits engages in a less obvious racial project – creating whiteness. Ania Loomba (1989) reminds us that "Debates over whether Othello was black, brown, or mulatto anxiously tried to recover the possibility of his whiteness from this ambiguity" (p. 49). Elits's insistence on the "purity" of their love resonates against his later connection of "Moors" with higher and nonmaterial endeavors – literature and art. In both his discussion of nationality and his discussion of the play's values, he insists on an immateriality and purity that are the hallmarks of whiteness. Richard Dyer's landmark work *White* (1997) notes that it is the movement from body to pure spirit that makes whiteness so vastly present, yet peculiarly difficult to identify: "What makes whites different, and at times uneasily locatable in terms of race, is their embodiment, their closeness to the pure spirit that was made flesh in Jesus, and their spirit of mastery over their and other bodies, in short, their potential to transcend their raced bodies" (p. 25). Purity, conquest, and transcendence become key elements in the ideology of whiteness and we see within Elits's earlier discussion an attribution of the properties of whiteness to Othello and Moors.

Located within this urge for transcendence is the problem of sexuality. Racial formations often have to grapple with what Dyer calls the "conundrum of sexuality" for whiteness: "To ensure the survival of the race, they have to have sex – but having sex and sexual desire, are not very white: the means of reproducing whiteness are not themselves pure white" (p. 26). Desire, particularly interracial desire, threatens the purity that is a quintessential drive of whiteness. If Desdemona, as the frankly desiring woman who Rymer found so objectionable, becomes increasingly objectionable to later audiences (Dash 1981: 115), her desire for a "black" or "Negro" man promises to sully the entire race. Frank sexual desire and blackness threaten to contaminate the nobility and purity of both the play and the playwright. The play, on many levels seen as too "gross" or barbaric, also becomes unable to secure critical claims of Shakespeare's universal genius. Rewriting the hero (and the play) as "white" creates the capacity for "transcendental claims to speak for everyone, while being itself everywhere and nowhere" (Hall 1988).

If my assertion that these critics whiten the play itself seems somewhat problematic, consider the links between Othello's color and the higher ideals of poetry in the words of theatre critic William Winter, who asserts that Shakespeare "anglicized the whole affair, leaving nothing barbaric in Othello but his capacity of animal delirium":

> It used to be the practice of the stage to paint the Moor quite black – to present him, in fact, as a Negro. There are expressions in the text which, taken quite literally, and without allowances for the moods and attitude of the speakers, would afford a warrant for this practice. But – since to make Othello a Negro is to unpoetize the character, and to deepen whatever grossness may already subsist in the tragedy – it seems the better way to remember that poetry has the privilege to idealize all it touches, and that expressions of opinion are not statements of fact – and may therefore be disregarded ... Besides, there is a clearly marked difference between a Moor and a Negro. The Moor should be painted a pale cinnamon colour, which is at once truthful and picturesque. (Winter 1897: 121)

Like other critics, Winter is at pains to dismiss both the stage history and the textual evidence to serve his supposition that a dark-complected "Negro" is inimical to the aesthetic ideals of poetry. If a "pale cinnamon colour" is "more truthful" to a more idealized Othello, then black is both more "real" – more "gross" and material – yet somehow less truthful to the spirit and poetry of the play. As in Patricia Williams's discussion of the black Rockette, a black Othello becomes "unaesthetic" and disruptive to an idealized form.

When referring to the "whatever grossness [that] may already subsist in the tragedy," Winter touches on a problem unique to *Othello* – the protagonist's color either exacerbates (or is seen as clarifying) all else that is disturbing about the play. *Othello*'s central themes – jealousy and adultery – are typically the purview of comedy rather than tragedy. Rather than answering such tensions through the resolution of comedy, *Othello*, with its violent murder of an innocent woman, forces one's attention to powerful extremes/intensity of emotion and sensuality in ways that audiences have found dreadfully moving and almost unbearable from its inception.[11] *Othello* thus stages many elements that discomfited its patriarchal, somewhat cloistered culture – the agency choice of women, sexual desire, the enduring nature of conversion, and the status of outsider. In the later era that subscribed to Romantic ideals of idealized refinement this horrific combination can only be made palatable by abstracting key elements – sexuality, blackness, and passion – out of the text.

"Your Son-in-Law Is Far More Fair than Black"

Although Othello's staged blackness is not a source of comment in its earliest history, in no way is the play *Othello* indifferent to Othello's blackness (Jordan 1968: 20). Virginia Vaughan (1994) rightfully asserts that *Othello* depends on the hero's darkness as "the visual signifier of his Otherness" (p. 51). The play is dominated by a dualist logic that shapes its central concerns with love and jealousy. Even if Othello's color or race cannot be fixed within a specific geographic location, it is apparent that a black/white imagery, which indelibly associates human bodies with cultural norms and values (as well as moral qualities), permeates *Othello*. Michelle Wallace (1990) argues that the "unrelenting logic of dualism, or polar opposition – such as black and white, good and evil, male and female – is basic to the discourse of the dominant culture" (p. 60) and is the basis for much of the culture's more negative thinking about race and gender. The insistence on vital oppositions that can never be reconciled leads to dilemmas such as the "Noble Moor" who contains nobility and jealous rage, and the allegedly submissive daughter who publicly declares her passionate love.

The dualist language of black and white provides an ideological and moral structure made visible in the range of crossings, substitutions, and splittings. Othello's perceptions are challenged throughout the play. He is asked to choose between his wife and his ancient, to choose between "his image of Desdemona and the image Iago offers" (Orkin 1987). In a like manner, the play demands that its audience consider its own perceptions about the alien Moor: we are from the outset offered two versions of Othello – an overtly racist one (bestial, carnal) proffered by Iago, Roderigo, and Brabantio, and the noble Moor (restrained and dignified) seen by Desdemona, Cassio, and Othello himself. Defenses of Othello make clear that he inhabits a potent ideological divide. The Duke's allegedly soothing words to Brabantio: "If virtue no delighted beauty lack, / Your son-in-law is far more fair than black" (1.3.290–1), operate on an assumption that nobility or virtue is opposed to black skin. Moreover, the first line seems to waver in resolution of the black/white contradiction. Beginning with a conditional "if," it rests on an odd pun on "light": Othello's virtue is either "delighted" or "de-lighted"/darkened. The dualist logic of these formulations means that Othello's contradictions cannot be reconciled; nevertheless the play in many ways disrupts the culture's polarities. According to Patricia Parker (1994), "the play produces a series of powerful chiastic splittings. Desdemona, the white, Venetian daughter becomes, as it proceeds, the sexually tainted woman traditionally condemned as 'black,' part of a representational schema that gives ironic resonance to the choice of the name 'Bianca' (white) for the character most explicitly linked to that taint" (p. 95). Preconceptions about gender play a large role in this – women were often seen as incipiently sexually unruly unless properly controlled. Attempts to make Othello become the stereotypically violent Moor run concurrently with attempts to make Desdemona seem tainted and unchaste, and both are articulated though a language of blackness.

Racial imagery and religious difference are inescapable factors in characterizing the couple's love. Part of Iago's arsenal is the ability to characterize Othello as hypersexual and their love as therefore monstrous ("an old black ram / Is tupping your white ewe!": 1.1.87–8). This characterization allows for a concomitant focus on Desdemona as a creature of changeable carnality. Iago reassures Roderigo of his plan's success by asserting that Desdemona will tire of her husband sexually: "She must change for youth. When she is / Sated with his body, she will find the error of her / Choice," and Othello, once persuaded, bemoans: "O curse of marriage, / That we can call these delicate creatures ours / And not their appetites." Desdemona's famous declaration of her love ("I saw Othello's visage in his mind": 1.3.253) implicitly responds to this impulse by simultaneously deflecting attention away from Othello's blackness (his visage) and insisting on a more transcendent love, a love not of flesh, but of mind and spirit. That this is an underlying motif in the play can be seen in the term "gross" that not only is evoked at key moments in *Othello*, but also becomes the term that in the critical history marks discomfort with sexuality and blackness. Roderigo's initial description of Desdemona's elopement is coded in a language of materiality: Desdemona was "Transported with no worse nor better guard / But with a knave of common hire, a gondolier / To the gross clasps of a lascivious Moor" (1.1.123–4). Just like Iago, Roderigo emphasizes the stereotypical lasciviousness of Moors and embeds it within a broader language of materiality. In his vision, once Desdemona leaves her father's house, she is surrounded by all that is common and fleshly – literally moving from a "knave of common hire" to Othello's "gross" and "lascivious" embrace.

Unlike the more easily recognizable racializing terms used by Iago, Roderigo, and Brabantio, "gross" speaks to similar fears of bodily and spiritual impurity and is used by a multitude of characters in reference to adultery and marriage. While the *OED* documents that "gross" at this time is primarily used when speaking of things that are "obvious," as in too large or significant to be ignored, a secondary meaning that comes to dominate suggests a rudeness or lack of refinement, particularly in contrast with spiritual immanence: "of things material or perceptible to the senses, as contrasted with what is spiritual, ethereal, or impalpable" (*OED* III.c.). Thus "grossness" is not simply a matter of manners, but marks a diminished spiritual state. When Satan's armies are pinned to the earth by the archangel Michael's in Milton's *Paradise Lost*, they are spiritually and physically grounded, "though Spirits of purest light, / Purest at first, now gross by sinning grown" (VI: 660–1). This line encapsulates a sense not only of the significant division between spirit and flesh, but also that sin moves one from heaven to earth, spirit to flesh. "Grossness" is a state of fleshly sin – fullness. If we imagine a Renaissance audience used to stage blackness as the sign of lasciviousness, sin, and demonic influence, and a stereotype of Moors as lecherous and potentially violent, we can imagine the suspense that might be built up in the first scene which circulates this host of associations without putting Othello on stage. He literally enters into an arena which has already assumed his spiritual and sexual "grossness" and which must have him publicly judged.

In *Race, Gender, Renaissance Drama* Ania Loomba (1989) asserts that the language of sin and errant sexuality for both figures assumes its charge from Othello's blackness: "Othello's blackness is central to any understanding of male or female sexuality or power structures in the play; secondly, the filtering of sexuality and race through each other's prism profoundly affects each of them" (p. 41). The dualist language of embodiment reveals how deep fears over the organization of gender, sexuality, and race feed each other: blackness positions not just dark-skinned peoples, but also unruly women and the lower classes, outside of culture and civilization. It is no coincidence that much of the criticism, like Rymer's, associates Desdemona's active attempts to defend her marriage with women of the lower classes (see above). Early modern culture's suspicion of women as inherently sinful subjects always puts them at risk of being labeled "black" and the "discourse of 'blackness' is mobilized in order to circumscribe female transgression" (Loomba 1994: 27).

In dualist logic the language of gross materiality/evil aligns with blackness to make visible the ways in which Othello's racial condition interacts with patriarchal interests in controlling women, thus making the pairing of black male/white female a potentially monstrous and explosive combination (Newman 1991). While Othello's color marks him as an avatar of sin and sexuality, women, as the primary bearers of cultural anxieties about sexuality, are continually represented as notoriously unstable in this regard. As Iago continually reminds the audience of the carnality and sinfulness of blackness, he makes Othello see Desdemona's "grossness" – to imagine her not as the wife of his heart, but as a dangerously desiring woman. The bestial language first used to alienate Brabantio from the couple is also used to inflame Othello's jealous suspicions of his wife: "Where's satisfaction? / It is impossible you should see this, / Were they as prime as goats, as hot as monkeys, / As salt as wolves in pride, and fools as gross / As ignorance made drunk" (3.3.406–8). I should note here that this truncated reading of the play focuses on Iago as generating the most potent racial language, but it is too easy to make him the sole bearer of the play's racial language (as many critics do). While I do agree that Iago certainly activates the language of black

and white in the most pernicious way, "black" and "fair," like "gross," appear throughout the play in a variety of contexts. For example, the "old paradoxes" Desdemona
and Iago exchange on the Cyprus waterfront (2.1.116–64) are based both on misogynist attitudes about white women and on a color schema which assumes an association of blackness with sin and errant sexuality (Wayne 1991).

Similarly, it becomes easy to examine the circulation of "race thinking" as linked
solely to blackness and thus more comfortably aligned with current conceptions of
race. However, Othello's blackness also queries the meanings and values associated
with fair/whiteness. The "chiastic splittings" Parker argues for also force attention to
the language of fair/lightness/whiteness and potentially destabilizes the comfort of
dualist logic. The many calls for "light" in the stage directions and by the characters
indicate a conceptual darkness in which the truth cannot be plainly known. While
black Moors are potent indices of evil in the culture and women are notoriously
accused of false seeming, in this particular play, the concupiscence and demonic
impulses of the other characters are both revealed and concealed. The audience clearly
sees Iago's methods (if not his motives), yet his demonic nature is quite hidden from
all the play's characters until the very end, when he is "revealed" and then tarred with
that language of sin and materiality. The wish to destroy and exclude evil is expressed
in terms of blackness and cultural difference. Othello's response to the structure of
impossibility that disallows his nobility and Desdemona's chastity is to "blacken"
himself and Desdemona: "Her name, that was as fresh / As Dian's visage, is now
begrimed and black / As mine own face" (3.3.380–91), and to render himself the conflicted foreign other ("turbaned Turk"; 5.2.351). However, few have noted how the
public revelation of Iago's crimes moves Cassio to proclaim him alien and sinful: "Most
heathenish and most gross" (5.2.310). Rymer's earlier insistence that Iago is "no blackamoor soldier" proves strangely compelling when we consider that Iago's theatrical
predecessors, the Vice figures from medieval morality plays, were often portrayed in
blackface or black disguise (Fryer 1984).[12] If the "white" courtesan, Bianca, is a sly
symbolic foil for the chaste Des/*demon*/a, Iago is the "white devil," whose seeming
"belonging" and adept directing of attention to others' transgressions (he accuses
Othello, Emilia, Desdemona, and Cassio of adultery) locates potent fears of "grossness" in others. Iago, the omniscient, controlling citizen, operates under the cover of
whiteness; he is the evil within who escapes notice by projecting sin onto others.

Contemporary critics are deeply concerned that students will misread race in the
play: asking whether the original play is racist or not anachronistically remakes the
text in order to exact a literary justice not always offered by society. It is true that the
postcolonial theory informing most discussions of race can make it too easy to recreate Shakespeare's England on the terms of later periods.[13] However, acknowledging
this point should not lead to a whitewashing of the text. It seems to me that one can
think about the play's alignment and questioning of sexuality, evil, and color without
proclaiming the play either racist or anti-racist – terms not known by Shakespeare.
Othello's original audiences inhabited a moment of historic beginnings which are, as
with any historic moment, blended with the centuries-old structures of everyday life.

Even though England was not in the early modern period systematically trafficking in slaves and certainly was not the empire that consolidated scientific racism, it is part of a confederation of countries that come to consider themselves Europe – white and Northern – in response to the threat of Islam that underpins the play.[14] It will also come to join freedom and whiteness against images of black servitude. These questions of belonging – of creating communities and alliances by "referring to different types of human bodies" – are part of a racial project. The "problem" of blackness – an outsideness that interrupts desired structures of order and belonging – is not the same as, but is certainly intimately related to, the "problem" that haunts Western cultures today. We inhabit a moment of similarly seismic change and we too must make the old contend with the new. It is important to see how *Othello* is embedded in older discourses of belonging and filiation, but it is equally important to think about the ways it can help us solve the "problem" of race today.

NOTES

1   This is by no means to suggest that other people of color are not discriminated against in the West. However, historically the transatlantic slave trade produced its own enduring codes, laws, and symbols that carry a particular resonance in Western culture.

2   For a sense of the arduousness of blackface, see Cowhig (134).

3   Informed by critical race theory in other fields, contemporary debates on Othello and race focus more on what constitutes race thinking in the period, rather than fixing Othello's identity. The work on race and *Othello* is too voluminous to cover in its entirety. Much is cited in this essay, but I direct the reader to Vaughan's thorough work in *Othello: A Contextual History* (1994).

4   It is widely thought that Shakespeare was familiar with this text. Leo may actually have been a model for Othello. See Johnson (1985) and Whitney (1992).

5   For a discussion of the methodological issues posed when examining blacks in Shakespeare's time, see Hall (1993).

6   For a concise discussion of Coleridge's role in Shakespeare criticism and its influence on twentieth-century Shakespeare criticism, see Drakakis (1985: 4–9).

7   I have omitted more overtly racist lines often attributed to Coleridge in contemporary criticism, but of doubtful provenance: "yet as we are constituted, and most surely as an English audience was disposed in the beginning of the seventeenth century, it would be something monstrous to conceive this beautiful Venetian girl falling in love with a veritable negro" (Coleridge 1960: 42). For a critique of these lines, see Newman (1991) and Neill (2000: 245–8). For a discussion of the difficulties in attributing this passage to Coleridge, see Pecter (1997).

8   I am avoiding several notorious instances of racist commentary on the play. For example, the comments by M. R. Ridley, the editor of the original Arden Shakespeare, have been amply scrutinized (see Newman 1991; Orkin 1987; Pecter 1997; Singh 1994).

9   This discussion of race theories is indebted to Banton (2000).

10 It is important to remember that "race" is different from individual prejudice against people different from oneself. Currently, when scholars discuss "race" they think in terms of ideologies and structures that shape human interaction and representation.

11 Unfortunately, there is not room to address fully how the play's generic hybridity interacts with its interest in foreign difference. Susan Snyder (1979) most prominently makes the point that *Othello* opens with all of the generic signals of comedy. Michael Neill (2000) discusses this hybridity in the context of the final bed scene (pp. 260–2). Joyce Green MacDonald (1994) argues Kean's erasure

of Othello's blackness is undone by the appearance of Ira Aldridge, a black man, in the role. One might draw from her research that, as slavery makes Othello's blackness increasingly disturbing, bronze Othellos dominate the tragedy while the comic structures of minstrelsy absorb and display the discomfort created by the tragic text.

12 For an in-depth discussion of the Vice tradition and its influence on *Othello* and later drama, see Spivack (1958).

13 Both Bartels (1977) and Matar (1999) level this charge.

14 Although there has been no extended analysis of this point, Lynda Boose (1994) and Michael Neill (2000) both raise the question in provocative ways.

REFERENCES AND FURTHER READING

Balibar, E. (2002). The Nation Form: History and Ideology. In P. Essed and D. T. Goldberg (eds.) *Race Critical Theories*. Oxford: Blackwell, 220–30.

Banton, M. (2000). The Idiom of Race: A Critique of Presentism. In L. Back and J. Solomos (eds.) *Theories of Race and Racism: A Reader*. London: Routledge, 51–63.

Barne, G. (1903–5). The Voyage of M. John Lok to Guinea, Anno 1554. In *The Principal Navigations, Voyages, Traffiques & Discoveries of the English Nation by Richard Hakluyt*, vol. 6. Glasgow: J. MacLehose.

Bartels, E. C. (1977). *Othello* and Africa: Postcolonialism Reconsidered. *William and Mary Quarterly*, 3rd series, 54, 45–64.

—— (1990). Making More of the Moor: Aaron, Othello and Renaissance Refashionings of Race. *Shakespeare Quarterly*, 41, 433–54.

Barthelemy, A. G. (1987). *Black Face, Maligned Race: The Representations of Blacks in English Drama from Shakespeare to Southerne*. Baton Rouge: Louisiana State University Press.

Benjamin, P. (1997). Did Shakespeare Intend Othello to Be Black? A Meditation on Blacks and the Bard. In M. Kaul (ed.) *Othello: New Essays by Black Writers*. Washington, DC: Howard University Press, 91–104.

Boose, L. E. (1994). "The Getting of a Lawful Race": Racial Discourses in Early Modern England and the Unrepresentable Black Woman. In M. Hendricks and P. Parker (eds.) *Women, "Race," and Writing in the Early Modern Period*. London: Routledge, 35–54.

Callaghan, D. (1996) Othello was a White Man: Properties of Race on Shakespeare's Stage. In T. Hawkes (ed.) *Alternative Shakespeares II*. London: Routledge.

Coleridge, S. T. (1960). Notes on the Tragedies of Shakespeare: *Othello*. In T. M. Raysor (ed.) *Shakespearean Criticism*, 2 vols. New York: Dutton.

Coles, P. (1968). *Ottoman Impact on Europe*. New York: Harcourt, Brace and World.

Cowhig, R. (n.d.). Actors, Black and Tawny, in the Role of Othello – and their Critics. *Theatre Journal International*.

D'Amico, J. (1991). *The Moor in English Renaissance Drama*. Tampa: University of South Florida Press.

Dash, I. G. (1981). *Wooing, Wedding and Power: Women in Shakespeare's Plays*. New York: Columbia University Press.

Drakakis, J. (1985). Introduction. In J. Drakakis (ed.) *Alternative Shakespeares*. London: Methuen, 1–25.

DuBois, W. E. B. (1996). *The Souls of Black Folk*. In E. Sundquist (ed.) *The Oxford W. E. B. DuBois Reader*. New York: Oxford University Press, 97–240.

Dyer, R. (1997). *White*. London: Routledge.

Elizabeth I (1977). Edict Arranging for the Expulsion from England of Negroes and Blackamoors. In R. McDonald (ed.) *The Bedford Companion to Shakespeare: An Introduction with Documents*. New York: Bedford/St. Martin's Press, 296.

Essed, P. and Goldberg, D. T. (2002). *Race Critical Theories*. Oxford: Blackwell.

Foakes, F. A. (ed.) (1989). *Coleridge's Criticism of Shakespeare*. Detroit, MI: Wayne State University Press.

Fryer, P. (1984). *Staying Power: The History of Black People in Britain*. London: Pluto Press.

Gildon, C. (1974). Some Reflections on Mr. Rymer's Short View of Tragedy and an Attempt at a Vindication of Shakespeare. In B. Vickers (ed.) *Shakespeare, The Critical Heritage: Vol. 2, 1693–1733*. London: Routledge and Kegan Paul, 63–85.

Hall, K. F. (1993). Reading What Isn't There: "Black" Studies in Early Modern England? *Stanford Humanities Re/View*, 3, 1, 23–33.

——(1995). *Things of Darkness: Economies of Race and Gender in Early Modern England*. Ithaca, NY: Cornell University Press.

—— (1999). Women and Race. In *Renaissance Women Online*. Brown Women Writers Project. Http://www.wwp.brown.edu/rwo/home.html.

Hall, S. (1988). New Ethnicities. In K. Mercer (ed.) *Black Film/British Cinema*. London: Institute for Contemporary Arts, 27–30.

Hankey, J. (ed.) (1987). *Othello*. Bristol: Bristol Classical Press.

Hawkins, F. W. (1869). *The Life of Edmund Kean. From Published and Original Sources*, 2 vols. London.

Hendricks, M. and Parker, P. (1994). *Women, "Race," and Writing in the Early Modern Period*. London: Routledge.

Honigmann, E. A. J. (1997). Introduction. *Othello*. The Arden Shakespeare, 3rd series. London: Thomas Nelson.

Johnson, R. (1985). African Presence in Shakespearean Drama: Parallels Between Othello and the Historical Leo Africanus. *African Presence in Early Europe (Journal of African Civilizations)*, 7, 276–87.

Jordan, W. (1968). *White Over Black: American Attitudes Toward the Negro, 1550–1812*. Chapel Hill: University of North Carolina Press.

Kaul, M. (ed.) (1996). *Othello: New Essays By Black Writers*. Washington, DC: Howard University Press.

Liu, T. (1995). Race. In R. W. Fox and J. Klopperman (eds.) *A Companion to American Thought*. Oxford: Blackwell, 564–7.

Loomba, A. (1989). *Race, Gender, Renaissance Drama*. Manchester: Manchester University Press.

——(1994). The Color of Patriarchy. In M. Hendricks and P. Barker (eds.) *Woman, "Race," and Writing in the Early Modern Period*. London: Routledge, 17–34.

MacDonald, J. G. (1994). Acting Black: *Othello*, *Othello* Burlesques and the Performance of Blackness. *Theater Journal*, 46, 231–49.

Matar, N. (1999). *Turks, Moors, and Englishmen in the Age of Discovery*. New York: Columbia University Press.

Milton, J. (1963). *Paradise Lost*. In J. T. Shawcross (ed.) *The Complete English Poetry of John Milton*. New York: New York University Press.

Neill, M. (2000). *Putting History to the Question: Power, Politics, and Society in English Renaissance Drama*. New York: Columbia University Press.

Newman, K. (1991). "And Wash the Ethiop White": Femininity and the Monstrous in *Othello*. In *Fashioning Femininity and English Renaissance Drama*. Chicago: University of Chicago Press.

Norris, C. (1985). Post-Structuralist Shakespeare: Text and Ideology. In J. Drakakis (ed.) *Alternative Shakespeares*. London: Methuen, 47–66.

Ogude, S. E. (1996). Literature and Racism: The Example of *Othello*. In M. Kaul (ed.) *Othello: New Essays By Black Writers*. Washington, DC: Howard University Press, 151–66.

Omi, M. and Winant, H. (1994). *Racial Formation in the United States: From the 1960s to the 1990s*. New York: Routledge.

Orkin, M. (1987). Othello and the "Plain Face" of Racism. *Shakespeare Quarterly*, 38, 166–88.

Parker, P. (1994). Fantasies of "Race" and "Gender": Africa, Othello and Bringing to Light. In M. Hendricks and P. Parker (eds.) *Women, "Race," and Writing in the Early Modern Period*. London: Routledge, 84–100.

Pecter, E. (1997). *Othello*, The Infamous Ripley and SHAKSPER. In J. Batchelor (ed.) *Shakespearean Continuities*. New York: Macmillan, 138–49.

Rosenberg, M. (1961). *Masks of Othello: The Search for the Identity of Othello, Iago, and Desdemona by Three Centuries of Actors and Critics*. Berkeley: University of California Press.

Rymer, T. (1693). *A Short View of Tragedy: Its Original, Excellency, and Corruption, With Some Reflections on Shakespear, and other Practitioners for the Stage*. London.

——(1956). *The Tragedies of the Last Age*. In C. A. Zimansky (ed.) *The Critical Works of Thomas Rymer*. New Haven, CT: Yale University Press, 17–76.

Said, E. (2002). Imaginative Geography and Its Representations: Orientalizing the Oriental. In P. Essed and D. T. Goldberg (eds.) *Race Critical Theories*. Oxford: Blackwell.

Singh, J. (1994). Othello's Identity, Postcolonial Theory, and Contemporary Rewritings of *Othello*. In M. Hendricks and P. Parker (eds.) *Women, "Race," and Writing in the Early Modern Period*. London: Routledge, 287–99.

Snyder, S. (1979). *The Comic Matrix of Shakespeare's Tragedies*. Princeton, NJ: Princeton University Press.

Spivack, B. (1958). *Shakespeare and the Allegory of Evil: The History of a Metaphor in Relation to his Major Villains*. New York: Columbia University Press.

Stallybrass, P. (1986). Patriarchal Territories: The Body Enclosed. In M. W. Ferguson, M. Quilligan, and N. J. Vickers (eds.) *Rewriting the Renaissance: The Discourses of Sexual Difference in Early Modern Europe*. Chicago, IL: University of Chicago Press, 123–42.

Stillé, A. (1887). *Othello and Desdemona: Their characters and the manner of Desdemona's death, with a notice of Calderon's debt to Shakespeare; a study by Dr. Ellits*. Philadelphia, PA: J. B. Lippincott.

Vaughan, V. M. (1994). *Othello: A Contextual History*. Cambridge, MA: Cambridge University Press.

Vickers, B. (1974–81). *Shakespeare: The Critical Heritage*. London: Routledge and Kegan Paul.

Vitkus, D. J. (1997). Turning Turk in Othello: The Conversion and Damnation of the Moor. *Shakespeare Quarterly*, 48, 2, 145–76.

Wallace, M. (1990). Variations on Negation and the Heresy of Black Feminist Creativity. In H. L. Gates, Jr. (ed.) *Reading Black, Reading Feminist*. New York: Penguin Books, 52–68.

Wayne, V. (1991). Historical Differences: Misogyny and *Othello*. In V. Wayne (ed.) *The Matter of Difference: Materialist Feminist Criticism of Shakespeare*. Ithaca, NY: Cornell University Press, 153–79.

Whitney, L. (1992). Did Shakespeare Know *Leo Africanus*? *Publications of the Modern Languages Association*, 37, 470–83.

Williams, P. (1991). *The Alchemy of Race and Rights*. Cambridge, MA: Harvard University Press.

Winter, W. (1897). *A Prompt-Book of Shakespeare's Tragedy of Othello as performed by Edwin Booth and Mr. Lawrence Barrett, season of 1888 and 1889 under the direction of Mr. Arthur B. Chase*. Philadelphia: Penn Publishing.

19

King Lear
Kiernan Ryan

Angling in the Lake of Darkness

Two hundred years ago Hazlitt judged *King Lear* to be "the best of all Shakespeare's plays" (Hazlitt 1930: 257), while Shelley had no doubt that it was "the most perfect specimen of the dramatic art existing in the world" (Shelley 1977: 489). Not all modern Shakespeare critics might go so far as Shelley, but most would probably subscribe to Hazlitt's view that it deserves to be dubbed Shakespeare's masterpiece. Securing critical agreement on the source of the play's supremacy, however, is quite another matter. Nor is this any wonder, if one considers how many commentators on *King Lear* have found it ultimately unfathomable. Hazlitt himself lost his nerve on the threshold of the task before him: "We wish that we could pass this play over, and say nothing about it. All that we can say must fall far short of the subject; or even of what we ourselves conceive of it" (Hazlitt 1930: 257). And at the close of the twentieth century Harold Bloom concluded that time had done nothing to diminish that task: "Hazlitt touches on the uncanniest aspect of *Lear*: something that we conceive of it hovers outside our expressive range," because it lies "beyond the categories of our critiques" (Bloom 1999: 484, 488).

This sense of *King Lear*'s elusiveness crops up repeatedly in the more perceptive latter-day accounts of the play. "Whatever the time and however subtle and diverse the analyses," writes Theodore Weiss, "*King Lear*, like Lear himself, gaily fleeing, trailing wild flowers and a mad lilt of syllables, refuses to be caught. To land this light-as-air Leviathan, a critic would have to be able to throw out a net as large, as subtle, as complex as the play itself" (Weiss 1981: 64). At the root of our frustration, Stephen Booth believes, is the awareness that "a governing idea for the play, a lodestone for our values, exists just beyond our mental reach, that the play is faithful to it, and that our responses would prove similarly faithful and consistent if only we could interpret the oracular truths we feel but cannot see" (Booth 1983: 22). As we read *King Lear* we can almost feel "Shakespeare's breath on the page," according to

John Jones: "We are extraordinarily, perhaps uniquely close; our *sense* of him as creative presence is importunate. But we can make no *sense* of what he is doing" (Jones 1995: 179–80).

Such testimonies to *Lear*'s resistance to criticism have done nothing, of course, to deter several generations of modern Shakespeare critics from making whatever sense of it they please. To review the dominant trends in criticism of *King Lear* during the last century is to confront a sustained attempt to evade the enigma at the heart of the play by settling for interpretations that buttress rather than baffle the critics' preconceptions. Up until the 1960s most criticism of *Lear* languished in the pious embrace of the Christian paradigm, which generated countless accounts of the tragedy as a parable of sin, suffering, sacrifice, and redemption, notwithstanding the blatant lack of supporting evidence in the text. Over the next two decades this paradigm collapsed under the pressure of the two new critical regimes that arose to take its place: on one hand, humanist views of the tragedy as affirming our capacity to endure and find significance in a godless universe; on the other, bleak Beckettian readings of *Lear* as Shakespeare's counsel of despair in the face of life's futility. Then, with the dawn of the 1980s and the advent of theory, this dispensation was displaced by a whole new spectrum of politicized criticism, for which the crucial issue was whether the play supported or sabotaged the structures of perception governing its world and our own.[1]

As a consequence, Shakespeare's mightiest tragedy is now colonized by most kinds of poststructuralist, new-historicist, cultural-materialist, feminist, and psychoanalytic criticism. It would certainly be dishonest to deny that we have learned a great deal about *Lear* from the leading exponents of these approaches. Deconstructive readings, such as those of Jonathan Goldberg (1988), Jackson Cope (1988), and Malcolm Evans (1986), have underscored the play's skepticism about the stability of meaning and the solidity of representation, even if few are inclined to dive after them into the void they discern at its core. Feminist critics like Kathleen McLuskie (1985), Coppélia Kahn (1986), and Janet Adelman (1992) have problematized the dimension of gender in the play, making it impossible to ignore the lethal alliance of patriarchy and misogyny that connives in the catastrophe. Interpretations of *Lear* informed by psychoanalysis, which include accounts by William F. Zak (1984) and Harry Berger, Jr. (1997) as well as the essays of Kahn and Adelman, have striven to exhume the buried motives of the characters' unconscious. Most influential of all, however, have been the reappraisals of *King Lear* by new historicists and cultural materialists, most notably Jonathan Dollimore (1984), Leonard Tennenhouse (1986), Leah Marcus (1988), Annabel Patterson (1989), and Stephen Greenblatt (1988b, 1990). Thanks to them, we have a fuller understanding of the play's anchorage in its epoch and the question of its complicity in bolstering or scuppering the Jacobean status quo.

Yet none of these new approaches to *King Lear* has succeeded in bringing us much closer to the solution of its mystery, which is still going begging because it still lies, as Bloom puts it, "beyond the categories of our critiques." There are, in my view, three main reasons why these approaches have proved unequal to the problem *Lear* poses. The first is their supposition that the tragedy is the symptom of some ulterior phenomenon, whether it be language, the unconscious, patriarchy, or power. The play's autonomy and integrity as a work of art are ditched by critics bent on recruiting it to confirm their theoretical assumptions or preconceptions of the past. The second reason is endemic to critics raring to immure *King Lear* in its early modern matrix: a blindness to the possibility that the tragedy may not be fully intelligible in terms of its time, because its gaze is fixed on horizons that still lie ahead of our time. Even when radical historicists like Patterson hold that *Lear* must have been subversive in Shakespeare's day, it remains the imprint of an obsolete era, the pawn of a purely retrospective viewpoint. And the third reason is the failure to engage in detail with the poetic language and dramatic form of *King Lear*, which in some cases, as Greenblatt's essays demonstrate, simply furnishes a pretext for expounding another text altogether. Nor should the habitual neglect of the play's aesthetic dimension come as any surprise, since it is by virtue of its formal grammar that *King Lear* defies theoretical abstraction and cuts itself adrift from its time.

Beyond Historicism

King Lear poses with unusual force the fundamental critical problems faced not only by Shakespeare studies, but also by the study of any great literature of the past, and especially the distant past, today. As Shakespeare's supreme accomplishment, the tragedy is widely regarded as the cornerstone of the canon and the gold standard of the entire discipline. It has consequently become an exemplary site on which the principal schools of criticism contend for priority. To contest the presiding perceptions of *King Lear* is thus to call the current critical regime into question; and to develop a more persuasive account of the play, which does not flinch from its elusiveness, would be to pave the way for an approach capable of transforming the study of Shakespeare and the practice of criticism itself.

I have written elsewhere about the exemplary impasse in which Shakespeare criticism finds itself, stalled between the equally unsatisfactory alternatives of historical retrospection and present appropriation (Ryan 2002a). What is needed to unlock this impasse, I have suggested, is a way of reading Shakespeare that involves a genuine dialogue between history and modernity, between us and him: a dialogue that allows Shakespeare's dispatches from the past to be judged by the present, but that places us in the dock as well, and calls the present to account through the plays' revelations of what we once were and what we might yet become. One of the least appealing features of literary studies today is the smug *diagnostic* attitude that has swept through them like foot-and-mouth disease through a fine herd of Friesians. It is this attitude that reduces Shakespeare's drama to an allegory or appendix of something else and then passes sentence on it from the supposedly superior vantage point of hindsight. It thereby denies the plays the power not only to arraign the world in which they were first forged *and* the world in which we now encounter them, but also to foreshadow futures that would otherwise remain intangible. It is an approach that goes hand in hand with a scorn for close reading, a contempt for the belief that there is something special about the creative use of language and form in imaginative writing at its best that sets it apart from other kinds of discourse and gives us ways of seeing the world which no other kind of writing can deliver.

Yet it is precisely in the unpredictable detail of diction and design that a work's impatience with the past and intolerance of the present find their most potent expression. That is why the development of a more dialogical approach to the historical study of Shakespeare needs to be accompanied by a return to his texts governed by a fresh perception of the relationship between texts and contexts, literature and history. What Flaubert wrote to George Sand in January 1869 remains just as true of academic criticism in the twenty-first century:

> Are you struck by how rare the literary sense is? A knowledge of languages, archaeology, history, etc. – all that should help. But not at all! So-called enlightened people are becoming more and more inept as regards art. Even what art *is* escapes them. Glosses are more important for them than the text. They value crutches more highly than legs. (Flaubert 1982: 123)

Nevertheless, the last thing I want to plead for is a relapse into sheer formalism, a reversion to the halcyon days before cultural materialists and new historicists rode roughshod through the tranquil dell of Shakespeare studies. I am more interested in what Roland Barthes had in mind when he insisted that "there is a special status of literary creation"; that "not only can we not treat literature like any other historical product," but "this special nature of the work is essentially paradoxical, being both the sign of a history, and the resistance to that history" (Barthes 1983: 155).

The aim should not be to divorce literature from history, but to redefine creative literature as a form of history in its own right – as a rival version of history, to which the future tense has been restored. A central task of a truly historical approach to Shakespeare would then be to decipher in the form and phrasing of his texts traces of what Ernst Bloch calls "the future in the past that is significant to the degree that the genuine agent (*Täter*) of cultural heritage reaches into the past, and in this very same act the past itself anticipates him, involves him and needs him" (Bloch 1988: 46–7). It is this notion of Shakespeare's ability, at his most powerful, to reach forward to us as we reach back to him, not merely prefiguring the concerns of the present, but giving us glimpses of what beckons from beyond our time, that strikes me as especially compelling.

There is no denying that the gains of the triumph of history in Shakespeare studies, as in literary studies at large, in recent decades have been immense. Cultural materialism, new historicism, and their various hybrid offshoots have enriched the realm of Shakespeare studies by letting other disciplines in on the act, plugging texts into incongruous contexts, probing the plays' collusion in social, racial, and sexual oppression, and giving Shakespeare criticism a political edge and pertinence it had hitherto lacked. The problem is that they have also closed things down insofar as they have trapped critics in a past-bound or a modernizing posture and put the aesthetic plane of the plays on the back burner, when they have put it on the stove at all.[2]

One of the most trenchant critiques of this kind of historicism is provided by Dominick LaCapra in *Rethinking Intellectual History*:

> The rhetoric of contextualization has often encouraged narrowly documentary readings in which the text becomes little more than a sign of the times or a straightforward expression of one larger phenomenon or another. At the limit, this indiscriminate approach to reading and interpretation becomes a detour around texts and an excuse for not really reading them at all. It simultaneously avoids the claims texts make on us as readers. (LaCapra 1983: 14)

The application of the "rhetoric of contextualization" to Shakespeare has indeed encouraged too many "narrowly documentary readings" of his plays, which shrink them into signs of the times or prestigious pegs on which cultural historians can hang the stuff about early modern medicine, maps, or money that they are really interested in. A genuinely historical hermeneutic, by contrast, should involve "the attempt to explore alternative possibilities in the past that are themselves suggested by the retrospective or deferred effects of later knowledge" (ibid: 18). And the quest for the "unrealized or even resisted possibilities" (ibid: 31) voiced by the literature of the past, and by the plays of Shakespeare *par excellence*, has to begin by analyzing afresh the strategies of style and form that govern each work's interpretation of its times. For to fail to do justice to the art of Shakespeare's plays, to the way they are shaped and the way they are worded, is to remain blind to Shakespeare's most profound and arresting quality, and the reason why our age is still enthralled by him: his *anachronism*, his refusal to coincide with the culture of early modern Britain, because his works are shaped as much by the pressure of futurity as they are by the world from which they sprang 400 years ago. From this standpoint, nothing could be more misguided than David Scott Kastan's belief that our chief aim should be to "restore Shakespeare's artistry to the earliest conditions of its realization and intelligibility: to the collaborations of the theater in which the plays were acted, to the practices of the book trade in which they were published, to the unstable political world of late Tudor and early Stuart England in which the plays were engaged by their various publics" (Kastan 1999: 16).[3]

I am not advocating the abandonment of history in our study of Shakespeare, but a rethinking of what it means to study Shakespeare historically. It is worth recalling that in the "Afterword" he supplied for the seminal collection *Political Shakespeare: New Essays in Cultural Materialism*, Raymond Williams concluded that the future of Shakespeare studies lay in a quite different direction from the one in which *Political Shakespeare* was heading: "the most practical and effective new direction," he predicted, "will be in analysis of the historically based conventions of language and representation: the plays themselves as socially and materially produced, within discoverable conditions; indeed *the texts themselves as history*" (Williams 1985: 239; emphasis added). And it is too often forgotten that, in the opening chapter of *Shakespearean Negotiations*, the founding father of new historicism, Stephen Greenblatt, wrote: "I believe that sustained, scrupulous attention to formal and linguistic design will remain at the center of literary teaching and study. But in the essays that follow I propose to do something different: to look less at the presumed center of the literary domain than at its borders." The cost of this "shift of attention," Greenblatt admitted, would be considerable, but the compensatory cultural insights it should produce would be sufficient, he hoped, to justify what he plainly regarded as a temporary departure from the main business of literary study (Greenblatt 1988a: 4).

I would suggest that the time is now ripe to shift our attention back to that main business in our study of Shakespeare, but on a new understanding of the texts themselves as history of a special kind. Because if we do, we just might find ourselves within reach of a way of studying Shakespeare in which aesthetic appreciation is inseparable from historical understanding, in which formal analysis is the instrument, not the antithesis, of political critique, and in which Shakespeare's plays are allowed to speak not only of the world as he found it, but of the world as we know it, and of worlds to come that we will never know. And none of Shakespeare's plays cries out for the development of such an approach more urgently than *King Lear*.

"This Prophecy Merlin Shall Make"

The enigma that flickers between the lines of *King Lear* is indivisible from what Winifred Nowottny described over forty years ago as "the magnitude of the stylistic mystery" of the play (Nowottny 1960: 49). That mystery is in turn inseparable from the text's complex reconfiguration of time. The Fool, predictably, has known this all along and turns our attention to it at the end of act 3, scene 2, the pivotal point of the play. As Lear and Kent exit in search of shelter from the storm, the Fool stays behind and steps out through the world and time of *King Lear* to address the audience directly in typically cryptic terms:

> This is a brave night to cool a courtesan. I'll speak a prophecy ere I go:
>   When priests are more in word than matter,
>   When brewers mar their malt with water,
>   When nobles are their tailors' tutors,
>   No heretics burned but wenches' suitors;
>   When every case in law is right,
>   No squire in debt, nor no poor knight;
>   When slanders do not live in tongues,
>   Nor cut-purses come not to throngs,
>   When usurers tell their gold i'the field,
>   And bawds and whores do churches build,
>   Then shall the realm of Albion

Come to great confusion:
Then comes the time, who lives to see't,
That going shall be used with feet.
This prophecy Merlin shall make, for I live before his time. (3.2.79–95)[4]

Pitched between wry satire and self-mocking parody, the Fool's vatic doggerel
fuses harsh Jacobean realities with millennial possibilities, deliberately dislocating and
confounding our temporal point of view. In a modern production a twenty-first-
century audience is addressed by a mercurial character in an early modern drama about
ancient Britain, who employs cod Chaucerian verse to make a prediction not due to
be delivered until the mythical reign of King Arthur several centuries later. Past,
future, and present are scrambled to activate their conflation in our response to the
play. The speech highlights the complex anachronistic construction of *King Lear*,
which uses every ruse of derangement and estrangement to stay out of sync with its
era.

The Romantics doubtless had little difficulty grasping what Shakespeare was up
to in *Lear*, since it was exactly what they were up to themselves. "Hear the voice of
the Bard!" proclaimed Blake, "Who Present, Past, & Future, sees" (Blake 1972: 210).
The poet, wrote Shelley, is someone who "not only beholds the present as it is, and
discovers those laws according to which present things ought to be ordered, but he
beholds the future in the present, and his thoughts are the germs of the flower and
the fruit of latest time." Poets are, Shelley added, in an awesome image, "the mirrors
of the gigantic shadows which futurity casts upon the present" (Shelley 1977: 482–3).
And Coleridge, with his customary critical acumen, quickly nosed out Shakespeare's
"fondness for presentiment" (Bate 1992: 323). With few exceptions, however, present-
day critics, doubly hobbled by unfamiliarity with the creation of poetry and the antiquarian bias of academia, have been immune to the spell of the subjunctive in
Shakespeare, and even fewer have taken the hint so conspicuously dropped by the Fool
in their accounts of *King Lear*.

In his pioneering essay "Past and Future in Shakespeare's Drama," Wolfgang
Clemen homed in on the history plays, *Hamlet*, and *The Tempest* to prove how central
these twin themes are to Shakespeare's art, and to show how he habitually "weaves
retrospect and prognostication into the action as it advances, into the dramatic discourse and conflict" (Clemen 1972: 128). Marjorie Garber delved further into the
subject in " 'What's Past is Prologue': Temporality and Prophecy in the History Plays."
Taking her cue from Derrida's discussion of the *futur antérieur*, or future perfect, in
Dissemination, Garber argued that "A similar logic of retrospective anticipation underlies the 'prior past that is still to come' in Shakespeare's histories. And the most con-
densed form of the temporal paradoxes of the historical *futur antérieur* occurs in the
form of the prophecy." The prophecies made in the imagined past of the histories pin-
point the "remarkable theatrical illusion" round which these plays revolve: "hindsight
masquerading as foresight . . . purporting to describe events taking place in the future
while actually chronicling developments from the past" (Garber 1986: 307, 308).

Harry Berger, Jr. has written fascinatingly, too, on the future perfect as the master tense of Richard II's imagination, as his means of commuting between present and future in order to fashion the past to which death is about to consign him (Berger 1989). And, more recently, Barbara Everett has discerned in the great tragedies a Shakespeare

> who so dissolves historical time as to find ways out of his own and into (we might almost say) the twentieth century. Little in our own time is as far from the Tudors as the latest advances in the philosophy of science. Quantum theory makes us accept the possibility of a universe with "black holes" in which time has to be said to go backwards. But, as Freud said about the Oedipus complex, "The poets have always known." Intelligences intense enough can find their way forward to metaphorical apprehensions that bring times together. (Everett 1998: 219)

Evidence of Shakespeare's proleptic cast of mind and propensity to fuse temporal horizons is actually so ubiquitous that it is remarkable that more critics have not cottoned on to it. The sonnets are packed with evidence of Shakespeare's possession by "the prophetic soul / Of the wide world dreaming on things to come" (sonnet 107).[5] Sonnet 81, for example, foretells with eerie confidence the poem's distant destiny:

> Your monument shall be my gentle verse,
> Which eyes not yet created shall o'er-read,
> And tongues to be your being shall rehearse
> When all the breathers of this world are dead.

The same certainty that, whatever eyes are viewing the author's work at the moment, other "eyes not yet created" will one day view them in the different light of a far-off future, is memorably voiced by Cassius as the conspirators stain their hands with Caesar's blood: "How many ages hence / Shall this our lofty scene be acted over, / In states unborn and accents yet unknown!" (*Julius Caesar*, 3.1.112–14). *Macbeth* is, of course, a protracted meditation on the dark side of the urge to be "transported . . . beyond / This ignorant present" and feel "The future in the instant" (1.5.54–6). And in *2 Henry IV* Warwick is given this striking speech about tracing the trajectory of the future in the contours of the past:

> There is a history in all men's lives
> Figuring the natures of the times deceased,
> The which observed, a man may prophesy,
> With a near aim, of the main chance of things
> As yet not come to life, who in their seeds
> And weak beginnings lie intreasurèd.
> Such things become the hatch and brood of time . . . (3.1.75–81)

A host of similar passages could be cited from Shakespeare's works.[6] But the bulk of the iceberg whose tip they form is yet to be uncovered, which leaves the prophetic proclivities of *King Lear* still to be fathomed, with a little help from a handful of trail-blazing critics and scholars. Taking his cue from the Fool's prophecy, Walter Cohen points out, for example, that "The prophecies of Merlin seem to have been linked to radicalism," and that "during the revolutionary years, but even before, fools and madmen were associated with revolutionary prophecy." In his "handy-dandy" speeches to Gloucester in 4.6, indeed, Lear "closely anticipates the Levellers" and "even the more radical positions of the Ranters and Diggers." And Cohen concludes that "Whatever the direct influence of the play on the Revolution, *King Lear* takes its place in a tradition of popular radicalism . . . that may extend without a break from the Peasants' Revolt of 1381 to the present" (Cohen 1985: 352–3, 354, 356). Malcolm Evans likewise sees a line directly linking *Lear*'s alignment with the dispossessed to the radical ideologies of the Revolution and the execution of "the great image of authority" (4.6.155) in 1649. He also recognizes "the indeterminate time of the Fool's prophecy" as central to the play's vision, finding in both the Fool's and the mad king's inverted logic "a figure not only of 'nothing' but also of the utopian plenitude associated with carnival and the Land of Cockaygne" (Evans 1986: 232, 228).

Shakespeare's fascination with foresight in *King Lear* and throughout his career was far from being peculiar to him. On the contrary, as Howard Dobin has shown in *Merlin's Disciples: Prophecy, Poetry, and Power in Renaissance England*, the whole period was consumed by the rage to prophesy, and the powers that be were in a permanent state of anxiety as a consequence:

> Private prophetic voices proclaiming alternate visions of the future rose to challenge the political, religious, and social institutions of the Elizabethan regime. Renaissance English society, despite the efforts of the church and state, consisted of a swelling cacophony of individual prophetic voices – almost a kind of Derridean "plurivocity" or Bakhtinian "heteroglossia" – rather than one univocal and authoritarian truth. (Dobin 1990: 33)

The Fool's prophecy and the tragedy that turns on it are products of this explosion of vatic activity, in which Old Testament prophecy, oracular utterance, Reformist protest, apocalyptic prediction, popular millenarianism, and astrological prognostication vied to control spiritual and secular expectations. Although Dobin only glances at *King Lear*, he has much to say about the nature of prophetic discourse in the period, especially as a feature of literary texts, that chimes with the play's deepest ambitions. His most important contention is that prophetic discourse becomes the epitome of poetic discourse in early modern culture. It does so because both kinds of discourse provoke, through their use of ambiguity and obliquity, an endless process of interpretation that opens them up to futurity. Poetic and prophetic texts ceaselessly solicit paraphrase by promising the delivery of an import that is perpetually deferred: they are designed to persist in saying one thing and meaning another. This is especially apparent, as Dobin demonstrates, in Jacobean literary texts that are overtly invaded by the prophetic voice, which "produces an increasing threat to both the ideological and formal integrity of these texts. The more the literature engages in dialogue with the inconclusive present, the more that inconclusiveness will pervade both the text's particular content and form" (Dobin 1990: 184). Nowhere in Jacobean literature is this effect more palpable than when, in the last line of his prophecy, the Fool transports himself from Lear's time and Shakespeare's time to speak to us in the inconclusive present of modern performance.

The extent of *King Lear*'s thraldom to the art of prescience is made clear by Joseph Wittreich's study, *"Image of that Horror": History, Prophecy, and Apocalypse in "King Lear."* Wittreich argues that in *Lear*, more than in any of Shakespeare's plays, the prophetic and apocalyptic are integral components of the dramatic perspective. The language and the strategies of prophecy are conscripted by the tragedy to release it from the deterministic grip of the given: to transmute the discourse of historicity into the dialect of possibility, the burden of what has been into a vista of what could be. In this sense, Wittreich suggests, *"Lear* is an historical mirror in which, beholding the past, we catch prophetic glimpses, however darkly, of the present and future" (Wittreich 1984: 11). The Fool, whose riddling prophecy encapsulates the larger riddle of *King Lear*, personifies the play's unshackling of time in the name of a new form of history – a history to which the prospect of transformation has been restored. Wittreich points out that in his sermon to the king and his court on Christmas Day, 1606, the day before they were entertained by *King Lear*, Lancelot Andrewes reminded his congregation that it is in the nature of prophecy to use the past to address the future, "speaking of things to come as if they were already past," as Andrewes put it (Wittreich 1984: 57). Even if one accepts that the Fool's prophecy may have played no part in this command performance (on the grounds that it features only in the 1623 Folio and not in the 1608 Quarto),[7] the consonance of the theme of the sermon with the thrust of the play is too uncanny to pass unremarked. It certainly does nothing to detract from Wittreich's conclusion that in *King Lear*

> Shakespeare edges history, tragedy and comedy toward, and then into, a prophetic mode. The play, repeatedly referring to prophecy, itself becomes a prophecy that would warn the present and wrest from it a new future; and in the last act, the play veers toward, seems to stand at the very verge of apocalypse. *Lear* is a prophecy not in the vulgar sense of predicting the future, but in the Renaissance sense of interpreting existing prophecy in order to bring mankind to a new stage of consciousness and increase the distance the "eyes may pierce." (Wittreich 1984: 105)

This brings us very close to the heart of the play's mystery. To move closer still, we need to rediscover what supposedly outmoded accounts of the tragedy can teach us about its formal art, which recent interdisciplinary, historicist criticism has elbowed aside as an irrelevance.

"Strange Mutations"

King Lear is an extremely deceptive play. In sharp contrast to *Hamlet*, which flaunts its perplexity at what it is about, *Lear* tells the relatively simple tale of two fathers and their families, and seems tailor-made for the moralizing constructions that generations of critics have been only too happy to place on it. In the main plot, an aged king's rejection of the daughter who loves him, and his misplaced trust in her malevolent sisters, strip him of his power and strand him in a wasteland of insanity and anguish. From this state death at last releases him, but not before the wicked sisters have met their deaths as well and the corpse of the loyal and loving daughter, with whom he has just been reunited, lies cold in his arms. In the parallel subplot, a nobleman is duped by his ruthless, illegitimate son into driving his legitimate son to flee for his life in the guise of a demented beggar. The nobleman suffers the torment of being blinded following his betrayal by his bastard and, like the king, is turned out to wander in despair, at the mercy of the elements. Death finally terminates his suffering too, after he has been reconciled with the faithful son he drove from home, and the latter dispatches his evil sibling in a climactic chivalric duel. At the end of the tragedy, all but three of the principal characters are dead, and the survivors show no sign of seeing a way forward.

But as soon as one examines the *way* the story of *King Lear* is told, the illusion of stark simplicity dissolves. The more deeply the structure and style of the play are analyzed, the clearer it becomes that its ostensible lucidity is a stalking horse for something altogether more obscure. The sense that *King Lear* harbors a hidden world within the patent world of its tragic narrative, that the action and dialogue conceal a darker poetic purpose, is exactly captured by John Bayley in *Shakespeare and Tragedy*. On the surface, the characters plainly act and react in a manner appropriate to their changing predicament, voicing views and sentiments suitable to their parts in the play and what they are undergoing: "nothing will come of nothing" (1.1.90), "The worst returns to laughter" (4.1.6), "Ripeness is all" (5.2.11), and so on. Yet, as Bayley observes, "the play slips out of every area for which there is something appropriate and intelligible to be said," because Shakespeare "has got hold of something that undermines the kind of expression that a play relies on" (Bayley 1981: 23, 27). It is as if the characters, confined as they are to the place, time, and words of the world of *King Lear*, are mouthing lines and going through the motions of behavior, oblivious to the real business of the play, which is being conducted behind their backs.

In fact, every aspect of the play's construction and style conspires to create a vision that cannot find full expression in the narrative, characters, and discourses with which it is obliged to work. The tragic double-plot, the dramatis personae, the location of the action, the period in which it is set, the social community to which the cast belong, the codes and conventions that bind them, and the modes of speech that clinch their fate in this particular imaginary universe: all of these elements converge to form a dramatic fiction that makes immediate, overt sense; but none of them is equal to the

articulation of the viewpoint from which *King Lear* is written. The play must therefore strive to resist entrapment in its own tragic narrative, to divorce itself from its
own discourse, by all the "strange mutations" (4.1.12) of its material it can muster.
Lear has to wrench from its world and from its words implications for which no adequate language is yet available.

Hence the play's confounding of times, which allows the present to pass for the past
and the past to secrete the future, is matched by its dislocation of persons and diffu-
sion of action. As Michael Goldman observes, "the sense of space in *King Lear* is unique
in the Shakespearean canon." The central characters spend the bulk of their time
wandering outdoors through a "vast, unlocalized, transitional space," drifting from one
nebulous locale to another, en route to no clear-cut, specific destination, such as
Dunsinane in *Macbeth*. "This sense of large, unorganized space and of errant, improvised movement through it," Goldman believes, "is fundamental to the play"
(Goldman 1981: 43, 44). Inextricable from this feature is the derailing of determinate
action, the constant sabotaging of linear narrative development. *King Lear* eschews the
kind of governing objective that is designed to generate and discharge suspense, to
excite and satisfy expectations of some climactic event, encounter, or revelation that
will deliver a denouement. As we watch the play, notes Emrys Jones, "We seem to
move from episode to episode without much sense of what the final destination is to
be . . . there is always an element of unpredictability in what comes next and the form
in which it comes." Furthermore, Shakespeare repeatedly inserts "scenes of a curiously
static nature, scenes of brooding, reflection, or, in a more impassioned style, of decla-
mation," whose effect is "to clog the onward movement of the action," in much the
same way as "the obsessively random use of iteration" in Lear's phrasing frustrates the
forward motion of the dramatic dialogue (Jones 1971: 155, 188, 156, 183).

"A turmoil of terms and things, drawn higgledy-piggledy from countless times
and places" (Weiss 1981: 65), *King Lear* defies circumscription, location, and closure
at every level, bridling at every restraint it imposes on itself. The play's generic instability has often been noted, mingling as it does tragedy and comedy in the first three
acts, where the heath serves as a bleak counterpart to the Forest of Arden, and tragedy
and tragicomedy in the last two, where Lear's reunion with Cordelia prefigures the
resonant recognition scenes of the romances. The fact that "the play refuses to fulfil
the generic promise inherent in its story," as Stephen Booth puts it, is merely one of
the myriad ways in which it transgresses boundaries and scorns distinction and limit.
Booth (1983) provides an invaluable conspectus of the techniques the play employs
to remain intractable and inconclusive, including digression, regression, repetition,
superfluity, and the creation of "a crazy quilt of frames of reference." *King Lear* culminates notoriously in a stammer of false endings and dashed hopes, which peter out
in ambiguity, leaving us uncertain whether Lear dies under the delusion that Cordelia
lives and unsure of who will take his place as ruler. But "the fact that *King Lear* ends
but does not stop," Booth maintains, "is only the biggest of a succession of similar
facts about the play," which "pushes inexorably beyond its own identity, rolling across
and crushing the very framework that enables its audience to endure the otherwise

terrifying explosion of all manner of ordinarily indispensable mental contrivances for isolating, limiting, and comprehending" (Booth 1983: 17, 28, 11).

This quality is equally apparent in the characteristic style of *King Lear*. Most accounts of the play have sidestepped the formidable challenge its language poses to the critic's powers of analysis. But in the brilliant essay which first drew attention to this facet of the tragedy, Winifred Nowottny nails the nub of the matter right at the outset. "The style alone," she writes, "might lead one to suppose that what happens in *King Lear* happens in some realm of the imagination beyond ear and eye." Like Bayley, Nowottny recognizes that language in the play is being subtly manipulated to deflect our attention away from its apparent import by implying more than it is at liberty to state. By analyzing the phrasing, shape, and rhythms of the verse, she anchors this perception in an "obscure sense that what is really peculiar about the language is the freedom and unexpectedness of its melodic line; Lear himself is unfailingly astonishing, and this property of his words is resistant to explanation in terms of the recurrence of patterns" (Nowottny 1960: 49). Both the protagonist and the play are engrossed in a titanic struggle with its discourse to communicate a vision which the current scope of language cannot encompass. As Goldman has shown in an acute analysis which complements Nowottny's, *Lear*'s language is packed with "densely recalcitrant chunks of meaning and sound," with "words and phrases that appear to be massively resistant to verse articulation, words like 'tender-hefted' or 'sea-monster' or 'sulph'rous,' which seem hard to move around in musical lines or paragraphs." What such effects presuppose, Goldman concludes, is "the operation of some dangerously unregulable power, something not quite contained by the procedures that seek to organize it" (Goldman 1981: 33).

The same resistance to regulation and containment in the prison-house of early modern discourse is manifest in the extemporized gibberish of Poor Tom – "Childe Rowland to the dark tower came" (3.4.178) – which dangles intimations of momentous import just beyond our reach. Tom's cryptic mutterings and the Fool's impromptu riddles and quibbles, like Lear's topsy-turvy "reason in madness" (4.6.171), expose the limits of conventional language in the act of transgressing them. They warn us to take not a word of the play at face value, to bracket everything that is said between quotation marks. By the same token, the chameleon key words of the play, most notably "natural," "fool," "kind," "fortune," and "nothing," change their meaning so often through multiple usage that they cease to signify anything in themselves, becoming opaque and impervious to translation. For Stanley Cavell, *King Lear* poses the fundamental question: "Is language such that expression and representation in it remain possible and survivable?" (Cavell 1998: 242). Given the poverty and perfidy of speech and writing, it is small wonder that the play repeatedly points to "the vast non-discursive regions that lie beyond mere words, and beyond an instrumental reason which claims to master them" (Hawkes 1995: 57); and still less of a wonder that it sets such store by the eloquent silence of Cordelia, who is "the embodiment of that aspect of *King Lear* which tends to elude and disappear from itself, from its status and form as tragedy" (Bayley 1981: 38). The whole play seems to speak through Gloucester when, at the harrowing climax of the storm on the heath, as he shepherds the bedraggled band of outcasts towards the hovel, he says simply: "No words, no words; hush" (3.4.177).

Prefiguring the Past

Through its framing, disruption, and estrangement of the language from which it weaves the tragedy, *King Lear* measures its distance from the world and time in which it was written. There is far more at stake here than mere disenchantment with the capacity of words and narratives to refract reality and transmit experience. On the contrary: words and narratives are all too capable of defining and perpetuating entrenched forms of experience by enshrining the assumptions and values that sustain them. The problem is to reveal the truth of the prevailing reality, using the dramatic and poetic codes that conventionally secure it, but in a way that registers the work's rejection of that reality and its rationale. *King Lear* succeeds in this task to a degree unsurpassed in the Shakespearean canon, and perhaps in the annals of world literature, because it is conceived in the future anterior and composed from a standpoint light-years ahead of the universe we still inhabit.

Grigori Kozintsev described *King Lear* as "a whole dead world galloping over the living earth beneath a sky full of stars" (Kozintsev 1977: 48). That dead world is not only Shakespeare's; it is also our own. The words of the play possess the same spectral quality as the characters who quote them. Its language, "ghostlike, the flicker of dead stars," consists of "haunting verbal relics from a world largely vanished" (Weiss 1981: 68). It is from this discourse of the dead, and the dispensation it preserves, that *King Lear* undertakes to deliver us. Its cathartic purpose is to free us "from enforced or stifled words, from enforced silence, from voices not our own, from falsifying accents, from the breath of words held too long" (Cavell 1998: 247). What these critical intuitions are tuned to is *Lear*'s premonition of the end of history as humanity *will have known* it, when it looks back on the modern epoch from a point far beyond it. In this sense *King Lear* is indeed "a veritable refuse heap: the wreckage of the ages, shadow-rich ruins, whispering in the wind" (Weiss 1981: 64–5). For it grants us a prophetic preview of the past, a vision of what the modern era, from its inception to its demise, might look like to the alien eyes of the era that will succeed it.

In the parallel fates of Lear's and Gloucester's families, Shakespeare offers us a parable that foretells the future in the language of the past. *King Lear* provides a compressed, foreshortened prospect of history, in which we witness the feudal age and ethos spawning the present age of rampant individualism, in which "Humanity must perforce prey on itself, / Like monsters of the deep" (4.2.50–1); and then the age of acquisitive egotism in turn destroying itself, leaving a handful of exhausted, bewildered survivors, who know that what has transpired dwarfs their comprehension and defies expression: "we that are young / Shall never see so much, nor live so long" (5.3.324–5). *King Lear* adumbrates the eclipse of modernity, moreover, with an unnerving mixture of contempt and compassion: compassion for the human creatures doomed to live and die on the inhuman terms of such a world; contempt for the parts history has obliged them to play in its brutal tragedy of division and domination. "There is a cruelty in the writing," observes Frank Kermode, "that echoes the cruelty of the story, a terrible calculatedness that puts one in mind of Cornwall's and Regan's. Suffering has to be protracted and intensified, as it were, without end" (Kermode 2000: 197). Only a pitiless hatred of life warped by subjection and injustice could account for the "authorial savagery" (ibid: 195) with which Shakespeare sets about the punitive humiliation and torture of King Lear, Gloucester, and Edgar, and the deliberate extermination of almost every one of the play's ruling-class protagonists. There is something vengeful, even vindictive, about the way the king in particular is robbed of his sanity, his royalty, and the roof over his head, forced to feel what the "poor naked wretches" (3.4.27) of his kingdom feel, and at last sadistically constrained to expire in agony after seeing his beloved daughter hanged. For Lear *as a king*, as the incarnation of an order programmed to produce "houseless heads and unfed sides" (3.4.30), the play has as little mercy as it has regard for the sentimental pieties of its audience.

Perhaps the hardest home truth to take from the play, however, is its indictment of familial love, the inviolable ideal of modern culture, the emotional touchstone of civilization. Harry Berger, Jr. (1997) has analyzed in deadly detail how *King Lear* reveals the serpent of self-interest coiled beneath the speech of every member of the Lear and Gloucester families. All the critical cant about Lear being redeemed by love has never been credible, because the fact is that, as Harold Bloom points out, "Love is no healer in *The Tragedy of King Lear*; indeed, it starts all the trouble, and is a tragedy in itself." Even in the restored relationships of Lear and Cordelia, and of Edgar and Gloucester, the play exposes without mercy "the mutually destructive nature of both paternal and filial love," engendering a "horror of generation that intensifies as the tragedy grows starker" (Bloom 1999: 484, 489). But what else could love be in a patriarchal culture wedded to hierarchy, where love is a euphemism for power, contaminated at the core by obligation, dependency, resentment, and guilt?

Through the deranged Lear, the blind Gloucester, and Edgar as Poor Tom, the play does, of course, foreshadow the possibility of relationships founded on what human beings have in common rather than on what divides them and subjects them to each other. When Lear perceives that beneath his royal robes and Poor Tom's rags shivers the same "poor, bare, forked animal" (3.4.105–6), a leveling alliance is forged with the mad, the poor, the voiceless, the powerless, the worthless – with all those of whom it may truly be said that "Freedom lives hence and banishment is here" (1.1.182), in history. But the play as a whole pushes beyond egalitarian compassion to anticipate the extinction of the world that creates the need for compassion in the first place. No wonder Christian and humanist critics have labored so long to twist *Lear* into a fable of forgiveness, enlightenment, and redemption. For what it actually seeks to do is to disengage us from a whole way of life whose death it already foresees. It is, as Bloom observes, "a play that divests all of us, male and female auditors and readers alike, of not less than everything" (Bloom 1999: 491).

King Lear can do this because it is not only a document of the past, but also a memory of the future. How can the historicist criticism that currently holds sway in literary studies begin to comprehend a work which, like all the greatest literature, is not back there behind us, awaiting our explanation and diagnosis, but way out ahead of us, waiting for us to catch up? *King Lear* prefigures the impending displacement and disappearance of its world, in which it invites us to recognize the prospective fate of our own. The magnitude of its achievement and the secret of its supremacy among Shakespeare's plays seem less of a mystery when seen in this light. *King Lear* catapults us forward to a time when "all the breathers of this world" are long since dead, and Shakespeare's age and our own can be seen for what they are, the barbaric prehistory of the genuine civilization that humanity still awaits.

NOTES

1 For a fuller account of recent criticism of *King Lear*, see Ryan (2002b).
2 For a critique of new historicism and cultural materialism on these grounds, see Ryan (1996: ix–xviii).
3 Kastan himself is rightly worried that "the focus on history, even the enabling conditions of literary activity, still deflects attention from the literary text itself," and disarmingly mocks the strain of historicism he commends as "The New Boredom" (Kastan 1999: 41, 18).
4 Textual references to *King Lear* are to Foakes (1997).
5 Textual references to Shakespeare's works other than *King Lear* are to Taylor and Wells (1988).
6 For further examples and a discussion of their implications, see Ryan (2001).
7 See Ryan (2002b) on the textual controversy surrounding *King Lear* and the case against "new revisionist" theories of the relationship between the Quarto and Folio versions.

REFERENCES AND FURTHER READING

Adelman, J. (1992). Suffocating Mothers in *King Lear*. In *Suffocating Mothers: Fantasies of Maternal Origin in Shakespeare's Plays, "Hamlet" to "The Tempest."* New York: Routledge, 103–29.

Barthes, R. (1983). *On Racine*, trans. R. Howard. New York: PAJ Publications.

Bate, J. (ed.) (1992). *The Romantics on Shakespeare*. Harmondsworth: Penguin Books.

Bayley, J. (1981). The King's Ship. In *Shakespeare and Tragedy*. London: Routledge and Kegan Paul, 7–48.

Berger, H., Jr. (1989). The Fight for the Future Perfect. In *Imaginary Audition: Shakespeare on Stage and Page*. Berkeley: University of California Press, 104–37.

——(1997). "*King Lear*: The Lear Family Romance" and "Text Against Performance: The Gloucester Family Romance." In *Making Trifles of Terrors: Redistributing Complicities in Shakespeare*. Stanford, CA: Stanford University Press, 25–49, 50–69.

Blake, W. (1972). *Songs of Experience*. In G. Keynes (ed.) *Blake: Complete Writings*. Oxford: Oxford University Press, 210–21.

Bloch, E. (1988). *The Utopian Function of Art and Literature: Selected Essays*, trans. J. Zipes and F. Mecklenburg. Cambridge, MA: MIT Press.

Bloom, H. (1999). *Shakespeare: The Invention of the Human*. London: Fourth Estate.

Booth, S. (1983). *"King Lear", "Macbeth", Indefinition, and Tragedy*. New Haven, CT: Yale University Press.

Cavell, S. (1998). Skepticism as Iconoclasm: The Saturation of the Shakespearean Text. In J. Bate et al. (eds.) *Shakespeare and the Twentieth Century*. Newark: University of Delaware Press, 231–47.

Cohen, W. (1985). *Drama of a Nation: Public Theater in Renaissance England and Spain*. Ithaca, NY: Cornell University Press.

Cope, J. (1988). Shakespeare, Derrida, and the End of Language in *King Lear*. In G. D. Atkins and D. M. Bergeron (eds.) *Shakespeare and Deconstruction*. New York: Peter Lang, 267–83.

Dobin, H. (1990). *Merlin's Disciples: Prophecy, Poetry, and Power in Renaissance England*. Stanford, CA: Stanford University Press.

Dollimore, J. (1984). *King Lear* and Essentialist Humanism. In *Radical Tragedy: Religion, Ideology and Power in the Drama of Shakespeare and his Contemporaries*. Brighton: Harvester Press, 189–203.

Evans, M. (1986). *Signifying Nothing: Truth's True Contents in Shakespeare's Text*. Brighton: Harvester Press.

Everett, B. (1998). Shakespeare in the Twentieth Century: Finding a Way Out. In J. Bate et al. (eds.) *Shakespeare and the Twentieth Century*. Newark: University of Delaware Press, 215–30.

Farrell, K. (1987). Prophetic Behaviour in Shakespeare's Histories. *Shakespeare Studies*, 19, 17–40.

Flaubert, G. (1982). *The Letters of Gustave Flaubert, 1857–1880*, ed. and trans. F. Steegmuller. Cambridge, MA: Harvard University Press.

Foakes, R. A. (ed.) (1997). *King Lear*. The Arden Shakespeare. Third series. Walton-on-Thames: Thomas Nelson.

Garber, M. (1986). "What's past is prologue": Temporality and Prophecy in the History Plays. In B. K. Lewalski (ed.) *Renaissance Genres: Essays on Theory, History, and Interpretation*. Cambridge, MA: Harvard University Press, 301–31.

Goldberg, J. (1988). Perspectives: Dover Cliff and the Conditions of Representation. In G. D. Atkins and D. M. Bergeron (eds.) *Shakespeare and Deconstruction*. New York: Peter Lang, 245–65.

Goldman, M. (1981). *King Lear*: Acting and Feeling. In L. Danson (ed.) *On "King Lear."* Princeton, NJ: Princeton University Press, 25–46.

Greenblatt, S. (1988a). The Circulation of Social Energy. In *Shakespearean Negotiations: The Circulation of Social Energy in Renaissance England*. Oxford: Clarendon Press, 1–20.

——(1988b). Shakespeare and the Exorcists. In *Shakespearean Negotiations: The Circulation of Social Energy in Renaissance England*. Oxford: Clarendon Press, 94–128.

——(1990). The Cultivation of Anxiety: King Lear and his Heirs. In *Learning to Curse: Essays in Early Modern Culture*. New York: Routledge, 80–98.

Hawkes, T. (1995). *William Shakespeare: "King Lear."* Plymouth: Northcote House.

Hazlitt, W. (1930). *Characters of Shakespeare's Plays*. In P. P. Howe (ed.) *The Complete Works of William Hazlitt*, 21 vols. (vol. 4). London: Dent.

Jones, E. (1971). *Scenic Form in Shakespeare*. Oxford: Clarendon Press.

Jones, J. (1995). *Shakespeare at Work*. Oxford: Clarendon Press.

Kahn, C. (1986). The Absent Mother in *King Lear*. In M. W. Ferguson et al. (eds.) *Rewriting the Renaissance: The Discourses of Sexual Difference in Early Modern Europe*. Chicago, IL: University of Chicago Press, 33–49.

Kastan, D. S. (1999). *Shakespeare After Theory*. New York: Routledge.

Kermode, F. (2000). *Shakespeare's Language*. London: Allen Lane.

Kozintsev, G. (1977). *"King Lear": The Space of Tragedy*, trans. M. Mackintosh. London: Heinemann.

LaCapra, D. (1983). *Rethinking Intellectual History: Texts, Contexts, Language*. Ithaca, NY: Cornell University Press.

McLuskie, K. (1985). The Patriarchal Bard: Feminist Criticism and Shakespeare: *King Lear* and *Measure for Measure*. In J. Dollimore and A. Sinfield (eds.) *Political Shakespeare: New Essays in Cultural Materialism*. Manchester: Manchester University Press, 88–108.

Marcus, L. (1988). Retrospective: *King Lear* on St Stephen's Night, 1606. In *Puzzling Shakespeare: Local Reading and its Discontents*. Berkeley: University of California Press, 148–59.

Nowottny, W. (1960). Some Aspects of the Style of *King Lear*. *Shakespeare Survey*, 13, 49–57.

Patterson, A. (1989). *Shakespeare and the Popular Voice*. Oxford: Blackwell, 106–16.

Ryan, K. (ed.) (1996). *New Historicism and Cultural Materialism: A Reader*. London: Edward Arnold.

——(2001). Shakespeare and the Future. In D. Cartmell and M. Scott (eds.) *Talking Shakespeare: Shakespeare into the Millennium*. Basingstoke: Palgrave, 187–200.

——(2002a). *Shakespeare*, 3rd edn. Basingstoke: Palgrave.

——(2002b). *King Lear:* A Retrospect, 1980–2000. *Shakespeare Survey*, 55, 1–11.

Shelley, P. B. (1977). A Defence of Poetry. In D. H. Reiman and S. B. Powers (eds.) *Shelley's Poetry and Prose*. New York: Norton, 480–508.

Taylor, G. and Wells, S. (eds.) (1988). *William Shakespeare: The Complete Works*. Oxford: Clarendon Press.

Tennenhouse, L. (1986). *Power on Display: The Politics of Shakespeare's Genres*. New York: Routledge, 134–42.

Weiss, T. (1981). As the Wind Sits: The Poetics of *King Lear*. In L. Danson (ed.) *On "King Lear."* Princeton, NJ: Princeton University Press, 61–90.

Williams, R. (1985). Afterword. In J. Dollimore and A. Sinfield (eds.) *Political Shakespeare: New Essays in Cultural Materialism*. Manchester: Manchester University Press, 231–9.

Willson, R. F. (1983). Shakespeare's Tragic Prefigurers. *Shakespeare Studies*, 16, 143–51.

Wittreich, J. (1984). *"Image of that Horror": History. Prophecy, and Apocalypse in "King Lear."* San Marino, CA: Huntington Library.

Zak, W. F. (1984). *Sovereign Shame: A Study of "King Lear."* Lewisburg: Bucknell University Press.

20

Macbeth, the Present, and the Past

Kathleen McLuskie

Shakespeare's *Macbeth* is a masterpiece of the English cultural heritage. The play appears continuously in theatre, film, and television repertories throughout the world; it is included in school curricula wherever "English" is taught and it continues to engage the attention of a surprising number of non-professional readers. These markers of the play's cultural provenance, however, do not in themselves explain the play's standing. That status has continually to be ratified by the experience of the play, by the mix of aesthetic and cultural impact that it continues to offer to readers and audiences as they encounter it.

That experience is, of course, continually mediated by the work of editors, critics, and theatrical performance. Like the archeological artifacts that appear, polished and gleaming, in museum collections, *Macbeth* appears in modern culture with its difficulties explained by editorial glosses, its inconsistencies smoothed out by textual emendation, and its historical specificity assimilated into its overall theatrical and literary effect. However, before we analyze and critique that process, it is as well to deal with the sources of aesthetic power that made that work of restoration seem necessary and appropriate.

The play presents a compelling narrative of a man seizing an opportunity for greatness offered by supernatural forces and then struggling desperately to resist the logic of those same inscrutable powers. Its speeches articulate the ethical and emotional implications of that struggle with an eloquence that gives its hero an intense dramatic authority and at the same time engages readers and audiences with sympathetic concern quite at odds with moral judgment of his actions. This paradoxical tension between moral judgment and sympathetic engagement is intensified by the role of his wife. She turns his temptation to greatness into a test of his masculinity, willfully deforming her own femininity in the process. She attempts to share his greatness and mitigate his psychic horror at his action but falls, in the end, to mental torment and death, leaving him to the final, futile, solitary stand against inevitable defeat.

For those trained to understand its language and theatrical effects, the experience of this play provides the combination of ethical and intellectual complexity and concentrated emotional affect that has been accorded the highest cultural value (Bradley 1969: ch. 1). That experience is created by the way that the play is structured through scenes and speeches that control the audience's perspective on the narrative. This narrative is structured in three movements. In the first, from the witches' prophecy to the murder of Duncan, attention is focused on Macbeth's agonized contemplation of the murder and his wife's eager embrace of the witches' prophecy. In the second, from the murder of Duncan to Macbeth's return to the witches, we witness the hero's realization that his triumph is fatally compromised by the second part of the witches' prophecy – that Banquo's heirs will succeed Macbeth. He attempts and fails to thwart their prophecy by killing Banquo and Fleance and is forced to contemplate the horror of that failure by the appearance of Banquo's ghost. In the third, the action moves from Scotland to England and back as Macbeth's enemies prepare their revenge.

This three-part structure drives the narrative forward to demonstrate how Macbeth is caught in the paradox that his success contains the seeds of his failure. However, the scope of the action is further complicated by its handling of place and time that widens the perspective on the action to include the fates of Scotland and the social world of which Macbeth is a part. During the first two phases, stage time parallels "real time" in the sequence of events from the arrival of Duncan to the death of Banquo. The focus is tight on Macbeth and his lady and actions such as the welcome banquet for Duncan and even his murder are kept off stage. In the final sequence, however, stage time and real time move apart. At the end of the scene with Banquo's ghost, Macbeth remembers that Macduff has refused the invitation to the feast (3.4.132–5). His suspicions open up a time loop in which he has set up a network of spies and Macduff has been identified as an enemy, actions which have not had any place in the narrative until then.

That offstage world in which Macbeth's actions have been experienced and responded to is dramatized in a scene between Lennox and the unnamed Lord. They announce that Macduff has fled to England "to pray the holy king," Edward the Confessor, for help against Macbeth. However, it is not until the end of 4.1, where Macbeth visits the witches, that he hears hoofbeats offstage and is told that they are from messengers who "bring you word / Macduff is fled to England." In the next scene Lady Macduff and her children are murdered. The action then moves to England and late in that scene Macduff is informed about the death of his family. This series of actions establishes the new narrative of Macduff's resistance and his flight to England. It also establishes Macbeth's increasing impotence in the face of the resistance of others, as well as the inexorable movement of time and the prophecies associated with it.

This sequence of scenes is vitally important for the momentum of the play's finale. It establishes the mix of personal and political motivation that will fuel Macduff's revenge and give shape to the play's final scenes. Macduff's move to England allows an oscillation between the stasis of the Scottish scenes in which Macbeth and his lady succumb to desperation and suicide, and the English scenes where the army gathers force and prepares the action which will avenge the tyrant as well as fulfill the witches' prophecies. The scenes as they appear in the Folio text offer a dramatic rhythm that works according to theatrical principles of suspense and interaction between and among characters. It was a method that was commonplace in early modern dramaturgy, but in the case of *Macbeth* the effect is reinforced by the hero's own commentary on his relationship to time.

He resolves to go "betimes" to the witches and when he finds, at the end of the witch scene, that Macduff is fled, he contemplates the connection between action and event:

> Time, thou anticipat'st my dread exploits;
> The flighty purpose never is o'ertook
> Unless the deed go with it. From this moment,
> The firstlings of my heart shall be
> The firstlings of my hand. And even now
> To crown my thoughts with acts, be it thought and done. (4.1)

His action in murdering Macduff's family, however, cannot redeem the time and from this point on he loses the initiative, until the final battle in which he is killed (Kermode 2000: 201–6).

This interaction between dramatic structures and poetic commentary is an important part of the play's affect. The audience is able not only to witness the action but is also engaged by a sense that it has wider significance. It offers the potential for a generalizing analysis of the relationship between thought and action, between conscience and resolve that is a major part of the intellectual pleasure that the play has afforded. These concepts had been introduced in the great soliloquies of the early part of the play. It is possible to contrast the agonized contemplation of a determining action elaborated in Macbeth's conscience-stricken speech when he leaves the banquet in 1.7 and the cold resolve with which he moves against Macduff. The psychic cost of that resolve is articulated in Macbeth's despairing speech (5.3.22–8) that offers a stark and simple contrast between the rewards of "Honour, love, obedience, troops of friends" and the "curses, not loud but deep" that surround him. It is further developed in the famous articulation of the despairing round of "tomorrow and tomorrow and tomorrow" (5.5.16–27) that Macbeth contemplates when he hears of the death of his wife.

This sense that the story of Macbeth is connected to larger psychic and ethical concerns is intensified by the involvement of witches. The witches in *Macbeth* are one of the play's most critically overdetermined aspects, attracting comment out of all proportion to the amount of time they take up in reading or performance. Within the play's structure of affect, however, they provide a brilliant dramatic device to increase the suspense, to drive the narrative to its conclusion, and to keep the audience on tenterhooks about how the action will be resolved. Achieving this theatrical end requires only three strategically placed scenes: at the beginning to start the action and alert the audience to the importance of Macbeth, who will not appear for another two scenes; towards the end of act 1 to deliver the all-important message to Macbeth and Banquo – a message which carries the action through the murders of Duncan and Banquo; and again in act 4 to provide a new momentum which will carry the action through to its climax. It was a structured use of the supernatural which Shakespeare had used in *Hamlet*; an instrumental, albeit brilliantly effective, device for securing particular theatrical and narrative effects.

The audience is placed in a situation where they must believe the witches' prophecies as a condition of engaging with the narrative. They have seen their actions from the beginning of the play and they know that the "two truths" of Macbeth's names of Glamis and Cawdor are ratified by experience. By witnessing the scene where Duncan strips the traitorous Thane of Cawdor of his title and confers it on Macbeth, they are in a position of superior knowledge to Macbeth. There is nothing supernatural about the witches' knowledge, since it is knowledge that the audience shares. The witches' narrative role is further emphasized in the letter that Macbeth sends to his lady. His account of how the witches' prophecy is corroborated by the award of the Thane of Cawdor's title reminds the audience, as it tells Macbeth's lady, that "they have more in them than mortal knowledge." It also connects that knowledge of the present to the knowledge of the future in which Macbeth is the "king that shall be" and provides the trigger for Lady Macbeth's deadly fantasy of demonic possession.

The audience's knowledge of the witches' truth can, however, be contrasted with Macbeth's. His anxious engagement with their prophecy presents it as a moral paradox, that "cannot be ill; cannot be good." Once again, the events of the narrative are set in counterpoint to a moral analysis. Macbeth ends his first consideration of the prophecy with a stoical acceptance of the workings of fate:

> If chance will have me King,
> Why chance may crown me
> Without my stir. (1.3.142–4)

The lineation of the Folio text, regularized in most modern editions, separates off the three concepts into discrete events. However, the action of the narrative prevents that separation. Duncan's election of his son, the Prince of Cumberland, to be his heir, closes off the possibility of a chance fulfillment of the witches' prophecy and leaves the connection to Macbeth. His translation of prophecy into regicidal ambition, "that suggestion / Whose horrid image doth unfix my hair" (1.3.135–7), appears to be based in a logical extension from known "truths," but the truths told by the witches and the truth of moral action are driven apart as the play proceeds.

Macbeth's final heroic stature depends upon his recognizing the distinction between the truth of the witches' prophecy and the truth of his own actions. At the end of the play, when Macduff tells him of his magical birth, Macbeth has finally to confront the gap between the truth of the witches' prophecy and his own potential for action. The pacing of that realization is brilliantly slowed down. Macbeth is initially dismayed:

> Accursed be that tongue that tells me so;
> For it hath cowed my better part of man.
> And be these juggling fiends no more believed
> That palter with us in a double sense,
> That keep the word of promise to our ear,
> And break it to our hope. I'll not fight with thee. (5.7.47–52)

Behind that speech lies a century of controversy over the efficacy of prophecy and the power of witches (Clark 1997; Farrell 1989). Its theatrical force, however, depends on the primary aesthetic pleasure of a narrative stopped in its tracks, of an ending that both had to be and might not have been. The significance of the literally show-stopping moment is enlarged and extended by the language and structure of the speech. The mysterious witches, described with such wonder in Macbeth's letter to his wife and seen as the source of reassurance after he has faced the ghost of Banquo (3.4.134–7), are denigrated as "juggling fiends" as his faith in them evaporates. And the antitheses in the final couplet between "keep" and "break," "ear" and "hope" potentially apply beyond the particular case of Macbeth to every failure of aspiration or wishful thinking. Macduff's challenge to Macbeth to yield breaks the moment of reflection. It returns the action to a conflict between men, a conflict that Macbeth responds to with a heroic denial of the inevitable, fighting to the last in a duel which offers both exciting physical display and a *psychomachia* of good and evil. That division between good and evil is paradoxical to the last. Macduff has the moral authority of the avenging victim of Macbeth's murderous aggression. However, the attention that the play has given to Macbeth's psychic and ethical torment, together with the courage of his final stand, compromises a simple attribution of moral judgment and creates once again the ethical and aesthetic complexity that is the marker of high art.

Critical accounts of *Macbeth* that emphasize the play's ethical and aesthetic complexity depend upon a consensus that the high seriousness of Shakesperean tragedy is axiomatic. They occlude the long theatrical and critical tradition in which the play was the object of comic travesty, theatrical spectacle, and childish trivialization (Rogers 1999; Bate 1989; Dobson 1992). When the play was revived, in Davenant's adaptation, after the Restoration of King Charles, it was deemed to be "still a lasting play," but its theatrical success was connected to its "new Cloath's, new Scenes, Machines (as flyings for the Witches), with all the Singing and Dancing in it" (Downes 1987: 33). Accounts of the play's theatrical history from the Restoration onwards demonstrate the instability of the relationship between the meaningful text and the range of intellectual and affective pleasures that it affords. It is perhaps possible to dismiss as aberrations the productions that added choruses of singing witches or the "grand and Terrific Caledonian Drama with National Marches, Choruses, Contests and Processions" (Trewin 1971: 28). However, even the canonical productions of Garrick and Sarah Siddons were recognized as depending as much on the creative work of performers as on the intrinsic meaning of the words in the text. Describing Garrick's performance in 1743–4, the author of the *Dramatic Miscellanies* observed:

> You heard what they spoke, but you learned more from the agitation of mind displayed in their action and deportment. (Davies 1784)

The theatrical performance was felt to encapsulate an emotional truth already internalized by the actor. The actions of individual performers were felt to give a life to the play which transcended its textual parameters. Writing of Mrs. Siddons's famous rendition of Lady Macbeth, William Hazlitt observed that

> it was in bursts of indignation, or grief, in sudden exclamations, in apostrophes and inarticulate sounds that she raised the soul of passion to its height, or sunk it in despair. (Bate 1989: 35)

Different performers could make the play their own, while simultaneously offering their version as a new truth to the infinite possibility of its meaning.

What is equally clear, however, is that it was the knowledge and sensibility of the critic that read these performances as meaningful renditions of the play. Hazlitt's admiration for Mrs. Siddons's performance was not shared by all those who saw it. As Jonathan Bate describes,

> In (a caricature called) *How to harrow up the Soul* the exclamation (in the sleepwalking scene) seems to result from the tight fit of her bodice. Mrs Siddons' attempt to squeeze the maximum passion from the moment is dismissed as fakery. (Bate 1989: 35)

The caricaturist's irreverent mockery of the actress's passion was shared by a long line of parodists who built on the familiarity of the play for comic and satirical purposes. Thomas Duffet, for example, entertained his audience at the Covent Garden theatre in 1674 with an Epilogue to his play, *The Empress of Morocco*. The Epilogue was "spoken by *Heccate* and three Witches, according to the famous Mode of Macbeth." Duffet mocked the theatrical effects of contemporary productions of *Macbeth* with the following display:

> Thunder and lightening is discover'd not behind Painted Tiffany to blind and amuse the Senses, but openly, by the most excellent way of Mustard-bowl and Saltpeter. Three witches fly over the Pit- Riding upon Beesomes. *Heccate* descends over the stage in a Glorious Charriot, adorn'd with Pictures of Hell and Devils, and made of a large Wicker Basket.

Duffet's witches are prostitutes, giving salaciously detailed accounts of sexual encounters with representatives of the gentlemen of the audience to Hecate, their madame. The familiar meter of the witches' speeches and the recognizable poetic tags were transformed into obscene ridicule:

> I pick'd Shop-keeper up, and went to th'Sun,
> He Houncht – and Houncht – and Houncht;
> And when h'had done,
> Pay me quoth I,
> Be damn'd you Whore: did fierce Mechanick cry;
> And most unlike a true bred Gentleman,
> Drunk as a Bitch he left me there in Pawn. (ll. 16–22)

Duffet's travesty was as much an attack on a rival theatre as a considered response to Shakespeare's play. Nevertheless it reveals the extent to which tragic seriousness and supernatural horror were not the only possible responses to the play's action. The eighteenth- and nineteenth-century critical history of the play and its performances can be read as a constant struggle to insist on its aesthetic power and to marginalize inappropriate responses as a low-life antithesis of its true meaning. In his account of Davenant's adapted production, Davies reported that the performance of music and dancing proved

> more agreeable to the taste of the audience who were pleased with the comic dress which the actors gave to the witches, contrary in the opinion of every person of taste to the original design of the author. (Davies 1784: 114–15)

Davies makes a distinction between the taste of those who responded to the immediate pleasures offered by particular theatrical representation and that of more discriminating "persons of taste" who had access to "the original design of the author."

The sense of the play's high seriousness depended upon invoking its historical moment, whether in the assumed intentions of the author or in the perceptions of the original audience. The need to control and exclude inappropriate reactions to the play by invoking its history was evident from the work of the earliest editors. Dr. Johnson, for example, began his 1765 edition of the play with a long and learned note on the opening stage direction, "Enter three witches." His note discussed King James VI and I's interest in witches and dealt with the evidence of James's personal involvement in the examination of the Witches of Berwick, described in the English publication, *Newes from Scotland*. His commentary was explicitly informed by the belief that

> In order to make a true estimate of the abilities and merit of a writer, it is always necessary to examine the genius of his age, and the opinions of his contemporaries. (Johnson, note on 1.1.0)

For Dr. Johnson, the witches presented an aesthetic problem that could be solved by historicizing the play. His Enlightenment audience's supposed disbelief in witches could be allayed by reference to "the system that was then universally admitted." Shakespeare could then be applauded for his skill in turning that system "to his advantage" in a way that "was far from overburthening the credulity of his audience." Dr. Johnson's insistence that early modern belief in witches was not to be relegated to credulous fools and infants was reinforced by his emphasis on James VI and I's interest in witchcraft. If the King of England and Scotland "believed" in witchcraft, the issue of the original audience's "belief" seemed to be solved (Larner 1973).

The effect of Johnson's commentary was to stabilize the play and to protect it from spontaneous and, in Johnson's view, inappropriate response. That process of critical commentary has continued to the present day and it has generated a critical consensus about the play's historical significance, insisting that it be read in terms of its relationship to the politics of James VI and I's accession to the throne and to the changing complex of witchcraft belief in the early modern period.

Since Dr. Johnson's time that work of critical commentary has produced some fascinating accounts of early modern patterns of thought. It has drawn on and contributed to wide-ranging accounts of the social and intellectual history of the period. However, much of that work is ancillary to the evidence about the play's provenance and it begs the difficult question of the relationship between a play performed at a professional theatre and other evidence of the mentalities of the time.

The argument about the historical existence of the play usually proceeds by attesting a known historical fact and then connecting it to the thematics of the play. The principal event that is invoked to support the proposed connection between *Macbeth* and King James is the establishment of the Chamberlain's Men, Shakespeare's playing company, as the King's Men in 1603. The impact of this event on the repertory and preoccupations of the company has often been overstated. As Susan Ceresano reminds us, we should not

> confuse the political interests expressed in a certain subgroup of Shakespeare's plays (*Henry V* and *Macbeth* are often discussed in this vein) with a company's interest in cultivating and maintaining the pleasure of its patron. (Ceresano 1997: 339)

Moreover, none of the documentary evidence of court performance names *Macbeth* as one of the plays performed at court in the reign of James I. This is not, in itself, proof that the Scottish play was not performed at court. Between fifteen and twenty-six plays were presented at court in each of the winter seasons and in the ten seasons between 1603/4 and 1612/13 only odd titles were listed in the Revels accounts. However, it is worth noting that in the 1611 court season, in the year in which the astrologer Simon Forman saw three Shakespeare plays at the Globe, two of the plays that Forman saw, *The Winter's Tale* and *The Tempest*, were transferred from the main Globe repertory to the court. One, *Macbeth*, was not (Astington 1999: 197).

Few critics now insist on a direct relationship between Shakespeare's play and the explicit preoccupations of James's policy and practice (Braunmuller 1997: 8–9). Nevertheless, the presentation of a Scottish play, including a procession of Stuart kings in act 4, the treatment of witches, and the flattering presentation of an English monarch as healer of his people, seems to require an explanation. The difficulty is to provide that explanation in ways that do not run counter to available documentary evidence. However, when critical views about the play are set against the documentary evidence of its seventeenth-century existence, the gap between the two kinds of analysis becomes all too evident.

Evidence for the historical existence of the play consists of a single text, printed in the Folio collected works of Shakespeare, together with an extraordinary eyewitness account by the physician and astrologer Simon Forman, who saw the play at the Globe Theatre in 1611, some twelve years before the Folio was published. Both documents need to be scrutinized in order to provide an image, however shadowy, of a play performed and published in the early years of the seventeenth century and associated with Shakespeare and his company performing at the Globe Theatre on the Bankside.

Forman's account is in many ways a frustrating document and responses to it reveal the difficulties of reading historical sources in relation to a Shakespearean text. It disrupts some of the most firmly held modern views about the seventeenth-century version of the play – that it was about witches and it was about kingship – especially the kingship of James VI and I. It does not, because it cannot, describe a *Macbeth* which will satisfy the modern critical imagination, and the details of Forman's account are at odds with the play in its Folio version. Macbeth is described as "king of Condon," not Thane of Cawdor, and Duncan "made Mackbeth [not Malcolm] forth with Prince of Northumberland" (not Cumberland). The prophecies which begin the play are made by "3 women feiries or Nimphes" and their appearance occurs when Macbeth and Banquo were "ridinge thorowe a wod." The image of Macbeth and Banquo on horseback confronted by women fairies or nymphs has been connected to the woodcut from the 1577 edition of Raphael Holinshed's *Chronicles of England and Scotland* (not the edition used by Shakespeare) that presents an encounter between two horsemen and three women dressed in classical costumes. This has led scholars to suggest that the chronicle "contaminates" Forman's diary entry (Braunmuller 1997: 58). Since, it is argued, horses did not appear on stage and since the Folio's figures are witches and not fairies, Forman's witness, they claim, cannot be regarded as completely reliable (Scragg 1973).

The coincidence between Holinshed's woodcut and Forman's account of the opening scene of the play is certainly intriguing. There is no evidence that Forman had read Holinshed, but Shakespeare certainly did, and Holinshed's account of Macbeth's reign is one of the principal sources for the play (Bullough 1957–75: 447–51). The connection between Forman and Holinshed could be an invention of critics drawing a circle between their knowledge and Forman's; it could be an example of the significance of images rather than words in early modern culture, or it could suggest that the King's Men might have drawn on Shakespeare's source rather than on Shakespeare's lines for the theatricalization of the opening scene. However, none of these problems really needs to be addressed. Forman's reference to Macbeth and Banquo "riding through a wood" need not imply that horses were on stage: there are many scenes in early modern drama, including in this play, when figures come on stage "as from horse back." In transposing a theatrical experience to a narrative one, Forman elides events seen onstage and heard offstage. His references to riding may have come from the attention the play gives to them, including the offstage sound of horses at the end of 4.2 which alerts Macbeth to Macduff's flight into England.

What is also clear is that for Forman the prophetic role of the "three fairies or nymphs" was more memorable than their particular supernatural qualities. This is unsurprising, since Forman was a doctor and astrologer who used similar models of prophetic explanation throughout his scientific diary, his notes on patients, and his autobiography. He is most concerned with a prophecy fulfilled, a murder discovered, and the murder of Macduff's wife and children requited in the final battle. He gives us some suggestion that he observed the relationship between motivation and action. Macbeth and Lady Macbeth were apparently "moch amazed & Affronted" by their inability to wash Duncan's blood from their hands and Macbeth's second murder was "for feare of Banko, his old companion, that he should beget kinges but be no kinge him selfe." Forman also notes particular theatrical moments, drawing attention to the bloody daggers and the sleepwalking scene and giving detailed attention to the appearance of Banquo's ghost. He provides an intriguing description of affective acting, though he does not indicate how far this affect was shared by him:

> And when Mack Beth had murdred the kinge, the blod on his handes could not be washed off by Any meanes, nor from his wives handes, which handled the bloddi daggers in hiding them, By which means they became both moch amazed and Affronted. (Braunmuller 1997: 57–8)

The principal problem with Forman's account is that it makes no reference to the witches' final appearance in which they prepare the magic potion and present Macbeth with the vision of the apparitions and the parade of kings. This might suggest that the text of the play that appears in the Folio represents a different version of the play from the one that Forman saw. Evidence of revision in the different texts of *King Lear* has encouraged modern scholars to suggest that Shakespeare's texts are characterized more by eclectic diversity than by a unitary authorial original that can be identified by bibliographical analysis (Ioppolo 1991). In the absence of any comparative text such as a Quarto version it is difficult to be certain about the extent of revision that might lie behind the Folio text. The text is remarkably "clean," with very little in the way of serious textual corruption in the sense of passages which cannot be deciphered because of syntactic confusion or incomprehensible words and phrases. It has none of the false starts and dead ends left over from previous versions that are the usual signs of a revised text (ibid: 131).

The most persuasive evidence for revision occurs in the directions for the witches' songs. The Folio text includes two marginal stage directions for songs, one in 3.5 – "*Music and a song, Come away, come away, within*" – and one in 4.1: "*Music, and a song, Black spirits, etc.*" A full text of songs with these first lines is included in Davenant's 1674 adaptation of the play and full texts of the songs also appear in Middleton's play *The Witch*. The possible explanation for these coincidences is summarized by Braunmuller in his Cambridge edition of the play:

> They may thus be: the result of Middleton, and/or Shakespeare, and/or a third party sharing a source or sources; borrowings (in any direction) among the known plays, other printed texts, and hypothetical unknown texts; the result of deliberate adaptation of one or the other surviving play. (Braunmuller 1997: 255–6)

In the absence of any further evidence it might be best to take an agnostic view of the relationship between the different occurrences of these songs. They are included in a collection of theatre music written by the lutenist Robert Johnson and could well have been part of a common stock of song material able to be drawn on when a song was needed.

The critical consequences of evidence of a revised text are rather more difficult to establish. Critics who emphasize the revisions that may lie behind the Folio text often do so in order to connect the provenance of the text to a larger thesis about Shakespeare's work. Diane Purkiss, for example, in anti-bardolatrous mode, describes Shakespeare "unblushingly strip-mining both popular culture and every learned text he can lay his hands on for the sake of creating an arresting stage event" (Purkiss 1996: 207). In order to give her thesis historical underpinning, Purkiss needs to assert (without textual analysis) that "the version of *Macbeth* which survives is the product of later revision" (p. 206). This categorical assumption of revision is necessary for Purkiss to make the connection between the Folio *Macbeth* and Jonson's *Masque of Queens*, performed at court in 1609. This allows her to elide the evidence for three quite different cultural phenomena: the performance of witchcraft before James during the trials of the Witches of Berwick in 1594, Jonson's masque in 1609, and a putative court performance of *Macbeth* at some later stage before the publication of the First Folio. All three events can then be subsumed into her overall thesis that the presentation of witchcraft in three quite different conditions of performance represented "a staging of violent misogyny for the benefit of a patriarchal absolutist paranoid about women's powers" (p. 206). Purkiss's judgment about the aesthetic and social impact of the representation of witches is the opposite of Dr. Johnson's, but the terms of the analysis, involving witchcraft, James VI and I, and Shakespeare's play, remain the same.

Purkiss is not alone in connecting textual revision to court performance and thence to critical judgment (see Mullaney 1980; Orgel 1999). It is a condition of the critical process that scholars use their understanding of the past to generate meanings that will make sense in terms established by the present – whether that present is the eighteenth or the twenty-first century. Stephen Orgel has mischievously suggested that the revision of the witch scenes was an attempt "to liven up an unpopular play" (ibid: 148). He nevertheless goes on to a persuasive account of the way that the supposed revisions, together with Davenant's adaptation, open a space for the consideration of the role of women in the play's world, an interpretation that builds on and corroborates contemporary feminist interests. The value of the past existence of the play lies in the meaning it is assumed to have for the present, the sense that it allows us access to what Jameson has called "the discursive constitution of a given social and historical formation" (Jameson 1989: 76–7), or gives us the opportunity, as Greenblatt has put it, to speak with the dead (Greenblatt 1988: 1). When we speak to the dead, however thoughtfully, they tell us what we want to hear.

There is no really satisfying alternative to this critical procedure. The forms of conservation and restoration that it depends upon are part of the aesthetic pleasure that is essential to the appreciation of a masterwork. However, just as some archeological conservators are beginning to make explicit their processes of restoration, often leaving objects in the states in which they were found, it might be interesting to contemplate a less stable literary artifact with its loose ends unconnected to definitive meaning, or at least with the process of creating meaning laid bare.

One way of doing this is to return to Simon Forman's account of the play as the only eyewitness account of a performance. As we have seen, Forman provides a stable account of a coherent narrative. Equally suggestive, however, are the theatrical moments he remembers. He gives the fullest attention to the appearance of Banquo's ghost:

> The next night, beinge at supper with his noblemen whom he had bid to a feaste . . . he began to speake of Noble Banco and to wish that he wer ther. And as he thus did, standing up to drincke a Carouse to him, the ghoste of Banco came and sate down in his cheier behind him. And he turninge About to sit down Again sawe the goste of Banco, which fronted him so, that he fell into a great passion of fear and fury, Utterynge many wordes about his murder . . .

The stage image of the ghost sitting in Macbeth's chair is incongruously redolent of a clown gag such as the one used in Heywood's *If You Know Not Me, You Know Nobody*, when the loyal clown pulls away a chair from behind jailor Bedingfield, knocking him to the ground. This, or a similar, theatrical structure was also remembered in other plays of the time. Middleton's *The Puritan* calls for "the ghost i'th white sheete sit at the upper end a'th Table" and Jasper in *The Knight of the Burning Pestle* suggests that a ghost appearing "When thou art at the Table with thy friends," "Shall make thee let the Cup fall from thy hand, / And stand as mute and pale as death itself" (Ingleby et al. 1932). The younger poets' reaction may have been part of the mockery of older forms which is found in a number of their plays, and some critics have been reluctant to connect these episodes to *Macbeth* (Holdsworth 1990). Nevertheless, they do reveal a gap between modern readings of the scene as a masterful representation of horror and suspense and the more simple narrative irony that Forman perceives.

The distinction between Forman's account and modern readings lies principally in the value accorded to the accompanying poetry. Forman's laconic reference to "many words about the murder" scarcely covers the eloquent desperation of Macbeth's reaction to the ghost. In the Folio text Macbeth's speeches seem to slow the pace of the scene, providing ten lines between the ghost's first appearance and Macbeth noticing him. The language spins the action out over two ghostly entrances, allowing Macbeth to recover his composure and then fall once more into terrified, guilt-stricken panic. Its dramatic effect in modern performances is dominated by Macbeth's double act as he vacillates with increasing desperation between the lords, the ghost, and a bewildered and angry Lady. It is presented as a summation of the psychic and moral costs of Macbeth's attempts to deflect the prophecy once it had fulfilled his own "deep and dark desires" and sets the tone for the final drive towards vengeance.

After the ghost's first exit, Macbeth reflects

> Blood has been shed e'er now, i'th'olden time,
> Ere humane statute purged the gentle weal;
> Ay, and since too, murders have been performed
> Too terrible for the ear. The time has been
> That when the brains were out, the man would die
> And there an end. But now they rise again
> With twenty mortal murders on their crowns
> And push us from our stools. (3.4.78–82)

The opening generalization allows the speech to connect the murder of Banquo to the atavistic violence of a precivilized past. That reflection, however, cannot completely banish the comic image, picked up in Middleton's and Beaumont's treatment, of a man pushed from his stool.

It is impossible to reconcile a modern critical sensibility, trained in the reading of poetry and culturally attuned to an interest in subjectivity, with Forman's bald account of the play's narrative. Nor is it sensible to turn Forman into a paradigm spectator with an authoritative insight into the state of the text and its impact across a whole culture. What Forman's observation can reveal is the way that the scene is built on a deep theatrical structure, part of a tool-kit of devices shared by all early modern dramatists. Its transformation by poetry into the Folio text opened wider possibilities of reading that have been elaborated by later critical activity. However, that analytical and interpretive activity belongs to a later time and a different sensibility than a 1611 performance of the play.

A similar critical chasm opens up between Forman's account of the witches' role and subsequent readings of their significance in the play. Forman's reference to "three women fairies or nimphes" who begin the action with their prophecy conveys none of the other-worldly horror or supernatural power that is associated with witches both in contemporary demonology and in historical accounts of witch belief. It restricts the witches' significance to their role in the narrative and raises the intriguing possibility that the witches in the play may not have been immediately identifiable as a representation of witches in the local communities of early modern England. This possibility is to some extent corroborated by additional historical evidence. In Barnaby Rich's *The Honestie of this Age* (1614) there occurs the following astonishing passage:

> My lady . . . holdeth on her way, perhaps to the Tyre maker's shope, where she shaketh out her crowns to bestowe upon some new fashion attire, that if we may say, there be deformitie in art, uppon such deformed perriwigs, that they were fitter to furnish a Theatre, or for her that in a stageplay, should represent some hagge of hell, then to be used by a Christian woman. (Rich 1614: sig B3v–4r)

In the midst of a commonplace misogynist trope about women's fashion, there seems to be a direct reference to a stage costume. Moreover, the stage costume referred to does not suggest a sinister representation of evil, or even sympathy for an oppressed woman, but a comic image of an actor in a bad wig. Braunmuller suggests that this passage offers "A hint of the witches' early costuming" and corroborates this by quoting Brome and Heywood's *Late Lancashire Witches* (1634), in which a daughter describes her mother's clothing as being "like one o'the Scottish wayward sisters" (Braunmuller 1997: 239). Braunmuller relegates this information to an appendix, for it is difficult to reconcile it with the poetic and narrative impact of the witches articulated in modern readings of the Folio text.

A significant part of that impact depends upon the long scene, apparently absent in the version that Forman saw, where the witches reinforce their magic power with the display of apparitions and kings. The opening speech around the cauldron stages the witches' power. It identifies them with poisonous and alien creatures and the body parts of demonized peoples, the Jew, Turk, and the Tartar. The very open-endedness of these references makes possible a wide range of connections to contemporary witch lore, but scholars have also used them as a starting point for an ethical and imaginative engagement with the social world of early modern England. The Jew, the Turk, and the Tartar are exemplars of the fearsome racialized alternatives to English nationhood. Their very lack of connection to the narrative of the play presents an intriguing gap that can be filled by accounts of early modern racial thinking. Those accounts reveal the dense complexity and pervasiveness of concerns about outsiders in early modern culture. Those analyses in turn deepen the sense that the poetry of the play has the potential to draw on the whole of that culture and synthesize it in a single evocative image.

Similarly, the "finger of birth-strangled babe / ditch delivered by a drab" can be read as a synecdoche for a grim social world in which infanticide is the desperate conclusion of oppressive sexual relations. The image can be linked back to the witches' account of killing swine and harassing the greedy sailor's wife (1.3.2–25) and seems to encapsulate the belief system of early modern England. The nature of that belief system has offered unlimited scope for debate. Social historians of witchcraft have debated the relationship between witch hunting and women hunting (Larner 1981: 84–8; Karlsen 1987; Sharpe 1991; Holmes 1993). They have analyzed the process of naming and trying a witch in which contentious social relationships moved from personal conflict, to public accusation, to the formal legal processes. Whether the actions of a particular witch were dismissed as superstition, tried as maleficium, or gloated over as a tall tale of village life, depended on who was telling the story and to whom it was told. Monolithic explanations of witch beliefs have been replaced by attention to the particularity of different cases, the importance of local conditions, such as the arrival of a new landowner, a reforming minister, or a commissioned witchfinder. Witch belief has been identified as a complex of intellectual traditions which included significant resistance to superstition and the varied local beliefs that implicated the victims as much as the accused. This analysis offers less a conflict between belief and skepticism than an understanding of the relative functions of belief and skepticism in emergent ideologies. It removes the issue of witchcraft from the credulous superstitions of early modern people into legitimate early modern modes of thought (Clark 1997).

The dense particularity of these accounts of witchcraft is fascinating in itself and it provides an alternative source of intellectual engagement that stands alongside the limited role of the witches in the play. In order to establish an interpretive connection between early modern witchcraft and *Macbeth*, critics need to invoke a connecting principle. As we have seen, for Dr. Johnson, that connecting principle was James VI and I. For more recent analysis, the connecting principle lies in the physical and poetic imagery of the play. The apparitions of the armed head, the bloody babe, and the crowned child act as physical symbols of the action's outcome. They can also be connected thematically to Macbeth's and his Lady's preoccupation with children and succession, as well as presenting a grim forecast of the fate of Macduff's child, murdered onstage in the following scene (Adelman 1992). In those analyses, the act 4 scene functions as an interpretive as well as a narrative pivot, cementing Macbeth's resolve to further evil deeds and connecting the witches, much more firmly than other witch scenes, to the finale and outcome of the play.

The critical impulse to interpret the witches beyond their narrative significance is endorsed because the characters who see the witches are themselves intensely preoccupied by their meaning. In act 4 the apparitions and the show of kings are offered up to be interpreted by Macbeth. When the apparitions rise, Macbeth is puzzled about what they might mean:

> What is this
> That rises like the issue of a king
> And wears upon his baby brow the round
> And top of sovereignty

he says, and the witches urge him to "listen, but speak not to't." Just before the procession of kings appears, the witches chant

> Show his eyes and grieve his heart
> Come, like shadows, so depart.

The significance of the representation of the kings lies in the effect they will have on Macbeth's heart, not merely on his eyes. As a result, Macbeth does not just tell us what he sees. His horrified reaction gives meaning to what is represented on the stage:

> Thou art too like the spirit of Banquo. Down.
> Thy crown does sear mine eyeballs . . .
> Filthy hags, why do you show me this . . .
> Start eyes . . . horrible sight . . .

The play's suspense turns on the tension between Macbeth's and the audience's interpretation of the witches, but the relationship between those interpretations is mediated by Banquo's views of the encounter he shares with Macbeth. Macbeth, as he indicates in his letter to his wife, presents the witches as having "more in them than mortal knowledge." It is Banquo who reminds him that

> to win us to our harm,
> The instruments of darkness tell us truths,
> Win us with honest trifles, to betray's
> In deepest consequence. (1.3.123–6)

Banquo's interpretation of the witches is then further complicated by Lady Macbeth's response to them. Her first line in the play – "They met me in the day of my success" – refers to Macbeth's account of their meeting. Her *reaction*, on the other hand, opens up another dynamic opposition between Macbeth's and Banquo's reception of the witches and her own eager embrace of the future they hold out.

The interpretive intensity that critics read into the cauldron scene is somewhat mitigated by its theatricality. It made full use of the technical potential of an early modern stage, using the trap-door for the apparitions and the cauldron to "descend" and the upstage doors as the beginning and end of the procession. It adds "Hecate and the other three witches" to the original prophetic trio and the seven witches *sing* (43), *dance and vanish* (131 s.d.). At the end of the scene the tone changes from the sinister to the charming as the first witch, somewhat disingenuously, enquires "why / Stands Macbeth thus amazedly" and suggests:

> Come sisters, cheer we up his sprites
> And show the best of our delights.

As we have seen, scholars have been at pains to distance Shakespeare from the "entertaining" elements of the scene, but both they and the apparitions are part of the theatrical traditions available to the author. The armed head prop that could reasonably be reused for Macbeth's at the end of the play had been seen in *Friar Bacon and Friar Bungay* and in Peele's play *The Old Wives Tale*; a procession of deadly sins had been brought by Lucifer from hell "to show . . . some passtime" to Dr. Faustus, in Marlowe's play, revived in 1609.

Given both the theatrical and the interpretive significance of this scene, it seems especially puzzling that it is absent from Forman's account. Scholars who accept the principle of revision seldom follow through the implications of the existence of a play without this scene. If this scene was added after 1611 it is doubtful that Shakespeare would have been involved in the revision. Yet the combination of poetry and theatricality, of action and commentary, are much less easily allocated to another hand than the more contingent effects of the songs and dances or the appearance of Hecate.

One possible explanation appears in Andrew Gurr's (1999) suggestions that there may have been a considerable gap between what he calls the "maximal" version of an early modern play – the full text licensed by the Master of the Revels – and the "minimal" version which offered variable parts appropriate for performance in different venues. Gurr cites the numerous references in printed texts that make clear that printed texts of early modern plays contained "more than hath been Publickely Spoken or Acted" (ibid: 80) and observes the contrasting attitude of modern editors:

On the principle that if it is Shakespeare it must be in every edition prepared for the reader is likely to incorporate more of the text than was heard in the early performances. (Ibid: 87)

It is no part of Gurr's intention to restore the fantasy of the authoritative authorial version of the play corrupted by performance. Rather, it reinforces the sense that early modern plays were made up of more or less discrete elements, theatrical devices, sequences, and speeches that could be dismantled and reconstituted in a variety of forms around a narrative core. That unstable model of drama adequately accounts for differences between the *Macbeth* that Forman described and the Folio text. However, it does present a challenge to critics who wish to validate their reading of the play by invoking its historical circumstances. The sense of this history behind every modern reading or performance is used to validate and endorse the modern experience of the play, correcting misinterpretation, disallowing perversity, ensuring a coherent aesthetic and intellectual experience. This model of an organic work of art, coherent in meaning and significance, occludes both the evidence of its reception – the possibility that Banquo's ghost or the witches might have been mocked – and the cumulative effect of centuries of reading and theatrical production that have marginalized that mockery and created the tradition of its ethical and aesthetic power. *Macbeth* needs the cohering effects of critical reading and historical significance to sustain its masterpiece status but, equally, the puzzling instability that lies behind it makes it dynamically available for the adaptation and interpretation that will ensure its future cultural power.

References and Further Reading

Adelman, J. (1992). Escaping the Matrix: The Construction of Masculinity in *Macbeth* and *Coriolanus*. In *Suffocating Mothers: Fantasies of Maternal Origin in Shakespeare's Plays*. London: Routledge, 130–64.

Astington, J. H. (1999). *English Court Theatre 1558–1642*. Cambridge: Cambridge University Press.

Bate, J. (1989). *Shakesperean Constitutions: Politics, Theatre, Criticism 1730–1830*. Oxford: Clarendon Press.

Bradley, A. C. (1969). *Shakesperean Tragedy*. London: Macmillan.

Braunmuller, A. R. (ed.) (1997). *Macbeth*. Cambridge: Cambridge University Press.

Bristol, M. (1996). *Big-Time Shakespeare*. London: Routledge.

Bullough, G. (ed.) (1957–75). *Narrative and Dramatic Sources of Shakespeare*, 8 vols. London: Routledge and Kegan Paul, vol. 7, 423–537.

Ceresano, S. (1997). The Chamberlain's–Kings Men. In J. Cox and D. S. Kastan (eds.) *A New History of Early English Drama*. New York: Columbia University Press.

Clark, S. (1997). *Thinking with Demons: The Idea of Witchcraft in Early Modern Europe*. Oxford: Oxford University Press.

Davies, T. (1784). *Dramatic Miscellanies: Consisting of Critical Observations on several Plays of Shakespeare*, 3 vols. Dublin: S. Price.

Dobson, M. (1992). *The Making of the National Poet: Shakespeare, Adaptation and Authorship, 1660–1769*. Oxford: Clarendon Press.

Downes, J. (1987) [1708]. *Roscius Anglicanus*, ed. J. Milhous and R. D. Hume. London: Society for Theatre Research.

Farrell, K. (1989). *Play, Death and Heroism in Shakespeare*. Chapel Hill: University of North Carolina Press.

Greenblatt, S. (1988). *Shakesperean Negotiations*. Oxford: Clarendon Press.

Gurr, A. (1999). Maximal and Minimal Texts: Shakespeare v. the Globe. *Shakespeare Survey*, 52, 68–87.

Holdsworth, R. V. (1990). *Macbeth and The Puritan*. N & Q, 235, 204–5.

Holmes, C. (1993). Women: Witnesses and Witches. *Past and Present*, 140, 45–78.

Ingleby, C. M. et al. (eds.) (1932). *The Shakespeare Allusion Book: A Collection of Allusions to Shakespeare from 1591–1700*, 2 vols. London.

Ioppolo, G. (1991). *Revising Shakespeare*. Cambridge, MA: Harvard University Press.

Jameson, F. (1989). *The Political Unconscious: Narrative as a Socially Symbolic Act*. London: Routledge.

Karlsen, C. F. (1987). *The Devil in the Shape of a Woman: Witchcraft in Colonial New England*. New York.

Kermode, F. (2000). *Shakespeare's Language*. London: Allen Lane.

Larner, C. (1973). James VI and I and Witchcraft. In A. G. R. Smith (ed.) *The Reign of James VI and I*. London: Macmillan, 74–90.

——(1981). *Enemies of God: The Witch-hunt in Scotland*. London: Chatto and Windus.

——(1984). *Witchcraft and Religion: The Politics of Popular Belief*. Oxford: Blackwell.

Mullaney, S. (1980). Lying like Truth: Riddle, Representation and Treason in Renaissance England. *English Literary History*, 47, 32–47.

Orgel, S. (1999). Macbeth and the Antic Round. *Shakespeare Survey*, 52, 143–53.

Purkiss, D. (1996). *The Witch in History: Early Modern and Twentieth Century Representations*. London: Routledge.

Rich, B. (1614). *The Honestie of the Age*.

Rogers, R. (1999). *Eighteenth Century Macbeths: The English Poet and the Scottish Play*. Ph.D. thesis, University of Southampton.

Scragg, L. (1973). Macbeth on Horseback. *Shakespeare Survey*, 26, 81–8.

Sharpe, J. A. (1991). Witchcraft and Women in Seventeenth Century England: Some Northern Evidence. *Continuity and Change*, 6, 179–99.

Trewin, J. C. (1971). Macbeth in the Nineteenth Century. *New Theatre Quarterly*, 1, 3, 26–31.

21

The Politics of Empathy in
Antony and Cleopatra: A View
from Below

Jyotsna G. Singh

I

Age cannot wither her, nor custom stale
Her infinite variety.[1]

"Who is Cleopatra?" This was the question addressed by a recent exhibition at the British Museum in London, entitled "Cleopatra of Egypt: From History to Myth" (summer 2001). The display of an array of material objects – coins, jewelry, maps, statues, and engravings – cohered around the question of Cleopatra's identity. The accompanying brochure described her as "Lady of the Two Lands": the Ptolemaic, Greek ruler of Egypt who was also identified with Isis and Hathor, major Egyptian goddesses. Attempting to convey her elusiveness and variety, the display emphasized how it is "notoriously difficult to identify portraits of Cleopatra." In fact, we were told that images purporting to represent the Egyptian queen on coins and busts could not be easily identified, since Cleopatra's presence in Rome fueled a minor Egypto-mania in fashion and style. Not surprisingly, of course, imitations of her style and idiom were carried over into the exhibition's lavish displays of twentieth-century, Hollywood incarnations of Cleopatra. She was a woman for all ages.

Despite the narrative frame that included the conquerors of antiquity – Alexander, Octavius, Antony – the Egyptian queen's mystique was in fact the subject of "Cleopatra of Egypt: From History to Myth," and the large crowds certainly demonstrated why the "figure of Cleopatra has survived so strongly as a term in cultural exchange and been reworked so often" (Hamer 1993: xvi). And the exhibition quite blithely conflated the historical images of the Ptolemaic and Egyptian Cleopatra with Hollywood representations of the queen, thus reinforcing a universal, timeless image of a powerful, though stereotypical, *femme fatale* belonging to all times. Overall, one came away feeling that whether one is casting a look at Cleopatra through history – via Plutarch and Shakespeare – or at the contemporary Hollywood embodiment

in Elizabeth Taylor, she seems perpetually conceived as an individual celebrity –
and it is as a celebrity that we are drawn to witness and define her role as a tragic
protagonist.

Shakespeare's *Antony and Cleopatra* and the critical responses that followed also
testify to the fact that the figure of "Cleopatra and her story have the weight of
originary myth in Western culture" (Hamer 1993: xvii). The cult of personality
evident in the British Museum exhibition underpins a long critical tradition
enthralled by Cleopatra and by the fate of the two lovers. This enthrallment has been
typically based on Cleopatra's power to generate strong feelings, whether empathy or
repulsion. While her changeable figure paradoxically embodies a sphinx-like opacity
to which her varied audiences have been drawn, it also has evoked a sense of her interiority. The critical history of Shakespeare's version, until recently, has manifested two
related though contradictory trends: an abiding fascination with Cleopatra's "infinite
variety" of seductiveness and beauty and a skepticism about the play's generic status
as a true tragedy. To sum up, the play has presented a "problem" for generations of
Anglo-American critics precisely because they have struggled to come to terms with
their own conflicting feelings toward her as a tragic protagonist. John Bayley (1981)
describes this critical ebb and flow quite aptly when he states: "The whole effect is
one of sexual rise and fall, endorsing and yet ironically contradicting the admiration
of Cleopatra for making hungry where most she satisfies" (p. 135). Perhaps with some
unwitting irony, Bayley is making visible the dilemma of several generations of masculine critics who acknowledged the play's artistic power, but who were uneasy about
their own ambivalent responses to Cleopatra's role in it.

This critical struggle is aptly summed up by A. P. Riemer in terms of two contradictory, yet related, critical interpretations of Shakespeare's play in the pre-
feminist era: "*Antony and Cleopatra* can be read as the fall of a great general, betrayed
in his dotage by a treacherous strumpet, or else it can be viewed as a celebration
of transcendent love" (cited in Fitz 1994: 182). Both the threat and allure of
Cleopatra are evoked in this statement. John Drakakis (1994) cites two important
nineteenth-century responses that point to the critical "fascination with [and focus
on] Cleopatra" going back to Samuel Johnson and ahead to A. C. Bradley and his
followers:

> In a manner which anticipates much of the subsequent masculine criticism of the
> play, both . . . Schlegel and Coleridge highlighted in their different ways the seductive
> power of Cleopatra. Schlegel regarded Antony as "Hercules in the chains of Omphale"
> . . . and Coleridge . . . identified the profound nature of "the art displayed in the char-
> acter of Cleopatra," but found that "the sense of criminality in her passion is lessened
> by our insight into its depth and energy, at the very moment that we cannot but per-
> ceive that the passion itself springs out of the habitual craving of a licentious nature."
> (Ibid: 2)

Such an essentializing focus on Cleopatra's shortcomings implicitly privileged
the Roman perspective on the Egyptian queen as a "strumpet," rather than on

Shakespeare's overall ambivalent response to an "official" reading of history. Such views quite consistently have been a staple of the earlier criticism that provided the basis for A. C. Bradley's refusal to admit *Antony and Cleopatra* to the supreme pantheon of Shakespearean tragedy. In part, their morally indignant responses to Cleopatra's mercurial role were framed within a view that the play's self-reflexive dramatic form militated against a coherent tragic progression and focus.[2]

Judgments of Cleopatra's failings, such as Riemer's, or a fascination with her charms, inevitably revealed the critics' desire for a natural *empathy* with a tragic protagonist. And since the universal audience is implicitly assumed to be male, it is taken for granted that Cleopatra, like women in general, is impossible for men to understand (Fitz 1994: 201). What is significant here, however, is that a desire for emotional identification and engagement was inevitably premised on realist and psychological assumptions of dramatic characters as "real" people.

Overall, the figure of Cleopatra that emerged from the Shakespearean critical tradition until the late 1970s and early 1980s seemed invested in the assumption of a universal human nature in which Cleopatra represented the archetypal, inscrutable "Woman." Furthermore, sexist stereotypes combined with the play's dialectical structure – evoking shifting responses – prevented Cleopatra from acquiring a tragic stature whereby critics could experience an emotional identification with her. Within their logic the impact of a tragedy was determined by the degree and nature of empathy evoked by the protagonist. Hence, the play lacked tragic authenticity.

Feminist critics, starting with Fitz, have freed the image of Cleopatra from stereotypical clichés, while stressing her role as a "co-protagonist" with Antony and insisting that in her journey of self-discovery we can find "the tragic hero's inner struggle" (Fitz 1994: 200). Yet Fitz also bases her recovery of Cleopatra on realist assumptions of identification and empathy with the tragic Egyptian queen. Thus, she explains the play's exclusion from the "holy circle of the 'big four'" – *Hamlet*, *Othello*, *King Lear*, and *Macbeth* – as a part of the sexist inflections of the earlier, male critics who could not relate to Cleopatra's emotions. According to Fitz, the earlier critics could not accept the play's status as a true tragedy and Cleopatra as a convincing tragic protagonist precisely because they looked for emotional identification as the main criterion for tragedy. Therefore, according to Riemer, for instance, Fitz explains, given that the play

> does not share [Cleopatra's] feelings and ideas, the audience does not participate in [her] emotional state to the extent it partakes of Hamlet's, Othello's, or Lear's emotions at the climactic point of the tragedies in which these characters appear . . . It is not possible for us to share her emotions. (p. 201)

More recent critics – coming in the wake of poststructuralist, new historicist, and psychoanalytical theories – have used Cleopatra for the larger feminist project of unfixing gender identity. Thus, in their eyes, Shakespeare's emphasis on the Egyptian queen's protean and androgynous manipulations of gender roles offers immense possibilities in rethinking gender politics. As one critic notes: "The play consistently locates Cleopatra at the juncture where categories collide and cannot comprehend one another: defect/perfection, satiety/hunger, vileness/holiness . . . In her infinite variety, Cleopatra['s] identity is the refusal of identity, of essence, of the kind of stability which can be made properly to serve Rome" (Cook 1996: 252).

Furthermore, in their reconsiderations of Cleopatra's role, feminist critics also recognize the complex issues of politics and desire at stake in her life. They do not naturalize her theatricality and histrionics as "feminine wiles," but rather point to their political ramifications in a variety of ways. In subverting Roman claims to a stable identity, for instance, Cleopatra reveals the "Roman myth of honor as a manipulable fiction" (Singh 1994: 320–1). In a related vein, another critic considers her androgynous play of identity as politically charged in its resemblances to Queen Elizabeth's own forays into powerful, androgynous self-representations (Jankowski 1992: 156–7).

From this brief survey of the critical history of Shakespeare's *Antony and Cleopatra* one can extrapolate some of the political implications of this history. For instance, in frequently using personal empathy as a criterion for defining the tragic experience in the play, many of the earlier critics seem far removed from the conventions and conditions of the Renaissance stage. To understand the shortcomings of this frequently personalized criticism of the play from the nineteenth century until the 1980s, one has only to look to Bertolt Brecht's reflections on the Elizabethan dramatic experience: "Compare the part played by empathy then [on the Elizabethan and Jacobean stage] and now. What a contradictory, complicated, and intermittent operation it was in Shakespeare's theatre!" (Willett 1964: 161).

Of course, the recent theoretically inflected feminist criticism is keenly sensitive to the constructed nature of gender identity, among other things. And such approaches remind us of the incompatibility between the traditional humanist notions of tragedy, which privileges the "Great Man" as hero, and the recent shifts toward a more inclusive perspective. But with the exception of a few essays (which I discuss later), the critical trend in general – with all its shifts and variety – still largely hinges on the centrality of Cleopatra as an individual protagonist – or even a co-protagonist with Antony. And in most instances, the "famous pair" enjoy a status of celebrity. Conversely, if one questions the central role of the lovers as tragic protagonists, then one is also led to reexamine the nature and ideological function of tragedy, both in the Renaissance and in our own times. In part, any consideration of tragedy may seem impossible in our postmodern era, given that traditionally, tragedy has been explained in terms of a permanent and universal human nature. But if one moves beyond this assumption, "tragedy is then not a single, permanent kind of fact, but a series of experiences and conventions and institutions" by which "we may measure experiences as tragic or accidental, and as bearing a general meaning or lacking ethical content" (Williams 1966: 44–6). And it is not necessary to interpret these experiences in terms of an unchanging humanity. Rather, the "varieties of tragic experience [can be] interpreted by reference to the changing conventions and institutions" (ibid: 46).

In this essay I wish to examine the varieties of tragic experience represented in Shakespeare's *Antony and Cleopatra* in the context of changing conventions and expectations. What kinds of suffering can be included or excluded by the tragic logic of the play? Can we, in the Bradleyan mode, only judge as tragic the suffering or misfortune that springs from the agency of the sufferers, here typically assumed as the two co-protagonists of the play with whom we are supposed to empathize? Or does the play's dialectical structure, conducive to alienating audiences, enable us to rethink connections between the tragedy of the individual(s) and the social and political realm? Such questions inevitably lead us to rethink the representations of the tragic in the play, especially in the context of Williams's critical history of Western ideas about tragedy.

Furthermore, in any consideration of the workings of the tragic genre, Bertolt Brecht's concept of "alienation" is particularly useful in revealing and disrupting the politics of empathy and identification with Cleopatra that have dominated the critical history of the play – and specifically the discussions of its status as a tragedy.[3] I use the term "alienation" drawn from Heinemann's discussion of Brecht's representation of Shakespearean theatre as "full of alienation effects" (Heinemann 1985: 208–18). According to Heinemann, the problem for Brecht in "presenting Shakespearean tragedy . . . is that it is based on the acceptance of evil and disaster as fated, unalterable, eternal" (p. 213). In response to this received tradition, Brecht's aim was to "open up and make explicit contradictions which are deep in [Shakespearean tragedy]" (p. 218).

In relation to contemporary attitudes of his own time towards classics such as Shakespeare's works, Brecht asked not how his work could serve the classics, but "how can the classics serve my work?"[4] According to Hortmann, "Brecht's theory of the 'Materialwert der Klassiker,' or the *material value of the classics*, was designed to cause trouble. The idea was that the prime value of the classics lay in their being raw material . . . a quarry to be plundered in the way the Vandals had sacked ancient Rome" (Hortmann 1998: 83). Thus, in Brecht's view, the epic style was the only contemporary style capable of "bringing out the true, namely the philosophical content of Shakespeare" (cited in Hortmann 1998: 82). In practical terms this meant that Brecht looked for alienation effects in order to counter the realistic illusionism of the theatre of his time, which he described as follows: "People go to the theatre to be carried away, spellbound . . . consoled . . . provided with illusions" (ibid). In countering this illusionist escape he called for different theatre arts that would not only help to interpret the world, but also help to change it (ibid: 83).

According to theatre historians, *Macbeth*, *King Lear*, and *Coriolanus* are Brecht's most frequently cited plays that he believed ought no longer to be performed unless means could be found to "stop the spectator from admiring and identifying with characters of such dubious . . . moral status [as heroic individuals]" (cited in Hortmann 1998: 83). Although *Antony and Cleopatra* did not seem to draw Brecht's attention in the same way as some of the other tragedies, it is clearly open to a "Brechtian" recuperation, given its dialectical structure in dramatizing inconsistencies and contradictions in the actions of the main characters and in the ensuing events.

II

> We think of tragedy as what happens to the hero, but the ordinary tragic action is what happens through the hero. When we confine our attention to the hero, we are unconsciously confining ourselves to one kind of experience, which in our own culture we tend to take as the whole. We are unconsciously confining ourselves to *the individual*. (Williams, 1966: 55)

> [The epic theatre] does not make the hero a victim of an inevitable fate, nor does it wish to make the spectator a victim, so to speak, of a hypnotic experience in the theatre. In fact, it has as a purpose the "teaching" of the spectator a certain quite practical attitude; we have to make it possible for him to take a critical attitude while he is in the theatre . . . (Willett 1964: 78)

It is generally understood that a main feature of Renaissance tragedy is an emphasis on the fall of a famous man. Thus, the tragic effect of a tragedy is premised on an assumption of a "noble" way to respond to suffering, while undergoing a process of growth and transformation at the end. Furthermore, in keeping with the general status of the man of rank, his "fate [is] the fate of the house or kingdom which he once ruled or embodied. In the person of . . . Lear [for instance], the fate of a house or kingdom is literally acted out" (Williams 1966: 50). At his destruction, then, there is a change in the power of the state with a new ruler or rulers. This is not to question that it is the death of the protagonist of high stature that is nonetheless central to the tragic catharsis of the audience. Rank remains the dividing line in Renaissance tragedy, whereby some deaths mattered more than others. "The death of a slave or retainer was no more than incidental and was certainly not tragic" (ibid: 49).

In Shakespeare's works, as we know, the deaths of secondary characters like Regan's servant, who is killed, or Charmian and Iras, who choose to commit suicide with their mistress, are not considered to have a larger tragic effect. Sidney's definition of tragedy in the Renaissance also clearly identifies men of rank covered with grandeur – kings or tyrants for instance – as central to the tragic experience: "The High and excellent Tragedy . . . openeth the greatest wounds, and sheweth forth the Ulcers that are covered with Tissue" (Sidney 1997: 105).

Despite the fact that Renaissance drama privileges the tragic experiences of personages of rank and nobility, paradoxically, it also affords space to the more general or public interests relating to the world it represents. And conversely, if modern tragedy includes the suffering of persons lacking rank and power, its stress on the fate of an individual may also have the effect of distancing his/her particular grief from our understanding of social and political life. Therefore, it is evident that if a work stresses the fate of the *individual*, the "general and public" character of tragedy may get lost (Williams 1966: 50). In this context, *Antony and Cleopatra* offers a particular challenge. How can critics illuminate the political and social dimensions of the tragedy given the long shadow cast by the presence of Cleopatra, or of the two co-protagonists? This is a question infrequently addressed in the rich and varied critical history of the play, ranging from the earlier humanist, character-based criticism to the more complex, anti-essentialist feminist readings that followed.[5]

A question some may ask is why should we expect critics to steer away from any empathy or preoccupation with the two protagonists in *Antony and Cleopatra*? Given that Shakespeare makes them articulate the tragic struggles of love, desire, and power that resonate in and propel the action of the play, shouldn't our focus remain on their extended poetic speeches, their feelings, their triumphs and trials? After all, they repeatedly attempt to create a private world of love by challenging the demands of duty: "Let Rome in Tiber melt." What is clearly dominant in terms of the plot and the poetic speeches has, not surprisingly, afforded generations of critics their point of entry into the play. I propose a reading from the margins, one that explores how *Antony and Cleopatra*'s dialectical, non-teleological structure approximates aspects of Brecht's "epic" theatre. Such an approach enables a politicized mediation into the politics of empathy, individualism, and identification so naturalized within Western representational practices in all areas of social, cultural, and political life. This was evident in the exhibition at the British Museum, which seamlessly elided the historical celebrity of Cleopatra with that of Elizabeth Taylor, given that the currency of individualism has such legitimacy in our media culture.

Of course, literary critics have productively analyzed the workings and effects of the play's distinctive structure, which Janet Adelman (1973) aptly defines as the play's "double perspective" (p. 52). "In tragedy," she notes, "everything usually tends to confirm the experience of the tragic hero . . . Comedy tends, on the other hand, to work toward a variety of experience, a multiplicity of versions, as tragedy does not" (p. 51). Thus, *Antony and Cleopatra*, according to Adelman, "is essentially a tragic experience embedded in a comic structure" (p. 52). Stage performances of the play cannot escape the comedy written into the play, and the recent (1999) Globe production in London, in fact, "mastered the play . . . with a light hand . . . not .. afraid to let the actors entertain us" (Duncan-Jones 1999: 18). In a production where a "fast pace and a tone . . . wobbles perpetually between tragedy and farce," one reviewer notes, "where scenes or speeches emerge as wholly or partly comic, they are allowed to be so" (ibid).

Highlighting the comic, farcical moments in this production, the director also prepared the audience for Mark Rylance's Cleopatra. One review captures the effect of his performance quite aptly as follows:

Mark Rylance may or may not have been the age of the now-unknown Jacobean actor who originally played one the greatest female roles of all time. It didn't matter; his performance as Cleopatra was a genuine revelation of . . . [an actor's version of] the role that I have ever seen or exploited before. It gained, for instance, from the audience's double awareness of character and actor, particularly when he was physically threatening other characters or doing one of Cleopatra's quick transitions between sinking into a faint and deciding not to bother at all. This Cleopatra, as several reviewers said, really did look as if she might decide at any time to hop forty paces through the public street . . . Following Plutarch's account, Rylance also gave us a Cleopatra who had shaved her head and lacerated her face in mourning for Antony, thus making the final transformation with robe and crown even more stunning than usual. (Potter 1999: 514)

Rylance's self-conscious manipulation of the "audience's double awareness of character and actor" certainly seemed to evoke some "alienation effects." For instance, the audience's constant recognition of the actor's actual sex prevented a sustained identification and empathy with Cleopatra as a tragic protagonist. Overall, Cleopatra's histrionics – evoking a mix of comedy, farce, and pathos – effectively distanced us from any sense of the timelessness of high tragedy. Was the final effect of this production tragic? Or "is it ever?" as one reviewer asks (ibid: 515). "The speed at which events moved, matched by that of the characters themselves as they danced and dashed across their world stage, made it easier to enjoy the comedy than to respond to the sense of 'greatness going off'" (ibid). All these distancing devices notwithstanding, it is questionable as to whether this production produced the desired "Brechtian" effects. In that context, to achieve the desired political ends, all distancing, alienating effects must be "deliberatively combative, *political* effects" (Heinemann 1985: 223). In fact, overall, this production was still dominated by the figure of Cleopatra as an individual, more so than as a social or political phenomenon. Ultimately "[the director], Giles Block, seems to . . . see the play as the triumph of a gloriously human couple" (Potter 1999: 515). And despite Rylance's theatrics that disrupted the audience's empathy, the production seemed entirely driven toward revealing the interiority of Cleopatra via her "infinite variety" of moods, demands, postures, and to some extent of Enobarbus, surprisingly even more so than Antony.

In terms of its politics, despite all the endless bustle of messengers on stage carrying news of love or war, the Globe production conveyed little sense of the way in which the politics of desire and war intersect with one another, leading to tragic consequences for many people in a vast kingdom. Neither did it consistently concern itself with the fate of the secondary or minor characters that suffer the consequences of the deeds of the mighty. One reviewer rightly notes that the "most moving part of the play was the mini tragedy of Enobarbus" (Potter 1999: 515); yet in evoking our empathy for this character, the director seemed to have no strategy of revealing the causal networks that led to this individual tragedy of a secondary figure. Finally, then, this theatrically successful and innovative production of the play revealed both the possibilities and limitations of capturing the dialectical, contradictory movements of the play, while allowing the figure of the Egyptian Cleopatra to take over as an embodiment of the structural flux and mutability that mark the text, though in a more comic than tragic vein.

Like this production, not surprisingly, other versions of the play as far back as the nineteenth century also focus on the performances of Cleopatra by famous celebrity actresses, so that it is not uncommon to identify a particular production with an actress playing the Egyptian queen in terms like "Suzman's Cleopatra" or "Lily Langtry's Cleopatra."[6] Of course, stage productions of the play often reflect and participate in the cultural and ideological worldviews of different periods; these range from the lavish, orientalist pageantry popular in the play's Victorian incarnations during the British empire, to Giles Block's campy version of "gender trouble," that was responsive to the sensibilities of the 1990s. And in the rich stage history of this play there have undoubtedly been many "Brechtian" moments, pushing at the edges of representation and its political effects. But the allure of Cleopatra's high-powered theatricality written into her role has probably also held the audiences – both within and outside the play – enthralled by varying modes of empathy towards her. Hence the lovers' story becomes the linchpin of the play's tragic experiences. But is there a way of interpreting *Antony and Cleopatra* less as a tragedy of individual interests and more as one in which audiences are encouraged to challenge the social, class, and gender attitudes implicit in valorization of the two protagonists' fate?

Two recent, proto-Brechtian readings of the play are particularly useful in addressing such questions from different perspectives. They do so initially by drawing attention to the ideological effects as well as political possibilities of the play's disjointed structure, its mingling of tragic and comic, and its representation of constant transmutation and disintegration (Loomba 1994: 280–91; Heinemann 1994: 166–71). Ania Loomba proposes a strategy of inserting the "dimension of gender more fully into . . . [the play's] proto-Brechtian multiplicity and montage," thereby emphasizing how "the epic structure is at least partly derived from and closely related to the drama's interrogation of gender roles and patriarchal authority" (Loomba 1994: 280–1). Thus the play's "non-teleological form itself," according to the critic, "becomes an important vehicle for resisting closure" (p. 281). It not only disrupts a smooth progression toward tragic catharsis, but also underscores the fluidity of racial and gender identity, "achieving a Brechtian alienation from character to posit a radical interrogation of the imperial and sexual drama" (p. 285).

Margot Heinemann's approach to the play's treatment of conflicting versions of history – the traditional Augustan historiography and the Tacitean critique of the triumphalist Augustan view – is also informed by "Brechtian" criteria of distance and alienation. She highlights the many "local conflicts" in the play to remind us that the final conflict of "Caesar against Antony, of Caesar's Rome against Cleopatra's Egypt," is often treated "as not only central but exclusive" in its significance (Heinemann 1994: 169).[7] In trying to get at Shakespeare's "wider rendering of the history as he found it in Plutarch" (p. 169), Heinemann identifies multiple trajectories of discord in the play showing how the alienating elements are incorporated into the very structure of the play:

> Disaster and collapse are shown as the outcome of multiple human, psychological, material and political contradictions in that world, dissected and exposed in the episodic action, cutting across one another, intersecting one with another and modifying one another with unforeseeable results . . . Too many local conflicts and insoluble contradictions are indeed observed and revealed for any to provide an overriding causal explanation of the global disorder. (pp. 168–9)

Since Heinemann's interest in the play lies in its engagement with competing versions of history and its "refusal of a single historical or ethical center," she is also aware of the local and particular effects of the larger sweep of history on the minor or secondary characters (p. 177). Observing the large cast-list of the play (35 speaking parts), she notes that it "allows the long and diffuse history to be *staged* in brief contrasting episodes" (p. 169). This structure gives "space for even minor characters to change . . . and allows an unforced sense of the price lower ranks have to pay in smaller personal tragedies for the grand designs and follies of those above them" (p. 169).

In the rest of this essay I wish to take up the cause of these minor or secondary characters – a profusion of messengers, servants, and followers of the protagonists and of the two warring camps, Rome and Egypt.[8] What price do they pay in the unfolding tragedy of war and conquest? Do their voices militate against the empathy for Antony and Cleopatra that is evoked by their poetic self-representations as lovers and as heroic, though failed, warriors? By forcing such questions onto the tragedy of the play, one can, I believe, articulate and evoke the urgency of our own times in which decisions about war and its political realignments are far removed from those who are its victims. Neither Loomba nor Heinemann address the function of minor and secondary characters in any detail. Nor do they radically interrogate the classical valorization of the tragic experiences of personages of rank and nobility. Loomba links the dialectical structure of the play to gender rather than class struggles, whereas Heinemann's more overtly "Brechtian" approach simply investigates the play's interventions in the dominant historiography of the period.

III

The acid test, probably, for a production that has assimilated the most important elements of Brecht's thinking is how it deals with crowds, servants, and the lower orders generally. The extra weight and attention given by him to these "famous forebears" in itself alters the dialectics of the plays. (Heinemann 1985: 255)

In describing his film version of *King Lear*, Grigori Kozintsev reminds us of the social dimensions of tragedy: "There is no 'desert' in *Lear*, the world of tragedy is densely populated . . . The scenes of courtly life, the life of politics, villages, war – tragedy takes place not among landscapes but among people" (cited in Heinemann 1985: 226). Who can forget the opening scene of Kozintsev's *King Lear* (1970), in which impoverished, bedraggled, anonymous crowds make their way to Lear's palace and wait outside in silence, while indoors the arbitrary power of the king reveals its full scope and force? The division of the kingdom is not simply a matter of family relationships, but has larger consequences for the silent, anonymous masses which have to eke out a living from the land – land which may carelessly be given away in this transaction. Also in the Kozintsev film, when Lear seeks shelter in the hovel, he has been forced to recognize his arbitrary power more poignantly when actually faced by those with "houseless heads" and "unfed sides." Kozintsev's strategy of taking the "imagery of beggars, outcasts, and oppressed peasants and [making] it into marvelous imagery of the masses" produced one of the most "Brechtian" productions till now, I believe, by accounting for the material existence of the oppressed, common people, who figure as mere images in the text of the play. The strategy clearly reveals the political use of the "raw material" of the play that Brecht proposed. Furthermore, as long as the presence of the commoners is noted, the director keeps alive the possibility of change and resistance, however tenuous. The tragedy of *King Lear* no longer seems to be set in an unequivocally stark world of unchanging evil.

Shakespeare's *Antony and Cleopatra*, unlike *King Lear*, is actually peopled by many secondary and minor characters, who are described variously in the dramatis personae as friends and followers of Antony and Caesar, ladies attendant upon Cleopatra, namely Iras and Charmian, and a host of figures known by their professions: soldiers, guards, messengers, courtiers, eunuchs, and a soothsayer, among numerous others. In varying degrees and forms the destinies of these characters are inextricably linked to the noble personages – Antony, Cleopatra, Caesar, Lepidus, Pompey – and in foregrounding their perspective, one can get to the more general and public nature of the ensuing tragedy. If, in keeping with traditional criteria of catharsis via identification, the deaths of Iras and Charmian, for instance, seem marginal to the grand tragedy of Cleopatra's death, one can nonetheless ask whether the play unquestioningly endorses their deaths, which I will address later.

One important function of several of the secondary characters is as choric figures, who are also bearers of historical knowledge. This knowledge includes a psychological understanding of the behavioral impulses and drives of the protagonists/rulers, as well as the larger political and military consequences of those drives on the common followers. According to Brecht, theatre is as much a means of knowledge as of pleasure. And "learning [or knowledge] has a very different function for different social strata" (Willett 1964: 72). The strata who are "waiting their turn, who are discontented with conditions, have a vast interest in the practical side of [knowledge], want at all costs to find out where they stand" (ibid). Benjamin echoes a similar stance when he states, "Not man or men but the struggling oppressed class is the depository of historical knowledge" (Benjamin 1983: 260). In this context, when we consider the minor characters' articulations of knowledge, we can observe that their interest in learning may often move beyond the psychological motivations of their rulers, and toward their history and material conditions. Taking such a "Brechtian" approach to the secondary and minor characters in *Antony and Cleopatra*, one can recognize the link between their choric commentaries on the actions of Antony, Cleopatra, Caesar, and others, and their concerns about the future of those who follow and serve, including themselves.

In the opening scene of the play, Demetrius and Philo, two Roman followers of Antony, act both as a chorus and stage audience for the ensuing scene between the lovers. Echoing Plutarch's account, they articulate the reductive Roman view of Cleopatra as a whore about to ensnare their Mars-like general, Antony:

> . . . this dotage of our General's
> O'erflows the measure: those his goodly eyes,
> That o'er the files and musters of the war
> Have glowed like plated Mars, now bend, now turn
> The office and devotion of their view
> Upon a tawny front; (1.1.1–5)

We quickly learn that their moral judgment of Cleopatra is based on an understanding of the historical moment in which the "triple-pillar of the world" – one of the three triumvirs who control the Roman empire – is about to become a "strumpet's fool." And by compromising his power, he will destabilize the empire. They are spectators of a scene in which Antony rejects Roman authority by declaring "let Rome in Tiber melt," and regret that his actions are living up to the "common liar who / Thus speaks of him at Rome" (1.1.63–4). More importantly, as Romans, whose destiny will be affected by Antony's actions, they can only hope for "better deeds tomorrow" (1.1.65).

The inevitability of war via the threat posed to Rome by Cleopatra's charms is more fully articulated by the most predominant secondary character, Enobarbus. As a commentator noted for the "double-sidedness of his sensibility," he constantly distances and estranges the audience, both within and outside the play, from the central characters (Neill 1994: 13). Quite notably, Enobarbus displays a knowledgeable understanding of the psychology of the main protagonists. He admires the seductive variety of Cleopatra – "she makes hungry / Where most she satisfies" (2.2.244–5) – while recognizing that when Antony spurns Octavia to return to "his Egyptian dish again," the familial bond that ties him to Caesar will "be the very strangler of their amity" (2.6.121, 125). Most importantly, and despite his paean to Cleopatra in his set-piece speech about her self-display in the water-pageant at Cydnus, Enobarbus "constantly strips away the hyperbolic rhetoric of love and martial prowess to expose in both the ungoverned play of mere appetite."[9] Thus, from his shifting perspective, we can observe how the main protagonists are engaged in constructing deity-like identities for themselves.

In revealing these entanglements of sexuality and power in a complex interplay of appetites embodied by the rulers, Enobarbus' vision reveals the causal networks underlying the larger tragedy of the war between Rome and Egypt. Ultimately, he reduces the whole action of the political world, the great epic of empire inscribed in history, to the grinding of voracious jaws:

> Then, world, thou hast a pair of chops, no more,
> And throw between them all the food thou hast,
> They'll grind the one the other. (3.5.12–14)

The ambitions of Antony and Caesar have "come to resemble the 'universal wolf' of self-devouring appetite in *Troilus and Cressida*" (Neill 1994: 230). By the end of the play we recognize the relevance of Enobarbus' misgivings. The names of the protagonists will remain inscribed in historical and mythical glory, while the war devours the commoners and soldiers. Win or lose, the stakes in waging war for Antony, Cleopatra, Caesar, and the other "world-sharers" are radically different from those of the followers. And in the annals of history the latter remain largely anonymous.

The chaos of the impending disorder and the complex dynamics of competing interests are frequently evoked by the minor characters. While the histrionic protagonists, especially Cleopatra, play to the hearts of the external and internal audiences, these marginal figures describe and participate in the material incidents of treachery, betrayal, and strategic error that constitute the war between Rome and Egypt. Thus, they demonstrate the rules of war beyond hyperbole in the unstable loyalty of subordinates and the gap between the power of rule and the decadent and weak men who wield it (Heinemann 1994: 170). For instance, in the course of the drunken bacchanals of the Roman leaders and rivals on Pompey's vessel, Menas, a friend and follower of Pompey, makes him a proposition of acquiring power through betrayal:

> These three world-sharers, these competitors
> Are in thy vessel. Let me cut the cable;
> And when we are put off, fall to their throats.
> All then is thine. (2.7.71–4)

Pompey's response reveals the machinations of power in which the relation between honor and profit is a devious one:

> Ah, this thou shouldst have done,
> And not spoken on't: in me 'tis villainy;
> In thee 't had been good service. Thou must know
> 'Tis not my profit that does lead mine honour;
> Mine honor it, it. Repent that e'er thy tongue
> Hath so betrayed thine act. Being done unknown,
> I should have found it afterwards well done . . . (2.7.74–81)

Here it is apparent that the followers and servers are agents of bloody actions of war or of political assassination, while their leaders take the guise of "honor." The lesson learnt by Menas is one of cynical self-preservation, when he vows to abandon Pompey: "For this, I'll never follow thy palled fortunes more" (2.7.82).

Choices between betrayal and self-preservation do not come as easily to the other followers of the Romans. For instance, Enobarbus also decides to leave Antony facing impending defeat. At the moment that the latter is flaunting his bravery, Enobarbus, once again, demonstrates his astute knowledge of the psychology of the general: "When valour preys on reason, / It eats the sword that it fights with. / I will

seek / Some way to leave him" (3.13.199–200). But later, when Antony sends him
his treasure, Enobarbus seeks death as a form of his remorse, dying of a broken heart
with his general's name on his lips.

Act 3.2 – a short scene often cut in modern productions for its seeming insignifi-
cance – further dramatizes the perspective of those who serve and follow in war. And
in doing so, it casts an ironic shadow over Antony's image as a heroic warrior. Figur-
ing the triumphal procession to mark Ventidius' victory over the Parthians (in
Antony's name), this scene was intended to "provide the most lavish spectacle in the
play . . . [and] to imitate the effect of a triumph *all'attica*; such a procession would
normally include (in addition to the ceremonially presented body of Pacorus) displays
of chained prisoners, captured weapons, and other trophies" (Neill 1994: Introduction, n. 2.219). Historically, this scene draws on Plutarch, who uses "Ventidius'
exploits in Parthia to illustrate that Antonius . . . enjoyed greater military success
through his subordinates than in his own person" (ibid: n. 3.1.219).

Shakespeare's rendering of this event juxtaposes the visual spectacle of triumph
with the hard-headed political realism of the victor, Ventidius. He reminds the soldier,
Sillius, of their "lower place" in the world and hence their inability to enjoy the fame
that they have earned with their blood and deeds, but must ascribe to their general,
Antony:

> O Sillius, Sillius,
> I have done enough. A lower place, note well,
> May make too great an act. For learn this, Sillius:
> Better to leave undone than by our deed
> Acquire too high a fame when him we serve's away.
> Caesar and Anthony have ever won
> More in their officer than person . . . (3.1.11–17)

Ventidius' realistic revelation of the inequities of glory in warfare offers an
ironic counterpoint to the earlier scene of the debauchery of the rulers in Pompey's
galleys. After his triumph, Ventidius' only aim is to inform Antony by "humbly
signify[ing] what in his name / That magical word of war, we have effected"
(3.1.30–1). Thus, through these seemingly marginal characters of less than noble
rank, Shakespeare points to the vast distance and alienation between the frontline
soldiers and commanders "at the borders of empire and all chairborne generals"
(Heinemann 1994: 170). In terms of staging choices, this scene lends itself to Brechtian alienation effects, whereby the stylized staging of death and pageantry could be
framed by film clips of close-ups of violent carnage – of mutilated bodies. Both the
artificiality of the triumph and effects of bloody war could be presented simultaneously in a conflation of the Jacobean stage with modern technological devices. The
aims of these alienating strategies would denaturalize war, while forcing an audience
to question the terms of its empathy, or lack of it, for nameless soldiers or lower-
ranked officers.

Within Shakespeare's play this brief triumphal scene gives way to undercutting scenes in which the war between Antony and Caesar develops in a haphazard way. During this growing division Antony's followers struggle with their loyalties and self-survival. They seem to have little agency and autonomy to change events, even though they repeatedly reveal their knowledge of the dynamics of war and political conflict. Scarrus, a loyal soldier under Antony, illustrates his powerless situation when he pleads with his general not to fight on sea:

> O noble Emperor, do not fight by sea;
> Trust not to rotten planks. Do you misdoubt
> This sword, and these my wounds? Let th'Egyptians
>   . . . go a-ducking – we
> Have used to conquer standing on the earth,
> And fighting foot to foot. (3.7.61–6)

Though he testifies to his loyalty in his "sword" and "wounds" of war, he can do little to influence Antony. His only choice is to follow his leader to a disastrous defeat at sea.

From the perspective of the common soldiers like Scarrus, the allure of Cleopatra, to whom Antony is drawn, can prove life-threatening for them. As one soldier declares, "our leader's led / And we are women's men" (3.7.68–9). While their image of Cleopatra reflects the Roman stereotypes articulated by Philo and Demetrius in the opening scene, they seem little concerned with her glamorous sexuality – neither demonizing nor exoticizing her; rather as soldiers their interest lies in the practical effects of bad military strategy. Since Antony follows Cleopatra in fighting at sea, they bemoan their personal losses in terms of a larger realignment of power, as Scarrus declares to his comrades in war: "the world is lost / With very ignorance; we have kissed away / Kingdoms and provinces" (3.10.6–7).

The cumulative effect of the comments of soldiers on the course and consequences of war is to reveal the processes of warfare – and implicitly to interrupt the sweeping perspective of Roman history as well as to alienate us from Cleopatra's histrionic tragedy. Thus, the chaos of war and ensuing defeat of Antony are not represented as a mystery of pure chance, and we can see his desertion by the god Hercules as the end of a long process, even though he believes that his "good stars" have left him (Heinemann 1994: 168). However, while some of his followers, like Scarrus, recognize the causes of his defeat, collectively Antony's army seems to share a sense of doom about his impending tragedy, one they cannot avert. This collective helplessness is vividly expressed by a group of anonymous soldiers who fear that "the god Hercules, whom Anthony loved, / Now leaves him" (4.3.13–14).

Not only do soldiers of Antony's defeated army in *Antony and Cleopatra* pay in smaller tragedies for the grand designs and foolish decisions of their leaders, but other minor functionaries, such as messengers, also suffer the consequences of casual and thoughtless cruelty. Cleopatra's petulant outburst at the messenger who brings her news of Octavia's marriage to Antony (2.5) is generally played for laughs on the stage, as evidence of Cleopatra's larger than life histrionics as well as her capacity for passion. On hearing his news, she strikes him, following with a threat:

> . . . I'll spurn thine eyes
> Like balls before me; I'll unhair thy head;
> Thou shalt be whipped with wire and stewed in brine,
> Smarting in lingering pickle. (2.5.64–7)

His comic retort – "I that do bring the news made not the match" – brings him no immediate release, though a calmer Cleopatra later states, "I will not hurt him," and later, calling him back (3.3) to employ him for a message to Antony, she rewards him: "There's gold for thee: / Thou must not take my former sharpness ill" (3.3.33–4). The whipping of Caesar's messenger, Thidias, at Antony's orders is another such instance of the punishment of innocents by the arbitrary fiat of their leaders. "Be thou sorry / To follow Caesar in his triumph," Antony tells Thidias, ". . . since / Thou hast been whipped for following him" (3.13.136–8). Thidias is punished, according to Antony, because the victorious Caesar "makes me angry." And in passing this message to the latter, Antony arbitrarily offers up his own slave, Hipparchus, for punishment if Caesar "mislike" his message:

> . . . tell him he has
> Hipparchus, my enfranched bondman, whom
> He may at pleasure whip, or hang, or torture,
> As he shall like, to quit me . . . (3.13.149–52)

While the appearances, commentaries, and interruptions of the secondary and minor characters, as sketched above, alienate and distance us from the ensuing tragedy of war, what impact do they have on the histrionic grandeur of the deaths of Antony and Cleopatra? Of course, the dying, suicidal moments of the two protagonists stir our empathy in their poetic expressions of grief and desire for each other. Thinking Cleopatra dead, Antony seeks "to run into [death] / As to a lover's bed" (4.15.100–1). Similarly, Cleopatra calls to him, "Husband, I come!" (5.2.286). Their deaths also attain a tragic grandeur in their transcendent vision of an afterlife reminiscent of another set of tragic lovers, Aeneas and Dido, although with some revisions.[10] And Caesar also memorializes them through a cathartic moment of "pity" accompanied by admiration for a "pair so famous."

Yet, as we know, the lovers do not die in isolation and their tragic deaths have social and political consequences, in that they mark a "change in the lives and relationships of others" (Williams 1966: 57). First, one has only to remember the chaos of war with its evocations of violence that precedes their deaths. More importantly, however, we cannot ascribe a totalizing, transcendent meaning to their tragedy if we consider the deaths of their three followers, Eros, Iras, and Charmian – who emulate

Antony and Cleopatra's suicidal moments in the most profound examples of loyalty. When ordered by Antony to kill him, Eros chooses his own death to "escape the sorrow of Anthony's death" (4.15.93–4). And Iras and Charmian share the stage with their mistress, Cleopatra, in being poisoned by the same asps as her, the former via Cleopatra's poisoned kiss and the latter by applying the aspic herself. For the Egyptian queen, Iras' poisoned swoon only takes on meaning as an image and metaphor of her own impending death: "Dost fall? / If thou and nature so gently part, / The stroke of death is as a lover's pinch / Which hurts, and is desired" (5.2.292–5). In this vein she even imagines Iras preceding her in a reunion with Antony in the afterlife: "If she first meet the curléd Anthony, / He'll make demand of her, and spend that kiss / Which is my heaven to have" (5.2.300–2). Charmian applies an aspic bite to herself, but in her dying moments, when Caesar's messenger asks "what work is here," she merges her own death into an image of Cleopatra, replying: "It is well done, and fitting for a princess / Descended of so many royal kings" (5.2.324–5).

Our response to the deaths of Charmian and Iras, as of Eros, would be to dismiss them as accidents of war and fortune. From this perspective, if Shakespeare's Antony and Cleopatra cannot avoid the historical inevitability of their deaths, then the accompanying suicide of royal attendants cannot be mourned as a tragedy. I would suggest that their deaths offer important interruptions and interventions in the heroic and tragic self-representations of the two protagonists. For instance, while Charmian and Iras unflinchingly embrace their shared destiny with their mistress, the inevitability of their tragic deaths gets undercut if we recall an earlier glimpse of their queries to the soothsayer. "Good sir, give me good fortune," pleads Charmian (1.2.14), who then asks, "Prithee, how many boys and wenches must I have?" (1.2.36). Equivocating in his answers, the soothsayer tells them both that "your fortunes are alike" (1.2.45), but does not raise their hopes for a husband or a future. If we recall this earlier scene – or if it is enacted in some kind of creative "flashback" on stage or on screen – then their deaths acquire more meaning than simply serving as a backdrop to Cleopatra's extravagant, posturing suicide. Or, if each of the two dead women are given a brief moment in a spotlight on an otherwise darkened stage, their presence could upstage Cleopatra, even though for a fleeting moment. Finally, like all the interruptions and interventions by other marginal and secondary characters through the play, their deaths challenge the supremacy of the notion of tragic inevitability, while reiterating once again the sufferings of those who follow and serve, but have little control over the processes of warfare. According to Benjamin's reading of Brecht, "epic theatre, then, does not reproduce conditions, rather [it] reveals them. The uncovering of conditions is brought about through processes of being interrupted" (Benjamin 1983: 4–5). The episodic, alienating structure of Shakespeare's *Antony and Cleopatra*, filled with intrusions of numerous minor and secondary characters, offers precisely such an uncovering of the conditions of warfare and political struggle, if, unlike generations of critics, we do not allow ourselves to be enthralled by Cleopatra and her tragic destiny.

NOTES

1 Shakespeare's *Anthony and Cleopatra* (1994), ed. Michael Neill. All further references to this play will be to this edition.

2 Drakakis (1994) cites Bradley to explain why the critic excluded *Antony and Cleopatra* from the other tragedies: "although *Antony and Cleopatra* may be for us as wonderful an achievement as the greatest of Shakespeare's plays, it has not an equal value to the four famous tragedies" (pp. 2–3). According to Drakakis, "Bradley felt that the emphasis on dramatic form distinguished the play from other major tragedies, which he argues, were more concerned with content" (p. 3). Furthermore, Bradley contrasted the play's relative lack of dramatic action with the play's non-tragic scenes, all involving Cleopatra: "Cleopatra coquetting, tormenting, beguiling, her lover to stay; Cleopatra left with her woman and longing for him, Cleopatra receiving news of his marriage" (pp. 2–3).

3 For a detailed reading of Brecht's responses to Shakespeare, see Heinemann (1985).

4 See Hortmann (1998: 81–6) for details about Brecht's theory about the "material value" or Materielwert of the classics.

5 My observation here is not meant to be definitive, but rather, simply to suggest a *trend* in the critical focus on the roles of the two co-protagonists.

6 For a stage history of the various actresses' interpretations of Cleopatra's role, see Neill (1994: 23–67).

7 In looking beyond the central conflict between Rome and Egypt – and between the values they represent – Heinemann (1994) charts the "complexities of [competing] interest[s], spread over three continents" (p. 70). These include the constant warfare in which everyone "competes for power, followers, and loot . . . [and] the unstable loyalty of subordinates . . . who depend on pillage and spoil . . . and must gravitate to the stronger side" (pp. 169–70).

8 While I am indebted to both Heinemann and Loomba, I extend their Brechtian reflections to include a sustained class analysis of the tragic experience of the play.

9 For a detailed analysis of Enobarbus' satiric, alienating vision, I am indebted to Neill (1994: 89–94). Especially relevant is the way he shows us how Enobarbus gives a "satiric edge" to the play's imagery of hunger and feeding.

10 See Bono (1984) for Antony's revision of "Vergil's great fiction of erotic abnegation. In place of Dido's harsh rejection of Aeneas in the underworld, Antony imagines Dido and Aeneas united in the underworld" (p. 187).

REFERENCES AND FURTHER READING

Adelman, J. (1973). *The Common Liar: An Essay on Antony and Cleopatra.* New Haven, CT: Yale University Press.

Archer, J. M. (1997). Antiquity and Degeneration in *Antony and Cleopatra.* In J. G. MacDonald (ed.) *Race, Ethnicity, and Power in the Renaissance.* Madison, NJ: Fairleigh Dickinson University Press.

Bayley, J. (1981). *Shakespeare and Tragedy.* London: Routledge. Kegan Paul.

Benjamin, W. (1969). *Illuminations: Essays and Reflections,* ed. H. Arendt. New York: Schocken Books.

——(1983). *Understanding Brecht,* trans. A. Bostock. London: Verso.

Bono, B. (1984). *Literary Transvaluation: From Vergilian Epic to Shakespearean Tragicomedy.* Berkeley: University of California Press.

Bradley, A. C. (1909). *Oxford Lectures on Poetry.* London: Macmillan.

Charnes, L. (1993). *Notorious Identity: Materializing the Subject in Shakespeare.* Cambridge, MA: Harvard University Press.

——(1996). What's Love Got To Do With It? Reading the Liberal Humanist Romance in *Antony and Cleopatra*. In S. N. Garner and M. Sprengnether (eds.) *Shakespearean Tragedy and Gender*. Bloomington: Indiana University Press, 268–85.

Cook, C. (1996). The Fatal Cleopatra. In S. N. Garner and M. Sprengnether (eds.) *Shakespearean Tragedy and Gender*. Bloomington: Indiana University Press, 241–67.

Danby, J. (1994). *Antony and Cleopatra*: A Shakespearean Adjustment. In J. Drakakis (ed.) *New Casebooks Antony and Cleopatra*. London: Macmillan, 33–55.

Drakakis, J. (ed.) (1994). Introduction. *New Casebooks Antony and Cleopatra*. London: Macmillan, 1–32.

Duncan-Jones, K. (1999). "Caught in the Coils of Old Nile": The Stale Custom and Infinite Variety of *Antony and Cleopatra*. *Times Literary Supplement*, August 6, 17–19.

Fitz, L. T. (1994). Egyptian Queens and Male Reviewers: Sexist Attitudes in *Antony and Cleopatra* Criticism. In J. Drakakis (ed.) *New Casebooks Antony and Cleopatra*. London: Macmillan, 182–211.

Gandrow, K. (2000). Review of *Antony and Cleopatra*. *Theatre Journal*, 52, March, 123–4.

Hamer, M. (1993). *Signs of Cleopatra: History, Politics, Representation*. London: Routledge.

Harris, J. G. (1994). "Narcissus in thy face": Roman Desire and the Difference it Fakes in *Antony and Cleopatra*. *Shakespeare Quarterly*, 45, winter, 408–25.

Heinemann, M. (1985). How Brecht Read Shakespeare. In *Political Shakespeare: New Essays in Cultural Materialism*. Ithaca, NY: Cornell University Press, 202–30.

——(1994). "Let Rome in Tiber Melt": Order and Disorder in *Antony and Cleopatra*. In J. Drakakis (ed.) *New Casebooks Antony and Cleopatra*. London: Macmillan, 166–81.

Hortmann, W. (1998). *Shakespeare on the German Stage: The Twentieth Century*. Cambridge: Cambridge University Press.

Jankowski, T. (1992). *Women in Power in Early Modern Drama*. Urbana: University of Illinois Press.

Loomba, A. (1994). "Travelling thoughts": Theatre and the Space of the Other. In J. Drakakis (ed.) *New Casebooks Antony and Cleopatra*. London: Macmillan, 279–307.

Miola, R. (1983). *Shakespeare's Rome*. Cambridge: Cambridge University Press.

Neill, M. (ed.) (1994). *Shakespeare's Antony and Cleopatra*. Oxford: Oxford University Press.

Potter, L. (1999). Shakespeare Performed: Roman Actors and Egyptian Travesties. *Shakespeare Quarterly*, 50, 509–17.

Rackin, P. (1994). Shakespeare's Boy Cleopatra, the Decorum of Nature and the Golden World of Poetry. In J. Drakakis (ed.) *New Casebooks Antony and Cleopatra*. London: Macmillan.

Royster, F. T. (1999). Cleopatra as Diva: African-American Women and Shakespearean Tactics In *Transforming Shakespeare: Contemporary Women's Re-Visions in Literature and Performance*. New York: St. Martin's Press, 103–25.

Sidney, P. (1997) [1595]. *Defence of Poesy, Astrophil and Stella and other Writings*, ed. E. P. Watson. London: Everyman.

Singh, J. G. (1994). Renaissance Antitheatricality, Antifeminism, and Shakespeare's *Antony and Cleopatra*. In J. Drakakis (ed.) *New Casebooks Antony and Cleopatra*. London: Macmillan, 308–29.

Weimann, R. (1978). *Shakespeare and the Popular Tradition in the Theatre*. Baltimore, MD: Johns Hopkins University Press.

Willett, J. (ed. and trans.) (1964). *Brecht on Theatre*. New York: Hill and Wang.

Williams, R. (1966). *Modern Tragedy*. Stanford, CA: Stanford University Press.

22

Timon of Athens: The Dialectic of Usury, Nihilism, and Art

Hugh Grady

Because of its singular status among the surviving texts of Shakespeare's works, *Timon of Athens* presents itself to many scholars as more of a puzzle than a play. Close analysis of the pagination of the 1623 First Folio – the only source for the text of this play – shows that *Timon* was a late addition to the collection. It takes up fewer pages than were allotted for it by the printers, throwing off the pagination of the "Tragedies" section of the Folio. It is easy to deduce that it took the place of another Shakespearean play with a setting in ancient Greece, *Troilus and Cressida*, about which there were apparently temporary copyright problems, since the text of *Troilus and Cressida* in the Folio is presented between the histories and the tragedies mispaginated, the page numbers indicating it was destined for the exact space that *Timon* failed to fill up.

This raises the question, of course, as to why *Timon* had not been included in the Folio before the last minute. One theory held that the play was not quite completed by Shakespeare. Evidence for this included irregular metrics in many scenes (even by the loose standards of the late Shakespeare), places where prose and verse were combined within a single speech, and what were perceived as loose ends in the play, from unanswered questions in the Alcibiades subplot to possible differences over the value of the biblical monetary unit, the talent, in different scenes.[1]

Another explanation for some of the same phenomena, however, is that two authors produced the text as we have it, thus accounting for differences in style and the inconsistencies and loose ends of the play, and also for the Folio editors' hesitation to include it in their first plans. Since the 1970s the case for this second theory has improved markedly as opinion has converged on the identity of the proposed second playwright as Thomas Middleton, a well-known younger author who would go on to his own successful dramatic career.[2] While the editor of the 2001 New Cambridge Shakespeare edition of *Timon of Athens*, Karl Klein, was unconvinced, internal stylistic evidence is strong for concluding that the play is a jointly written work by Shakespeare and Middleton. For example, the "irregular" meter in scenes like 3.5, with a number of

9-syllable, 12-syllable or even longer lines, is like nothing elsewhere in Shakespeare – but it does fit Middleton's versifying habits. Similarly, statistical analysis of such stylistic markers as the use of contractions, oaths and exclamations, grammatical preferences, stage directions, spelling, rare vocabulary, and "function words" (conjunctions, prepositions, and so on) produces distinct portions of the text, one portion corresponding to Shakespeare's writing habits, the other to Middleton's.[3] Using such methods, John Jowett estimates that Shakespeare wrote about two-thirds of the text, Middleton the remaining third. The co-authors apparently each agreed on specific scenes to write, although each may have inserted revisions into the other's scenes, judging by a number of ambiguous passages within several scenes. In what is reported to be the fullest study of the technicalities of the issue, Holdsworth attributes the following scenes and passages to Middleton (line numbering as in Evans): (a) 1.2; (b) 3.1–3.6 (with the exception of the middle section of 3.6, perhaps ll. 25–105); (c) 4.2.30–50; (d) 4.3.458–536. He adds a few passages that he regards as of collaborative or uncertain authorship: (a) 1.1.272–83; (b) 2.2.1–45; (c) 2.2.120–233; (d) 42.1–29.

Middleton's portions thus encompass the banquet scene (1.2), the scenes in the middle of the play in which Timon interacts with his creditors and in which his steward Flavius denounces his profligate unthriftiness and mourns for him, and the scene of Alcibiades at the Senate (3.5).[4] Shakespeare concentrated on the rest, roughly the beginning and the end of the play.

The themes I am focusing on in what follows are most developed in the Shakespearean portions of the text, and I will refer to Shakespeare as author of those passages to emphasize their connections with other Shakespearean works. I will refer to the play as a whole, however, as by Shakespeare and Middleton, in deference to the strong case which has been made for this attribution. But the fact that this play seems to have been written by two writers presents few difficulties for critical analysis. Just after his critique of the two-author theory of the play, Karl Klein approvingly quoted the single-author views of A. D. Nuttal: *"Timon of Athens* is one play, not two, superficially disfigured by technical inconsistencies but conceptually and imaginatively coherent" (Nuttal 1989: 39; quoted in Klein 2001: 66). I couldn't agree more – but such a conclusion in no way invalidates a theory of dual authorship. Creative writing is never a matter of an author's creating a text *ex nihilo*, and single authorship has never been a criterion for artistic coherence, as any number of other works of Shakespeare's era and our own attest. Aesthetic creation always involves dialogue with the surrounding culture and its history, so that in an important sense there is never just a single author for any work. In addition, almost all of Shakespeare's plays are dialogic productions in which radically opposed viewpoints are enunciated and clash with each other. While it is true that *Timon* has a large degree of what German reader-response theorist Wolfgang Iser calls "indeterminacy" – that is, resistance to a clear, singular interpretation – it offers a powerful imaginative and intellectual experience for those who accept its challenges to comprehension. And if there are possible inconsistencies in such matters as the value of the talent, the play at a deeper level is worked out with great intellectual clarity and boldness. The two portions of the play, as John Jowett argued, work together quite coherently, but they each have discernibly different thematic emphases. Speaking broadly, Middleton stresses issues of waste and unthriftiness, evincing a culturally Puritan, middle-class sensibility toward aristocratic extravagance. The long critical tradition which has pointed out Timon's folly, his share in his own downfall, finds much of its evidence in Middleton's portions of the play. In Shakespeare's portions, themes of ingratitude, loyalty and disloyalty, and misanthropy and its problems are highlighted, in a sensibility that is at once conservative in its evocation of older, "feudal" values, and radical in its representation of a God-deserted universe and in its denunciations of the cash nexus of emerging capitalism. For some readers these differences in emphasis might seem discordant, but for anyone who has worked through the clashing discourses of plays like *1 and 2 Henry IV*, *The Merchant of Venice*, *Hamlet*, *Othello*, or *King Lear*, the interplay of discordant discourses can be seen to enrich rather than undermine the drama. And this play builds to a strong conceptual conclusion, as we will see.

In short, *Timon* is a play which repays study and one which adds new dimensions to our understanding of Shakespeare as a tragic author. Most strikingly for us at the beginning of the twenty-first century, it is a play which reveals Shakespeare to have been a keen and insightful participant in and critic of modernity, establishing in this play a historically novel category of the aesthetic and a related critique of the capitalist economic system which was developing in the London around him in its preindustrial stage. The play's very end also seems to assert the necessity of machiavellian *realpolitik*, as a kind of supplement to the more symbolic aesthetic register, to deal with the corruptions of society which art alone cannot erase. Shakespeare of course developed his concepts and critique within the terms of his own day, and our attempt to define how his vision and our own interact give the play much of its interest.

Athens and Modernity

The first step in the creation of modernity, as Frankfurt School theory in particular has stressed, is the clearing away of the older religious and cosmological worldviews which constituted the mental frameworks of premodern cultures. Shakespeare and several of his contemporaries effected such a clearing in the imaginative space of theatre and book, if not in a cultural reality which remained deeply invested in religion. As Hegel first suggested, and as Stephen Greenblatt (1980) has described much more concretely for the case of sixteenth-century England, it was the deepening religiosity of the Protestant Reformation which set the conditions requiring a secular sphere within Western culture. Once the external, universal religious framework of medieval Catholicism was replaced by competing and inconsistent centers of religious authority, and once such authority was called into question by the private interpretations of scripture associated with Protestantism, a new non-religious social contract would ultimately be required (Grady 2000). Well before it was institutionally established, skeptical Renaissance intellectuals were able to find a model through which to imagine secularity in the works of ancient Rome (and secondarily Greece) which proved to be the cultural harbingers of modernity throughout Western Europe. Shakespeare's classical plays, very much including *Timon of Athens*, can be considered as a series of thought experiments investigating an imagined secular culture well before its actual historical construction.

Timon of Athens is one of a group of Shakespearean plays which are set in republics, preeminently Rome (*Julius Caesar*, *Coriolanus*, *Antony and Cleopatra*), but also, specifically in this play, Athens, which is unhistorically given a Roman-style Senate rather than its historical institutions of direct democracy. Republics are associated in Shakespeare with commerce, wealth, and commodities, and with power, warfare, and politics – in brief with emerging modernity and its constituent institutions, a capitalist economy, and a nation-state/empire system. Athens in this play is a site for all of these associations, and they are interconnected.

But we have to get outside our own post-Romantic idealizations to understand how Shakespeare's age understood "the glory that was Greece." Classical Greek literature was known primarily by reputation and Roman references rather than directly. In Elizabethan slang the associations of the word "Greek" were anything but grand. "Merrygreeks" were rowdy, licentious revelers, for example. And Shakespeare's two plays with classical Greek settings, *Troilus and Cressida* and *Timon of Athens*, are excellent examples of these negative associations (Spencer 1962). Robert Miola (1980) cataloged numerous instances of Renaissance humanists denouncing Athens as a decadent historical example, its democracy a frightening and ill-conceived aberration. Miola does less justice to the pro-republican discourse exemplified, for example, in Machiavelli's *Discourses* and widespread among his English admirers, and he doesn't take into account Shakespeare and Middleton's treatment of Athens as a republic, not a direct democracy, but he clearly establishes the suspicion of Greek political forms rampant in Elizabethan and Jacobean England.

These negative associations of the Greek political world throw light on the atmosphere of Shakespeare's two forays into depicting Greek history, *Timon* and *Troilus and Cressida*. This last play, written about 1602, is well known for its darkness or nihilism. It is a play with a relentless, puncturing, deflating strategy, and what it subjects to deflation are two of the most valued themes of Western literature (and Elizabeth's court), romantic love and heroic chivalry. The Homeric heroes Shakespeare had apparently encountered through Chapman's translation of *The Iliad* are treated as vainglorious, contemptible, and brutal. The love between Troilus and Cressida which he discovered in Chaucer's poem becomes a sordid liaison between a self-deceiving, extravagantly idealizing Troilus and a realist, materialist Cressida at the mercy of the powerful, instrumentalizing men around her.[5] All is lechery and war, we are continually reminded by the play's *de facto* choral commentator, Thersites. He speaks a naturalistic, materialist discourse in which all values are diagnosed as in the service of those drives which a post-Freudian age calls aggression and sexuality. His characterization of the cause of the Trojan war, for example, is as follows:

All the argument is a whore and a cuckold. A good quarrel to draw emulous factions and bleed to death upon. Now the dry serpigo on the subject, and war and lechery confound all. (2.3.65–8)

The Trojans in this play fare somewhat better than the Greeks, but only superficially. In one of the day's much repeated commonplaces, Troy was a figure for mercantile London, and the Trojans in *Troilus* speak a language fraught with mercantile terms and concepts. Troilus' extravagantly idealizing discourse is revealed to be not merely his, but that of all the Trojans. Their idealization is depicted as a product of the marketplace and its quantifying of the irrationalities of human desire in the form of the prices of commodities. Many critics (myself included) have concluded that *Troilus and Cressida* embodies an early critique of mercantile, proto-capitalist commodification.[6] In the end, the Trojans' romantic discourses do not keep them from acting very much like the Greeks.

Ancient Greece, in short, is a very nasty place in *Troilus and Cressida*. It is clearly allegorical for contemporary London as well, of course, and that helps give point and bite to the deflation so relentlessly pursued in the play. And in *Timon* ancient Greece in the form of classical Athens is evoked with similar affect and topical function. Composed by Shakespeare and Middleton sometime between 1605 and 1608,[7] at least four years after *Troilus*, *Timon of Athens* re-presents the earlier play's picture of an ancient Greece dominated by instrumental reason and mercantile calculation, but it also recapitulates themes and motifs from Jonson's and Middleton's city comedies, with their evocations of contemporaneous London. *Timon*'s Athenian society is shown to consist of a hypocritical exterior of entertainment, friendship, and (oddly female-less) domestic life actually organized to enrich a class of merchants and usurers and corrode ancient bonds of loyalty and service, clearly indicting its own social context. Timon's transformation from an idealizing, generous patron to a bitter, railing misanthrope serves among other things as a vehicle to puncture Athenian/London pretensions to civility, much as was the case for Troy in *Troilus and Cressida*. This play, however, is far more than a recapitulation of the critique of mercantile capitalism of *Troilus*. It explores not just commodification and capital (in the form of loans with interest); it probes that other form of autotelic human practice, the aesthetic, a socially critical form which simultaneously participates in the corruptions of commercialism as a commodity. And it follows Timon's denunciations of corruption to their logical extremes, only to subject Timon's critique to its own interrogations and assert at the very end of the play an alternative to it in an unusual combination of harsh political reform and a separate world of aesthetic perceptions.

Art and Capital in 1.1

In the first scene of *Timon of Athens* we are introduced to a painter and a poet. While Shakespeare alludes to artistic creation throughout his work, it is very unusual for him to present creative artists as characters in his plays. Cinna the poet in *Julius Caesar* comes to mind, but he might have had another profession. We hear of the skill of the sculptor and painter Giulio Romano in *The Winter's Tale*, and there are various amateur poets among Shakespeare's characters, but those references are brief and relatively undeveloped. Furthermore in the opening dialogue of *Timon* the two engage in a dialogue about the nature of art that is also relatively unique but which, perhaps because of textual problems, perhaps because of the relative obscurity of the play itself, has been little discussed in Shakespeare studies. In this discussion poetry and painting are, in the great Renaissance tradition first defined in the ancient world by Horace, linked as cognate, mimetic art-forms. Perhaps because of the associations of both arts with lying or feigning, they are also linked to a practice which in post-Romantic thought has been designated as very nearly the opposite of art – the lending of money with interest, or usury, as it was referred to in Shakespeare's day. The productions of the painter and the poet are not only works of art, but they are also commodities, with monetary values. This point is emphasized when the poet and painter are joined by a jeweler and a merchant, and all four are tied together in their pursuit of a profitable sale of merchandise to Lord Timon. They are all drawn by what the poet calls the "magic of bounty," the endless flow of wealth from Timon's coffers to them and a herd of their fellows. The poet in fact personifies this force and addresses it:

> See
> Magic of bounty, all these spirits thy power
> Hath conjured to attend! (1.1.5–7)[8]

As Coppélia Kahn (1987) emphasized in her insightful psychoanalytic and new historicist reading of the play, Timon's suppliers – and ultimately Timon himself – fantasize an endless fecundity, the creation of wealth from nothing through magic. We will discover later in the play the true source of this illusion, created by the paradoxical, delusive properties of financial interest, which becomes in Marx's sense no longer simply money but capital; that is, money expended not for tangible commodities but for profits. For any post-Marxist reader the figure of the "magic of bounty," in the words of John Jowett, is a fantasizing figure for capitalism itself.

But the poet and painter also insist on other functions of their work, which they resist reducing to the status of an empty commodity. The poet, for example, praises the production of the painter:

> Admirable! How this grace
> Speaks his own standing! What a mental power
> This eye shoots forth! How big imagination
> Moves in this lip! To th'dumbness of the gesture
> One might interpret.
> *Painter.* It is a pretty mocking of the life.
> Here is a touch; is't good?

> *Poet.*   I will say of it,
> It tutors nature; artificial strife
> Lives in these touches, livelier than life. (1.1.37–9)

This dialogue is attention-getting on two levels. First, it establishes a category of the aesthetic, a concept of connoisseurship about properties of artistic production which go beyond received ideas of didacticism and the simple imitation of nature. In the praise of the poet is an implied concept of art as a mode of knowledge, a conveyer of information and nuanced judgment not available through any other medium. The "touches" of the painter produce knowledge of and judgments about the subject of the painting that can only be approximated in ordinary language ("mental power," "big imagination") and which are present in the artistic representation of the subject but not in the subject "in nature." Hence, the artwork "tutors nature" and is "Livelier than life."

Something similar is true, we are given to understand, about the productions of the poet. Poetry is "a speaking picture," Sir Philip Sidney had famously written in his *Defense of Poesy* (1595), a kind of imitation of reality which, like painting, encodes moral and subjective interpretations within its representations, and it, too, provides knowledge which escapes more unilinear discourses. The poet gives us an interpretation of Timon's situation which no one else in the play at this point seems to have thought of. Timon is described as one among a multitude "of all deserts, all kind of nature," laboring beneath a hill on which the lady Fortune sits enthroned. She "wafts" Timon to come to her, privileging him over his rivals (1.1.66–75). After this, Timon is pictured as surrounded by followers seeking to share his good fortune (1.1.8–86). Finally, presciently, we are informed:

> When Fortune in her shift and change of mood
> Spurns down her late beloved, all his dependants
> Which laboured after him to the mountain's top
> Even on their knees and hands, let him slip down,
> Not one accompanying his declining foot. (1.1.87–91)

Here, momentarily, art emerges as the carrier of an insight into Timon's precarious position which not even the skeptical philosophy of Apemantus (to which I will turn below) completely encompasses. The poet's work has enunciated a truth which neither the poet nor the painter seems completely to grasp in its concrete applicability to Timon.

Secondly, beyond this rare Shakespearean treatment of aesthetic ideas, these passages take on additional significance because they are self-referential and allude to the self-enclosed aesthetic space we normally associate with post-Romantic poetry. That is, not only does the poet's poem-within-the-play present us with a moral interpretation of Timon and his situation, but also the play which I am discussing does precisely the same thing, incorporating the poet's images of Fortune and Timon for its own artistic and rhetorical purposes. Indeed, Coppélia Kahn, followed by other contemporary critics, approvingly quoted Maurice Charney's characterization of this series of images as "the central fable of the play" (Charney 1972: 1368; quoted in Kahn 1987: 36). In short, what is true of the poet's work in this case is true as well of the play *Timon of Athens*. In characterizing the work of the poet and painter, these lines characterize the play we are reading as well and make it self-consciously aesthetic. Rather than crude and unfinished, this work is subtly conceived and evocative of aesthetic ideas which would not be articulated in theoretical language for another two hundred years after Shakespeare.

The opening scene of the play, then, presents us with two opposing ideas of artistic production. On the one hand, the work of art is a commodity, like any other, with monetary value like that of other commodities and in fact sharing some of the characteristics of that "magic," self-breeding commodity, mercantile capital. On the other hand, it is a special kind of commodity, one which embodies truths, evaluations, and insights into reality which no other mode of knowledge possesses.

Both of these functions of art are glanced at in the odd, elusive definition of poetry given by the poet as he describes the work he has produced in hopes of patronage from Timon, in lines which have troubled editors because of their obscurity and possible status as typographical errors:

> A thing slipp'd idly from me.
> Our poesy is as a gown which uses
> From whence 'tis nourished. The fire i'th'flint
> Shows not till it be struck. Our gentle flame
> Provokes itself, and like the current flies
> Each bound it chases. (1.1.21–6)

In an innovation followed by numerous subsequent editions of the play, including that of Wells and Taylor, Samuel Johnson had emended the first simile as given in the Folio to the following:

> Our poesy is as a gum which oozes
> From whence 'tis nourished.

But in this Johnsonian reading there is a subtle shift to an eighteenth-century, proto-Romantic notion of art as self-expression. In the Folio's reading the emphasis is on poetry as a kind of commodity which can wear out through use, like a gown which, as it is repeatedly worn, frays and thins. At the same time, and with an almost opposite meaning whose relevance to this play turns out to be central, the term *uses* evokes as well the practice of usury. The classic critique of usury, evoked repeatedly in Shakespeare's *Merchant of Venice* and in some of the sonnets, indicted the "unnatural" practice of allowing sterile money to reproduce itself like a living thing. Here, poetry "uses" in the sense of money in an interest-bearing loan, that is, it gains in

value of itself, an instance of the magic of bounty evoked earlier by the poet. We can
see a similar usage of *use* in a dialogue in *The Merchant* between Shylock and Antonio.
Shylock says:

> Methought you said you neither lend nor borrow
> Upon advantage. (1.3.65–6)

Antonio replies, "I do never use it" (1.3.66),[9] with *use* clearly here referring to the
practice of usury in lending. Similar instances of *use* as a verb occur in the sonnets,
for example in sonnet 4:

> Profitless usurer, why doest thou use
> So great a sum of sums yet canst not live.[10]

Given the prominence of usury to the story of Timon of Athens, and the explanation
of a crux which this gloss provides, the case is strong for reading a similar meaning
in the obscure line of the poet.

With this double meaning of *uses*, then, poetry is like the world itself which the
painter at the beginning of the scene said, "wears, sir, as it grows" (1.1.3) – that is,
it wears out at one level while it grows at another. This second sense of self-growth
is restated by the two following comparisons: poetry is like a "gentle flame" arising
of itself, not needing to be struck with a flint, and it is like a stream which overflows
each barrier which tries to contain it. The world and poetry are both usurious commodities for the poet and painter, and their works share in the "magic." Poetry has
become exhibit "a" in the long list of commodifications which this play will catalog
for us.

The theme of usurious loans as the material force explaining the apparent magic
of bounty is picked up and enhanced by Middleton in the following scene and given
a new emphasis which had not been developed by Shakespeare in the first scene. First
the disillusioned philosopher Apemantus, then the steward Flavius, are the voices for
a discourse on wastefulness which punctures the illusions about the magic of bounty
we had witnessed in the first scenes (1.2.29–48, 186–9). This is the first indication
of what every audience of the previous scenes has been surmising, that Timon's
apparently limitless bounty is in reality finite. Beyond that, we learn that he is now
in debt to usurers, his lands collateral to his loans. And later Flavius reports, "The
greatest of your having lacks a half / To pay your present debts" (2.2.138–9). Timon's
private bubble economy has burst, and the text underlines two interacting causes.
First, in passages by both poets, the foolishness of Timon's self-deception and denial
are eloquently emphasized. Shakespeare apparently wrote the lines of a Senator who
realizes that the time has come to call in his earlier loan to Timon:

> It cannot hold, it will not.
> If I want gold, steal but a beggar's dog

> And give it Timon, why, the dog coins gold.
> If I would sell my horse and buy twenty more
> Better than he, why, give my horse to Timon,
> Ask nothing, give it him, it foals me straight
> And able horses. No porter at his gate,
> But rather one that smiles and still invites
> All that pass by. It cannot hold, no reason
> Can sound his state in safety. (2.1.4–13)

Similarly, but with different emphasis, we read in one of Middleton's passages:

> When all our offices have been oppressed
> With riotous feeders, when our vaults have wept
> With drunken spilth of wine, when every room
> Hath blazed with lights, and brayed with minstrelsy,
> I have retired me to a wasteful cock,
> And set mine eyes at flow. (2.2.152–6)

Both poets, however, underline usury as the instrument which exploits Timon's foolishness to effect his undoing.[11] Shakespeare inaugurated the theme of usury in scene 1.1 subtly but decisively, as I argued above. The next scene by Shakespeare, 2.1, replaces subtlety with directness, using the Cynical philosopher Apemantus and an underdeveloped accompanying Fool to drive home the point. The usurers' servants are said to be fools and bawds: fools for serving manifestly evil masters and bawds for pandering to the wants of others with damaging relief. The dialogue here makes the first of many connections in the play between usury and the sex trade. The Fool works for a brothel and notes:

> I think no usurer but has a fool to his servant. My mistress is one, and I am her fool. When men come to borrow of your masters, they approach sadly, and go away merry; but they enter my master's house merrily, and go away sadly. (2.2.96–9)

Shakespeare made a similar connection in another dark play, *Measure for Measure*, when the comic figure Pompey wittily says, "'Twas never merry world since, of two usuries, the merriest was put down, and the worser allowed by order of laws" (3.1.263–4). In *Timon*, though, the "second usury," sexual reproduction, is less than merry because it leads to venereal disease. Sexuality in this play is always presented in its commodity form, just like art. The sexuality, as in Dante's *Inferno*, is like usury because it is a parallel perversion of natural reproduction, and also, as numerous allusions throughout the play attest, because it leads to disease, as usurious loans lead Timon to financial ruin. When bandits come to Timon in the wilderness, giving the occasion for his great lines on universal thievery (4.3.429–42), one last and crucial implication of the critique of usury is in place:

> Break open shops; nothing you can steal
> But thieves do lose it. (4.3.440–1)

The practice of usury in *Timon of Athens*, then, is far more than incidental to the play's other concerns. It is a central motif, metaphorically connected to the play's other themes: art, commodities, prostitution, theft, venereal disease, gold, and politics. All these connections are made explicit in the play's stylistic highpoint, the great invectives of Timon in act 4, when he has renounced the company of mankind in a rage and proclaimed himself "Misanthropos, hater of man." Famously, the central passage – unmistakably Shakespearean in provenance – was also a favorite of Karl Marx. It occurs after Timon, digging for roots, discovers instead gold in the soil of the Athenian countryside:

> Gold? Yellow, glittering, precious gold?
> No, gods, I am no idle votarist.
> Roots, you clear heavens! Thus much of this will make
> Black, white; foul, fair; wrong, right;
> Base, noble; old, young; coward, valiant.
> Ha, you gods? Why this? What this, you gods? Why, this
> Will lug our priests and servants from your sides,
> Pluck stout men's pillows from below their heads.
> This yellow slave
> Will knit and break religions, bless th'accursed,
> Make the hoar leprosy adored, place thieves,
> And give them title, knee, and approbation
> With senators on the bench. This is it
> That makes the wappened widow wed again;
> She whom the spital-house and ulcerous sores
> Would cast the gorge at, this imbalms and spices
> To th'April day again. Come, damnèd earth,
> Thou common whore of mankind, that puts odds
> Among the rout of nations, I will make thee
> Do thy right nature. (4.3.26–45)

Ben Jonson, in the opening scene of *Volpone*, had famously represented his title character worshiping gold. Shakespeare here deepens by reversing Jonson's opening, giving us not an ironic instance of gold-worship but an impassioned, analytic denunciation of it. As in Jonson the gold is both literal and metonymic, invoking not just itself as legal tender but the whole fantastic network of commodities, credit, capital, and the desire underlying the whole system. The new economic criticism has taught us much about the mechanics of finance in Shakespeare's day, and we now know that gold itself, despite the Spanish plunder of the New World, was in relatively short supply. Elizabethan lords and sovereigns distributed much of their wealth and benefits through a system of credit, which created obligations and networks of its own.

We are a century or more from a modern financial system of banks and stocks in England, and thus the credit system which Shakespeare and Middleton have in mind in their depictions of Timon's financial situation is still premodern and pre-capitalist in many ways. For example, most financial transactions took place through credit, without an exchange of money (Jowett 2001).

Nevertheless, Marx's comments on the passage on gold quoted above are still of great relevance to our understanding of this play because it is the long-run, philosophical, system-creating properties of money that Timon denounces, and as Marx saw, Shakespeare had got to the heart of the matter, giving us a description not just of his own day's financial follies, but of the logic of any commercial civilization under the sway of the circulation of capital. Of this and a later, related passage (4.3.381–92), Marx wrote,

> Shakespeare excellently depicts the real nature of money . . . Shakespeare stresses especially two properties of money: (1) It is the visible divinity – the transformation of all human and natural properties into their contraries, the universal confounding and overturning of things; it makes brothers of impossibilities. (2) It is the common whore, the common pimp of people and nations.
>
> The overturning and confounding of all human and natural qualities, the fraternization of impossibilities – the divine power of money – lies in its *character* as men's estranged, alienating, and self-disposing *species-nature*. Money is the *alienated ability of mankind*. (Marx 1964: 167–8)

The peculiar terminology used here in this 1844 manuscript is borrowed from the German philosopher of alienation Ludwig Feuerbach, and its relation to the work of the older Marx has been a much debated issue; however, Marx quoted *Timon* again at a climactic moment of *Capital* (I: 132), and he again asserts something very similar in a more popular language, beginning with a hoarded quote from Christopher Columbus:

> "Gold is a wonderful thing! Whoever possesses it is lord of all he wants. By means of gold one can even get souls into Paradise." (Columbus in his letter from Jamaica, 1503). Since gold does not disclose what has been transformed into it, everything, commodity or not, is convertible into gold . . . Just as every qualitative difference between commodities is extinguished in money, so money, on its side, like the radical leveler that it is, does away with all distinctions. But money itself is a commodity, an external object, capable of becoming the private power of private persons. The ancients therefore denounced money as subversive of the economic and moral order of things. Modern society, which, soon after its birth, pulled Plutus by the hair of his head from the bowels of the earth, greets gold as its Holy Grail, as the glittering incarnation of the very principle of its own life. (Marx 1967: 132–3)

Here, clearly, Marx is a Shakespearean, just as, in other contexts, Freud was. For both social critics, money is not merely a mammon of iniquity to make friends with, but the central organizing principle of societies of ethically inverted values and practices. The young Marx expressed the idea as an alienation of human species-being, that is, as an organization of the totality of human wants and capabilities into a vast abstraction – money – given control over every individual and of society as a whole. The older Marx wrote of the private expropriation of a universal human capability. But both passages are explications of Shakespeare's *Timon of Athens.* And the startling convergence in viewpoints between the nineteenth-century radical socialist and the early seventeenth-century pragmatic royalist can help us penetrate some of the layers of assumptions about what Shakespeare could and could not have believed and help us see this remarkable play afresh.

In what follows I want to focus on what Marx saw in this play, its social criticism and its great insight into the nature of commodities, money, and capital. But the ending, I believe, goes beyond what Marx saw, working out not just the logic of a society organized around capital, but something of its potentiality for creating negative, critical institutions for the preservation of what otherwise is suppressed by commodification. Shakespeare, like Marx in some of his scattered remarks on art and literature, but perhaps more like his twentieth-century developers in the Frankfurt School, Theodor Adorno and Walter Benjamin, saw art as contributing to a possible secular redemption of a world utterly corrupted by the common whore of mankind.

Timon in the Woods

The falling action of the play, constituting the second of its two main divisions, encompasses what modern editors have designated acts 4 and 5 and is almost entirely by Shakespeare, with the exception of two fairly clear interpolations by Middleton and an ambiguous passage at 4.2.1–29, all three involving the faithful steward Flavius. Although the action builds towards Timon's suicide and the conquest of Athens by Alcibiades, dramatic suspense as such gives way to something more like a series of philosophical dialogues. If there is precedent for this practice elsewhere in Shakespeare, it would be in the middle of *As You Like It*, when plot development is also sacrificed to a series of encounters of the various characters in a complex discursive dialogue. In *Timon*, however, Timon is at the center of each of the encounters, and each of the visitors can be considered a kind of dramatic foil designed to throw light on one or another facet of Timon's new misanthropy. Timon is visited in turn by Alcibiades and his two accompanying prostitutes, by Apemantus, by the Banditti or thieves, by the steward Flavius, by the poet and painter, and by two Senators (with Flavius). The procession of these characters recapitulates the major rhetorical figures connected with the central motif of usury built up in the play's first half and thus constructs the diptych-like structure alluded to by critics. Power, prostitution, diseased sex, Cynicism, theft, and art all parade before the now misanthropic Timon. Several of the encounters work to reinforce the condemnatory vectors toward specific social ills established in the play's first half. Alcibiades' prostitutes Timandra and Phrynia are darkly comic instances of the corrupting power of gold, emblematic figures evoking simultaneously the infections of venereal disease and the socially corrupting influences of the usury which diseased sex has consistently signified. The painter and poet reestablish their earlier practice of corrupted, commodified art, and the Senators reinforce the theme of money's corruption of power. Three of the visits, however – those of Alcibiades himself, Apemantus, and Flavius – perform a different function, measuring for us in their different ways the inadequacy of Timon's misanthropy as a response to corruption. The ending movement of the play, if I may anticipate my argument, reinforces the diagnosis of profound corruption in Athens, but it undermines Timon's misanthropy as an adequate response to it. The longest of these darkly comic episodes involves the visit of the philosopher Apemantus.

Before Timon's change, Apemantus had foreshadowed elements of the bitter misanthropy which Timon ultimately adopts, but after the change, he also represents a contrast. Apemantus helps define the limits of Timon's misanthropy by contrasting it with his own more measured, less logically self-destructing philosophy, although by the end of the scene his own consistency is also called in doubt.

A character named Apemantus was mentioned in Plutarch's brief comments on Timon – the only source we can be sure Shakespeare used since he took specific wording from it. Apemantus was linked with Timon as one "much like to his nature and condition and also followed him in his manner of life" (Bullough 1966: 251). But the many allusions to dogs in the language of those talking to and about Apemantus in the play, as well as Apemantus' demeanor and argumentation, clearly indicate that Shakespeare had picked up from one of several possible sources a tradition of associating Apemantus with the Cynics, whose name derives from the Greek word for dog, which in turn was either a reference to a gymnasium where the sect developed or the nickname of its best-known figure, Diogenes of Sinope (412?–323 BC), famous for his disdain of comforts and his search in the streets of Athens for one honest man. Despite his aggressive bluntness, Diogenes was generally admired in the classical world for his principled consistency. Our own most common associations with the term *cynic* – in the sense of a person who believes that other people are motivated in all their actions by selfishness – seem to come to prominence later. At this period such a meaning seems rather an implication of the term, but not its main signification. The main uses of the term from Shakespeare's era given in the *OED* link cynicism with asceticism or the disdaining of pleasure, with railing against society and those accepting its ordinary customs, and with an unpleasant disposition or churlishness. And we can see admiration for the Cynics in another author from whom Shakespeare borrowed at least once. There is an interesting passage in Montaigne's short essay "Of Democritus and Heraclitus" (Montaigne 1965, I: 50), which makes a distinction involving Diogenes and Timon[12] that is relevant here, distinguishing between Diogenes' cynicism and Timon's misanthropy. Shakespeare in 1605–9, when *Timon* was written, would have had access to John Florio's 1603 translation of Montaigne;

he certainly had read in Florio's Montaigne by 1611, the date of *The Tempest*, with its verbal borrowing from Florio's translation. Near the end of this brief essay Montaigne proposes to consider the contrast between two ancient philosophers and the general stance each took before the world. Both found "the condition of man vain and ridiculous" (p. 220), but each responded in his own way. Diogenes "never went out in public but with a mocking and laughing face; whereas Heraclitus, having pity and compassion on this same condition of ours, wore a face perpetually sad, and eyes filled with tears" (p. 220).

Montaigne writes that he judges Diogenes' stance to be superior, and he clinches his argument not with a reference to Heraclitus, but to the legendary figure of Timon:

> Timon wished us ill, passionately desired our ruin, shunned association with us as dangerous, as with wicked men depraved by nature. Diogenes esteemed us so little that contact with us could neither disturb him nor affect him, and avoided our company, not through fear of association with us, but through disdain of it; he considered us incapable of doing either good or evil. (p. 221)

Thus Apemantus, or Cynicism, was a foil for Timon in the already existing material on him before Shakespeare and Middleton took up the legend, and the earlier material tended to see Apemantus as positive. The Apemantus of the first half of the play seems to be taken from this mold, as he does much to win over the audience even while he alienates us (and his fictional fellows) with his rudeness and verbal aggression. As the exposition of the play makes clearer Timon's foolishness, Apemantus emerges less ambiguously as a voice of perception and moral integrity, particularly in the banquet scene by Middleton when he penetrates the illusion and hypocrisy with his remark:

> O you gods! What a number of men eats Timon, and he sees 'em not. It grieves me to see so many dip their meat in one man's blood, and all the madness is, he cheers them up too. (1.2.39–41)

Apemantus continues his double role as unsocial churl and truth-teller in his appearance in the second act. Just like the Fool in Lear (and the association may explain why he has a Fool as a companion briefly in a clearly Shakespearean portion of 2.2) and like Thersites of *Troilus*, he is colored by the very negativity of his own judgments, becoming a character completely taken up by a certain stance or role, the very opposite of Shakespeare's myriad-minded protagonists who most engage audiences sympathetically.

When the complexly developed Apemantus pays his visit to misanthrope Timon in the woods, our expectations are whetted. What follows is an intricate dance, akin, as William O. Scott (1984) wrote, to the logical puzzle of the liar's paradox. Timon has followed Cynicism to the extent of withdrawing from an artificial society, living a natural, austere life without the comforts of civilization, and cursing men for their hypocrisy. But Cynicism offers an alternative, a mode of life which its disciples can adopt to remain virtuous amid corruption, and an important part of that life involves seeking converts. Timon rejects this aspect of Cynicism with great verbal hostility, and begins to question Apemantus' own motives. The debate continues through a few more turns, then ends in an exchange of mutual insults.

The effect is darkly comic. The alienation of each man from his society finally transforms a philosophical debate into a schoolboy's mutual taunting contest. But Apemantus, on balance, scores the better points, and he also provides the audience with an aphorism which gets reaffirmed as the rest of the play develops, again distancing and contextualizing Timon's misanthropy:

> The middle of humanity thou never knewest, but the extremity of both ends. When thou was in thy gilt and thy perfume, they mocked thee for too much curiosity; in thy rags thou know'st none, but art despised for the contrary. (4.3.307–10)

And he is able to offer Timon what he desperately needs, a friendship based on shared values and perceptions, not flattery and sponging. Timon refuses this offer, as he does all the others, and drives his would-be philosopher-friend away in anger.

From this point on, the play turns against misanthropy and even Cynicism as philosophies. Both are valuable up to a point, as critical tools to perceive society's hypocrisy. Beyond that point, however, death is the only logical outcome of each, and more pragmatic men, the artists and politician-soldiers, are more constructive agents in the world than these universalizing philosophers. In the course of the debate, Apemantus had said to Timon, "Thou should'st desire to die, being miserable" (4.3.255). At the end of the scene, after Apemantus has left and before the painter and poet arrive, Timon seems to have seen Apemantus' logic. He realizes that the only logically cogent outcome of his misanthropy is suicide. Even being a "beast among the beasts" involves him in corruption and domination, as he had earlier proven in his argument against Apemantus (4.3.330–44).

Thus Apemantus' encounter with Timon in the woods, while it makes its own philosophical points, has comic aspects which relativize and distance the alienation from society of each of these deep-seeing, foul-speaking characters. In contrast, Timon's two faithful friends, Alcibiades and Flavius, lead us in a different direction. Both treat Timon's misanthropy as a kind of madness or disease into which Timon has fallen and ask their companions to take it likewise. Alcibiades repeats this idea in the very last speech of the play.

Thus, it is to a certain point only that Timon takes the audience in his great invectives early in act 4 denouncing the transformative power of money. As he begins to universalize his anger, to become "Misanthropos, hater of Mankind," and as we begin to see that such universalism makes no distinctions between true and false friends, the satire of the play is turned against the satirist, the denouncer is implicitly denounced – or pitied as stricken with madness – because of the absurdity of his own blanket condemnations. Early in his exile, Timon had prayed,

> The gods confound – hear me, you good gods all –
> Th'Athenians both within and out that wall!
> And grant, as Timon grows, his hate may grow
> To the whole race of mankind, high and low!
> Amen. (4.1.37–41)

We watch as Timon undergoes such growth. But if we remember the early associations of growth in 1.1 – the world, growing as it wears, the spontaneous growth of bounty which proves illusory and destructive, the perverse growth of a usurious loan, even the paradoxical growth of poetry, which wears like a gown as it "uses" – we will be suspicious of the growth wished for by Timon here. Earlier, in lines by Middleton, the steward Flavius had forced Timon into a concession against his universalizing (4.3.483–530), and in the context of his earlier prayer, it is clear that Flavius and his fellow servants rebuff by example Timon's project of hating mankind "high and low." In a short scene apparently penned by Middleton, but echoing themes from *As You Like It* and *King Lear*, the servants form a utopian counter-society and embrace fellowship and communalism in the face of the atomization and individualism of Timon's erstwhile wealthy friends:

> Good fellows all,
> The latest of my wealth I'll share amongst you.
> Wherever we shall meet, for Timon's sake
> Let's yet be fellows. Let's shake our heads, and say,
> As 'twere a knell unto our master's fortunes,
> "We have seen better days." (4.2.22–7)

Immediately following come Shakespearean lines echoing the theme of the good servant and clearly functioning, as does this whole scene, as a counterpoint to Timon's unmeasured response to his grief.

Timon's misanthropy, then, is like the poet's inspiration: it "like the current flies / Each bound it chases" (1.1.25–6). It is a kind of madness recognized as such by the most trustworthy of Timon's friends, Alcibiades and Flavius. As a number of critics have recognized, this madness of Timon's parallels in many ways that of that other great wielder of universalizing invective against mankind, the mad King Lear of the heath scenes. In a critical classic from the 1920s the novelist and painter Wyndham Lewis (whose illustrations of *Timon* in Cubist style are among the greatest of all illustrations to Shakespeare) argued that madness in Shakespearean tragedy always signals an exploration of nihilism – the perception of a God-deserted cosmos in which there are no intrinsic values and in which human nature itself is seen to sway between possibilities of benevolence and malevolence. And Lewis was certainly right to group *Timon of Athens* with *Hamlet*, *Troilus and Cressida*, and *King Lear* as his chief examples of this phenomenon (Lewis 1927: 247–56). In this play, as in most of Shakespeare after about 1595, there is no revelation of the voice of God in the emptiness – Ken Jackson's (2001) Derrida-influenced reading of the play notwithstanding. Instead, like the exiles in the Forest of Arden or on the heath with Lear, like Richard II in his prison, like Antony and Cleopatra after their defeat, we and the remaining characters of *Timon* are left to our own devices to make what we can out of the unenviable circumstances of life under conditions of modernity. Like so many Shakespearean tragic heroes, Timon chooses suicide – a decision presented as the only logical outcome of his universalizing misanthropy. But his suicide is a singular one – offstage, undramatic, and accompanied by some of the most lyrical language of the entire play. Timon's last movement is twofold: it is the culmination of his misanthropy, but at the same time it is the inauguration of a new mode of perception that responds to the critique of misanthropy we have had performed before us. This new theme had been artfully and subtly introduced in the first scene of the play but left to bide its time until the very end. Timon at the end makes of his death – and specifically his final resting place – a work of art. At the end of the play, in passages entirely written by Shakespeare, he goes beyond misanthropy and into the aesthetic – a realm, of course, which had not yet been conceptualized in philosophical language, but which had begun to be conceptualized by Shakespeare (and a few others) in self-constituting poetry and drama, nowhere more explicitly than in this play.

The play's shift in tone at the very end comes from a marked shift in Timon's mood. After one of his most devastating expressions of universal hatred – his invitation to all Athenians to use his tree to hang themselves – his focus on death brings him to a different word-tone altogether:

> Come not to me again, but say to Athens,
> Timon hath made his everlasting mansion
> Upon the beachèd verge of the salt flood,
> Who once a day with his embossèd froth
> The turbulent surge shall cover, thither come;
> And let my grave-stone be your oracle.
> Lips, let four words go by and language end;
> What is amiss, plague and infection mend.
> Graves only be men's works, and death their gain;
> Sun, hide thy beams, Timon hath done his reign.

The sentiment is hardly beneficent, with its references to plague, infection, and graves, but the elegiac tone is new, as is the charged description of the seaside. The same emotional heightening, in fact, is present in each of the descriptions of or allusions to this gravesite by the sea. Alcibiades presents another of them as a moment of his own order-restoring, nearly machiavellian pronouncements in the play's very last scene:

> . . . yet rich conceit
> Taught thee to make vast Neptune weep for aye
> On thy low grave, on faults forgiven. Dead
> Is noble Timon, of whose memory
> Hereafter more. (5.4.77)

Timon's mad misanthropy is preserved in the epitaph which Alcibiades reads, but it
is then distanced:

> These well express in thee thy latter spirits.
> Though thou abhorest in us our human griefs,
> Scornst our brains' flow and those our droplets
> Which from niggard nature fall . . . (5.4.74–7)

The result is to create a forgiving frame around the madness, which becomes an aspect
of the new aesthetic object, the "rich conceit" in which Timon's misanthropic vision
is both contained and recontextualized.

   This is the moment of the play which opens out into the whole extravagant reading
by G. Wilson Knight (1949), so impressed by this rare moment of Shakespearean
aestheticism that he pronounced it the apex of all that Shakespeare had written. Of
course in doing so Knight inserted into this brief, subtle opening a world of post-
Romantic aestheticism which is latent at best in Shakespeare's singular poetry. And
in the process he lost sight of much of the play's searing social criticism, relevant to
Knight's, our own, and Shakespeare's day in different ways. The same might be said
of Ken Jackson's stimulating article (Jackson 2001), which opens up from this
moment into Derrida's meditations on a religion beneath religion. Nevertheless, it is
also true that the political criticism of our own recent era has evolved to a point
where it must confront some of its own enabling blindspots – its lack of an adequare
concept of the aesthetic perhaps the chief among them[13] – and this play is a key case
in point. Timon at the end undergoes one more transition, and it is a transition into
art. The agents of this transition were not the poet and the painter, who when they
returned to Timon manifested even more unambiguously than before their own mer-
cantilism, their treatment of their art as mere commodities for profit. Instead Timon
introduces the last stage of his extraordinary development, as a dialectical leap from
his own despair and spite. The movement from the climax of his misanthropy in
his invitation to mass suicide to the idea of his death as an aesthetic act is almost
instantaneous.

   In contrast, Alcibiades becomes an agent of reform, along the lines Machiavelli
described in *The Discourses* in his account of the earliest days of the Roman republic.
Alcibiades ends the play with an instance of that inevitable cycle of republics growing
corrupt and requiring the strong arm of a harsh reformer to reestablish their ancient
virtues and liberties (Machiavelli 1950: 124–270; 1.6–90). The play concludes, then,
with an extraordinary balance, simultaneously affirming the efficacy of pragmatic
politics as Alcibiades enters Athens to "use the olive with my sword" (5.4.82) and
the preserving qualities of the aesthetic as Timon's grave creates a form adequate
to contain and qualify the great insights of his mad misanthropy. The Timon who
in his last phase spurned all human contact and sought only solitude bombards the
world with a number of last messages: two epitaphs and the gravesite itself. All
three of these "letters to the world" utilize a self-destructing rhetoric that conveys

two contradictory messages. Timon hates humanity and wants no notice of his grave. But Timon speaks out to humanity and asserts his presence to us. Montaigne had noted that the misanthrope is involved in a double bind, "for what we hate we take seriously. Timon wished us ill, passionately desired our ruin, shunned association with us as dangerous, as with wicked men depraved by nature." Shakespeare at the end of this play finishes Montaigne's thought for him. Timon reconciles his impulses by aestheticizing his hate and leaving it as a gift within a work of environmental art.

This gesture lacks the transcendent intentions of full-fledged late nineteenth-century aestheticism. This version of the aesthetic is not necessarily the ultimate, truth/illusion about reality which Nietzsche defined and which has been a potent – and of course much criticized – final resting place of so many works of twentieth-century modernism. It is more modest and apparently inadequate without the pragmatic accompaniment provided by Alcibiades. Precisely because of those differences, however, it is a version of the aesthetic that speaks to us with renewed urgency at the very beginning of the twenty-first century.

Timon of Athens is one of Shakespeare's probings of an imagined, fully formed modernity and one which is deeply condemnatory of the values of a developing commercial society. The almost complete negativity of an earlier treatment of these themes in *Troilus and Cressida*, however, gives way here to something more meditated and at once more pragmatic and more idealistic. The idealism behind Timon's generosity is not simply denounced, at least in the Shakespearean portions of this play; it is preserved in the aesthetic form of Timon's gravesite, while it is qualified – by the suggestion that art by itself is unable to transform the world – by the machiavellian pragmatics of a harsh republican reformer. The result is a quiet masterpiece of great philosophical insight and import that speaks freshly to us almost four hundred years after its origins.

NOTES

1   The most influential argument for incompleteness has been that of Ellis-Fermor (1942), but a very recent critic, Ken Jackson (2001), has reasserted this position – and holds it compatible with a two-author theory of the play. Klein (2001) puts it forward as an alternative to the two-author theory, however.

2   The two-author hypothesis was first put forward in 1843 by Charles Knight. Proponents of Middleton as second author since the 1970s include Lake (1975), Jackson (1979), Holdsworth (1982), Wells and Taylor (1997), and Jowett (2001).

3   I am summarizing the argument of Jowett (2001), who is in turn drawing on the unpublished dissertation of Holdsworth (1982), which I was unable to consult. The argument overlaps to a large degree with that of Wells and Taylor (1997), to which Jowett contributed. My thanks to John Jowett for providing me with a transcript of his conference presentation and for additional details about the two-author case.

4   For details of the allocation, including ambiguous passages, see Wells and Taylor (1997: 501), who are summarizing Holdsworth (1982).

5　See my earlier treatment of this play in Grady (1996: 58–94).
6　See, for example, Grady (1996), Bruster (1992), Mallin (1996), and Engle (1993).
7　The evidence for dating is wholly internal. No records of its performance or other allusions to it survive, although that is the case for a few other plays as well, so a performance is not precluded. It has been almost universally dated among the later tragedies on stylistic and thematic grounds, with interconnections to *King Lear* (1605–6), *Antony and Cleopatra* (1606), and *Coriolanus* (1608); these dates of composition are from Wells and Taylor (1997), who assign *Timon* to 1605 based on stylistic tests.
8　Unless otherwise indicated, all quotations from *Timon of Athens* are from Klein (2001).
9　Here and for all works by Shakespeare other than *Timon*, the text used is Greenblatt (1997). My thanks to John Drakakis for alerting me to this line from *Merchant*.
10　Additional related usage of *use* in the sonnets occurs at 4.13–14, 6.5, 20.14, 40.6, 48.3, and 134.10. My thanks to David Hawkes for alerting me to these lines.
11　The interest of both playwrights in issues of usury, with its commonplace associations with breeding, would explain what Klein (2001: 63–4) took to be a weakness in Taylor and Wells's argument (subsequently amplified by Jowett), that images of "breeding" appeared in portions Wells and Taylor assigned to Shakespeare and Middleton separately. Such common use of a commonplace is unexceptional.
12　The relevance of this essay to *Timon* was first pointed out by Farnham (1950: 65–7).
13　See Joughin (2000) for a succinct articulation of this position.

References and Further Reading

Bradbrook, M. C. (1966). *The Tragic Pageant of "Timon of Athens."* Cambridge: Cambridge University Press.
Brill, L. (1979). Truth and *Timon of Athens*. *Modern Language Quarterly*, 40, 1, 17–36.
Bruster, D. (1992). *Drama and the Market in the Age of Shakespeare*. Cambridge: Cambridge University Press.
Bullough, G. (ed.) (1966). *Narrative and Dramatic Sources of Shakespeare*, vol. 6. London: Routledge.
Charney, M. (1972). Introduction to *Timon of Athens*. In S. Barnet (ed.) *The Complete Signet Shakespeare*. New York: Harcourt.
Chorost, M. (1991). Biological Finance in Shakespeare's *Timon of Athens*. *English Literary Renaissance*, 21, 349–70.
Ellis-Fermor, U. (1942). "Timon of Athens": An Unfinished Play. *The Review of English Studies*, 18, 270–83.
Engle, L. (1993). *Shakespearean Pragmatism: Market of his Time*. Chicago, IL: University of Chicago Press, 147–63.
Evans, G. B. et al. (eds.) (1974). *The Riverside Shakespeare*. Boston, MA: Houghton Mifflin.
Farnham, W. (1950). *Shakespeare's Tragic Frontier: The World of his Final Tragedies*. Berkeley: University of California Press.
Grady, H. (1996). *Shakespeare's Universal Wolf: Studies in Early Modern Reification*. Oxford: Clarendon Press, 58–94.
——(2000). Introduction: Shakespeare and Modernity. In H. Grady (ed.) *Shakespeare and Modernity: From Early Modern to Millennial*. London: Routledge, 1–19.
Greenblatt, S. (1980). *Renaissance Self-Fashioning: From More to Shakespeare*. Chicago, IL: University of Chicago Press.
Greenblatt, S. et al. (eds.) (1997). *The Norton Shakespeare: Based on the Oxford Shakespeare*. New York: Norton.
Holdsworth, R. V. (1982). Middleton and Shakespeare: The Case for Middleton's Hand in "Timon of Athens." Unpublished dissertation, University of Manchester.

Hoy, C. (1973). Jacobean Tragedy and the Mannerist Style. *Shakespeare Survey*, 26, 49–67.

Jackson, K. (2001). "One wish" or the Possibility of the Impossible: Derrida, the Gift, and God in *Timon of Athens*. *Shakespeare Quarterly*, 52, 1, 34–66.

Jackson, M. P. (1979). *Studies in Attribution: Middleton and Shakespeare*. Jacobean Drama Studies 79. Salzburg Studies in English Literature. Salzburg: Institut für Anglistik und Amerikanistik Universität Salzburg.

Joughin, J. J. (2000). Shakespeare, Modernity, and the Aesthetic. In H. Grady (ed.) *Shakespeare and Modernity: Early Modern to Millennium*. London: Routledge, 61–84.

Jowett, J. (2001). Middleton and Debt in *Timon of Athens*. Presentation, Annual Meeting, Shakespeare Association of America, April, Miami, FL.

Kahn, C. (1987). "Magic of Bounty": *Timon of Athens*, Jacobean Patronage, and Maternal Power. *Shakespeare Quarterly*, 38, 1, 34–57.

Kernan, A. (1959). *The Cankered Muse: Satire of the English Renaissance*. New Haven, CT: Yale University Press, 192–246.

Klein, K. (ed.) (2001). *Timon of Athens*. Cambridge: Cambridge University Press.

Knight, C. (1843). Introduction to William Shakespeare, *Timon of Athens*. In C. Knight (ed.) *The Comedies, Histories, Tragedies, and Poems of William Shakespeare*, 2nd edn., vol. 10. London: Charles Knight.

Knight, G. W. (1949). *The Wheel of Fire: Interpretations of Shakespearean Tragedy*, revd. edn. London: Methuen, 207–39.

Lake, D. J. (1975). *The Canon of Thomas Middleton's Plays: Internal Evidence for the Major Problems of Authorship*. Cambridge: Cambridge University Press.

Lewis, W. (1927). *The Lion and the Fox: The Role of the Hero in the Plays of Shakespeare*. London: G. Richards.

Machiavelli, N. (1950). *The Prince and The Discourses*. New York: Modern Library.

Mallin, E. S. (1996). *Inscribing the Time: Shakespeare and the End of Elizabethan England*. Berkeley: University of California Press.

Marx, K. (1964). *Economic and Philosophic Manuscripts of 1844*, ed. D. J. Struik, trans. M. Milligan. New York: International.

——(1967). *Capital: A Critical Analysis of Capitalist Production*, ed. F. Engels, trans. S. Moore and E. Aveling, vol. 1. New York: International.

Miola, R. S. (1980). Timon in Shakespeare's Athens. *Shakespeare Quarterly*, 31, 21–30.

Montaigne, M. de (1965). *The Complete Essays of Montaigne*, trans. D. M. Frame. Palo Alto, CA: Stanford University Press.

Nuttal, A. D. (1989). *Timon of Athens*. Harvester New Critical Introductions to Shakespeare. New York: Harvester Wheatsheaf.

O'Dair, S. (2000). *Class, Critics, and Shakespeare: Bottom Lines on the Culture Wars*. Ann Arbor: University of Michigan Press, 43–66.

Paster, G. K. (1985). *The Idea of the City in the Age of Shakespeare*. Athens, GA: University of Georgia Press, 91–108.

Scott, W. O. (1984). The Paradox of Timon's Self-Cursing. *Shakespeare Quarterly*, 35, 3, 290–304.

Slights, W. W. E. (1977). "Genera mixta" and *Timon of Athens*. *Studies in Philology*, 74, 1, 36–62.

Soellner, R. (1979). *"Timon of Athens": Shakespeare's Pessimistic Tragedy*. Columbus: Ohio State University Press.

Spencer, T. (1953). Shakespeare Learns the Value of Money: The Dramatist at Work on *Timon of Athens*. *Shakespeare Survey*, 6, 75–8.

Spencer, T. J. B. (1962). "Greeks" and "Merrygreeks": A Background to *Timon of Athens* and *Troilus and Cressida*. In R. Hosley (ed.) *Essays on Shakespeare and Elizabethan Drama in Honor of Hardin Craig*. Columbia: University of Missouri Press, 223–33.

Wells, S. and Taylor, G. (1997). *Shakespeare: A Textual Companion*. New York: Norton.

23

Coriolanus and the Politics of Theatrical Pleasure

Cynthia Marshall

> History does not offer return tickets, and before we enter the halls to admire what we are offered, we should perhaps reflect on [the] extraordinary practical joke played on us by our good taste.
>
> Agamben (1999: 22)

In a highly charged scene late in act 1, Martius Caius Coriolanus is hoisted aloft by a band of enthusiastic followers as he exclaims "O, me alone! Make you a sword of me?"[1] If this is the hero's "happiest moment," as Michael Goldman has called it, the parallel with his assassination – "the only other moment in the play when Marcius allows a group of men to touch him" – is especially interesting (Goldman 1981: 80). As Goldman implies, the issues of Martius' singularity and his troubled relation to a social world are most vividly enacted in these two scenes. In the first, Martius seeks recruits by urging any man who judges "his country's dearer than himself" to "Let him . . . follow Martius." He outlines a formulation whereby honor derives from loyalty to the state, not from any assertion of individual glory. Although the scene confirms Martius' own superiority ("O, me alone!"), he wins this distinction peculiarly, by being transformed into an implement of war ("Make you a sword of me?"), surrendering control and autonomy to the evidently greater reward of becoming the transitive tool of the Roman war effort. It is a strange moment, prompting inquiry into the delight taken by this most active of heroes in becoming the passive tool of others, and into the pleasure audiences presumably take in the hero's momentary transformation. Engaging these questions will take this essay from consideration of the play's text to its troubled critical reception and then to several key theatrical productions. Centrally at issue, I will argue, is Shakespeare's act of turning a violent political history to the uses of theatrical pleasure. *Coriolanus* helps to inaugurate a modern culture of entertainment, in which political questions of social discord and harmony are subordinated to individual questions of autonomy and pleasure. Indeed, the play foreshadows the way that, in certain domains, even violence and pain will come eventually to dwell under the aegis of pleasure.

Shakespeare's creative appropriation of elements of early modern culture has been a central tenet of recent criticism. New historicists have traced the theatrical uses of religious concerns, political disputes, colonialist energies, sex and gender anxieties, changing notions of madness, and myriad other elements of social life in the early modern world. As historical analysis has sharpened its economic edge, this process has ceased to be imagined as the innocent "circulation of social energy" by which Shakespeare stood welcomingly at the theatre door granting entry to unhoused cultural concerns and free-ranging practices (Greenblatt 1988). The fact of early modern capitalism has become increasingly unavoidable, so that Shakespeare's theatre appears less the recipient of stray social energies than a powerful machine of appropriation, moving through popular culture and its various practices and discourses like a talent scout with an eye toward good material.[2] Tracing the route from social origin to theatrical destination has done much to fill in a picture of early modern culture and a developed sense of where the plays stood in their own milieu. However, inadequate attention has been paid to the formal transformations involved in, or incurred by, these appropriations. From our belated perspective, it has often seemed sufficient to track down the cultural origins of events and practices. By instead proceeding forward — tending to the movement *from* source, origin, or early version *to* theatrical event — we can gain a crucial sense of the effect and the pleasure a play was created to instill in viewers. I have examined elsewhere the structural changes in notions of character occasioned by Shakespeare's adaptation of Plutarchan narrative histories for the dramatic stage (Marshall, 2000). Here I am concerned with the formal and psychological dimensions of pleasure. Scrutinizing the powerful energies of self-negation that are adopted from the Plutarchan political narrative and put to theatrical use in *Coriolanus*, I am picking up an argument about catharsis Kenneth Burke raised years ago and reconsidering it in light of contemporary critical and theoretical practice.

Few plays are so intense in their scrutiny of the nature and exercise of power, so deliberate in their focus on social discord, so single-minded in directing domestic and personal issues toward those of public concern as *Coriolanus*. Debate over the character of the hero — seen at one extreme as a man of valor and integrity, at the other as a selfish and dimensionless boy — is necessarily inflected by politics: the more manipulable the plebeians and corrupt the tribunes, the higher Coriolanus' disdain is justified in soaring. Nevertheless, while the play demands attention to political structures and while the history of theatrical performance confirms the recurring expectation that its stagings should engage political themes, the nature and essence of *Coriolanus'* politics remain inscrutable. Perhaps this was most famously illustrated by René-Louis Piachaud's production at the Comédie Française in 1933–4 that incited both the left and the right to riot in the streets — some judging the play to glorify fascism (it had, after all, been recommended to school children in emergent Nazi Germany for its "examples of valour and heroism": Brockbank 1976: 86), others deeming it an attack on the socialist government. In the charged atmosphere of Paris between the wars, it could hardly be surprising that responses to *Coriolanus* were so polemical. Yet the play's capacity to heat passions on both sides underscores a perception that its power is not precisely or specifically allied with a particular ideology, but is instead "political" in some other, looser way.[3]

Shakespeare's Roman and English history plays generally represent political stories for their early modern audience while also deconstructing their source material, and *Coriolanus* in particular uses self-reflexive encoding of theatricality to displace the heft and significance of Roman affairs. The discomfiture the play produces in its audiences derives from the absence of any obviously correct view of events. Rather than attempting to indoctrinate viewers into a political perspective, or to gather their enthusiasms behind a (nationalist or other) cause, *Coriolanus* works the rift opened by the *performance* of politics.[4] Demonstrating the gap between subjective identity and shaping ideological codes, and then holding out this gap to viewers as a site of pleasure, *Coriolanus* spans "the stretch between theatrical and deconstructive meanings of 'performative.'"[5] In doing so it anticipates modern debates about the theatrical dimension of political life and about the political valency of entertainment. Annexing the political into the domain of pleasure, the work of art loses its ability to shock its viewer into a sense of wholeness and completion. As Giorgio Agamben describes, the advent of culture and good taste means that "the spectator . . . does not in any way recover a determinate content and concrete measure of his existence, but recovers simply his own self in the form of absolute alienation, and he can possess himself only inside this split" (Agamben 1999: 37). *Coriolanus* instances an early step in the process that would later include the writings of Sade and Masoch, that of representing politics for the pleasure of audiences.

I

According to logical economies that emerged during the Enlightenment, human political affairs are situated in the public domain, where they are conducted according to rational standards. Personal affairs, by contrast, are relegated to the private or domestic sphere, along with the emotions and physical needs and pleasures. Disconcertingly, these distinctions are not maintained in *Coriolanus*. Affairs of state are a personal matter manipulated by ranking aristocrats. The hero's body is less a site of personal experience and identity than one invested with political consequence; his wounds are tallied fetishistically and their display to the populace is a significant act. As a character, Martius troubles the terms through which Western subjectivity has come to be defined. He would be separate, unique, godlike in his superiority, but the play undoes this dream of singularity by exposing his troubled quest for this position and by plotting his loss of it. As I have shown elsewhere, a modern notion of masculinity suffers from the insistence that Martius' dependency on others renders his identity as permeable as his wounds show his body to be (Marshall 1996).

The relationship between the human body and political or social truth is insistently pondered in the play. The presentation so early on of Menenius' fable of the belly is sometimes taken as overt advertisement for a conservative analogy between the individual and the state. But Menenius is obviously partial in his sympathies and manipulative in his rhetoric:

> The senators of Rome are this good belly,
> And you the mutinous members; for examine
> Their counsels and their cares, digest things rightly
> Touching the weal o' th' common, you shall find
> No public benefit which you receive
> But it proceeds or comes from them to you,
> And no way from yourselves. (1.1.147–54)

The body as Menenius describes it functions mechanically to digest and distribute caloric energy. In fact, the fable takes on greatest vividness when the First Citizen interrupts to ask about "The kingly crown'd head, the vigilant eye, / The counsellor heart, the arm our soldier, / Our steed the leg, the tongue our trumpeter . . ." (114–16); his imagination animates the body as Menenius, with his studied purpose, refrains from doing. If viewers were not otherwise inclined to be suspicious of easy analogies, Martius, only a few lines after Menenius' conclusion, lights on the issue of rhetoric that purposefully flatters, telling the First Citizen: "He that will give good words to thee, will flatter / Beneath abhorring" (1.1.166–7). Rather than simply instructing viewers with a seamless analogy between the body and the state, the belly fable highlights the politically charged nature of such rhetoric, indicating the complexity of the individual's place in society.

Martius himself functions like an automaton within his chosen sphere of war: "before him he carries noise, and behind him he leaves tears" (2.1.157–8); "when he walks, he moves like an engine and the ground shrinks before his treading" (5.4.18–19). Serving as an "engine of war" simplifies human existence (Kermode 1974: 1393), severely reducing possibility and complexity. Martius is eclipsed as the invisible force between noise and tears. The martial code therefore appears at least as limited a story of human operation and existence as the belly fable. Moreover, as Frank Kermode points out, beyond the sphere of combat Martius is "reduced to a mere actor" (ibid). He resists campaigning before the citizens, calling it "a part / That I shall blush in acting" (2.2.144–5) and rejecting his own expected lines like a bad script: "What must I say? – 'I pray, sir,' – Plague upon't! I cannot bring / My tongue to such a pace" (2.3.51–3). The trope of acting carries a suggestion of inner truth or identity falsified by a role or disguise, as when Martius proclaims, "Would you have me / False to my nature? Rather say I play / The man I am" (3.2.14–16). Urging him to reconsider, Volumnia likewise differentiates between "th'matter which your heart prompts you" and the more politic "words that are but roted in Your tongue" (3.2.54, 55–6).

Crucially, however, the notion that the subject carries truth within himself does not hold up in the play. Stanley Fish (1980) has argued that *Coriolanus* demonstrates the degree to which truth is socially derived and validated through community norms and speech acts. The claim of inner truth is problematized by attention to the performativity of social behavior and by demonstration of the emptiness or lack on which the hero is constituted. The displacement of interiority can be seen in Volumnia's advocation of expediency over authenticity. For Volumnia, no firm distinction exists between military and political campaigns; she argues:

> If it be honour in your wars to seem
> The same you are not, which, for your best ends
> You adopt your policy, how is it less or worse
> That it shall hold companionship in peace
> With honour, as in war, since that to both
> It stands in like request? (3.2.46–51)

In her machiavellian view there is no field of innocent, unmediated action. In war and peace alike, it may be honorable to use policy because both are political spheres. Accordingly, she bolsters her point that "action is eloquence" (3.2.76) by offering specific instructions on posture ("this bonnet in thy hand," "thy knee bussing the stones," "waving thy head"; 3.2.73, 75, 77) and rhetoric ("say to them, 'Thou art their soldier, and being bred in broils, / Hast not the soft way . . .'"; 3.2.80–2). Martius briefly consents by adopting her rhetoric of performance: "You have put me now to such a part which never / I shall discharge to th'life" (3.2.105–6); and Cominius punctuates the theatricality of the role: "Come, come, we'll prompt you" (3.2.106). But Martius quickly changes his mind, reverting once more to his claim of interior validity:

> I will not do't,
> Lest I surcease to honour mine own truth,
> And by my body's action teach my mind
> A most inherent baseness. (3.2.120–3)

Tellingly, Martius here endorses the power of performativity: the "body's action" is no longer merely a false exterior role, but is granted the power to "teach" or alter the mind.

Martius fails at the part his mother has scripted and stage directed for him, largely because the tribunes manage to manipulate him into another role, knowing as they do that

> Being once chaf'd, he cannot
> Be rein'd again to temperance; then he speaks
> What's in his heart . . . (3.3.27–9)

They script a scene in which Martius is called "traitor" (3.3.66) and he basically accepts the role. The result, of course, is his banishment from Rome. Martius' rejection of Volumnia's instructions does not prove the ascendancy of what he calls his "own truth" and Brutus calls "what's in his heart." Instead it demonstrates a man moving from one political scenario, in which he plays the humble and obliging defender of the state, to another, in which he mocks the people, defies their law, and seeks to win "a power tyrannical" (3.3.65). Lest we doubt that Volumnia is correct in her view of the effectiveness of political performance, the play's grand emotional climax shows her own use of eloquent action. By kneeling to her son at the Volscian camp outside Rome, she makes an irresistible appeal, prompting him to action that he knows will be "most mortal" to him (5.3.189).

Demonstrating the instability of the hero's claim to an interior zone of truth, *Coriolanus* displaces the Cartesian idea of an inner self. This seems a classic instance of deconstruction: no stable truth can exist within language or symbolic systems; the individual subject is the effect of discursive forces and hence far from being self-determining. *Coriolanus* illustrates a principle of performative legitimacy, according to which the "right" action is determined through context, not intentionality. John Plotz has argued that the play shows the moral failure of performativity. In his view, Rome offers "a morass of deception" that Coriolanus correctly rejects (Plotz 1996: 812). To resolve the settled impasse between Coriolanus' claim to self-authorizing truth and the general Roman embrace of pragmatic politics, Plotz proposes "radical theatricality," a mode of imaginative interaction through which the citizens might "enter fully, unabashedly, into the theater of Coriolanus's spectacular body" (p. 824). This is a productive move, because it points toward the theatrical dimension as not only the "destiny" of a playtext, but also as the embedded model for the interactions it explores (Serpieri 1985: 122). Plotz, however, does not pursue the play's course into the theatre; instead he imagines Coriolanus as a kind of Christ figure whose sacrificial body might reunite the fragmented *polis*, an argument that substitutes a nostalgia for order for the proposed "radical theatricality." By contrast, productions that have staged the play with reference to political movements or causes often thought of as coercive (Nazi Germany, Napoleonic France, or, in the arena of gender politics, gay biker culture) suggest a provocative link between the performance of culture (in Judith Butler's sense – that is, through the repetition of behaviors) and performance on stage.[6]

Nevertheless, deconstruction alone cannot account for the intensity of the play's concern with violence against the human body. Here the body is not only a source of metaphysical interest but also a particular site of disputed subjectivity. By scrutinizing the notion of interior truth in such a visceral way, *Coriolanus* accords with psychoanalytic models of split subjectivity. In the terms of Lacanian psychoanalytic theory, there can be no "truth of the subject" because the subject consists precisely of lack or division, and truth does not reside in the body, which constitutes the "blind spot" in the subject's self-understanding. Against the formulation *cogito ergo sum*, Lacan maintains that the subject "emerges only when a key aspect of [his] *phenomenal* (self-) experience . . . becomes *inaccessible* to him" (Žižek, 1997: 121). Both the deconstructive and the Lacanian approaches have relevance for the play, although the psychoanalytic view holds particular potency because of the play's concern not just with signifying systems but with the body as a problematic domain of truth. Significantly, this approach can help us understand not only the represented content of the play, but also the theatrical effect it aims to produce.

As is frequently noted, the hero's hurt body is the focus of inordinate attention in the play. Virgilia quails at the thought of blood, although Volumnia says "it more becomes a man / Than gilt his trophy" (1.3.39–40); Volumnia and Menenius proudly (or obsessively) tally the number and location of his wounds (2.1.146–55). Martius' downfall in Rome is caused by his refusal to display his wounds in the marketplace – an episode Shakespeare clearly means to highlight, since he alters it from his Plutarchan source. And Martius appears drenched in blood at the battle of Corioles; the extremity of his appearance is several times commented upon:

> *Enter Martius, bleeding, assaulted by the enemy.* (1.4.61s.d.)
>   Worthy sir, thou bleed'st;
> Thy exercise hath been too violent
> For a second course of fight. (1.5.14–16)
>   Who's yonder,
> That does appear as he were flay'd? (1.6.21–2)

We should ponder the peculiarities of Coriolanus' association with blood, which extends beyond that of any other Shakespearean tragic hero (with the early exception of Titus Andronicus). By his mature period Shakespeare creates relatively cerebral heroes whose valorous deeds in battle are more likely to be reported (Othello, Macbeth) than staged; age (Lear), disposition (Hamlet), or scruples (Othello) prevent them from shedding blood until late in the action, if at all. When Macbeth appears bloodied from the attack on Duncan, he is horrified by the vestiges of his own deed and accordingly weakened by it; and Julius Caesar's status as victim rather than hero is confirmed by the sheer bloodiness of his fall in act 3. In her seminal work on the meanings attached to the humoral body, Gail Kern Paster articulates the gendered terms of blood and bleeding on the early modern stage, noting that Caesar's bloody body bears the valency of "a passivity, uncontrol, and bodily wastefulness gendered female" (Paster 1993: 104). Paster points out Coriolanus' attempt (in 1.5.17–19) to define his bleeding "as both voluntary and therapeutic," and acknowledges the "psychic precariousness" of his effort, especially given that "the autonomy Coriolanus has claimed in shedding blood in battle is threatened by his inability to forgo displaying his wounds" (pp. 96, 97). Nevertheless, the gendered associations of blood are complicated by an important distinction between Martius' active, upright bloodiness and the fallen posture of a victim such as Caesar (a posture into which Martius himself eventually is forced). Although any appearance of blood instances a breach in the bodily surface and therefore a breach in social decorum, Martius pursues violent confrontations, seeking, like the future Henry V, "a garment all of blood" (*1 Henry IV*, 3.2.135). Blood is central to his image and identity, and in the theatre, to the actor's makeup – as is emphasized by textual reference to it as "painting" (1.6.68), something with which he is "mask'd" (1.8.10).

Putting on and displaying a garment comprised of the body's interior, Martius recalls the mythic Marsyas, the satyr who was flayed alive for defeating Apollo in a contest. Submerged reference to the satyr is made in the description of Martius as "flay'd" (1.6.21–2) (Brockbank 1976: 136n., citing Poisson), and a rich if indirect set of associations links the two homonymic figures. A statue of Marsyas stood at the entrance to the Forum in Rome, where it was intended to deter litigants, and the image has long been used in theatrical productions of *Coriolanus* – it appeared in the backdrop of Macready's production of *Coriolanus* in 1838. In the early modern period the flayed Marsyas became an icon of anatomical speculation and presented a special challenge to visual artists; the image was attempted by numerous painters, including Giulio Romano, Raphael, and, most successfully, Titian. Jonathan Sawday identifies Marsyas as the probable model for the self-dissecting corpses of sixteenth-century anatomy manuals, those figures who so graciously expose their musculature to the curious eye, granting access to the bodily interior (Sawday 1995: 186–7). Like Martius Caius Coriolanus, these figures advertise their physicality while revealing nothing of themselves as individuals. We might compare the practice of contemporary body-builders, who seek to display their hypertrophic musculature through a stylized "inside-out" body.

> After months of hard training and force-feeding, they spend the final weeks starving themselves to achieve the 'inside-out' look by the day of competition. That's the skin shrunk like Saran Wrap, the body ripped and stripped . . . today's bodybuilders inject diuretics until their skin . . . is so translucent one can visibly see raw tissue and striated muscle swimming in a bowl of veins beneath. (Fussell 1993: 583)

The element of homoerotic display in the bodybuilders' practice invites attention, especially as it coincides with the affiliation between *Coriolanus* and gay politics and theatre, in recent decades. The thematic interest in bodily interiors and exteriors also carries philosophical stakes.

The play's fascination with rupturing the smooth surface of the classical body recalls Gilles Deleuze's definition of Baroque architecture as a

> severing of the facade from the inside, of the interior from the exterior, and the auton-omy of the interior from the independence of the exterior, but in such conditions that each of the two terms thrusts the other forward. (Deleuze 1993: 28)

Although it seems reasonable to associate *Coriolanus* with an incipient Baroque aes-thetic, the relevant point for my argument is Baroque's ontology, the way it responds to a collapse of reason and a loss of principles by offering a paradoxical "solution": "we shall multiply principles – we can always slip a new one out from under our cuffs

– and in this way we will change their use." It is a "game . . . of inventing principles," "the splendid moment when Some Thing is kept rather than nothing" (Deleuze
1993: 67, 68). With multiple principles in play, weighted valuations of established
terms are cast into confusion, like the interior and the exterior each "thrust[ing] the
other forward." We might compare Coriolanus' tragic effort to "stand as if a man were
author of himself" (5.3.35–6) within a complex social world requiring adjustments
and concessions, a Baroque incursion of performativity into the certainty of tragic
action.

There is an affinity between Deleuze's postmodern concept of Baroque and the goal
of a feminism such as Paster's, which seeks to break down inscribed positions of male
and female by exposing the feminine traces within male heroes such as Caesar and
Coriolanus. So too, the performative display of masculinity – in *Coriolanus*, in Renaissance drawings of anatomized bodies, in contemporary bodybuilders – explodes the
myth of bodily display as a feminine behavior. These deconstructions of established
gender terms convey the force of Baroque's "multiple perspectives." This is not a
matter of pluralistic tolerance for different viewpoints, but the radical, postmodern
rebuttal of universality before the claim that each perspective bears on every other.
Following Leibniz, Deleuze envisions the world as "the infinite curve that touches at
an infinity of points an infinity of curves" (Deleuze 1993: 24). The curve, or, in other
formulations, the fold, images the proximity of points and their implication in and
for one another. Both the curve and the fold imagistically countervail the Enlightenment oppositions of inner and outer, forward and back. More generally in Deleuze's
thought, radically horizontal formulations of truth and value are favored over vertical, hierarchical ones.

Ovid reports that as Marsyas is tortured by Apollo, the wretched satyr groans,
"Who is it that tears me from myself?" (cited in Sawday 1995: 185). Shakespeare's
Martius reaches a parallel crisis when he cries, "Oh mother, mother! What have you
done?" (5.3.182–3) after Volumnia convinces (forces?) him to abandon his attack on
Rome. The physical rendering of Marsyas' skin from himself, or what to him seems
a tearing of self from self, is matched in Shakespeare's more political terms by Martius'
exile from Rome. His banishment entails the division of his political and familial
identities from his personal identification of himself as a warrior. As Fish points out,
Martius' bizarre rejoinder, "I banish you!" (3.3.123), breaks the codes for an ordinary
speech act, by reappropriating the position of legal authority (Fish 1980: 214–18),
thus tearing apart the ground on which he is himself constituted. The proud assertive-
ness of his effort to "stand as if a man were author of himself and knew no other kin"
(5.3.35–7) becomes as perverse and impossible an act of severance from his bonds as
the flaying of Marsyas, each tearing self from self. Martius' binary logic, which structures his thinking about himself, his family, the Roman citizens, the tribunes, and
the Volscians, is revealed by the play as inadequate to a tragic degree; the terms of
above and beneath, for and against, inside and outside, true and false, do not provide
the stability Martius seeks. Instead they shift in relation, like points upon a curve, or
points seen from different perspectives. The hero's claim of an unchanging inner truth

is undermined by the play's demonstration of performative truth, and by the Deleuzean pattern of the fold or the curve that compounds depth and surface. Martius' truth is written on his body and written through the actions he takes – not lodged, jewel-like, within him.

Martius is subjected to ideological forces whose pressure he is unable to withstand, and "what the subjectivation masks is . . . a lack in the structure, a lack which is the subject" (Žižek 1989: 175). Although Martius strikes many critics as a hero without dimensions or depth, his troubled identity as a social creature reveals him to be a paradigmatic split subject. Martius is torn between dependence on others who will validate his existence simply by requiring his heroic services in combat, and his utter disdain for those whom he judges to be less worthy than himself. In this Lacanian formulation the plebeians play the crucial role of The Thing (*Das Ding*), or "the absolute Other of the subject."[7] Martius structures his existence around his rejection of the plebs. He must demonstrate his superiority to them in order to maintain the role he has constructed. And yet he obviously requires their admiration at the same time that he despises them for being in a position to give it.

To the extent that an audience – in its group presence and its dependency on the enacted spectacle – will have at least as much in common with the plebs as with the patricians, Martius' explosive disdain for the crowd creates an odd theatrical dynamic, like that of Miles Davis diffidently playing with his back to his fans. It seems an understatement to call Martius an unlikeable hero; the character pointedly dislikes those who would admire or require him, as well as those who make accommodations to social existence – in short, most of us. Jane Adelman, observing the parallel between the position of the common people in the play's fiction and that of the audience in the theatre, notes that "Coriolanus seems to find our love as irrelevant, as positively demeaning, as theirs" (Adelman 1980: 144). Where does this leave an audience? Some have found in the play the rubrics of a brief for democratic action. Bertolt Brecht famously deemed Coriolanus himself altogether dispensable outside of war and the tragedy therefore one "of Rome, and specifically of the plebs" who fail to gain control of their fate (Brecht 1972: 374). More often, *Coriolanus* has been seen as making a nostalgic appeal to a truth inscribed within the individual and as advocating an ordered social hierarchy that staves off chaos. Kenneth Burke attempted to solve the problem of audience appeal by defining *Coriolanus* as a play directed toward an elite audience, although his approach, to which I now turn, leaves a number of issues unresolved.

II

In his classic essay "*Coriolanus* – and the Delights of Faction" Kenneth Burke ponders the issue of catharsis in relation to the play. He endorses a traditional interpretation of dramatic catharsis, understanding it as a tool for social hygiene, whereby tragedy purges the tensions of group existence and restores political harmony. For

Burke, *Coriolanus* alleviates "the *malaise* of the conflict between the privileged and the underprivileged" (Burke 1966: 82). He locates the play in historical terms at a moment when the medieval synthesis of thought and culture had broken apart, and emergent structures (economic systems, religious beliefs, ethical codes) became more particularized and therefore divisive. The rise of nationalism, for instance, entailed a "transvaluation" of traditional ethical standards; Machiavelli was controversial because he successfully represented these new standards of political expediency and competitiveness to his early modern readers. Such an ethical "transvaluation was called for, because *religion* aimed at *universal* virtues, whereas the virtues of *nationalism* would necessarily be *factional*, insofar as they pitted nation against nation." A play like *Coriolanus* had particular relevance in the context of this unraveling social fabric, in which traditional appeals to common humanity were newly complicated in the light of competing factions. As the static structures of feudalism gave way to turbulent emerging economies, there was a rise in "*class* factionalism" as well (ibid: 90; original emphases).

In Burke's view, *Coriolanus* "exploits" these tensions "to the ends of dramatic entertainment" (p. 88). He offers his "formula for tragic catharsis":

> Take some pervasive unresolved tension typical of a given social order (or of life in general). While maintaining the 'thought' of it in its overall importance, reduce it to terms of personal conflict (conflict between friends, or members of the same family). Feature some prominent figure who, in keeping with his character, though possessing admirable qualities, carries this conflict to excess. Put him in a situation that points up the conflict. (p. 94)

What is complex and abstract ("pervasive unresolved tension") becomes vivid and immediate. The argument is powerful in granting a force and effect to drama, rather than seeing it as a mimetic reflection of society. As theorists have increasingly pointed out in recent years, any critical practice that neglects the formal dimensions of literature risks discounting the power that made the texts interesting in the first place.[8] Burke understands catharsis to be achieved in two ways. First, by means of the plot, Martius is made a scapegoat who ultimately receives violent punishment for his disdainful attitude toward the populace. Second, through his scurrilous invective, he expresses anger and "untoward tendencies" normally repressed in civilized society. Although one might anticipate that the lower classes would be the main beneficiaries of any pleasure taken in Martius' violent death, Burke implies that both sources of catharsis appeal primarily to the upper classes (the usual theatregoing crowd in modern society). Thanks to Martius' late change of heart, at his death viewers "pity him even while we resent his exaggerated ways of representing our own less admirable susceptibilities" (p. 89). The second, more freely poetic, catharsis would involve those sharing Martius' scorn for the commoners. In other words, Burke understands *Coriolanus* as a tool for accommodating the privileged classes to their own privilege. More specifically and more radically, Burke shows Shakespeare positioning his audience to indulge in negative emotions, to enjoy anger and suffering, and to do so without the imposition of positive, unifying terms at the conclusion.

Shuli Barzilai (1998) has proposed that *Coriolanus* is Shakespeare's dramatization of the death instinct. Noting the conjunction in Freud's theory of death instinct and destructive impulses, she brilliantly connects the hero's destructive behavior toward others with a plot in which he is actively complicit in his own death. Essentially, Barzilai identifies a sadomasochistic aspect of Martius' character, a gratification derived both from giving and receiving suffering. Linking this reading with Burke's attention to the "delight" or cathartic pleasure of painful emotion experienced by the play's audience suggests that *Coriolanus* accords with an aesthetic of masochism, a formal structure identified by Leo Bersani (1986: 107). Bersani draws from Jean Laplanche's reading of Freud a concept of the ego or sense of self as formed in response to a wish for its own dissolution (the death instinct) and constituted through that wish. Emphasizing, as Burke does, the dimension of audience pleasure, Bersani locates that pleasure in psychic shattering or emotional release. The masochism he posits in art "has nothing to do with self-punishment" (Bersani 1990: 38). Instead it is an adaptive mechanism, a way of elaborating and interpreting the pleasurable tensions of violence, toward which viewers are inevitably drawn. As I have argued elsewhere, this aesthetic had particular currency for the early modern period, when emerging notions of individualism were in tension with older, more dispersive modes of self-understanding (Marshall 2002).

The masochistic aesthetic appears formally in the peculiar teleology of *Coriolanus'* structure. On the one hand, the plot moves with a certain relentlessness toward the hero's destruction, or as Barzilai suggests, his self-destruction. Martius' propensity to throw himself into battle, to plunge alone into the enemy city, to antagonize those whom he would court, establishes his masochistic drive as a narrative element. On the other hand, the play contains, as Burke observes, a striking number of plot reversals (Burke 1966: 85–6). Martius changes names, allegiances, loyalties; he is and is not Rome's protector. The peripeteia interrupts and slows down the movement toward the tragic conclusion; the reversals loosen Martius' identity from its structuring bonds, emphasizing the lability of his supposedly fixed identity. This structure accords with sadomasochism's aim of subverting established hierarchies by uncoupling roles and behaviors from identities. *Coriolanus* moves in the direction of sadomasochism by merging political reality with political performance. It offers viewers the simulation of battle, blood, and violence, and reflexively calls attention to its own theatricality. The point is not to convince them of any particular position or idea, but rather to entertain, to offer delight through the simulation of violence. The masochism of viewers, not that of Martius, is at stake.

Burke was no fan of psychoanalytic criticism and would probably resist my assimilation of his reading to a masochistic aesthetic. Still, the evidence of unresolved tensions within his essay engenders a sense that something has not been fully articulated. For example, its attention to factionalism seems incomplete. As I have suggested, Burke raises the issue of class conflict within the play but does not pursue it as a factor in terms of audience response. Indeed, Burke avoids discussion of class so much that he risks allegorizing the play by assimilating it to his "formula," whereby the social is "reduced" to the personal. In light of contemporary theories of ideological construction, such clearcut division between the social and the personal seems distinctly problematic. Both Bruce Smith and Coppélia Kahn have demonstrated how Roman ideologies shape gender roles as imaged in *Coriolanus* (Smith 2000; Kahn 1997). Martius, of course, refuses social norms in rejecting his scripted role as candidate for consul, and as we have seen above, the play encodes this refusal in terms of both a theatrical type of performativity and a deconstruction of the norms themselves: Martius wishes to "play the man I am," rather than the part urged by Volumnia and Menenius. Given that Martius' conflict is *with the political* – with the requirements of life in a social group – not with Volumnia or Menenius personally, Burke's view, in which the struggle is "reduced" to a "personal conflict" (between friends or family members), overly domesticates the play.

The "Comments" appended to Burke's essay in its appearance in *Language as Symbolic Action* evince further tension. Ranging widely, these remarks address, among other things, "the 'fecal' nature of invective" (Burke 1966: 97). Although within the essay proper Burke writes of symbolic purgation, in the appendix he indulges the fixation on anal and scatological themes that is central to his thinking about catharsis elsewhere.[9] For Jonathan Goldberg, the "Comments" suggest Burke's alertness to the play's anal eroticism; he points out the way that Stanley Cavell picks up the theme of anality "in a similarly well-positioned postscript" (Goldberg 2000: 261). Burke's engagement with anality indicates a level of response grounded in the body and its economies that is otherwise missing from his notion of purgation. Still, anality would seem only one element within the play's encompassing structure of masochism. The pleasure of viewing *Coriolanus* does not reside in factionalism *per se*, nor in the mimetic representation of political themes or erotic intensities. It is rather a question of how viewers interact with the enacted events. The play's foregrounding of performativity enables catharsis, by presenting viewers with multiple possibilities for psychic identification and response. Martius' aggression and disdain, and his withering invective, act out an audience's "less admirable susceptibilities," in Burke's polite phrase. The terror and humiliation Martius causes his enemies, and his own emotional surrender to Volumnia, followed by his physical surrender to the Volsces, enable or even invite a more purely masochistic set of responses, and the emphasis on his wounded body suggests an unsettling reminder of physical abjection. Indeed, Martius' emphatic emotional coldness and mechanical behavior ("When he walks, he moves like an engine"; 5.4.1–19) suggest the dehumanizing rituals of sadomasochistic practices. No wonder the play has repeatedly been staged as an affair of metal-studded black leather. "Make you a sword of me?": Martius' transformation into a tool of war is paradigmatic of the process through which performative roleplaying enables a satisfying release of autonomy. Martius' "happiest moment" is one in which he trades heroic self-control for the pleasure of personal relinquishment.[10] *Coriolanus* urges the same on its audience, inviting their investment in an emotionally cold hero whose enthusiasm for punishment cuts both ways.

III

To demonstrate how this tragedy works, how it gains meaning through its emotional effect on viewers, I turn in this final section to the record of *Coriolanus*' performance in the modern theatre. I am particularly interested in analyzing the rhetoric of reviewers' comments, as it encodes their assessment of theatrical reception and response. Revisiting earlier arguments through reference to their theatrical realization, this section is meant as a coda of sorts to the rest of the essay, a structure that belies the extent to which the performance history informs my argument, but that serves heuristically to illustrate the movement of political representation into a world of performance and performativity.

Again, *Coriolanus* carries the reputation of being a keenly political drama; many call it Shakespeare's *most* overtly political play. Traditionally its theatrical performance was linked with political events: in George C. D. Odell's words, the play "seemed destined to be launched, with new trimmings, during or after each of England's successive politico-civic upheavals" (Odell 1921, I: 59–60). As we have noted, the play was embraced by fascist causes in Germany in the 1930s. Twenty years later in East Germany it was adapted by Bertolt Brecht to reveal what he saw as its hidden theme of revolution. In Brecht's view the bourgeois theatre heroicized Martius because it identified with the patricians' cause; a more enlightened and properly historical view would realize that the tragedy lay in the plebeians' failure of self-awareness. In general, continental theatre tends to be more overtly political than its British or American counterparts, and Philip Brockbank suggests that "in translation . . . the propaganda potentials of [the play's] political myth can be more manifest" (Brockbank 1976: 84). For whatever reasons, the history of twentieth-century performances of *Coriolanus* in England and America indicates "a disengagement from the nakedly political aspects of the text" (Berry 1981: 31). On the contemporary stage the "menacing crowd" has lost its fascination and attention has turned instead toward "the relationship of man with man, with whatever emphasis of sexuality and group that the actors and directors impart" (ibid: 34). By far the dominant trend among modern productions has been a romantic, character-based interpretation of the play. Alternatively, there have been overtly political versions (Brecht's redaction, presented by the Berliner Ensemble in Berlin in 1964 and in London the following year; Brian Bedford's effort to show "the debasement of contemporary democratic politics" in his 1981 production at Stratford, Ontario: Ripley 1998: 312) and those which have explored the play's gender politics (Tyrone Guthrie's exploration of the "hysterical and homosexual" passion between Coriolanus and Aufidius in his 1963 staging at the Nottingham Playhouse: Ripley 1998: 304; Steven Berkoff's study of male bonding in his 1989 production at New York's Public Theatre, with Christopher Walken as a leatherclad "bike-gang leader": Wills 1989: 46). Yet the most noteworthy productions of the twentieth century were those in which the sensational effects of the play's masochistic aesthetic dominated over any deeper meaning involving political history or contemporary reference.

This foregrounding of the personal has carried a peculiar cost: a nagging sense of dissatisfaction with productions that do not feature overtly political themes. Politics hangs like a shadow over modern interpretations of *Coriolanus*. Even with theatre in modern Britain and America becoming increasingly less engaged with partisan events, more a matter of bourgeois entertainment, *Coriolanus* presents a special instance because it is a recognizably political play. Some productions have attempted to appease the looming shadow by featuring the trappings of political theatre – references that are more a matter of style than of substance. As Lee Bliss notes, "contemporary directors' interest in the play's often-neglected political argument runs the danger of imposing a topical but ultimately superficial 'concept' that distorts more than it illuminates" (Bliss 2000: 93). However, in the striking instances of Laurence Olivier's two performances in the role, theatricality openly usurped historical reference or political concept, and performativity itelf was foregrounded as a motif within the play. As a result, whatever nagging feeling of loss viewers experienced from the displacement of political valency was turned to thematic purpose. Viewers who felt themselves deprived of a classical world of grand and simple truths were offered instead the vestiges of theatre. Compensation worked here less straightforwardly than in the formula Greenblatt identified in his eloquent New Historicist account of *King Lear*, whose "force," he said, "is to make us love the theater" (Greenblatt 1988: 127). Instead, Coriolanus' passionate indignity, as translated by Olivier, fed the audience's own sense of accepting a lesser thing. Their abasement was formally appropriated into the theatrical dynamic, as the actor punished the crowd for being no better than viewers – in effect, plebs – and they loved it.

At Stratford in 1933, just after Hitler had been appointed chancellor, William Bridges-Adams staged a resolutely apolitical *Coriolanus* that signaled "the retreat of British Shakespeare from the external conditions of the world" (Kennedy 1993: 126). Six years later, "as Mussolini invaded Albania, Hitler threatened Poland, . . . and Britain introduced conscription" (Ripley 1998: 276), Ben Iden Payne returned to the play with no more activist an agenda. By 1939 the Shakespeare Memorial Theatre's choice of *Coriolanus* was hailed for its timeliness,

> since it deals with the clash of states, the making and breaking of treaties and alliances, the bitter, indissoluble antipathies of the autocrat and the demagogue, the reactions of the common people to various methods of incitement and appeasement, and the unending struggle of private affection against public hate.[11]

But the "quaintly pictorial" Jacobean costumes, the excision of political references in the text, and the surging crowd of plebeians who were robbed of ideological purpose demonstrated that Iden Payne had "made no attempt to draw modern comparisons."[12] This seemed to critics not merely a missed opportunity but a refusal of the play's presumed obligation to deal with political currents.

It may have been the contrast with the production at the Old Vic the year before that prompted such criticism of Payne's *Coriolanus*. Although director Lewis Casson did not foreground contemporary reference, Laurence Olivier as Martius suggested an "embryo Fascist dictator" (Berry 1981: 28). Olivier stunned with his power as an actor: Desmond MacCarthy called his performance "a masterpiece . . . We watch him with moments of exhilarating wonder, but without acute sympathy, stumbling blindly to his end."[13] In Olivier's 1938 *Coriolanus* the politics of performativity had substituted for the performance of politics. Rather than playing, or suggesting, figures redolent of actual events, Olivier's political statement sprang from the extreme control he exercised from the stage. I am identifying, that is, the emphasis on performativity that is particular to Shakespeare's *Coriolanus* with a wider cultural movement in which theatrical roles become more and more indistinguishable from politically honed identities.

When Olivier played the part again twenty-one years later, this time at Stratford, there could be no question that masterful acting had trumped historical reference as the means to authority in staging *Coriolanus*. Philip Hope-Wallace wrote that the performance "keeps the audience in thrall," and the swooning sense of subjugation to a higher power characterizes reviewers' language.[14] W. A. Darlington called it "as powerful a display of an actor's authority as I remember to have seen."[15] A. Alvarez wrote of Olivier's "innate command": "his presence dominates the stage no matter what is happening or who is talking."[16] Laurence Kitchin famously described Olivier's Coriolanus cursing the plebeians as "one man lynching a crowd" (Wells 1997: 265). As Kitchin makes clear, Olivier took enormous liberties with the part, "mountebanking" whole scenes, an effect Kitchin was willing to grant as "Olivier's exclusive privilege," won through the abundant evidence that the actor was in control. As he put it, "one of the attractions of such great acting is the confidence you have that the current of expression could be switched off at any moment and the effect just made survive a searching scrutiny" (Wells 1997: 263, 262, 265).

Inevitably, a few found the production, and especially Olivier's performance, over the top. T. C. Worsely judged it to have "too many trick throwaways" and Alan Brien objected to the presentation of "a Coriolanus far more sophisticated and self-critical than the text warrants." Elaborating his criticism, Brien resorted to a standard trope of antitheatrical rhetoric – a despised feminization:

> Perhaps it was only that one costume with the brief skirt and the flattering neckline that would have seemed provocative on Gina Lollobrigida, topped by a handsome curly head and supported by the loveliest pair of thighs in show business, but too often here and there Olivier seemed to be giving a Green Room parody of the role. Surely there can be no interpretation of Coriolanus that justifies him, even for a moment, suddenly rolling a saucy eye and bending his right knee in to his left in a Windmill curtsy?[17]

Olivier's Coriolanus was no drag queen, so it is interesting that where other reviewers write of mastery and authority and dominance, Brien diagnoses a fatal indulgence in spectacle, refusing the bargain the production implicitly offered: a great actor's mesmerizing power in place of the play's political depth. One reviewer wrote: "The politics – and, oh, this is such a political play – remain, but we are mainly concerned with Coriolanus the warrior."[18] Another elaborated further: "Experts are not even sure what the play is about. Some say that it's a political treatise, some that it is not; some say that Shakespeare was on the side of Coriolanus in his contempt for the people; others deny it . . . Sir Laurence by-passes these difficulties by being firmly himself, a virile self."[19]

Nevertheless, the "virile self" was that of an actor – exactly what Martius Coriolanus agonizingly refuses to be. When Olivier played Coriolanus, a performer sometimes accused of overacting took on the character of a man who would be nothing but "the thing I am." While Olivier would warp roles and even whole plots in an effort to command attention with *tour de force* emotional displays, Coriolanus sacrifices position, family, and finally his life rather than adjust his behavior to social norms. This might seem a doomed assignment were it not for the final twist of performativity: by making Coriolanus' proclaimed authenticity a role within a play, Shakespeare unsettled his claim to truth, and Olivier exploited this to maximum effect.

Olivier's 1959 Coriolanus established the standard for a modern staging of the play, foregrounding the performative aspects of the role as a theatrical event. Thirty years later Michael Billington criticized Charles Dance's Coriolanus by noting its contrast with Olivier's and complained that "although Mr. Dance dutifully turns over tables in the Forum and hurls people to the ground, he does not give off that palpable sense of danger the role requires."[20] In an era like the present one, when increased demand for audience involvement has meant that actors are not hesitant to spray fluids on the crowd and Hamlet may turn a pistol on viewers rather than point a bodkin at himself, the notion of theatrical "danger" has become easier to visualize. The power Olivier exerted was more metaphysical, that of the actor as egoist, insisting that others submit to his will. Just as significantly, the powerful energy required to hold the audience "in thrall" was surrendered at key moments. After sealing his pact with Aufidius, "whatever integration the character of Marcius had possessed fell apart," and "the rest was crumble, detonation and collapse" (Wells 1997: 261). A more strikingly visual display of submission was the terrifying death leap in which Olivier hurled himself backward from the high "Tarpeian rock" on stage, to be caught at the last second by the ankles, and left dangling head down. One reviewer quoted Lauren Bacall: "I thought Larry had really killed himself. It was so exciting."[21] This pattern of dominance and submission, with the actor bringing the audience to heel, and then submitting the character's integration and his own physical safety to a cruelly punishing ordeal, enacts a profoundly sadomasochistic rhythm.

The complex political vision in *Coriolanus* rightly engages many critics, but ultimately we need to remember that here Shakespeare was not writing political theory. He was doing almost the opposite: by staging histories for popular entertainment in a way that emphasizes performativity over essence, Shakespeare drains political process of any clear claim to authenticity. The play encourages viewers to respond to character and spectacle more than to any underlying ideological significance. At the dawn of what Lacan calls the "era of the ego," theatrical images functioned as the mirror or screen in which viewers might glimpse their own projected identities (Lacan 1977: 71). As the displacement of self born of such projection/reflection became more and more disconcertingly evident, so too did the hunger for a *jouissance* that would dissolve structuring bonds. It would be a mistake to hold Shakespeare responsible for the development of a culture hungry for sensational effects (much less for an entertainment industry eager to supply them in every tawdry and excessive variety), but clearly he understood the pleasure audiences would derive from the theatrical dissolution of established norms and identities.

NOTES

1 *The Riverside Shakespeare*, 1.6.76. I follow Philip Brockbank's Arden edition for all other references to the text of *Coriolanus*, but Brockbank goes against the Folio in assigning this line to the soldiers. References to Shakespeare's plays other than *Coriolanus* follow the Riverside.

2 In his most recent formulation, Stephen Greenblatt describes "something magnificently opportunistic, appropriative, absorptive, even cannibalistic about Shakespeare's art" (Greenblatt 2001: 254).

3 Cf. A. P. Rossiter's remark that "*Coriolanus* plays on political feeling: the capacity to be not only intellectually, but emotionally and purposively, engaged by the management of public affairs; the businesses of groups of men in (ordered) communities; the contrivance or maintenance of agreement; the establishment of a will-in-common; and all the exercises of suasion, pressure, concession and compromise which achieve that *will* (a mind to *do*) in place of a chaos of confused appetencies" (Rossiter 1961: 239).

4 Bryan Reynolds (2000) shares my interest in the play's performative dimension, which in his view "compels the audience's awareness and contemplation of performance as an operative sociopolitical mechanism in the real world" (p. 117). Reynolds maintains that Shakespeare's play, like Brecht's *Coriolan*, supports the plebeians' cause. See also Terence Hawkes's (1992) demonstration of the linkage between a performance of *Coriolanus* in 1926 at Stratford and the political upheaval of the General Strike.

5 Parker and Sedgwick (1995: 2). The contemporary debate on performativity has its locus in the following texts: John Austin, *How to Do Things With Words* (Oxford: Oxford University Press, 1962); Jacques Derrida, "Signature, Event, Context" (1972), *Margins of Philosophy*, trans. Alan Bass (Chicago, IL: University of Chicago Press, 1982); John Searle, "Reiterating the Differences: A Reply to Derrida," *Glyph*, 1 (1977): 198–208; Jacques Derrida, "Limited Inc: abc . . ." *Glyph*, 2 (1977): 162–254.

6 According to Judith Butler's (1997) notion of the performative, social norms are rehearsed by a group's members, each of whom reaffirms and maintains the norm by his or her consensual act of participation.

7   Lacan (1992: 52). Bruce Fink describes the role of *Das Ding* in subject formation in terms evocative of Martius' attitude toward the plebeians: *"the subject comes into being as a defense against it, against the primal experience of pleasure/pain associated with it."* See *The Lacanian Subject: Between Language and Jouissance.* Princeton, NJ: Princeton University Press, 1995, p. 95; original emphasis).

8   See, for instance, Agamben (1999); Michael P. Clark (ed.) *Revenge of the Aesthetic: The Place of Literature in Theory Today* (Berkeley: University of California Press, 2000); Susan J. Wolfson, "Reading for Form," *Modern Language Quarterly*, 61, 1 (2000): 1–16; Ellen Rooney, "Form and Contentment," *Modern Language Quarterly*, 61, 1 (2000): 17–40.

9   See "The Thinking of the Body: Comments on the Imagery of Catharsis in Literature," in Burke (1966).

10 The motif is repeated in the assassination scene, where, as Bruce Smith points out, Martius "actively begs for the violence that is visited upon him seconds later" (Smith 1995: 423).

11 *Birmingham Mail*, May 10, 1939.

12 Ripley (1998: 277); *Birmingham Evening Dispatch*, May 10, 1939.

13 Desmond MacCarthy, *New Statesman and Nation*, May 14, 1938, quoted in Ripley (1998: 273).

14 Philip Hope-Wallace, *Manchester Guardian*, July 9, 1959.

15 W. A. Darlington, *Daily Telegraph*, July 8, 1959.

16 A. Alvarez, *New Statesman and Nation*, July 18, 1959.

17 T. C. Worsely, *Financial Times*, July 8, 1959; Alan Brien, *Spectator*, July 17, 1959.

18 *Stratford-upon-Avon Herald*, July 10, 1959.

19 Alan Pryce-Jones, *Observer*, July 12, 1959.

20 Michael Billington, *Country Life*, December 14, 1989. Billington makes reference to Kitchin's line about "one man lynching a crowd."

21 *Daily Express*, July 8, 1959.

References and Further Reading

Adelman, J. (1980). "Anger's My Meat": Feeding, Dependency, and Aggression in *Coriolanus*. In M. M. Schwartz and C. Kahn (eds.) *Representing Shakespeare*. Baltimore, MD: Johns Hopkins University Press, 129–49.

Agamben, G. (1999). *The Man Without Content*, trans. G. Albert. Stanford, CA: Stanford University Press.

Barzilai, S. (1998). *Coriolanus* and the Compulsion to Repeat. In A. Oz (ed.) *Strands Afar Remote: Israeli Perspectives on Shakespeare*. Newark: University of Delaware Press, 232–54.

Berry, R. (1981). *Changing Styles in Shakespeare*. London: Allen and Unwin.

Bersani, L. (1986). *The Freudian Body: Psychoanalysis and Art*. New York: Columbia University Press.

——(1990). *The Culture of Redemption*. Cambridge, MA: Harvard University Press.

Bliss, L. (ed.) (2000). *Coriolanus, by William Shakespeare*. New Cambridge Shakespeare. Cambridge: Cambridge University Press.

Brecht, B. (1972). *Bertolt Brecht: Plays, Poetry, & Prose*, vol. 9, ed. R. Manheim and J. Willett. New York: Random–Pantheon.

Brockbank, P. (ed.) (1976). *Coriolanus, by William Shakespeare*. Arden Shakespeare. London: Methuen.

Burke, K. (1966). *Language as Symbolic Action: Essays on Life, Literature, and Method*. Berkeley: University of California Press.

Butler, J. (1997). *Excitable Speech: A Politics of the Performative*. New York: Routledge.

Cavell, S. (1987). *Disowning Knowledge in Six Plays of Shakespeare*. New York: Cambridge University Press.

DeBois, P. (1985). A Disturbance of Syntax at the Gates of Rome. *Stanford Literature Review*, 2, 185–208.

Deleuze, G. (1993). *The Fold: Leibniz and the Baroque*, trans. T. Conley. Minneapolis: University of Minnesota Press.

Evans, G. B. (ed.) (1974). *The Riverside Shakespeare*. Boston, MA: Houghton Mifflin.

Fish, S. (1980). How To Do Things with Austin and Searle. In *Is There a Text in this Class?* Cambridge, MA: Harvard University Press, 197–245.

Fussell, S. (1993). Bodybuilder Americanus. *Michigan Quarterly Review*, 32, 4, 577–96.

Goldberg, J. (2000). The Anus in *Coriolanus*. In C. Mazzio and D. Trevor (eds.) *Historicism, Psychoanalysis, and Early Modern Culture*. New York: Routledge, 260–71.

Goldman, M. (1981). Characterizing Coriolanus. *Shakespeare Survey*, 34, 73–84.

Gordon, D. J. (1975). Name and Fame: Shakespeare's *Coriolanus*. In S. Orgel (ed.) *The Renaissance Imagination: Essays and Lectures*. Berkeley: University of California Press, 203–19.

Greenblatt, S. (1988). *Shakespearean Negotiations: The Circulation of Social Energy in Renaissance England*. Berkeley: University of California Press.

——(2001). *Hamlet in Purgatory*. Princeton, NJ: Princeton University Press.

Hawkes, T. (1992). *Meaning By Shakespeare*. New York: Routledge.

Jagendorf, Z. (1990). Coriolanus: Body Politic and Private Parts. *Shakespeare Quarterly*, 41, 4, 455–69.

Kahn, C. (1992). Mother of Battles: Volumnia and Her Son in Shakespeare's *Coriolanus*. *Differences: A Journal of Feminist Cultural Studies*, 4, 2, 154–70.

——(1997). *Roman Shakespeare: Warriors, Wounds, and Women*. New York: Routledge.

Kennedy, D. (1993). *Looking at Shakespeare: A Visual History of Twentieth-Century Performance*. Cambridge: Cambridge University Press.

Kermode, F. (1974). Introduction to *Coriolanus*. In G. B. Evans (ed.) *The Riverside Shakespeare*. Boston, MA: Houghton Mifflin, 1392–5.

Lacan, J. (1977). *Écrits: A Selection*, trans. A. Sheridan. New York: Norton.

——(1992). *The Seminar of Jacques Lacan, Book VII: The Ethics of Psychoanalysis, 1959–1960*, ed. J.-A. Miller, trans. D. Porter. New York: Norton.

Marshall, C. (1996). Wound-man: *Coriolanus*, Gender, and the Theatrical Construction of Interiority. In V. Traub, M. L. Kaplan, and D. Callaghan (eds.) *Feminist Readings of Early Modern Culture: Emerging Subjects*. Cambridge: Cambridge University Press, 93–118.

——(2000). Shakespeare, Crossing the Rubicon. *Shakespeare Survey*, 53, 73–88.

——(2002). *The Shattering of the Self: Violence, Subjectivity, and Early Modern Texts*. Baltimore, MD: Johns Hopkins University Press.

Odell, G. C. D. (1921). *Shakespeare from Betterton to Irving*, 2 vols. London: Constable.

Parker. A. and Sedgwick, E. K. (eds.) (1995). *Performativity and Performance*. New York: Routledge.

Paster, G. K. (1993). *The Body Embarrassed: Drama and the Disciplines of Shame in Early Modern England*. Ithaca, NY: Cornell University Press.

Plotz, J. (1996). *Coriolanus* and the Failure of Performatives. *English Literary History*, 63, 4, 809–32.

Reynolds, B. (2000). "What is the city but the people?" Transversal Performance and Radical Politics in Shakespeare's *Coriolanus* and Brecht's *Coriolan*. In D. Hedrick and B. Reynolds (eds.) *Shakespeare Without Class: Misappropriations of Cultural Capital*. New York: Palgrave, 107–32.

Ripley, J. (1998). *Coriolanus on Stage in England and America, 1609–1994*. Cranbury, NJ: Fairleigh Dickinson University Press.

Rossiter, A. P. (1961). *Angels with Horns, and Other Shakespeare Lectures*, ed. G. Storey. London: Longmans.

Sawday, J. (1995). *The Body Emblazoned: Dissection and the Human Body in Renaissance Culture*. New York: Routledge.

Serpieri, A. (1985). Reading the Signs: Towards a Semiotics of Shakespearean Drama, trans. K. Elam. In J. Drakakis (ed.) *Alternative Shakespeares*. New York: Routledge, 119–43.

Sicherman, C. M. (1972). *Coriolanus*: The Failure of Words. *English Literary History*, 39, 2, 189–207.

Smith, B. R. (1995). Rape, Rap, Rupture, Rapture: R-rated Futures on the Global Market. *Textual Practice*, 9, 3, 421–44.

——(2000). *Shakespeare and Masculinity.* Oxford: Oxford University Press.

Wells, S. (ed.) (1997). Kitchin on Olivier as Coriolanus. In *Shakespeare in the Theatre: An Anthology of Criticism.* Oxford: Clarendon Press.

Wills, G. (1989). Coriolanus Without Rome. *New York Review of Books*, January 19, 46.

Žižek, S. (1989). *The Sublime Object of Ideology.* London: Verso.

——(1997). *The Plague of Fantasies.* London: Verso.

Index